Access the entire book in PDF!

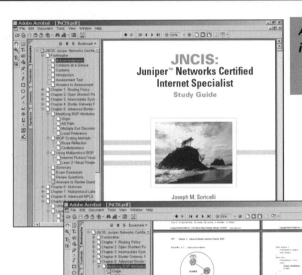

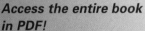

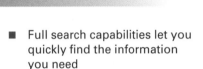

- Full search capabilities let you quickly find the information you need

- Complete with tables and illustrations

- Adobe Acrobat Reader 6 with Search included

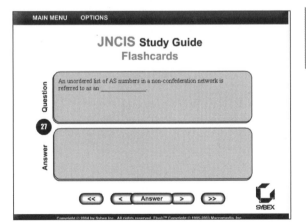

Reinforce understanding of key topics with flashcards for your PC, Pocket PC, or Palm handheld!

- Contains over 150 flashcard questions

- Runs on multiple platforms for usability and portability

- Quiz yourself anytime, anywhere!

JNCIS: Juniper Networks Certified Internet Specialist Study Guide

Juniper Networks Certified Internet Specialist, M-series, T-series Routers (JNCIS-M)

Exam JN0-302

OBJECTIVE	CHAPTER
ROUTING POLICY	
Describe JUNOS software routing policy design considerations—import; export; terms; match criteria; actions; default actions.	1
Identify the operation of community regular expressions.	1
Identify the operation of AS path regular expressions.	1
Evaluate the outcome of a policy using a subroutine.	1
Evaluate the outcome of a policy using a policy expression.	1
OPEN SHORTEST PATH FIRST (OSPF)	
Define the functions of the following OSPF area designations and functions—backbone area; non-backbone area; stub area; not-so-stubby area.	2
Identify OSPF authentication types.	2
Identify the configuration of OSPF route summarization.	2
Determine route selection based on IGP route metrics and the Shortest Path Algorithm.	2
Identify the routing policy capabilities of OSPF.	2
Describe the functionality of the OSPF LSA types.	2
Describe the relationship between the loopback address and the router ID.	2
Define the capabilities and operation of graceful restart.	2
Identify the operation and configuration of a virtual link.	2
INTERMEDIATE SYSTEM TO INTERMEDIATE SYSTEM (IS-IS)	
Define the functions of the following IS-IS parameters—authentication; mesh groups; wide metrics; route preferences; IS-IS levels; LSP lifetime; overload; routing policy.	3
Describe characteristics of IS-IS adjacencies.	3
Describe inter-area routing in IS-IS.	3

SYBEX

SYBEX

JNCIS:
Juniper Networks Certified Internet Specialist
Study Guide

JNCIS:
Juniper™ Networks Certified Internet Specialist
Study Guide

Joseph M. Soricelli

San Francisco • London

Associate Publisher: Neil Edde
Acquisitions and Developmental Editor: Maureen Adams
Production Editor: Leslie E.H. Light
Technical Editors: Steven T.Y. Wong, Douglas Marschke
Copyeditor: Liz Welch
Compositor: Craig Woods, Happenstance Type-O-Rama
Graphic Illustrator: Happenstance Type-O-Rama
CD Coordinator: Dan Mummert
CD Technician: Kevin Ly
Proofreaders: Laurie O'Connell, Nancy Riddiough
Indexer: Jack Lewis
Cover Designer: Archer Design
Cover Illustrator/Photographer: Bruce Heinemann, PhotoDisc

Library of Congress Card Number: 2003115676

ISBN: 0-7821-4072-6

Manufactured in the United States of America

10 9 8 7 6 5 4 3 2

SYBEX

To Our Valued Readers:

As internetworking technologies continue to pervade nearly every aspect of public and private industry worldwide, the demand grows for individuals who can demonstrate that they possess the skills needed to manage these technologies. Recognizing this need, Juniper Networks—the leading provider of Internet infrastructure solutions that enable ISPs and other telecommunications companies to meet the demands of Internet growth—recently restructured its certification program to provide a clear path for the acquisition of these skills. Sybex is proud to have partnered with Juniper Networks and worked closely with members of the Juniper Networks Technical Certification Program to develop this Official Study Guide for the Juniper Networks Certified Internetworking Associate certification.

Just as Juniper Networks is committed to establishing measurable standards for certifying those professionals who work in the cutting-edge field of internetworking, Sybex is committed to providing those professionals with the means of acquiring the skills and knowledge they need to meet those standards. It has long been Sybex's desire to help individuals acquire the technical knowledge and skills necessary to excel in the IT industry.

The authors and editors have worked hard to ensure that this Official Juniper Networks Study Guide is comprehensive, in-depth, and pedagogically sound. We're confident that this book will exceed the demanding standards of the certification marketplace and help you, the Juniper Networks certification candidate, succeed in your endeavors.

Good luck in pursuit of your Juniper Networks certification!

Neil Edde
Associate Publisher—Certification
Sybex Inc.

This book is dedicated to my wife, Christine, whose patience and love has allowed me to pursue those things in my life that interest me. In addition, my family and friends have provided encouragement beyond words that have helped me accomplish numerous things in my life.

Acknowledgments

There are numerous people who deserve a round of thanks for assisting with this book. I would first like to thank Jason Rogan and Patrick Ames, who got this project started and kept it going through thick and thin. I would also like to thank Colleen Strand, Leslie Light, Liz Welch, and Maureen Adams at Sybex. Without their assistance and guidance, this book would still be a figment of my imagination. A very large thank-you goes out to the technical editors, Steven Wong and Doug Marschke. Both of them worked very hard to make this book as accurate and complete as possible.

I would be remiss without acknowledging the colleagues and cohorts I've known and met throughout the years. You all know who you are, but I'll name just few: Terry, Pete, John, Renee, Noel, Chris, Jim, Dante, Matt, Sush, Terence, Andy, Jeff, Chris, Rajah, Colby, Wayne, Jamie, Dave, Jeff, and Trey.

Finally, a special thank-you belongs to all of the folks at Juniper Networks. The ES crew (Matt, Todd, Jason, Harry, Doug, Will), the PS crew (Gary, Drew, Pete, Eural, Ken, John, Taher, Tom, Steve, Bob, Glenn), the JTAC crew (Mark, Scott, Jim, Sunny, Derek, Alex, Siew, Robert, Steven), and others (Mary, Susan, Sheila, Chris, Andrew, Dennis, Alan) have made Juniper an organization that I feel truly blessed to belong to.

Contents at a Glance

Bonus Chapters

Contents

Bonus Chapters

Introduction

Welcome to the world of Juniper Networks. This Introduction serves as a location to pass on to you some pertinent information about the Juniper Networks Technical Certification Program. In addition, you'll learn how the book itself is laid out and what it contains. Also, we'll review what you should already know before you start reading this book.

Juniper Networks Technical Certification Program

The Juniper Networks Technical Certification Program (JNTCP) consists of two platform-specific, multitiered tracks. Each exam track allows participants to demonstrate their competence with Juniper Networks technology through a combination of written proficiency and hands-on configuration exams. Successful candidates demonstrate a thorough understanding of Internet technology and Juniper Networks platform configuration and troubleshooting skills.

The two JNTCP tracks focus on the M-series Routers and T-series Routing Platforms and the ERX Edge Routers, respectively. While some Juniper Networks customers and partners work with both platform families, it is most common to find individuals working with only one or the other platform. The two certification tracks allow candidates to pursue specialized certifications, which focus on the platform type most pertinent to their job functions and experience. Candidates wishing to attain a certification on both platform families are welcome to do so, but they are required to pass the exams from each track for their desired certification level.

 This book covers the M-series and T-series track. For information on the ERX Edge Routers certification track, please visit the JNTCP website at www.juniper.net/certification.

M-series Routers and T-series Routing Platforms

The M-series routers certification track consists of four tiers:

Juniper Networks Certified Internet Associate (JNCIA)   The Juniper Networks Certified Internet Associate, M-series, T-series Routers (JNCIA-M) certification does not have any prerequisites. It is administered at Prometric testing centers worldwide.

Juniper Networks Certified Internet Specialist (JNCIS)   The Juniper Networks Certified Internet Specialist, M-series, T-series Routers (JNCIS-M) certification also does not have any prerequisites. Like the JNCIA-M, it is administered at Prometric testing centers worldwide.

Juniper Networks Certified Internet Professional (JNCIP)   The Juniper Networks Certified Internet Professional, M-series, T-series Routers (JNCIP-M) certification requires that candidates first obtain the JNCIS-M certification. The hands-on exam is administered at Juniper Networks offices in select locations throughout the world.

Juniper Networks Certified Internet Expert (JNCIE)   The Juniper Networks Certified Internet Expert, M-series, T-series Routers (JNCIE-M) certification requires that candidates first obtain the JNCIP-M certification. The hands-on exam is administered at Juniper Networks offices in select locations throughout the world.

FIGURE 1.1 JNTCP M-series Routers and T-series Routing Platforms certification track

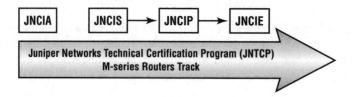

The JNTCP M-series Routers and T-series Routing Platforms certification track covers the M-series and T-series routing platforms as well as the JUNOS software configuration skills required for both platforms. The lab exams are conducted using M-series routers only.

Juniper Networks Certified Internet Associate

The JNCIA-M certification is the first of the four-tiered M-series Routers and T-series Routing Platforms track. It is the entry-level certification designed for experienced networking professionals with beginner-to-intermediate knowledge of the Juniper Networks M-series and T-series routers and the JUNOS software. The JNCIA-M (exam code JN0-201) is a computer-based, multiple-choice exam delivered at Prometric testing centers globally for $125 USD. It is a fast-paced exam that consists of 60 questions to be completed within 60 minutes. The current passing score is set at 70 percent.

JNCIA-M exam topics are based on the content of the Introduction to Juniper Networks Routers, M-series (IJNR-M) instructor-led training course. Just as IJNR-M is the first class most students attend when beginning their study of Juniper Networks hardware and software, the JNCIA-M exam should be the first certification exam most candidates attempt. The study topics for the JNCIA-M exam include

- System operation, configuration, and troubleshooting
- Routing protocols—BGP, OSPF, IS-IS, and RIP
- Protocol-independent routing properties
- Routing policy
- MPLS
- Multicast

Please be aware that the JNCIA-M certification is *not* a prerequisite for further certification in the M-series Routers and T-series Routing Platform track. The purpose of the JNCIA-M is to validate a candidate's skill set at the Associate level and is meant to be a stand-alone certification fully recognized and worthy of pride of accomplishment. Additionally, it can be used as a steppingstone before attempting the JNCIS-M exam.

Juniper Networks Certified Internet Specialist

The JNCIS-M was originally developed as the exam used to prequalify candidates for admittance to the practical hands-on certification exam. While it still continues to serve this purpose, this certification has quickly become a sought-after designation in its own right. Depending on candidates' job functions, many have chosen JNCIS-M as the highest level of JNTCP certification needed to validate their skill set. Candidates also requiring validation of their hands-on configuration and troubleshooting ability on the M-series and T-series routers and the JUNOS software use the JNCIS-M as the required prerequisite to the JNCIP-M practical exam.

The JNCIS-M exam tests for a wider and deeper level of knowledge than does the JNCIA-M exam. Question content is drawn from the documentation set for the M-series routers, the T-series routers, and the JUNOS software. Additionally, on-the-job product experience and an understanding of Internet technologies and design principles are considered to be common knowledge at the Specialist level.

The JNCIS-M (exam code JN0-303) is a computer-based, multiple-choice exam delivered at Prometric testing centers globally for $125 USD. It consists of 75 questions to be completed in 90 minutes. The current passing score is set at 70 percent.

The study topics for the JNCIS-M exam include

- Advanced system operation, configuration, and troubleshooting
- Routing protocols—BGP, OSPF, and IS-IS
- Routing policy
- MPLS
- Multicast
- Router and network security
- Router and network management
- VPNs
- IPv6

 There are no prerequisite certifications for the JNCIS-M exam. While JNCIA-M certification is a recommended steppingstone to JNCIS-M certification, candidates are permitted to go straight to the Specialist (JNCIS-M) level.

Juniper Networks Certified Internet Professional

The JNCIP-M is the first of the two one-day practical exams in the M-series Routers and T-series Routing Platforms track of the JNTCP. The goal of this challenging exam is to validate a candidate's ability to successfully build an ISP network consisting of seven M-series routers and multiple EBGP neighbors. Over a period of eight hours, the successful candidate will perform system configuration on all seven routers, install an IGP, implement a well-designed IBGP, establish connections with all EBGP neighbors as specified, and configure the required routing policies correctly.

This certification establishes candidates' practical and theoretical knowledge of core Internet technologies and their ability to proficiently apply that knowledge in a hands-on environment. This exam is expected to meet the hands-on certification needs of the majority of Juniper Networks customers and partners. The more advanced JNCIE-M exam focuses on a set of specialized skills and addresses a much smaller group of candidates. You should carefully consider your certification goals and requirements, for you may find that the JNCIP-M exam is the highest-level certification you need.

The JNCIP-M (exam code CERT-JNCIP-M) is delivered at one of several Juniper Networks offices worldwide for $1,250. The current passing score is set at 80 percent.

The study topics for the JNCIP-M exam include

- Advanced system operation, configuration, and troubleshooting
- Routing protocols—BGP, OSPF, IS-IS, and RIP
- Routing policy
- Routing protocol redistribution
- VLANs
- VRRP

The JNCIP-M certification is a prerequisite for attempting the JNCIE-M practical exam.

Juniper Networks Certified Internet Expert

At the pinnacle of the M-series Routers and T-series Routing Platforms track is the one-day JNCIE-M practical exam. The *E* stands for Expert and they mean it—the exam is the most challenging and respected of its type in the industry. Maintaining the standard of excellence established over two years ago, the JNCIE-M certification continues to give candidates the opportunity to distinguish themselves as the truly elite of the networking world. Only a few have dared attempt this exam, and fewer still have passed.

The new 8-hour format of the exam requires that candidates troubleshoot an existing and preconfigured ISP network consisting of 10 M-series routers. Candidates are then presented with additional configuration tasks appropriate for an expert-level engineer.

The JNCIE-M (exam code CERT-JNCIE-M) is delivered at one of several Juniper Networks offices worldwide for $1,250 USD. The current passing score is set at 80 percent.

The study topics for the JNCIE-M exam *may* include

- Expert-level system operation, configuration, and troubleshooting
- Routing protocols—BGP, OSPF, IS-IS, and RIP
- Routing protocol redistribution
- Advanced routing policy implementation
- Firewall filters

- Class of service
- MPLS
- VPNs
- IPv6
- IPSec
- Multicast

 Since the JNCIP-M certification is a prerequisite for attempting this practical exam, all candidates who pass the JNCIE-M will have successfully completed two days of intensive practical examination.

Registration Procedures

JNTCP written exams are delivered worldwide at Prometric testing centers. To register, visit Prometric's website at www.2test.com (or call 1-888-249-2567 in North America) to open an account and register for an exam.

The JNTCP Prometric exam numbers are

- JNCIA-M—JN0-201
- JNCIS-M—JN0-303
- JNCIA-E—JN0-120
- JNCIS-E—JN0-130

JNTCP lab exams are delivered by Juniper Networks at select locations. Currently the testing locations are

- Sunnyvale, CA
- Herndon, VA
- Westford, MA
- Amsterdam, Holland

Other global locations are periodically set up as testing centers based on demand. To register, send an e-mail message to Juniper Networks at certification-testreg@juniper.net and place one of the following exam codes in the subject field. Within the body of the message indicate the testing center you prefer and which month you would like to attempt the exam. You will be contacted with the available dates at your requested testing center. The JNTCP lab exam numbers are

- JNCIP-M—CERT-JNCIP-M
- JNCIE-M—CERT-JNCIE-M
- JNCIP-E—CERT-JNCIP-E

Recertification Requirements

To maintain the high standards of the JNTCP certifications, and to ensure that the skills of those certified are kept current and relevant, Juniper Networks has implemented the following recertification requirements, which apply to both certification tracks of the JNTCP:

- All JNTCP certifications are valid for a period of two years.

- Certification holders who do not renew their certification within this two-year period will have their certification placed in *suspended mode*. Certifications in suspended mode are not eligible as prerequisites for further certification and cannot be applied to partner certification requirements.

- After being in suspended mode for one year, the certification is placed in *inactive mode*. At that stage, the individual is no longer certified at the JNTCP certification level that has become inactive and the individual will lose the associated certification number. For example, a JNCIP holder placed in inactive mode will be required to pass both the JNCIS and JNCIP exams in order to regain JNCIP status; such an individual will be given a new JNCIP certification number.

- Renewed certifications are valid for a period of two years from the date of passing the renewed certification exam.

- Passing an exam at a higher level renews all lower-level certifications for two years from the date of passing the higher-level exam. For example, passing the JNCIP exam will renew the JNCIS certification (and JNCIA certification if currently held) for two years from the date of passing the JNCIP exam.

- JNCIA holders must pass the current JNCIA exam in order to renew the certification for an additional two years from the most recent JNCIA pass date.

- JNCIS holders must pass the current JNCIS exam in order to renew the certification for an additional two years from the most recent JNCIS pass date.

- JNCIP and JNCIE holders must pass the current JNCIS exam in order to renew these certifications for an additional two years from the most recent JNCIS pass date.

 The most recent version of the JNTCP Online Agreement must be accepted for the recertification to become effective.

JNTCP Nondisclosure Agreement

Juniper Networks considers all written and practical JNTCP exam material to be confidential intellectual property. As such, an individual is not permitted to take home, copy, or re-create the entire exam or any portions thereof. It is expected that candidates who participate in the JNTCP will not reveal the detailed content of the exams.

For written exams delivered at Prometric testing centers, candidates must accept the online agreement before proceeding with the exam. When taking practical exams, candidates are provided with a hard-copy agreement to read and sign before attempting the exam. In either case, the agreement can be downloaded from the JNTCP website for your review prior to the testing date. Juniper Networks retains all signed hard-copy nondisclosure agreements on file.

Candidates must accept the online JNTCP Online Agreement in order for their certifications to become effective and to have a certification number assigned. You do this by going to the CertManager site at www.certmanager.net/juniper.

Resources for JNTCP Participants

Reading this book is a fantastic place to begin preparing for your next JNTCP exam. You should supplement the study of this volume's content with related information from various sources. The following resources are available for free and are recommended to anyone seeking to attain or maintain Juniper Networks certified status.

JNTCP Website

The JNTCP website (www.juniper.net/certification) is the place to go for the most up-to-date information about the program. As the program evolves, this website is periodically updated with the latest news and major announcements. Possible changes include new exams and certifications, modifications to the existing certification and recertification requirements, and information about new resources and exam objectives.

The site consists of separate sections for each of the certification tracks. The information you'll find there includes the exam number, passing scores, exam time limits, and exam topics. A special section dedicated to resources is also provided to supply you with detailed exam topic outlines, sample written exams, and study guides. The additional resources listed next are also linked from the JNTCP website.

CertManager

The CertManager system (www.certmanager.net/juniper) provides you with a place to track your certification progress. The site requires a username and password for access, and you typically use the information contained on your hard-copy score report from Prometric the first time you log in. Alternatively, a valid login can be obtained by sending an e-mail message to certification@juniper.net with the word **certmanager** in the subject field.

Once you log in, you can view a report of all your attempted exams. This report includes the exam dates, your scores, and a progress report indicating the additional steps required to attain a given certification or recertification. This website is where you accept the online JNTCP agreement, which is a required step to become certified at any level in the program. You can also use the website to request the JNTCP official certification logos to use on your business cards, resumes, and websites.

Perhaps most important, the CertManager website is where all your contact information is kept up to date. Juniper Networks uses this information to send you certification benefits, such as your certificate of completion, and to inform you of important developments regarding your certification status. A valid company name is used to verify a partner's compliance with certification requirements. To avoid missing out on important benefits and information, you should ensure that your contact information is kept current.

Juniper Networks Training Courses

Juniper Networks training courses (`www.juniper.net/training`) are the best source of knowledge for seeking a certification and to increase your hands-on proficiency with Juniper Networks equipment and technologies. While attendance of official Juniper Networks training courses doesn't guarantee a passing score on the certification exam, it does increase the likelihood of your successfully passing it. This is especially true when you seek to attain JNCIP or JNCIE status, where hands-on experience is a vital aspect of your study plan.

Juniper Networks Technical Documentation

You should be intimately familiar with the Juniper Networks technical documentation set (`www.juniper.net/techpubs`). During the JNTCP lab exams (JNCIP and JNCIE), these documents are provided in PDF format on your PC. Knowing the content, organizational structure, and search capabilities of these manuals is a key component for a successful exam attempt. At the time of this writing, hard-copy versions of the manuals are provided only for the hands-on lab exams. All written exams delivered at Prometric testing centers are closed-book exams.

Juniper Networks Solutions and Technology

To broaden and deepen your knowledge of Juniper Networks products and their applications, you can visit `www.juniper.net/techcenter`. This website contains white papers, application notes, frequently asked questions (FAQ), and other informative documents, such as customer profiles and independent test results.

Group Study

The Groupstudy mailing list and website (`www.groupstudy.com/list/juniper.html`) is dedicated to the discussion of Juniper Networks products and technologies for the purpose of preparing for certification testing. You can post and receive answers to your own technical questions or simply read the questions and answers of other list members.

JNCIS Study Guide

Now that you know a lot about the JNTCP, we now need to provide some more information about this text. The most important thing you can do to get the most out of this book is to read the *JNCIA Study Guide*. I don't say this to get you to purchase another book. In reality, both the *JNCIA Study Guide* and this book form a complete set of knowledge that you'll need while pursuing the JNTCP. In fact, the chapters in this book assume that you have read the *JNCIA Study Guide*.

What Does This Book Cover?

This book covers what you need to know to pass the JNCIS-M exam. It teaches you advanced topics related to the JUNOS software. While this material is helpful, we also recommend gaining some hands-on practice. We understand that accessing a live Juniper Networks router in a

Tips for Taking Your Exam

Many questions on the exam have answer choices that at first glance look identical. Remember to read through all the choices carefully because "close" doesn't cut it. Although there is never any intent on the part of Juniper Networks to trick you, some questions require you to think carefully before answering. Also, never forget that the right answer is the *best* answer. In some cases, you may feel that more than one appropriate answer is presented, but the best answer is the *correct* answer.

Here are some general tips for exam success:

- Arrive early at the exam center, so you can relax and review your study materials.

- Read the questions *carefully*. Don't just jump to conclusions. Make sure that you're clear about *exactly* what each question asks.

- Don't leave any questions unanswered. They count against you.

- When answering multiple-choice questions that you're not sure about, use a process of elimination to eliminate the obviously incorrect answers first. Doing this greatly improves your odds if you need to make an educated guess.

- Mark questions that you're not sure about. If you have time at the end, you can review those marked questions to see if the correct answer "jumps out" at you.

After you complete the exam, you'll get immediate, online notification of your pass or fail status, a printed Examination Score Report that indicates your pass or fail status, and your exam results by section. (The test administrator will give you the printed score report.) Test scores are automatically forwarded to Juniper Networks within five working days after you take the test, so you don't need to send your score to them.

lab environment is difficult, but if you can manage it you'll retain this knowledge far longer in your career.

Each chapter begins with a list of the exams objectives covered, so make sure you read them over before getting too far into the chapter. The chapters end with some review questions that are specifically designed to help you retain the knowledge we discussed. Take some time to carefully read through the questions and review the sections of the chapter relating to any question you miss. The book consists of the following material:

- Chapter 1: Routing policy
- Chapter 2: OSPF
- Chapter 3: IS-IS
- Chapter 4: BGP
- Chapter 5: Advanced BGP

- Chapter 6: Multicast
- Chapter 7: MPLS
- Chapter 8: Advanced MPLS
- Chapter 9: VPN

How to Use This Book

This book can provide a solid foundation for the serious effort of preparing for the Juniper Networks Certified Internet Specialist M-series routers (JNCIS-M) exam. To best benefit from this book, we recommend the following study method:

1. Take the Assessment Test immediately following this Introduction. (The answers are at the end of the test.) Carefully read over the explanations for any question you get wrong, and note which chapters the material comes from. This information should help you to plan your study strategy.

2. Study each chapter carefully, making sure that you fully understand the information and the test topics listed at the beginning of each chapter. Pay extra-close attention to any chapter where you missed questions in the Assessment Test.

3. Answer the review questions found at the conclusion of each chapter. (The answers appear at the end of the chapter, after the review questions.)

4. Note the questions that you answered correctly but that confused you. Also make note of any questions you answered incorrectly. Go back and review the chapter material related to those questions.

5. Before taking the exam, try your hand at the two bonus exams that are included on the CD accompanying this book. The questions in these exams appear only on the CD. This gives you a complete overview of what you can expect to see on the real thing. After all, the authors of this book are the people who wrote the actual exam questions!

6. Remember to use the products on the CD that is included with this book. The electronic flashcards and the EdgeTest exam-preparation software have all been specifically selected to help you study for and pass your exam.

7. Take your studying on the road with the *JNCIS Study Guide* eBook in PDF format. You can also test yourself remotely with the electronic flashcards.

The electronic flashcards can be used on your Windows computer or on your Palm device.

8. Make sure you read the glossary. It includes all of the terms used in the book (as well as others), along with an explanation for each term.

To learn all the material covered in this book, you'll have to apply yourself regularly and with discipline. Try to set aside the same amount of time every day to study, and select a comfortable and quiet place to do so. If you work hard, you will be surprised at how quickly you learn this material. Before you know it, you'll be on your way to becoming a JNCIE. Good luck and may the Force be with you!

What's on the CD?

We worked very hard to provide some really great tools to help you with your certification process. All of the following tools should be loaded on your workstation when you're studying for the test.

Bonus Chapters

The accompanying CD contains three bonus chapters which cover additional JNCIS exam topics. These include an introductory level examination of Class of Service, the use of security for securing network resources and preventing network attacks, and a basic IP version 6 discussion.

The Sybex Test Preparation Software for the JNCIS-M Exam

This test-preparation software prepares you to successfully pass the JNCIS-M exam. In this test engine, you'll find all of the questions from the book, plus two additional Bonus Exams that appear exclusively on the CD. You can take the Assessment Test, test yourself by chapter, or take the two Bonus Exams that appear on the CD.

To find more test-simulation software for the Juniper Networks exams, explore the information at www.boson.com.

Electronic Flashcards for PC and Palm Devices

After you read the *JNCIS Study Guide*, read the review questions at the end of each chapter and study the practice exams included in the book and on the CD. But wait, there's more! Test yourself with the flashcards included on the CD. If you can get through these difficult questions and understand the answers, you'll know you'll be ready for the actual exam.

The flashcards include over 150 questions specifically written to hit you hard and make sure you are ready for the exam. Between the review questions, practice exam, and flashcards, you'll be more than prepared for the exam.

JNCIS Study Guide in PDF

Sybex is now offering the Juniper Networks Certification books on CD so you can read the book on your PC or laptop. The *JNCIS Study Guide* is in Adobe Acrobat format. Acrobat Reader 4 with Search is also included on the CD.

This will be extremely helpful to readers who travel and don't want to carry a book, as well as to readers who find it more comfortable to read from their computer.

JUNOS Software Documentation in PDF

Finally, the Juniper Networks documentation set for version 5.6 is included on the CD so that you can read these manuals on your PC or laptop. The documentation set is in Adobe Acrobat format. Acrobat Reader 4 with Search is also included on the CD.

About the Author and Technical Editors

You can reach the author and the technical editors through the Core Routing website at www.corerouting.net. This website includes links to e-mail the authors, a list of known errata, and other study material to aid in your pursuit of all the Juniper Networks certifications.

Joseph M. Soricelli

Joseph M. Soricelli is a Professional Services Engineer at Juniper Networks Inc. He is a Juniper Networks Certified Internet Expert (#14), a Juniper Networks Authorized Trainer, and a Cisco Certified Internet Expert (#4803). He is the editor of and a contributing author to the *Juniper Networks Certified Internet Associate Study Guide*, as well as a contributing author to the *Juniper Networks Routers: The Complete Reference*. In addition to writing numerous training courses, he has worked with and trained network carriers, telecommunications providers, and Internet service providers (ISPs) throughout his 10-year career in the networking industry.

Steven Wong (Technical Editor)

Steven Wong, Tze Yeung, is currently a Customer Support Engineer in Juniper Networks Technical Assistance Center (JTAC), where he provides technical support to major ISPs. Before joining Juniper Networks, he worked in a regional system integrator and was responsible for providing consulting and technical support services to multinational enterprise customers as well as ISPs. He is a Juniper Networks Certified Internet Expert (JNCIE #0010) and a Cisco Certified Internetwork Expert (CCIE #4353). He also holds an M.S. and a B.S. in Electrical and Electronic Engineering, both from the Hong Kong University of Science and Technology.

Douglas Marschke (Technical Editor)

Douglas J. Marschke is an Education Services Engineer at Juniper Networks Inc. He has a B.S. in Electrical Engineering from the University of Michigan. He is a Juniper Networks Certified Internet Expert (#41) and a Juniper Networks Authorized Trainer. He has been electrifying audiences worldwide since joining Juniper Networks in January 2001.

Assessment Test

1. What forms of authentication does the JUNOS software utilize for BGP?

    A. None

    B. Simple

    C. Plain-text

    D. MD5

2. The regular expression `^65.*:*$` matches which community value(s)?

    A. 64:123

    B. 65:1234

    C. 64512:123

    D. 65512:1234

3. What value is used within the final two octets of the LDP ID to signify that the local router is using a per-node label allocation method?

    A. 0

    B. 1

    C. 10

    D. 100

4. How many bits are used in an IPv6 address?

    A. 32

    B. 64

    C. 128

    D. 256

5. A PIM domain is using a static configuration to learn the RP address. Which type of forwarding tree is created from the RP to the last-hop router?

    A. Rendezvous point tree

    B. Reverse-path forwarding tree

    C. Shortest-path tree

    D. Source-based tree

6. After the CSPF algorithm runs through the information in the TED, what is passed to RSVP to signal the LSP?

    A. A single loose-hop ERO listing the egress address

    B. A single strict-hop ERO listing the first router in the path

    C. A complete loose-hop ERO listing each router in the path

    D. A complete strict-hop ERO listing each router in the path

7. In a stable network environment, by default how often does the JUNOS software refresh its locally generated LSAs?

    A. Every 20 minutes

    B. Every 30 minutes

    C. Every 50 minutes

    D. Every 60 minutes

8. What is the maximum number of area addresses supported by the JUNOS software for IS-IS?

    A. 1

    B. 2

    C. 3

    D. 4

9. Your local AS value is 1234. Your EBGP peer is expecting you to establish the peering session using AS 6789. What JUNOS software command allows this session to be established successfully?

    A. `as-override`

    B. `as-loops`

    C. `local-as`

    D. `remove-private`

10. Which JUNOS software command is used to allocate the amount of memory space used for queuing?

    A. `transmit-rate`

    B. `drop-profile`

    C. `priority`

    D. `buffer-size`

11. Which Layer 2 VPN access technology connects different data-link encapsulations on either side of the provider network?

    A. Frame Relay

    B. ATM

    C. Ethernet VLAN

    D. IP Interworking

12. By default, how many attempts does the JUNOS software make to a configured RADIUS server?

    A. 1

    B. 2

    C. 3

    D. 4

13. What two functions are supported by an opaque LSA within the JUNOS software?

    A. Virtual link

    B. Graceful restart

    C. Authentication

    D. Traffic engineering

14. What is the default JUNOS software method for using the MED attribute?

    A. Deterministic MED

    B. Always compare MEDs

    C. Never compare MEDs

    D. Cisco compatibility mode

15. Which two sources of routing information automatically populate the inet.2 routing table with unicast routes to be used for RPF validation checks?

    A. MBGP

    B. Multi-topology IS-IS

    C. OSPF

    D. Static routes

16. What MPLS feature allows for the protection of traffic already transmitted into the LSP by the ingress router?

    A. Adaptive mode

    B. Fast reroute

    C. Primary path

    D. Secondary path

17. Which JUNOS software configuration component associates a specific interface queue with a human-friendly name?

    A. Forwarding class

    B. Scheduler

    C. Rewrite rule

    D. Code-point alias

18. Which IPv6 header is used by a host to source-route a packet through the network?

    A. Hop-by-hop options

    B. Destination options

    C. Fragment

    D. Routing

19. You have three import policies configured on your router. The **alter-lp** policy has an action of then local-preference 200, the **delete-comms** policy has an action of then community delete all-comms, and the **set-nhs** policy has an action of then set next-hop self. Each policy has no configured match criteria and no other actions configured. In what order should these policies be applied?

    A. import [alter-lp delete-comms set-nhs]

    B. import [delete-comms set-nhs alter-lp]

    C. import [set-nhs alter-lp delete-comms]

    D. All of the above

20. What is the default IS-IS interface metric assigned to all non-loopback interfaces in the JUNOS software?

    A. 0

    B. 1

    C. 10

    D. 20

21. In a BGP confederation network, what type of peering session is used within an individual sub-AS?

    A. IBGP

    B. CBGP

    C. EBGP

    D. MBGP

22. Which RSVP object contains the tunnel ID value assigned by the ingress router to identify the egress router for the LSP?

    A. Sender-Template

    B. Sender-Tspec

    C. Session

    D. Session Attribute

23. What is the default value of the OSPF domain ID within the JUNOS software?

    A. 0.0.0.0

    B. 10.10.10.1

    C. 172.16.1.1

    D. 192.168.1.1

24. Which TACACS message type contains the user's login name and is sent by the router to the server?

    A. Start

    B. End

    C. Reply

    D. Continue

25. Which graceful restart mode signifies that the local router has set the RR bit in its graceful restart TLV?

   A. Restart candidate

   B. Possible helper

   C. Helper

   D. Disabled helper

26. When a CE router in a Layer 3 VPN is forwarding Internet-bound traffic across its VRF interface, what command should be configured in the [edit routing-instances VPN routing-options static] hierarchy on the PE router?

   A. set route 0/0 next-table inet.0

   B. set route 0/0 discard

   C. set route 0/0 reject

   D. set route 0/0 lsp-next-hop to-Internet

27. Which bit in the router LSA is set to signify that the local router is an ASBR?

   A. V bit

   B. E bit

   C. B bit

   D. N/P bit

28. Which BGP attribute is added by a route reflector to describe the router that first advertised a route to a BGP route reflector ?

   A. Cluster ID

   B. Cluster List

   C. Originator ID

   D. Router ID

29. During a failure mode, the ingress router can protect MPLS traffic flows when which feature is configured?

   A. Adaptive mode

   B. Optimization

   C. Primary path

   D. Secondary path

30. Which RADIUS message type is sent by the server to signal that a user is allowed to log into the router?

   A. Access-Accept

   B. Access-Reject

   C. Access-Authenticate

   D. Access-Request

31. When it is applied to a policy, which route(s) matches the prefix list called ***these-routes***?

```
prefix-list these-routes{
        192.168.1.0/24;
        192.168.2.0/24;
        192.168.3.0/24;
        192.168.4.0/24;
}
```

   A. 192.168.0.0 /16

   B. 192.168.1.0 /24

   C. 192.168.2.0 /28

   D. 192.168.3.32 /30

32. You're examining the output of the show route detail command and see a BGP path advertisement with an inactive reason of Update source. What selection criterion caused this route to not be selected?

   A. MED

   B. EBGP vs. IBGP

   C. IGP Cost

   D. Peer ID

33. An MPLS transit router receives a Path message and finds that the first hop listed in the ERO is strictly assigned. Additionally, the address listed in the ERO doesn't match the local interface address the message was received on. What does the router do at this point?

   A. Generates a PathErr message and forwards it upstream

   B. Processes the Path message and forwards it downstream

   C. Generates a PathTear message and forwards it upstream

   D. Generates a Resv message and forwards it downstream

34. Which JUNOS software configuration component is used to allocate resources to a particular queue?

   A. Forwarding class

   B. Scheduler

   C. Rewrite rule

   D. Code-point alias

35. What is the second bootstrap router election criterion?

   A. Lowest configured priority value

   B. Highest configured priority value

   C. Lowest IP address

   D. Highest IP address

Answers to Assessment Test

1. A, D.   By default, BGP sessions are not authenticated. The use of the `authentication-key` command enables MD5 authentication. For more information, see Chapter 4.

2. B, D.   The first portion of the expression requires an AS value to begin with a 65 and contain any other values. Only Options B and D fit that criterion. The second portion of the expression can be any possible value. This means that both Options B and D match the expression. For more information, see Chapter 1.

3. A.   When a value of 0 is used with the router ID to identify the local router's label space, it means that the router is using a per-node label allocation mechanism. For more information, see Chapter 7.

4. C.   An IPv6 address uses 128 bits to fully address a host. This provides for a substantial increase in addressing space over IPv4. For more information, see Bonus Chapter C on the CD.

5. A.   A PIM-SM domain always creates a rendezvous point tree (RPT) from the RP to the last hop router. The shortest-path tree is created between the first-hop and last-hop routers, while a source-based tree is used in a dense-mode PIM domain. Multicast networks don't use reverse-path forwarding trees. The reverse-path concept is used to prevent forwarding loops in the network. For more information, see Chapter 6.

6. D.   The result of a CSPF calculation is a complete strict-hop ERO of all routers in the path of the LSP. This information is sent to the RSVP process, which signals the path and establishes it in the network. For more information, see Chapter 8.

7. C.   The MaxAge of an LSA is 60 minutes (3600 seconds). Before reaching the MaxAge, the JUNOS software refreshes the locally generated LSAs at 50-minute intervals. For more information, see Chapter 2.

8. C.   The JUNOS software supports up to three area addresses per router. For more information, see Chapter 3.

9. C.   The `local-as` command allows the BGP peering session to be established using an AS value other than the value configured within the `routing-options` hierarchy. For more information, see Chapter 5.

10. D.   The `buffer-size` command is used by an individual queue to determine the amount of space to use for storing information. For more information, see Bonus Chapter A on the CD.

11. D.   By default, the data-link encapsulations must match on either side of the provider network. Only the use of IP Interworking relaxes this restriction by allowing this dissimilar connection. For more information, see Chapter 9.

12. C.   By default, the JUNOS software makes three attempts to reach a configured RADIUS server. For more information, see Bonus Chapter B on the CD.

13. B, D.   The JUNOS software currently uses opaque LSAs to support graceful restart and traffic engineering. The link-local (type 9) opaque LSA is used with graceful restart, and the area-local (type 10) opaque LSA is used with traffic engineering. For more information, see Chapter 2.

14. A.   The JUNOS software always groups incoming path advertisements by the neighboring AS and evaluates the MED values within each group. This process is called *deterministic* MED. For more information, see Chapter 4.

15. A, B.   Both BGP and IS-IS are capable of automatically populating the inet.2 routing table with unicast routes. These routes are designed for use within the context of a multicast RPF check. For more information, see Chapter 6.

16. B.   Fast reroute is a temporary solution to a failure scenario in which each router protects traffic already traveling through the LSP. For more information, see Chapter 8.

17. A.   A forwarding class is the mapping of a human-readable name to a specific interface queue within the JUNOS software. For more information, see Bonus Chapter A on the CD.

18. D.   The routing header in an IPv6 packet is used to source-route the packet across the network. It contains a list of addresses through which the packet must pass. For more information, see Bonus Chapter C on the CD.

19. D.   Since each of the policies contains no terminating action, they can be applied in any order desired. The BGP default policy will accept all incoming BGP routes. For more information, see Chapter 1.

20. C.   Each IS-IS interface receives a default metric value of 10 for all interfaces. The exception to this rule is the loopback interface, which receives a metric value of 0. For more information, see Chapter 3.

21. A.   Each sub-AS in a BGP confederation network maintains an IBGP full mesh. For more information, see Chapter 5.

22. C.   The ingress router of an RSVP LSP assigns a unique value to the tunnel through the tunnel ID. This value is contained in the Session object. For more information, see Chapter 7.

23. A.   By default, all routing instances operating OSPF are not assigned a domain ID value. This is interpreted as 0.0.0.0 by all PE routers. For more information, see Chapter 9.

24. A.   After receiving the user's login name at the router prompt, the router sends it to the TACACS server in a Start message. For more information, see Bonus Chapter B on the CD.

25. A.   An IS-IS router sets the restart request (RR) bit in its restart TLV to signify that it has recently experienced a restart event and that each neighbor should maintain an Up adjacency with the local router. This moves the restarting router into the restart candidate mode. For more information, see Chapter 3.

26. A.   The VRF routing instance requires the configuration of a static default route to allow packets to reach Internet destinations. The key attribute assigned to that route is the next-table option, which allows the PE router to consult inet.0 for route destinations. For more information, see Chapter 9.

27. B.   The E bit in the router LSA is set when the local router has a configured routing policy applied to its OSPF configuration. For more information, see Chapter 2.

28. C. The Originator ID describes the router that first advertised a route into a route reflection network. It is added by the route reflector and provides a second level of protection of loop avoidance. For more information, see Chapter 5.

29. D. When an ingress router has a secondary path configured for an LSP, it establishes that path and begins forwarding traffic during a failure of the primary path. For more information, see Chapter 8.

30. A. Once the username and password are validated by the server, an Access-Accept message is sent to the router. This allows the user to log into the device. For more information, see Bonus Chapter B on the CD.

31. B. A prefix list within a routing policy always assumes a route-filter match type of exact. Therefore, only routes explicitly listed in the prefix list will match. Only the 192.168.1.0 /24 route fits this criterion. For more information, see Chapter 1.

32. D. The source of any BGP update represents the Peer ID route selection criterion. This is used when multiple advertisements are received from the same router (constant router ID). This causes the inactive reason to be displayed as Update source. For more information, see Chapter 4.

33. A. When any MPLS router encounters the situation described in the question, the Path message is not processed any further. In addition, a PathErr message is generated and sent upstream to the ingress router, informing it of the incorrect address within the ERO. For more information, see Chapter 7.

34. B. A scheduler allows a network administrator to allocate resources, such as transmission bandwidth, to a queue in the router. For more information, see Bonus Chapter A on the CD.

35. D. When multiple candidate bootstrap routers are sharing the same priority value, the router with the highest router ID is elected the BSR for the domain. For more information, see Chapter 6.

Chapter 1

Routing Policy

JNCIS EXAM OBJECTIVES COVERED IN THIS CHAPTER:

- ✓ Describe JUNOS software routing policy design considerations—import; export; terms; match criteria; actions; default actions
- ✓ Identify the operation of community regular expressions
- ✓ Identify the operation of AS Path regular expressions
- ✓ Evaluate the outcome of a policy using a subroutine
- ✓ Evaluate the outcome of a policy using a policy expression

Before reading this chapter, you should be very familiar with the functionality of a routing policy in the JUNOS software and when it might be appropriate to use one. You should also understand how a multiterm policy uses match criteria and actions to perform its functions. Finally, the use of route filters and their associated match types is assumed knowledge.

In this chapter, we'll explore the use of routing policies within the JUNOS software. We first examine the multiple methods of altering the processing of a policy, including policy chains, sub-routines, and expressions. We then discuss the use of a routing policy to locate routes using Border Gateway Protocol (BGP) community values and Autonomous System (AS) Path information.

Throughout the chapter, we see examples of constructing and applying routing policies. We also explore some methods for verifying the effectiveness of your policies before implementing them on the router using the test policy command.

Routing policy basics are covered extensively in *JNCIA: Juniper Networks Certified Internet Associate Study Guide* (Sybex, 2003).

Routing Policy Processing

One of the advantages (or disadvantages depending on your viewpoint) of the JUNOS software policy language is its great flexibility. Generally speaking, you often have four to five methods for accomplishing the same task. A single policy with multiple terms is one common method for constructing an advanced policy. In addition, the JUNOS software allows you to use a policy chain, a subroutine, a prefix list, and a policy expression to complete the same task. Each of these methods is unique in its approach and attacks the problem from a different angle. Let's examine each of these in some more detail.

Policy Chains

We first explored the concept of a *policy chain* in the *JNCIA Study Guide*. Although it sounds very formal, a policy chain is simply the application of multiple policies within a specific section of the configuration. An example of a policy chain can be seen on the Merlot router as:

```
[edit protocols bgp]
user@Merlot# show
```

```
group Internal-Peers {
    type internal;
    local-address 192.168.1.1;
    export [ adv-statics adv-large-aggregates adv-small-aggregates ];
    neighbor 192.168.2.2;
    neighbor 192.168.3.3;
}
```

The *adv-statics*, *adv-large-aggregates*, and *adv-small-aggregates* policies, in addition to the default BGP policy, make up the policy chain applied to the BGP peers of Merlot. When we look at the currently applied policies, we find them to be rather simple:

```
[edit policy-options]
user@Merlot# show
policy-statement adv-statics {
    term statics {
        from protocol static;
        then accept;
    }
}
policy-statement adv-large-aggregates {
    term between-16-and-18 {
        from {
            protocol aggregate;
            route-filter 192.168.0.0/16 upto /18;
        }
        then accept;
    }
}
policy-statement adv-small-aggregates {
    term between-19-and-24 {
        from {
            protocol aggregate;
            route-filter 192.168.0.0/16 prefix-length-range /19-/24;
        }
        then accept;
    }
}
```

You could easily make an argument for just converting this policy chain into a single multi-term policy for the internal BGP (IBGP) peers. While this is certainly true, one of the advantages of a policy chain would be lost: the ability to reuse policies for different purposes.

Figure 1.1 displays the Merlot router with its IBGP peers of Muscat and Chablis. There are also external BGP (EBGP) connections to the Cabernet router in AS 65010 and the Zinfandel router in AS 65030. The current administrative policy within AS 65020 is to send the customer static routes only to other IBGP peers. Any EBGP peer providing transit service should only receive aggregate routes whose mask length is smaller than 18 bits. Any EBGP peer providing peering services should receive all customer routes and all aggregates whose mask length is larger than 19 bits. Each individual portion of these administrative policies is coded into a separate routing policy within the [edit policy-opitons] configuration hierarchy. They then provide the administrators of AS 65020 with a multitude of configuration options for advertising routes to its peers.

FIGURE 1.1   Policy chain network map

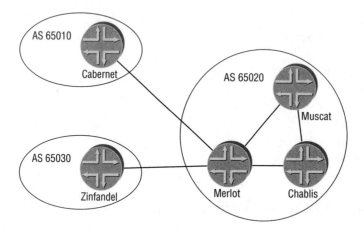

NOTE   Cabernet is providing transit service to AS 65020, which allows it to advertise their assigned routing space to the Internet at large. On the other hand, the peering service provided by Zinfandel allows AS 65020 to route traffic directly between the Autonomous Systems for all customer routes.

The EBGP peering sessions to Cabernet and Zinfandel are first configured and established:

```
[edit]
user@Merlot# show protocols bgp
group Internal-Peers {
    type internal;
    local-address 192.168.1.1;
    export [ adv-statics adv-large-aggregates adv-small-aggregates ];
    neighbor 192.168.2.2;
    neighbor 192.168.3.3;
```

```
}
group Ext-AS65010 {
    type external;
    peer-as 65010;
    neighbor 10.100.10.2;
}
group Ext-AS65030 {
    type external;
    peer-as 65030;
    neighbor 10.100.30.2;
}
```

```
[edit]
user@Merlot# run show bgp summary
Groups: 3 Peers: 4 Down peers: 0
Table           Tot Paths  Act Paths  Suppressed    History Damp State    Pending
inet.0               12         10          0           0          0            0
Peer            AS      InPkt    OutPkt    OutQ    Flaps Last Up/Dwn State
192.168.2.2     65020    170      172        0        0   1:22:50 5/6/0
192.168.3.3     65020    167      170        0        0   1:21:39 5/6/0
10.100.10.2     65010     30       32        0        0     12:57 0/0/0
10.100.30.2     65030     55       57        0        0     24:49 0/0/0
```

The **adv-large-aggregates** policy is applied to Cabernet to advertise the aggregate routes with a subnet mask length between 16 and 18 bits. After committing the configuration, we check the routes being sent to AS 65010:

```
[edit protovols bgp]
user@Merlot# set group Ext-AS65010 export adv-large-aggregates
```

```
[edit protovols bgp]
user@Merlot# commit
```

```
[edit protocols bgp]
user@Merlot# run show route advertising-protocol bgp 10.100.10.2
```

```
inet.0: 32 destinations, 36 routes (32 active, 0 holddown, 0 hidden)
Prefix                  Nexthop              MED     Lclpref     AS path
192.168.0.0/16          Self                                     I
192.168.2.0/24          Self                                     I
192.168.2.16/28         Self                                     I
192.168.2.32/28         Self                                     I
```

```
192.168.2.48/28            Self                                I
192.168.2.64/28            Self                                I
192.168.3.0/24             Self                                I
192.168.3.16/28            Self                                I
192.168.3.32/28            Self                                I
192.168.3.48/28            Self                                I
192.168.3.64/28            Self                                I
```

The 192.168.0.0 /16 aggregate route is being sent as per the administrative policy, but a number of other routes with larger subnet masks are also being sent to Cabernet. Let's first verify that we have the correct policy applied:

```
[edit protocols bgp]
user@Merlot# show group Ext-AS65010
type external;
export adv-large-aggregates;
peer-as 65010;
neighbor 10.100.10.2;
```

The **adv-large-aggregates** policy is correctly applied. Let's see if we can find where the other routes are coming from. The show route command provides a vital clue:

```
[edit]
user@Merlot# run show route 192.168.3.16/28


inet.0: 32 destinations, 36 routes (32 active, 0 holddown, 0 hidden)
+ = Active Route, - = Last Active, * = Both


192.168.3.16/28     *[BGP/170] 05:51:24, MED 0, localpref 100, from 192.168.3.3
                       AS path: I
                     > via so-0/1/1.0
```

Merlot has learned this route via its BGP session with Chablis. Since it is an active BGP route, it is automatically advertised by the BGP default policy. Remember that the default policy is always applied to the end of every policy chain in the JUNOS software. What we need is a policy to block the more specific routes from being advertised. We create a policy called **not-larger-than-18** that rejects all routes within the 192.168.0.0 /16 address space that have a subnet mask length greater than or equal to 19 bits. This ensures that all aggregates with a mask between 16 and 18 bits are advertised—exactly the goal of our administrative policy.

```
[edit policy-options]
user@Merlot# show policy-statement not-larger-than-18
term reject-greater-than-18-bits {
```

```
    from {
        route-filter 192.168.0.0/16 prefix-length-range /19-/32;
    }
    then reject;
}

[edit policy-options]
user@Merlot# top edit protocols bgp

[edit protocols bgp]
user@Merlot# set group Ext-AS65010 export not-larger-than-18

[edit protocols bgp]
user@Merlot# show group Ext-AS65010
type external;
export [ adv-large-aggregates not-larger-than-18 ];
peer-as 65010;
neighbor 10.100.10.2;

[edit protocols bgp]
user@Merlot# commit
commit complete

[edit protocols bgp]
user@Merlot# run show route advertising-protocol bgp 10.100.10.2

inet.0: 32 destinations, 36 routes (32 active, 0 holddown, 0 hidden)
Prefix                  Nexthop            MED    Lclpref   AS path
192.168.0.0/16          Self                                I
```

It appears as if our policy chain is working correctly—only the 192.168.0.0 /16 route is advertised to Cabernet. In fact, as long as the **not-larger-than-18** policy appears before the BGP default policy in our policy chain we achieve the desired results.

We now shift our focus to Zinfandel, our EBGP peer in AS 65030. Our administrative policy states that this peer should receive only aggregate routes larger than 18 bits in length and all customer routes. In anticipation of encountering a similar problem, we create a policy called **not-smaller-than-18** that rejects all aggregates with mask lengths between 16 and 18 bits. In addition, we apply the **adv-statics** and **adv-small-aggregates** policies to announce those particular routes to the peer:

```
[edit policy-options]
user@Merlot# show policy-statement not-smaller-than-18
```

```
term reject-less-than-18-bits {
    from {
        protocol aggregate;
        route-filter 192.168.0.0/16 upto /18;
    }
    then reject;
}
```

```
[edit policy-options]
user@Merlot# top edit protocols bgp
```

```
[edit protocols bgp]
user@Merlot# set group Ext-AS65030 export adv-small-aggregates
user@Merlot# set group Ext-AS65030 export adv-statics
user@Merlot# set group Ext-AS65030 export not-smaller-than-18
```

```
[edit protocols bgp]
user@Merlot# show group Ext-AS65030
type external;
export [ adv-small-aggregates adv-statics not-smaller-than-18 ];
peer-as 65030;
neighbor 10.100.30.2;
```

```
[edit protocols bgp]
user@Merlot# commit
commit complete
```

```
[edit protocols bgp]
user@Merlot# run show route advertising-protocol bgp 10.100.30.2
```

```
inet.0: 32 destinations, 36 routes (32 active, 0 holddown, 0 hidden)
```

Prefix	Nexthop	MED	Lclpref	AS path
192.168.1.0/24	Self			I
192.168.1.16/28	Self	0		I
192.168.1.32/28	Self	0		I
192.168.1.48/28	Self	0		I
192.168.1.64/28	Self	0		I
192.168.2.0/24	Self			I
192.168.2.16/28	Self			I
192.168.2.32/28	Self			I

192.168.2.48/28	Self	I
192.168.2.64/28	Self	I
192.168.3.0/24	Self	I
192.168.3.16/28	Self	I
192.168.3.32/28	Self	I
192.168.3.48/28	Self	I
192.168.3.64/28	Self	I
192.168.20.0/24	Self	0	I

It looks like this policy chain is working as designed as well. In fact, after configuring our individual policies, we can use them in any combination on the router. Another useful tool for reusing portions of your configuration is a policy subroutine, so let's investigate that concept next.

Policy Subroutines

The JUNOS software policy language is similar to a programming language. This similarity also includes the concept of nesting your policies into a *policy subroutine*. A subroutine in a software program is a section of code that you reference on a regular basis. A policy subroutine works in the same fashion—you reference an existing policy as a match criterion in another policy. The router first evaluates the subroutine and then finishes its processing of the main policy. Of course, there are some details that greatly affect the outcome of this evaluation.

First, the evaluation of the subroutine simply returns a true or false Boolean result to the main policy. Because you are referencing the subroutine as a match criterion, a true result means that the main policy has a match and can perform any configured actions. A false result from the subroutine, however, means that the main policy does not have a match. Let's configure a policy called *main-policy* that uses a subroutine:

```
[edit policy-options policy-statement main-policy]
user@Merlot# show
term subroutine-as-a-match {
    from policy subroutine-policy;
    then accept;
}
term nothing-else {
    then reject;
}
```

Of course, we can't commit our configuration since we reference a policy we haven't yet created. We create the *subroutine-policy* and check our work:

```
[edit policy-options policy-statement main-policy]
user@Merlot# commit
Policy error: Policy subroutine-policy referenced but not defined
```

```
error: configuration check-out failed

[edit policy-options policy-statement main-policy]
user@Merlot# up

[edit policy-options]
user@Merlot# edit policy-statement subroutine-policy

[edit policy-options policy-statement subroutine-policy]
user@Merlot# set term get-routes from protocol static
user@Merlot# set term get-routes then accept

[edit policy-options policy-statement subroutine-policy]
user@Merlot# show
term get-routes {
    from protocol static;
    then accept;
}

[edit policy-options policy-statement subroutine-policy]
user@Merlot# commit
commit complete
```

The router evaluates the logic of *main-policy* in a defined manner. The match criterion of from policy subroutine-policy allows the router to locate the subroutine. All terms of the subroutine are evaluated, in order, following the normal policy processing rules. In our example, all static routes in the routing table match the subroutine with an action of accept. This returns a true result to the original, or calling, policy which informs the router that a positive match has occurred. The actions in the calling policy are executed and the route is accepted. All other routes in the routing table do not match the subroutine and should logically return a false result to the calling policy. The router should evaluate the second term of *main-policy* and reject the routes.

Keep in mind that the actions in the subroutine do not actually accept or reject a specific route. They are only translated into a true or a false result. Actions that modify a route's attribute, however, are applied to the route regardless of the outcome of the subroutine.

Figure 1.2 shows AS 65020 now connected to the Chardonnay router in AS 65040. The policy subroutine of *main-policy* is applied as an export policy to Chardonnay. After establishing the BGP session, we verify that Merlot has static routes to send:

FIGURE 1.2   Policy subroutine network map

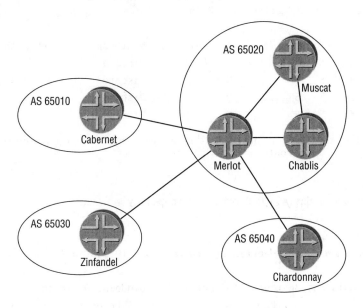

```
[edit]
user@Merlot# show protocols bgp group Ext-AS65040
type external;
peer-as 65040;
neighbor 10.100.40.2;

[edit]
user@Merlot# run show bgp summary
Groups: 4 Peers: 5 Down peers: 0
Table          Tot Paths  Act Paths Suppressed   History Damp State     Pending
inet.0               12        10          0         0    0     0           0
Peer             AS     InPkt    OutPkt    OutQ   Flaps Last Up/Dwn State
192.168.2.2    65020    2284      2285       0       0    19:00:15 5/6/0
192.168.3.3    65020    2275      2275       0       0    18:55:29 5/6/0
10.100.10.2    65010    2292      2294       0       0    19:03:50 0/0/0
10.100.30.2    65030    2293      2295       0       0    19:03:46 0/0/0
10.100.40.2    65040      23        25       0       0        9:01 0/0/0

[edit]
user@Merlot# run show route protocol static terse
```

```
inet.0: 33 destinations, 37 routes (33 active, 0 holddown, 0 hidden)
+ = Active Route, - = Last Active, * = Both
```

```
A Destination        P Prf  Metric 1  Metric 2  Next hop      AS path
* 192.168.1.16/28    S   5         0             Discard
* 192.168.1.32/28    S   5         0             Discard
* 192.168.1.48/28    S   5         0             Discard
* 192.168.1.64/28    S   5         0             Discard
```

After applying the policy subroutine to Chardonnay, we check to see if only four routes are sent to the EBGP peer:

```
[edit protocols bgp]
user@Merlot# set group Ext-AS65040 export main-policy
```

```
[edit]
user@Merlot# run show route advertising-protocol bgp 10.100.40.2
```

```
inet.0: 32 destinations, 36 routes (32 active, 0 holddown, 0 hidden)
Prefix                 Nexthop           MED      Lclpref   AS path
192.168.1.16/28        Self              0                  I
192.168.1.32/28        Self              0                  I
192.168.1.48/28        Self              0                  I
192.168.1.64/28        Self              0                  I
192.168.2.0/24         Self                                 I
192.168.2.16/28        Self                                 I
192.168.2.32/28        Self                                 I
192.168.2.48/28        Self                                 I
192.168.2.64/28        Self                                 I
192.168.3.0/24         Self                                 I
192.168.3.16/28        Self                                 I
192.168.3.32/28        Self                                 I
192.168.3.48/28        Self                                 I
192.168.3.64/28        Self                                 I
```

The four local static routes are being sent to Chardonnay, but additional routes are being advertised as well. Let's see if we can figure out where these routes are coming from:

```
[edit]
user@Merlot# run show route 192.168.2.16/28
```

```
inet.0: 32 destinations, 36 routes (32 active, 0 holddown, 0 hidden)
+ = Active Route, - = Last Active, * = Both
```

```
192.168.2.16/28    *[BGP/170] 19:06:01, MED 0, localpref 100, from 192.168.2.2
                     AS path: I
                   > via so-0/1/0.0
```

The 192.168.2.16/28 route is in the routing table as an IBGP-learned route from the Muscat router. We saw a similar problem in the "Policy Chains" section earlier in the chapter when the BGP default policy was advertising "extra" routes. The default policy is affecting the outcome in this case as well, but not in the way that you might think.

The currently applied policy chain for Chardonnay is **main-policy** followed by the BGP default policy. The terms of **main-policy** account for all routes with an explicit accept or reject action, so the BGP default policy is not evaluated as a part of the policy chain. It is being evaluated, however, as a part of the subroutine, which brings up the second important concept concerning a policy subroutine. The default policy of the protocol where the subroutine is applied is always evaluated as a part of the subroutine itself. In our case, the BGP default policy is evaluated along with **subroutine-policy** to determine a true or false result.

The actions of the default policy within the subroutine mean that you are actually evaluating a policy chain at all times. When you combine the BGP default policy with the terms of **subroutine-policy**, we end up with a subroutine that looks like the following:

```
policy-options {
    policy-statement subroutine-policy {
        term get-routes {
            from protocol static;
            then accept;
        }
        term BGP-default-policy-part-1 {
            from protocol bgp;
            then accept;
        }
        term BGP-default-policy-part-2 {
            then reject;
        }
    }
}
```

Using this new concept of a subroutine alters the logic evaluation of the subroutine. All static and BGP routes in the routing table return a true result to the calling policy while all other routes return a false result to the calling policy. This clearly explains the routes currently being advertised to Chardonnay. To achieve the result we desire, we need to eliminate the BGP default policy from being evaluated within the subroutine. This is easily accomplished by adding a new term to **subroutine-policy** as follows:

```
[edit policy-options policy-statement subroutine-policy]
user@Merlot# show
```

```
term get-routes {
    from protocol static;
    then accept;
}
term nothing-else {
    then reject;
}
```

When we check the results of this new subroutine, we see that only the local static routes are advertised to Chardonnay:

```
[edit]
user@Merlot# run show route advertising-protocol bgp 10.100.40.2
```

```
inet.0: 32 destinations, 36 routes (32 active, 0 holddown, 0 hidden)
Prefix                Nexthop              MED      Lclpref     AS path
192.168.1.16/28       Self                 0                    I
192.168.1.32/28       Self                 0                    I
192.168.1.48/28       Self                 0                    I
192.168.1.64/28       Self                 0                    I
```

Determining the Logic Result of a Subroutine

It is worth noting again that the configured actions within a subroutine do not in any way affect whether a particular route is advertised by the router. The subroutine actions are used only to determine the true or false result. To illustrate this point, assume that *main-policy* is applied as we saw in the "Policy Subroutines" section. In this instance, however, the policies are altered as so:

```
[edit policy-options]
user@Merlot# show policy-statement main-policy
term subroutine-as-a-match {
    from policy subroutine-policy;
    then accept;
}
```

```
[edit policy-options]
user@Merlot# show policy-statement subroutine-policy
term get-routes {
    from protocol static;
    then accept;
}
```

```
term no-BGP-routes {
    from protocol bgp;
    then reject;
}
```

We are now aware of the protocol default policy being evaluated within the subroutine, so *subroutine-policy* now has an explicit term rejecting all BGP routes. Because they are rejected within the subroutine, there is no need within *main-policy* for an explicit then reject term. You may already see the flaw in this configuration, but let's follow the logic.

The router evaluates the first term of *main-policy* and finds a match criterion of from policy subroutine-policy. It then evaluates the first term of the subroutine and finds that all static routes have an action of then accept. This returns a true result to *main-policy*, where the *subroutine-as-a-match* term has a configured action of then accept. The static routes are now truly accepted and are advertised to the EBGP peer.

When it comes to the BGP routes in the routing table, things occur a bit differently. When the router enters the subroutine, it finds the *no-BGP-routes* term where all BGP routes are rejected. This returns a false result to *main-policy*, which means that the criterion in the *subroutine-as-a-match* term doesn't match. This causes the routes to move to the next configured term in *main-policy*, which has no other terms. The router then evaluates the next policy in the policy chain—the BGP default policy. The default policy, of course, accepts all BGP routes, and they are advertised to the EBGP peer. We can prove this logic with a show route command on Merlot:

```
user@Merlot> show route advertising-protocol bgp 10.100.40.2

inet.0: 32 destinations, 36 routes (32 active, 0 holddown, 0 hidden)
  Prefix                Nexthop         MED     Lclpref    AS path
  192.168.1.16/28       Self            0                  I
  192.168.1.32/28       Self            0                  I
  192.168.1.48/28       Self            0                  I
  192.168.1.64/28       Self            0                  I
  192.168.2.0/24        Self                               I
  192.168.2.16/28       Self                               I
  192.168.2.32/28       Self                               I
  192.168.2.48/28       Self                               I
  192.168.2.64/28       Self                               I
  192.168.3.0/24        Self                               I
  192.168.3.16/28       Self                               I
  192.168.3.32/28       Self                               I
  192.168.3.48/28       Self                               I
  192.168.3.64/28       Self                               I
```

Prefix Lists

The use of the policy subroutine in the previous section was one method of advertising a set of routes by configuring a single section of code. The JUNOS software provides other methods of accomplishing the same task, and a *prefix list* is one of them. A prefix list is a listing of IP prefixes that represent a set of routes that are used as match criteria in an applied policy. Such a list might be useful for representing a list of customer routes in your AS.

A prefix list is given a name and is configured within the [`edit policy-options`] configuration hierarchy. Using Figure 1.2 as a guide, each router in AS 65020 has customer routes that fall into the 24-bit subnet defined by their loopback address. This means that Merlot, whose loopback address is 192.168.1.1 /32, assigns customer routes within the 192.168.1.0 /24 subnet. The Muscat and Chablis routers assign customer routes within the 192.168.2.0 /24 and 192.168.3.0 /24 subnets, respectively.

Merlot has been designated the central point in AS 65020 to maintain a complete list of customer routes. It configures a prefix list called **all-customers** as so:

```
[edit]
user@Merlot# show policy-options prefix-list all-customers
192.168.1.16/28;
192.168.1.32/28;
192.168.1.48/28;
192.168.1.64/28;
192.168.2.16/28;
192.168.2.32/28;
192.168.2.48/28;
192.168.2.64/28;
192.168.3.16/28;
192.168.3.32/28;
192.168.3.48/28;
192.168.3.64/28;
```

As you look closely at the prefix list you see that there are no match types configured with each of the routes (as you might see with a route filter). This is an important point when using a prefix list in a policy. The JUNOS software evaluates each address in the prefix list as an exact route filter match. In other words, each route in the list must appear in the routing table exactly as it is configured in the prefix list. You reference the prefix list as a match criterion within a policy like this:

```
[edit]
user@Merlot# show policy-options policy-statement customer-routes
term get-routes {
```

```
    from {
        prefix-list all-customers;
    }
    then accept;
}
term nothing-else {
    then reject;
}
```

All the routes in the ***all-customers*** prefix list appear in the current routing table:

```
[edit]
user@Merlot# run show route 192.168/16 terse
```

```
inet.0: 32 destinations, 36 routes (32 active, 0 holddown, 0 hidden)
+ = Active Route, - = Last Active, * = Both
```

A	Destination	P	Prf	Metric 1	Metric 2	Next hop	AS path
*	192.168.0.0/16	A	130			Reject	
		B	170	100		>so-0/1/0.0	I
		B	170	100		>so-0/1/1.0	I
*	192.168.1.0/24	A	130			Reject	
*	192.168.1.1/32	D	0			>lo0.0	
*	192.168.1.16/28	S	5	0		Discard	
*	192.168.1.32/28	S	5	0		Discard	
*	192.168.1.48/28	S	5	0		Discard	
*	192.168.1.64/28	S	5	0		Discard	
*	192.168.2.0/24	B	170	100		>so-0/1/0.0	I
*	192.168.2.2/32	O	10	1		>so-0/1/0.0	
*	192.168.2.16/28	B	170	100	0	>so-0/1/0.0	I
*	192.168.2.32/28	B	170	100	0	>so-0/1/0.0	I
*	192.168.2.48/28	B	170	100	0	>so-0/1/0.0	I
*	192.168.2.64/28	B	170	100	0	>so-0/1/0.0	I
*	192.168.3.0/24	B	170	100		>so-0/1/1.0	I
*	192.168.3.3/32	O	10	1		>so-0/1/1.0	
*	192.168.3.16/28	B	170	100	0	>so-0/1/1.0	I
*	192.168.3.32/28	B	170	100	0	>so-0/1/1.0	I
*	192.168.3.48/28	B	170	100	0	>so-0/1/1.0	I
*	192.168.3.64/28	B	170	100	0	>so-0/1/1.0	I

After applying the ***customer-routes*** policy to the EBGP peer of Zinfandel, as seen in Figure 1.2, we see that only the customer routes are advertised:

```
[edit protocols bgp]
user@Merlot# show group Ext-AS65030
type external;
export customer-routes;
peer-as 65030;
neighbor 10.100.30.2;

[edit protocols bgp]
user@Merlot# run show route advertising-protocol bgp 10.100.30.2

inet.0: 32 destinations, 36 routes (32 active, 0 holddown, 0 hidden)
Prefix                Nexthop            MED      Lclpref    AS path
192.168.1.16/28       Self               0                   I
192.168.1.32/28       Self               0                   I
192.168.1.48/28       Self               0                   I
192.168.1.64/28       Self               0                   I
192.168.2.16/28       Self                                   I
192.168.2.32/28       Self                                   I
192.168.2.48/28       Self                                   I
192.168.2.64/28       Self                                   I
192.168.3.16/28       Self                                   I
192.168.3.32/28       Self                                   I
192.168.3.48/28       Self                                   I
192.168.3.64/28       Self                                   I
```

Policy Expressions

In the "Policy Subroutines" section earlier in the chapter, we compared the JUNOS software policy language to a programming language. This comparison also holds true when we discuss a *policy expression*. A policy expression within the JUNOS software is the combination of individual policies together with a set of logical operators. This expression is applied as a portion of the policy chain. To fully explain how the router uses a policy expression, we need to discuss the logical operators themselves as well as the evaluation logic when each operator is used. Then, we look at some examples of policy expressions in a sample network environment.

Logical Operators

You can use four logical operators in conjunction with a policy expression. In order of precedence, they are a logical NOT, a logical AND, a logical OR, and a group operator. You can think of the precedence order as being similar to arithmetic, where multiplication is performed before addition. In the case of the logical operators, a NOT is performed before an OR. Let's look at the function of each logical operator, as well as an example syntax:

Logical NOT   The *logical NOT* (!) reverses the normal logic evaluation of a policy. A true result becomes a false and a false result becomes a true. This is encoded in the JUNOS software as `!policy-name`.

Logical AND   The *logical AND* (&&) operates on two routing policies. Should the result of the first policy be a true result, then the next policy is evaluated. However, if the result of the first policy is a false result, then the second policy is skipped. This appears as `policy-1 && policy-2`.

Logical OR   The *logical OR* (||) also operates on two routing policies. It skips the second policy when the first policy returns a true result. A false result from the first policy results in the second policy being evaluated. This appears as `policy-1 || policy-2`.

Group operator   The *group operator*, represented by a set of parentheses, is used to override the default precedence order of the other logical operators. For example, a group operator is useful when you want to logically OR two policies and then AND the result with a third policy. The JUNOS software views this as `(policy-1 || policy-2) && policy-3`.

WARNING   When parentheses are not used to group policy names, such as `policy-1 || policy-2 && policy-3`, the JUNOS software evaluates the expression using the default precedence order. This order requires all logical NOT operations to be performed first, then all logical AND operations, and finally all logical OR operations. For clarity, we recommend using group operators when more than two policies are included in an expression.

Logical Evaluation

When the router encounters a policy expression, it must perform two separate steps. The logical evaluation is calculated first, followed by some actual action on the route. In this respect, the policy expression logic is similar to a policy subroutine. The two are very different, however, when it comes to using the protocol default policy. Because the policy expression occupies a single place in the normal policy chain, the protocol default policy is not evaluated within the expression. It is evaluated only as a part of the normal policy chain applied to the protocol.

When the router evaluates the individual policies of an expression, it determines whether the policy returns a true or false result. A true result is found when either the `accept` or `next policy` action is found. The `next policy` action is either encountered by its explicit configuration within the policy or when the route does not match any terms in the policy. A logical false result is encountered when the `reject` action is encountered within the policy.

After determining the logical result of the expression, the router performs some action on the route. This action results from the policy that guaranteed the logical result. This might sound a bit confusing, so let's look at some examples to solidify the concept.

OR Operations

The normal rules of OR logic means that when either of the policies returns a true value, then the entire expression is true. When configured as `policy-1 || policy-2`, the router first evaluates `policy-1`. If the result of this policy is a true value, then the entire expression becomes true as per the OR evaluation rules. In this case, `policy-2` is not evaluated by the router. The route being evaluated through the expression has the action defined in `policy-1` applied to it since `policy-1` guaranteed the result of the entire expression.

Should the evaluation of `policy-1` return a false result, then `policy-2` is evaluated. If the result of `policy-2` is true, the entire expression is true. Should the evaluation of `policy-2` result in a false, the entire expression becomes false as well. In either case, `policy-2` has guaranteed the result of the entire expression. Therefore, the action in `policy-2` is applied to the route being evaluated through the expression.

AND Operations

The rules of AND logic states that both of the policies must return a true value to make the entire expression true. If either of the policies returns a false value, then the entire expression becomes false. The configuration of `policy-1 && policy-2` results in the router first evaluating `policy-1`. If the result of this policy is true, then `policy-2` is evaluated since the entire expression is not yet guaranteed. Only when the result of `policy-2` is true does the expression become true. Should the evaluation of `policy-2` return a false, the entire expression then becomes false. Regardless, `policy-2` guarantees the result of the entire expression and the action in `policy-2` is applied to the route being evaluated.

Should the evaluation of `policy-1` return a false result, then the expression is guaranteed to have a false result since both policies are not true. In this case, the action in `policy-1` is applied to the route.

NOT Operations

The operation of a logical NOT is performed only on a single policy. When the result of a NOT evaluation is true, the router transforms that into a false evaluation. This false result tells the router to reject the route being evaluated. The exact opposite occurs when the NOT evaluation is false. The router transforms the false into a true result and accepts the route being evaluated.

An Example of Expressions

A policy expression in the JUNOS software occupies a single position in a protocol's policy chain, so the protocol in use is an important factor in determining the outcome of the expression. We'll use BGP as our protocol using the information in Figure 1.3.

The Merlot router in AS 65020 is peering both with its internal peers of Muscat and Chablis and with the Cabernet router in AS 65010. The customer routes within the subnets of 192.168.2.0 /24 and 192.168.3.0 /24 are being advertised from Muscat and Chablis, respectively. Two policies are configured on Merlot to locate these routes:

FIGURE 1.3   Policy expression network map

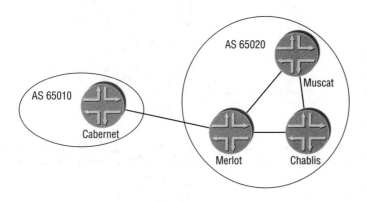

```
[edit policy-options]
user@Merlot# show policy-statement Muscat-routes
term find-routes {
    from {
        route-filter 192.168.2.0/24 longer;
    }
    then accept;
}
term nothing-else {
    then reject;
}

[edit policy-options]
user@Merlot# show policy-statement Chablis-routes
term find-routes {
    from {
        route-filter 192.168.3.0/24 longer;
    }
    then accept;
}
```

By default, the BGP policy advertises the customer routes to Cabernet:

```
[edit]
user@Merlot# run show route advertising-protocol bgp 10.100.10.2

inet.0: 30 destinations, 32 routes (30 active, 0 holddown, 0 hidden)
Prefix                  Nexthop              MED     Lclpref    AS path
192.168.2.16/28         Self                                    I
```

```
192.168.2.32/28          Self                                    I
192.168.2.48/28          Self                                    I
192.168.2.64/28          Self                                    I
192.168.3.16/28          Self                                    I
192.168.3.32/28          Self                                    I
192.168.3.48/28          Self                                    I
192.168.3.64/28          Self                                    I
```

An OR Example

A logical OR policy expression is configured on the Merlot router. This means that the policy chain applied to Cabernet becomes the expression followed by the default BGP policy:

```
[edit protocols bgp]
lab@Merlot# show group Ext-AS65010
type external;
export ( Muscat-routes || Chablis-routes );
peer-as 65010;
neighbor 10.100.10.2;
```

To illustrate the operation of the expression, we select a route from each neighbor. Merlot evaluates the 192.168.2.16 /28 route against the ***Muscat-routes*** policy first. The route matches the criteria in the ***find-routes*** term, where the action is accept. This means that the first policy is a true result and the entire logical OR expression is also true. The configured action of accept in the ***Muscat-routes*** policy is applied to the route and it is sent to Cabernet. We can verify this with the show route command:

```
user@Merlot> show route advertising-protocol bgp 10.100.10.2 192.168.2.16/28

inet.0: 30 destinations, 32 routes (30 active, 0 holddown, 0 hidden)
Prefix                   Nexthop              MED      Lclpref      AS path
192.168.2.16/28          Self                                       I
```

The 192.168.3.16 /28 route is selected from the Chablis router. As before, Merlot evaluates the ***Muscat-routes*** policy first. This route matches the ***nothing-else*** term and returns a false result to the expression. Because the expression result is not guaranteed yet, Merlot evaluates the ***Chablis-routes*** policy. The route matches the ***find-routes*** term in that policy and returns a true result to the expression. The ***Chablis-routes*** policy guaranteed the expression result, so the action of accept from that policy is applied to the route. Again, we verify that the route is sent to Cabernet:

```
user@Merlot> show route advertising-protocol bgp 10.100.10.2 192.168.3.16/28

inet.0: 30 destinations, 32 routes (30 active, 0 holddown, 0 hidden)
Prefix                   Nexthop              MED      Lclpref      AS path
192.168.3.16/28          Self                                       I
```

An AND Example

Using the same sample routes and policies, we can explore a logical AND policy expression on the Merlot router. Again, the expression occupies a single slot in the policy chain:

```
[edit protocols bgp]
lab@Merlot# show group Ext-AS65010
type external;
export ( Muscat-routes && Chablis-routes );
peer-as 65010;
neighbor 10.100.10.2;
```

Merlot first evaluates the 192.168.2.16 /28 route against the ***Muscat-routes*** policy. The route matches the criteria in the ***find-routes*** term and returns a true result to the policy expression. The expression result is not guaranteed, so the ***Chablis-routes*** policy is evaluated. The route doesn't match any terms in this policy, which means that the implicit next policy action is used. This action is interpreted by the expression as a true result. The expression itself is true, as both policies in the expression are true. The ***Chablis-routes*** policy guaranteed the expression result, so its action is applied to the route. The action was next policy, so Merlot takes the 192.168.2.16 /28 route and evaluates it against the next policy in the policy chain— the BGP default policy. The BGP default policy accepts all BGP routes, so the route is advertised to Cabernet:

```
user@Merlot> show route advertising-protocol bgp 10.100.10.2 192.168.2.16/28

inet.0: 30 destinations, 32 routes (30 active, 0 holddown, 0 hidden)
Prefix                  Nexthop          MED    Lclpref    AS path
192.168.2.16/28         Self                               I
```

The evaluation of the 192.168.3.16 /28 route returns a different result. Merlot evaluates the ***Muscat-routes*** policy first, where the route matches the ***nothing-else*** term. This returns a false result to the expression and guarantees a result of false for the entire expression. Since the ***Muscat-routes*** policy guaranteed the result, its action of reject is applied to the route and it is not advertised to Cabernet:

```
user@Merlot> show route advertising-protocol bgp 10.100.10.2 192.168.3.16/28


user@Merlot>
```

A NOT Example

The evaluation and use of the logical NOT operator is a little more straightforward than the OR and AND operators. As such, we apply only a single policy to the Merlot router:

```
[edit protocols bgp]
lab@Merlot# show group Ext-AS65010
```

```
type external;
export ( ! Muscat-routes );
peer-as 65010;
neighbor 10.100.10.2;
```

Merlot evaluates the 192.168.2.16 /28 route against the ***Muscat-routes*** policy, where it matches the ***find-routes*** term and returns a true result. The NOT operator converts this result to a false and applies the `reject` action to the route. It is not advertised to the Cabernet router:

user@Merlot> **show route advertising-protocol bgp 10.100.10.2 192.168.2.16/28**

user@Merlot>

The 192.168.3.16 /28 route is evaluated by Merlot against the ***Muscat-routes*** policy, where it matches the ***nothing-else*** term. This return of a false result by the policy is converted into a true result by the NOT operator. The true evaluation implies that the `accept` action is applied to the route and it is advertised to Cabernet:

user@Merlot> **show route advertising-protocol bgp 10.100.10.2 192.168.3.16/28**

```
inet.0: 30 destinations, 32 routes (30 active, 0 holddown, 0 hidden)
Prefix                   Nexthop           MED      Lclpref    AS path
192.168.3.16/28          Self                                  I
```

A Group Example

The purpose of the logical group operator is to override the default precedence of the OR and AND operators. We can see the functionality of this operator within the network of Figure 1.3. The administrators of AS 65020 would like to advertise only certain customer routes to the EBGP peer of Cabernet. These routes are designated by the BGP community value of ***adv-to-peers*** attached to the route. We can see these routes in the local routing table:

user@Merlot> **show route terse community-name adv-to-peers**

```
inet.0: 30 destinations, 32 routes (30 active, 0 holddown, 0 hidden)
+ = Active Route, - = Last Active, * = Both
```

A	Destination	P	Prf	Metric 1	Metric 2	Next hop	AS path
*	192.168.2.48/28	B	170	100	0	>so-0/1/0.0	I
*	192.168.2.64/28	B	170	100	0	>so-0/1/0.0	I
*	192.168.3.48/28	B	170	100	0	>so-0/1/1.0	I
*	192.168.3.64/28	B	170	100	0	>so-0/1/1.0	I

 We discuss the definition and use of communities within a policy in more detail in the "Communities" section later in this chapter.

Both *Muscat-routes* and *Chablis-routes* now guarantee a true or false result within the policy through the use of the *nothing-else* term. We've also created a policy called *Check-for-Community* to look for the *adv-to-peers* community value.

```
[edit policy-options]
user@Merlot# show policy-statement Muscat-routes
term find-routes {
    from {
        route-filter 192.168.2.0/24 longer;
    }
    then accept;
}
term nothing-else {
    then reject;
}


[edit policy-options]
user@Merlot# show policy-statement Chablis-routes
term find-routes {
    from {
        route-filter 192.168.3.0/24 longer;
    }
    then accept;
}
term nothing-else {
    then reject;
}


[edit policy-options]
user@Merlot# show policy-statement Check-for-Community
term find-routes {
    from community adv-to-peers;
    then accept;
}
term nothing-else {
    then reject;
}
```

In human terms, we want to advertise only routes that match either the *Muscat-routes* or the *Chablis-routes* policy as well as the *Check-for-Community* policy. To illustrate the usefulness of the group operator, we first apply the policies using just the OR and AND operators to create a single policy expression (that also occupies a single policy chain spot):

```
[edit protocols bgp group Ext-AS65010]
lab@Merlot# show
type external;
export ( Muscat-routes || Chablis-routes && Check-for-Community );
peer-as 65010;
neighbor 10.100.10.2;
```

If we assume that our thought process is correct, then the 192.168.2.64 /28 route from the Muscat router should be advertised to Cabernet by Merlot. Because the AND operator has precedence over the OR operator, the *Chablis-routes* and *Check-for-Community* policies are evaluated together first. The route doesn't match the *Chablis-routes* policy and returns a false result. This guarantees the result of the expression itself, so the action of reject from that policy is applied to the route and it is not advertised to Cabernet:

```
user@Merlot> show route advertising-protocol bgp 10.100.10.2 192.168.2.64/28

user@Merlot>
```

This is clearly not the result we intended, so it appears that the group operator has some usefulness after all! Let's alter the policy expression on Merlot:

```
[edit protocols bgp group Ext-AS65010]
lab@Merlot# show
type external;
export (( Muscat-routes || Chablis-routes ) && Check-for-Community );
peer-as 65010;
neighbor 10.100.10.2;
```

The group operator now causes Merlot to evaluate the *Muscat-routes* and *Chablis-routes* policies together before evaluating the *Check-for-Community* policy. Using the same 192.168.2.64 /28 route, Merlot evaluates the *Muscat-routes* policy and gets a true result. This guarantees a true result for the first portion of the expression, so the *Chablis-routes* policy is skipped and Merlot evaluates the *Check-for-Community* policy. This policy also returns a true result based on the *find-routes* term, because the route does indeed have the community attached. The *Check-for-Community* policy guaranteed the result of the expression, so its action of accept is applied to the route and it is advertised to the Cabernet router:

```
user@Merlot> show route advertising-protocol bgp 10.100.10.2 192.168.2.64/28

inet.0: 30 destinations, 32 routes (30 active, 0 holddown, 0 hidden)
Prefix                  Nexthop             MED     Lclpref     AS path
192.168.2.64/28         Self                                    I
```

The logic of the group operator applies to all of the routes in the local routing table of Merlot. Only the four routes with the correct community value of ***adv-to-peers*** attached are advertised to Cabernet:

```
user@Merlot> show route advertising-protocol bgp 10.100.10.2

inet.0: 30 destinations, 32 routes (30 active, 0 holddown, 0 hidden)
Prefix                  Nexthop              MED    Lclpref    AS path
192.168.2.48/28         Self                                    I
192.168.2.64/28         Self                                    I
192.168.3.48/28         Self                                    I
192.168.3.64/28         Self                                    I
```

Communities

A *community* is a route attribute used by BGP to administratively group routes with similar properties. We won't be discussing how to use communities in conjunction with BGP in this chapter; we cover these details in Chapter 4, "Border Gateway Protocol." Here we explore how to define a community, apply or delete a community value, and locate a route using a defined community name.

Regular Communities

A community value is a 32-bit field that is divided into two main sections. The first 16 bits of the value encode the AS number of the network that originated the community, while the last 16 bits carry a unique number assigned by the AS. This system attempts to guarantee a globally unique set of community values for each AS in the Internet.

The JUNOS software uses a notation of `AS-number:community-value`, where each value is a decimal number. The AS values of 0 and 65,535 are reserved, as are all of the community values within those AS numbers. Each community, or set of communities, is given a name within the `[edit policy-options]` configuration hierarchy. The name of the community uniquely identifies it to the router and serves as the method by which routes are categorized. For example, a route with a community value of 65010:1111 might belong to the community named ***AS65010-routes***, once it is configured. The community name is also used within a routing policy as a match criterion or as an action. The command syntax for creating a community is:

```
policy-options {
    community name members [community-ids];
}
```

The *community-ids* field is either a single community value or multiple community values. When more than one value is assigned to a community name, the router interprets this as a logical AND of the community values. In other words, a route must have all of the configured values before being assigned the community name.

FIGURE 1.4   Communities sample network

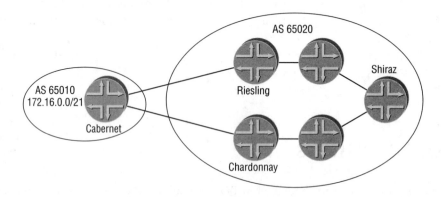

Figure 1.4 shows the Riesling, Chardonnay, and Shiraz routers as IBGP peers in AS 65020. The Cabernet router is advertising the 172.16.0.0 /21 address space from AS 65010. The specific routes received by Riesling include:

```
user@Riesling> show route receive-protocol bgp 10.100.10.1
```

```
inet.0: 28 destinations, 36 routes (28 active, 0 holddown, 0 hidden)
Prefix                  Nexthop           MED     Lclpref     AS path
172.16.0.0/24           10.100.10.1       0                   65010 I
172.16.1.0/24           10.100.10.1       0                   65010 I
172.16.2.0/24           10.100.10.1       0                   65010 I
172.16.3.0/24           10.100.10.1       0                   65010 I
172.16.4.0/24           10.100.10.1       0                   65010 I
172.16.5.0/24           10.100.10.1       0                   65010 I
172.16.6.0/24           10.100.10.1       0                   65010 I
172.16.7.0/24           10.100.10.1       0                   65010 I
```

You view the community values attached to each route, if there are any, by adding the detail option to the show route command:

```
user@Riesling> show route receive-protocol bgp 10.100.10.1 detail
```

```
inet.0: 28 destinations, 36 routes (28 active, 0 holddown, 0 hidden)
172.16.0.0/24 (2 entries, 1 announced)
```

```
    Nexthop: 10.100.10.1
    MED: 0
    AS path: 65010 I
Communities: 65010:1111 65010:1234


172.16.1.0/24 (2 entries, 1 announced)
    Nexthop: 10.100.10.1
    MED: 0
    AS path: 65010 I
Communities: 65010:1111 65010:1234


172.16.2.0/24 (2 entries, 1 announced)
    Nexthop: 10.100.10.1
    MED: 0
    AS path: 65010 I
Communities: 65010:1234 65010:2222


172.16.3.0/24 (2 entries, 1 announced)
    Nexthop: 10.100.10.1
    MED: 0
    AS path: 65010 I
Communities: 65010:1234 65010:2222


172.16.4.0/24 (2 entries, 1 announced)
    Nexthop: 10.100.10.1
    MED: 0
    AS path: 65010 I
Communities: 65010:3333 65010:4321


172.16.5.0/24 (2 entries, 1 announced)
    Nexthop: 10.100.10.1
    MED: 0
    AS path: 65010 I
Communities: 65010:3333 65010:4321


172.16.6.0/24 (2 entries, 1 announced)
    Nexthop: 10.100.10.1
    MED: 0
    AS path: 65010 I
Communities: 65010:4321 65010:4444
```

```
172.16.7.0/24 (2 entries, 1 announced)
     Nexthop: 10.100.10.1
     MED: 0
     AS path: 65010 I
 Communities: 65010:4321 65010:4444
```

Match Criteria Usage

The administrators of AS 65010 attached a community value of 65010:1234 to all routes for which they would like to receive user traffic from Riesling. The community value of 65010:4321 is attached to routes for which AS 65010 would like to receive user traffic from Chardonnay. Routing policies within AS 65020 are configured using a community match criterion to effect this administrative goal. The policies change the Local Preference of the received routes to new values that alter the BGP route-selection algorithm. The policies and communities on Riesling look like this:

```
[edit]
user@Riesling# show policy-options
policy-statement alter-local-preference {
    term find-Riesling-routes {
        from community out-via-Riesling;
        then {
            local-preference 200;
        }
    }
    term find-Chardonay-routes {
        from community out-via-Chardonnay;
        then {
            local-preference 50;
        }
    }
}
community out-via-Chardonnay members 65010:4321;
community out-via-Riesling members 65010:1234;
```

A similar policy is configured on Chardonnay with the Local Preference values reversed. The policy on Riesling is applied as an import policy to alter the attributes as they are received from Cabernet:

```
[edit protocols bgp]
user@Riesling# show group Ext-AS65010
type external;
import alter-local-preference;
peer-as 65010;
neighbor 10.100.10.1;
```

We check the success of the policy on the Shiraz router. The 172.16.0.0 /24 route should use the advertisement from Riesling (192.168.1.1), while the 172.16.4.0 /24 route should use the advertisement from Chardonnay (192.168.3.3):

```
user@Shiraz> show route 172.16.0/24

inet.0: 28 destinations, 31 routes (28 active, 0 holddown, 0 hidden)
+ = Active Route, - = Last Active, * = Both

172.16.0.0/24      *[BGP/170] 00:08:30, MED 0, localpref 200, from 192.168.1.1
                      AS path: 65010 I
                    > via so-0/1/0.0

user@Shiraz> show route 172.16.4/24

inet.0: 28 destinations, 31 routes (28 active, 0 holddown, 0 hidden)
+ = Active Route, - = Last Active, * = Both

172.16.4.0/24      *[BGP/170] 00:04:58, MED 0, localpref 200, from 192.168.3.3
                      AS path: 65010 I
                    > via so-0/1/1.0
```

It appears the policies are working as designed. We've successfully located the BGP routes using a single community value in the ***alter-local-preference*** policies. The JUNOS software also allows you to locate routes containing multiple community values. One method of accomplishing this is to create two community names and reference those names in your routing policies. Or, you create a single community name with both values and reference that single name in the policy. Let's see how these two options work on the Shiraz router.

The administrators of AS 65020 decide that they would like to reject all routes on Shiraz containing both the 65010:4321 and 65010:4444 community values. We first create three separate community names: one each for the single values and one for the combined values.

```
[edit policy-options]
user@Shiraz# show
community both-comms members [ 65010:4321 65010:4444 ];
community just-4321 members 65010:4321;
community just-4444 members 65010:4444;
```

We locate the current routes in the routing table that have these values by using the `community` or `community-name` options of the `show route` command. The `community` option allows you to enter a numerical community value and the router outputs all routes containing that value.

```
user@Shiraz> show route terse community 65010:4321

inet.0: 28 destinations, 31 routes (28 active, 0 holddown, 0 hidden)
```

```
+ = Active Route, - = Last Active, * = Both

A Destination          P Prf   Metric 1   Metric 2  Next hop       AS path
* 172.16.4.0/24        B 170      200            0 >so-0/1/1.0     65010 I
* 172.16.5.0/24        B 170      200            0 >so-0/1/1.0     65010 I
* 172.16.6.0/24        B 170      200            0 >so-0/1/1.0     65010 I
* 172.16.7.0/24        B 170      200            0 >so-0/1/1.0     65010 I
```

user@Shiraz> **show route terse community 65010:4444**

```
inet.0: 28 destinations, 31 routes (28 active, 0 holddown, 0 hidden)
+ = Active Route, - = Last Active, * = Both

A Destination          P Prf   Metric 1   Metric 2  Next hop       AS path
* 172.16.6.0/24        B 170      200            0 >so-0/1/1.0     65010 I
* 172.16.7.0/24        B 170      200            0 >so-0/1/1.0     65010 I
```

It appears that the 172.16.6.0 /24 and 172.16.7.0 /24 routes have both community values attached to them. We can confirm this with the `show route detail` command to view the actual values, but we have another method at our disposal. The `community-name` option allows you to specify a configured name and have the router output the routes matching that community value. The ***both-comms*** community is configured with multiple members so that only routes currently containing both community values match this community name.

user@Shiraz> **show route terse community-name both-comms**

```
inet.0: 28 destinations, 31 routes (28 active, 0 holddown, 0 hidden)
+ = Active Route, - = Last Active, * = Both

A Destination          P Prf   Metric 1   Metric 2  Next hop       AS path
* 172.16.6.0/24        B 170      200            0 >so-0/1/1.0     65010 I
* 172.16.7.0/24        B 170      200            0 >so-0/1/1.0     65010 I
```

We create two different policies on Shiraz and apply them separately as an import policy for the IBGP peer group. The first policy uses the single community match criteria of ***both-comms***:

```
[edit policy-options]
user@Shiraz# show
policy-statement single-comm-match {
    term use-just-one-comm {
        from community both-comms;
        then reject;
    }
}
```

```
}
community both-comms members [ 65010:4321 65010:4444 ];
community just-4321 members 65010:4321;
community just-4444 members 65010:4444;

[edit protocols bgp]
user@Shiraz# set group Internal-Peers import single-comm-match

[edit]
user@Shiraz# commit and-quit
commit complete
Exiting configuration mode

user@Shiraz> show route 172.16.5/24

inet.0: 28 destinations, 31 routes (26 active, 0 holddown, 2 hidden)
+ = Active Route, - = Last Active, * = Both

172.16.5.0/24        *[BGP/170] 01:27:54, MED 0, localpref 200, from 192.168.3.3
                        AS path: 65010 I
                     > via so-0/1/1.0

user@Shiraz> show route 172.16.6/24

inet.0: 28 destinations, 31 routes (26 active, 0 holddown, 2 hidden)

user@Shiraz> show route 172.16.7/24

inet.0: 28 destinations, 31 routes (26 active, 0 holddown, 2 hidden)

user@Shiraz>
```

The routes are no longer in the inet.0 routing table on Shiraz. The logical AND within the community definition correctly located only the routes containing both community values. We now create a second policy, called ***double-comm-match***, using the individual community names:

```
[edit policy-options policy-statement double-comm-match]
user@Shiraz# show
term two-comms {
    from community [ just-4321 just-4444 ];
    then reject;
}
```

```
[edit policy-options policy-statement double-comm-match]
user@Shiraz# top edit protocols bgp

[edit protocols bgp]
user@Shiraz# show group Internal-Peers
type internal;
local-address 192.168.7.7;
import double-comm-match;
neighbor 192.168.1.1;
neighbor 192.168.2.2;
neighbor 192.168.3.3;
neighbor 192.168.4.4;
neighbor 192.168.5.5;
neighbor 192.168.6.6;
```

After committing our configuration, we check the success of our new policy:

```
user@Shiraz> show route 172.16.5/24

inet.0: 28 destinations, 31 routes (24 active, 0 holddown, 4 hidden)

user@Shiraz> show route 172.16.6/24

inet.0: 28 destinations, 31 routes (24 active, 0 holddown, 4 hidden)

user@Shiraz> show route 172.16.7/24

inet.0: 28 destinations, 31 routes (24 active, 0 holddown, 4 hidden)
```

As you can see, something isn't right. The 172.16.5.0 /24 route should be active in the routing table, but it is not there. In addition, we now have four hidden routes whereas we had only two hidden routes using the *single-comm-match* policy. Let's see what routes are now hidden:

```
user@Shiraz> show route terse hidden

inet.0: 28 destinations, 31 routes (24 active, 0 holddown, 4 hidden)
+ = Active Route, - = Last Active, * = Both
```

A	Destination	P	Prf	Metric 1	Metric 2	Next hop	AS path
	172.16.4.0/24	B		200		0 >so-0/1/1.0	65010 I
	172.16.5.0/24	B		200		0 >so-0/1/1.0	65010 I

```
172.16.6.0/24        B          200         0 >so-0/1/1.0       65010 I
172.16.7.0/24        B          200         0 >so-0/1/1.0       65010 I
```

Something in the ***double-comm-match*** policy is rejecting more routes than we would like. The policy currently is configured like this:

```
user@Shiraz> show configuration policy-options
policy-statement single-comm-match {
    term use-just-one-comm {
        from community both-comms;
        then reject;
    }
}
policy-statement double-comm-match {
    term two-comms {
        from community [ just-4321 just-4444 ];
        then reject;
    }
}
community both-comms members [ 65010:4321 65010:4444 ];
community just-4321 members 65010:4321;
community just-4444 members 65010:4444;
```

The highlighted portion of the policy is where our problems are arising. Listing multiple values in square brackets ([]) within the community configuration itself is a logical AND of the values. We proved this with the ***both-comms*** community. The same theory doesn't hold true within a routing policy itself, where listing multiple values within a set of square brackets results in a logical OR operation. The ***double-comm-match*** policy is actually locating routes with either the ***just-4321*** community or the ***just-4444*** community value attached. To effectively locate the correct routes using the individual community values, we actually require two policies applied in a policy chain. The first policy locates routes with one of the communities attached and moves their evaluation to the next policy in the chain. The first policy then accepts all other routes. The second policy in the chain locates routes with the second community value attached and rejects them while also accepting all routes. The relevant policies are configured as so:

```
[edit policy-options]
user@Shiraz# show policy-statement find-4321
term 4321-routes {
    from community just-4321;
    then next policy;
}
term all-other-routes {
    then accept;
```

```
}

[edit policy-options]
user@Shiraz# show policy-statement find-4444
term 4444-routes {
    from community just-4444;
    then reject;
}
term all-other-routes {
    then accept;
}
```

We apply the policies to the IBGP peer group in the proper order and verify that the correct routes are rejected:

```
[edit protocols bgp]
user@Shiraz# show group Internal-Peers
type internal;
local-address 192.168.7.7;
import [ find-4321 find-4444 ];
neighbor 192.168.1.1;
neighbor 192.168.2.2;
neighbor 192.168.3.3;
neighbor 192.168.4.4;
neighbor 192.168.5.5;
neighbor 192.168.6.6;

[edit]
user@Shiraz# commit and-quit
commit complete
Exiting configuration mode

user@Shiraz> show route 172.16.5/24

inet.0: 28 destinations, 31 routes (26 active, 0 holddown, 2 hidden)
+ = Active Route, - = Last Active, * = Both

172.16.5.0/24      *[BGP/170] 02:00:58, MED 0, localpref 200, from 192.168.3.3
                      AS path: 65010 I
                    > via so-0/1/1.0
```

```
user@Shiraz> show route 172.16.6/24

inet.0: 28 destinations, 31 routes (26 active, 0 holddown, 2 hidden)

user@Shiraz> show route 172.16.7/24

inet.0: 28 destinations, 31 routes (26 active, 0 holddown, 2 hidden)

user@Shiraz>
```

The 172.16.5.0 /24 route is active in the routing table and neither the 172.16.6.0 /24 or 172.16.7.0 /24 routes are present. The router output of two hidden routes also provides a hint that the policies are working as designed. While this application might seem a bit complex, the use of regular expressions (as outlined in the "Regular Expressions" section later in this chapter) makes the routing policy configuration more straightforward.

Modifying Current Values

Altering the current values attached to a route is the other main use of a community in a routing policy. You can perform three main actions: you can add, delete, or set a community value. Here are the details of each policy action:

add   The policy action then community add *community-name* maintains the current list of communities on the route and adds to it the community values defined in *community-name*.

delete   The policy action then community delete *community-name* also maintains the current list of communities on the route while removing all community values defined in *community-name*.

set   The policy action then community set *community-name* deletes all of the current communities assigned to the route. In its place, the router installs the community values defined in *community-name*.

The administrators of AS 65010 in Figure 1.4 want to alter the community values on the routes they receive from Riesling. The routes currently in the routing table include:

```
user@Cabernet> show route protocol bgp

inet.0: 20 destinations, 20 routes (20 active, 0 holddown, 0 hidden)
+ = Active Route, - = Last Active, * = Both

192.168.1.0/24     *[BGP/170] 00:07:34, localpref 100
                      AS path: 65020 I
                    > to 10.100.10.2 via at-0/1/0.100
192.168.2.0/24     *[BGP/170] 00:07:34, localpref 100
                      AS path: 65020 I
                    > to 10.100.10.2 via at-0/1/0.100
```

```
192.168.3.0/24      *[BGP/170] 00:07:34, localpref 100
                        AS path: 65020 I
                     > to 10.100.10.2 via at-0/1/0.100
```

Cabernet wants to add a community value of 65010:1 to the 192.168.1.0 /24 route. We configure the appropriate policy and apply it to Riesling after examining the current community values on the route:

```
[edit]
user@Cabernet# run show route 192.168.1/24 detail

inet.0: 20 destinations, 20 routes (20 active, 0 holddown, 0 hidden)
192.168.1.0/24 (1 entry, 1 announced)
        *BGP    Preference: 170/-101
                Source: 10.100.10.2
                Next hop: 10.100.10.2 via at-0/1/0.100, selected
                State: <Active Ext>
                Local AS: 65010 Peer AS: 65020
                Age: 11:15
                Task: BGP_65020.10.100.10.2+2698
                Announcement bits (2): 0-KRT 1-BGP.0.0.0.0+179
                AS path: 65020 I
                Communities: 65020:1 65020:10 65020:100 65020:1000
                Localpref: 100
                Router ID: 192.168.1.1

[edit]
user@Cabernet# show policy-options
policy-statement add-a-community {
    term add-comm {
        from {
            route-filter 192.168.1.0/24 exact;
        }
        then {
            community add comm-1;
        }
    }
}
community comm-1 members 65010:1;

[edit]
user@Cabernet# show protocols bgp
```

```
group Ext-AS65020 {
    type external;
    import add-a-community;
    peer-as 65020;
    neighbor 10.100.10.2;
}
```

```
user@Cabernet> show route 192.168.1/24 detail
```

```
inet.0: 20 destinations, 20 routes (20 active, 0 holddown, 0 hidden)
192.168.1.0/24 (1 entry, 1 announced)
        *BGP    Preference: 170/-101
                Source: 10.100.10.2
                Next hop: 10.100.10.2 via at-0/1/0.100, selected
                State: <Active Ext>
                Local AS: 65010 Peer AS: 65020
                Age: 12:11
                Task: BGP_65020.10.100.10.2+2698
                Announcement bits (2): 0-KRT 1-BGP.0.0.0.0+179
                AS path: 65020 I
                Communities: 65010:1 65020:1 65020:10 65020:100 65020:1000
                Localpref: 100
                Router ID: 192.168.1.1
```

The router output clearly shows the 65010:1 community value added to the 192.168.1.0 /24 route as a result of the ***add-a-community*** policy. We back out our changes and create a policy to remove the 65020:200 community value from the 192.168.2.0 /24 route. As before, we view the route before and after the policy application:

```
[edit]
user@Cabernet# run show route 192.168.2/24 detail
```

```
inet.0: 20 destinations, 20 routes (20 active, 0 holddown, 0 hidden)
192.168.2.0/24 (1 entry, 1 announced)
        *BGP    Preference: 170/-101
                Source: 10.100.10.2
                Next hop: 10.100.10.2 via at-0/1/0.100, selected
                State: <Active Ext>
                Local AS: 65010 Peer AS: 65020
                Age: 18:23
                Task: BGP_65020.10.100.10.2+2698
                Announcement bits (2): 0-KRT 1-BGP.0.0.0.0+179
```

```
                    AS path: 65020 I
                    Communities: 65020:2 65020:20 65020:200 65020:2000
                    Localpref: 100
                    Router ID: 192.168.1.1


[edit]
user@Cabernet# show policy-options
policy-statement delete-a-community {
    term delete-comm {
        from {
            route-filter 192.168.2.0/24 exact;
        }
        then {
            community delete comm-2;
        }
    }
}
community comm-2 members 65020:200;


[edit]
user@Cabernet# show protocols bgp
group Ext-AS65020 {
    type external;
    import delete-a-community;
    peer-as 65020;
    neighbor 10.100.10.2;
}


user@Cabernet> show route 192.168.2/24 detail

inet.0: 20 destinations, 20 routes (20 active, 0 holddown, 0 hidden)
192.168.2.0/24 (1 entry, 1 announced)
        *BGP    Preference: 170/-101
                Source: 10.100.10.2
                Next hop: 10.100.10.2 via at-0/1/0.100, selected
                State: <Active Ext>
                Local AS: 65010 Peer AS: 65020
                Age: 18:53
                Task: BGP_65020.10.100.10.2+2698
                Announcement bits (2): 0-KRT 1-BGP.0.0.0.0+179
```

```
                    AS path: 65020 I
                    Communities: 65020:2 65020:20 65020:2000
                    Localpref: 100
                    Router ID: 192.168.1.1
```

The **delete-a-community** policy removed the 65020:200 community value from the 192.168.2.0 /24 route without deleting the other existing values as we expected. We again back out our changes and use the set community action to remove all community values attached to the 192.168.3.0 /24 route. In their place, Cabernet adds the 65010:33 community value to the route:

```
[edit]
user@Cabernet# run show route 192.168.3/24 detail

inet.0: 20 destinations, 20 routes (20 active, 0 holddown, 0 hidden)
192.168.3.0/24 (1 entry, 1 announced)
        *BGP    Preference: 170/-101
                    Source: 10.100.10.2
                    Next hop: 10.100.10.2 via at-0/1/0.100, selected
                    State: <Active Ext>
                    Local AS: 65010 Peer AS: 65020
                    Age: 23:29
                    Task: BGP_65020.10.100.10.2+2698
                    Announcement bits (2): 0-KRT 1-BGP.0.0.0.0+179
                    AS path: 65020 I
                    Communities: 65020:3 65020:30 65020:300 65020:3000
                    Localpref: 100
                    Router ID: 192.168.1.1

[edit]
user@Cabernet# show policy-options
policy-statement set-a-community {
    term set-comm {
        from {
            route-filter 192.168.3.0/24 exact;
        }
        then {
            community set comm-3;
        }
    }
}
community comm-3 members 65010:33;
```

```
[edit]
user@Cabernet# show protocols bgp
group Ext-AS65020 {
    type external;
    import set-a-community;
    peer-as 65020;
    neighbor 10.100.10.2;
}

user@Cabernet> show route 192.168.3/24 detail

inet.0: 20 destinations, 20 routes (20 active, 0 holddown, 0 hidden)
192.168.3.0/24 (1 entry, 1 announced)
        *BGP    Preference: 170/-101
                Source: 10.100.10.2
                Next hop: 10.100.10.2 via at-0/1/0.100, selected
                State: <Active Ext>
                Local AS: 65010 Peer AS: 65020
                Age: 23:49
                Task: BGP_65020.10.100.10.2+2698
                Announcement bits (2): 0-KRT 1-BGP.0.0.0.0+179
                AS path: 65020 I
                Communities: 65010:33
                Localpref: 100
                Router ID: 192.168.1.1
```

As we expected, the ***set-a-community*** policy removed the existing community values and in its place inserted the 65010:33 value.

Extended Communities

Recent networking enhancements, such as virtual private networks (VPN), have functionality requirements that can be satisfied by an attribute such as a community. (We discuss VPNs in more detail in Chapter 9, "Layer 2 and Layer 3 Virtual Private Networks.") However, the existing 4-octet community value doesn't provide enough expansion and flexibility to accommodate the requirements that would be put on it. This leads to the creation of extended communities. An *extended community* is an 8-octet value that is also divided into two main sections. The first 2 octets of the community encode a type field while the last 6 octets carry a unique set of data in a format defined by the type field.

Figure 1.5 shows the format of the extended community attribute. The individual fields are defined as:

Type (2 octets)   The type field designates both the format of the remaining community fields as well as the actual kind of extended community being used.

The high-order octet uses the two defined values of 0x00 and 0x01. A value of 0x00 denotes a 2-octet administrator field and a 4-octet assigned number field. The 0x01 value results in the opposite: a 4-octet administrator field and a 2-octet assigned number field.

The low-order octet determines the kind of community used. Two common values are 0x02 (a route target community) and 0x03 (a route origin community).

Administrator (Variable)   The variable-sized administrator field contains information designed to guarantee the uniqueness of the extended community. The AS number of the network originating the community is used when 2 octets are available, and an IPv4 prefix is used when 4 octets are available. The prefix is often the router ID of the device originating the community.

Assigned Number (Variable)   The assigned number field is also variably sized to either 2 or 4 octets. It contains a value assigned by the originating network. When combined with the administrator field, the community value is designed to be unique in the Internet.

FIGURE 1.5   Extended community format

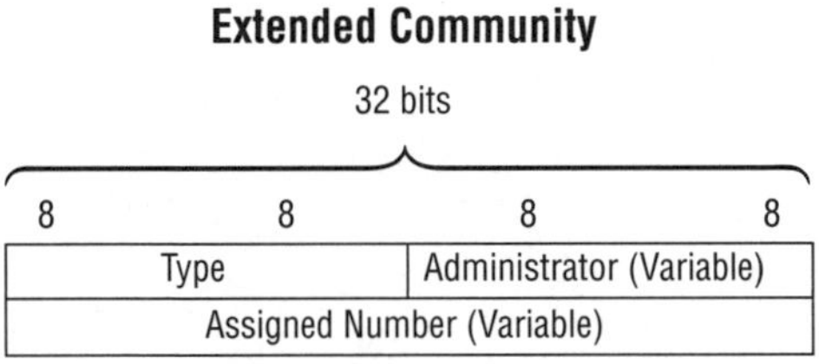

Extended Community

32 bits

8	8	8	8
Type		Administrator (Variable)	
Assigned Number (Variable)			

The JUNOS software provides the same command syntax for an extended community as a regular community. The difference is in the *community-id* value supplied. An extended community uses a notation of `type:administrator:assigned-number`. The router expects you to use the words `target` or `origin` to represent the type field. The administrator field uses a decimal number for the AS or an IPv4 address, while the assigned number field expects a decimal number no larger than the size of the field (65,535 for 2 octets or 4,294,967,295 for 4 octets).

You use the defined community name for an extended community in the same manner as for a regular community. You can match on a route or modify the route attributes using the `add`, `delete`, or `set` keywords. Refer back to Figure 1.4 and the Shiraz router in AS 65020. Shiraz has local static routes representing customer networks, which have existing regular community values assigned to them. Shiraz adds extended community values to the routes before advertising them via BGP. The existing routes are:

```
[edit]
user@Shiraz# show routing-options
static {
```

```
    route 192.168.1.0/24 {
        next-hop 10.222.6.1;
        community 65020:1;
    }
    route 192.168.2.0/24 {
        next-hop 10.222.6.1;
        community 65020:2;
    }
    route 192.168.3.0/24 {
        next-hop 10.222.6.1;
        community 65020:3;
    }
    route 192.168.4.0/24 {
        next-hop 10.222.6.1;
        community 65020:4;
    }
}
```

Shiraz creates four extended communities: one for each possible combination of type, administrator field size, and assigned number field size. The communities are associated on a one-to-one basis with a route using an export policy:

```
[edit]
user@Shiraz# show policy-options
policy-statement set-ext-comms {
    term route-1 {
        from {
            route-filter 192.168.1.0/24 exact;
        }
        then {
            community add target-as;
            accept;
        }
    }
    term route-2 {
        from {
            route-filter 192.168.2.0/24 exact;
        }
        then {
            community add target-ip;
            accept;
        }
    }
```

```
    term route-3 {
        from {
            route-filter 192.168.3.0/24 exact;
        }
        then {
            community add origin-as;
            accept;
        }
    }
    term route-4 {
        from {
            route-filter 192.168.4.0/24 exact;
        }
        then {
            community add origin-ip;
            accept;
        }
    }
}
community origin-as members origin:65020:3;
community origin-ip members origin:192.168.7.7:4;
community target-as members target:65020:1;
community target-ip members target:192.168.7.7:2;

[edit]
user@Shiraz# show protocols bgp
group Internal-Peers {
    type internal;
    local-address 192.168.7.7;
    export set-ext-comms;
    neighbor 192.168.1.1;
    neighbor 192.168.2.2;
    neighbor 192.168.3.3;
    neighbor 192.168.4.4;
    neighbor 192.168.5.5;
    neighbor 192.168.6.6;
}
```

The routes are received on the Riesling router with the correct community values attached:

```
user@Riesling> show route protocol bgp 192.168/16 detail
```

```
inet.0: 32 destinations, 32 routes (32 active, 0 holddown, 0 hidden)
192.168.1.0/24 (1 entry, 1 announced)
        *BGP    Preference: 170/-101
                Source: 192.168.7.7
                Next hop: 10.222.4.2 via fe-0/0/2.0, selected
                Protocol next hop: 10.222.6.1 Indirect next hop: 85a3000 62
                State: <Active Int Ext>
                Local AS: 65020 Peer AS: 65020
                Age: 1:58      Metric2: 3
                Task: BGP_65020.192.168.7.7+1562
                Announcement bits (3): 0-KRT 1-BGP.0.0.0.0+179 4-Resolve inet.0
                AS path: I
                Communities: 65020:1 target:65020:1
                Localpref: 100
                Router ID: 192.168.7.7


192.168.2.0/24 (1 entry, 1 announced)
        *BGP    Preference: 170/-101
                Source: 192.168.7.7
                Next hop: 10.222.4.2 via fe-0/0/2.0, selected
                Protocol next hop: 10.222.6.1 Indirect next hop: 85a3000 62
                State: <Active Int Ext>
                Local AS: 65020 Peer AS: 65020
                Age: 1:58      Metric2: 3
                Task: BGP_65020.192.168.7.7+1562
                Announcement bits (3): 0-KRT 1-BGP.0.0.0.0+179 4-Resolve inet.0
                AS path: I
                Communities: 65020:2 target:192.168.7.7:2
                Localpref: 100
                Router ID: 192.168.7.7


192.168.3.0/24 (1 entry, 1 announced)
        *BGP    Preference: 170/-101
                Source: 192.168.7.7
                Next hop: 10.222.4.2 via fe-0/0/2.0, selected
                Protocol next hop: 10.222.6.1 Indirect next hop: 85a3000 62
                State: <Active Int Ext>
                Local AS: 65020 Peer AS: 65020
                Age: 1:58      Metric2: 3
                Task: BGP_65020.192.168.7.7+1562
```

```
            Announcement bits (3): 0-KRT 1-BGP.0.0.0.0+179 4-Resolve inet.0
            AS path: I
            Communities: 65020:3 origin:65020:3
            Localpref: 100
            Router ID: 192.168.7.7

192.168.4.0/24 (1 entry, 1 announced)
        *BGP    Preference: 170/-101
            Source: 192.168.7.7
            Next hop: 10.222.4.2 via fe-0/0/2.0, selected
            Protocol next hop: 10.222.6.1 Indirect next hop: 85a3000 62
            State: <Active Int Ext>
            Local AS: 65020 Peer AS: 65020
            Age: 1:58       Metric2: 3
            Task: BGP_65020.192.168.7.7+1562
            Announcement bits (3): 0-KRT 1-BGP.0.0.0.0+179 4-Resolve inet.0
            AS path: I
            Communities: 65020:4 origin:192.168.7.7:4
            Localpref: 100
            Router ID: 192.168.7.7
```

Regular Expressions

The definition of your community within [edit policy-options] can contain decimal values, as we've already done, or a regular expression. A *regular expression* (regex) uses nondecimal characters to represent decimal values. This allows you the flexibility of specifying any number of community values in a single community name. When used with communities, as opposed to a BGP AS Path, the JUNOS software uses two different forms—simple and complex. Let's explore the difference between these regex types.

Simple Community Expressions

A simple community regular expression uses either the asterisk (*) or the dot (.) to represent some value. The asterisk represents an entire AS number or an entire community value. Some examples of a regular expression using the asterisk are:

*:1111   Matches a community with any possible AS number and a community value of 1111.

65010:*   Matches a community from AS 65010 with any possible community value.

The dot represents a single decimal place in either the AS number or the community value. Examples of regular expressions using the dot are:

65010:100.   Matches a community with an AS of 65010 and a community value that is four digits long, whereas the community value begins with 100. These values include 1000, 1001, 1002, ..., 1009.

65010:2...4   Matches a community from AS 65010 with a community value that is five digits long. The first digit of the community value must be 2 and the last digit must be 4. Some possible values are 23754, 21114, and 29064.

650.0:4321   Matches a community with a community value of 4321 and an AS number that is five digits long. The fourth digit of the AS number can be any value. The AS numbers include 65000, 65010, 65020, ..., 65090.

> To classify as a simple regular expression, the asterisk and the dot must be used separately. Using them together (.*) results in a complex community regular expression. We discuss complex expressions in the "Complex Community Expressions" section later in the chapter.

Refer back to Figure 1.4 as a guide. Here, the Shiraz router is receiving routes within the 172.16.0.0 /21 address space from AS 65010. Those routes currently have the following community values assigned to them:

```
user@Shiraz> show route 172.16.0/21 detail | match Communities
            Communities: 65010:1111 65010:1234
            Communities: 65010:1111 65010:1234
            Communities: 65010:1234 65010:2222
            Communities: 65010:1234 65010:2222
            Communities: 65010:3333 65010:4321
            Communities: 65010:3333 65010:4321
            Communities: 65010:4321 65010:4444
            Communities: 65010:4321 65010:4444
```

At this point we don't know which values are attached to which routes; we only know the list of possible values within the address range. We use the show route community *community-value* command in conjunction with some simple regular expressions to accomplish this:

```
user@Shiraz> show route community *:1111

inet.0: 32 destinations, 35 routes (32 active, 0 holddown, 0 hidden)
+ = Active Route, - = Last Active, * = Both

172.16.0.0/24      *[BGP/170] 22:41:39, MED 0, localpref 200, from 192.168.1.1
                      AS path: 65010 I
                    > via so-0/1/0.0
172.16.1.0/24      *[BGP/170] 22:41:39, MED 0, localpref 200, from 192.168.1.1
                      AS path: 65010 I
                    > via so-0/1/0.0
```

The 172.16.0.0 /24 and the 172.16.1.0 /24 routes have a community attached with a community value of 1111. The asterisk regex allows the AS number to be any value, although our previous capture tells us it is 65010. We see the actual communities by adding the `detail` option to the command:

```
user@Shiraz> show route community *:1111 detail

inet.0: 32 destinations, 35 routes (32 active, 0 holddown, 0 hidden)
172.16.0.0/24 (1 entry, 1 announced)
        *BGP    Preference: 170/-201
                Source: 192.168.1.1
                Next hop: via so-0/1/0.0, selected
                Protocol next hop: 192.168.1.1 Indirect next hop: 8570738 120
                State: <Active Int Ext>
                Local AS: 65020 Peer AS: 65020
                Age: 22:43:48   Metric: 0       Metric2: 65536
                Task: BGP_65020.192.168.1.1+179
                Announcement bits (2): 0-KRT 4-Resolve inet.0
                AS path: 65010 I
                Communities: 65010:1111 65010:1234
                Localpref: 200
                Router ID: 192.168.1.1

172.16.1.0/24 (1 entry, 1 announced)
        *BGP    Preference: 170/-201
                Source: 192.168.1.1
                Next hop: via so-0/1/0.0, selected
                Protocol next hop: 192.168.1.1 Indirect next hop: 8570738 120
                State: <Active Int Ext>
                Local AS: 65020 Peer AS: 65020
                Age: 22:43:48   Metric: 0       Metric2: 65536
                Task: BGP_65020.192.168.1.1+179
                Announcement bits (2): 0-KRT 4-Resolve inet.0
                AS path: 65010 I
                Communities: 65010:1111 65010:1234
                Localpref: 200
                Router ID: 192.168.1.1
```

The routes on Shiraz with a community from AS 65010 and a community value four digits long that begins with 4 are:

```
user@Shiraz> show route community 65010:4...
```

```
inet.0: 32 destinations, 35 routes (32 active, 0 holddown, 0 hidden)
+ = Active Route, - = Last Active, * = Both

172.16.4.0/24       *[BGP/170] 20:32:12, MED 0, localpref 50, from 192.168.1.1
                       AS path: 65010 I
                     > via so-0/1/0.0
172.16.5.0/24       *[BGP/170] 20:32:12, MED 0, localpref 50, from 192.168.1.1
                       AS path: 65010 I
                     > via so-0/1/0.0
172.16.6.0/24       *[BGP/170] 20:32:12, MED 0, localpref 50, from 192.168.1.1
                       AS path: 65010 I
                     > via so-0/1/0.0
172.16.7.0/24       *[BGP/170] 20:32:12, MED 0, localpref 50, from 192.168.1.1
                       AS path: 65010 I
                     > via so-0/1/0.0
```

The JUNOS software also provides the ability to combine the asterisk and dot regular expressions. For example, Shiraz displays the routes whose community is from any AS and whose value is four digits long ending with 1:

```
user@Shiraz> show route terse community *:...1

inet.0: 32 destinations, 35 routes (32 active, 0 holddown, 0 hidden)
+ = Active Route, - = Last Active, * = Both
```

A	Destination	P	Prf	Metric 1	Metric 2	Next hop	AS path
*	172.16.0.0/24	B	170	200	0	>so-0/1/0.0	65010 I
*	172.16.1.0/24	B	170	200	0	>so-0/1/0.0	65010 I
*	172.16.4.0/24	B	170	50	0	>so-0/1/0.0	65010 I
*	172.16.5.0/24	B	170	50	0	>so-0/1/0.0	65010 I
*	172.16.6.0/24	B	170	50	0	>so-0/1/0.0	65010 I
*	172.16.7.0/24	B	170	50	0	>so-0/1/0.0	65010 I

Complex Community Expressions

A complex community regular expression allows for a more varied set of combinations than a simple expression does. The complex regex uses both a *regular expression term* in conjunction with a *regular expression operator*. The regex term is any single character within the community, including both the actual decimal digits and the simple dot (.) regex. The operator is an optional character that applies to a single term and usually follows that term. The JUNOS software allows you to combine multiple term-operator pairs within a single community definition. Table 1.1 displays the regular expression operators supported by the router.

TABLE 1.1 Community Regular Expression Operators

Operator	Description
{m,n}	Matches at least m and at most n instances of the term.
{m}	Matches exactly m instances of the term.
{m,}	Matches m or more instances of the term, up to infinity.
*	Matches 0 or more instances of the term, which is similar to {0,}.
+	Matches one or more instances of the term, which is similar to {1,}.
?	Matches 0 or 1 instances of the term, which is similar to {0,1}.
|	Matches one of the two terms on either side of the pipe symbol, similar to a logical OR.
^	Matches a term at the beginning of the community attribute.
$	Matches a term at the end of the community attribute.
[]	Matches a range or an array of digits. This occupies the space of a single term within the community attribute.
(…)	Groups terms together to be acted on by an additional operator.

An Effective Use of a Simple Expression

The format and design of the community attribute means that each community should be globally unique. Router implementations, however, don't provide a sanity check on received routes looking for communities belonging to your local AS. In other words, some other network may attach a community value that "belongs" to you. To combat this, some network administrators remove all community values from each received BGP route. Of course, this is helpful only when your local administrative policy is not expecting community values from a peer. When this is not the case, you should honor the expected community values before removing the unexpected values.

A typical configuration that might accomplish the removal of all community values is shown in the *delete-all-comms* policy:

```
[edit policy-options]
user@Muscat# show
```

```
policy-statement delete-all-comms {
    term remove-comms {
        community delete all-comms;
    }
}
community all-comms members *:*;
```

This policy doesn't contain any match criteria, so all possible routes match the *remove-comms* term. The action is then to delete all communities that match the *all-comms* community name. The named community uses a regular expression to match all possible AS numbers and all possible community values. After applying the *delete-all-comms* policy as an import from its EBGP peers, the Muscat router can test its effectiveness:

```
user@Muscat> show route receive-protocol bgp 10.222.45.1 detail

inet.0: 35 destinations, 35 routes (35 active, 0 holddown, 0 hidden)
* 172.16.1.0/24 (1 entry, 1 announced)
      Nexthop: 10.222.45.1
      AS path: 65030 65020 65010 I
  Communities: 65010:1111 65010:1234


user@Muscat> show route 172.16.1/24 detail

inet.0: 35 destinations, 35 routes (35 active, 0 holddown, 0 hidden)
172.16.1.0/24 (1 entry, 1 announced)
        *BGP    Preference: 170/-101
                Source: 10.222.45.1
                Next hop: 10.222.45.1 via so-0/1/1.0, selected
                State: <Active Ext>
                Local AS: 65040 Peer AS: 65030
                Age: 1:42:14
                Task: BGP_65030.10.222.45.1+179
                Announcement bits (2): 0-KRT 1-BGP.0.0.0.0+179
                AS path: 65030 65020 65010 I
                Localpref: 100
                Router ID: 192.168.4.4
```

The lack of communities in the local inet.0 routing table proves the effectiveness of the regular expression. If the administrators of Muscat want to use communities within their own AS, they can easily apply them in a second term or another import policy.

The use of the caret (^) and dollar sign ($) operators as anchors for your community regular expression is optional. However, we recommend their use for clarity in creating and using expressions with BGP communities.

Examples of complex regular expressions include the following:

^65000:.{2,3}$ This expression matches a community value where the AS number is 65000. The community value is any two- or three-digit number. Possible matches include 65000:123, 65000:16, and 65000:999.

^65010:45.{2}9$ This expression matches a community value where the AS number is 65010. The community value is a five-digit number that begins with 45 and ends with 9. The third and fourth digits are any single number repeated twice. Possible matches include 65010:45119, 65010:45999, and 65010:45339.

^65020:.*$ This expression matches a community value where the AS number is 65020. The community value is any possible combination of values from 0 through 65,535. The .* notation is useful for representing any value any number of times.

^65030:84+$ This expression matches a community value where the AS number is 65030. The community value must start with 8 and include between one and four instances of 4. Matches are 65030:84, 65030:844, 65030:8444, and 65030:84444.

^65040:234?$ This expression matches a community value where the AS number is 65040. The community value is either 23 or 234, which results in the matches being 65040:23 and 65040:234.

^65050:1|2345$ This expression matches a community value where the AS number is 65050. The community value is either 1345 or 2345, which results in the matches being 65050:1345 and 65050:2345. You can also write the regex as ^65050:(1|2)345$ for added clarity.

^65060:1[357]9$ This expression matches a community value where the AS number is 65060. The community value is 139, 159, or 179, which results in the matches being 65060:139, 65060:159, and 65060:179.

^65070:1[3-7]9$ This expression matches a community value where the AS number is 65070. The community value is a three-digit number that starts with 1 and ends with 9. The second digit is any single value between 3 and 7. The matches for this regex are 65070:139, 65070:149, 65070:159, 65070:169, and 65060:179.

While we explored complex regular expressions only within the community value, the JUNOS software also allows expressions within the AS number. For example, ^65.{3}:1234$ matches any private AS number starting with 65 and a community value of 1234.

The Shiraz router in Figure 1.4 has local customer static routes it is advertising to its IBGP peers. These routes and their communities are:

user@Shiraz> **show route protocol static detail**

```
inet.0: 32 destinations, 35 routes (32 active, 0 holddown, 0 hidden)
192.168.1.0/24 (1 entry, 1 announced)
        *Static Preference: 5
                Next hop: 10.222.6.1 via so-0/1/2.0, selected
                State: <Active Int Ext>
                Local AS: 65020
                Age: 1:21
                Task: RT
                Announcement bits (3): 0-KRT 3-BGP.0.0.0.0+179 4-Resolve inet.0
                AS path: I
                Communities: 65020:1 65020:10 65020:11 65020:100 65020:111


192.168.2.0/24 (1 entry, 1 announced)
        *Static Preference: 5
                Next hop: 10.222.6.1 via so-0/1/2.0, selected
                State: <Active Int Ext>
                Local AS: 65020
                Age: 1:21
                Task: RT
                Announcement bits (3): 0-KRT 3-BGP.0.0.0.0+179 4-Resolve inet.0
                AS path: I
                Communities: 65020:2 65020:20 65020:22 65020:200 65020:222


192.168.3.0/24 (1 entry, 1 announced)
        *Static Preference: 5
                Next hop: 10.222.6.1 via so-0/1/2.0, selected
                State: <Active Int Ext>
                Local AS: 65020
                Age: 1:21
                Task: RT
                Announcement bits (3): 0-KRT 3-BGP.0.0.0.0+179 4-Resolve inet.0
                AS path: I
                Communities: 65020:3 65020:30 65020:33 65020:300 65020:333


192.168.4.0/24 (1 entry, 1 announced)
        *Static Preference: 5
```

```
Next hop: 10.222.6.1 via so-0/1/2.0, selected
State: <Active Int Ext>
Local AS: 65020
Age: 1:21
Task: RT
Announcement bits (3): 0-KRT 3-BGP.0.0.0.0+179 4-Resolve inet.0
AS path: I
Communities: 65020:4 65020:40 65020:44 65020:400 65020:444
```

To adequately test complex regular expressions, Shiraz creates a policy called **_test-regex_** that locates routes by using a complex regular expression and rejects all other routes. The policy is configured like this:

```
[edit]
user@Shiraz# show policy-options policy-statement test-regex
term find-routes {
    from community complex-regex;
    then accept;
}
term reject-all-else {
    then reject;
}
```

The complex regular expression is currently set to match on community values beginning with either 1 or 3. Here's the configuration:

```
[edit]
user@Shiraz# show policy-options | match members
community complex-regex members "^65020:[13].*$";
```

The 192.168.1.0 /24 and 192.168.3.0/24 routes both have communities attached that should match this expression. We test the regex and its policy by using the test policy *policy-name* command:

```
user@Shiraz> test policy test-regex 0/0

inet.0: 32 destinations, 35 routes (32 active, 0 holddown, 0 hidden)
+ = Active Route, - = Last Active, * = Both

192.168.1.0/24      *[Static/5] 00:31:44
                     > to 10.222.6.1 via so-0/1/2.0
192.168.3.0/24      *[Static/5] 00:31:44
                     > to 10.222.6.1 via so-0/1/2.0
```

```
Policy test-regex: 2 prefix accepted, 30 prefix rejected
```

The complex regular expression is altered to match on any community value containing any number of instances of the digit 2. The new expression configuration and the associated routes are shown here:

```
[edit]
user@Shiraz# show policy-options | match members
community complex-regex members "^65020:2+$";

user@Shiraz> test policy test-regex 0/0

inet.0: 32 destinations, 35 routes (32 active, 0 holddown, 0 hidden)
+ = Active Route, - = Last Active, * = Both

192.168.2.0/24     *[Static/5] 00:40:28
                    > to 10.222.6.1 via so-0/1/2.0

Policy test-regex: 1 prefix accepted, 31 prefix rejected
```

Autonomous System Paths

An *AS Path* is also a route attribute used by BGP. The AS Path is used both for route selection and to prevent potential routing loops. As with the communities, we won't discuss the details of using AS Paths within BGP in this chapter; those details are covered in Chapter 4. The topics concerning us in this chapter are defining regular expressions and using those expressions to locate a set of routes.

Regular Expressions

An AS Path regular expression also uses a term-operator format similar to the complex community regular expressions. Unlike the community term, the AS Path regular expression term is an entire AS number, such as 65000 or 65432. This translates into the simple dot (.) regex representing an entire AS number. Table 1.2 displays the AS Path regular expression operators supported by the router.

Examples of AS Path regular expressions include:

65000   This expression matches an AS Path with a length of 1 whose value is 65000. The expression uses a single term with no operators.

TABLE 1.2 AS Path Regular Expression Operators

Operator	Description
{m,n}	Matches at least m and at most n instances of the term.
{m}	Matches exactly m instances of the term.
{m, }	Matches m or more instances of the term, up to infinity.
*	Matches 0 or more instances of the term, which is similar to {0,}.
+	Matches one or more instances of the term, which is similar to {1,}.
?	Matches 0 or 1 instances of the term, which is similar to {0,1}.
|	Matches one of the two terms on either side of the pipe symbol, similar to a logical OR.
-	Matches an inclusive range of terms.
^	Matches the beginning of the AS Path. The JUNOS software uses this operator implicitly and its use is optional.
$	Matches the end of the AS Path. The JUNOS software uses this operator implicitly and its use is optional.
(...)	Groups terms together to be acted on by an additional operator.
( )	Matches a null value as a term.

65010 . 65020   This expression matches an AS Path with a length of 3 where the first AS is 65010 and the last AS is 65020. The AS in the middle of the path can be any single AS number.

65030?   This expression matches an AS Path with a length of 0 or 1. A path length of 0 is represented by the null AS Path. If a value appears, it must be 65030.

. (65040|65050)?   This expression matches an AS Path with a length of 1 or 2. The first AS in the path can be any value. The second AS in the path, if appropriate, must be either 65040 or 65050.

65060 .*   This expression matches an AS Path with a length of at least 1. The first AS number must be 65060, and it may be followed by any other AS number any number of times or no AS numbers. This expression is often used to represent all BGP routes from a particular neighboring AS network.

.* 65070   This expression matches an AS Path with a length of at least 1. The last AS number must be 65070, and it may be preceded by any other AS number any number of times or no AS numbers. This expression is often used to represent all BGP routes that originated from a particular AS network.

.* 65080 .* This expression matches an AS Path with a length of at least 1. The 65080 AS number must appear at least once in the path. It may be followed by or preceded by any other AS number any number of times. This expression is often used to represent all BGP routes that have been routed by a particular AS network.

.* (64512-65535) .* This expression matches an AS Path with a length of at least 1. One of the private AS numbers must appear at least once in the path. It may be followed by or preceded by any other AS number any number of times. This expression is useful at the edge of a network to reject routes containing private AS numbers.

() This expression matches an AS Path with a length of 0. The *null AS Path* represents all BGP routes native to your local Autonomous System.

FIGURE 1.6   An AS Path sample network map

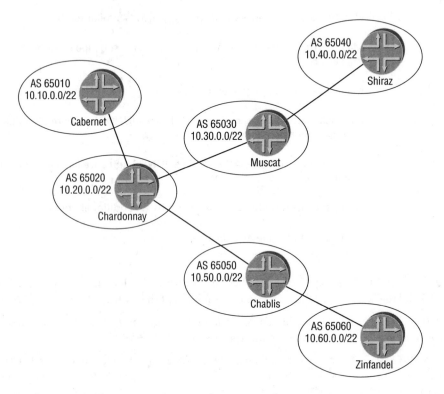

Figure 1.6 shows several Autonomous Systems connected via EBGP peering sessions. Each router is generating customer routes within their assigned address space. The Cabernet router in AS 65010 uses the `aspath-regex` option of the `show route` command to locate routes using regular expressions.

The routes originated by the Zinfandel router in AS 65060 include:

```
user@Cabernet> show route terse aspath-regex ".* 65060"
```

```
inet.0: 27 destinations, 27 routes (27 active, 0 holddown, 0 hidden)
+ = Active Route, - = Last Active, * = Both

A Destination     P Prf  Metric 1  Metric 2  Next hop      AS path
* 10.60.1.0/24    B 170     100              >10.100.10.6  65020 65050 65060 I
* 10.60.2.0/24    B 170     100              >10.100.10.6  65020 65050 65060 I
* 10.60.3.0/24    B 170     100              >10.100.10.6  65020 65050 65060 I
```

The routes originating in either AS 65040 or AS 65060 include:

```
user@Cabernet> show route terse aspath-regex ".* (65040|65060)"

inet.0: 27 destinations, 27 routes (27 active, 0 holddown, 0 hidden)
+ = Active Route, - = Last Active, * = Both

A Destination     P Prf  Metric 1  Metric 2  Next hop      AS path
* 10.40.1.0/24    B 170     100              >10.100.10.6  65020 65030 65040 I
* 10.40.2.0/24    B 170     100              >10.100.10.6  65020 65030 65040 I
* 10.40.3.0/24    B 170     100              >10.100.10.6  65020 65030 65040 I
* 10.60.1.0/24    B 170     100              >10.100.10.6  65020 65050 65060 I
* 10.60.2.0/24    B 170     100              >10.100.10.6  65020 65050 65060 I
* 10.60.3.0/24    B 170     100              >10.100.10.6  65020 65050 65060 I
```

The routes using AS 65030 as a transit network include:

```
user@Cabernet> show route terse aspath-regex ".* 65030 .+"

inet.0: 27 destinations, 27 routes (27 active, 0 holddown, 0 hidden)
+ = Active Route, - = Last Active, * = Both

A Destination     P Prf  Metric 1  Metric 2  Next hop      AS path
* 10.40.1.0/24    B 170     100              >10.100.10.6  65020 65030 65040 I
* 10.40.2.0/24    B 170     100              >10.100.10.6  65020 65030 65040 I
* 10.40.3.0/24    B 170     100              >10.100.10.6  65020 65030 65040 I
```

Locating Routes

An AS Path regular expression is used within a routing policy as a match criterion to locate routes of interest. Much as you saw with communities in the "Match Criteria Usage" section earlier, you associate an expression with a name in the [edit policy-options] configuration hierarchy. You then use this name in the from section of the policy to locate your routes.

The administrators of AS 65010 would like to reject all routes originating in AS 65030. An AS Path regular expression called ***orig-in-65030*** is created and referenced in a policy called ***reject-AS65030***. The routing policy is then applied as an import policy on the Cabernet router. The relevant portions of the configuration are:

```
[edit]
user@Cabernet# show protocols bgp
export adv-statics;
group Ext-AS65020 {
    type external;
    import reject-AS65030;
    peer-as 65020;
    neighbor 10.100.10.6;
}
```

```
[edit]
user@Cabernet# show policy-options
policy-statement adv-statics {
    from protocol static;
    then accept;
}
policy-statement reject-AS65030 {
    term find-routes {
        from as-path orig-in-65030;
        then reject;
    }
}
as-path orig-in-65030 ".* 65030";
```

The Muscat router in AS 65030 is advertising the 10.30.0.0 /22 address space. After committing the configuration on Cabernet, we check for those routes in the inet.0 routing table:

```
user@Cabernet> show route protocol bgp 10.30.0/22

inet.0: 27 destinations, 27 routes (24 active, 0 holddown, 3 hidden)

user@Cabernet>
```

No routes in that address range are present in the routing table. Additionally, we see that Cabernet has three hidden routes, which indicates a successful rejection of incoming routes. We verify that the hidden routes are in fact from the Muscat router:

```
user@Cabernet> show route hidden terse
```

```
inet.0: 27 destinations, 27 routes (24 active, 0 holddown, 3 hidden)
+ = Active Route, - = Last Active, * = Both

A Destination      P Prf  Metric 1  Metric 2  Next hop      AS path
  10.30.1.0/24     B          100             >10.100.10.6  65020 65030 I
  10.30.2.0/24     B          100             >10.100.10.6  65020 65030 I
  10.30.3.0/24     B          100             >10.100.10.6  65020 65030 I
```

The Cabernet router also wants to reject routes originating in AS 65040 and the Shiraz router. A new AS Path expression called ***orig-in-65040*** is created and added to the current import routing policy:

```
user@Cabernet> show configuration policy-options
policy-statement adv-statics {
    from protocol static;
    then accept;
}
policy-statement reject-AS65030 {
    term find-routes {
        from as-path [ orig-in-65030 orig-in-65040 ];
        then reject;
    }
}
as-path orig-in-65040 ".* 65040";
as-path orig-in-65030 ".* 65030";
```

The router interprets the configuration of multiple expressions in the ***reject-AS65030*** policy as a logical OR operation. This locates routes originating in either AS 65030 or AS 65040. We verify the effectiveness of the policy on the Cabernet router:

```
user@Cabernet> show route 10.30.0/22

inet.0: 27 destinations, 27 routes (21 active, 0 holddown, 6 hidden)


user@Cabernet> show route 10.40.0/22

inet.0: 27 destinations, 27 routes (21 active, 0 holddown, 6 hidden)


user@Cabernet> show route hidden terse

inet.0: 27 destinations, 27 routes (21 active, 0 holddown, 6 hidden)
+ = Active Route, - = Last Active, * = Both
```

A Destination	P Prf	Metric 1	Metric 2	Next hop	AS path
10.30.1.0/24	B	100		>10.100.10.6	65020 65030 I
10.30.2.0/24	B	100		>10.100.10.6	65020 65030 I
10.30.3.0/24	B	100		>10.100.10.6	65020 65030 I
10.40.1.0/24	B	100		>10.100.10.6	65020 65030 65040 I
10.40.2.0/24	B	100		>10.100.10.6	65020 65030 65040 I
10.40.3.0/24	B	100		>10.100.10.6	65020 65030 65040 I

Once again, it appears we've successfully used an expression to locate and reject advertised BGP routes. Should the administrators in AS 65010 continue this process, they can reject routes from multiple regular expressions. A potential configuration readability issue does arise, however, when multiple expressions are referenced in a policy. The output of the router begins to wrap after reaching the edge of your terminal screen, and reading a policy configuration might become more difficult. To alleviate this potential issue, the JUNOS software allows you to group expressions together into an *AS Path group*.

An AS Path group is simply a named entity in the [edit policy-options] hierarchy within which you configure regular expressions. The Cabernet router has configured a group called **from-65030-or-65040**. Its configuration looks like this:

```
[edit]
user@Cabernet# show policy-options | find group
as-path-group from-65030-or-65040 {
    as-path from-65030 ".* 65030";
    as-path from-65040 ".* 65040";
}
```

The group currently contains two expressions—**from-65030** and **from-65040**—which locate routes originating in each respective AS. The router combines each expression in the AS Path group together using a logical OR operation. In this fashion, it is identical to referencing each expression separately in a policy term. The group is used in a routing policy term to locate routes, and its configuration is similar to a normal regular expression:

```
[edit]
user@Cabernet# show policy-options
policy-statement adv-statics {
    from protocol static;
    then accept;
}
policy-statement reject-AS65030 {
    term find-routes {
        from as-path [ orig-in-65030 orig-in-65040 ];
        then reject;
    }
```

```
}
policy-statement reject-65030-or-65040 {
    term find-routes {
        from as-path-group from-65030-or-65040;
        then reject;
    }
}
as-path orig-in-65040 ".* 65040";
as-path orig-in-65030 ".* 65030";
as-path-group from-65030-or-65040 {
    as-path from-65030 ".* 65030";
    as-path from-65040 ".* 65040";
}
```

After replacing the current BGP import policy with the ***reject-65030-or-65040*** policy, we find that the same routes are rejected on the Cabernet router:

```
user@Cabernet> show configuration protocols bgp
export adv-statics;
group Ext-AS65020 {
    type external;
    import reject-65030-or-65040;
    peer-as 65020;
    neighbor 10.100.10.6;
}

user@Cabernet> show route 10.30.0/22

inet.0: 27 destinations, 27 routes (21 active, 0 holddown, 6 hidden)

user@Cabernet> show route 10.40.0/22

inet.0: 27 destinations, 27 routes (21 active, 0 holddown, 6 hidden)

user@Cabernet> show route hidden terse

inet.0: 27 destinations, 27 routes (21 active, 0 holddown, 6 hidden)
+ = Active Route, - = Last Active, * = Both

A Destination       P Prf  Metric 1  Metric 2  Next hop      AS path
  10.30.1.0/24      B         100              >10.100.10.6  65020 65030 I
  10.30.2.0/24      B         100              >10.100.10.6  65020 65030 I
```

10.30.3.0/24	B	100	>10.100.10.6	65020 65030 I
10.40.1.0/24	B	100	>10.100.10.6	65020 65030 65040 I
10.40.2.0/24	B	100	>10.100.10.6	65020 65030 65040 I
10.40.3.0/24	B	100	>10.100.10.6	65020 65030 65040 I

Summary

In this chapter, you saw how the JUNOS software provides multiple methods for processing routing policies. We explored policy chains in depth and discovered how a policy subroutine works. We then looked at how to advertise a set of routes using a prefix list. Finally, we discussed the concept of a policy expression using logical Boolean operators. This complex system allows you the ultimate flexibility in constructing and advertising routes.

We concluded our chapter with a discussion of two BGP attributes, communities and AS Paths, and some methods of interacting with those attributes with routing policies. Both attributes are used as match criteria in a policy, and community values are altered as a policy action. Regular expressions are an integral part of locating routes, and we examined the construction of these expressions with respect to both communities and AS Paths.

Exam Essentials

Be able to identify the default processing of a policy chain. Multiple polices can be applied to a particular protocol to form a policy chain. The router evaluates the chain in a left-to-right fashion until a terminating action is reached. The protocol's default policy is always implicitly evaluated at the end of each chain.

Know how to evaluate a policy subroutine. A common policy configuration is referenced from within another policy as a match criterion. The router processes the subroutine and the protocol's default policy to determine a true or false result. This result is returned to the original policy where a true result is a match and a false result is not a match for the term.

Understand the logical evaluation of a policy expression. Logical Boolean operations of AND, OR, and NOT are used to combine multiple policies. Each expression occupies one space in a policy chain. The router first evaluates the expression to determine a true or false result and then uses that result to take various actions.

Know how to evaluate a prefix list. A prefix list is a set of routes which is applied to a routing policy as a match criterion. The prefix list is evaluated as a series of exact route matches.

Be able to construct a community regular expression. A regular expression is a pattern-matching system consisting of a term and an operator. The term for a community is a single character, which can be combined with an operator. An expression is used to locate routes as a match criterion in a policy and to modify the list of communities attached to a BGP route.

Be able to construct an AS Path regular expression.   Regular expressions can also be built to locate routes using the BGP AS Path attribute. The term for an AS Path expression is an entire AS number, not an individual character. The expression is used as a routing policy match criterion either by itself or within an AS Path group.

Review Questions

1. Which policy is always evaluated last in a policy chain?

    A. The first configured import policy

    B. The last configured import policy

    C. The first configured export policy

    D. The last configured export policy

    E. The protocol default policy

2. What is a possible result of evaluating *called-policy* when the router encounters a configuration of from policy called-policy?

    A. The route is accepted by *called-policy*.

    B. The route is rejected by *called-policy*.

    C. A true or false result is returned to the original policy.

    D. Nothing occurs by this evaluation.

3. The policy called *outer-policy* is applied as an export policy to BGP. What happens to the 10.10.10.0 /24 static route when it is evaluated by this policy?

    ```
    outer-policy {
        term find-routes {
            from policy inner-policy;
            then accept;
        }
        term reject-all-else {
            then reject;
        }
    }
    inner-policy {
        term find-routes {
            from protocol static;
            then reject;
        }
    }
    ```

    A. It is accepted by *outer-policy*.

    B. It is rejected by *outer-policy*.

    C. It is accepted by *inner-policy*.

    D. It is rejected by *inner-policy*.

4. Which route filter match type is assumed when a policy evaluates a prefix list?

 A. exact

 B. longer

 C. orlonger

 D. upto

5. The policy expression of (`policy-1 && policy-2`) is applied as an export within BGP. Given the following policies, what happens when the local router attempts to advertise the 172.16.1.0 /24 BGP route?

```
policy-1 {
    term accept-routes {
        from {
            route-filter 172.16.1.0/24 exact;
        }
        then accept;
    }
}
policy-2 {
    term reject-routes {
        from {
            route-filter 172.16.1.0/24 exact;
        }
        then reject;
    }
}
```

 A. It is accepted by *policy-1*.

 B. It is rejected by *policy-2*.

 C. It is accepted by the BGP default policy.

 D. It is rejected by the BGP default policy.

6. The policy expression of (`policy-1 || policy-2`) is applied as an export within BGP. Given the following policies, what happens when the local router attempts to advertise the 172.16.1.0 /24 BGP route?

```
policy-1 {
    term accept-routes {
        from {
            route-filter 172.16.1.0/24 exact;
        }
        then accept;
    }
```

```
    }
policy-2 {
    term reject-routes {
        from {
            route-filter 172.16.1.0/24 exact;
        }
        then reject;
    }
}
```

    A. It is accepted by *policy-1*.

    B. It is rejected by *policy-2*.

    C. It is accepted by the BGP default policy.

    D. It is rejected by the BGP default policy.

7.   The regular expression ^6[45][5-9]..:.{2,4}$ matches which community value(s)?

    A. 6455:123

    B. 64512:1234

    C. 64512:12345

    D. 65536:1234

8.   The regular expression ^*:2+345?$ matches which community value(s)?

    A. 65000:12345

    B. 65010:2234

    C. 65020:22345

    D. 65030:23455

9.   The regular expression 64512 .+ matches which AS Path?

    A. Null AS Path

    B. 64512

    C. 64512 64567

    D. 64512 64567 65000

10. The regular expression 64512 .* matches which AS Path?

    A. Null AS Path

    B. 64512

    C. 64513 64512

    D. 65000 64512 64567

Answers to Review Questions

1. E. The default policy for a specific protocol is always evaluated last in a policy chain.

2. C. The evaluation of a policy subroutine only returns a true or false result to the calling policy. A route is never accepted or rejected by a subroutine policy.

3. B. The policy subroutine returns a false result to **outer-policy** for the 10.10.10.0 /24 static route. The **find-routes** term in that policy then doesn't have a match, so the route is evaluated by the **reject-all-else** term. This term matches all routes and rejects them. This is where the route is actually rejected.

4. A. A routing policy always assumes a match type of exact when it is evaluating a prefix list as a match criterion.

5. B. The result of **policy-1** is true, but the result of **policy-2** is false. This makes the entire expression false, and **policy-2** guaranteed its result. Therefore, the action of then reject in **policy-2** is applied to the route and it is rejected.

6. A. The result of **policy-1** is true, which makes the entire expression true. Because **policy-1** guaranteed its result, the action of then accept in **policy-1** is applied to the route and it is accepted.

7. B. The first portion of the expression requires a five-digit AS value to be present. Option A doesn't fit that criterion. While Option D does, it is an invalid AS number for a community. The second portion of the expression requires a value between two and four digits long. Of the remaining choices, only Option B fits that requirement.

8. B and C. The first portion of the expression can be any AS value, so all options are still valid at this point. The second portion of the expression requires that it begin with one or more instances of the value 2. Option A begins with 1, so it is not correct. Following that must be 3 and 4, which each of the remaining options have. The final term requires a value of 5 to be present zero or one times. Options B and C fit this requirement, but Option D has two instances of the value 5. Therefore, only Options B and C are valid.

9. C. The expression requires an AS Path length of at least 2, which eliminates Options A and B. The second AS in the path may be repeated further, but a new AS number is not allowed. Option D lists two different AS values after 64512, so it does not match the expression. Only Option C fits all requirements of the regex.

10. B. The expression requires an AS Path length of at least 1, which must be 64512. Other AS values may or may not appear after 64512. Only Option B fits this criterion.

Chapter

2

Open Shortest Path First

JNCIS EXAM OBJECTIVES COVERED IN THIS CHAPTER:

✓ Define the functions of the following OSPF area designations and functions—backbone area; non-backbone area; stub area; not-so-stubby area

✓ Identify OSPF authentication types

✓ Identify the configuration of OSPF route summarization

✓ Determine route selection based on IGP route metrics and the Shortest Path Algorithm

✓ Identify the routing policy capabilities of OSPF

✓ Describe the functionality of the OSPF LSA types

✓ Describe the relationship between the loopback address and the router ID

✓ Define the capabilities and operation of graceful restart

✓ Identify the operation and configuration of a virtual link

In this chapter, we explore the operation of the Open Shortest Path First (OSPF) routing protocol in depth. Because you are reading this book, we assume that you are already familiar with OSPF basics, so we'll jump right into the details. We discuss OSPF link-state advertisements and explain how each represents a portion of the link-state database. After compiling a complete database, we examine the operation of the shortest path first (SPF) algorithm and see how the router determines the best path to each destination.

Next, we configure a sample network for both stub and not-so-stubby operation, and discuss the effects these area types have on the link-state database. We also explore options for controlling the operation of the area. This chapter concludes with a look at various OSPF configuration knobs available within the JUNOS software.

Link-State Advertisements

OSPF is a link-state protocol that uses a least-cost algorithm to calculate the best path for each network destination. Once an OSPF-speaking router forms an adjacency with a neighbor, it generates a link-state update and floods this packet into the network. Each update packet contains one or more *link-state advertisements* (LSA), which contain information the local router is injecting into the network. Each specific LSA type encodes particular data from the viewpoint of the local router.

The Common LSA Header

Each LSA advertised by an OSPF router uses a common 20-octet header format. The header contains information that allows each receiving router to determine the LSA type as well as other pertinent information.

Figure 2.1 displays the fields of the LSA header, which includes the following:

Link-State Age (2 octets)   The Link-State Age field displays the time since the LSA was first originated in the network. The age is incremented in seconds beginning at a value of 0 and increasing to a value of 3600 (1 hour). The 3600-second upper limit is defined as the *MaxAge* of the LSA, after which time it is removed from the database. The originating router is responsible for reflooding its LSAs into the network before they reach the MaxAge limit, which the JUNOS software accomplishes at an age of 3000 seconds (50 minutes), by default.

FIGURE 2.1 LSA header format

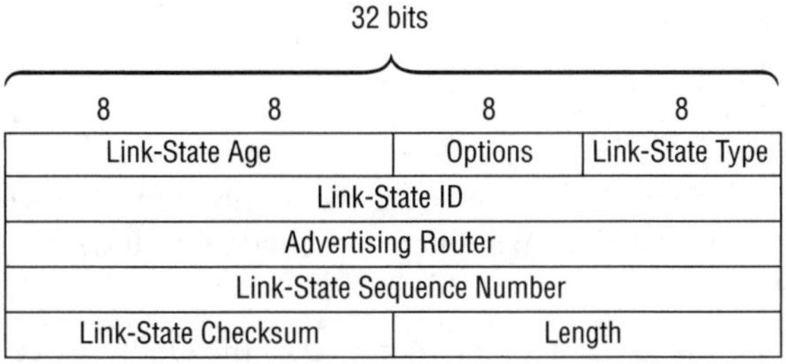

Options (1 octet) The local router advertises its capabilities in this field, which also appears in other OSPF packets. Each bit in the Options field represents a different function. The various bit definitions are:

Bit 7 The DN bit is used for loop prevention in a virtual private network (VPN) environment. An OSPF router receiving an update with this bit set does not forward that update.

Bit 6 The O bit indicates that the local router supports opaque LSAs. The JUNOS software uses opaque LSAs to support graceful restart and traffic engineering capabilities.

Bit 5 The DC bit indicates that the local router supports demand circuits. The JUNOS software does not use this feature.

Bit 4 The EA bit indicates that the local router supports the external attributes LSA for carrying Border Gateway Protocol (BGP) information in an OSPF network. The JUNOS software does not use this feature.

Bit 3 The N/P bit describes the handling and support of not-so-stubby LSAs.

Bit 2 The MC bit indicates that the local router supports multicast OSPF LSAs. The JUNOS software does not use this feature.

Bit 1 The E bit describes the handling and support of Type 5 external LSAs.

Bit 0 The T bit indicates that the local router supports type of service (TOS) routing functionality. The JUNOS software does not use this feature.

Link-State Type (1 octet) This field displays the type of LSA following the common header. The possible type codes are:

- 1—Router LSA
- 2—Network LSA
- 3—Network summary LSA
- 4—ASBR summary LSA
- 5—AS external LSA
- 6—Group membership LSA

- 7—NSSA external LSA
- 8—External attributes LSA
- 9—Opaque LSA (link-local scope)
- 10—Opaque LSA (area-local scope)
- 11—Opaque LSA (AS-wide scope)

Link-State ID (4 octets)   The Link-State ID field describes the portion of the network advertised by the LSA. Each LSA type uses this field in a different manner, which we discuss within the context of that specific LSA.

Advertising Router (4 octets)   This field displays the router ID of the OSPF device that originated the LSA.

Link-State Sequence Number (4 octets)   The Link-State Sequence Number field is a signed 32-bit field used to guarantee that each router has the most recent version of the LSA in its database. Each new instance of an LSA uses a sequence number of 0x80000001, which increments up to 0x7fffffff.

Link-State Checksum (2 octets)   This field displays a standard IP checksum for the entire LSA, excluding the Link-State Age field.

Length (2 octets)   This field displays the length of the entire LSA, including the header fields.

The Router LSA

Each OSPF router in the network generates a *router LSA* (Type 1) to describe the status and cost of its interfaces. The Type 1 LSA has an area-flooding scope, so it propagates no further than the area border router (ABR) for its area. The fields of a router LSA are shown in Figure 2.2 and include the following:

V/E/B Bits (1 octet)   This field contains five leading zeros followed by the V, E, and B bits. These bits convey the characteristics of the local router. The various bit definitions are:

V bit   The *V bit* is set when the local router is an endpoint for one or more fully operational virtual links. We discuss virtual links in more detail in the "Virtual Links" section later in this chapter.

E bit   The *E bit* is set when the local router is configured as an AS boundary router (ASBR) to inject external routes into the network.

B bit   The *B bit* is set when the local router has configured interfaces in more than one OSPF area, thereby turning the router into an ABR.

Reserved (1 octet)   This field is set to a constant value of 0x00.

Number of Links (2 octets)   This field displays the total number of links represented in the router LSA. The remaining fields in the LSA are repeated for each advertised link.

Link ID (4 octets)   This field displays information about the far end of the advertised interface. The information encoded here depends on the individual link type.

Link ID and Link Data Fields

The contents of the Link ID and Link Data fields within a router LSA are linked with the type of interface advertised. Each interface type places different types of information in these fields. The various interface types and their corresponding values are:

Point-to-point   An OSPF router always forms an adjacency over a point-to-point link using an unnumbered interface. This causes the Link ID field to contain the router ID of the adjacent peer. The Link Data field contains the IP address of the local router's interface or the local interface index value for unnumbered interfaces.

Transit   Transit links are interfaces connected to a broadcast segment, such as Ethernet, that contain other OSPF-speaking routers. The Link ID field is set to the interface address of the segment's designated router (DR). The Link Data field contains the IP address of the local router's interface.

Stub   Each operational OSPF interface that doesn't contain an adjacency is defined as a *stub network*. The router's loopback address and all interfaces configured in passive mode are considered stub networks. In addition, each subnet configured on a point-to-point interface is advertised as a stub network, since the actual adjacency is formed over the unnumbered interface. The Link ID field for a stub network contains the network number of the subnet, and the Link Data field contains the subnet mask.

Virtual link   A virtual link is a logical connection between two ABRs, one of which is not physically connected to the backbone. As with a point-to-point interface, the Link ID field contains the router ID of the adjacent peer and the Link Data field contains the IP address of the local router's interface used to reach the remote ABR.

FIGURE 2.2   The router LSA

32 bits			
8	8	8	8
V/E/B bits	Reserved	Number of Links	
Link ID			
Link Data			
Link Type	# of TOS Metrics	Metric	
Additional TOS Data			

Link Data (4 octets)   This field displays information about the near end of the advertised interface. Its value also is connected to the individual link type.

Link Type (1 octet)   The specific type of link advertised is encoded in this field. Possible values are:

- 1—Point-to-point
- 2—Transit
- 3—Stub
- 4—Virtual link

Number of TOS Metrics (1 octet)   This field displays the number of various TOS metrics for use with the interface. The JUNOS software uses only the basic link metric, which prompts this field to be set to a constant value of 0x00.

FIGURE 2.3   A sample OSPF network

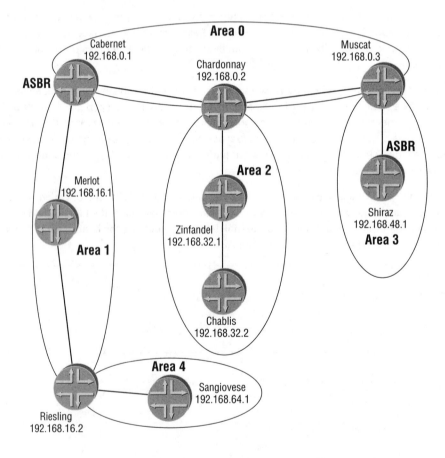

Metric (2 octets)   This field displays the cost, or metric, of the local interface. Possible values range from 0 to 65,535.

Additional TOS Data (4 octets)   These fields contain the TOS-specific information for the advertised link. The JUNOS software does not use these fields, and they are not included in any advertised LSAs.

Figure 2.3 displays a sample network using OSPF. The Cabernet, Chardonnay, and Muscat routers are all ABRs in area 0. Area 1 contains both the Merlot and Riesling routers, and area 2 encompasses the Zinfandel and Chablis routers. The Shiraz router is the only internal router in area 3, and the Sangiovese router is the only internal router in area 4. Both Cabernet and Shiraz are configured as ASBRs and they are injecting routes within the 172.16.0.0 /16 address space.

 We explore the connectivity of area 4 in the "Virtual Links" section later in this chapter.

The Chardonnay router has the following router LSAs within its area 0 database:

```
user@Chardonnay> show ospf database router area 0 extensive

    OSPF link state database, area 0.0.0.0
 Type       ID                   Adv Rtr           Seq        Age  Opt  Cksum  Len
 Router    192.168.0.1      192.168.0.1       0x80000002   422  0x2  0x1c94  60
   bits 0x3, link count 3
   id 192.168.0.2, data 192.168.1.1, type PointToPoint (1)
   TOS count 0, TOS 0 metric 1
   id 192.168.1.0, data 255.255.255.0, type Stub (3)
   TOS count 0, TOS 0 metric 1
   id 192.168.0.1, data 255.255.255.255, type Stub (3)
   TOS count 0, TOS 0 metric 0
   Aging timer 00:52:58
   Installed 00:06:56 ago, expires in 00:52:58, sent 00:06:44 ago
 Router   *192.168.0.2      192.168.0.2       0x80000006   399  0x2  0x635c  72
   bits 0x1, link count 4
   id 192.168.0.1, data 192.168.1.2, type PointToPoint (1)
   TOS count 0, TOS 0 metric 1
   id 192.168.1.0, data 255.255.255.0, type Stub (3)
   TOS count 0, TOS 0 metric 1
   id 192.168.2.2, data 192.168.2.1, type Transit (2)
   TOS count 0, TOS 0 metric 1
   id 192.168.0.2, data 255.255.255.255, type Stub (3)
   TOS count 0, TOS 0 metric 0
```

```
Gen timer 00:09:13
Aging timer 00:53:21
Installed 00:06:39 ago, expires in 00:53:21, sent 00:06:39 ago
Ours
Router    192.168.0.3       192.168.0.3       0x80000003    400  0x2  0x23fc  48
  bits 0x1, link count 2
  id 192.168.2.2, data 192.168.2.2, type Transit (2)
  TOS count 0, TOS 0 metric 1
  id 192.168.0.3, data 255.255.255.255, type Stub (3)
  TOS count 0, TOS 0 metric 0
  Aging timer 00:53:20
  Installed 00:06:39 ago, expires in 00:53:20, sent 00:06:39 ago
```

Compare this output to the information you saw in Figure 2.3. Both Chardonnay and Muscat are advertising that they are ABRs by setting the B bit—bits 0x1. Cabernet is an ABR, but it is injecting external routes into the network, making it an ASBR as well. Both of these capabilities are shown by the bits 0x3 setting within Cabernet's router LSA. Each of those routers is also advertising its loopback address as a stub network, type 3, as you'd expect. A point-to-point link exists between Cabernet and Chardonnay as each router lists its neighbor's router ID in the Link ID field. Muscat is connected to Chardonnay over a broadcast segment for which it is the DR. We verify this by noting that each router reports a link ID of 192.168.2.2 associated with the interface. Finally, each router lists its Options support (Opt) as 0x2, which signifies support for external LSAs, a requirement for the backbone.

 Each LSA in the link-state database originated by the local router is noted with an asterisk (*). This notation is often useful for troubleshooting your network's operation.

The router LSAs seen on the Chablis router in area 2 reveal information similar to what we saw in area 0:

user@Chablis> **show ospf database router extensive**

```
    OSPF link state database, area 0.0.0.2
Type       ID               Adv Rtr           Seq       Age  Opt  Cksum  Len
Router    192.168.0.2       192.168.0.2       0x80000003  409  0x2  0x87c5  60
  bits 0x1, link count 3
  id 192.168.32.1, data 192.168.33.1, type PointToPoint (1)
  TOS count 0, TOS 0 metric 1
  id 192.168.33.0, data 255.255.255.0, type Stub (3)
  TOS count 0, TOS 0 metric 1
  id 192.168.0.2, data 255.255.255.255, type Stub (3)
  TOS count 0, TOS 0 metric 0
  Aging timer 00:53:11
```

```
Installed 00:06:42 ago, expires in 00:53:11, sent 2w3d 19:51:02 ago
Router    192.168.32.1       192.168.32.1       0x80000003   406  0x2  0x2c1f  84
 bits 0x0, link count 5
 id 192.168.32.2, data 192.168.34.1, type PointToPoint (1)
 TOS count 0, TOS 0 metric 1
 id 192.168.34.0, data 255.255.255.0, type Stub (3)
 TOS count 0, TOS 0 metric 1
 id 192.168.0.2, data 192.168.33.2, type PointToPoint (1)
 TOS count 0, TOS 0 metric 1
 id 192.168.33.0, data 255.255.255.0, type Stub (3)
 TOS count 0, TOS 0 metric 1
 id 192.168.32.1, data 255.255.255.255, type Stub (3)
 TOS count 0, TOS 0 metric 0
 Aging timer 00:53:13
 Installed 00:06:45 ago, expires in 00:53:14, sent 2w3d 19:51:02 ago
Router   *192.168.32.2       192.168.32.2       0x80000003   408  0x2  0x9654  60
 bits 0x0, link count 3
 id 192.168.32.1, data 192.168.34.2, type PointToPoint (1)
 TOS count 0, TOS 0 metric 1
 id 192.168.34.0, data 255.255.255.0, type Stub (3)
 TOS count 0, TOS 0 metric 1
 id 192.168.32.2, data 255.255.255.255, type Stub (3)
 TOS count 0, TOS 0 metric 0
 Gen timer 00:43:11
 Aging timer 00:53:11
 Installed 00:06:48 ago, expires in 00:53:12, sent 00:06:48 ago
 Ours
```

The Zinfandel and Chablis routers are not ABR or ASBR routers, so they set neither the E nor the B bit (`bits 0x0`) in their LSAs. Again, each router advertises its loopback address as a stub network.

The Network LSA

The DR on a broadcast segment sends a *network LSA* (Type 2) to list the operational OSPF routers on the segment. The Type 2 LSA also has an area-flooding scope, so it propagates no further than the ABR. The Link-State ID field in the LSA header is populated with the IP interface address of the DR. The fields of the network LSA itself are displayed in Figure 2.4 and include the following:

Network Mask (4 octets)   This field displays the subnet mask for the broadcast segment. It is combined with the interface address of the DR in the Link-State ID field of the LSA header to represent the subnet for the segment.

Attached Router (4 octets)   This field is repeated for each router connected to the broadcast segment and contains the router ID of the routers.

FIGURE 2.4   The network LSA

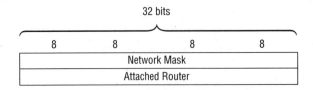

Using the sample OSPF network in Figure 2.3 we examine the link-state database for Type 2 LSAs. As you can see, area 0 contains a broadcast segment. Here's the output from the Chardonnay router:

```
user@Chardonnay> show ospf database network area 0 extensive

   OSPF link state database, area 0.0.0.0
Type     ID              Adv Rtr          Seq       Age  Opt  Cksum  Len
Network  192.168.2.2     192.168.0.3      0x80000002 369  0x2  0x7a2d 32
  mask 255.255.255.0
  attached router 192.168.0.3
  attached router 192.168.0.2
  Aging timer 00:53:51
  Installed 00:06:07 ago, expires in 00:53:51, sent 2w3d 19:53:30 ago
```

Both the Cabernet (192.168.0.2) and Muscat (192.168.0.3) routers are attached to the broadcast segment. By combining the Link-State ID field in the LSA header with the advertised network mask within the LSA, we find that the segment address is 192.168.2.0 /24. Recall that the segment's DR always generates the network LSA, making it the advertising router. This particular LSA is advertised by 192.168.0.3, meaning that Muscat is the current DR for the segment.

The Network Summary LSA

Router and network LSAs have an area-flooding scope, which means that routers in other OSPF areas require a different method for reaching the addresses advertised in those LSA types. This is the function of the *network summary LSA* (Type 3), which is generated by an ABR. A single Type 3 LSA is generated for each router and network LSA in the area.

The ABR advertises local routing knowledge (router and network LSAs) in both directions across the area boundary. Non-backbone routes are sent into area 0, and local area 0 routes are sent to the non-backbone area. In addition, the ABR generates a network summary LSA for every Type 3 LSA received from a remote ABR through the backbone. These latter network summary LSAs are advertised only in the non-backbone areas and provide routing knowledge to subnets in a remote OSPF non-backbone area.

The Link-State ID field in the LSA header displays the network being advertised across the area boundary. The fields of the network summary LSA itself are shown in Figure 2.5 and include the following:

Network Mask (4 octets)   This field displays the subnet mask for the advertised network. When combined with the network listed in the Link-State ID field of the LSA header, it represents the entire address being announced.

Reserved (1 octet)   This field is set to a constant value of 0x00.

Metric (3 octets)   This field displays the metric of the advertised network. The ABR uses its local total cost for the route as the advertised metric in the LSA. If several addresses are aggregated into the Type 3 LSA, the largest metric of the summarized routes is placed in this field.

Type of Service (1 octet)   This field displays the specific TOS the following metric refers to. The JUNOS software does not use this field, and it is not included in any LSAs.

TOS Metric (3 octets)   This field contains the TOS metric for the advertised route. The JUNOS software does not use this field, and it is not included in any LSAs.

FIGURE 2.5   The network summary LSA

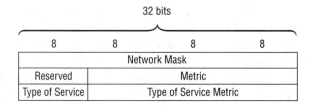

We'll use Figure 2.3 as a reference for examining the link-state database information in the network. The Muscat router is an ABR for area 3, so let's begin there. The local routes from area 3 are advertised in the backbone as follows:

```
user@Muscat> ... netsummary area 0 extensive advertising-router 192.168.0.3

    OSPF link state database, area 0.0.0.0
Type        ID               Adv Rtr          Seq        Age  Opt  Cksum  Len
Summary *192.168.48.1    192.168.0.3      0x80000001   434  0x2  0x89cb  28
  mask 255.255.255.255
  TOS 0x0, metric 1
```

```
Gen timer 00:08:33
Aging timer 00:52:46
Installed 00:07:14 ago, expires in 00:52:46, sent 00:06:56 ago
Ours
Summary *192.168.49.0    192.168.0.3    0x80000001  439  0x2  0x88cc  28
mask 255.255.255.0
TOS 0x0, metric 1
Gen timer 00:02:59
Aging timer 00:52:41
Installed 00:07:19 ago, expires in 00:52:41, sent 00:06:56 ago
Ours
```

The 192.168.48.1 /32 route is the loopback address of Shiraz, while the 192.168.49.0 /24 route is the subnet of the Muscat-Shiraz link. Both of the routes are advertised in the backbone using Type 3 LSAs. The Link-State ID field is combined with the Network Mask field to represent the network addresses. The other key field in the network summary LSA is the Metric field. The ABR always places its current metric for the route in this field. A quick look at the network map reveals that, from Muscat's perspective, the Shiraz router and the intermediate link should have a cost of 1 (the default OSPF metric for almost all interface types).

We see much more interesting information when we examine Muscat's advertisements in area 3. These LSAs are currently in the link-state database as:

```
user@Muscat> show ospf database netsummary area 3


    OSPF link state database, area 0.0.0.3
Type       ID           Adv Rtr          Seq        Age  Opt  Cksum  Len
Summary *192.168.0.1    192.168.0.3    0x80000001  411  0x2  0xa5de  28
Summary *192.168.0.2    192.168.0.3    0x80000001  411  0x2  0x91f2  28
Summary *192.168.1.0    192.168.0.3    0x80000001  411  0x2  0xa4df  28
Summary *192.168.2.0    192.168.0.3    0x80000001  456  0x2  0x8ff4  28
Summary *192.168.16.1   192.168.0.3    0x80000001  312  0x2  0xfe74  28
Summary *192.168.16.2   192.168.0.3    0x80000001  312  0x2  0xfe72  28
Summary *192.168.17.0   192.168.0.3    0x80000001  411  0x2  0xfd75  28
Summary *192.168.18.0   192.168.0.3    0x80000001  312  0x2  0xfc74  28
Summary *192.168.32.1   192.168.0.3    0x80000001  377  0x2  0x4420  28
Summary *192.168.32.2   192.168.0.3    0x80000001  377  0x2  0x441e  28
Summary *192.168.33.0   192.168.0.3    0x80000001  386  0x2  0x4321  28
Summary *192.168.34.0   192.168.0.3    0x80000001  377  0x2  0x4220  28
```

Muscat is advertising the local backbone routes as well as routes from the other non-backbone areas. For example, the loopback address of Cabernet (192.168.0.1 /32) is a router LSA within area 0:

```
user@Muscat> show ospf database area 0 lsa-id 192.168.0.1
```

```
OSPF link state database, area 0.0.0.0
Type      ID              Adv Rtr         Seq        Age  Opt  Cksum  Len
Router  192.168.0.1     192.168.0.1     0x80000002  226  0x2  0x1c94  60
```

The loopback address of the Riesling router in area 1 (192.168.16.2 /32) is a network summary LSA within area 0:

user@Muscat> **show ospf database area 0 lsa-id 192.168.16.2**

```
OSPF link state database, area 0.0.0.0
Type      ID              Adv Rtr         Seq        Age  Opt  Cksum  Len
Summary  192.168.16.2    192.168.0.1     0x80000001  223  0x2  0xf67e  28
```

We use the extensive option of the show ospf database command to view the LSAs before and after Muscat advertises them in area 3:

user@Muscat> **show ospf database area 0 lsa-id 192.168.0.1 extensive**

```
OSPF link state database, area 0.0.0.0
Type      ID              Adv Rtr         Seq        Age   Opt  Cksum  Len
Router  192.168.0.1     192.168.0.1     0x80000004  1130  0x2  0x1896  60
  bits 0x1, link count 3
  id 192.168.0.2, data 192.168.1.1, type PointToPoint (1)
  TOS count 0, TOS 0 metric 1
  id 192.168.1.0, data 255.255.255.0, type Stub (3)
  TOS count 0, TOS 0 metric 1
  id 192.168.0.1, data 255.255.255.255, type Stub (3)
  TOS count 0, TOS 0 metric 0
  Aging timer 00:41:09
  Installed 00:18:44 ago, expires in 00:41:10, sent 4w6d 19:03:15 ago
```

user@Muscat> **show ospf database area 3 lsa-id 192.168.0.1 extensive**

```
OSPF link state database, area 0.0.0.3
Type      ID              Adv Rtr         Seq        Age  Opt  Cksum  Len
Summary *192.168.0.1     192.168.0.3     0x80000003  670  0x2  0xa1e0  28
  mask 255.255.255.255
  TOS 0x0, metric 2
  Gen timer 00:35:24
  Aging timer 00:48:50
  Installed 00:11:10 ago, expires in 00:48:50, sent 00:11:08 ago
  Ours
```

```
user@Muscat> show ospf database area 0 lsa-id 192.168.16.2 extensive

    OSPF link state database, area 0.0.0.0
 Type       ID              Adv Rtr          Seq       Age  Opt  Cksum  Len
Summary  192.168.16.2    192.168.0.1      0x80000002  1736  0x2  0xf47f  28
  mask 255.255.255.255
  TOS 0x0, metric 2
  Aging timer 00:31:03
  Installed 00:28:50 ago, expires in 00:31:04, sent 4w6d 19:03:21 ago

user@Muscat> show ospf database area 3 lsa-id 192.168.16.2 extensive

    OSPF link state database, area 0.0.0.3
 Type       ID              Adv Rtr          Seq       Age  Opt  Cksum  Len
Summary *192.168.16.2    192.168.0.3      0x80000002  1577  0x2  0xfc73  28
  mask 255.255.255.255
  TOS 0x0, metric 4
  Gen timer 00:18:24
  Aging timer 00:33:43
  Installed 00:26:17 ago, expires in 00:33:43, sent 00:26:15 ago
  Ours
```

By paying particular attention to the metrics carried within the LSAs, we gain a unique insight into the operation of the protocol. Muscat receives a router LSA from Cabernet with an advertised metric of 0. After running the SPF algorithm, Muscat determines that the Cabernet router is a metric of 2 away from it. Muscat then adds the advertised metric in the LSA to the calculated SPF metric to determine the total cost to the router, which it places in the routing table. The total cost of the router is also used as the advertised metric within the network summary LSA Muscat advertises in area 3, as seen in the router output earlier. This allows the Shiraz router in area 3 to calculate the total cost to Cabernet's loopback address in a similar manner. Shiraz's SPF metric to Muscat is 1, which is added to the advertised metric of 2 for a total metric cost of 3.

A similar process occurs for the loopback address of the Riesling router, 192.168.16.2 /32. Cabernet is advertising a metric of 2 in its network summary LSA in area 0. Like the Muscat router, Cabernet uses its total cost to the route as the advertised metric. We've already determined that Muscat is a metric of 2 away from Cabernet, so the advertised metric in the LSA is added to this value to determine the total cost to reach Riesling. This metric value is 4, which Muscat advertises in its own network summary LSA within area 3. As before, the Shiraz router adds its SPF metric of 1 (to reach Muscat) to the advertised LSA metric to determine its total metric cost of 5 to reach the Riesling router's loopback address.

The ASBR Summary LSA

Before an OSPF-speaking router uses an advertised external route, it first verifies that it has local knowledge of the ASBR itself. When the ASBR is in the same area as the router, it uses the V/E/B bits within the ASBR's router LSA as its method for determining its existence. When a routing policy is configured on the ASBR, the E bit is set within the LSA, allowing all other routers in the area to know that it is now an ASBR. The same method is not available when the ASBR is in a remote OSPF area, however, because the ASBR's router LSA is not transmitted across the area boundary. To allow routers in a remote area to use external routes from the ASBR, the area's ABR generates an *ASBR summary LSA* (Type 4) that contains the router ID of the ASBR as well as the metric cost to reach that same router.

The JUNOS software generates a Type 4 LSA when one of two conditions is met. The first condition is the receipt of an ASBR summary LSA from within the backbone. This means that an ASBR exists in a remote non-backbone area and that remote area's ABR has generated the Type 4 LSA. The second condition is the receipt of a router LSA within a connected area that has the E bit set (indicating the router is an ASBR). The router LSA may be located in either the backbone or a connected non-backbone area. In either case, the ABR generates an ASBR summary LSA to represent the ASBR and floods it into the appropriate area.

The ASBR summary LSA uses the same format as the network summary LSA. The key difference between the two is the information appearing in the Link-State ID field in the LSA header. An ASBR summary LSA contains the router ID of the ASBR in this field. The remaining fields of the ASBR summary LSA are shown in Figure 2.6 and include the following:

Network Mask (4 octets)   This field has no meaning to an ASBR summary LSA and is set to a constant value of 0.0.0.0.

Reserved (1 octet)   This field is set to a constant value of 0x00.

Metric (3 octets)   This field displays the cost to reach the ASBR. The ABR uses its local total cost for the ASBR as the advertised metric in the LSA.

Type of Service (1 octet)   This field displays the specific TOS the following metric refers to. The JUNOS software does not use this field, and it is not included in any LSAs.

TOS Metric (3 octets)   This field contains the TOS metric for the advertised route. The JUNOS software does not use this field, and it is not included in any LSAs.

FIGURE 2.6   The ASBR summary LSA

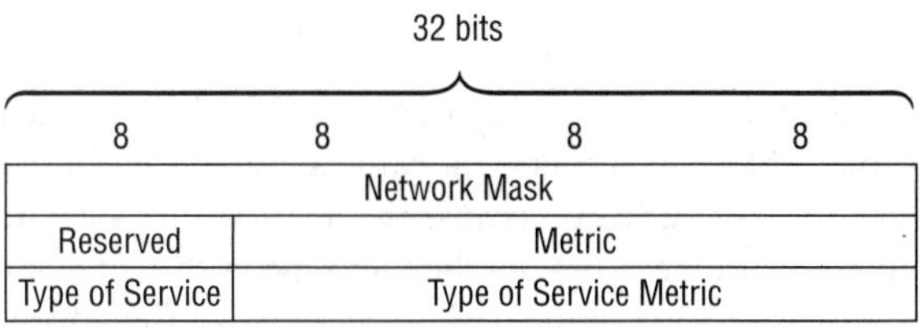

Both the Cabernet router and the Shiraz router you saw in Figure 2.3 are now configured as ASBRs and are injecting external routes into the network. The presence of the E bit in the router LSA from Shiraz causes the Muscat router to generate an ASBR summary LSA and flood it into area 0:

```
user@Muscat> show ospf database area 3 lsa-id 192.168.48.1 extensive

    OSPF link state database, area 0.0.0.3
 Type        ID            Adv Rtr           Seq      Age  Opt  Cksum  Len
 Router   192.168.48.1     192.168.48.1    0x80000005    4  0x2  0xe3ed  48
   bits 0x2, link count 2
   id 192.168.49.0, data 255.255.255.0, type Stub (3)
   TOS count 0, TOS 0 metric 1
   id 192.168.48.1, data 255.255.255.255, type Stub (3)
   TOS count 0, TOS 0 metric 0
   Aging timer 00:59:55
   Installed 00:00:01 ago, expires in 00:59:56, sent 00:00:03 ago


user@Muscat> show ospf database area 0 lsa-id 192.168.48.1 extensive

    OSPF link state database, area 0.0.0.0
 Type        ID            Adv Rtr           Seq      Age  Opt  Cksum  Len
 Summary *192.168.48.1     192.168.0.3     0x80000002   18  0x2  0x87cc  28
   mask 255.255.255.255
   TOS 0x0, metric 1
   Gen timer 00:49:42
   Aging timer 00:59:42
   Installed 00:00:18 ago, expires in 00:59:42, sent 00:00:18 ago
   Ours
 ASBRSum *192.168.48.1     192.168.0.3     0x80000001   18  0x2  0x7bd8  28
   mask 0.0.0.0
   TOS 0x0, metric 1
   Gen timer 00:49:42
   Aging timer 00:59:42
   Installed 00:00:18 ago, expires in 00:59:42, sent 00:00:18 ago
   Ours
```

Muscat is advertising two LSAs with the Link-State ID field set to 192.168.48.1 a Type 3 and a Type 4 LSA. Notice that the format of the two LSAs is the same and that the contents are very similar. The metric values in both LSAs are identical because the method for calculating them is the same. The largest distinction between the two, besides the LSA type, is the contents of the Network Mask field. The network summary LSA contains the subnet mask of the advertised route, 255.255.255.255 in this case. The ASBR summary LSA is always set to the value 0.0.0.0, because it is advertising only a 32-bit router ID that is contained wholly within the Link-State ID field.

Should we shift our focus to the Chardonnay router in area 0, we see an example of the second reason for generating a Type 4 LSA. In this case, Chardonnay receives an ASBR summary LSA from Muscat for the ASBR of Shiraz. Chardonnay generates a new ASBR summary LSA and floods it into area 2:

```
user@Chardonnay> show ospf database area 0 lsa-id 192.168.48.1 extensive

    OSPF link state database, area 0.0.0.0
 Type      ID                 Adv Rtr           Seq       Age  Opt  Cksum  Len
Summary  192.168.48.1    192.168.0.3       0x80000002  1025  0x2  0x87cc  28
  mask 255.255.255.255
  TOS 0x0, metric 1
  Aging timer 00:42:55
  Installed 00:17:04 ago, expires in 00:42:55, sent 00:17:04 ago
ASBRSum  192.168.48.1    192.168.0.3       0x80000001  1025  0x2  0x7bd8  28
  mask 0.0.0.0
  TOS 0x0, metric 1
  Aging timer 00:42:55
  Installed 00:17:04 ago, expires in 00:42:55, sent 00:17:04 ago


user@Chardonnay> show ospf database area 2 lsa-id 192.168.48.1 extensive

    OSPF link state database, area 0.0.0.2
 Type      ID                 Adv Rtr           Seq       Age  Opt  Cksum  Len
Summary *192.168.48.1    192.168.0.2       0x80000002  1027  0x2  0x97bc  28
  mask 255.255.255.255
  TOS 0x0, metric 2
  Gen timer 00:25:20
  Aging timer 00:42:52
  Installed 00:17:07 ago, expires in 00:42:53, sent 00:17:07 ago
  Ours
ASBRSum *192.168.48.1    192.168.0.2       0x80000001  1027  0x2  0x8bc8  28
  mask 0.0.0.0
  TOS 0x0, metric 2
  Gen timer 00:27:59
  Aging timer 00:42:52
  Installed 00:17:07 ago, expires in 00:42:53, sent 00:17:07 ago
  Ours
```

Once again, we see the Metric fields in the ASBR summary LSAs increment across the area boundary. This allows all routers in the network to calculate a total metric cost to each ASBR should multiple routers advertise the same external route. In that situation, each router chooses the metrically closest ASBR to forward user traffic to.

The AS External LSA

External routing information is advertised within an OSPF network using an *AS external LSA* (Type 5). The AS external LSAs are unique within the protocol in that they have a domain-wide flooding scope. This means that, by default, each OSPF-speaking router receives the same LSA which was advertised by the ASBR. The network portion of the advertised external route is placed in the Link-State ID field in the LSA header. The remaining fields of the AS external LSA are shown in Figure 2.7 and include the following:

Network Mask (4 octets)   This field displays the subnet mask for the advertised network and is combined with the network listed in the Link-State ID field of the LSA header to represent the entire address being announced.

E Bit (1 octet)   The description of this field may sound a bit unusual since it doesn't take an entire octet to describe a single bit. This portion of the LSA contains a single bit, the E bit. It is followed by 7 bits, all set to a constant value of 0. The E bit represents the type of metric encoded for the external route.

When the E bit is set to the value 1 (the default), it is considered a Type 2 external metric. This means that all OSPF routers use the metric advertised in the LSA as the total cost for the external route.

When the E bit is set to the value 0, the advertised route is a Type 1 external metric. To find the total cost for the external route, each OSPF router combines the metric in the LSA with the cost to reach the ASBR.

Metric (3 octets)   This field displays the metric of the external route as set by the ASBR. The value is used with the E bit to determine the total cost for the route.

Forwarding Address (4 octets)   This field displays the IP address each OSPF router forwards traffic to when it desires to reach the external route. An address of 0.0.0.0 means the ASBR itself is the forwarding address and is the default value within the JUNOS software for native Type 5 LSAs.

External Route Tag (4 octets)   This field contains a 32-bit value that may be assigned to the external route. The OSPF routing protocol itself does not use this field, but other routing protocols might use the information located here. The JUNOS software sets this field to the value 0.0.0.0 by default.

FIGURE 2.7   The AS external LSA

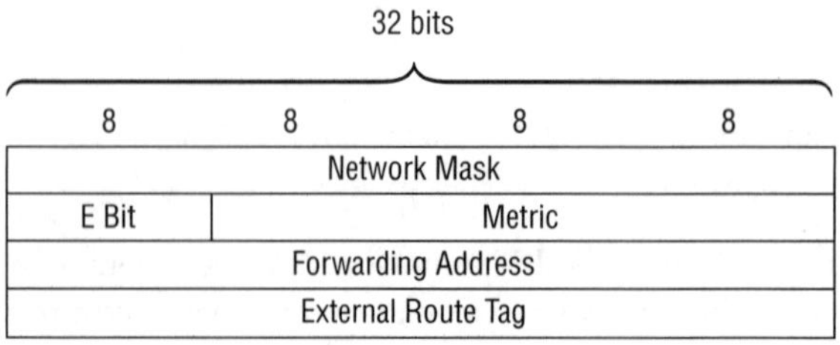

32 bits

8	8	8	8
Network Mask			
E Bit	Metric		
Forwarding Address			
External Route Tag			

Both the Cabernet and Shiraz routers you saw in Figure 2.3 are configured as ASBRs and are injecting external routes into the network. Let's view the details of the Type 5 LSAs on the Chablis router:

```
user@Chablis> show ospf database extern extensive lsa-id 172.16.1.0
    OSPF AS SCOPE link state database
 Type      ID               Adv Rtr           Seq      Age  Opt  Cksum  Len
 Extern   172.16.1.0       192.168.0.1       0x80000002 1583 0x2  0x3e6b  36
   mask 255.255.255.0
   Type 2, TOS 0x0, metric 0, fwd addr 0.0.0.0, tag 0.0.0.0
   Aging timer 00:33:36
   Installed 00:26:13 ago, expires in 00:33:37, sent 4w6d 20:14:35 ago
```

The Link-State ID field contains the network being advertised by the LSA—172.16.1.0 in this case. We combine this value with the Network Mask field of 255.255.255.0 to conclude that the advertised route is 172.16.1.0 /24. The E bit in the Type 5 LSA is currently set (the router output shows the LSA as a Type 2). This causes the Chablis router to use the advertised metric of 0 as the total metric cost of the route. Both the fwd addr and tag fields are set to their default values of 0.0.0.0. User traffic from Chablis is then sent to the ASBR itself (192.168.0.1), using the information contained in the Adv rtr field.

Provided that Chablis has an ASBR summary LSA in its area 2 database for 192.168.0.1, it installs the 172.16.1.0 /24 route in its routing table as an OSPF external route with a metric of 0:

```
user@Chablis> show ospf database asbrsummary lsa-id 192.168.0.1

    OSPF link state database, area 0.0.0.2
 Type      ID               Adv Rtr           Seq      Age  Opt  Cksum  Len
 ASBRSum  192.168.0.1      192.168.0.2       0x80000002 400  0x2  0x91f2  28

user@Chablis> show route 172.16.1/24

inet.0: 28 destinations, 29 routes (28 active, 0 holddown, 0 hidden)
+ = Active Route, - = Last Active, * = Both

172.16.1.0/24       *[OSPF/150] 00:46:34, metric 0, tag 0
                     > via so-0/1/0.0
```

The NSSA External LSA

External routing information in an OSPF network injected into a not-so-stubby area (NSSA) is advertised in an *NSSA external LSA* (Type 7). These LSAs use the same format as the AS external LSAs but have an area-flooding scope. Each ABSR within the NSSA generates a Type 7 LSA and floods it into the area. Each router in the NSSA already has a router LSA from the ASBR, so the Type 7 LSAs are installed in the database as well as the routing table.

A potential problem arises, however, when we examine the operation of the rest of the network. None of the other OSPF-speaking routers have any knowledge of the NSSA's existence. Furthermore, these routers don't comprehend the concept and usage of the NSSA external LSAs. As with most of the other "issues" we've encountered thus far in OSPF, the ABR again plays a role in resolving our apparent contradiction. Because the Type 7 LSAs have an area-flooding scope, they are advertised no further than the ABR. To provide network reachability for the backbone and other remote areas, the ABR generates an AS external LSA for each received NSSA external LSA. This translation is facilitated through the identical formats of the Type 5 and Type 7 LSAs.

When multiple ABRs are present in the NSSA, only the ABR with the highest router ID performs the 5-to-7 LSA translation.

The network portion of the advertised NSSA external route is placed in the Link-State ID field in the LSA header. The remaining fields of the NSSA external LSA are shown in Figure 2.8 and include the following:

Network Mask (4 octets)   This field displays the subnet mask for the advertised network and is combined with the network listed in the Link-State ID field of the LSA header to represent the entire address being announced.

E Bit (1 octet)   This field contains the E bit followed by 7 bits, all set to a constant value of 0. The E bit represents the type of metric encoded for the external route.

When the E bit is set to the value 1 (the default), it is considered a Type 2 NSSA external metric. This means that all OSPF routers use the metric advertised in the LSA as the total cost for the external route.

When the E bit is set to the value 0, the advertised route is a Type 1 NSSA external metric. To find the total cost for the external route, each OSPF router combines the metric in the LSA with the cost to reach the ASBR.

Metric (3 octets)   This field displays the metric of the external route as set by the ASBR. The value is used with the E bit to determine the total cost for the route.

FIGURE 2.8   The NSSA external LSA

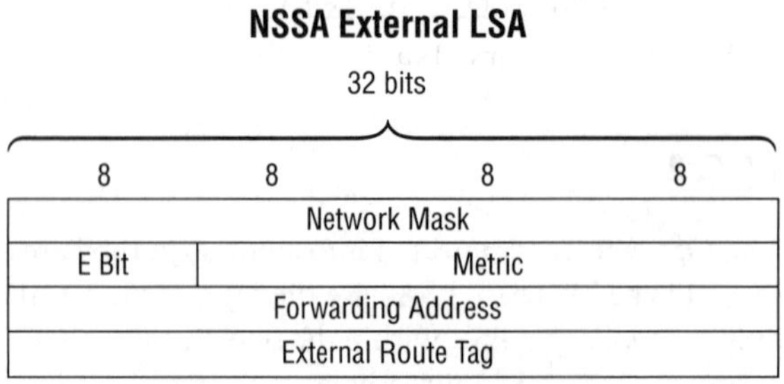

NSSA External LSA

32 bits

8	8	8	8
Network Mask			
E Bit	Metric		
Forwarding Address			
External Route Tag			

Forwarding Address (4 octets)   This field displays the IP address an OSPF router forwards traffic to when it desires to reach the external route. By default, the JUNOS software places the router ID of the ASBR in this field.

External Route Tag (4 octets)   This field contains a 32-bit value that may be assigned to the external route. The OSPF routing protocol itself does not use this field, but other routing protocols might use the information located here. The JUNOS software sets this field to the value 0.0.0.0 by default.

Area 3 in the sample network you saw in Figure 2.3 is now configured as a not-so-stubby area, with the Shiraz router still injecting external routes as an ASBR. (We discuss the configuration and operation of an NSSA in the "Not-So-Stubby Areas" section later in this chapter.) The Muscat router displays the external routes from Shiraz in its area 3 link-state database like this:

```
user@Muscat> show ospf database nssa

    OSPF link state database, area 0.0.0.3
 Type     ID              Adv Rtr          Seq        Age  Opt  Cksum  Len
 NSSA     172.16.4.0      192.168.48.1     0x80000008  139  0x8  0xf9d3  36
 NSSA     172.16.5.0      192.168.48.1     0x80000006  139  0x8  0xf2db  36
 NSSA     172.16.6.0      192.168.48.1     0x80000006  139  0x8  0xe7e5  36
 NSSA     172.16.7.0      192.168.48.1     0x80000005  139  0x8  0xdeee  36
```

Each of the NSSA external LSAs advertised by the Shiraz router is translated by Muscat into an AS external LSA. These Type 5 LSAs are then advertised to the rest of the network using a domain-flooding scope. These "new" Type 5 LSAs, in addition to the appropriate ASBR summary LSA, are seen on the Chablis router in area 2:

```
user@Chablis> show ospf database extern advertising-router 192.168.0.3
    OSPF AS SCOPE link state database
 Type     ID              Adv Rtr          Seq        Age  Opt  Cksum  Len
 Extern   172.16.4.0      192.168.0.3      0x8000000c  418  0x2  0xad52  36
 Extern   172.16.5.0      192.168.0.3      0x8000000a  418  0x2  0xa65a  36
 Extern   172.16.6.0      192.168.0.3      0x80000005  418  0x2  0xa55f  36
 Extern   172.16.7.0      192.168.0.3      0x8000000e  418  0x2  0x8872  36

user@Chablis> show ospf database asbrsummary lsa-id 192.168.0.3

    OSPF link state database, area 0.0.0.2
 Type     ID              Adv Rtr          Seq        Age  Opt  Cksum  Len
 ASBRSum  192.168.0.3     192.168.0.2      0x80000003  431  0x2  0x7b06  28
```

You might notice that in the Type 5 LSAs seen on the Chablis router the advertising router field lists 192.168.0.3 (Muscat) as the ASBR. This change occurs during the translation process on the NSSA ABR. Let's examine a single route advertised from Shiraz, 172.16.6.0 /24, as it is translated at the edge of area 3:

```
user@Muscat> show ospf database lsa-id 172.16.6.0 extensive

    OSPF link state database, area 0.0.0.3
 Type       ID              Adv Rtr           Seq       Age   Opt  Cksum  Len
NSSA     172.16.6.0      192.168.48.1     0x80000006   931   0x8  0xe7e5  36
  mask 255.255.255.0
  Type 2, TOS 0x0, metric 0, fwd addr 192.168.48.1, tag 0.0.0.0
  Aging timer 00:44:29
  Installed 00:15:28 ago, expires in 00:44:29, sent 00:39:51 ago


    OSPF AS SCOPE link state database
 Type       ID              Adv Rtr           Seq       Age   Opt  Cksum  Len
Extern   *172.16.6.0      192.168.0.3      0x80000005   919   0x2  0xa55f  36
  mask 255.255.255.0
  Type 2, TOS 0x0, metric 0, fwd addr 192.168.48.1, tag 0.0.0.0
  Gen timer 00:29:49
  Aging timer 00:44:41
  Installed 00:15:19 ago, expires in 00:44:41, sent 00:15:17 ago
  Ours
```

The differences between the Type 7 and Type 5 LSAs are highlighted in this router output. The LSA type code in the header is changed from 7 (NSSA) to 5 (Extern). The setting 0x8 in the Opt field of the NSSA external LSA informs the Muscat router that it can perform the translation. After generating the AS external LSA, Muscat sets this field to the normal value of 0x2, as seen in other Type 5 LSAs. Finally, Muscat places its own router ID in the Adv Rtr field because it is the originating router for the Type 5 LSA. Although not configured with a routing policy, the act of translating the Type 7 LSAs into Type 5 LSAs turns the Muscat router into an ASBR. As such, it sets the E bit in its router LSA to indicate this fact to the rest of the network:

```
user@Muscat> show ospf database router area 0 lsa-id 192.168.0.3 extensive

    OSPF link state database, area 0.0.0.0
 Type       ID              Adv Rtr           Seq       Age  Opt  Cksum  Len
Router   *192.168.0.3     192.168.0.3      0x80000014   992  0x2  0x706   48
  bits 0x3, link count 2
   id 192.168.2.2, data 192.168.2.2, Type Transit (2)
   TOS count 0, TOS 0 metric 1
   id 192.168.0.3, data 255.255.255.255, Type Stub (3)
   TOS count 0, TOS 0 metric 0
```

```
Gen timer 00:25:58
Aging timer 00:43:27
Installed 00:16:32 ago, expires in 00:43:28, sent 00:16:30 ago
Ours
```

The Opaque LSA

Thus far in our exploration of OSPF, we've created a new LSA type to account for extensions and enhancements to the protocol. The prime example of this is the NSSA external LSA. The creation and acceptance of new LSA types can be a lengthy process, which leads us to the creation of *opaque LSAs* (Types 9, 10, and 11). These three LSA types, all called opaque, are intended to allow for future expandability of the protocol. In fact, the specification for opaque LSAs defines the format of only certain LSA header fields. The body of the LSA is defined as "Opaque Information."

The difference in the type of opaque LSA lies in its flooding scope in the network. The three options are:

Link-local scope   LSAs with the type code 9 are considered to be *link-local opaque LSAs*. This means that the LSA must be flooded no further than the attached routers on a network segment. This is similar to the flooding of an OSPF hello packet between neighbors.

Area-local scope   LSAs with the type code 10 are considered to be *area-local opaque LSAs*. This means that the LSA can be flooded throughout the originating OSPF area but no further. This is similar to the area-flooding scope of router and network LSAs.

AS-wide scope   LSAs with the type code 11 are considered to be *AS-wide opaque LSAs*. This means that the LSA can be flooded to all routers in the domain in a similar fashion to AS external LSAs.

The JUNOS software, in addition to other popular vendor implementations, currently supports the use of link-local and area-local opaque LSAs only. Link-local LSAs are used within the context of a graceful restart environment, and area-local LSAs are used to support traffic-engineering capabilities.

We discuss graceful restart in the "Graceful Restart" section later in this chapter. The traffic-engineering capabilities of OSPF are discussed in Chapter 8, "Advanced MPLS."

The Link-State ID field in the LSA header of an opaque LSA is defined as having two distinct portions. The first 8 bits of the 32-bit field designate the *opaque type*, while the remaining 24 bits represent a unique *opaque ID*. The Internet Assigned Numbers Authority (IANA) is responsible for assigning opaque type codes 0 through 127, with the remaining values (128–255) set aside for private and experimental usage.

The Link-State Database

We've looked at portions of the link-state database in our discussion of the various LSA types, but let's now take a step back and observe the operation of the database from a macro point of view. The two main sections we examine are the flooding and maintenance of the database and the SPF algorithm run against its contents.

Database Integrity

To ensure the proper operation of the OSPF network, each router maintains a link-state database for each area to which it connects. In addition, a separate database is maintained for external routes and other AS-wide information. Let's view an example of an entire database on the Chardonnay router from Figure 2.3:

```
user@Chardonnay> show ospf database
```

OSPF link state database, area 0.0.0.0

Type	ID	Adv Rtr	Seq	Age	Opt	Cksum	Len
Router	192.168.0.1	192.168.0.1	0x8000000d	1326	0x2	0xc97	60
Router	*192.168.0.2	192.168.0.2	0x8000001a	2192	0x2	0x3b70	72
Router	192.168.0.3	192.168.0.3	0x80000016	377	0x2	0xfc10	48
Network	192.168.2.2	192.168.0.3	0x80000011	131	0x2	0x5c3c	32
Summary	192.168.16.1	192.168.0.1	0x8000000b	1184	0x2	0xe28a	28
Summary	192.168.16.2	192.168.0.1	0x8000000b	1168	0x2	0xe288	28
Summary	192.168.17.0	192.168.0.1	0x8000000c	1026	0x2	0xdf8c	28
Summary	192.168.18.0	192.168.0.1	0x8000000b	883	0x2	0xe08a	28
Summary	*192.168.32.1	192.168.0.2	0x8000000c	842	0x2	0x2a31	28
Summary	*192.168.32.2	192.168.0.2	0x8000000c	692	0x2	0x2a2f	28
Summary	*192.168.33.0	192.168.0.2	0x8000000b	542	0x2	0x2b31	28
Summary	*192.168.34.0	192.168.0.2	0x8000000b	392	0x2	0x2a30	28
Summary	192.168.48.1	192.168.0.3	0x8000000a	371	0x2	0x77d4	28
Summary	192.168.49.0	192.168.0.3	0x8000000f	376	0x2	0x6cda	28
ASBRSum	192.168.48.1	192.168.0.3	0x80000008	371	0x2	0x6ddf	28

OSPF link state database, area 0.0.0.2

Type	ID	Adv Rtr	Seq	Age	Opt	Cksum	Len
Router	*192.168.0.2	192.168.0.2	0x8000000f	1142	0x2	0x6fd1	60
Router	192.168.32.1	192.168.32.1	0x80000009	146	0x2	0x2025	84
Router	192.168.32.2	192.168.32.2	0x80000008	147	0x2	0x8c59	60
Summary	*192.168.0.1	192.168.0.2	0x8000000e	242	0x2	0x87f1	28
Summary	*192.168.0.3	192.168.0.2	0x80000004	2042	0x2	0x87f9	28
Summary	*192.168.1.0	192.168.0.2	0x8000000e	992	0x2	0x86f2	28

Summary	*192.168.2.0	192.168.0.2	0x80000005	1892	0x2	0x8df3 28
Summary	*192.168.16.1	192.168.0.2	0x8000000e	92	0x2	0xe087 28
Summary	*192.168.16.2	192.168.0.2	0x8000000c	2792	0x2	0xe483 28
Summary	*192.168.17.0	192.168.0.2	0x8000000b	2642	0x2	0xe585 28
Summary	*192.168.18.0	192.168.0.2	0x8000000b	2492	0x2	0xe484 28
Summary	*192.168.48.1	192.168.0.2	0x80000003	370	0x2	0x95bd 28
Summary	*192.168.49.0	192.168.0.2	0x80000004	1592	0x2	0x92bf 28
ASBRSum	*192.168.0.1	192.168.0.2	0x80000007	2342	0x2	0x87f7 28
ASBRSum	*192.168.48.1	192.168.0.2	0x80000003	370	0x2	0x87ca 28

OSPF AS SCOPE link state database

Type	ID	Adv Rtr	Seq	Age	Opt	Cksum	Len
Extern	172.16.1.0	192.168.0.1	0x80000008	868	0x2	0x3271	36
Extern	172.16.2.0	192.168.0.1	0x80000008	726	0x2	0x277b	36
Extern	172.16.3.0	192.168.0.1	0x80000008	583	0x2	0x1c85	36
Extern	172.16.4.0	192.168.48.1	0x80000001	387	0x2	0xcda9	36
Extern	172.16.5.0	192.168.48.1	0x80000001	387	0x2	0xc2b3	36
Extern	172.16.6.0	192.168.48.1	0x80000001	387	0x2	0xb7bd	36
Extern	172.16.7.0	192.168.48.1	0x80000001	387	0x2	0xacc7	36

The LSA information in each area must be identical on each router in that area. Each LSA is uniquely defined by the combination of the Link-State ID, Advertising Router, and Link-State Type fields. Newer versions of each LSA have their Link-State Sequence Number field updated and replace older versions of the same LSA. An individual LSA is reflooded into the network by the originating router based on a topology or network change. For example, if you change the metric value on an OSPF interface, a new version of the router LSA is flooded.

The Shortest Path First Algorithm

An OSPF-speaking router translates the information in the database into usable routes for the routing table by using the Dijkstra, or shortest path first (SPF), algorithm. This computation is performed within the context of each OSPF area, and the results are compiled and presented to the routing table on the router. Generally speaking, the SPF algorithm locates the best (metrically shortest) path to each unique destination. When the router encounters two paths to the same destination learned through different means, intra-area versus inter-area, it has some tie-breaking rules to follow to determine which version to use. The order of precedence for using a route is as follows:

- Routes learned from within the local area

- Routes learned from a remote area

- External routes marked as Type 1 routes

- External routes marked as Type 2 routes

The router maintains some conceptual tables (databases) in its memory for use with the SPF algorithm. Let's explore these in some detail as well as look at an example of an SPF calculation.

SPF Components

One of the key portions of an SPF calculation is the creation of a (router ID, neighbor ID, cost) tuple. Each router examines the information in the link-state database and builds a map of the network connectivity using this tuple notation. Both the router ID and the neighbor ID values represent the routers connected to a network link. The cost value is the metric cost to transmit data across the link. For example, suppose that router A, with a router ID of 1.1.1.1, and router B, with a router ID of 2.2.2.2, are connected on a point-to-point link. Each router has a configured metric of 5 within OSPF for that intervening interface. Each router builds two tuples for use within the SPF calculation. The first represents the connectivity from router A to router B and is (1.1.1.1, 2.2.2.2, 5). The second is for the opposite connectivity of router B to router A and is (2.2.2.2, 1.1.1.1, 5). By using this method of representation, each router in the network can populate the internal memory tables needed by the SPF algorithm.

Each router constructs three conceptual databases during the process of running the SPF calculation. Those tables include:

Link-state database   This data structure, the *SPF link-state database*, should not be confused with the OSPF link-state database viewed with the `show ospf database` command. We use the same name for this table because it contains the same data as the OSPF link-state database in the (router ID, neighbor ID, cost) tuple format.

Candidate database   The *candidate database* also contains network data in the tuple format. Its function is a bit different than the SPF link-state database in that the cost from the root of the SPF tree (the local router) to the neighbor ID of each tuple is calculated. It is within this table that the shortest path to each end node is determined.

Tree database   The *tree database* is the data structure that most closely matches the information in the routing table. Only the network paths representing the shortest cost are placed in this database. In essence, this is the result of the SPF calculation. After completing its calculation, the algorithm passes the information in the tree database to the routing table on the router for its use.

When the local router operates the SPF algorithm, it first moves its own local tuple (router ID, router ID, 0) to the candidate database and calculates the total cost to the root (itself) from the neighbor ID in the tuple (itself). This cost is always 0 because no other router has a better way to reach the local router than itself. The router then moves its local tuple to the tree database and places itself at the root of the SPF network map. All tuples in the link-state database containing the local router in the router ID field are then moved to the candidate database. The following steps are performed by the local router until the candidate database is empty:

1. For each new entry in the candidate database, determine the cost to the root from each neighbor ID. After calculating the total cost, move the tuple with the lowest cost from the candidate database to the tree database. If multiple equal-cost tuples exist, choose one at random and move it to the tree database.

2. When a new neighbor ID appears in the tree database, locate all tuples in the link-state database with a router ID equal to the new tree database entry. Move these tuples to the candidate database and calculate the total cost to the root from each neighbor ID.

3. Evaluate each entry in the candidate database and delete all tuples whose neighbor ID is already located in the tree database and whose cost from the root is greater than the current entry in the tree database. Return to Step 1.

These steps continue processing until all entries in the link-state and candidate databases are empty, leaving only the tree database remaining. The results of the calculation are then passed to the routing table for potential use in forwarding user data traffic.

An SPF Calculation Example

To better comprehend the process of running the SPF algorithm, let's explore an example. Figure 2.9 shows a network consisting of four routers; RTR A, RTR B, RTR C, and RTD D. The interface metrics configured within OSPF are also displayed on the network map.

FIGURE 2.9   An SPF sample network map

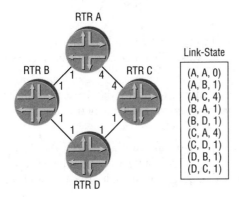

The network recently converged onto this view of connectivity, and the SPF algorithm is being run on RTR A to determine the shortest path to each node in the network. The following steps illustrate how the algorithm operates on our sample network:

1. RTR A begins by moving its own local database tuple (A, A, 0) to the candidate database. The total cost from the root to the neighbor ID is calculated, which results in the value 0. In other words, RTR A is directly connected to itself and no other router has a better path to RTR A.

2. The tuple with the lowest cost in the candidate database, the only tuple at this point, is moved to the tree database and the new neighbor ID (RTR A) is placed on the network map. Figure 2.10 shows Steps 1 and 2 in operation.

3. The neighbor ID of RTR A is the most recent entry to the tree database. Therefore, all tuples listing RTR A in the router ID field are moved from the link-state database to the candidate database. This includes tuples (A, B, 1) and (A, C, 4).

4. The cost from each neighbor ID to the root is calculated for all new entries in the candidate database. The first new tuple in the database is (A, B, 1). The total cost of reaching RTR A, the router ID, is already known to be 0. The cost in the tuple to reach the neighbor ID from the

router ID is 1. These costs are added together to determine that the total cost to the root from RTR B is 1. A similar calculation is performed for the second tuple and RTR C. The total cost to the root from RTR C is 4, and this value is placed in the candidate database.

FIGURE 2.10   RTR A is added to the SPF tree.

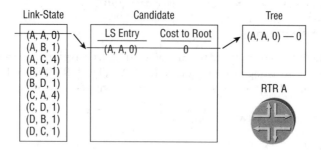

5. The candidate database is then examined to determine whether a shortest path is already known to any neighbor IDs—RTR A in our case. There are currently no such tuples in the candidate database.

6. The tuple with the lowest cost to the root is moved to the tree database: (A, B, 1) with a total cost of 1. RTR B is placed on the network map showing its final metric cost. Steps 3 through 6 are shown in Figure 2.11.

7. The candidate database is not empty, so the algorithm continues. RTR B is the most recent entry to the tree database, so all tuples listing RTR B in the Router ID field are moved from the link-state database to the candidate database. This includes (B, A, 1) and (B, D, 1).

FIGURE 2.11   RTR B is added to the SPF tree.

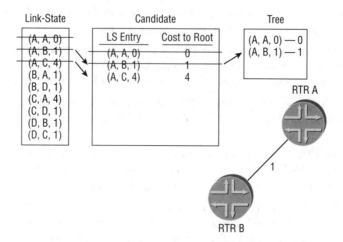

8. The cost from each neighbor ID to the root is calculated for all new tuples in the candidate database. For tuple (B, A, 1), there is a cost of 1 to reach RTR B on the SPF tree, and it costs RTR B a value of 1 to reach RTR A. The total cost to reach RTR A through RTR B is then calculated as 2. The same process occurs for the (B, D, 1) tuple, with a total cost of 2 calculated to reach RTR D through RTR B.

9. All neighbor IDs in the candidate database for which a path exists in the tree database are deleted. This results in the (B, A, 1) tuple being removed because RTR A already has a shortest path to RTR A.

10. The lowest-cost tuple in the candidate database, (B, D, 1), is moved to the tree database and RTR D is placed on the network map. Figure 2.12 shows Steps 7 through 10.

FIGURE 2.12   RTR D is added to the SPF tree.

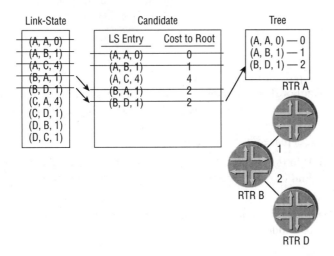

11. The candidate database is not empty, so the algorithm continues. RTR D is now the most recent entry to the tree database, so its tuples are moved from the link-state database to the candidate database. This includes (D, B, 1) and (D, C, 1).

12. The cost from each neighbor ID to the root is calculated for all new neighbor IDs. It costs a value of 2 to reach RTR D, and it costs RTR D a value of 1 to reach RTR B. The total cost to reach RTR B through RTR D is then 3. As before, the same is done for RTR C. It costs a value of 3 to reach RTR C through RTR D.

13. All known neighbor IDs in the tree database are removed from the candidate database. This includes (D, B, 1) because RTR A already has a path to RTR B.

14. The lowest-cost tuple in the candidate database, (D, C, 1), is moved to the tree database and RTR C is placed on the network map. Steps 11 through 14 are shown in Figure 2.13.

15. The candidate database is not empty, so the algorithm continues. RTR C is the most recent entry to the tree database, and its tuples of (C, A, 4) and (C, D, 1) are moved from the link-state database to the candidate database.

FIGURE 2.13   RTR C is added to the SPF tree.

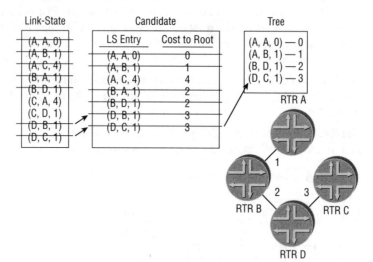

16. The cost from each neighbor ID to the root is calculated. It costs a value of 3 to reach RTR C, and it costs RTR C a value of 4 to reach RTR A. The total cost of 7 to reach RTR A through RTR C is placed in the candidate database. Similarly, the total cost of 4 to reach RTR C through RTR C is placed in the candidate database.

17. All known neighbor IDs in the tree database are removed from the candidate. The tuples of (A, C, 4), (C, A, 4), and (C, D, 1) are removed because paths already exist to RTR C, RTR A, and RTR D.

18. The candidate database is now empty, so the algorithm stops at this point. Figure 2.14 shows these final steps.

FIGURE 2.14   Final SPF calculations

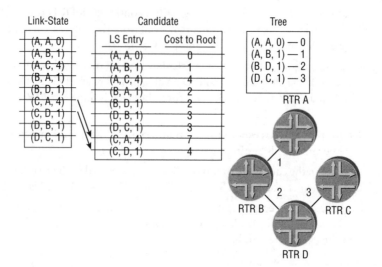

Configuration Options

While the title of this section may appear to be quite broad, we'll be focusing our attention on a few select topics. We start with an exploration of using graceful restart as a method for maintaining network stability. We then examine authentication within OSPF, altering the metric values used on the router interfaces, and connecting OSPF areas using a virtual link.

Graceful Restart

When an OSPF-speaking router restarts its routing process, it has the potential to disrupt the network's operation. For example, each of its neighbors stops receiving hello packets from the restarting router. When this condition occurs for a long enough period of time, the neighbors expire their dead timer for the restarting router, causing the OSPF adjacency between them to transition to the Down state. This forces each of the neighboring routers to regenerate their router or network LSAs to reflect this new adjacency, which in turn causes new SPF calculations to occur throughout the network. The SPF calculations could result in new routing paths through the network and the "migration" of user data traffic from one set of network links to another. This traffic shift could potentially lead to oversubscribed and congested links in the network.

Of course, if the restarting router has a catastrophic failure then this process is unavoidable. But what happens when the routing process returns to operation in a short time period, say 60 to 90 seconds? The neighboring routers reacquire their OSPF adjacencies, reflood their LSAs, and rerun the SPF algorithm. In essence, the process we just described occurs again, with network traffic returning to the links it was previously using.

From the perspective of the routing protocol, everything occurred as it should. After all, OSPF was designed to be responsive to failures and recover automatically. Unfortunately, the perspective of the network's users is not so forgiving. The brief network instability caused by the restarting router can mean delays in transmissions or dropped user data packets. In short, the end user sees a slow, unresponsive, and poorly operational network. Recent developments in the networking industry have led to the introduction of methods designed to avoid this particular situation.

Graceful restart, or *hitless restart*, is the common name for the ability to restart a routing process without causing network instability. Each of the major routing protocols has the capability to perform a graceful restart. We'll focus on how OSPF accomplishes this functionality according to the current standard, Request for Comments 3623.

Some preconditions must be met before an OSPF router can perform a graceful restart. First, the restarting router must be able to continuously forward user data packets while the software process is restarting. This can occur only when the routing and forwarding planes of the router are separated, a central design principle of Juniper Networks routers. Second, other portions of the network topology must be stable. In other words, physical links and other network devices must remain operational during the restart period. Finally, the OSPF neighbors of the restarting router must support the ability to assist in the graceful restart process. Neighboring routers help the restarting device by not transitioning the adjacency of the restarting router to the Down state. Neighbors must also not flood new LSAs into the network that alter the network map or announce a topology change.

The Restart Operation

Let's now examine the functionality of the OSPF graceful restart procedure from a high-level perspective. The restarting router is alerted to a restart event by some means. This can be a command-line interface (CLI) command, such as restart routing, or an internal signal from the routing software. The restarting router stores the current forwarding table in memory in addition to its current adjacencies and network configuration. It asks each of its neighbors for assistance during the restart process. Finally, it restarts the routing software for OSPF. After the restart event, the local router announces to its neighbors that it has returned and waits for a specified amount of time for each of the neighbors to reflood their databases back to the local router. After receiving a complete database, the local router returns to its normal OSPF operational mode.

Each router capable of supporting graceful restart operates in one of three modes:

Restart candidate   When an OSPF router is operating in *restart candidate mode*, it is actually attempting to perform a graceful restart. The router generates notification messages to its neighbors, stores its local protocol state, and performs its restart event. The restart candidate mode is mutually exclusive with the other restart modes. In other words, a router can't be both a restart candidate and a helper router at the same time.

Possible helper   The *possible helper restart mode* is the default operational mode of a restart-capable OSPF router. In this mode, the local router is able to assist neighbors with a restart event, or it may transition to the restart candidate mode upon its own restart event. An individual router may be a possible helper for some neighbors while it is in helper mode for other neighbors.

Helper   When a restart-capable router receives a notification message from a neighbor, it transitions into *helper mode*. In this mode, the helper router maintains an adjacency in the Full state with the restarting router. It also does not flood new LSAs announcing a topology or network change into its local areas.

Grace LSA

The messages exchanged between restart candidate and helper routers are carried within a *grace LSA* (Type 9). The grace LSA uses the format defined for a link-local opaque LSA, which limits the flooding scope to the two directly connected routers. This is precisely the type of communication needed to support graceful restart. Recall from the "Opaque LSA" section earlier that the Link-State ID field in the LSA header is defined as having an 8-bit opaque type field and a 24-bit opaque ID field. When used to support graceful restart, the Type 9 LSA header uses an opaque type code of 3 and an opaque ID value of 0. The information carried in the body of the LSA is encoded using a type, length, value (TLV) system, as shown in Figure 2.15. The details of the TLV fields are:

Type (2 octets)   This field displays the type of information contained in the value portion of the TLV. Three possible type values are currently defined to support graceful restart:

- Grace period—1
- Hitless restart reason—2
- IP interface address—3

Length (2 octets)   This field displays the length of the value portion of the TLV. Each of the defined type codes has a fixed length associated with it:

- Grace period—4 octets
- Hitless restart reason—1 octet
- IP interface address—4 octets

Value (Variable)   This field contains the value carried within the TLV. The defined type codes carry information used by restarting routers in their operations:

Grace Period   The time period (in units of seconds) for the restart event is placed in this field. Helper routers use this value to determine whether the restarting router is in service after the restart. Upon its expiration, the helper routers flush their adjacency to the restarting router and flood new LSAs into the network. The grace period TLV is required in all grace LSAs.

Hitless Restart Reason   The reason for the graceful restart is encoded in this one-octet field. The possible reasons for a restart are: unknown (0), software restart (1), software upgrade or reload (2), or a switch to a redundant control processor (3). The hitless restart reason TLV is required in all grace LSAs.

IP Interface Address   When the restarting router transmits a grace LSA on a broadcast or non-broadcast multiaccess (NBMA) network, it includes the IP interface address TLV. This TLV encodes the address of the interface connected to the segment, which allows the neighboring helper routers to identify the restarting device.

F I G U R E   2 . 1 5   A Grace LSA

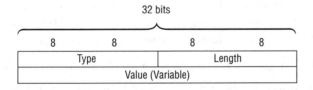

Both the Zinfandel and Chablis routers in Figure 2.3 are configured to support graceful restart. When Chablis encounters a restart event, it sends a grace LSA to Zinfandel:

```
user@Zinfandel> show ospf database link-local extensive
```

OSPF Link-Local link state database, interface so-0/1/0.0

```
Type        ID                  Adv Rtr           Seq       Age  Opt  Cksum   Len
OpaqLoc   3.0.0.0            192.168.32.2      0x80000001   46   0x2  0xf16a  36
   Grace 90
   Reason 1
   Aging timer 00:59:14
   Installed 00:00:45 ago, expires in 00:59:14, sent 2w1d 17:24:34 ago
```

When it received the grace LSA from Chablis, the Zinfandel router created a separate database, keyed off its so-0/1/0.0 interface, to store the LSA. By using the extensive option, we see some of the details advertised by Chablis. The link-state ID reports this as a grace LSA with the setting of 3.0.0.0, a type code of 3. Both the grace period and hitless restart reason TLVs are sent within the LSA. Chablis is requesting a grace period of 90 seconds and reports that it is requesting assistance based on a software restart event.

Restart Configuration

The JUNOS software supports graceful restart for all of the major routing protocols. As such, the configuration of this feature occurs within the [edit routing-options] configuration hierarchy. In addition, each of the protocols has the ability to disable graceful restart using configuration options within the protocol itself. The Zinfandel router is currently configured to support graceful restart:

```
user@Zinfandel> show configuration routing-options
graceful-restart;
```

Within the [edit protocols ospf] hierarchy, a graceful-restart directory exists as well:

```
[edit protocols ospf]
user@Zinfandel# set graceful-restart ?
Possible completions:
+ apply-groups        Groups from which to inherit configuration data
  disable             Disable OSPF graceful-restart capability
  helper-disable      Disable graceful restart helper capability
  notify-duration     Time to send all max-aged grace LSAs (1..3600 seconds)
  restart-duration    Time for all neighbors to become full (1..3600 seconds)
```

The individual options alter the graceful restart process in specific ways. Here are the details:

disable   The disable option prevents the local router from performing any graceful restart functions. This includes both performing a local restart as well as providing help to a neighboring router for its restart.

helper-disable   The helper-disable option prevents the local router from assisting with a restart event on a neighboring router. The local router, however, is still able to perform a restart with assistance from its neighbors.

notify-duration   The notify-duration timer runs after the expiration of the restart-duration timer. Once it reaches 0, the local router purges the grace LSAs from the database for the devices that failed to restart properly. The JUNOS software sets this value to 30 seconds, by default, with a possible range between 1 and 3600 seconds.

`restart-duration`   The `restart-duration` timer begins running immediately as the restart event occurs. It is the amount of time that the router requires to reestablish its adjacencies. The JUNOS software sets this value to 60 seconds, by default, with a possible range between 1 and 3600 seconds. When combined with the `notify-duration` timer, an OSPF router has 90 seconds to gracefully restart.

Authentication

OSPF, by its very nature, is a very trusting protocol. Once a neighbor relationship is established, each router believes all information sent to it by that neighbor. This trusting nature might lead to serious network problems should bad information be injected into the link-state database, either by mistake or by intentional means. To help avoid such issues, many network administrators enable authentication mechanisms within their protocols. This not only ensures that your local routers form adjacencies with trusted routers, but also helps to ensure that only unintentional mistakes cause network problems.

The JUNOS software supports three methods of authenticating OSPF packets: none, simple authentication, and MD5. By default, the protocol operates with no authentication in place across all interfaces. Plain-text password authentication is useful for protecting your network against an inadvertent configuration mistake. Basically, it keeps your routers from forming a neighbor relationship with any device that doesn't have the correct password configured. The problem with using plain-text authentication is that the password itself is placed in the transmitted OSPF packets, which allows it to be viewed by a packet-capture device. To provide real security in your network, use the MD5 authentication mechanism. MD5 uses a standard algorithm to generate an encrypted checksum from your configured password, which is then transmitted in the OSPF packets themselves. All receiving routers compare their locally generated checksum against the received value to verify that the packet is genuine.

If you want to add authentication to your configuration, you should know about two locations where information is enabled. The first is within the OSPF area portion of the configuration hierarchy. This is where the *type* of authentication is configured; all routers in that area are required to support the same authentication type. The second location for configuring authentication options is within the individual interfaces running OSPF. This is where you place the actual password used to authenticate and verify all protocol packets. In fact, while each router in an area must use the same type of authentication, it is the password on the interface that actually enables the authentication function. This gives you the flexibility to enable authentication only on some interfaces and not others. As long as the neighbors agree on the configured password value (or lack of a value), the authentication mechanism operates normally.

Simple Authentication

The Chablis and Zinfandel routers are connected across a point-to-point link in area 2 of our sample network in Figure 2.3. Each of the routers configures simple password authentication as the type to be used within area 2, but only Chablis configures a password of **test1**. This causes the adjacency to drop between the neighbors:

```
[edit protocols ospf]
user@Chablis# show
area 0.0.0.2 {
    authentication-type simple; # SECRET-DATA
    interface so-0/1/0.0 {
        authentication-key "$9$9SwLCORrlMXNbvWaZ"; # SECRET-DATA
    }
}

[edit protocols ospf]
user@Zinfandel# show
area 0.0.0.2 {
    authentication-type simple; # SECRET-DATA
    interface so-0/1/0.0;
    interface at-0/2/0.0;
    interface lo0.0;
}
```

```
user@Zinfandel> show ospf neighbor
```

Address	Interface	State	ID	Pri	Dead
192.168.33.1	at-0/2/0.0	Full	192.168.0.2	128	35
192.168.34.2	so-0/1/0.0	Full	192.168.32.2	128	20

```
user@Zinfandel> show ospf neighbor
```

Address	Interface	State	ID	Pri	Dead
192.168.33.1	at-0/2/0.0	Full	192.168.0.2	128	39
192.168.34.2	so-0/1/0.0	Full	192.168.32.2	128	5

```
user@Zinfandel> show ospf neighbor
```

Address	Interface	State	ID	Pri	Dead
192.168.33.1	at-0/2/0.0	Full	192.168.0.2	128	30

The adjacency with the Chardonnay router, 192.168.33.1, remains at the Full state although no authentication information has been configured on the router:

```
user@Chardonnay> show configuration protocols ospf
area 0.0.0.0 {
    interface fe-0/0/1.0;
    interface fe-0/0/2.0;
```

```
    interface lo0.0;
}
area 0.0.0.2 {
    interface at-0/1/0.0;
}
```

After applying an authentication key on the so-0/1/0.0 interface of Zinfandel, the adjacency with Chablis returns to the Full state:

```
[edit protocols ospf]
user@Zinfandel# show
area 0.0.0.2 {
    authentication-type simple; # SECRET-DATA
    interface so-0/1/0.0 {
        authentication-key "$9$dQVgJiHmTF/.PO1"; # SECRET-DATA
    }
    interface at-0/2/0.0;
    interface lo0.0;
}
```

```
user@Zinfandel> show ospf neighbor
  Address         Interface       State     ID            Pri  Dead
  192.168.33.1    at-0/2/0.0      Full      192.168.0.2   128  36
  192.168.34.2    so-0/1/0.0      Full      192.168.32.2  128  36
```

MD5 Authentication

The configuration of MD5 requires the addition of a value known as the *key ID*, which is used in conjunction with the configured password to generate the encrypted checksum. The key ID, an integer value between 0 and 255, is a one-octet field that defaults to the value 0 when omitted from the configuration. Without this value, the configuration does not commit and MD5 authentication does not operate.

The Muscat and Shiraz routers in area 3 of Figure 2.3 have configured MD5 authentication within their area. Although they have used the same password (test), the key ID values don't match. This causes the adjacency between the neighbors to fail:

```
[edit protocols ospf]
user@Muscat# show
area 0.0.0.0 {
    interface fe-0/0/2.0;
}
area 0.0.0.3 {
    authentication-type md5; # SECRET-DATA
    interface fe-0/0/1.0 {
```

```
            authentication-key "$9$Hk5FCA0Ihru0" key-id 25; # SECRET-DATA
    }
}

[edit protocols ospf]
user@Shiraz# show
export adv-statics;
area 0.0.0.3 {
    authentication-type md5; # SECRET-DATA
    interface fe-0/0/0.0 {
        authentication-key "$9$CFB2ABEleWx-wM8" key-id 50; # SECRET-DATA
    }
}

user@Shiraz> show ospf neighbor
  Address         Interface         State      ID           Pri  Dead
  192.168.49.1    fe-0/0/0.0        Full       192.168.0.3   128  34

user@Shiraz> show ospf neighbor
  Address         Interface         State      ID           Pri  Dead
  192.168.49.1    fe-0/0/0.0        Full       192.168.0.3   128  6

user@Shiraz> show ospf neighbor

user@Shiraz>
```

We've now verified the requirement that the key ID values match. After we configure the correct key ID of 25 on the Shiraz router, the adjacency with Muscat returns to the Full state:

```
[edit protocols ospf]
user@Shiraz# show
export adv-statics;
area 0.0.0.3 {
    authentication-type md5; # SECRET-DATA
    interface fe-0/0/0.0 {
        authentication-key "$9$vcCM7Vg4ZjkPJG" key-id 25; # SECRET-DATA
    }
}

user@Shiraz> show ospf neighbor
  Address         Interface         State      ID           Pri  Dead
  192.168.49.1    fe-0/0/0.0        Full       192.168.0.3   128  37
```

Interface Metrics

Each operational interface running OSPF automatically calculates a metric value using the pre-defined formula of *10 ^ 8 ÷ bandwidth (BW) of the interface in bits/second*. The portion 10 ^ 8 is also represented as 100,000,000, which equals the speed (in bits per second) of a Fast Ethernet interface. This means that all Fast Ethernet interfaces have a metric value of 1 (10 ^ 8 ÷ 100,000,000). When an interface has a higher bandwidth than a Fast Ethernet interface, the result of the metric formula is less than 1. For example, an OC-3c interface has a bandwidth of 155,000,000 bps, which results in a metric of .065 (10 ^ 8 ÷ 155,000,000). The metric field within the OSPF LSAs account for only integer values, so any calculated metric less than 1 is rounded up to a metric of 1. In fact, all interfaces operating at a bandwidth higher than a Fast Ethernet interface receive a metric value of 1 by default. The JUNOS software provides two methods for calculating or assigning metric values to OSPF interfaces. You can manually configure the interface metric, or you can alter the reference bandwidth used in the metric formula. Let's look at each of these options in further detail.

Manual Configuration

Each configured interface within the [edit protocols ospf] configuration hierarchy has the ability to have a metric value assigned to it between 1 and 65,535. Each interface on the router may receive a different metric value, and any configured values override the use of the automatic metric formula. The Merlot router in our sample network in Figure 2.3 currently has a metric value of 1 assigned to each interface by the automatic formula:

```
user@Merlot> show configuration protocols ospf
area 0.0.0.1 {
    interface fe-0/0/0.0;
    interface fe-0/0/1.0;
    interface lo0.0;
}


user@Merlot> show ospf interface detail
Interface            State    Area        DR ID          BDR ID      Nbrs
fe-0/0/0.0           DR       0.0.0.1     192.168.16.1   192.168.16.2  1
Type LAN, address 192.168.18.1, mask 24, MTU 1500, cost 1
DR addr 192.168.18.1, BDR addr 192.168.18.2, adj count 1, priority 128
Hello 10, Dead 40, ReXmit 5, Not Stub
fe-0/0/1.0           BDR      0.0.0.1     192.168.0.1    192.168.16.1  1
Type LAN, address 192.168.17.2, mask 24, MTU 1500, cost 1
DR addr 192.168.17.1, BDR addr 192.168.17.2, adj count 1, priority 128
Hello 10, Dead 40, ReXmit 5, Not Stub
lo0.0                DR       0.0.0.1     192.168.16.1   0.0.0.0       0
Type LAN, address 192.168.16.1, mask 32, MTU 65535, cost 0
```

```
DR addr 192.168.16.1, BDR addr (null), adj count 0, priority 128
Hello 10, Dead 40, ReXmit 5, Not Stub
```

Merlot has connectivity to the loopback address of Riesling (192.168.16.2 /32) across the fe-0/0/0.0 interface with a metric of 1:

```
user@Merlot> show route 192.168.16.2

inet.0: 29 destinations, 29 routes (29 active, 0 holddown, 0 hidden)
+ = Active Route, - = Last Active, * = Both

192.168.16.2/32    *[OSPF/10] 00:01:12, metric 1
                    > to 192.168.18.2 via fe-0/0/0.0
```

We configure a metric value of 15 on the fe-0/0/0.0 interface and a metric value of 20 on the fe-0/0/1.0 interface. These values are then used as the cost of each respective interface and are advertised to the network in Merlot's router LSA:

```
[edit protocols ospf]
user@Merlot# show
area 0.0.0.1 {
    interface fe-0/0/0.0 {
        metric 15;
    }
    interface fe-0/0/1.0 {
        metric 20;
    }
    interface lo0.0;
}

user@Merlot> show ospf interface detail
Interface            State    Area         DR ID         BDR ID      Nbrs
fe-0/0/0.0           DR       0.0.0.1      192.168.16.1  192.168.16.2  1
Type LAN, address 192.168.18.1, mask 24, MTU 1500, cost 15
DR addr 192.168.18.1, BDR addr 192.168.18.2, adj count 1, priority 128
Hello 10, Dead 40, ReXmit 5, Not Stub
fe-0/0/1.0           BDR      0.0.0.1      192.168.0.1   192.168.16.1  1
Type LAN, address 192.168.17.2, mask 24, MTU 1500, cost 20
DR addr 192.168.17.1, BDR addr 192.168.17.2, adj count 1, priority 128
Hello 10, Dead 40, ReXmit 5, Not Stub
lo0.0                DR       0.0.0.1      192.168.16.1  0.0.0.0        0
Type LAN, address 192.168.16.1, mask 32, MTU 65535, cost 0
DR addr 192.168.16.1, BDR addr (null), adj count 0, priority 128
```

```
Hello 10, Dead 40, ReXmit 5, Not Stub
```

user@Merlot> **show ospf database router lsa-id 192.168.16.1 extensive**

```
    OSPF link state database, area 0.0.0.1
 Type        ID               Adv Rtr          Seq      Age  Opt  Cksum  Len
Router  *192.168.16.1     192.168.16.1     0x80000014   18  0x2  0xf0ad  60
  bits 0x0, link count 3
  id 192.168.18.1, data 192.168.18.1, type Transit (2)
  TOS count 0, TOS 0 metric 15
  id 192.168.17.1, data 192.168.17.2, type Transit (2)
  TOS count 0, TOS 0 metric 20
  id 192.168.16.1, data 255.255.255.255, type Stub (3)
  TOS count 0, TOS 0 metric 0
  Gen timer 00:49:41
  Aging timer 00:59:41
  Installed 00:00:18 ago, expires in 00:59:42, sent 00:00:18 ago
  Ours
```

The information in the routing table for Riesling's loopback address is now changed as well:

user@Merlot> **show route 192.168.16.2**

```
inet.0: 29 destinations, 29 routes (29 active, 0 holddown, 0 hidden)
+ = Active Route, - = Last Active, * = Both

192.168.16.2/32    *[OSPF/10] 00:00:52, metric 15
                    > to 192.168.18.2 via fe-0/0/0.0
```

Reference Bandwidth

The automatic metric formula uses the numerator value of 10 ^ 8 as the default reference bandwidth. We've seen that this equals the bandwidth of a Fast Ethernet interface. The JUNOS software allows you to alter the reference bandwidth used in the formula by using the reference-bandwidth command at the global OSPF configuration hierarchy level. Changing the reference bandwidth affects all OSPF interfaces on the router, except for those configured with a manual metric value.

You should configure the same reference bandwidth value on all routers to distinguish between the slowest and fastest interfaces in your network. This helps to ensure a consistent calculation of network paths and routing topologies across your network.

The Chardonnay router in Figure 2.3 has three operational interfaces: fe-0/0/1.0, fe-0/0/2.0, and at-0/1/0.0. Each of the interfaces is currently using a metric cost of 1:

```
user@Chardonnay> show ospf interface detail
Interface            State   Area         DR ID          BDR ID       Nbrs
fe-0/0/1.0           BDR     0.0.0.0      192.168.0.1    192.168.0.2   1
Type LAN, address 192.168.1.2, mask 24, MTU 1500, cost 1
DR addr 192.168.1.1, BDR addr 192.168.1.2, adj count 1, priority 128
Hello 10, Dead 40, ReXmit 5, Not Stub
fe-0/0/2.0           DR      0.0.0.0      192.168.0.2    192.168.0.3   1
Type LAN, address 192.168.2.1, mask 24, MTU 1500, cost 1
DR addr 192.168.2.1, BDR addr 192.168.2.2, adj count 1, priority 128
Hello 10, Dead 40, ReXmit 5, Not Stub
lo0.0                DR      0.0.0.0      192.168.0.2    0.0.0.0        0
Type LAN, address 192.168.0.2, mask 32, MTU 65535, cost 0
DR addr 192.168.0.2, BDR addr (null), adj count 0, priority 128
Hello 10, Dead 40, ReXmit 5, Not Stub
at-0/1/0.0           PtToPt  0.0.0.2      0.0.0.0        0.0.0.0        1
Type P2P, address (null), mask 0, MTU 4470, cost 1
DR addr (null), BDR addr (null), adj count 1
Hello 10, Dead 40, ReXmit 5, Not Stub
at-0/1/0.0           PtToPt  0.0.0.2      0.0.0.0        0.0.0.0        0
Type P2P, address 192.168.33.1, mask 24, MTU 4470, cost 1
DR addr (null), BDR addr (null), adj count 0,  passive
Hello 10, Dead 40, ReXmit 5, Not Stub
```

Remember that an OSPF router forms an adjacency across an unnumbered interface and advertises the configured subnet as a passive stub network. This accounts for the "double" listing of the interface at-0/1/0.0.

A reference bandwidth value of 1,000,000,000 (1Gbps) is configured on the router. This alters the metric values for all interfaces in the router:

```
[edit protocols ospf]
user@Chardonnay# show
reference-bandwidth 1g;
area 0.0.0.0 {
    interface fe-0/0/1.0;
    interface fe-0/0/2.0;
    interface lo0.0;
}
```

```
area 0.0.0.2 {
    interface at-0/1/0.0;
}
```

```
user@Chardonnay> show ospf interface detail
Interface              State   Area        DR ID          BDR ID       Nbrs
fe-0/0/1.0             BDR     0.0.0.0     192.168.0.1    192.168.0.2   1
Type LAN, address 192.168.1.2, mask 24, MTU 1500, cost 10
DR addr 192.168.1.1, BDR addr 192.168.1.2, adj count 1, priority 128
Hello 10, Dead 40, ReXmit 5, Not Stub
fe-0/0/2.0             DR      0.0.0.0     192.168.0.2    192.168.0.3   1
Type LAN, address 192.168.2.1, mask 24, MTU 1500, cost 10
DR addr 192.168.2.1, BDR addr 192.168.2.2, adj count 1, priority 128
Hello 10, Dead 40, ReXmit 5, Not Stub
lo0.0                 DR      0.0.0.0     192.168.0.2    0.0.0.0       0
Type LAN, address 192.168.0.2, mask 32, MTU 65535, cost 0
DR addr 192.168.0.2, BDR addr (null), adj count 0, priority 128
Hello 10, Dead 40, ReXmit 5, Not Stub
at-0/1/0.0            PtToPt   0.0.0.2     0.0.0.0        0.0.0.0       1
Type P2P, address (null), mask 0, MTU 4470, cost 6
DR addr (null), BDR addr (null), adj count 1
Hello 10, Dead 40, ReXmit 5, Not Stub
at-0/1/0.0            PtToPt   0.0.0.2     0.0.0.0        0.0.0.0       0
Type P2P, address 192.168.33.1, mask 24, MTU 4470, cost 6
DR addr (null), BDR addr (null), adj count 0,  passive
Hello 10, Dead 40, ReXmit 5, Not Stub
```

```
user@Chardonnay> show ospf database router lsa-id 192.168.0.2 extensive
```

```
    OSPF link state database, area 0.0.0.0
 Type      ID               Adv Rtr            Seq       Age  Opt  Cksum  Len
 Router  *192.168.0.2      192.168.0.2       0x8000001a   25  0x2  0x49ca  60
   bits 0x1, link count 3
   id 192.168.1.1, data 192.168.1.2, type Transit (2)
   TOS count 0, TOS 0 metric 10
   id 192.168.2.1, data 192.168.2.1, type Transit (2)
   TOS count 0, TOS 0 metric 10
   id 192.168.0.2, data 255.255.255.255, type Stub (3)
   TOS count 0, TOS 0 metric 0
   Gen timer 00:49:35
```

```
  Aging timer 00:59:35
  Installed 00:00:25 ago, expires in 00:59:35, sent 00:00:25 ago
  Ours


    OSPF link state database, area 0.0.0.2
 Type        ID                  Adv Rtr            Seq       Age  Opt  Cksum  Len
 Router  *192.168.0.2       192.168.0.2       0x80000018    25  0x2  0xa9f   48
    bits 0x1, link count 2
    id 192.168.32.1, data 192.168.33.1, type PointToPoint (1)
    TOS count 0, TOS 0 metric 6
    id 192.168.33.0, data 255.255.255.0, type Stub (3)
    TOS count 0, TOS 0 metric 6
    Gen timer 00:49:35
    Aging timer 00:59:35
    Installed 00:00:25 ago, expires in 00:59:35, sent 00:00:25 ago
    Ours
```

Individual interfaces may still have a metric value manually configured when using the reference-bandwidth command. In our example, the Chardonnay router decides to set the metric of the fe-0/0/1.0 interface to the value 34. Each of the other interfaces on the router retains its configured metric using the reference bandwidth of 1Gbps:

```
[edit protocols ospf]
user@Chardonnay# show
reference-bandwidth 1g;
area 0.0.0.0 {
    interface fe-0/0/1.0 {
        metric 34;
    }
    interface fe-0/0/2.0;
    interface lo0.0;
}
area 0.0.0.2 {
    interface at-0/1/0.0;
}
```

```
user@Chardonnay> show ospf interface detail
Interface           State     Area          DR ID            BDR ID     Nbrs
fe-0/0/1.0          BDR       0.0.0.0       192.168.0.1      192.168.0.2  1
Type LAN, address 192.168.1.2, mask 24, MTU 1500, cost 34
DR addr 192.168.1.1, BDR addr 192.168.1.2, adj count 1, priority 128
Hello 10, Dead 40, ReXmit 5, Not Stub
fe-0/0/2.0          DR        0.0.0.0       192.168.0.2      192.168.0.3  1
```

```
Type LAN, address 192.168.2.1, mask 24, MTU 1500, cost 10
DR addr 192.168.2.1, BDR addr 192.168.2.2, adj count 1, priority 128
Hello 10, Dead 40, ReXmit 5, Not Stub
lo0.0                    DR       0.0.0.0        192.168.0.2      0.0.0.0       0
Type LAN, address 192.168.0.2, mask 32, MTU 65535, cost 0
DR addr 192.168.0.2, BDR addr (null), adj count 0, priority 128
Hello 10, Dead 40, ReXmit 5, Not Stub
at-0/1/0.0               PtToPt   0.0.0.2        0.0.0.0          0.0.0.0       1
Type P2P, address (null), mask 0, MTU 4470, cost 6
DR addr (null), BDR addr (null), adj count 1
Hello 10, Dead 40, ReXmit 5, Not Stub
at-0/1/0.0               PtToPt   0.0.0.2        0.0.0.0          0.0.0.0       0
Type P2P, address 192.168.33.1, mask 24, MTU 4470, cost 6
DR addr (null), BDR addr (null), adj count 0,  passive
Hello 10, Dead 40, ReXmit 5, Not Stub
```

Virtual Links

So far, we've been examining the operation of OSPF using the sample network in Figure 2.3. You might have noticed that area 4, containing the Sangiovese router, is not connected directly to the backbone. Although this type of configuration is not considered a best design practice, we've done it for a reason—to illustrate the use of a virtual link. An OSPF *virtual link* is a method for connecting a remote OSPF area, like area 4, to the backbone.

Operation of a Remote Area

When an OSPF network has a remote area not physically connected to the backbone, you might be surprised by the operation of the network. In short, each router connected to more than one area views itself as an ABR. As with all ABRs, the router and network LSAs are translated into network summary LSAs. The end result of this operation is the appearance of a partially functional network.

Figure 2.16 shows our sample network with the addition of a virtual link between the Cabernet and Riesling routers in area 1. We examine the configuration of this link in the "Configuring a Virtual Link" section later in this chapter. At this point, let's explore how the current network is operating without the virtual link in place. The configuration of the Riesling router is currently set to:

```
user@Riesling> show configuration protocols ospf
area 0.0.0.4 {
    interface fe-0/0/0.0;
}
area 0.0.0.1 {
    interface fe-0/0/1.0;
}
```

FIGURE 2.16 A virtual link connecting a remote OSPF area

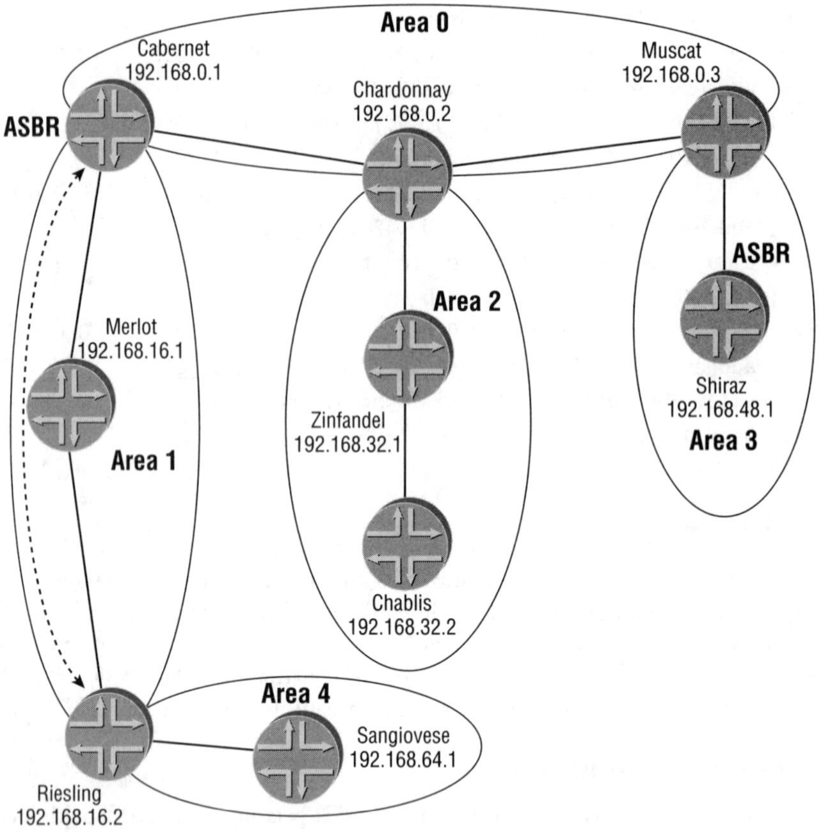

With interfaces configured and operational in multiple OSPF areas, although neither of which is the backbone, Riesling sets the B bit in its router LSAs:

user@Riesling> **show ospf database router lsa-id 192.168.16.2 extensive**

```
    OSPF link state database, area 0.0.0.1
 Type      ID              Adv Rtr          Seq      Age  Opt  Cksum  Len
Router  *192.168.16.2    192.168.16.2     0x80000021 1337 0x2  0x684d  48
  bits 0x1, link count 2
  id 192.168.18.1, data 192.168.18.2, type Transit (2)
  TOS count 0, TOS 0 metric 1
  id 192.168.16.2, data 255.255.255.255, type Stub (3)
  TOS count 0, TOS 0 metric 0
  Gen timer 00:22:43
```

```
Aging timer 00:37:43
Installed 00:22:17 ago, expires in 00:37:43, sent 00:22:15 ago
Ours


    OSPF link state database, area 0.0.0.4
Type        ID                 Adv Rtr              Seq        Age  Opt  Cksum  Len
Router  *192.168.16.2      192.168.16.2       0x80000021   2237  0x2  0x72e4  48
    bits 0x1, link count 2
    id 192.168.65.2, data 192.168.65.1, type Transit (2)
    TOS count 0, TOS 0 metric 1
    id 192.168.16.2, data 255.255.255.255, type Stub (3)
    TOS count 0, TOS 0 metric 0
    Gen timer 00:07:43
    Aging timer 00:22:43
    Installed 00:37:17 ago, expires in 00:22:43, sent 00:37:15 ago
    Ours
```

This set of circumstances causes Riesling to advertise local area routes from area 4 to area 1, and vice versa. The current router and network LSAs in area 4 are sent as network summary LSAs in area 1:

```
user@Riesling> show ospf database router area 4

    OSPF link state database, area 0.0.0.4
Type        ID                 Adv Rtr              Seq        Age  Opt  Cksum  Len
Router  *192.168.16.2      192.168.16.2       0x80000021   2319  0x2  0x72e4  48
Router   192.168.64.1      192.168.64.1       0x8000001e   1999  0x2  0xebe   48


user@Riesling> show ospf database network area 4

    OSPF link state database, area 0.0.0.4
Type        ID                 Adv Rtr              Seq        Age  Opt  Cksum  Len
Network  192.168.65.2      192.168.64.1       0x8000001b   2010  0x2  0xd9e8  32


user@Riesling> ...abase netsummary area 1 advertising-router 192.168.16.2

    OSPF link state database, area 0.0.0.1
Type        ID                 Adv Rtr              Seq        Age  Opt  Cksum  Len
Summary  *192.168.64.1      192.168.16.2       0x8000001f   2074  0x2  0x32e5  28
Summary  *192.168.65.0      192.168.16.2       0x80000020   1774  0x2  0x2fe7  28
```

The Merlot router in area 1 has a route to the loopback address of the Sangiovese router, 192.168.64.1 /32. Network connectivity between the loopbacks of these two routers is also established:

```
user@Merlot> show route 192.168.64.1 terse

inet.0: 29 destinations, 29 routes (29 active, 0 holddown, 0 hidden)
+ = Active Route, - = Last Active, * = Both

A Destination        P Prf   Metric 1   Metric 2  Next hop        AS path
* 192.168.64.1/32    0  10         16             >192.168.18.2

user@Merlot> ping 192.168.64.1 source 192.168.16.1 rapid
PING 192.168.64.1 (192.168.64.1): 56 data bytes
!!!!!
--- 192.168.64.1 ping statistics ---
5 packets transmitted, 5 packets received, 0% packet loss
round-trip min/avg/max/stddev = 0.876/0.946/1.210/0.132 ms
```

The same set of circumstances doesn't exist for the backbone area and the Chardonnay router. It doesn't have a route for the loopback address of Sangiovese:

```
user@Chardonnay> show route 192.168.64.1

user@Chardonnay> ping 192.168.64.1
PING 192.168.64.1 (192.168.64.1): 56 data bytes
ping: sendto: No route to host
ping: sendto: No route to host
^C
--- 192.168.64.1 ping statistics ---
2 packets transmitted, 0 packets received, 100% packet loss
```

Conversely, the Sangiovese router in area 4 has reachability to the loopback addresses in area 1 only. No other route in the 192.168.0.0 /16 address range is in the routing table:

```
user@Sangiovese> show route protocol ospf 192.168/16 terse

inet.0: 14 destinations, 14 routes (14 active, 0 holddown, 0 hidden)
+ = Active Route, - = Last Active, * = Both

A Destination        P Prf   Metric 1   Metric 2  Next hop        AS path
* 192.168.0.1/32     0  10         22             >192.168.65.1
```

```
*  192.168.16.1/32    0  10        2            >192.168.65.1
*  192.168.16.2/32    0  10        1            >192.168.65.1
*  192.168.17.0/24    0  10       22            >192.168.65.1
*  192.168.18.0/24    0  10        2            >192.168.65.1
```

Now that you have a good feeling for how the network is operating, let's try to determine exactly why things are operating in this fashion. Using the 192.168.64.1 /32 route as our test case, we examine the link-state database and routing table as the information flows into the network. The first router in that path is Riesling. It contains both a router LSA in the database and a usable route in the routing table:

```
user@Riesling> show ospf database router lsa-id 192.168.64.1 extensive

    OSPF link state database, area 0.0.0.1
 Type       ID              Adv Rtr          Seq       Age  Opt  Cksum  Len

    OSPF link state database, area 0.0.0.4
 Type       ID              Adv Rtr          Seq       Age  Opt  Cksum  Len
Router   192.168.64.1    192.168.64.1    0x8000001e 2857  0x2  0xebe   48
  bits 0x0, link count 2
  id 192.168.65.2, data 192.168.65.2, type Transit (2)
  TOS count 0, TOS 0 metric 1
  id 192.168.64.1, data 255.255.255.255, type Stub (3)
  TOS count 0, TOS 0 metric 0
  Aging timer 00:12:23
  Installed 00:47:34 ago, expires in 00:12:23, sent 2w2d 12:47:43 ago

user@Riesling> show route 192.168.64.1 terse

inet.0: 15 destinations, 15 routes (15 active, 0 holddown, 0 hidden)
+ = Active Route, - = Last Active, * = Both

A Destination        P Prf   Metric 1   Metric 2  Next hop        AS path
*  192.168.64.1/32   0  10        1               >192.168.65.2
```

As we just saw, the Riesling router is an ABR between areas 1 and 4. The 192.168.64.1 /32 route is advertised to area 1 using a network summary LSA:

```
user@Riesling> show ospf database netsummary lsa-id 192.168.64.1 extensive

    OSPF link state database, area 0.0.0.1
 Type       ID              Adv Rtr          Seq       Age  Opt  Cksum  Len
```

```
Summary *192.168.64.1     192.168.16.2     0x80000020   289  0x2  0x30e6  28
  mask 255.255.255.255
  TOS 0x0, metric 1
  Gen timer 00:45:11
  Aging timer 00:55:11
  Installed 00:04:49 ago, expires in 00:55:11, sent 00:04:47 ago
  Ours

    OSPF link state database, area 0.0.0.4
Type       ID              Adv Rtr          Seq      Age  Opt  Cksum  Len
```

We verify that the next router in the path, Merlot, receives the network summary LSA and installs the route in its routing table:

```
user@Merlot> show ospf database netsummary lsa-id 192.168.64.1 extensive

    OSPF link state database, area 0.0.0.1
Type       ID              Adv Rtr          Seq      Age  Opt  Cksum  Len
Summary  192.168.64.1     192.168.16.2     0x80000020   382  0x2  0x30e6  28
  mask 255.255.255.255
  TOS 0x0, metric 1
  Aging timer 00:53:38
  Installed 00:06:19 ago, expires in 00:53:38, sent 00:06:17 ago

user@Merlot> show route 192.168.64.1 terse

inet.0: 29 destinations, 29 routes (29 active, 0 holddown, 0 hidden)
+ = Active Route, - = Last Active, * = Both

A Destination      P Prf   Metric 1   Metric 2  Next hop       AS path
* 192.168.64.1/32  O  10         16              >192.168.18.2
```

The operation of the network so far looks good, so we check the next router in the path. The Cabernet router is also an ABR between area 1 and the backbone. It receives the network summary LSA from Riesling in its area 1 database:

```
user@Cabernet> show ospf database netsummary lsa-id 192.168.64.1 extensive

    OSPF link state database, area 0.0.0.0
Type       ID              Adv Rtr          Seq      Age  Opt  Cksum  Len
```

```
    OSPF link state database, area 0.0.0.1
 Type        ID               Adv Rtr            Seq       Age  Opt  Cksum  Len
 Summary  192.168.64.1     192.168.16.2     0x80000020   522  0x2  0x30e6  28
    mask 255.255.255.255
    TOS 0x0, metric 1
    Aging timer 00:51:18
    Installed 00:08:36 ago, expires in 00:51:18, sent 2w2d 12:54:21 ago
```

However, the Cabernet router doesn't have a route in its routing table:

```
user@Cabernet> show route 192.168.64.1 terse

user@Cabernet>
```

It seems we've found where the "problem" lies. An examination of the router LSAs within area 1 might provide some valuable information:

```
user@Cabernet> show ospf database router area 1 extensive

    OSPF link state database, area 0.0.0.1
 Type        ID               Adv Rtr            Seq       Age  Opt  Cksum  Len
 Router   *192.168.0.1     192.168.0.1      0x8000002a   575  0x2  0x2de   48
    bits 0x3, link count 2
    id 192.168.17.1, data 192.168.17.1, type Transit (2)
    TOS count 0, TOS 0 metric 1
    id 192.168.0.1, data 255.255.255.255, type Stub (3)
    TOS count 0, TOS 0 metric 0
    Gen timer 00:38:10
    Aging timer 00:50:25
    Installed 00:09:35 ago, expires in 00:50:25, sent 00:09:33 ago
    Ours
 Router   192.168.16.1     192.168.16.1     0x80000024  2532  0x2  0xd0bd  60
    bits 0x0, link count 3
    id 192.168.18.1, data 192.168.18.1, type Transit (2)
    TOS count 0, TOS 0 metric 15
    id 192.168.17.1, data 192.168.17.2, type Transit (2)
    TOS count 0, TOS 0 metric 20
    id 192.168.16.1, data 255.255.255.255, type Stub (3)
    TOS count 0, TOS 0 metric 0
    Aging timer 00:17:47
    Installed 00:42:09 ago, expires in 00:17:48, sent 2w2d 12:56:49 ago
 Router   192.168.16.2     192.168.16.2     0x80000022    70  0x2  0x664e  48
```

```
bits 0x1, link count 2
id 192.168.18.1, data 192.168.18.2, type Transit (2)
TOS count 0, TOS 0 metric 1
id 192.168.16.2, data 255.255.255.255, type Stub (3)
TOS count 0, TOS 0 metric 0
Aging timer 00:58:50
Installed 00:01:04 ago, expires in 00:58:50, sent 2w2d 12:56:49 ago
```

Both the Cabernet router (192.168.0.1) and the Riesling router (192.168.16.2) have the B bit set in their router LSAs, designating them as ABRs. Of course, we can look at the network map in Figure 2.16 and see that Riesling is not a "real" ABR because it isn't connected to the backbone. However, the routers themselves don't have that knowledge. Each assumes that the other is connected to area 0 and doesn't use the network summary LSAs advertised from the remote router. In fact, this is the main method used in OSPF to prevent routing loops. An ABR never creates a network summary LSA to represent a network summary LSA from a non-backbone area. In addition, the non-backbone summary LSA is not included in the SPF calculation on the local router.

To adequately provide reachability and connectivity in our network, we must configure a virtual link between Cabernet and Riesling. Let's see how this process works.

Configuring a Virtual Link

From a high-level viewpoint, a virtual link connects a remote router to the backbone. As such, the configuration of the link always occurs within the area 0 portion of the OSPF configuration. The end result is an operational interface within area 0 on both routers. The virtual link configuration requires two pieces of information: the router ID of the remote router and the OSPF transit area the two routers have in common. We first configure the Cabernet router:

```
[edit protocols ospf]
user@Cabernet# show
export adv-statics;
area 0.0.0.0 {
    virtual-link neighbor-id 192.168.16.2 transit-area 0.0.0.1;
    interface fe-0/0/0.0;
}
area 0.0.0.1 {
    interface fe-0/0/2.0;
}
```

After committing our configuration, we have an operational interface (v1-192.168.16.2) within area 0 on the Cabernet router. No adjacency is formed because the Riesling router is not configured:

```
user@Cabernet> show ospf interface
```

```
Interface              State    Area         DR ID            BDR ID      Nbrs
fe-0/0/0.0             DR       0.0.0.0      192.168.0.1      192.168.0.2  1
vl-192.168.16.2       PtToPt   0.0.0.0      0.0.0.0          0.0.0.0      0
fe-0/0/2.0            DR       0.0.0.1      192.168.0.1      192.168.16.1 1

user@Cabernet> show ospf neighbor
  Address         Interface          State    ID            Pri  Dead
  192.168.1.2     fe-0/0/0.0         Full     192.168.0.2   128  39
  192.168.17.2    fe-0/0/2.0         Full     192.168.16.1  128  39
```

The Riesling router is now configured to support its virtual link:

```
[edit protocols ospf]
user@Riesling# show
area 0.0.0.4 {
    interface fe-0/0/0.0;
}
area 0.0.0.1 {
    interface fe-0/0/1.0;
}
area 0.0.0.0 {
    virtual-link neighbor-id 192.168.0.1 transit-area 0.0.0.1;
}
```

We now have a fully established adjacency between Riesling and Cabernet:

```
user@Riesling> show ospf neighbor
  Address         Interface          State    ID            Pri  Dead
  192.168.18.1    fe-0/0/1.0         Full     192.168.16.1  128  32
  192.168.65.2    fe-0/0/0.0         Full     192.168.64.1  128  32
  192.168.17.1    vl-192.168.0.1     Full     192.168.0.1   0    39
```

Some interesting things occur at this point within the contents of the link-state database. The Riesling router is now virtually connected to the backbone, so it populates an area 0 portion of the link-state database:

```
user@Riesling> show ospf database area 0

  OSPF link state database, area 0.0.0.0
 Type       ID                Adv Rtr           Seq         Age  Opt  Cksum  Len
 Router     192.168.0.1       192.168.0.1       0x8000002e  272  0x2  0x5df  60
 Router     192.168.0.2       192.168.0.2       0x80000031  931  0x2  0xcc18 60
 Router     192.168.0.3       192.168.0.3       0x80000025  1073 0x2  0xd42a 48
```

Router	*192.168.16.2	192.168.16.2	0x80000002	266	0x2	0x8b45	48
Network	192.168.1.1	192.168.0.1	0x80000027	534	0x2	0x3d4b	32
Network	192.168.2.1	192.168.0.2	0x8000002b	1080	0x2	0x3c44	32
Summary	*192.168.0.1	192.168.16.2	0x80000002	271	0x2	0xf769	28
Summary	192.168.16.1	192.168.0.1	0x80000029	604	0x2	0xa6a8	28
Summary	*192.168.16.1	192.168.16.2	0x80000002	271	0x2	0x7ee6	28
Summary	192.168.16.2	192.168.0.1	0x8000002a	604	0x2	0x310d	28
Summary	192.168.17.0	192.168.0.1	0x8000002a	604	0x2	0xa3aa	28
Summary	*192.168.17.0	192.168.16.2	0x80000002	271	0x2	0x460b	28
Summary	192.168.18.0	192.168.0.1	0x8000002b	604	0x2	0x2d10	28
Summary	*192.168.18.0	192.168.16.2	0x80000002	271	0x2	0x72f1	28
Summary	192.168.32.1	192.168.0.2	0x80000027	1980	0x2	0x2615	28
Summary	192.168.32.2	192.168.0.2	0x80000022	1830	0x2	0x300e	28
Summary	192.168.33.0	192.168.0.2	0x8000002c	1680	0x2	0x1b1b	28
Summary	192.168.34.0	192.168.0.2	0x8000002b	1680	0x2	0x1c19	28
Summary	192.168.48.1	192.168.0.3	0x8000001b	773	0x2	0x55e5	28
Summary	192.168.49.0	192.168.0.3	0x80000024	633	0x2	0x42ef	28
Summary	*192.168.64.1	192.168.16.2	0x80000002	271	0x2	0x6cc8	28
Summary	*192.168.65.0	192.168.16.2	0x80000002	271	0x2	0x6bc9	28
ASBRSum	*192.168.0.1	192.168.16.2	0x80000004	266	0x2	0xe578	28
ASBRSum	192.168.48.1	192.168.0.3	0x8000001b	473	0x2	0x47f2	28

The router output shows that Riesling has generated a router LSA within area 0. Within that LSA, the virtual link interface is reported to the network. The cost of the interface is the actual metric value used by Riesling to reach Cabernet. Cabernet's router LSA contains similar information:

```
user@Riesling> show ospf database area 0 router extensive
```

```
    OSPF link state database, area 0.0.0.0
Type      ID              Adv Rtr         Seq        Age  Opt  Cksum  Len
Router   192.168.0.1     192.168.0.1     0x8000002e  471  0x2  0x5df  60
  bits 0x3, link count 3
  id 192.168.1.1, data 192.168.1.1, type Transit (2)
  TOS count 0, TOS 0 metric 1
  id 192.168.16.2, data 192.168.17.1, type Virtual (4)
  TOS count 0, TOS 0 metric 16
  id 192.168.0.1, data 255.255.255.255, type Stub (3)
  TOS count 0, TOS 0 metric 0
  Aging timer 00:52:09
  Installed 00:07:45 ago, expires in 00:52:09, sent 2w2d 14:03:01 ago
```

```
Router    192.168.0.2       192.168.0.2       0x80000031 1130 0x2  0xcc18  60
  bits 0x1, link count 3
  id 192.168.1.1, data 192.168.1.2, type Transit (2)
  TOS count 0, TOS 0 metric 34
  id 192.168.2.1, data 192.168.2.1, type Transit (2)
  TOS count 0, TOS 0 metric 10
  id 192.168.0.2, data 255.255.255.255, type Stub (3)
  TOS count 0, TOS 0 metric 0
  Aging timer 00:41:10
  Installed 00:07:50 ago, expires in 00:41:10, sent 2w2d 14:03:01 ago
Router    192.168.0.3       192.168.0.3       0x80000025 1272 0x2  0xd42a  48
  bits 0x1, link count 2
  id 192.168.2.1, data 192.168.2.2, type Transit (2)
  TOS count 0, TOS 0 metric 1
  id 192.168.0.3, data 255.255.255.255, type Stub (3)
  TOS count 0, TOS 0 metric 0
  Aging timer 00:38:48
  Installed 00:07:50 ago, expires in 00:38:48, sent 2w2d 14:03:01 ago
Router    *192.168.16.2     192.168.16.2      0x80000002  465 0x2  0x8b45  48
  bits 0x1, link count 2
  id 192.168.0.1, data 192.168.18.2, type Virtual (4)
  TOS count 0, TOS 0 metric 21
  id 192.168.16.2, data 255.255.255.255, type Stub (3)
  TOS count 0, TOS 0 metric 0
  Gen timer 00:19:30
  Aging timer 00:52:15
  Installed 00:07:45 ago, expires in 00:52:15, sent 00:07:45 ago
  Ours
```

The router LSAs within area 1 for Cabernet and Riesling contain some valuable information as well. Each router is now reporting the active virtual link by setting the V bit to a value of 1:

```
user@Riesling> show ospf database area 1 router extensive

    OSPF link state database, area 0.0.0.1
  Type      ID                Adv Rtr           Seq       Age  Opt  Cksum  Len
  Router    192.168.0.1       192.168.0.1       0x8000002d  108 0x2  0x8d1  48
    bits 0x7, link count 2
    id 192.168.17.1, data 192.168.17.1, type Transit (2)
    TOS count 0, TOS 0 metric 1
```

```
  id 192.168.0.1, data 255.255.255.255, type Stub (3)
  TOS count 0, TOS 0 metric 0
  Aging timer 00:58:12
  Installed 00:01:46 ago, expires in 00:58:12, sent 2w2d 13:56:57 ago
Router   192.168.16.1    192.168.16.1    0x80000026   195  0x2  0xccbf  60
  bits 0x0, link count 3
  id 192.168.18.1, data 192.168.18.1, type Transit (2)
  TOS count 0, TOS 0 metric 15
  id 192.168.17.1, data 192.168.17.2, type Transit (2)
  TOS count 0, TOS 0 metric 20
  id 192.168.16.1, data 255.255.255.255, type Stub (3)
  TOS count 0, TOS 0 metric 0
  Aging timer 00:56:44
  Installed 00:03:12 ago, expires in 00:56:45, sent 2w2d 13:56:57 ago
Router   *192.168.16.2    192.168.16.2    0x80000026   101  0x2  0x6a42  48
  bits 0x5, link count 2
  id 192.168.18.1, data 192.168.18.2, type Transit (2)
  TOS count 0, TOS 0 metric 1
  id 192.168.16.2, data 255.255.255.255, type Stub (3)
  TOS count 0, TOS 0 metric 0
  Gen timer 00:48:19
  Aging timer 00:58:19
  Installed 00:01:41 ago, expires in 00:58:19, sent 00:01:41 ago
  Ours
```

Remember that the end goal of this configuration was reachability for the area 4 routes, in particular the loopback address of the Sangiovese router. Riesling, still an ABR, generates a network summary LSA for the area 4 routes and injects them into the area 0 database:

```
user@Riesling> show ospf database router area 4

    OSPF link state database, area 0.0.0.4
 Type      ID             Adv Rtr          Seq       Age  Opt  Cksum  Len
 Router   *192.168.16.2   192.168.16.2   0x80000026   468  0x2  0x68e9  48
 Router    192.168.64.1   192.168.64.1   0x80000020  1745  0x2  0xac0   48

user@Riesling> show ospf database network area 4

    OSPF link state database, area 0.0.0.4
 Type      ID             Adv Rtr          Seq       Age  Opt  Cksum  Len
 Network  192.168.65.2   192.168.64.1   0x8000001d  1753  0x2  0xd5ea  32
```

```
user@Riesling> ...abase area 0 netsummary advertising-router 192.168.16.2

    OSPF link state database, area 0.0.0.0
Type      ID                Adv Rtr           Seq        Age  Opt  Cksum  Len
Summary *192.168.0.1        192.168.16.2      0x80000003  279  0x2  0xf56a  28
Summary *192.168.16.1       192.168.16.2      0x80000003  165  0x2  0x7ce7  28
Summary *192.168.17.0       192.168.16.2      0x80000002  847  0x2  0x460b  28
Summary *192.168.18.0       192.168.16.2      0x80000002  847  0x2  0x72f1  28
Summary *192.168.64.1       192.168.16.2      0x80000002  847  0x2  0x6cc8  28
Summary *192.168.65.0       192.168.16.2      0x80000002  847  0x2  0x6bc9  28
```

The presence of the Type 3 LSAs within the backbone means that the routes should now be populated on the routing table of each router in the network. We verify this, and check our connectivity, from the Shiraz router in area 3:

```
user@Shiraz> show route 192.168.64.1 terse

inet.0: 29 destinations, 29 routes (29 active, 0 holddown, 0 hidden)
+ = Active Route, - = Last Active, * = Both

A Destination       P Prf   Metric 1   Metric 2  Next hop       AS path
* 192.168.64.1/32   O  10        53               >192.168.49.1

user@Shiraz> ping 192.168.64.1 source 192.168.48.1 rapid
PING 192.168.64.1 (192.168.64.1): 56 data bytes
!!!!!
--- 192.168.64.1 ping statistics ---
5 packets transmitted, 5 packets received, 0% packet loss
round-trip min/avg/max/stddev = 1.059/1.143/1.418/0.138 ms
```

Stub Areas

The OSPF specification details the reason for creating a stub area: reducing the database size and the memory requirements of the internal area routers. While the Juniper Networks routers do not have restrictions in this manner, it is still useful to understand the operation of a stub area and its effect on the link-state database. Recall that a *stub area* prevents the use of AS external LSAs by not allowing the ABR to re-flood these LSAs into the area from the backbone. Additionally, the ABR also stops generating ASBR summary LSAs.

FIGURE 2.17 A stub area sample network

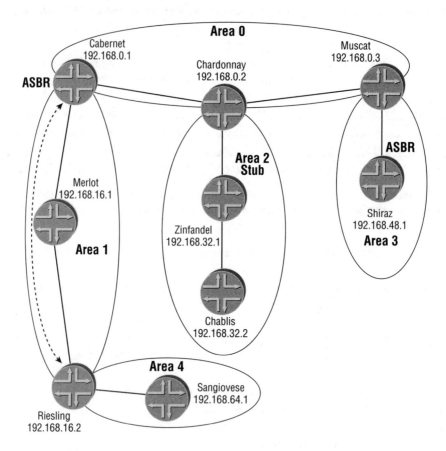

Figure 2.17 shows that area 2 in our sample network is a stub area. Before we actually configure the routers in this area, let's first establish a baseline of the area's operation. The Chablis router currently has several AS external LSAs in its database, as well as the appropriate corresponding Type 4 LSAs:

```
user@Chablis> show ospf database extern
     OSPF AS SCOPE link state database
  Type       ID              Adv Rtr        Seq        Age  Opt  Cksum   Len
  Extern     172.16.1.0      192.168.0.1    0x8000002d 1238 0x2  0xe796  36
  Extern     172.16.2.0      192.168.0.1    0x8000002d 1103 0x2  0xdca0  36
  Extern     172.16.3.0      192.168.0.1    0x8000002d 1073 0x2  0xd1aa  36
  Extern     172.16.4.0      192.168.48.1   0x80000036 1702 0x2  0x63de  36
  Extern     172.16.5.0      192.168.48.1   0x80000036  802 0x2  0x58e8  36
  Extern     172.16.6.0      192.168.48.1   0x80000036  502 0x2  0x4df2  36
```

```
Extern    172.16.7.0        192.168.48.1      0x80000036   202  0x2  0x42fc  36

user@Chablis> show ospf database asbrsummary

    OSPF link state database, area 0.0.0.2
 Type      ID              Adv Rtr           Seq        Age  Opt  Cksum  Len
ASBRSum  192.168.0.1       192.168.0.2       0x8000002b  183  0x2  0x8aaf  28
ASBRSum  192.168.48.1      192.168.0.2       0x80000025  153  0x2  0x9d89  28
```

Configuring a Stub Area

A quick look at the network map shows that the ABR of Chardonnay is the only exit point from area 2. Therefore, the need for explicit routing knowledge on the area 2 routers is not required because all paths lead to the ABR—a perfect candidate for a stub area configuration. Each router in the area must be configured to support the operation of the stub process. The support is signaled by setting the E bit in the Options field of the OSPF header to the value 0 (known as *clearing* the bit). Let's configure the Chablis router to make area 2 a stub area:

```
[edit protocols ospf]
user@Chablis# show
area 0.0.0.2 {
    stub;
    authentication-type simple; # SECRET-DATA
    interface so-0/1/0.0 {
        authentication-key "$9$9SwLCORrlMXNbvWaZ"; # SECRET-DATA
    }
}
```

After committing the configuration, we can verify that the E bit is cleared by examining the router LSA of Chablis in area 2. The other routers in the area still have the E bit set in their hello packets, so the adjacency to the Zinfandel router goes away:

```
user@Chablis> show ospf database router lsa-id 192.168.32.2 extensive

    OSPF link state database, area 0.0.0.2
 Type      ID              Adv Rtr           Seq        Age  Opt  Cksum  Len
Router  *192.168.32.2      192.168.32.2      0x80000001   22  0x0  0x52c3  48
  bits 0x0, link count 2
  id 192.168.34.0, data 255.255.255.0, type Stub (3)
  TOS count 0, TOS 0 metric 1
  id 192.168.32.2, data 255.255.255.255, type Stub (3)
  TOS count 0, TOS 0 metric 0
```

```
Gen timer 00:49:38
Aging timer 00:59:38
Installed 00:00:22 ago, expires in 00:59:38, sent 2w2d 15:36:30 ago
Ours
```

```
user@Chablis> show ospf neighbor
```

```
user@Chablis>
```

In fact, every OSPF packet received from Zinfandel is discarded. In addition, Chablis purges its OSPF database of all LSAs from other routers:

```
user@Chablis> show ospf database
```

```
    OSPF link state database, area 0.0.0.2
 Type      ID             Adv Rtr          Seq       Age  Opt  Cksum  Len
 Router  *192.168.32.2    192.168.32.2    0x80000002  143  0x0  0x50c4  48
```

We now configure the other area 2 routers, Zinfandel and Chardonnay, to support the stub network operation:

```
[edit protocols ospf]
user@Zinfandel# show
area 0.0.0.2 {
    stub;
    authentication-type simple; # SECRET-DATA
    interface so-0/1/0.0 {
        authentication-key "$9$dQVgJiHmTF/.PO1"; # SECRET-DATA
    }
    interface at-0/2/0.0;
    interface lo0.0;
}
```

```
[edit protocols ospf]
user@Chardonnay# show
reference-bandwidth 1g;
area 0.0.0.0 {
    interface fe-0/0/1.0 {
        metric 34;
    }
    interface fe-0/0/2.0;
    interface lo0.0;
```

```
}
area 0.0.0.2 {
    stub;
    interface at-0/1/0.0;
}
```

The adjacency between Zinfandel and Chablis is now functional again and a full link-state database exists on the Chablis router. In addition, the routers in the area agree on their use of AS external LSAs:

```
user@Chablis> show ospf neighbor
  Address        Interface        State      ID          Pri  Dead
  192.168.34.1   so-0/1/0.0       Full       192.168.32.1  128  37

user@Chablis> show ospf interface detail
Interface          State    Area       DR ID        BDR ID       Nbrs
so-0/1/0.0         PtToPt   0.0.0.2    0.0.0.0      0.0.0.0      1
Type P2P, address (null), mask 0, MTU 4470, cost 1
DR addr (null), BDR addr (null), adj count 1
Hello 10, Dead 40, ReXmit 5, Stub
so-0/1/0.0         PtToPt   0.0.0.2    0.0.0.0      0.0.0.0      0
Type P2P, address 192.168.34.2, mask 24, MTU 4470, cost 1
DR addr (null), BDR addr (null), adj count 0,   passive
Hello 10, Dead 40, ReXmit 5, Stub

user@Chablis> show ospf database router detail

    OSPF link state database, area 0.0.0.2
  Type       ID             Adv Rtr           Seq       Age  Opt  Cksum   Len
Router    192.168.0.2     192.168.0.2      0x80000002   188  0x0  0x546d  48
   bits 0x1, link count 2
   id 192.168.32.1, data 192.168.33.1, type PointToPoint (1)
   TOS count 0, TOS 0 metric 6
   id 192.168.33.0, data 255.255.255.0, type Stub (3)
   TOS count 0, TOS 0 metric 6
Router    192.168.32.1    192.168.32.1     0x80000004   171  0x0  0x123a  84
   bits 0x0, link count 5
   id 192.168.0.2, data 192.168.33.2, type PointToPoint (1)
   TOS count 0, TOS 0 metric 1
   id 192.168.33.0, data 255.255.255.0, type Stub (3)
   TOS count 0, TOS 0 metric 1
   id 192.168.32.1, data 255.255.255.255, type Stub (3)
```

```
      TOS count 0, TOS 0 metric 0
      id 192.168.32.2, data 192.168.34.1, type PointToPoint (1)
      TOS count 0, TOS 0 metric 1
      id 192.168.34.0, data 255.255.255.0, type Stub (3)
      TOS count 0, TOS 0 metric 1
Router  *192.168.32.2     192.168.32.2     0x80000003    209  0x0  0xb438  60
      bits 0x0, link count 3
      id 192.168.32.1, data 192.168.34.2, type PointToPoint (1)
      TOS count 0, TOS 0 metric 1
      id 192.168.34.0, data 255.255.255.0, type Stub (3)
      TOS count 0, TOS 0 metric 1
      id 192.168.32.2, data 255.255.255.255, type Stub (3)
      TOS count 0, TOS 0 metric 0

user@Chablis> show ospf database extern

user@Chablis>
```

While we've successfully eliminated the AS external LSAs from the databases of the area 2 internal routers, we have also lost some information. Primarily, both Chablis and Zinfandel no longer have reachability to the routes in the 172.16.0.0 /16 address range as advertised by the ASBRs in the network—specifically the 172.16.1.1 and 172.16.4.1 addresses:

```
user@Zinfandel> show route 172.16.1.1

user@Zinfandel> show route 172.16.4.1

user@Zinfandel>

user@Chablis> show route 172.16.1.1

user@Chablis> show route 172.16.4.1

user@Chablis>
```

This reachability is replaced by a default 0.0.0.0 /0 route advertised by the ABR. The default route is carried in a network summary LSA generated by the ABR with a metric value you configure. As the Type 3 LSA has only an area-flooding scope, just the routers in the stub area use this route.

Within the JUNOS software, the generation of the default route is a manual configuration step to provide for the greatest administrator flexibility and control. For example, you might want only a single ABR to advertise the default route instead of two or more ABRs. In addition, multiple ABRs could advertise the route with different metric values attached.

The `default-metric` command within the ABR's stub configuration generates the Type 3 LSA. The configuration of the Chardonnay router is altered to support this functionality:

```
[edit protocols ospf]
user@Chardonnay# show
reference-bandwidth 1g;
area 0.0.0.0 {
    interface fe-0/0/1.0 {
        metric 34;
    }
    interface fe-0/0/2.0;
    interface lo0.0;
}
area 0.0.0.2 {
    stub default-metric 20;
    interface at-0/1/0.0;
}
```

The details of the network summary LSA generated for the default route are:

```
user@Chardonnay> show ospf database area 2 lsa-id 0.0.0.0 extensive


    OSPF link state database, area 0.0.0.2
 Type        ID               Adv Rtr          Seq        Age  Opt  Cksum  Len
 Summary *0.0.0.0            192.168.0.2      0x80000001   71  0x0  0x3aa5  28
   mask 0.0.0.0
   TOS 0x0, metric 20
   Gen timer 00:48:48
   Aging timer 00:58:48
   Installed 00:01:11 ago, expires in 00:58:49, sent 00:01:11 ago
   Ours
```

The Link-State ID and Network Mask fields are each set to a value of 0.0.0.0. When they are combined, the resulting route is 0.0.0.0 /0, our default route. The ABR set the metric value in the LSA to 20. Each internal area router adds this advertised metric to their cost to reach the ABR in order to determine the final metric cost of the default route. After receiving the default LSA from Chardonnay, both Zinfandel and Chablis have a valid route for the 172.16.0.0 /16 address range. When the Chardonnay router receives those user packets, it uses its explicit routing knowledge of the address space to forward the packets to their final destination:

```
user@Zinfandel> show route 172.16.1.1

inet.0: 23 destinations, 25 routes (23 active, 0 holddown, 0 hidden)
```

```
+ = Active Route, - = Last Active, * = Both

0.0.0.0/0               *[OSPF/10] 00:00:08, metric 21
                        > via at-0/2/0.0


user@Chablis> show route 172.16.4.1

inet.0: 23 destinations, 24 routes (23 active, 0 holddown, 0 hidden)
+ = Active Route, - = Last Active, * = Both

0.0.0.0/0               *[OSPF/10] 00:00:24, metric 22
                        > via so-0/1/0.0


user@Chardonnay> show route 172.16.1.1

inet.0: 30 destinations, 31 routes (30 active, 0 holddown, 0 hidden)
+ = Active Route, - = Last Active, * = Both

172.16.1.0/24          *[OSPF/150] 00:00:29, metric 0, tag 0
                        > to 192.168.1.1 via fe-0/0/1.0


user@Chardonnay> show route 172.16.4.1

inet.0: 30 destinations, 31 routes (30 active, 0 holddown, 0 hidden)
+ = Active Route, - = Last Active, * = Both

172.16.4.0/24          *[OSPF/150] 00:00:32, metric 0, tag 0
                        > to 192.168.2.2 via fe-0/0/2.0
```

Configuring a Totally Stubby Area

The concept of reducing the size of the database in an area with a single exit point can be taken a step further with the creation of a *totally stubby area*. To see the effectiveness of this type of OSPF area, let's continue examining area 2 in Figure 2.17, which is already configured as a stub area. The Zinfandel router currently has connectivity to each of the other routers in the network:

```
user@Zinfandel> show route protocol ospf 192.168/16 terse

inet.0: 23 destinations, 25 routes (23 active, 0 holddown, 0 hidden)
+ = Active Route, - = Last Active, * = Both
```

A	Destination	P	Prf	Metric 1	Metric 2	Next hop	AS path
*	192.168.0.1/32	O	10	35		>at-0/2/0.0	
*	192.168.0.2/32	O	10	1		>at-0/2/0.0	
*	192.168.0.3/32	O	10	11		>at-0/2/0.0	
*	192.168.1.0/24	O	10	35		>at-0/2/0.0	
*	192.168.2.0/24	O	10	11		>at-0/2/0.0	
*	192.168.16.1/32	O	10	36		>at-0/2/0.0	
*	192.168.16.2/32	O	10	51		>at-0/2/0.0	
*	192.168.17.0/24	O	10	36		>at-0/2/0.0	
*	192.168.18.0/24	O	10	51		>at-0/2/0.0	
*	192.168.32.2/32	O	10	1		>so-0/1/0.0	
	192.168.33.0/24	O	10	1		>at-0/2/0.0	
	192.168.34.0/24	O	10	1		>so-0/1/0.0	
*	192.168.48.1/32	O	10	12		>at-0/2/0.0	
*	192.168.49.0/24	O	10	12		>at-0/2/0.0	
*	192.168.64.1/32	O	10	52		>at-0/2/0.0	
*	192.168.65.0/24	O	10	52		>at-0/2/0.0	

With the exception of the 192.168.32.2 /32 route, the loopback address of Chablis, each of the active OSPF routes has a next-hop interface of at-0/2/0.0. This is the interface connecting Zinfandel to Chardonnay, the ABR for the area. The current operation of the area has very explicit routing knowledge to each of the internal destinations, each with the same exit point out of the area. This is similar to the "issue" we saw with configuring a stub area in the first place. The benefit of explicit routing is not outweighed by the potential of reduced processing on the internal area routers.

The main difference between a stub and a totally stubby area is the absence of network summary LSAs in the link-state database of the area. These LSAs are generated by the ABR for local backbone routes as well as routes from other non-backbone areas. To convert a stub area into a totally stubby area, we simply inform the ABR to stop generating these Type 3 LSAs.

WARNING   The injection of a default Type 3 LSA from the ABR is critical to the operation of a totally stubby area.

The Chardonnay router is configured with the no-summaries command to support the operation of area 2 as a totally stubby area:

```
[edit protocols ospf]
user@Chardonnay# show
reference-bandwidth 1g;
area 0.0.0.0 {
    interface fe-0/0/1.0 {
        metric 34;
    }
```

```
    interface fe-0/0/2.0;
    interface lo0.0;
}
area 0.0.0.2 {
    stub default-metric 20 no-summaries;
    interface at-0/1/0.0;
}
```

The link-state database on the Chablis router is now greatly reduced. The router has explicit routing knowledge of the local area routes and uses the default route to reach all other networks in other portions of the OSPF domain:

```
userChablis> show ospf database

    OSPF link state database, area 0.0.0.2
   Type      ID              Adv Rtr         Seq         Age  Opt  Cksum  Len
   Router    192.168.0.2     192.168.0.2     0x8000000b  112  0x0  0x4276  48
   Router    192.168.32.1    192.168.32.1    0x8000000b  116  0x0  0x441   84
   Router   *192.168.32.2    192.168.32.2    0x80000006  1142 0x0  0xae3b  60
   Summary   0.0.0.0         192.168.0.2     0x80000003  117  0x0  0x36a7  28


user@Chablis> show route protocol ospf terse

inet.0: 10 destinations, 11 routes (10 active, 0 holddown, 0 hidden)
+ = Active Route, - = Last Active, * = Both


A Destination        P Prf  Metric 1  Metric 2  Next hop        AS path
* 0.0.0.0/0          0  10     22               >so-0/1/0.0
* 192.168.32.1/32    0  10      1               >so-0/1/0.0
* 192.168.33.0/24    0  10      2               >so-0/1/0.0
  192.168.34.0/24    0  10      1               >so-0/1/0.0
* 224.0.0.5/32       0  10      1                MultiRecv
```

Not-So-Stubby Areas

One of the core tenets of using an OSPF stub area is the exclusion of an ASBR within the area. There are times, however, when a network administrator might find it useful to have an ASBR in an otherwise stub area. Often this occurs when you're connecting your network to an external partner network. Regardless of the requirements, this type of situation is handled through the use of a *not-so-stubby area* (NSSA). An NSSA allows for the injection of external routing knowledge by an ASBR using an NSSA external LSA, type code 7.

FIGURE 2.18   An NSSA sample network

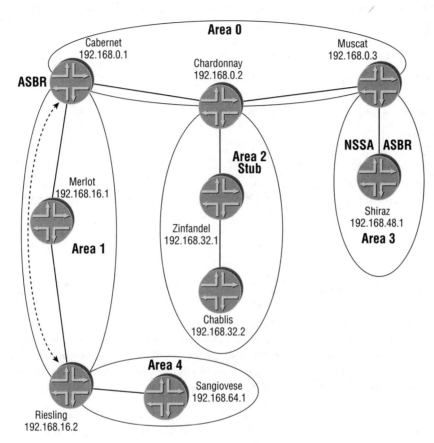

Our sample network in Figure 2.18 displays area 3, with its ASBR, as a not-so-stubby area. To effectively operate an NSSA, each router in the area must be configured to support the flooding of Type 7 LSAs. As with the stub area operation, this support is signaled through the use of the Options field in the OSPF hello packet header. The E bit is cleared (set to the value 0), while the N/P bit is set to the value 1. Let's configure both the Muscat and Shiraz routers to convert area 3 to an NSSA:

```
[edit protocols ospf]
user@Muscat# show
area 0.0.0.0 {
    interface fe-0/0/2.0;
}
area 0.0.0.3 {
    nssa;
    authentication-type md5; # SECRET-DATA
```

```
    interface fe-0/0/1.0 {
        authentication-key "$9$Hk5FCAOIhruO" key-id 25; # SECRET-DATA
    }
}

[edit protocols ospf]
user@Shiraz# show
export adv-statics;
area 0.0.0.3 {
    nssa;
    authentication-type md5; # SECRET-DATA
    interface fe-0/0/0.0 {
        authentication-key "$9$vcCM7Vg4ZjkPJG" key-id 25; # SECRET-DATA
    }
}
```

Checking for NSSA Support

The N/P bit in the Options field plays two roles within a not-so-stubby area. In an OSPF hello packet, the N bit signifies whether the local router supports Type 7 LSAs. One effective method for viewing this field in the hello packet is through the use of the JUNOS software `traceoptions` functionality. The following router output from the Shiraz router shows hello packets being sent and received with the N bit set and the E bit cleared:

```
Feb 26 20:24:11 OSPF sent Hello 192.168.49.2 -> 224.0.0.5 (fe-0/0/0.0, IFL 3)
Feb 26 20:24:11   Version 2, length 48, ID 192.168.48.1, area 0.0.0.3
Feb 26 20:24:11   checksum 0x0, authtype 0
Feb 26 20:24:11   mask 255.255.255.0, hello_ivl 10, opts 0x8, prio 128
Feb 26 20:24:11   dead_ivl 40, DR 192.168.49.2, BDR 192.168.49.1
Feb 26 20:24:13 OSPF rcvd Hello 192.168.49.1 -> 224.0.0.5 (fe-0/0/0.0, IFL 3)
Feb 26 20:24:13   Version 2, length 48, ID 192.168.0.3, area 0.0.0.3
Feb 26 20:24:13   checksum 0x0, authtype 2
Feb 26 20:24:13   mask 255.255.255.0, hello_ivl 10, opts 0x8, prio 128
Feb 26 20:24:13   dead_ivl 40, DR 192.168.49.2, BDR 192.168.49.1
```

Within the header of an NSSA external LSA, the P bit set to 1 tells the ABR with the highest router ID to translate the Type 7 LSA into a Type 5 LSA. Should the bit be clear (set to 0), the ABR should not perform the translation. The NSSA external LSAs sent by Shiraz have the bit set and should be translated:

```
user@Shiraz> show ospf database nssa
```

```
      OSPF link state database, area 0.0.0.3
    Type       ID              Adv Rtr          Seq       Age  Opt  Cksum  Len
    NSSA    *172.16.4.0     192.168.48.1     0x8000000e  1241  0x8  0xedd9  36
    NSSA    *172.16.5.0     192.168.48.1     0x8000000d   941  0x8  0xe4e2  36
    NSSA    *172.16.6.0     192.168.48.1     0x8000000d   641  0x8  0xd9ec  36
    NSSA    *172.16.7.0     192.168.48.1     0x8000000d   341  0x8  0xcef6  36
```

We verify that each of the routers supports the NSSA functionality and that the adjacency between them is operational:

```
user@Shiraz> show ospf interface detail
Interface              State    Area          DR ID          BDR ID        Nbrs
fe-0/0/0.0             DR       0.0.0.3       192.168.48.1   192.168.0.3   1
Type LAN, address 192.168.49.2, mask 24, MTU 1500, cost 1
DR addr 192.168.49.2, BDR addr 192.168.49.1, adj count 1, priority 128
Hello 10, Dead 40, ReXmit 5, Stub NSSA
```

```
user@Shiraz> show ospf neighbor
 Address          Interface           State      ID            Pri  Dead
192.168.49.1      fe-0/0/0.0          Full       192.168.0.3   128  31
```

As with the stub area, an NSSA ABR should inject a default route into the area to provide connectivity for the external routes injected by the Cabernet router. Unlike the stub area, however, the default route is injected as a Type 7 LSA:

```
[edit protocols ospf]
user@Muscat# show
area 0.0.0.0 {
    interface fe-0/0/2.0;
}
area 0.0.0.3 {
    nssa {
        default-lsa default-metric 25;
    }
    authentication-type md5; # SECRET-DATA
    interface fe-0/0/1.0 {
        authentication-key "$9$Hk5FCAOIhruO" key-id 25; # SECRET-DATA
    }
}
```

```
user@Muscat> show ospf database lsa-id 0.0.0.0 extensive

    OSPF link state database, area 0.0.0.0
 Type        ID              Adv Rtr           Seq      Age  Opt  Cksum  Len

    OSPF link state database, area 0.0.0.3
 Type        ID              Adv Rtr           Seq      Age  Opt  Cksum  Len
NSSA    *0.0.0.0           192.168.0.3       0x80000001   11  0x0  0x3e8f  36
  mask 0.0.0.0
  Type 1, TOS 0x0, metric 25, fwd addr 0.0.0.0, tag 0.0.0.0
  Gen timer 00:49:49
  Aging timer 00:59:49
  Installed 00:00:11 ago, expires in 00:59:49, sent 00:00:11 ago
  Ours


user@Shiraz> show route 172.16.1.1

inet.0: 27 destinations, 27 routes (27 active, 0 holddown, 0 hidden)
+ = Active Route, - = Last Active, * = Both


0.0.0.0/0           *[OSPF/150] 00:06:31, metric 26, tag 0
                    > to 192.168.49.1 via fe-0/0/0.0
```

Should the Muscat router stop injecting network summary LSAs into the NSSA (to create a totally stubby not-so-stubby area), the default route begins to be injected using a Type 3 LSA:

```
[edit protocols ospf]
user@Muscat# show
area 0.0.0.0 {
    interface fe-0/0/2.0;
}
area 0.0.0.3 {
    nssa {
        default-lsa default-metric 25;
        no-summaries;
    }
    authentication-type md5; # SECRET-DATA
    interface fe-0/0/1.0 {
        authentication-key "$9$Hk5FCA0Ihru0" key-id 25; # SECRET-DATA
    }
}
```

```
user@Muscat> show ospf database lsa-id 0.0.0.0 extensive

    OSPF link state database, area 0.0.0.0
Type        ID                Adv Rtr          Seq       Age  Opt  Cksum  Len

    OSPF link state database, area 0.0.0.3
Type        ID                Adv Rtr          Seq       Age  Opt  Cksum  Len
Summary  *0.0.0.0             192.168.0.3      0x80000001  12  0x0  0x6673  28
  mask 0.0.0.0
  TOS 0x0, metric 25
  Gen timer 00:49:47
  Aging timer 00:59:47
  Installed 00:00:12 ago, expires in 00:59:48, sent 00:00:12 ago
  Ours

user@Shiraz> show route 172.16.1.1

inet.0: 13 destinations, 13 routes (13 active, 0 holddown, 0 hidden)
+ = Active Route, - = Last Active, * = Both

0.0.0.0/0           *[OSPF/10] 00:04:23, metric 26
                    > to 192.168.49.1 via fe-0/0/0.0
```

The use of the network summary LSA is the default action in an NSSA with the no-summaries command configured. A network administrator can inject the default route using a Type 7 LSA again by configuring the type-7 option within the nssa portion of the OSPF configuration:

```
[edit protocols ospf]
user@Muscat# show
area 0.0.0.0 {
    interface fe-0/0/2.0;
}
area 0.0.0.3 {
    nssa {
        default-lsa {
            default-metric 25;
            type-7;
        }
        no-summaries;
    }
    authentication-type md5; # SECRET-DATA
```

```
    interface fe-0/0/1.0 {
        authentication-key "$9$Hk5FCAOIhruO" key-id 25; # SECRET-DATA
    }
}
```

user@Muscat> **show ospf database lsa-id 0.0.0.0 extensive**

```
    OSPF link state database, area 0.0.0.0
 Type      ID                Adv Rtr            Seq     Age  Opt  Cksum  Len

    OSPF link state database, area 0.0.0.3
 Type      ID                Adv Rtr            Seq     Age  Opt  Cksum  Len
 NSSA    *0.0.0.0            192.168.0.3      0x80000001  22  0x0  0x3e8f  36
    mask 0.0.0.0
    Type 1, TOS 0x0, metric 25, fwd addr 0.0.0.0, tag 0.0.0.0
    Gen timer 00:49:38
    Aging timer 00:59:38
    Installed 00:00:22 ago, expires in 00:59:38, sent 00:00:22 ago
    Ours
```

Address Summarization

The use of stub, totally stubby, and not-so-stubby areas in an OSPF network is designed to help reduce the size of the link-state database for internal area routers. None of these concepts, however, shield the routers in the backbone area from a potentially large number of network summary LSAs generated by the ABRs. This large data size occurs as a new Type 3 LSA is generated on a one-for-one basis for each router and network LSA in a non-backbone area.

The method for solving this "issue" is to perform some *address summarization* on the ABR. One example of summarization is combining the area routes sent into the backbone into a few network summary LSAs. A second possibility is the combination of multiple Type 7 LSAs combined into a fewer number of Type 5 LSAs before they are advertised into the backbone. Let's examine each of these options in some further detail.

Area Route Summarization

The effectiveness of summarizing the area routes in a non-backbone area depends greatly on the method you use to allocate your internal address space. If portions of your address block are spread across your network, you'll find it challenging to create a summarization scheme that greatly reduces the database size in the backbone.

FIGURE 2.19   Area route summarization

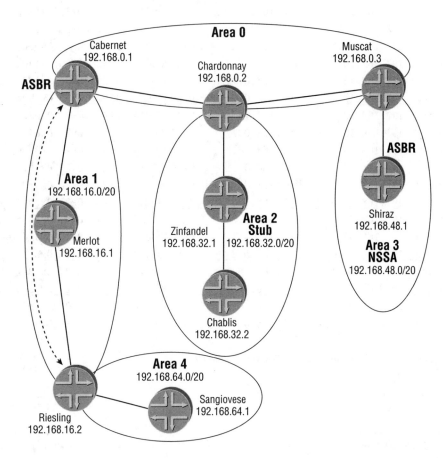

Figure 2.19 shows our sample network and the address ranges assigned to each OSPF area. For example, area 1 currently uses the 192.168.16.0 /20 range for router loopback address and network link addresses. A look at the area 0 database on the Chardonnay router shows a great number of network summary LSAs, representing the routes from the non-backbone areas. In fact, there are 16 such LSAs currently in the database:

user@Chardonnay> **show ospf database area 0**

```
      OSPF link state database, area 0.0.0.0
  Type       ID               Adv Rtr           Seq      Age  Opt  Cksum  Len
  Router     192.168.0.1      192.168.0.1       0x80000053  549  0x2  0xba05  60
  Router    *192.168.0.2      192.168.0.2       0x80000059  2024 0x2  0x7c40  60
  Router     192.168.0.3      192.168.0.3       0x80000055  104  0x2  0x7a52  48
  Router     192.168.16.2     192.168.16.2      0x8000001e  1842 0x2  0x5361  48
```

```
Network   192.168.1.1     192.168.0.1     0x8000004b  1020  0x2  0xf46f  32
Network  *192.168.2.1     192.168.0.2     0x8000004f  2324  0x2  0xf368  32
Summary   192.168.0.1     192.168.16.2    0x8000001f   542  0x2  0xbd86  28
Summary   192.168.16.1    192.168.0.1     0x8000004d  2049  0x2  0x5ecc  28
Summary   192.168.16.1    192.168.16.2    0x8000001f    42  0x2  0x4404  28
Summary   192.168.16.2    192.168.0.1     0x8000004e  1920  0x2  0xe831  28
Summary   192.168.17.0    192.168.0.1     0x8000004e  1792  0x2  0x5bce  28
Summary   192.168.17.0    192.168.16.2    0x8000001e  2742  0x2  0xe27   28
Summary   192.168.18.0    192.168.0.1     0x8000004f  1749  0x2  0xe434  28
Summary   192.168.18.0    192.168.16.2    0x8000001e  2542  0x2  0x3a0e  28
Summary  *192.168.32.1    192.168.0.2     0x8000001f   824  0x2  0x360d  28
Summary  *192.168.32.2    192.168.0.2     0x8000001f   524  0x2  0x360b  28
Summary  *192.168.33.0    192.168.0.2     0x80000052  1724  0x2  0xce41  28
Summary  *192.168.34.0    192.168.0.2     0x8000001f   224  0x2  0x340d  28
Summary   192.168.48.1    192.168.0.3     0x8000001d   677  0x2  0x51e7  28
Summary   192.168.49.0    192.168.0.3     0x80000053   674  0x2  0xe31f  28
Summary   192.168.64.1    192.168.16.2    0x8000001e  2342  0x2  0x34e4  28
Summary   192.168.65.0    192.168.16.2    0x8000001e  2142  0x2  0x33e5  28
ASBRSum   192.168.0.1     192.168.16.2    0x80000020   942  0x2  0xad94  28
ASBRSum   192.168.48.1    192.168.0.3     0x8000001c   374  0x2  0x45f3  28

user@Chardonnay> show ospf database summary
Area 0.0.0.0:
    4 Router LSAs
    2 Network LSAs
    16 Summary LSAs
    2 ASBRSum LSAs
Area 0.0.0.2:
    3 Router LSAs
    1 Summary LSAs
Externals:
    7 Extern LSAs
Interface at-0/1/0.0:
Interface at-0/1/0.0:
Interface fe-0/0/1.0:
Interface fe-0/0/2.0:
Interface lo0.0:
```

The network summary LSAs highlighted in the router output from Chardonnay represent some example routes we can use to check the effectiveness of our summarization. The area-range command performs the summarization process on the ABR. You supply the range of addresses you wish to summarize and place the command within the area portion of your OSPF configuration. The ABR locates any router and network LSAs in the respective area that fall within the configured summary address and does not advertise them into the backbone. In their place, a single network summary LSA representing the summary address is advertised. The summary address of 192.168.32.0 /20 is configured on the Chardonnay router:

```
[edit protocols ospf]
user@Chardonnay# show
reference-bandwidth 1g;
area 0.0.0.0 {
    interface fe-0/0/1.0 {
        metric 34;
    }
    interface fe-0/0/2.0;
    interface lo0.0;
}
area 0.0.0.2 {
    stub default-metric 20 no-summaries;
    area-range 192.168.32.0/20;
    interface at-0/1/0.0;
}
```

The newly created network summary LSA is now present in the area 0 link-state database. The more specific Type 3 LSAs have been purged by Chardonnay, leaving just 13 Type 3 LSAs in the database:

```
user@Chardonnay> show ospf database area 0
```

```
        OSPF link state database, area 0.0.0.0
 Type      ID              Adv Rtr         Seq         Age  Opt  Cksum  Len
Router    192.168.0.1     192.168.0.1     0x80000053  1043 0x2  0xba05  60
Router   *192.168.0.2     192.168.0.2     0x8000005b    51 0x2  0x7842  60
Router    192.168.0.3     192.168.0.3     0x80000055   598 0x2  0x7a52  48
Router    192.168.16.2    192.168.16.2    0x8000001e  2336 0x2  0x5361  48
Network   192.168.1.1     192.168.0.1     0x8000004b  1514 0x2  0xf46f  32
Network  *192.168.2.1     192.168.0.2     0x80000050   418 0x2  0xf169  32
Summary   192.168.0.1     192.168.16.2    0x8000001f  1036 0x2  0xbd86  28
Summary   192.168.16.1    192.168.0.1     0x8000004e   186 0x2  0x5ccd  28
Summary   192.168.16.1    192.168.16.2    0x8000001f   536 0x2  0x4404  28
Summary   192.168.16.2    192.168.0.1     0x8000004f   143 0x2  0xe632  28
Summary   192.168.17.0    192.168.0.1     0x8000004f    14 0x2  0x59cf  28
Summary   192.168.17.0    192.168.16.2    0x8000001f   336 0x2  0xc28   28
```

```
Summary   192.168.18.0     192.168.0.1     0x8000004f  2243  0x2  0xe434  28
Summary   192.168.18.0     192.168.16.2    0x8000001f   136  0x2  0x380f  28
Summary  *192.168.32.0     192.168.0.2     0x80000001    51  0x2  0x3b35  28
Summary   192.168.48.1     192.168.0.3     0x8000001d  1171  0x2  0x51e7  28
Summary   192.168.49.0     192.168.0.3     0x80000053  1168  0x2  0xe31f  28
Summary   192.168.64.1     192.168.16.2    0x8000001e  2836  0x2  0x34e4  28
Summary   192.168.65.0     192.168.16.2    0x8000001e  2636  0x2  0x33e5  28
ASBRSum   192.168.0.1      192.168.16.2    0x80000020  1436  0x2  0xad94  28
ASBRSum   192.168.48.1     192.168.0.3     0x8000001c   868  0x2  0x45f3  28
```

```
user@Chardonnay> show ospf database summary
Area 0.0.0.0:
    4 Router LSAs
    2 Network LSAs
   13 Summary LSAs
    2 ASBRSum LSAs
Area 0.0.0.2:
    3 Router LSAs
    1 Summary LSAs
Externals:
    7 Extern LSAs
Interface at-0/1/0.0:
Interface at-0/1/0.0:
Interface fe-0/0/1.0:
Interface fe-0/0/2.0:
Interface lo0.0:
```

A closer examination of the details of this new network summary LSA reveals some interesting information:

```
user@Chardonnay> ...spf database netsummary lsa-id 192.168.32.0 extensive

    OSPF link state database, area 0.0.0.0
 Type        ID              Adv Rtr          Seq      Age  Opt  Cksum  Len
Summary *192.168.32.0     192.168.0.2     0x80000001   276  0x2  0x3b35  28
   mask 255.255.240.0
   TOS 0x0, metric 7
   Gen timer 00:45:24
   Aging timer 00:55:24
   Installed 00:04:36 ago, expires in 00:55:24, sent 00:04:36 ago
   Ours
```

The correct summary address, 192.168.32.0 /20, is advertised, and a metric value has been calculated for the LSA. When the ABR was generating the Type 3 LSAs for every area route, the metric cost from the ABR to that route was used for the metric in the Type 3 LSA. This process doesn't work so well for the summary address since there is no existing route to calculate a metric for. Instead, the ABR uses the highest metric available for the routes being summarized as the metric for the network summary LSA. The routing table on Chardonnay shows two routes with a current metric value of 7:

```
user@Chardonnay> show route protocol ospf 192.168.32/20

inet.0: 31 destinations, 32 routes (31 active, 0 holddown, 0 hidden)
+ = Active Route, - = Last Active, * = Both

192.168.32.0/20    *[OSPF/10] 00:05:21, metric 16777215
                    Discard
192.168.32.1/32    *[OSPF/10] 00:05:21, metric 6
                    > via at-0/1/0.0
192.168.32.2/32    *[OSPF/10] 00:05:21, metric 7
                    > via at-0/1/0.0
192.168.33.0/24     [OSPF/10] 00:05:21, metric 6
                    > via at-0/1/0.0
192.168.34.0/24    *[OSPF/10] 00:05:21, metric 7
                    > via at-0/1/0.0
```

The output of the show route command contains some additional interesting information. A new route representing the summary address is installed in the routing table with a next-hop address of Discard. This ensures that any received packets matching the summary address as a longest match (a more-specific route doesn't exist) are dropped to prevent potential loops in the network. The 16,777,215 metric assigned to the route is the maximum value available for a network summary LSA ($2 \wedge 24 - 1$).

Each of the other ABRs in the network (Cabernet, Muscat, and Riesling) now configures its summary addresses within OSPF. The area 0 database now contains eight network summary LSAs:

```
user@Chardonnay> show ospf database area 0
```

```
    OSPF link state database, area 0.0.0.0
Type        ID            Adv Rtr         Seq        Age  Opt  Cksum  Len
Router   192.168.0.1      192.168.0.1    0x80000055  210  0x2  0xb607  60
Router  *192.168.0.2      192.168.0.2    0x8000005c  1064 0x2  0x7643  60
Router   192.168.0.3      192.168.0.3    0x80000057  195  0x2  0x7654  48
Router   192.168.16.2     192.168.16.2   0x80000020  177  0x2  0x4f63  48
Network  192.168.1.1      192.168.0.1    0x8000004d   23  0x2  0xf071  32
Network *192.168.2.1      192.168.0.2    0x80000051  1364 0x2  0xef6a  32
```

Summary	192.168.0.1	192.168.16.2	0x80000020	177	0x2	0xbb87	28
Summary	192.168.16.0	192.168.0.1	0x80000001	210	0x2	0x4c2c	28
Summary	192.168.16.1	192.168.16.2	0x80000020	177	0x2	0x4205	28
Summary	192.168.17.0	192.168.16.2	0x80000020	177	0x2	0xa29	28
Summary	192.168.18.0	192.168.16.2	0x80000020	177	0x2	0x3610	28
Summary	*192.168.32.0	192.168.0.2	0x80000002	164	0x2	0x3936	28
Summary	192.168.48.0	192.168.0.3	0x80000001	195	0x2	0x481d	28
Summary	192.168.64.0	192.168.16.2	0x80000001	178	0x2	0x2d19	28
ASBRSum	192.168.0.1	192.168.16.2	0x80000022	177	0x2	0xa996	28
ASBRSum	192.168.48.1	192.168.0.3	0x8000001e	195	0x2	0x41f5	28

```
user@Chardonnay> show ospf database summary
Area 0.0.0.0:
    4 Router LSAs
    2 Network LSAs
    8 Summary LSAs
    2 ASBRSum LSAs
Area 0.0.0.2:
    3 Router LSAs
    1 Summary LSAs
Externals:
    7 Extern LSAs
Interface at-0/1/0.0:
Interface at-0/1/0.0:
Interface fe-0/0/1.0:
Interface fe-0/0/2.0:
Interface lo0.0:
```

Even though the Riesling router is not physically connected to the backbone, it is still injecting LSAs into area 0 using its virtual link to Cabernet. This configuration required us to place an area-range command for the area 4 internal routes on that ABR to truly summarize those routes.

Curiously, the link-state database still reports Type 3 LSAs within the address range configured on the Cabernet router in area 1. We verify that the configuration is correct:

```
user@Cabernet> show configuration protocols ospf
export adv-statics;
area 0.0.0.0 {
    virtual-link neighbor-id 192.168.16.2 transit-area 0.0.0.1;
```

```
        interface fe-0/0/0.0;
}
area 0.0.0.1 {
    area-range 192.168.16.0/20;
    interface fe-0/0/2.0;
}
```

The configuration of Cabernet appears correct; in fact, it is. A closer look at the `show ospf database` output from Chardonnay leads us in another direction. The Type 3 LSAs in question are being advertised from the 192.168.16.2 router—Riesling:

```
user@Riesling> show configuration protocols ospf
area 0.0.0.4 {
    area-range 192.168.64.0/20;
    interface fe-0/0/0.0;
}
area 0.0.0.1 {
    interface fe-0/0/1.0;
}
area 0.0.0.0 {
    virtual-link neighbor-id 192.168.0.1 transit-area 0.0.0.1;
}
```

An `area-range` command is correctly configured within area 4 for that area's internal routes. However, Riesling also has an operational interface in area 1, which makes it an ABR for that area as well. This requires us to place a summary address within the area 1 portion of Riesling's configuration as well:

```
[edit protocols ospf]
user@Riesling# show
area 0.0.0.4 {
    area-range 192.168.64.0/20;
    interface fe-0/0/0.0;
}
area 0.0.0.1 {
    area-range 192.168.16.0/20;
    interface fe-0/0/1.0;
}
area 0.0.0.0 {
    virtual-link neighbor-id 192.168.0.1 transit-area 0.0.0.1;
}
```

The link-state database for area 0 now appears as we would expect it to, with only five network summary LSAs present:

```
user@Chardonnay> show ospf database area 0

    OSPF link state database, area 0.0.0.0
 Type       ID            Adv Rtr        Seq         Age  Opt  Cksum  Len
 Router    192.168.0.1    192.168.0.1    0x8000005b   21  0x2  0xea9   60
 Router   *192.168.0.2    192.168.0.2    0x8000005e   34  0x2  0x7245  60
 Router    192.168.0.3    192.168.0.3    0x80000059   35  0x2  0x7256  48
 Router    192.168.16.2   192.168.16.2   0x80000025   26  0x2  0x4568  48
 Network   192.168.1.1    192.168.0.1    0x8000004e   35  0x2  0xee72  32
 Network  *192.168.2.1    192.168.0.2    0x80000053   34  0x2  0xeb6c  32
 Summary   192.168.16.0   192.168.0.1    0x80000005   28  0x2  0x4430  28
 Summary   192.168.16.0   192.168.16.2   0x80000003   30  0x2  0x45c   28
 Summary  *192.168.32.0   192.168.0.2    0x80000003   34  0x2  0x3737  28
 Summary   192.168.48.0   192.168.0.3    0x80000002   35  0x2  0x461e  28
 Summary   192.168.64.0   192.168.16.2   0x80000004   35  0x2  0x271c  28
 ASBRSum   192.168.0.1    192.168.16.2   0x80000027   20  0x2  0x9f9b  28
 ASBRSum   192.168.48.1   192.168.0.3    0x80000020   35  0x2  0x3df7  28

user@Chardonnay> show ospf database summary
Area 0.0.0.0:
    4 Router LSAs
    2 Network LSAs
    5 Summary LSAs
    2 ASBRSum LSAs
Area 0.0.0.2:
    3 Router LSAs
    1 Summary LSAs
Externals:
    7 Extern LSAs
Interface at-0/1/0.0:
Interface at-0/1/0.0:
Interface fe-0/0/1.0:
Interface fe-0/0/2.0:
Interface lo0.0:
```

NSSA Route Summarization

The summarization of internal area routes is easily accomplished as the ABR is generating new LSAs before flooding the information into the backbone. This same concept is carried forward when we talk about NSSA external routes. Although these routes are not carried in router or network LSAs, the ABR is still generating a new LSA on a one-for-one basis to represent these routes to the backbone. The difference in this case is that the newly created LSAs are external LSAs.

FIGURE 2.20   NSSA route summarization

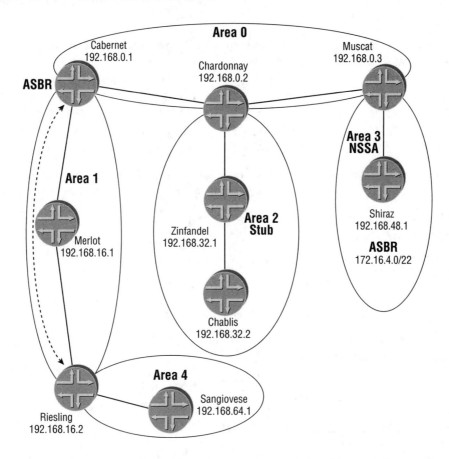

The Shiraz router in area 3 is an ASBR injecting external routes in the address range of 172.16.4.0 /22, as shown in Figure 2.20. These routes are advertised using Type 7 LSAs within the area:

```
user@Shiraz> show ospf database nssa
```

```
    OSPF link state database, area 0.0.0.3
 Type       ID               Adv Rtr          Seq        Age   Opt   Cksum   Len
 NSSA    0.0.0.0          192.168.0.3      0x8000001f    771   0x0   0x2ad    36
 NSSA    *172.16.4.0      192.168.48.1     0x8000002d    371   0x8   0xaff8   36
 NSSA    *172.16.5.0      192.168.48.1     0x8000002c     71   0x8   0xa602   36
 NSSA    *172.16.6.0      192.168.48.1     0x8000002b   1571   0x8   0x9d0b   36
 NSSA    *172.16.7.0      192.168.48.1     0x8000002b    671   0x8   0x9215   36
```

The ABR for area 3, the Muscat router, translates these routes into Type 5 LSAs and advertises them into the network:

```
user@Muscat> show ospf database extern advertising-router 192.168.0.3
    OSPF AS SCOPE link state database
 Type       ID               Adv Rtr          Seq        Age   Opt   Cksum   Len
 Extern   *172.16.4.0      192.168.0.3      0x80000030   1432   0x2   0x6576   36
 Extern   *172.16.5.0      192.168.0.3      0x8000002f   1432   0x2   0x5c7f   36
 Extern   *172.16.6.0      192.168.0.3      0x8000002f   1432   0x2   0x5189   36
 Extern   *172.16.7.0      192.168.0.3      0x8000002e   1432   0x2   0x4892   36
```

We again use the `area-range` command to summarize these NSSA routes into a single AS external LSA. However, we place the summary address within the NSSA portion of the OSPF configuration:

```
[edit protocols ospf]
user@Muscat# show
area 0.0.0.0 {
    interface fe-0/0/2.0;
}
area 0.0.0.3 {
    nssa {
        default-lsa {
            default-metric 25;
            type-7;
        }
        no-summaries;
        area-range 172.16.4.0/22;
    }
    area-range 192.168.48.0/20;
    authentication-type md5; # SECRET-DATA
    interface fe-0/0/1.0 {
        authentication-key "$9$Hk5FCA0Ihru0" key-id 25; # SECRET-DATA
    }
}
```

The configuration of the Muscat router shows the `area-range` command configured twice within area 3. The subtle difference in its placement causes different summarization actions. The `area-range 192.168.48.0/20` usage within the area hierarchy itself summarizes the intra-area routes. The `area-range 172.16.4.0/22` usage in the NSSA hierarchy summarizes only the external NSSA routes. Please take care when using this type of configuration.

Muscat advertises only a single AS external LSA of 172.16.4.0 /22 into the network at this point. The other backbone routers receive the LSA and install the route in their routing tables:

```
user@Muscat> show ospf database extern lsa-id 172.16.4.0 extensive
    OSPF AS SCOPE link state database
 Type       ID              Adv Rtr         Seq        Age  Opt  Cksum  Len
 Extern  *172.16.4.0        192.168.0.3     0x80000032   44  0x2  0xabca 36
   mask 255.255.252.0
   Type 2, TOS 0x0, metric 1, fwd addr 0.0.0.0, tag 0.0.0.0
   Gen timer 00:49:15
   Aging timer 00:59:15
   Installed 00:00:44 ago, expires in 00:59:16, sent 00:00:44 ago
   Ours

user@Chardonnay> show ospf database extern
    OSPF AS SCOPE link state database
 Type       ID              Adv Rtr         Seq        Age  Opt  Cksum  Len
 Extern   172.16.1.0        192.168.0.1     0x80000053  1289 0x2  0x9bbc 36
 Extern   172.16.2.0        192.168.0.1     0x80000053  1120 0x2  0x90c6 36
 Extern   172.16.3.0        192.168.0.1     0x80000053   989 0x2  0x85d0 36
 Extern   172.16.4.0        192.168.0.3     0x80000032   155 0x2  0xabca 36

user@Chardonnay> show route 172.16/16

inet.0: 24 destinations, 25 routes (24 active, 0 holddown, 0 hidden)
+ = Active Route, - = Last Active, * = Both

172.16.1.0/24      *[OSPF/150] 01:20:08, metric 0, tag 0
                    > to 192.168.1.1 via fe-0/0/1.0
172.16.2.0/24      *[OSPF/150] 01:20:08, metric 0, tag 0
                    > to 192.168.1.1 via fe-0/0/1.0
172.16.3.0/24      *[OSPF/150] 01:20:08, metric 0, tag 0
                    > to 192.168.1.1 via fe-0/0/1.0
172.16.4.0/22      *[OSPF/150] 00:02:45, metric 1, tag 0
                    > to 192.168.2.2 via fe-0/0/2.0
```

Summary

In this chapter, we took a very detailed look at the operation of OSPF. We discussed each of the link-state advertisement types, including packet formats, and showed an example of their use in a sample network. We then explored the shortest path first (SPF) algorithm and how it calculates the path to each destination in the network. We performed an example of the calculation on a small network sample.

We then examined the configuration options within the protocol. We looked at the router's ability to use graceful restart to avoid network outages. We then discussed authentication in the network and altering the metric values advertised in the router LSAs. Finally, we described the uses of virtual links and saw an example of their configuration.

We concluded the chapter with configuration examples of a stub and a not-so-stubby area. We explored the effect of these area types on the link-state database as well as methods for maintaining reachability in the network. Finally, we looked at summarizing internal area and NSSA routes on the ABRs before advertising those routes into the OSPF backbone.

Exam Essentials

Be able to identify the format and function of the OSPF link-state advertisements.   The JUNOS software uses the following link-state advertisements: router, network, network summary, ASBR summary, AS external, NSSA external, and opaque. Each LSA performs a separate function within the protocol. When they are combined, each portion of the network is uniquely described in the link-state database.

Understand the preference of OSPF routes within the database.   An OSPF router always prefers intra-area routes learned from within its own area over all other routes. Intra-area routes learned from another area are preferred next, followed by external routes. Type 1 external routes are always preferred over type 2 external routes.

Be familiar with the three data structures used by the SPF algorithm.   During the operation of the SPF algorithm, the router constructs three tables to represent network routes and their metrics. These tables are the link-state, candidate, and tree databases.

Be able to describe the uses and configuration of a virtual link.   A virtual link is used to either reconnect a discontiguous backbone area or to connect a physically separated non-backbone area to area 0. The virtual link configuration is always placed within the area 0 portion of the configuration and includes the remote neighbor's router ID as well as the transit area used to reach the neighbor.

Understand the effect a stub or not-so-stubby area has on the link-state database.   Both a stub area and an NSSA restrict the flooding of AS external LSAs within the area. When a large number of external routes exist in the backbone area, these types reduce the size of the link-state database. A smaller database results in memory processing savings as less information is passed through the SPF algorithm.

Be able to configure address summarization within OSPF.   Address summarization is accomplished in the JUNOS software through the use of the `area-range` command. You place this command at either the area or NSSA level of the OSPF configuration. When used at the area level, it summarizes internal area routes to the backbone. The application within the NSSA portion of the configuration summarizes NSSA external routes.

Review Questions

1.   What is the MaxAge of an OSPF LSA?

   A. 1200 seconds

   B. 2400 seconds

   C. 3600 seconds

   D. 4800 seconds

2.   Which bit in the router LSA is set to signify that the local router is an ABR?

   A. V bit

   B. E bit

   C. B bit

   D. N/P bit

3.   Before using an advertised AS external LSA, an OSPF router must verify reachability to the ASBR. Which two LSA types can be used for this reachability?

   A. Router LSA

   B. Network LSA

   C. Network summary LSA

   D. ASBR summary LSA

4.   Which authentication command is placed at the area hierarchy level and describes the method of authentication used?

   A. `authentication-type`

   B. `authentication-key`

   C. `key-id`

   D. `key-value`

5.   Which SPF algorithm database contains the result of the calculation and whose results are passed to the routing table on the router?

   A. Root database

   B. Link-state database

   C. Candidate database

   D. Tree database

6.   The total cost from each neighbor to the root of the tree is calculated in which SPF algorithm database?

   A. Root database

   B. Link-state database

   C. Candidate database

   D. Tree database

7. How is the metric of a network summary LSA selected when it represents a router LSA in the non-backbone area?

   A. The advertised metric in the router LSA is used.

   B. It is always set to the minimum value of 0.

   C. It is always set to the maximum value of 16,777,215.

   D. The ABR's current cost for the route is used.

8. What capability is the local router advertising through its router LSA?

```
Router   192.168.0.2        192.168.0.2        0x80000063   793  0x2  0x684a   60
bits 0x1, link count 3
id 192.168.1.1, data 192.168.1.2, type Transit (2)
TOS count 0, TOS 0 metric 34
id 192.168.2.1, data 192.168.2.1, type Transit (2)
TOS count 0, TOS 0 metric 10
id 192.168.0.2, data 255.255.255.255, type Stub (3)
TOS count 0, TOS 0 metric 0
```

   A. It is currently an ABR.

   B. It is currently an ASBR.

   C. It is currently supporting a virtual link.

   D. It is currently configured within a stub area.

9. What capabilities is the local router advertising through its router LSA?

```
Router   192.168.0.2        192.168.0.2        0x80000063   793  0x2  0x684a   60
bits 0x5, link count 3
id 192.168.1.1, data 192.168.1.2, type Transit (2)
TOS count 0, TOS 0 metric 34
id 192.168.2.1, data 192.168.2.1, type Transit (2)
TOS count 0, TOS 0 metric 10
id 192.168.0.2, data 255.255.255.255, type Stub (3)
TOS count 0, TOS 0 metric 0
```

   A. It is currently an ABR.

   B. It is currently an ASBR.

   C. It is currently supporting a virtual link.

   D. It is currently configured within a stub area.

10. How many physical interfaces are configured for OSPF on the local router?

```
Router    192.168.32.1      192.168.32.1      0x80000027   126  0x0  0xcb5d   84
bits 0x0, link count 5
id 192.168.0.2, data 192.168.33.2, type PointToPoint (1)
TOS count 0, TOS 0 metric 1
id 192.168.33.0, data 255.255.255.0, type Stub (3)
TOS count 0, TOS 0 metric 1
id 192.168.32.1, data 255.255.255.255, type Stub (3)
TOS count 0, TOS 0 metric 0
id 192.168.32.2, data 192.168.34.1, type PointToPoint (1)
TOS count 0, TOS 0 metric 1
id 192.168.34.0, data 255.255.255.0, type Stub (3)
TOS count 0, TOS 0 metric 1
```

A. 2

B. 3

C. 4

D. 5

Answers to Review Questions

1. C. The Age field in an LSA is initialized to a value of 0 and counts up to a MaxAge of 3600 seconds.

2. C. The B bit in the router LSA is set when the local router has operational interfaces in more than one OSPF area.

3. A and D. When an ASBR is in the same area as the local router, the router LSA of the ASBR is used to provide the needed reachability. When the ASBR is in another area, the ASBR summary LSA is used.

4. A. Each router in the area must agree on the form of authentication used in the area by configuring the `authentication-type` command at the area configuration hierarchy level.

5. D. The end result of the SPF calculation is stored in the tree database. When the algorithm completes, this information is passed to the routing table on the router for possible use in forwarding user data packets.

6. C. As tuples are moved into the candidate database, the cost from each newly installed neighbor ID to the root is calculated. The tuple with the lowest cost is then moved to the tree database.

7. D. The metric value placed into a network summary LSA is always the ABR's current cost for the route. This occurs whether the Type 3 LSA represents a router LSA, a network LSA, or another network summary LSA. Routers that receive this new Type 3 LSA add their cost to the ABR to the advertised metric in order to determine their total cost for the route.

8. A. The `bits` setting in the router LSA displays the router's V/E/B settings. Currently this value reads `0x1`, which means that the router is advertising itself as an ABR.

9. A and C. The `bits` setting in the router LSA displays the router's V/E/B settings. Currently this value reads `0x5`, which means that the router is an ABR that has an established virtual link with another router in a non-backbone area.

10. A. An OSPF router always forms an adjacency over a point-to-point link using an unnumbered interface and reports that connection in its router LSA using a link type of 1 (`PointToPoint`). The subnets configured on those interfaces are then advertised as `Stub` networks. In addition, the loopback interface of the router is always advertised as a `Stub` network. This means that the router represented in the LSA shown here has only two physical interfaces configured for OSPF.

Chapter

3

Intermediate System to Intermediate System (IS-IS)

JNCIS EXAM OBJECTIVES COVERED IN THIS CHAPTER:

- ✓ Define the functions of the following IS-IS parameters—authentication; mesh groups; wide metrics; route preferences; IS-IS levels; LSP lifetime; overload; routing policy
- ✓ Describe characteristics of IS-IS adjacencies
- ✓ Describe inter-area routing in IS-IS
- ✓ Identify the operation and database characteristics of a multi-area IS-IS network
- ✓ Describe the functionality of the IS-IS protocol data units
- ✓ Describe the functionality of the defined IS-IS TLVs
- ✓ Describe ISO network addressing as it applies to IS-IS
- ✓ Determine route selection based on IGP route metrics and the Shortest Path Algorithm
- ✓ Define the capabilities and operation of graceful restart
- ✓ Identify the configuration of IS-IS route summarization

In this chapter, we present a detailed examination of the operation of the Intermediate System to Intermediate System (IS-IS) routing protocol. We first discuss the type, length, value (TLV) formats used to represent protocol information. Many of the transmitted TLVs are used to compile a complete link-state database, and we discuss the operation of the Shortest Path First (SPF) algorithm on that database.

We then explore some configuration options used with an IS-IS network, including graceful restart, interface metrics, and authentication. A detailed discussion of the operation and configuration of a multilevel IS-IS network follows. We conclude the chapter with an examination of network address summarization at the borders of an IS-IS level.

IS-IS TLV Details

Each IS-IS PDU used in a network contains one or more data structures encoded in a *type, length, value (TLV)* format. Table 3.1 displays some common IS-IS TLV codes, the name of each TLV, and which Protocol Data Units (PDUs) contain the TLV.

TABLE 3.1 Common IS-IS TLVs

TLV Name	TLV #	Protocol Data Unit Usage
Area Address	1	L1 LAN Hello, L2 LAN Hello, P2P Hello, L1 LSP, L2 LSP
IS Reachability	2	L1 LSP, L2 LSP
IS Neighbors	6	L1 LAN Hello, L2 LAN Hello
Padding	8	L1 LAN Hello, L2 LAN Hello, P2P Hello,
LSP Entry	9	L1 CSNP, L2 CSNP, L1 PSNP, L2 PSNP
Authentication	10	L1 LAN Hello, L2 LAN Hello, P2P Hello, L1 LSP, L2 LSP, L1 CSNP, L2 CSNP, L1 PSNP, L2 PSNP
Checksum	12	L1 LAN Hello, L2 LAN Hello, P2P Hello, L1 CSNP, L2 CSNP, L1 PSNP, L2 PSNP

TABLE 3.1   Common IS-IS TLVs *(continued)*

TLV Name	TLV #	Protocol Data Unit Usage
Extended IS Reachability	22	L1 LSP, L2 LSP
IP Internal Reachability	128	L1 LSP, L2 LSP
Protocols Supported	129	L1 LAN Hello, L2 LAN Hello, P2P Hello, L1 LSP, L2 LSP
IP External Reachability	130	L1 LSP, L2 LSP
IP Interface Address	132	L1 LAN Hello, L2 LAN Hello, P2P Hello, L1 LSP, L2 LSP
Traffic Engineering IP Router ID	134	L1 LSP, L2 LSP
Extended IP Reachability	135	L1 LSP, L2 LSP
Dynamic Host Name	137	L1 LSP, L2 LSP
Graceful Restart	211	L1 LAN Hello, L2 LAN Hello, P2P Hello
Point-to-Point Adjacency State	240	P2P Hello

The details of each TLV, as well as their packet formats, are contained in the following sections.

Area Address TLV

The *area address TLV* (type code 1) is transmitted in all Hello and link-state PDUs. It describes the current areas configured on the local router, up to the maximum of three addresses. Both the area length and area ID fields are repeated for each address. Figure 3.1 displays the fields of the area address TLV, which include the following:

TLV Type (1 octet)   This field displays the type of information encoded in the TLV. A constant value of 1 (0x0001) is placed in this octet.

TLV Length (1 octet)   The length of the remaining TLV fields is placed in this field. Possible values for the TLV length can range from 2 (a single area with a length of 1) to 42 (3 areas each with a length of 13).

Area Length (1 octet)   This area length field displays the size of the area address in the following field.

Area ID (Variable)   The area ID field contains the actual area address encoded within the router's network entity title (NET). The length of the area ID can range from 1 to 13 bytes.

FIGURE 3.1 Area address TLV (1)

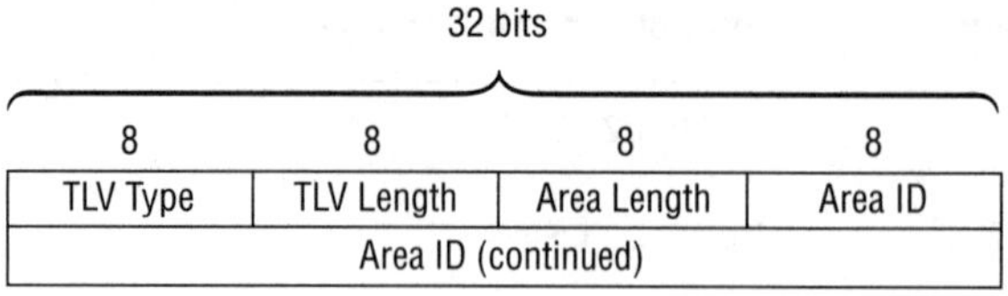

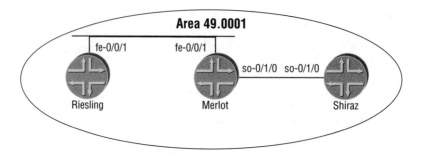

FIGURE 3.2 IS-IS sample network

Figure 3.2 shows the Riesling, Merlot, and Shiraz routers in an IS-IS network. A broadcast segment connects Riesling to Merlot, while a point-to-point link connects Merlot to Shiraz. Each router is configured to operate at Level 2 within area 49.0001. Hello PDUs are captured on the Merlot-Shiraz link using the `monitor traffic` command:

```
user@Merlot> monitor traffic interface so-0/1/0 size 1514 detail
Listening on so-0/1/0, capture size 1514 bytes

07:40:32.671912 Out OSI IS-IS, length: 58
        hlen: 20, v: 1, pdu-v: 1, sys-id-len: 6 (0), max-area: 3 (0),
          pdu-type: p2p IIH, source-id: 1921.6800.2002, holding time: 27s,
          circuit-id: 0x01, Level 2 only, PDU length: 58
            Point-to-point Adjacency State TLV #240, length: 15
              Adjacency State: Up
              Extended Local circuit ID: 0x00000043
              Neighbor SystemID: 1921.6800.3003
              Neighbor Extended Local circuit ID: 0x00000042
            Protocols supported TLV #129, length: 2
              NLPID(s): IPv4, IPv6
            IPv4 Interface address(es) TLV #132, length: 4
              IPv4 interface address: 192.168.20.1
```

```
Area address(es) TLV #1, length: 4
  Area address (length: 3): 49.0001
Restart Signaling TLV #211, length: 3
  Restart Request bit clear, Restart Acknowledgement bit clear
  Remaining holding time: 0s
```

 The router output above extends beyond the limit of an 80-character screen. The fields of the IS-IS header have been moved for readability.

The value portion of the TLV is a total of 4 bytes, as seen by the `length: 4` router output. This includes the single area length octet and the three octets containing the actual area address. Merlot is reporting (based on this outbound PDU) a configured area of 49.0001.

IS Reachability TLV

The *IS reachability TLV* (type code 2) is transmitted in all link-state PDUs to inform all routers in the network which systems are adjacent with the local router. Each set of metric fields and the neighbor ID field are repeated for every neighbor. The fields of the IS reachability TLV, which are displayed in Figure 3.3, include:

TLV Type (1 octet)   This field displays the type of information encoded in the TLV. A constant value of 2 (0x0002) is placed in this octet.

TLV Length (1 octet)   The length of the remaining TLV fields is placed in this field. Each neighbor and its associated metrics consume 11 octets worth of space. Therefore, the length encoded in this field minus 1 octet (for the virtual flag field) should be divisible by 11. This computation results in the number of neighbors advertised in the TLV.

Virtual Flag (1 octet)   This field is used to signal the repair of a broken (discontiguous) Level 2 area. The JUNOS software doesn't support this feature and the field is set to a constant value of 0x00.

R Bit, I/E Bit, Default Metric (1 octet)   This field contains information regarding the default metric used to reach the advertised neighbor. The R (reserved) bit is set to a constant value of 0. The I/E bit is used to support internal and external metrics. A value of 0 represents an internal metric, while a value of 1 represents an external metric (We discuss the various metric types in the section "Multi-Level IS-IS" later in the chapter). The final 6 bits in this field encode the metric cost to reach the neighbor, with possible values ranging from 0 to 63. The limitation of this metric space is often referred to as "old-style" or "small" metrics.

S Bit, I/E Bit, Delay Metric (1 octet)   This field represents the type of service (ToS) metric of delay between the local router and the neighbor. This feature is not supported by the JUNOS software, so the S (supported) bit is set to the value 1. Both the I/E bit and the metric bits are set to the value 0.

S Bit, I/E Bit, Expense Metric (1 octet)   This field represents the ToS metric of expense between the local router and the neighbor. This feature is not supported by the JUNOS software, so the S bit is set to the value 1. Both the I/E bit and the metric bits are set to the value 0.

S Bit, I/E Bit, Error Metric (1 octet)   This field represents the ToS metric of error between the local router and the neighbor. This feature is not supported by the JUNOS software, so the S bit is set to the value 1. Both the I/E bit and the metric bits are set to the value 0.

Neighbor ID (7 octets)   The neighbor ID field displays the adjacent neighbor of the local router. It is set to the 6-byte system ID and 1-byte circuit ID representing the neighbor.

FIGURE 3.3   IS reachability TLV (2)

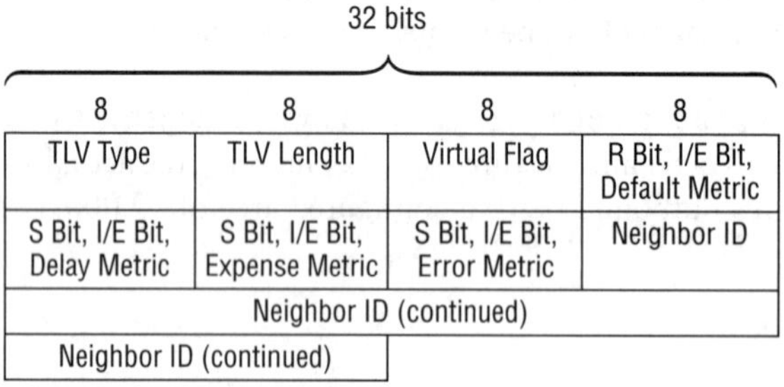

32 bits

8	8	8	8
TLV Type	TLV Length	Virtual Flag	R Bit, I/E Bit, Default Metric
S Bit, I/E Bit, Delay Metric	S Bit, I/E Bit, Expense Metric	S Bit, I/E Bit, Error Metric	Neighbor ID
Neighbor ID (continued)			
Neighbor ID (continued)			

We use the Merlot router to capture a Link-State PDU (LSP) transmitted on the network. In addition, the information in the IS reachability TLV is viewed in the output of the show isis database command:

```
user@Merlot> monitor traffic interface so-0/1/0 size 1514 detail
Listening on so-0/1/0, capture size 1514 bytes

08:04:42.986302  In OSI IS-IS, length: 141
        hlen: 27, v: 1, pdu-v: 1, sys-id-len: 6 (0), max-area: 3 (0),
          pdu-type: L2 LSP, lsp-id: 1921.6800.3003.00-00, seq: 0x000000b0,
          lifetime:  1198s, chksum: 0x2358 (correct), PDU length: 141, L1L2 IS
          Area address(es) TLV #1, length: 4
            Area address (length: 3): 49.0001
          Protocols supported TLV #129, length: 2
            NLPID(s): IPv4, IPv6
          Traffic Engineering Router ID TLV #134, length: 4
            Traffic Engineering Router ID: 192.168.3.3
          IPv4 Interface address(es) TLV #132, length: 4
            IPv4 interface address: 192.168.3.3
          Hostname TLV #137, length: 6
            Hostname: Shiraz
          IS Reachability TLV #2, length: 12
            IsNotVirtual
```

        <u>IS Neighbor: 1921.6800.2002.00, Default Metric: 10, Internal</u>
      Extended IS Reachability TLV #22, length: 23
        IS Neighbor: 1921.6800.2002.00, Metric: 10, sub-TLVs present (12)
          IPv4 interface address: 192.168.20.2
          IPv4 neighbor address: 192.168.20.1
      IPv4 Internal reachability TLV #128, length: 24
        IPv4 prefix: 192.168.3.3/32, Distribution: up, Metric: 0, Internal
        IPv4 prefix: 192.168.20.0/24, Distribution: up, Metric: 10, Internal
      Extended IPv4 reachability TLV #135, length: 17
        IPv4 prefix: 192.168.3.3/32, Distribution: up, Metric: 0
        IPv4 prefix: 192.168.20.0/24, Distribution: up, Metric: 10

user@Merlot> **show isis database Shiraz.00-00 extensive level 2**
IS-IS level 2 link-state database:

Shiraz.00-00 Sequence: 0xb0, Checksum: 0x2358, Lifetime: 862 secs
   IS neighbor: Merlot.00 Metric: 10
   IP prefix: 192.168.3.3/32 Metric: 0 Internal Up
   IP prefix: 192.168.20.0/24 Metric: 10 Internal Up

  Header: LSP ID: Shiraz.00-00, Length: 141 bytes
   Allocated length: 141 bytes, Router ID: 192.168.3.3
   Remaining lifetime: 862 secs, Level: 2,Interface: 67
   Estimated free bytes: 0, Actual free bytes: 0
   Aging timer expires in: 862 secs
   Protocols: IP, IPv6

  Packet: LSP ID: Shiraz.00-00, Length: 141 bytes, Lifetime : 1196 secs
   Checksum: 0x2358, Sequence: 0xb0, Attributes: 0x3 <L1 L2>
   NLPID: 0x83, Fixed length: 27 bytes, Version: 1, Sysid length: 0 bytes
   Packet type: 20, Packet version: 1, Max area: 0

  TLVs:
   Area address: 49.0001 (3)
   Speaks: IP
   Speaks: IPv6
   IP router id: 192.168.3.3
   IP address: 192.168.3.3
   Hostname: Shiraz
   <u>IS neighbor: Merlot.00, Internal, Metric: default 10</u>

```
  IS extended neighbor: Merlot.00, Metric: default 10
    IP address: 192.168.20.2
    Neighbor's IP address: 192.168.20.1
  IP prefix: 192.168.3.3/32, Internal, Metric: default 0, Up
  IP prefix: 192.168.20.0/24, Internal, Metric: default 10, Up
  IP extended prefix: 192.168.3.3/32 metric 0 up
  IP extended prefix: 192.168.20.0/24 metric 10 up
No queued transmissions
```

Merlot receives this Level 2 LSP from the Shiraz router. The IS reachability TLV reports that Shiraz has a single IS neighbor of 1921.6800.2002.00 (Merlot.00). Shiraz is using the default metric field to announce a cost of 10 to reach Merlot. Finally, the advertised adjacency is of an internal type.

 The output of the show isis database command displays Merlot.00 instead of the system ID of 1921.6800.2002.00 since the router is supporting dynamic hostname resolution.

IS Neighbors TLV

Each IS-IS LAN Hello PDU contains an *IS neighbors TLV* (type code 6) to report all remote peers from which the local router has received a hello packet. The *sub-network point of attachment* (SNPA) is repeated for each neighbor on the broadcast segment. The JUNOS software uses the Media Access Control (MAC) address of the outgoing interface to represent the SNPA. Figure 3.4 displays the fields of the IS neighbors TLV.

TLV Type (1 octet)   This field displays the type of information encoded in the TLV. A constant value of 6 (0x0006) is placed in this octet.

TLV Length (1 octet)   The length of the remaining TLV fields is placed in this field. Because each neighbor's address is 6 octets in length, the local router divides the value in this field to determine the total number of neighbors on the segment.

Neighbor SNPA (6 octets)   This field contains the MAC address of the neighbor.

FIGURE 3.4   IS neighbors TLV (6)

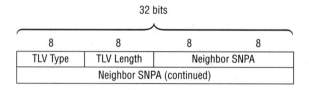

The Merlot router in Figure 3.2 is connected to Riesling over a broadcast segment. A Level 2 LAN Hello PDU is captured using the `monitor traffic` command:

```
user@Merlot> monitor traffic interface fe-0/0/1 size 1514 detail
Listening on fe-0/0/1, capture size 1514 bytes

12:13:55.457603 Out OSI 0:90:69:67:b4:1 > 1:80:c2:0:0:15, IS-IS, length: 56
        hlen: 27, v: 1, pdu-v: 1, sys-id-len: 6 (0), max-area: 3 (0),
        pdu-type: L2 Lan IIH, source-id: 1921.6800.2002,  holding time: 9s,
        Flags: [Level 2 only], lan-id:    1921.6800.2002.02,
        Priority: 64, PDU length: 56
            IS Neighbor(s) TLV #6, length: 6
              IS Neighbor: 0090.6967.4401
            Protocols supported TLV #129, length: 2
              NLPID(s): IPv4, IPv6
            IPv4 Interface address(es) TLV #132, length: 4
              IPv4 interface address: 192.168.10.2
            Area address(es) TLV #1, length: 4
              Area address (length: 3): 49.0001
            Restart Signaling TLV #211, length: 3
              Restart Request bit clear, Restart Acknowledgement bit clear
              Remaining holding time: 0s
```

Once Riesling receives this hello and finds it's local MAC address (0090.6967.4401) in the IS neighbor's TLV, it then knows that bidirectional communication is established between itself and Merlot.

Padding TLV

Each interface in an IS-IS network must support a maximum transmission unit (MTU) of 1492 bytes. To verify this support, each IS-IS router pads its Hello PDUs to the maximum MTU size. Should an interface not support 1492 bytes' worth of data payload, the PDU is not received by the neighbor and the adjacency is not established. The JUNOS software performs a process of "smart" padding whereby the PDUs are only padded until the adjacency is in an Up state.

The *padding TLV* (type code 8) allows the routers to increase the length of the Hello PDU to the 1492 byte limit. Each TLV contains 255 bytes, at most, so multiple padding TLVs are often transmitted in each PDU. The fields of the padding TLV are shown in Figure 3.5 and include the following:

TLV Type (1 octet)   This field displays the type of information encoded in the TLV. A constant value of 8 (0x0008) is placed in this octet.

TLV Length (1 octet)   The length of the remaining TLV fields is placed in this field. Possible entries in this field range from 1 to 255.

Padding Data (Variable)   This field is set to a constant value of 0x00.

FIGURE 3.5   Padding TLV (8)

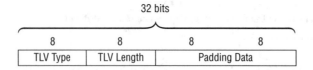

As the adjacency forms between the Riesling and Merlot routers in Figure 3.2, we see the padding TLVs used:

```
user@Riesling> monitor traffic interface fe-0/0/1 size 1514 detail
Listening on fe-0/0/1, capture size 1514 bytes

16:20:39.105403 Out OSI 0:90:69:67:44:1 > 1:80:c2:0:0:15, IS-IS, length: 1492
        hlen: 27, v: 1, pdu-v: 1, sys-id-len: 6 (0), max-area: 3 (0),
        pdu-type: L2 Lan IIH, source-id: 1921.6800.1001,  holding time: 27s,
        Flags: [Level 2 only], lan-id:    1921.6800.1001.02, Priority: 64,
        PDU length: 1492
            IS Neighbor(s) TLV #6, length: 6
              IS Neighbor: 0090.6967.b401
            Protocols supported TLV #129, length: 2
              NLPID(s): IPv4, IPv6
            IPv4 Interface address(es) TLV #132, length: 4
              IPv4 interface address: 192.168.10.1
            Area address(es) TLV #1, length: 4
              Area address (length: 3): 49.0001
            Restart Signaling TLV #211, length: 3
              Restart Request bit clear, Restart Acknowledgement bit clear
              Remaining holding time: 0s
            Padding TLV #8, length: 255
            Padding TLV #8, length: 255
            Padding TLV #8, length: 255
            Padding TLV #8, length: 255
            Padding TLV #8, length: 255
            Padding TLV #8, length: 149
```

LSP Entry TLV

When an IS-IS router sends either a Complete Sequence Number PDU (CSNP) or a Partial Sequence Number PDU (PSNP), it contains summary information about the entries in its local copy of the link-state database. These summaries are encoded in the *LSP entry TLV* (type code 9). The fields contained in the value portion of the TLV (remaining lifetime, LSP ID, sequence number, and checksum) are repeated for each LSP summary sent by the local router. Figure 3.6 displays the fields of the LSP entry TLV.

TLV Type (1 octet)   This field displays the type of information encoded in the TLV. A constant value of 9 (0x0009) is placed in this octet.

TLV Length (1 octet)   The length of the remaining TLV fields is placed in this field. Each LSP contains 16 octets of data, which allows the receiving router to divide this value by 16 to arrive at the number of entries contained in the TLV.

Remaining Lifetime (2 octets)   This field lists the amount of time, in seconds, each router should consider the LSP active. The JUNOS software assigns each new LSP a lifetime value of 1200 seconds, by default.

LSP ID (8 octets)   This field uniquely identifies the LSP throughout the network. The value is a combination of the system ID (6 bytes), circuit ID (1 byte), and LSP Number value (1 byte).

Sequence Number (4 octets)   This field is set to the current version number of the LSP. The initial number is 0x00000001 and it is incremented each time the originating router updates the LSP to a maximum value of 0xffffffff.

Checksum (2 octets)   This field contains the checksum value of the PDU fields after the Remaining Lifetime.

FIGURE 3.6   LSP entry TLV (9)

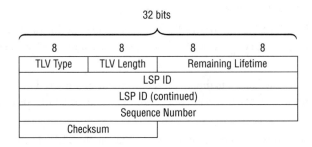

A complete sequence number PDU is received from Merlot on the fe-0/0/1.0 interface:

```
user@Riesling> monitor traffic interface fe-0/0/1 size 1514 detail
Listening on fe-0/0/1, capture size 1514 bytes

16:37:06.917690  In OSI 0:90:69:67:b4:1 > 1:80:c2:0:0:15, IS-IS, length: 99
        hlen: 33, v: 1, pdu-v: 1, sys-id-len: 6 (0), max-area: 3 (0),
        pdu-type: L2 CSNP, source-id: 1921.6800.2002.00, PDU length: 99
          start lsp-id: 0000.0000.0000.00-00
          end lsp-id:   ffff.ffff.ffff.ff-ff
```

```
LSP entries TLV #9, length: 64
   lsp-id: 1921.6800.1001.00-00, seq: 0x000000d7,
     lifetime:   968s, chksum: 0x0960
   lsp-id: 1921.6800.2002.00-00, seq: 0x000000d8,
     lifetime:  1192s, chksum: 0x7961
   lsp-id: 1921.6800.2002.02-00, seq: 0x000000d3,
     lifetime:  1192s, chksum: 0x34f4
   lsp-id: 1921.6800.3003.00-00, seq: 0x000000d9,
     lifetime:   947s, chksum: 0xd081
```

Again, watch out for output wrapping on terminals with 80-character screen widths.

Authentication TLV

The JUNOS software supports IS-IS authentication using both plain-text passwords and MD5 one-way hashes. Configuring authentication causes the *authentication TLV* (type code 10) to be included in certain PDUs. (We discuss authentication in the "Authentication" section later in this chapter.) Figure 3.7 shows the fields of the authentication TLV, which include the following:

TLV Type (1 octet)   This field displays the type of information encoded in the TLV. A constant value of 10 (0x000a) is placed in this octet.

TLV Length (1 octet)   The length of the remaining TLV fields is placed in this field. While the length of a plain-text password may vary, the use of MD5 causes the router to place a constant value of 17 in this field.

Authentication Type (1 octet)   This field lists the method of authentication used in the TLV. A value of 1 indicates that a plain-text password is encoded, while a value of 54 means that MD5 authentication is in use.

Password (Variable)   This field contains the authentication data for the TLV. The configured password is displayed in this field when plain-text authentication is used. The result of the one-way hash is placed here to "secure" the PDU with MD5 authentication. The hash result is always 16 bytes in length.

FIGURE 3.7   Authentication TLV (10)

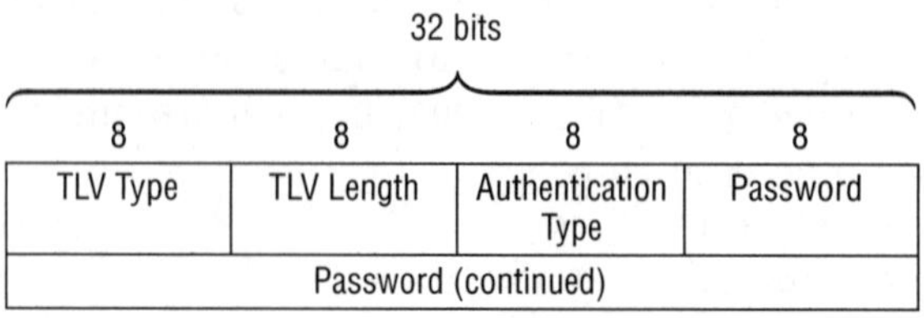

32 bits

8	8	8	8
TLV Type	TLV Length	Authentication Type	Password
Password (continued)			

All routers in the sample IS-IS network in Figure 3.2 are configured to perform authentication on their Hello PDUs. Plain-text passwords are used between the Riesling and Merlot routers while MD5 authentication is used from Merlot to Shiraz. A Level 2 LAN Hello PDU is captured on Merlot's fe-0/0/1.0 interface to Riesling:

```
user@Merlot> monitor traffic interface fe-0/0/1 size 1514 detail
Listening on fe-0/0/1, capture size 1514 bytes

16:57:08.887134  In OSI 0:90:69:67:44:1 > 1:80:c2:0:0:15, IS-IS, length: 79
        hlen: 27, v: 1, pdu-v: 1, sys-id-len: 6 (0), max-area: 3 (0),
        pdu-type: L2 Lan IIH, source-id: 1921.6800.1001,  holding time: 27s,
        Flags: [Level 2 only], lan-id: 1921.6800.2002.02, Priority: 64,
        PDU length: 79
            IS Neighbor(s) TLV #6, length: 6
              IS Neighbor: 0090.6967.b401
            Protocols supported TLV #129, length: 2
              NLPID(s): IPv4, IPv6
            IPv4 Interface address(es) TLV #132, length: 4
              IPv4 interface address: 192.168.10.1
            Area address(es) TLV #1, length: 4
              Area address (length: 3): 49.0001
            Restart Signaling TLV #211, length: 3
              Restart Request bit clear, Restart Acknowledgement bit clear
              Remaining holding time: 0s
            Authentication TLV #10, length: 21
              simple text password: this-is-the-password
```

From the router output, you can clearly see that this-is-the-password is the configured password used between Merlot and Riesling. This lack of security from snooped PDUs is avoided when MD5 authentication is used between Merlot and Shiraz. A point-to-point Hello PDU is captured on the Merlot's so-0/1/0.0 interface to Shiraz:

```
user@Merlot> monitor traffic interface so-0/1/0 size 1514 detail
Listening on fe-0/0/1, capture size 1514 bytes

16:57:57.667488  In OSI IS-IS, length: 77
        hlen: 20, v: 1, pdu-v: 1, sys-id-len: 6 (0), max-area: 3 (0), pdu-type:
p2p IIH
            source-id: 1921.6800.3003, holding time: 27s, circuit-id: 0x01, Level
2 only, PDU length: 77
                Point-to-point Adjacency State TLV #240, length: 15
                  Adjacency State: Up
                  Extended Local circuit ID: 0x00000042
```

```
        Neighbor SystemID: 1921.6800.2002
        Neighbor Extended Local circuit ID: 0x00000043
     Protocols supported TLV #129, length: 2
        NLPID(s): IPv4, IPv6
     IPv4 Interface address(es) TLV #132, length: 4
        IPv4 interface address: 192.168.20.2
     Area address(es) TLV #1, length: 4
        Area address (length: 3): 49.0001
     Restart Signaling TLV #211, length: 3
        Restart Request bit clear, Restart Acknowledgement bit clear
        Remaining holding time: 0s
     Authentication TLV #10, length: 17
        HMAC-MD5 password: 694960f5855ff8b00ff9c1d2f1cde494
```

Checksum TLV

An IS-IS interface can be configured with the checksum command to force the calculation of a 2-byte checksum. This result is placed in the *checksum TLV* (type code 12) in Hello and sequence number PDUs to provide a check against faulty transmission equipment. The fields of the checksum TLV are shown in Figure 3.8 and include the following:

TLV Type (1 octet)   This field displays the type of information encoded in the TLV. A constant value of 12 (0x000c) is placed in this octet.

TLV Length (1 octet)   The length of the remaining TLV fields is placed in this field. A constant value of 2 is encoded here.

Checksum (2 octets)   This field displays the computed checksum value for the PDU sent across the configured interface.

FIGURE 3.8   Checksum TLV (12)

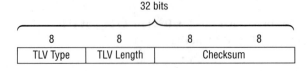

The point-to-point link between Merlot and Shiraz is configured to support the addition of the checksum TLV in transmitted Hello PDUs. Shiraz receives hellos from Merlot as:

```
user@Shiraz> monitor traffic interface so-0/1/0 size 1514 detail
Listening on so-0/1/0, capture size 1514 bytes
```

```
17:18:24.112419  In OSI IS-IS, length: 81
        hlen: 20, v: 1, pdu-v: 1, sys-id-len: 6 (0), max-area: 3 (0),
        pdu-type: p2p IIH, source-id: 1921.6800.2002, holding time: 27s,
        circuit-id: 0x01, Level 2 only, PDU length: 81
            Point-to-point Adjacency State TLV #240, length: 15
                Adjacency State: Up
                Extended Local circuit ID: 0x00000043
                Neighbor SystemID: 1921.6800.3003
                Neighbor Extended Local circuit ID: 0x00000042
            Protocols supported TLV #129, length: 2
                NLPID(s): IPv4, IPv6
            IPv4 Interface address(es) TLV #132, length: 4
                IPv4 interface address: 192.168.20.1
            Area address(es) TLV #1, length: 4
                Area address (length: 3): 49.0001
            Restart Signaling TLV #211, length: 3
                Restart Request bit clear, Restart Acknowledgement bit clear
                Remaining holding time: 0s
            Checksum TLV #12, length: 2
                checksum: 0x7eb5 (correct)
```

The combination of the checksum command and MD5 authentication results in the checksum result of 0x0000 (incorrect). This is due to the fact that the authentication hash is performed last, leaving the checksum value empty.

Extended IS Reachability TLV

In the original Open Standards Interconnect (OSI) specification, IS reachability (TLV 2) uses just 6 bits for a metric value. Modern network designers and engineers find this metric space too small to provide adequate granularity for operating a network. In addition, TLV 2 doesn't provide support for traffic engineering (TE) capabilities used with Multiprotocol Label Switching (MPLS).

The *Extended IS reachability TLV* (type code 22) addresses these shortcomings by providing support for TE and allowing for a larger metric range to be advertised to the network. The extended range begins at 0 and ends at 16,777,215 by using 24 bits to advertise the metric. The extended IS reachability TLV uses a construct of sub-TLVs to announce TE information into the network. An individual extended IS reachability TLV may or may not have sub-TLVs encoded within it. This allows individual routers in the network to participate in the forwarding of MPLS packets, if they are so configured. Each of the sub-TLVs is placed into the traffic engineering database (TED) on the local router, with some sub-TLVs also being placed into the local link-state database.

Each field in the extended IS reachability TLV following the TLV length field is repeated for each adjacent neighbor. The specific fields defined for the TLV are displayed in Figure 3.9 and include the following:

TLV Type (1 octet)   This field displays the type of information encoded in the TLV. A constant value of 22 (0x0016) is placed in this octet.

TLV Length (1 octet)   The length of the remaining TLV fields is placed in this field.

System ID (7 octets)   This field displays the system ID of the adjacent neighbor. It consists of the 6-byte system ID and 1-byte circuit ID for that peer.

Wide Metric (3 octets)   This field represents the metric cost to reach the adjacent peer. Possible values for the metric are between 0 and 16,777,215. This larger metric space is often referred to as "new-style" or *wide metrics*.

Sub-TLV Length (1 octet)   This field displays the length of any optional sub-TLVs contained within the TLV. If no sub-TLVs are present, this field is set to a value of 0.

Sub-TLVs (Variable)   This field contains any included sub-TLVs. Each sub-TLV uses a TLV format to advertise its information. The available sub-TLVs, as well as their type codes, are:

- 3—Administrative group (color)
- 6—IPv4 interface address
- 8—IPv4 neighbor address
- 9—Maximum link bandwidth
- 10—Maximum reservable link bandwidth
- 11—Unreserved bandwidth
- 18—Traffic engineering metric

FIGURE 3.9   Extended IS reachability TLV (22)

32 bits			
8	8	8	8
TLV Type	TLV Length	System ID	
System ID (continued)			
System ID (continued)	Wide Metric		
Sub-TLV Length	Sub-TLVs		

The information transmitted in the extended IS reachability TLV is viewed in the link-state database using the `show isis database extensive` command. The Merlot router in Figure 3.2 is adjacent with both the Riesling and Shiraz routers. Each router is the network is supporting the IS-IS extensions for TE, which is the default JUNOS software behavior:

```
user@Merlot> show isis database Merlot.00-00 extensive | find TLV
  TLVs:
    Area address: 49.0001 (3)
    Speaks: IP
    Speaks: IPv6
    IP router id: 192.168.2.2
    IP address: 192.168.2.2
    Hostname: Merlot
    IS neighbor: Merlot.02, Internal, Metric: default 10
    IS neighbor: Shiraz.00, Internal, Metric: default 10
    IS extended neighbor: Merlot.02, Metric: default 10
      IP address: 192.168.10.2
    IS extended neighbor: Shiraz.00, Metric: default 10
      IP address: 192.168.20.1
      Neighbor's IP address: 192.168.20.2
    IP prefix: 192.168.10.0/24, Internal, Metric: default 10, Up
    IP prefix: 192.168.2.2/32, Internal, Metric: default 0, Up
    IP prefix: 192.168.20.0/24, Internal, Metric: default 10, Up
    IP extended prefix: 192.168.10.0/24 metric 10 up
    IP extended prefix: 192.168.2.2/32 metric 0 up
    IP extended prefix: 192.168.20.0/24 metric 10 up
  No queued transmissions
```

Merlot is advertising an IS-IS connection to the system IDs of `Merlot.02` and `Shiraz.00`. Both TLVs use sub-TLV 6 (IPv4 interface address) to report their local address. This is represented as `IP address:` in the router's output. In addition, the connection to Shiraz.00 also reports the neighbor's address (`Neighbor's IP address`) using sub-TLV 8. A similar advertisement isn't present for Merlot.02 as this is a connection to the pseudonode (designated intermediate system) for the segment.

IP Internal Reachability TLV

The *IP internal reachability TLV* (type code 128) is used to advertise locally connected IP subnets to the IS-IS network. Each advertised subnet contains the network prefix and the subnet mask of the route. In addition, 2 bits are associated with each route: the Up/Down (U/D) bit and the Internal/External (I/E) bit. Each bit can be used to support address advertisements in a multilevel IS-IS network. The metric associated with the advertised routes uses the 6-bit "small" metrics.

Each field in the IP internal reachability TLV after the TLV length field is repeated for each advertised prefix. Figure 3.10 displays the fields in the TLV; these fields include:

TLV Type (1 octet)   This field displays the type of information encoded in the TLV. A constant value of 128 (0x0080) is placed in this octet.

TLV Length (1 octet)   The length of the remaining TLV fields is placed in this field. Each route consumes 12 bytes of space, allowing the local router to determine the number of encoded routes by dividing the length of the TLV by 12.

U/D Bit, I/E Bit, Default Metric (1 octet)   This field contains information regarding the default metric associated with the advertised route. The U/D bit signifies whether the route can be advertised into a specific level. A value of 0 means the route is able to be advertised up to a higher level; a value of 1 means the route is not able to be advertised to a higher level. The I/E bit is used to support internal and external metrics. A value of 0 represents an internal metric; a value of 1 represents an external metric. The final 6 bits in this field encode the metric cost to reach the neighbor, with possible values ranging from 0 to 63—"small" metrics.

S Bit, R Bit, Delay Metric (1 octet)   This field represents the ToS metric of delay for the advertised route. This feature is not supported by the JUNOS software, so the S (supported) bit is set to the value 1. Both the R (reserved) bit and the metric bits are set to the value 0.

S Bit, R Bit, Expense Metric (1 octet)   This field represents the ToS metric of expense for the advertised route. This feature is not supported by the JUNOS software, so the S bit is set to the value 1. Both the R bit and the metric bits are set to the value 0.

S Bit, R Bit, Error Metric (1 octet)   This field represents the ToS metric of error for the advertised route. This feature is not supported by the JUNOS software, so the S bit is set to the value 1. Both the R bit and the metric bits are set to the value 0.

IP Address (4 octets)   This field displays the network prefix advertised by the local router.

Subnet Mask (4 octets)   This field displays the subnet mask for the advertised route.

FIGURE 3.10   IP internal reachability TLV (128)

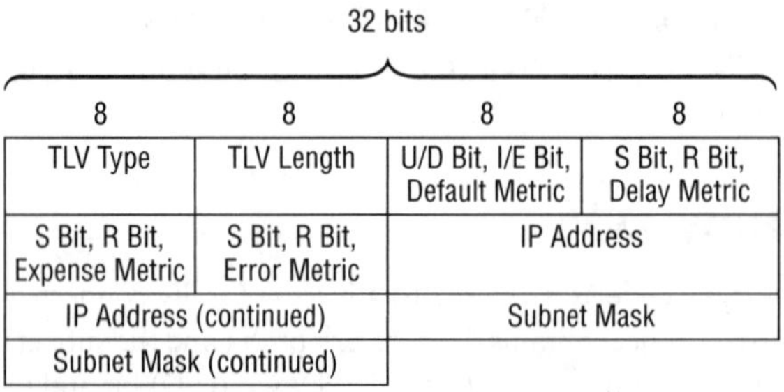

32 bits

8	8	8	8
TLV Type	TLV Length	U/D Bit, I/E Bit, Default Metric	S Bit, R Bit, Delay Metric
S Bit, R Bit, Expense Metric	S Bit, R Bit, Error Metric	IP Address	
IP Address (continued)		Subnet Mask	
Subnet Mask (continued)			

Using the sample network in Figure 3.2, we examine the link-state PDU advertised by the Riesling router:

```
user@Riesling> show isis database Riesling.00-00 extensive | find TLV
  TLVs:
    Area address: 49.0001 (3)
    Speaks: IP
    Speaks: IPv6
    IP router id: 192.168.1.1
    IP address: 192.168.1.1
    Hostname: Riesling
    IS neighbor: Merlot.02, Internal, Metric: default 10
    IS extended neighbor: Merlot.02, Metric: default 10
      IP address: 192.168.10.1
    IP prefix: 192.168.10.0/24, Internal, Metric: default 10, Up
    IP prefix: 192.168.1.1/32, Internal, Metric: default 0, Up
    IP extended prefix: 192.168.10.0/24 metric 10 up
    IP extended prefix: 192.168.1.1/32 metric 0 up
  No queued transmissions
```

Riesling is advertising both its local loopback address and the segment connecting it to Merlot. These fields are marked with the `IP prefix:` notation in the router's output. The I/E bit is currently set to a 0 value as seen by the `Internal` notation. In addition, the `Up` notation signifies that this address can be advertised to other Level 2 areas but not into a Level 1 area.

Protocols Supported TLV

The Layer 3 protocols supported by an IS-IS router are advertised to the network using the *protocols supported TLV* (type code 129). The TLV lists the network layer protocol ID of each supported protocol. The fields of the TLV are shown in Figure 3.11 and include the following:

TLV Type (1 octet)   This field displays the type of information encoded in the TLV. A constant value of 129 (0x0081) is placed in this octet.

TLV Length (1 octet)   The length of the remaining TLV fields is placed in this field. Each supported protocol consumes 1 octet of space.

Network Layer Protocol ID (1 octet)   This field displays the supported Layer 3 protocols. The JUNOS software supports only IPv4 (0xCC) and IPv6 (0x8E).

FIGURE 3.11   Protocols supported TLV (129)

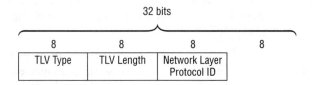

An examination of the link-state database on the Shiraz router shows the supported Layer 3 protocols in our sample network:

```
user@Shiraz> show isis database Shiraz.00-00 extensive | find TLV
  TLVs:
    Area address: 49.0001 (3)
    Speaks: IP
    Speaks: IPv6
    IP router id: 192.168.3.3
    IP address: 192.168.3.3
    Hostname: Shiraz
    IS neighbor: Merlot.00, Internal, Metric: default 10
    IS extended neighbor: Merlot.00, Metric: default 10
      IP address: 192.168.20.2
      Neighbor's IP address: 192.168.20.1
    IP prefix: 192.168.3.3/32, Internal, Metric: default 0, Up
    IP prefix: 192.168.20.0/24, Internal, Metric: default 10, Up
    IP extended prefix: 192.168.3.3/32 metric 0 up
    IP extended prefix: 192.168.20.0/24 metric 10 up
  No queued transmissions
```

IP External Reachability TLV

The *IP external reachability TLV* (type code 130) uses the same packet format as the IP internal reachability TLV. The main difference between the two is the type of information advertised to the network. The IP external reachability TLV is used to announce routes that are not native to the IS-IS domain—in other words, external routes. For completeness, we outline the fields of the IP external reachability TLV in Figure 3.12.

TLV Type (1 octet)   This field displays the type of information encoded in the TLV. A constant value of 130 (0x0082) is placed in this octet.

TLV Length (1 octet)   The length of the remaining TLV fields is placed in this field. Each route consumes 12 bytes of space, allowing the local router to determine the number of encoded routes by dividing the length of the TLV by 12.

U/D Bit, I/E Bit, Default Metric (1 octet)   This field contains information regarding the default metric associated with the advertised route. The U/D bit signifies whether the route can be advertised into a specific level. A value of 0 means the route is able to be advertised up to a higher level; a value of 1 means the route is not able to be advertised to a higher level. The I/E bit is used to support internal and external metrics. A value of 0 represents an internal metric; a value of 1 represents an external metric. The final 6 bits in this field encode the metric cost to reach the neighbor with possible values ranging from 0 to 63—"small" metrics.

S Bit, R Bit, Delay Metric (1 octet)   This field represents the ToS metric of delay for the advertised route. This feature is not supported by the JUNOS software, so the S (supported) bit is set to the value 1. Both the R (reserved) bit and the metric bits are set to the value 0.

S Bit, R Bit, Expense Metric (1 octet)   This field represents the ToS metric of expense for the advertised route. This feature is not supported by the JUNOS software, so the S bit is set to the value 1. Both the R bit and the metric bits are set to the value 0.

S Bit, R Bit, Error Metric (1 octet)   This field represents the ToS metric of error for the advertised route. This feature is not supported by the JUNOS software, so the S bit is set to the value 1. Both the R bit and the metric bits are set to the value 0.

IP Address (4 octets)   This field displays the network prefix advertised by the local router.

Subnet Mask (4 octets)   This field displays the subnet mask for the advertised route.

FIGURE 3.12   IP external reachability TLV (130)

32 bits			
8	8	8	8
TLV Type	TLV Length	U/D Bit, I/E Bit, Default Metric	S Bit, R Bit, Delay Metric
S Bit, R Bit, Expense Metric	S Bit, R Bit, Error Metric	IP Address	
IP Address (continued)		Subnet Mask	
Subnet Mask (continued)			

The Shiraz router in Figure 3.2 has a local static route configured for the 172.16.3.0 /24 subnet. A routing policy inserts this route into the IS-IS network using the IP external reachability TLV:

```
user@Shiraz> show isis database Shiraz.00-00 extensive | find TLV
  TLVs:
    Area address: 49.0001 (3)
    Speaks: IP
    Speaks: IPv6
    IP router id: 192.168.3.3
    IP address: 192.168.3.3
    Hostname: Shiraz
    IS neighbor: Merlot.00, Internal, Metric: default 10
    IS extended neighbor: Merlot.00, Metric: default 10
      IP address: 192.168.20.2
      Neighbor's IP address: 192.168.20.1
    IP prefix: 192.168.3.3/32, Internal, Metric: default 0, Up
    IP prefix: 192.168.20.0/24, Internal, Metric: default 10, Up
    IP extended prefix: 192.168.3.3/32 metric 0 up
    IP extended prefix: 192.168.20.0/24 metric 10 up
```

```
    IP external prefix: 172.16.3.0/24, Internal, Metric: default 0, Up
    IP extended prefix: 172.16.3.0/24 metric 0 up
  No queued transmissions
```

The route is advertised with a metric value of 0. It can be advertised to other Level 2 areas as the U/D bit is set to the value 0 (Up). The route is also marked as `Internal`, as the I/E bit is also set to the value 0.

You might be confused as to why an external route advertised in the IP external reachability TLV is marked with the I/E bit set for `Internal`. We discuss this situation, as well as other uses of the U/D and I/E bits, in the section "Multilevel IS-IS" later in this chapter.

IP Interface Address TLV

Each IPv4 address configured on an IS-IS router may be advertised in the *IP interface address TLV* (type code 132). While a minimum of one address must be included, an individual implementation may include all of the local router's addresses. The JUNOS software default is to advertise just the address configured on the loopback interface within the TLV. Figure 3.13 displays the fields of the IP interface address TLV.

TLV Type (1 octet)   This field displays the type of information encoded in the TLV. A constant value of 132 (0x0084) is placed in this octet.

TLV Length (1 octet)   The length of the remaining TLV fields is placed in this field. Each advertised address consumes 4 octets of space.

IPv4 Address (4 octets)   This field displays the advertised IPv4 interface address.

FIGURE 3.13   IP interface address TLV (132)

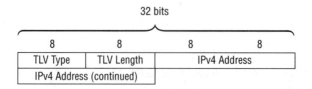

The Riesling router advertises an IP interface address of 192.168.1.1 /.32.

```
user@Riesling> show isis database Riesling.00-00 extensive | find TLV
  TLVs:
    Area address: 49.0001 (3)
    Speaks: IP
    Speaks: IPv6
    IP router id: 192.168.1.1
```

```
  IP address: 192.168.1.1
  Hostname: Riesling
  IS neighbor: Merlot.02, Internal, Metric: default 10
  IS extended neighbor: Merlot.02, Metric: default 10
    IP address: 192.168.10.1
  IP prefix: 192.168.10.0/24, Internal, Metric: default 10, Up
  IP prefix: 192.168.1.1/32, Internal, Metric: default 0, Up
  IP extended prefix: 192.168.10.0/24 metric 10 up
  IP extended prefix: 192.168.1.1/32 metric 0 up
No queued transmissions
```

Traffic Engineering IP Router ID TLV

Each IS-IS router configured to support TE, which is the JUNOS software default, uses the *traffic engineering IP router ID TLV* (type code 134) to advertise its local router ID. Each router in the network places this ID value in both the link-state database as well as the TED. The fields of the TE IP router ID TLV are displayed in Figure 3.14 and include the following:

TLV Type (1 octet)   This field displays the type of information encoded in the TLV. A constant value of 134 (0x0086) is placed in this octet.

TLV Length (1 octet)   The length of the remaining TLV fields is placed in this field. Only a single router ID is advertised by each router, so this field contains a constant value of 4.

Router ID (4 octets)   This field displays the advertised router ID of the local router.

FIGURE 3.14   TE IP router ID TLV (134)

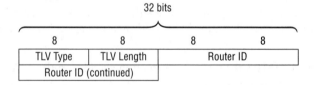

Using Figure 3.2 as a guide, we see the Riesling router advertising a TE router ID of 192.168.1.1:

```
user@Riesling> show isis database Riesling.00-00 extensive | find TLV
  TLVs:
    Area address: 49.0001 (3)
    Speaks: IP
    Speaks: IPv6
    IP router id: 192.168.1.1
    IP address: 192.168.1.1
```

```
Hostname: Riesling
IS neighbor: Merlot.02, Internal, Metric: default 10
IS extended neighbor: Merlot.02, Metric: default 10
  IP address: 192.168.10.1
IP prefix: 192.168.10.0/24, Internal, Metric: default 10, Up
IP prefix: 192.168.1.1/32, Internal, Metric: default 0, Up
IP extended prefix: 192.168.10.0/24 metric 10 up
IP extended prefix: 192.168.1.1/32 metric 0 up
No queued transmissions
```

Extended IP Reachability TLV

In the "Extended IS Reachability TLV" section earlier, we saw that the need for a larger metric space and support for TE prompted the addition of a new TLV. That extended TLV simply advertised a connection to another IS-IS router. Additionally, we've seen how the original IS-IS specification used two TLVs for advertising internal and external IP routes to the network. Over time, network engineers have found this separate TLV structure wasteful; both TLVs are now advertised in all IS-IS levels.

 The reason for the separate TLVs, as well as the history behind their use, is outside the scope of this book.

The *Extended IP reachability TLV* (type code 135) is a single defined method for advertising IP routing information to the network using the wide metric space defined for TE. The TLV also uses a sub-TLV paradigm for announcing additional information to the network. As before, an individual extended IP reachability TLV may or may not have sub-TLVs encoded within it. Each TLV field following the TLV length is repeated for each advertised route. The fields of the extended IP reachability TLV are shown in Figure 3.15 and include the following:

TLV Type (1 octet) This field displays the type of information encoded in the TLV. A constant value of 135 (0x0087) is placed in this octet.

TLV Length (1 octet) The length of the remaining TLV fields is placed in this field.

Metric (4 octets) This field displays the metric for the advertised prefix. Possible values range between 0 and 16,777,215, the current wide metric range. Although the actual field supports a higher metric, this is reserved for future use.

U/D Bit, Sub Bit, Prefix Length (1 octet) This field contains information regarding the advertised prefix. The U/D bit signifies whether the route can be advertised into a specific level. A value of 0 means the route is able to be advertised up to a higher level; a value of 1 means the route is not able to be advertised to a higher level. The sub-bit is used to indicate whether any optional sub-TLVs are present. A value of 0 means no sub-TLVs are used; a value of 1 indicates the presence of some sub-TLVs. The final 6 bits in this field encode the length of the network portion of the advertised route.

Prefix (Variable)   This field displays the route advertised by the local router. The variable length functionality of this field potentially saves space in an LSP when large numbers of routes are advertised.

Optional Sub-TLV Type (1 octet)   This field displays the type of information encoded in the sub-TLV. The JUNOS software supports a single sub-TLV: a 32-bit administrative tag (type code 1).

Sub-TLV Length (1 octet)   This field displays the length of any optional sub-TLVs contained within the TLV.

Sub-TLVs (Variable)   This field contains the applied administrative tag for the route.

FIGURE 3.15   Extended IP reachability TLV (135)

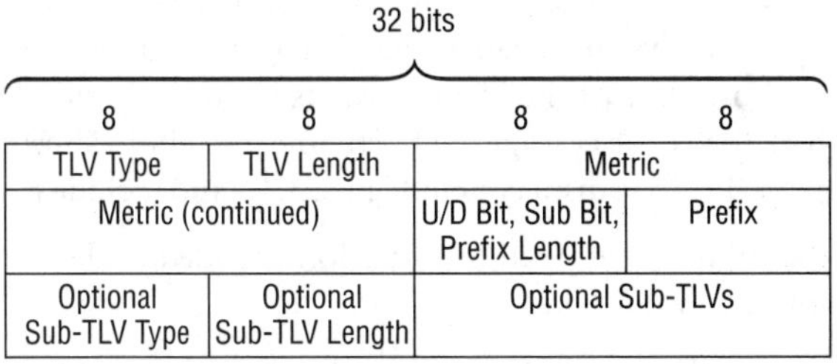

The Shiraz router in Figure 3.2 is advertising three routes to the IS-IS network: 192.168.3.3 /32, 192.168.20.0 /24, and 172.16.3.0 /24. The advertised routes are viewed with the **show isis database** command:

```
user@Shiraz> show isis database Shiraz.00-00 extensive | find TLV
  TLVs:
    Area address: 49.0001 (3)
    Speaks: IP
    Speaks: IPv6
    IP router id: 192.168.3.3
    IP address: 192.168.3.3
    Hostname: Shiraz
    IS neighbor: Merlot.00, Internal, Metric: default 10
    IS extended neighbor: Merlot.00, Metric: default 10
      IP address: 192.168.20.2
      Neighbor's IP address: 192.168.20.1
    IP prefix: 192.168.3.3/32, Internal, Metric: default 0, Up
    IP prefix: 192.168.20.0/24, Internal, Metric: default 10, Up
    IP extended prefix: 192.168.3.3/32 metric 0 up
```

```
   IP extended prefix: 192.168.20.0/24 metric 10 up
   IP external prefix: 172.16.3.0/24, Internal, Metric: default 0, Up
   IP extended prefix: 172.16.3.0/24 metric 0 up
      6 bytes of subtlvs
      Administrative tag 1: 1234
No queued transmissions
```

Each route contains a setting for the U/D bit, and each is set to Up, as well as an advertised metric value. The 172.16.3.0/24 route has an administrative tag of 1234 assigned to it using an optional sub-TLV.

Dynamic Host Name TLV

The identification of IS-IS routers in your network is accomplished through each router's unique system ID. Traditionally, these system ID values are displayed in all IS-IS show commands. Network operators, however, find it easier to reference routers using a symbolic name rather than a hexadecimal value, so the *dynamic host name TLV* (type code 137) is advertised in a router's LSP. The configured hostname of the local router is included in this TLV, which allows other routers in the network to use the configured hostname in all IS-IS show commands. The fields of the dynamic host name TLV are displayed in Figure 3.16 and include the following:

TLV Type (1 octet)   This field displays the type of information encoded in the TLV. A constant value of 137 (0x0089) is placed in this octet.

TLV Length (1 octet)   The length of the remaining TLV field is placed in this field.

Hostname (Variable)   This field displays the hostname of the local router.

FIGURE 3.16   Dynamic host name TLV (137)

The LSP advertised by the Riesling router shows the advertised hostname of Hostname: Riesling:

```
user@Riesling> show isis database Riesling.00-00 extensive | find TLV
  TLVs:
    Area address: 49.0001 (3)
    Speaks: IP
    Speaks: IPv6
    IP router id: 192.168.1.1
    IP address: 192.168.1.1
    Hostname: Riesling
```

```
   IS neighbor: Merlot.02, Internal, Metric: default 10
   IS extended neighbor: Merlot.02, Metric: default 10
     IP address: 192.168.10.1
   IP prefix: 192.168.10.0/24, Internal, Metric: default 10, Up
   IP prefix: 192.168.1.1/32, Internal, Metric: default 0, Up
   IP extended prefix: 192.168.10.0/24 metric 10 up
   IP extended prefix: 192.168.1.1/32 metric 0 up
 No queued transmissions
```

Graceful Restart TLV

IS-IS routers use the *graceful restart TLV* (type code 211) to advertise graceful restart capabilities to their neighbors within the Hello PDU. The TLV contains flags to alert the peer routers as to what the current state of the router is. In addition, a hold time is included as a countdown timer until the restart process is completed. (We discuss graceful restart in the section "Graceful Restart" later in this chapter). The fields of the graceful restart TLV are displayed in Figure 3.17 and include:

TLV Type (1 octet)   This field displays the type of information encoded in the TLV. A constant value of 211 (0x00D3) is placed in this octet.

TLV Length (1 octet)   The length of the remaining TLV fields is placed in this field. A constant value of 3 appears in this field.

Flags (1 octet)   This field contains bits used to inform neighboring routers about the current restart status. The bit flags are:

- 2 through 7—Reserved
- 1—Restart acknowledgement
- 0—Restart request

Remaining Time (2 octets)   This field contains the time until the restart event should be completed.

FIGURE 3.17   Graceful restart TLV (211)

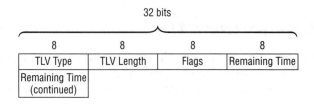

The Merlot router receives a Hello PDU from Shiraz. The monitor traffic command provides us with the details of the PDU:

```
user@Merlot> monitor traffic interface so-0/1/0 size 1514 detail
Listening on so-0/1/0, capture size 1514 bytes


13:27:02.551853  In OSI IS-IS, length: 81
        hlen: 20, v: 1, pdu-v: 1, sys-id-len: 6 (0), max-area: 3 (0),
        pdu-type: p2p IIH, source-id: 1921.6800.3003, holding time: 27s,
        circuit-id: 0x01, Level 2 only, PDU length: 81
            Point-to-point Adjacency State TLV #240, length: 15
              Adjacency State: Up
              Extended Local circuit ID: 0x00000042
              Neighbor SystemID: 1921.6800.2002
              Neighbor Extended Local circuit ID: 0x00000043
            Protocols supported TLV #129, length: 2
              NLPID(s): IPv4, IPv6
            IPv4 Interface address(es) TLV #132, length: 4
              IPv4 interface address: 192.168.20.2
            Area address(es) TLV #1, length: 4
              Area address (length: 3): 49.0001
            Restart Signaling TLV #211, length: 3
              Restart Request bit clear, Restart Acknowledgement bit clear
              Remaining holding time: 0s
            Checksum TLV #12, length: 2
              checksum: 0x0000 (incorrect)
            Authentication TLV #10, length: 17
              HMAC-MD5 password: 9fa99b2af49b49b8c364e63e46c66c05
```

The router output represents a steady state in an IS-IS network using graceful restart. Shiraz is reporting both the restart request and restart acknowledgement bits clear (set to the value 0). In addition, the remaining time is set to a value of 0 seconds.

Point-to-Point Adjacency State TLV

The IS reachability TLV (type code 6) describes a method for allowing an IS-IS router to determine whether a neighbor has seen the local router before moving the adjacency to an Up state. This TLV is only used in a broadcast LAN environment, which leaves routers on a point-to-point link without a similar method of verifying bidirectional communications. The *point-to-point adjacency state TLV* (type code 240) provides this functionality by containing the extended circuit ID of the local router, the system ID of the neighbor, and the neighbor's extended circuit ID.

NOTE   The JUNOS software sets the circuit ID of all point-to-point interfaces to 0x01. Therefore, using this value is not useful for uniquely identifying a neighbor—hence the use of the extended circuit ID.

Figure 3.18 displays the fields of the point-to-point adjacency state TLV, which include:

TLV Type (1 octet)   This field displays the type of information encoded in the TLV. A constant value of 240 (0x00F0) is placed in this octet.

TLV Length (1 octet)   The length of the remaining TLV fields is placed in this field. A constant value of 15 appears in this field.

Adjacency State (1 octet)   This field contains the current state of the adjacency from the perspective of the local router. Possible values are:

- 0—Up
- 1—Initializing
- 2—Down

Extended Local Circuit ID (4 octets)   This field displays the extended circuit ID of the local router's interface. The JUNOS software places the interface index (ifIndex) of the point-to-point interface in this field.

Neighbor System ID (6 octets)   This field displays the system ID of the adjacent neighbor; it consists of the 6-byte system ID for that peer.

Neighbor Extended Local Circuit ID (4 octets)   This field displays the extended circuit ID of the neighbor's interface. The JUNOS software places the interface index (ifIndex) of the point-to-point interface in this field.

FIGURE 3.18   Point-to-point adjacency state TLV (240)

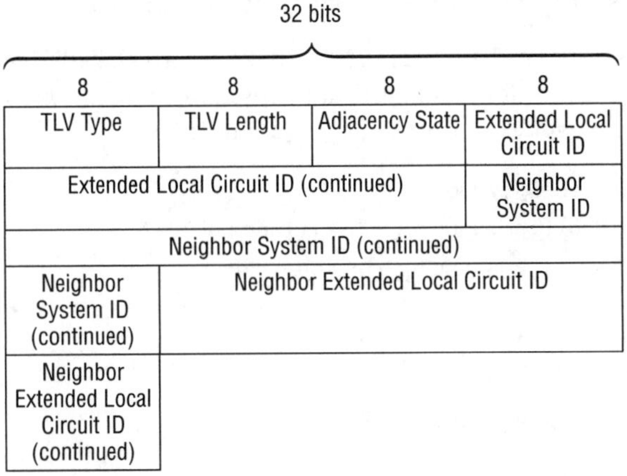

32 bits

8	8	8	8
TLV Type	TLV Length	Adjacency State	Extended Local Circuit ID
Extended Local Circuit ID (continued)			Neighbor System ID
Neighbor System ID (continued)			
Neighbor System ID (continued)	Neighbor Extended Local Circuit ID		
Neighbor Extended Local Circuit ID (continued)			

The point-to-point adjacency state TLV is only present in Hello PDUs on a point-to-point link. In Figure 3.2, we have such a link between the Merlot and Shiraz routers, where we capture a Hello PDU sent by Shiraz:

```
user@Merlot> monitor traffic interface so-0/1/0 size 1514 detail
Listening on so-0/1/0, capture size 1514 bytes

13:27:02.551853  In OSI IS-IS, length: 81
        hlen: 20, v: 1, pdu-v: 1, sys-id-len: 6 (0), max-area: 3 (0),
        pdu-type: p2p IIH, source-id: 1921.6800.3003, holding time: 27s,
        circuit-id: 0x01, Level 2 only, PDU length: 81
            Point-to-point Adjacency State TLV #240, length: 15
            Adjacency State: Up
            Extended Local circuit ID: 0x00000042
            Neighbor SystemID: 1921.6800.2002
            Neighbor Extended Local circuit ID: 0x00000043
            Protocols supported TLV #129, length: 2
            NLPID(s): IPv4, IPv6
            IPv4 Interface address(es) TLV #132, length: 4
            IPv4 interface address: 192.168.20.2
            Area address(es) TLV #1, length: 4
            Area address (length: 3): 49.0001
            Restart Signaling TLV #211, length: 3
              Restart Request bit clear, Restart Acknowledgement bit clear
              Remaining holding time: 0s
            Checksum TLV #12, length: 2
            checksum: 0x0000 (incorrect)
            Authentication TLV #10, length: 17
            HMAC-MD5 password: 9fa99b2af49b49b8c364e63e46c66c05
```

The Shiraz router (Neighbor SystemID: 1921.6800.2002) reports the adjacency to be in an Up state with Merlot. The extended local circuit ID advertised by Shiraz is 0x00000042, which corresponds to the interface index of the so-0/1/0.0 interface:

```
user@Shiraz> show interfaces so-0/1/0.0
  Logical interface so-0/1/0.0 (Index 66) (SNMP ifIndex 67)
    Flags: Point-To-Point SNMP-Traps Encapsulation: PPP
    Protocol inet, MTU: 4470
      Flags: None
      Addresses, Flags: Is-Preferred Is-Primary
        Destination: 192.168.20/24, Local: 192.168.20.2
    Protocol iso, MTU: 4470
      Flags: Is-Primary
```

The neighbor extended local circuit ID, Merlot's interface, is listed as 0x00000043. This value matches the interface index of the so-0/1/0.0 interface on Merlot:

```
user@Merlot> show interfaces so-0/1/0.0
  Logical interface so-0/1/0.0 (Index 67) (SNMP ifIndex 43)
    Flags: Point-To-Point SNMP-Traps Encapsulation: PPP
    Protocol inet, MTU: 4470
      Flags: None
      Addresses, Flags: Is-Preferred Is-Primary
        Destination: 192.168.20/24, Local: 192.168.20.1
    Protocol iso, MTU: 4470
      Flags: None
```

Link-State Database

To this point, we've been examining individual LSPs in the link-state database. While it is important to understand how the various TLVs appear in the database, we now need to take a step back and examine the database from a larger viewpoint. We first discuss the flooding and maintenance of the database as well as the SPF algorithm run against its contents. We then explore the differences between an IS-IS area and a level from the perspective of what information is placed into the link-state database.

Database Integrity

Each router in the IS-IS network maintains a complete link-state database for each of its configured levels. We can view all database entries in the sample network shown in Figure 3.2 by using the show isis database command:

```
user@Riesling> show isis database
IS-IS level 1 link-state database:
  0 LSPs

IS-IS level 2 link-state database:
LSP ID                   Sequence Checksum Lifetime Attributes
Riesling.00-00            0x217    0xb770      1031 L1 L2
Merlot.00-00             0x217    0xf6a3       983 L1 L2
Merlot.02-00             0x20f    0xb734       788 L1 L2
Shiraz.00-00             0x218    0xded2      1027 L1 L2
  4 LSPs
```

The advertised LSPs in each level must be identical on each router. Each LSP in the database is uniquely identified by its 8-byte LSP ID, which contains the system ID, circuit ID, and LSP number fields. New versions of each LSP begin with a sequence number of 0x00000001 and count up to a maximum value of 0xffffffff. If an IS-IS router receives an LSP with a known LSP ID and an updated sequence number, it assumes that the received LSP is more up-to-date than the current LSP and installs it in the database.

To maintain an accurate link-state database, LSPs have a defined lifetime, during which they are considered active and usable. The LSP header contains a configurable remaining lifetime field, which counts down to a value of 0. By default, the JUNOS software sets the beginning lifetime of all LSPs to 1200 seconds (20 minutes). The originating router is responsible for reflooding its own LSP before the remaining lifetime reaches 0 seconds. The JUNOS software accomplishes this task when the lifetime reaches approximately 317 seconds.

Shortest Path First Algorithm

Each IS-IS router translates the information in the database into usable routes by implementing the Shortest Path First (SPF) algorithm. This computation is performed separately within each IS-IS level, and the results are compiled together and presented to the routing table on the router. The algorithm locates the metrically shortest path to each unique destination in the network. On occasion, the result of the calculation encounters multiple paths to the same destination learned through different means. To decide which path to use, the protocol has some tie-breaking rules to follow. The order of precedence for using a route is:

1. Level 1 intra-area routes with an internal metric
2. Level 1 external routes with an internal metric
3. Level 2 intra-area routes with an internal metric
4. Level 2 external routes with an internal metric
5. Inter-area routes (Level 1 to Level 2) with an internal metric
6. Inter-area external routes (Level 1 to Level 2) with an internal metric
7. Inter-area routes (Level 2 to Level 1) with an internal metric
8. Inter-area external routes (Level 2 to Level 1) with an internal metric
9. Level 1 external routes with an external metric
10. Level 2 external routes with an external metric
11. Inter-area external routes (Level 1 to Level 2) with an external metric
12. Inter-area external routes (Level 2 to Level 1) with an external metric

The components and operation of the SPF algorithm within IS-IS are identical to those of an OSPF network. We explored this operation in great detail in Chapter 2, within the section titled "The Shortest Path First Algorthm," so we won't repeat the process here. If you haven't read through Chapter 2 yet, we encourage you to locate that section for a full explanation of how the SPF algorithm operates.

IS-IS Areas and Levels

Perhaps one of the most confusing things about learning how IS-IS operates is the correlation between areas and levels. After all, OSPF and IS-IS are somewhat similar and OSPF has areas— so IS-IS areas *should* work in a similar manner. Unfortunately, that's not exactly the case. An OSPF area controls the flooding scope of link-state advertisements, whereas an IS-IS area is only used to regulate the formation of adjacencies and the setting of the Attached bit in a Level 1 LSP. The flooding scope of an LSP is controlled by an IS-IS level. Each set of contiguous Level 2 areas share a common Level 2 link-state database. In fact, the same is true for a set of Level 1 areas, but this configuration is not very common.

FIGURE 3.19   Flooding scope of LSPs

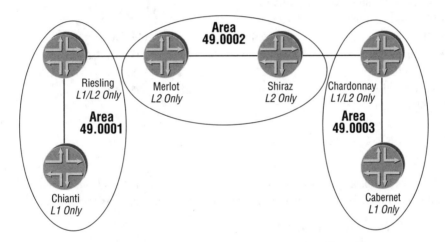

Figure 3.19 shows an IS-IS network with three configured areas; 49.0001, 49.0002, and 49.0003. The area assignments regulate that the Level 1 routers of Chianti and Cabernet only form adjacencies with Level 1 routers in their own areas. Riesling and Chardonnay are configured to operate at both Level 1 and Level 2. In terms of an LSP's flooding scope, these L1/L2 routers perform a function akin to an OSPF area border router (ABR). Both the Merlot and Shiraz routers are operating only at Level 2, so they form adjacencies with all other Level 2 routers. The current set of IS-IS adjacencies in the network appear as so:

```
user@Riesling> show isis adjacency
Interface           System       L State      Hold (secs) SNPA
fe-0/0/1.0          Merlot       2 Up                   6 0:90:69:67:b4:1
fe-0/0/2.0          Chianti      1 Up                   6 0:90:69:6e:fc:1

user@Merlot> show isis adjacency
Interface           System       L State      Hold (secs) SNPA
fe-0/0/1.0          Riesling     2 Up                  26 0:90:69:67:44:1
so-0/1/0.0          Shiraz       2 Up                  24
```

```
user@Chardonnay> show isis adjacency
Interface          System        L State      Hold (secs) SNPA
fe-0/0/2.0         Cabernet      1 Up                   7 0:90:69:9b:d0:2
so-0/1/1.0         Shiraz        2 Up                  25
```

Each of the routers has formed the appropriate adjacencies according to their current IS-IS area configuration. A quick look at Figure 3.19 reveals that the network has three flooding scopes. The first is a Level 1 scope between Chianti and Riesling; a second Level 2 scope encompasses the Riesling, Merlot, Shiraz, and Chardonnay routers. The final scope includes the Chardonnay and Cabernet routers for Level 1 LSPs. One of the Level 1 flooding scopes is easily verified by examining the link-state databases on the Chianti router:

```
user@Chianti> show isis database
IS-IS level 1 link-state database:
LSP ID                   Sequence Checksum Lifetime Attributes
Riesling.00-00              0xd5   0x1f83     1053 L1 L2 Attached
Chianti.00-00              0xd5   0xc8fc     1057 L1
Chianti.02-00             0xd3   0xa1ef     1057 L1
  3 LSPs


IS-IS level 2 link-state database:
  0 LSPs
```

Chianti's database contains no Level 2 LSPs and only Level 1 LSPs from routers in the local 49.0001 IS-IS area. A similar situation exists in the other Level 1 area, as seen by the Cabernet router:

```
user@Cabernet> show isis database
IS-IS level 1 link-state database:
LSP ID                   Sequence Checksum Lifetime Attributes
Chardonnay.00-00           0xd6   0x96b0      618 L1 L2 Attached
Cabernet.00-00            0xd4   0x30d5      442 L1
Cabernet.02-00           0xd2   0xbd3b      657 L1
  3 LSPs


IS-IS level 2 link-state database:
  0 LSPs
```

Thus far, we don't see much difference between the IS-IS areas and levels, which is quite typical for the operation of Level 1 IS-IS. When we look at the Level 2 areas, however, we see things quite differently. Each of the routers operating at Level 2 generates an LSP and injects it into the flooding topology where the other Level 2 routers receive it, regardless of their configured IS-IS area. The current database on the Merlot router appears as so:

```
user@Merlot> show isis database
IS-IS level 1 link-state database:
  0 LSPs
```

```
IS-IS level 2 link-state database:
LSP ID                     Sequence Checksum Lifetime Attributes
Riesling.00-00               0xd8    0x745d      690 L1 L2
Merlot.00-00                 0xd9    0x15c3      875 L1 L2
Merlot.02-00                 0xd4    0x32f5      579 L1 L2
Shiraz.00-00                 0xd9    0xf2d3     1171 L1 L2
Chardonnay.00-00             0xd7    0xe0c3      429 L1 L2
  5 LSPs
```

Clearly, the set of contiguous Level 2 areas constitutes a single Level 2 flooding topology. A similar flooding topology can be constructed using a contiguous set of Level 1 areas.

FIGURE 3.20   Contiguous set of Level 1 areas

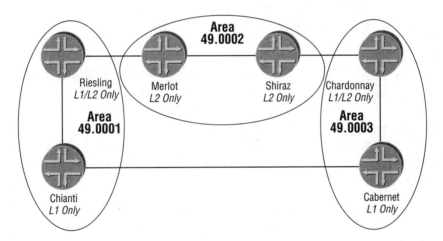

Figure 3.20 connects the Level 1 routers of Chianti and Cabernet. The addition of an ISO address within area 49.0003 on Chianti allows these devices to become adjacent at Level 1:

```
user@Chianti> show configuration interfaces lo0
unit 0 {
    family inet {
        address 192.168.5.5/32;
    }
    family iso {
        address 49.0001.1921.6800.5005.00;
        address 49.0003.1921.6800.5005.00;
    }
}
```

```
user@Chianti> show isis adjacency
Interface          System         L State       Hold (secs) SNPA
fe-0/0/0.0         Cabernet       1 Up                    8 0:90:69:9b:d0:1
fe-0/0/1.0         Riesling       1 Up                   23 0:90:69:67:44:2
```

WARNING   We do not recommend using this type of network configuration. It is not common in operational networks and is used here only for demonstration and learning purposes.

The operational adjacency between Chianti and Cabernet generates a larger Level 1 flooding topology in our sample network. The link-state database on Cabernet now appears as:

```
user@Cabernet> show isis database
IS-IS level 1 link-state database:
LSP ID                     Sequence Checksum Lifetime Attributes
Riesling.00-00                0xdb   0x1389     1123 L1 L2 Attached
Chardonnay.00-00              0xdc   0x8ab6     1069 L1 L2 Attached
Chianti.00-00                 0xdf   0xe47d     1041 L1
Chianti.02-00                 0xdb   0x91f7     1030 L1
Cabernet.00-00                0xdb   0x7780     1043 L1
Cabernet.02-00                0xd9   0xaf42     1043 L1
Cabernet.03-00                 0x1   0xe4c2     1043 L1
   7 LSPs

IS-IS level 2 link-state database:
   0 LSPs
```

While not recommended for an operational network, the Level 1 connection of area 49.0001 and 49.0003 clearly proves our earlier statement. An IS-IS area only affects the formation of adjacencies between two routers, while a level controls the flooding scope of LSPs.

Configuration Options

A discussion of every IS-IS configuration option within the JUNOS software would take an entire book unto itself. Instead, we'll focus on just a few select topics. These include an examination of using graceful restart to maintain stability in the network and a discussion of how authentication is used to secure network transmissions. After exploring the various options for metric values in an IS-IS network, we conclude the section with two notions unique to IS-IS: mesh groups and the overload bit.

Graceful Restart

The restart of the IS-IS routing process on a router has a potentially damaging effect on the operation of the network and the flow of user data traffic across it. The neighboring routers stop receiving Hello PDUs from the restarting router and eventually change the state of the IS-IS adjacency to Down. This, in turn, causes the regeneration of LSPs into the network reflecting a topology change. Each router receiving the LSP reruns the SPF algorithm, which could lead to new routing paths through the network. This process helps ensure the reliability and resiliency of a link-state protocol to a network failure.

The "problem" with this process occurs when the IS-IS restart time is of a short duration. The neighboring routers reacquire their previous adjacency and reflood their LSPs. The resulting SPF calculations return user traffic to their original links in short order. Unfortunately, the users of the network experience a degradation of performance from the network, and they see unresponsiveness from their applications. These negative aspects of a restarting router can be mitigated, or eliminated, when the restart time is short enough to be covered under the operation of *graceful restart*.

Graceful restart is the common name for the process of allowing a routing process to restart without stopping the forwarding of user data traffic through the router. Let's explore the operation of graceful restart in an IS-IS network and discuss the use of the graceful restart TLV. In addition, we'll look at configuring this option on the router.

Restart Operation

The high-level operation of the IS-IS graceful restart procedure is quite simple. The restarting router is alerted to a restart event and stores the current forwarding table in memory on the Packet Forwarding Engine. After the router returns to service, it announces to its neighbors that it has returned and asks for their assistance in regenerating its local link-state database. Each restart-capable neighbor that has an Up adjacency with the restarting router maintains that adjacency state and sends CSNPs to the restarting router to rebuild the database contents. The restarting router generates a PSNP, if needed, to receive the full information in the form of an LSP. After building a complete database, the local router returns to its normal IS-IS operational mode.

Each IS-IS router capable of supporting graceful restart operates in one of three modes:

Restart candidate An IS-IS router in *restart candidate mode* is currently attempting to perform a graceful restart. The router stores its local protocol state and performs the restart event. This mode is mutually exclusive with other restart modes; a single router can't be restarting and helping a neighbor restart at the same time.

Possible helper The *possible helper restart mode* is the default operational mode of a restart-capable IS-IS router. The local router is able to assist neighbors with their own restart events, or it may transition to the restart candidate mode based on a local restart event. An individual IS-IS router can be in possible helper mode for some neighbors and be actively helping other neighbors restart.

Helper Upon the receipt of a restart message from a neighbor, an IS-IS router transitions to *helper mode*. In this mode, the helper router maintains an Up adjacency with the restarting router and doesn't flood new LSPs indicating a topology change. It generates CSNPs to the restarting neighbor and responds to any received PSNPs with the appropriate LSP.

> If any operational interface on the restarting router does not have a helper, the graceful restart process is aborted and all routers revert to a non-graceful restart operation.

Graceful Restart TLV

The messages exchanged during a restart event are carried within the graceful restart TLV (type code 211). In a normal operating environment, both the restart request (RR) and restart acknowledgement (RA) bits are cleared (value of 0). Once the restarting router has returned to service, it sets the RR bit to the value 1 within the TLV. This alerts the neighbor that a restart is in process and that the neighbor should maintain its Up adjacency with the local router.

The Riesling and Merlot routers in Figure 3.19 have been configured to support graceful restart. After causing a restart event using the restart routing command on Merlot, we see the received restart TLV on Riesling:

```
user@Riesling> monitor traffic interface fe-0/0/1 size 1514 detail
Listening on fe-0/0/1, capture size 1514 bytes

13:25:15.038594  In OSI 0:90:69:67:b4:1 > 1:80:c2:0:0:15, IS-IS, length: 48
        hlen: 27, v: 1, pdu-v: 1, sys-id-len: 6 (0), max-area: 3 (0),
        pdu-type: L2 Lan IIH, source-id: 1921.6800.2002,  holding time: 90,
        Level 2 only, lan-id: 1921.6800.2002.02, Priority: 64, PDU length: 48
            Protocols supported TLV #129, length: 2
                NLPID(s): IPv4, IPv6
            IPv4 Interface address(es) TLV #132, length: 4
                IPv4 interface address: 192.168.10.2
            Area address(es) TLV #1, length: 4
                Area address (length: 3): 49.0002
            Restart Signaling TLV #211, length: 3
                Restart Request bit set, Restart Acknowledgement bit clear
                Remaining holding time: 0s
```

The Riesling router responds by altering the values in its transmitted restart TLV to Merlot:

```
user@Riesling> monitor traffic interface fe-0/0/1 size 1514 detail
Listening on fe-0/0/1, capture size 1514 bytes

13:25:15.039208  Out OSI 0:90:69:67:44:1 > 1:80:c2:0:0:15, IS-IS, length: 56
        hlen: 27, v: 1, pdu-v: 1, sys-id-len: 6 (0), max-area: 3 (0),
        pdu-type: L2 Lan IIH, source-id: 1921.6800.1001,  holding time: 27,
        Level 2 only, lan-id: 1921.6800.2002.02, Priority: 64, PDU length: 56
```

```
        IS Neighbor(s) TLV #6, length: 6
          IS Neighbor: 0090.6967.b401
        Protocols supported TLV #129, length: 2
          NLPID(s): IPv4, IPv6
        IPv4 Interface address(es) TLV #132, length: 4
          IPv4 interface address: 192.168.10.1
        Area address(es) TLV #1, length: 4
          Area address (length: 3): 49.0001
        Restart Signaling TLV #211, length: 3
            Restart Request bit clear, Restart Acknowledgement bit set
            Remaining holding time: 90s
```

Riesling acknowledges the restart event by setting the RA bit in its TLV and making the restart hold time 90 seconds. Once the exchange of database information between the neighbors is complete, they perform their normal operation of transmitting the restart TLV with all bits cleared:

```
user@Riesling> monitor traffic interface fe-0/0/1 size 1514 detail
Listening on fe-0/0/1, capture size 1514 bytes


13:41:54.661574  In OSI 0:90:69:67:b4:1 > 1:80:c2:0:0:15, IS-IS, length: 56
        hlen: 27, v: 1, pdu-v: 1, sys-id-len: 6 (0), max-area: 3 (0),
        pdu-type: L2 Lan IIH, source-id: 1921.6800.2002,  holding time: 9,
        Level 2 only, lan-id: 1921.6800.2002.02, Priority: 64, PDU length: 56
          IS Neighbor(s) TLV #6, length: 6
            IS Neighbor: 0090.6967.4401
          Protocols supported TLV #129, length: 2
            NLPID(s): IPv4, IPv6
          IPv4 Interface address(es) TLV #132, length: 4
            IPv4 interface address: 192.168.10.2
          Area address(es) TLV #1, length: 4
            Area address (length: 3): 49.0002
          Restart Signaling TLV #211, length: 3
              Restart Request bit clear, Restart Acknowledgement bit clear
              Remaining holding time: 0s

13:41:56.624185 Out OSI 0:90:69:67:44:1 > 1:80:c2:0:0:15, IS-IS, length: 56
        hlen: 27, v: 1, pdu-v: 1, sys-id-len: 6 (0), max-area: 3 (0),
        pdu-type: L2 Lan IIH, source-id: 1921.6800.1001,  holding time: 27,
        Level 2 only, lan-id: 1921.6800.2002.02, Priority: 64, PDU length: 56
          IS Neighbor(s) TLV #6, length: 6
            IS Neighbor: 0090.6967.b401
          Protocols supported TLV #129, length: 2
```

```
              NLPID(s): IPv4, IPv6
       IPv4 Interface address(es) TLV #132, length: 4
           IPv4 interface address: 192.168.10.1
       Area address(es) TLV #1, length: 4
           Area address (length: 3): 49.0001
       Restart Signaling TLV #211, length: 3
           Restart Request bit clear, Restart Acknowledgement bit clear
           Remaining holding time: 0s
```

Restart Configuration

The JUNOS software supports graceful restart for all of the major routing protocols. As such, the configuration of this feature occurs within the [edit routing-options] configuration hierarchy:

```
user@Riesling> show configuration routing-options
graceful-restart;
```

In addition, each IS-IS router may selectively set any of the following options:

```
[edit protocols isis]
user@Riesling# set graceful-restart ?
Possible completions:
  disable              Disable graceful restart
  helper-disable       Disable graceful restart helper capability
  restart-duration     Maximum time for graceful restart to finish (seconds)
```

These options alter the graceful restart process in specific ways:

disable   The disable option prevents the local router from performing any graceful restart functions within IS-IS. Both a local restart and helper mode are covered by this configuration option.

helper-disable   The helper-disable option prevents the local router from assisting with a restart event on a neighboring router. The local router, however, is still able to perform a local restart with assistance from its neighbors.

restart-duration   The restart-duration timer begins running as soon as the restart event occurs. It is the amount of time that the helper router sets to complete the restart event. The JUNOS software sets this value to 90 seconds by default.

Authentication

The JUNOS software supports three methods of authenticating IS-IS PDUs: none, simple authentication, and MD5. By default, the router doesn't perform authentication on any operational interfaces. To protect your network from a configuration mistake, you might use plaintext password authentication. This will help ensure that adjacencies are formed only with other routers using the same password. Additionally, authentication ensures that the LSPs generated by an authenticating router are placed into the database on a remote router only after they have passed an authentication check. The main issue with using plain-text authentication, however, is the lack of security it provides since the actual password is placed in the PDUs. This allows the configured secret value to be viewed by a packet capture device in the network. To provide better security in your network, use the MD5 authentication mechanism, which places an encrypted checksum into the transmitted PDUs. Each router receiving this value compares a locally generated checksum against it to verify that the PDU is genuine.

Authentication is configured in multiple places within the [edit protocols isis] hierarchy. Each IS-IS level has the ability to support both plain-text and MD5 authentication. When used in this fashion, every PDU generated by the router (Hello, link-state, and sequence number) contains the authentication information. The second location for configuring authentication within IS-IS is for each individual interface. This configuration adds the authentication TLV just to Hello PDUs. All link-state and sequence number PDUs are sent without the authentication TLV. In essence, this controls the routers you form an adjacency with, but doesn't control the contents of the link-state database.

Simple Level Authentication

All operational interfaces within a specific IS-IS level use the same method of authentication. Using the network in Figure 3.19 as a guide, the Cabernet and Chardonnay routers in area 49.0003 configure simple authentication within their Level 1 configurations:

```
[edit protocols isis]
user@Cabernet# show
level 2 disable;
level 1 {
    authentication-key "$9$Mn5WNbJZjHqfJGQFn90B7-VwgoUjq.PQdbjH"; # SECRET-DATA
    authentication-type simple; # SECRET-DATA
}
interface fe-0/0/2.0;
interface lo0.0;
```

```
[edit protocols isis]
user@Chardonnay# show
level 1 {
    authentication-key "$9$q.QnOORhSeOBM8XNY2Tz36Ap1RSylMFnRhcSW"; # SECRET-DATA
    authentication-type simple; # SECRET-DATA
}
interface fe-0/0/2.0 {
    level 2 disable;
}
interface so-0/1/1.0 {
    level 1 disable;
}
interface lo0.0;
```

The monitor traffic command shows the authentication TLV received by Cabernet on its fe-0/0/2.0 interface:

```
user@Cabernet> monitor traffic interface fe-0/0/2 size 1514 detail
Listening on fe-0/0/2, capture size 1514 bytes

15:45:38.280668  In OSI 0:90:69:68:80:2 > 1:80:c2:0:0:14, IS-IS, length: 79
        hlen: 27, v: 1, pdu-v: 1, sys-id-len: 6 (0), max-area: 3 (0),
        pdu-type: L1 Lan IIH, source-id: 1921.6800.4004, holding time: 27,
        Level 1 only, lan-id: 1921.6800.6006.02, Priority: 64, PDU length: 79
            IS Neighbor(s) TLV #6, length: 6
                IS Neighbor: 0090.699b.d002
            Protocols supported TLV #129, length: 2
                NLPID(s): IPv4, IPv6
            IPv4 Interface address(es) TLV #132, length: 4
                IPv4 interface address: 192.168.50.1
            Area address(es) TLV #1, length: 4
                Area address (length: 3): 49.0003
            Restart Signaling TLV #211, length: 3
                Restart Request bit clear, Restart Acknowledgement bit clear
                Remaining holding time: 0s
            Authentication TLV #10, length: 21
                simple text password: this-is-the-password
```

The configuration of simple authentication within the Level 1 hierarchy means that all LSPs are authenticated as well. This is clearly seen in the output of show isis database on the Cabernet router:

```
user@Cabernet> show isis database Chardonnay.00-00 extensive | find TLV
  TLVs:
    Area address: 49.0003 (3)
    Speaks: IP
    Speaks: IPv6
    IP router id: 192.168.4.4
    IP address: 192.168.4.4
    Hostname: Chardonnay
    IS neighbor: Cabernet.02, Internal, Metric: default 10
    IS neighbor: Cabernet.02, Metric: default 10
      IP address: 192.168.50.1
    IP prefix: 192.168.4.4/32, Internal, Metric: default 0, Up
    IP prefix: 192.168.50.0/24, Internal, Metric: default 10, Up
    IP prefix: 192.168.4.4/32 metric 0 up
```

```
    IP prefix: 192.168.50.0/24 metric 10 up
    Authentication data: 21 bytes
  No queued transmissions
```

While the actual password is not displayed in this output, as we saw in the received hello, the presence of the `Authentication data` notation allows us to see that the TLV is included in the received LSP as well.

MD5 Level Authentication

The configuration of MD5 is very similar to that of simple authentication. The main difference is the use of the *md5* option with the `authentication-type` command and the use of the encrypted checksum in the authentication TLV.

All Level 2–capable routers in Figure 3.19 are now configured for MD5 authentication at Level 2. As a sample, the configuration of the Riesling router is as follows:

```
[edit protocols isis]
user@Riesling# show
level 2 {
    authentication-key "$9$ewMKLNdVYoZjwYF/tOcSwYg4aU"; # SECRET-DATA
    authentication-type md5; # SECRET-DATA
}
interface fe-0/0/1.0 {
    level 1 disable;
}
interface fe-0/0/2.0 {
    level 2 disable;
}
interface lo0.0;
```

As before, we can view the authentication TLV by using the `monitor traffic` command on the Shiraz router:

```
user@Shiraz> monitor traffic interface so-0/1/2 size 1514 detail
Listening on so-0/1/2, capture size 1514 bytes

15:05:02.386026  In OSI IS-IS, length: 77
        hlen: 20, v: 1, pdu-v: 1, sys-id-len: 6 (0), max-area: 3 (0),
        pdu-type: p2p IIH, source-id: 1921.6800.4004, holding time: 27s,
        circuit-id: 0x01, Level 2 only, PDU length: 77
            Point-to-point Adjacency State TLV #240, length: 15
                Adjacency State: Up
                Extended Local circuit ID: 0x00000006
                Neighbor SystemID: 1921.6800.3003
```

```
            Neighbor Extended Local circuit ID: 0x00000006
        Protocols supported TLV #129, length: 2
            NLPID(s): IPv4, IPv6
        IPv4 Interface address(es) TLV #132, length: 4
            IPv4 interface address: 192.168.30.2
        Area address(es) TLV #1, length: 4
            Area address (length: 3): 49.0003
        Restart Signaling TLV #211, length: 3
            Restart Request bit clear, Restart Acknowledgement bit clear
            Remaining holding time: 0s
        Authentication TLV #10, length: 17
            HMAC-MD5 password: e0703170ea1c3bdd1fc557916ed79cc9
```

As we saw before, each router configured for Level 2 authentication does so for all PDUs. Riesling's LSP, as received by Shiraz, contains the authentication TLV, as we would expect:

```
user@Shiraz> show isis database Riesling.00-00 extensive | find TLV
  TLVs:
    Area address: 49.0001 (3)
    Speaks: IP
    Speaks: IPv6
    IP router id: 192.168.1.1
    IP address: 192.168.1.1
    Hostname: Riesling
    IP prefix: 192.168.1.1/32, Internal, Metric: default 0, Up
    IP prefix: 192.168.5.5/32, Internal, Metric: default 10, Up
    IP prefix: 192.168.10.0/24, Internal, Metric: default 10, Up
    IP prefix: 192.168.40.0/24, Internal, Metric: default 10, Up
    IP prefix: 192.168.1.1/32 metric 0 up
    IP prefix: 192.168.5.5/32 metric 10 up
    IP prefix: 192.168.10.0/24 metric 10 up
    IP prefix: 192.168.40.0/24 metric 10 up
    IS neighbor: Merlot.02, Internal, Metric: default 10
    IS neighbor: Merlot.02, Metric: default 10
      IP address: 192.168.10.1
    Authentication data: 17 bytes
  No queued transmissions
```

Hello Authentication

Configuring authentication at the IS-IS interface level secures only the Hello PDUs transmitted by the local router and is used in two different situations. The first of these is a case where the network operator only needs to ensure that trusted sources become adjacent with each other.

The inclusion of the authentication TLV in just the Hello PDU meets this need without adding overhead to the other PDU types. The second situation where only using hello authentication is beneficial is in a multivendor operating environment. Not every router vendor supports the authentication of the link-state and sequence-number PDUs within IS-IS. However, the authentication of the Hello PDUs is widely used. As such, the JUNOS software provides this configuration option for flexibility.

Within area 49.0001 in Figure 3.19, the Chianti and Riesling routers configure hello authentication on their connected Level 1 interface:

```
[edit protocols isis interface fe-0/0/2.0]
user@Riesling# show
level 2 disable;
level 1 {
    hello-authentication-key "$9$6gr2/u1SyK8xdevs2g4jik.PQ6AOBEK"; # SECRET-DATA
    hello-authentication-type md5; # SECRET-DATA
}
```

```
[edit protocols isis interface fe-0/0/1.0]
user@Chianti# show
level 1 {
    hello-authentication-key "$9$2hgGiPfz6CuQF1REhvM8X7V2aUjqznC"; # SECRET-DATA
    hello-authentication-type md5; # SECRET-DATA
}
```

The adjacency between the routers remains in the Up state:

```
user@Chianti> show isis adjacency
Interface          System        L State      Hold (secs) SNPA
fe-0/0/1.0         Riesling      1 Up                  23  0:90:69:67:44:2
```

All received Hello PDUs on the Chianti router have the authentication TLV included:

```
user@Chianti> monitor traffic interface fe-0/0/1 size 1514 detail
Listening on fe-0/0/1, capture size 1514 bytes

22:27:30.543550  In OSI 0:90:69:67:44:2 > 1:80:c2:0:0:14, IS-IS, length: 75
        hlen: 27, v: 1, pdu-v: 1, sys-id-len: 6 (0), max-area: 3 (0),
        pdu-type: L1 Lan IIH, source-id: 1921.6800.1001,  holding time: 27,
        Level 1 only, lan-id: 1921.6800.5005.02, Priority: 64, PDU length: 75
            IS Neighbor(s) TLV #6, length: 6
                IS Neighbor: 0090.696e.fc01
            Protocols supported TLV #129, length: 2
                NLPID(s): IPv4, IPv6
```

```
           IPv4 Interface address(es) TLV #132, length: 4
               IPv4 interface address: 192.168.40.1
           Area address(es) TLV #1, length: 4
               Area address (length: 3): 49.0001
           Restart Signaling TLV #211, length: 3
               Restart Request bit clear, Restart Acknowledgement bit clear
               Remaining holding time: 0s
           Authentication TLV #10, length: 17
               HMAC-MD5 password: 01ac8c51e239d0f44176fd1a11c3bd69
```

The use of `hello-authentication-type` keeps the authentication TLV out of the LSP, which Chianti sends into the network:

```
user@Chianti> show isis database Chianti.00-00 extensive | find TLV
  TLVs:
    Area address: 49.0001 (3)
    Speaks: IP
    Speaks: IPv6
    IP router id: 192.168.5.5
    IP address: 192.168.5.5
    Hostname: Chianti
    IS neighbor: Chianti.02, Internal, Metric: default 10
    IS neighbor: Chianti.02, Metric: default 10
      IP address: 192.168.40.2
    IP prefix: 192.168.5.5/32, Internal, Metric: default 0, Up
    IP prefix: 192.168.40.0/24, Internal, Metric: default 10, Up
    IP prefix: 192.168.5.5/32 metric 0 up
    IP prefix: 192.168.40.0/24 metric 10 up
  No queued transmissions
```

Altering the Default Authentication Methods

The JUNOS software provides several other configuration options related to authentication. Each of them provides network operators with flexibility to run their authentication configuration in the method best suited for their environment. The various options include:

`no-authentication-check`   This option is configured at the [edit protocols isis] hierarchy level and stops the local router from performing authentication verification on all received PDUs. All transmitted PDUs, however, still include the authentication TLV for verification by a remote system. This configuration option allows for an easy migration path for a network altering their authentication setup.

`no-hello-authentication`   This option is configured at the [edit protocols isis level *level-value*] hierarchy level. It removes the authentication TLV from all transmitted Hello

PDUs when authentication is configured for the appropriate level. This option is useful in a multivendor environment when other implementations of IS-IS don't authenticate all PDUs.

no-csnp-authentication   This option is configured at the [`edit protocols isis level` **_level-value_**] hierarchy level. It removes the authentication TLV from all transmitted complete sequence number PDUs when authentication is configured for the appropriate level. This option is also useful in a multivendor environment where all PDUs are not authenticated.

no-psnp-authentication   This option is configured at the [`edit protocols isis level` **_level-value_**] hierarchy level. It removes the authentication TLV from all transmitted partial sequence number PDUs when authentication is configured for the appropriate level. Again, a multivendor environment might not authenticate all PDUs and this option provides the ability to selectively not provide authentication for PSNPs.

Interface Metrics

Each interface running IS-IS receives a metric value of 10, by default, for both Level 1 and Level 2. The exception to this rule is the loopback interface, which has a metric value of 0. These default values are changeable in one of two methods: manual configuration for each interface or the use of a formula for automatic calculation. Let's explore these options further.

Manual Configuration

Each interface in the [`edit protocols isis`] configuration hierarchy has the ability to have a metric value (between 1 and 16,277,215) assigned to it for each operational IS-IS level. Additionally, each interface may receive a different metric value for either Level 1 or Level 2. The Shiraz router in Figure 3.19 currently has the default metric value of 10 assigned to each transit interface and a value of 0 on its loopback interface:

```
user@Shiraz> show configuration protocols isis
level 1 disable;
level 2 {
    authentication-key "$9$DXj.5Qz6Au136MX-waJ369CtO"; # SECRET-DATA
    authentication-type md5; # SECRET-DATA
}
interface so-0/1/0.0;
interface so-0/1/2.0;
interface lo0.0;
```

```
user@Shiraz> show isis interface
IS-IS interface database:
```

Interface	L	CirID	Level 1 DR	Level 2 DR	L1/L2 Metric
lo0.0	0	0x1	Passive	Passive	0/0
so-0/1/0.0	2	0x1	Disabled	Point to Point	10/10
so-0/1/2.0	2	0x1	Disabled	Point to Point	10/10

Shiraz has connectivity to the loopback address of Merlot (192.168.2.2 /32) across the so-0/1/0.0 interface. The current metric for this route is 10:

```
user@Shiraz> show route 192.168.2.2

inet.0: 17 destinations, 17 routes (17 active, 0 holddown, 0 hidden)
Restart Complete
+ = Active Route, - = Last Active, * = Both

192.168.2.2/32      *[IS-IS/18] 00:54:39, metric 10
                    > to 192.168.20.1 via so-0/1/0.0
```

We configure interface so-0/1/0.0 with a metric value of 25 for Level 1. While this changes the value of this interface, the route to 192.168.2.2 /32 doesn't change since Shiraz isn't using a Level 1 adjacency to reach the Merlot router:

```
user@Shiraz> show configuration protocols isis
level 1 disable;
level 2 {
    authentication-key "$9$DXj.5Qz6Au136MX-waJ369Ct0"; # SECRET-DATA
    authentication-type md5; # SECRET-DATA
}
interface so-0/1/0.0 {
    level 1 metric 25;
}
interface so-0/1/2.0;
interface lo0.0;


user@Shiraz> show isis interface
IS-IS interface database:
Interface           L CirID Level 1 DR     Level 2 DR      L1/L2 Metric
lo0.0               0  0x1 Passive         Passive         0/0
so-0/1/0.0          2  0x1 Disabled        Point to Point  25/10
so-0/1/2.0          2  0x1 Disabled        Point to Point  10/10


user@Shiraz> show route 192.168.2.2

inet.0: 17 destinations, 17 routes (17 active, 0 holddown, 0 hidden)
Restart Complete
+ = Active Route, - = Last Active, * = Both

192.168.2.2/32      *[IS-IS/18] 00:57:29, metric 10
                    > to 192.168.20.1 via so-0/1/0.0
```

The metric cost to reach 192.168.2.2 /32 is increased when the so-0/1/0.0 interface has its Level 2 metric set to 30:

```
user@Shiraz> show configuration protocols isis
level 1 disable;
level 2 {
    authentication-key "$9$DXj.5Qz6Au136MX-waJ369Ct0"; # SECRET-DATA
    authentication-type md5; # SECRET-DATA
}
interface so-0/1/0.0 {
    level 1 metric 25;
    level 2 metric 30;
}
interface so-0/1/2.0;
interface lo0.0;

user@Shiraz> show isis interface
IS-IS interface database:
Interface          L CirID Level 1 DR     Level 2 DR      L1/L2 Metric
lo0.0              0  0x1 Passive         Passive              0/0
so-0/1/0.0         2  0x1 Disabled        Point to Point      25/30
so-0/1/2.0         2  0x1 Disabled        Point to Point      10/10

user@Shiraz> show route 192.168.2.2

inet.0: 17 destinations, 17 routes (17 active, 0 holddown, 0 hidden)
Restart Complete
+ = Active Route, - = Last Active, * = Both

192.168.2.2/32     *[IS-IS/18] 00:00:06, metric 30
                    > to 192.168.20.1 via so-0/1/0.0
```

The costs for other routes in our sample network are also altered by the configuration changes made on the Shiraz router as these values are transmitted in an updated LSP to the network:

```
user@Shiraz> show isis database Shiraz.00-00 extensive | find TLV
  TLVs:
    Area address: 49.0002 (3)
    Speaks: IP
    Speaks: IPv6
    IP router id: 192.168.3.3
    IP address: 192.168.3.3
```

```
   Hostname: Shiraz
   IS neighbor: Merlot.00, Internal, Metric: default 30
   IS neighbor: Chardonnay.00, Internal, Metric: default 10
   IS neighbor: Merlot.00, Metric: default 30
     IP address: 192.168.20.2
     Neighbor's IP address: 192.168.20.1
   IS neighbor: Chardonnay.00, Metric: default 10
     IP address: 192.168.30.1
     Neighbor's IP address: 192.168.30.2
   IP prefix: 192.168.3.3/32, Internal, Metric: default 0, Up
   IP prefix: 192.168.20.0/24, Internal, Metric: default 30, Up
   IP prefix: 192.168.30.0/24, Internal, Metric: default 10, Up
   IP prefix: 192.168.3.3/32 metric 0 up
   IP prefix: 192.168.20.0/24 metric 30 up
   IP prefix: 192.168.30.0/24 metric 10 up
   Authentication data: 17 bytes
 No queued transmissions
```

Reference Bandwidth

The JUNOS software has the ability to automatically calculate the metric for an interface based on the bandwidth of that interface. The formula used for this calculation is (`reference-bandwidth` ÷ bandwidth (BW) of the interface in bits per second, or bps). You supply the numerator value for the equation by using the `reference-bandwidth` command at the global IS-IS configuration hierarchy level. When the router calculates the metric for an interface, it supplies only whole integer values to be used in the LSP; all calculated results less than 1 are rounded up to a value of 1. For example, suppose that the supplied `reference-bandwidth` is that of a Fast Ethernet interface (10,000,000 bps). This means that the calculated value for an OC-3c interface is .065 (10,000,000 ÷ 155,000,000). This result is rounded up to a metric of 1.

The use of the `reference-bandwidth` command affects all operational IS-IS interfaces on the router, with the exception of those manually configured with a metric value.

> You should configure the same reference bandwidth value on all routers in your network. This helps to ensure a consistent calculation of network paths and routing topologies across the network.

We once again configure the Shiraz router, which currently has a manual metric assigned to its `so-0/1/0.0` interface:

```
user@Shiraz> show isis interface
IS-IS interface database:
Interface          L CirID Level 1 DR       Level 2 DR       L1/L2 Metric
```

```
lo0.0                    0    0x1 Passive          Passive                0/0
so-0/1/0.0               2    0x1 Disabled         Point to Point        25/30
so-0/1/2.0               2    0x1 Disabled         Point to Point        10/10
```

We configure a reference bandwidth value of 1,000,000,000 (1Gbps) at the global IS-IS hierarchy level. The metric value for the other transit interface (so-0/1/2.0) is now changed to a value of 6:

```
user@Shiraz> show configuration protocols isis
reference-bandwidth 1g;
level 1 disable;
level 2 {
    authentication-key "$9$DXj.5Qz6Au136MX-waJ369CtO"; # SECRET-DATA
    authentication-type md5; # SECRET-DATA
}
interface so-0/1/0.0 {
    level 1 metric 25;
    level 2 metric 30;
}
interface so-0/1/2.0;
interface lo0.0;


user@Shiraz> show isis interface
IS-IS interface database:
Interface            L CirID Level 1 DR      Level 2 DR        L1/L2 Metric
lo0.0                0    0x1 Passive         Passive                0/0
so-0/1/0.0           2    0x1 Disabled        Point to Point        25/30
so-0/1/2.0           2    0x1 Disabled        Point to Point         6/6
```

The configured Level 2 metric value of 30 is still used for the so-0/1/0.0 interface even after using the reference-bandwidth command.

Wide Metrics

The original IS-IS specification defines the IS reachability (2), IP internal reachability (128), and IP external reachability (130) TLVs as methods for advertising information into the network. Each method supports a maximum metric of 63 through use of a 6-bit field in the TLV. In addition, these original TLVs don't have the capability to support TE extensions for advertising information such as reserved and available bandwidth. These limitations led to the creation of the IS extended reachability (22) and IP extended reachability (135) TLVs, which each use a 24-bit metric field and support sub-TLVs. The JUNOS software implementation of IS-IS uses the TE extensions by default. This means that both the extended TLVs, as well as the original TLVs, are advertised in all LSPs.

FIGURE 3.21   Wide metrics sample network

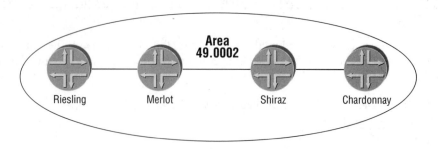

Figure 3.21 shows a simple Level 2 only network using the default metric value of 10 for all transit interfaces. The Riesling router advertises its network reachability using both the small metric (2 and 128) and wide metric (22 and 135) TLVs:

```
user@Riesling> monitor traffic interface fe-0/0/1 size 1514 detail
Listening on fe-0/0/1, capture size 1514 bytes

11:09:47.755684 Out OSI 0:90:69:67:44:1 > 1:80:c2:0:0:15, IS-IS, length: 137
        hlen: 27, v: 1, pdu-v: 1, sys-id-len: 6 (0), max-area: 3 (0),
        pdu-type: L2 LSP, lsp-id: 1921.6800.1001.00-00, seq: 0x0000015a,
        lifetime:   925s, chksum: 0x08dc (correct), PDU length: 137, L1L2 IS
            Area address(es) TLV #1, length: 4
                Area address (length: 3): 49.0002
            Protocols supported TLV #129, length: 2
                NLPID(s): IPv4, IPv6
            Traffic Engineering Router ID TLV #134, length: 4
                Traffic Engineering Router ID: 192.168.1.1
            IPv4 Interface address(es) TLV #132, length: 4
                IPv4 interface address: 192.168.1.1
            Hostname TLV #137, length: 8
                Hostname: Riesling
            IPv4 Internal reachability TLV #128, length: 24
                IPv4 prefix: 192.168.10.0/24
                  Default Metric: 10, Internal, Distribution: up
                IPv4 prefix: 192.168.1.1/32
                  Default Metric: 00, Internal, Distribution: up
            Extended IPv4 reachability TLV #135, length: 17
                IPv4 prefix: 192.168.10.0/24
                  Metric: 10, Distribution: up, no sub-TLVs present
                IPv4 prefix: 192.168.1.1/32
                  Metric: 0, Distribution: up, no sub-TLVs present
```

```
      IS Reachability TLV #2, length: 12
          IsNotVirtual
          IS Neighbor: 1921.6800.2002.02, Default Metric: 10, Internal
      Extended IS Reachability TLV #22, length: 17
          IS Neighbor: 1921.6800.2002.02, Metric: 10, sub-TLVs present (6)
            IPv4 interface address: 192.168.10.1
```

The default metric of 10 on all network links provides the Chardonnay router with a route to Riesling's loopback address (192.168.1.1 /32) having a total cost of 30:

```
user@Chardonnay> show route 192.168.1.1

inet.0: 12 destinations, 12 routes (12 active, 0 holddown, 0 hidden)
+ = Active Route, - = Last Active, * = Both

192.168.1.1/32      *[IS-IS/18] 01:03:47, metric 30
                    > to 192.168.30.1 via so-0/1/1.0
```

The metric for the loopback address on Riesling is set to a value of 1,000. This updates the LSP from Riesling in the link-state database of each router in the network:

```
user@Riesling> show configuration protocols isis
level 1 disable;
interface fe-0/0/1.0;
interface lo0.0 {
    level 2 metric 1000;
}

user@Chardonnay> show isis database Riesling.00-00 extensive | find TLV
  TLVs:
    Area address: 49.0002 (3)
    Speaks: IP
    Speaks: IPv6
    IP router id: 192.168.1.1
    IP address: 192.168.1.1
    Hostname: Riesling
    IS neighbor: Merlot.02, Internal, Metric: default 10
    IS neighbor: Merlot.02, Metric: default 10
      IP address: 192.168.10.1
    IP prefix: 192.168.1.1/32, Internal, Metric: default 63, Up
    IP prefix: 192.168.10.0/24, Internal, Metric: default 10, Up
    IP prefix: 192.168.1.1/32 metric 63 up
    IP prefix: 192.168.10.0/24 metric 10 up
  No queued transmissions
```

The router output details the default behavior of the JUNOS software—a configured metric greater than 63 results in an advertised metric of 63 within the LSP. Other routers in the network use the advertised metric to calculate the total cost for each route. This leads the Chardonnay router to install a metric of 93 for Riesling's loopback address:

```
user@Chardonnay> show route 192.168.1.1

inet.0: 12 destinations, 12 routes (12 active, 0 holddown, 0 hidden)
+ = Active Route, - = Last Active, * = Both

192.168.1.1/32     *[IS-IS/18] 00:04:44, metric 93
                    > to 192.168.30.1 via so-0/1/1.0
```

The maximum metric allowed in the routing table using small metrics is 1023.

To properly advertise the metric value of 1000, Riesling uses the `wide-metrics-only` command within the appropriate IS-IS level. This command informs the local router to only send the wide metric TLVs (22 and 135):

```
[edit protocols isis]
user@Riesling# show
level 1 disable;
level 2 wide-metrics-only;
interface fe-0/0/1.0;
interface lo0.0 {
    level 2 metric 1000;
}

user@Riesling> monitor traffic interface fe-0/0/1 size 1514 detail
Listening on fe-0/0/1, capture size 1514 bytes

12:49:50.730794 Out OSI 0:90:69:67:44:1 > 1:80:c2:0:0:15, IS-IS, length: 97
        hlen: 27, v: 1, pdu-v: 1, sys-id-len: 6 (0), max-area: 3 (0),
        pdu-type: L2 LSP, lsp-id: 1921.6800.1001.00-00, seq: 0x00000163,
        lifetime:  1162s, chksum: 0x8f45 (correct), PDU length: 97, L1L2 IS
            Area address(es) TLV #1, length: 4
                Area address (length: 3): 49.0002
            Protocols supported TLV #129, length: 2
                NLPID(s): IPv4, IPv6
```

```
        Traffic Engineering Router ID TLV #134, length: 4
            Traffic Engineering Router ID: 192.168.1.1
        IPv4 Interface address(es) TLV #132, length: 4
            IPv4 interface address: 192.168.1.1
        Hostname TLV #137, length: 8
            Hostname: Riesling
        Extended IS Reachability TLV #22, length: 17
            IS Neighbor: 1921.6800.2002.02, Metric: 10, sub-TLVs present (6)
              IPv4 interface address: 192.168.10.1
        Extended IPv4 reachability TLV #135, length: 17
            IPv4 prefix: 192.168.1.1/32
              Metric: 1000, Distribution: up, no sub-TLVs present
            IPv4 prefix: 192.168.10.0/24
              Metric: 10, Distribution: up, no sub-TLVs present
```

When the JUNOS software operates in this mode, the full 24-bit metric space is visible in the link-state LSP and is usable by all routers in the network:

```
user@Chardonnay> show isis database Riesling.00-00 extensive | find TLV
  TLVs:
    Area address: 49.0002 (3)
    Speaks: IP
    Speaks: IPv6
    IP router id: 192.168.1.1
    IP address: 192.168.1.1
    Hostname: Riesling
    IS neighbor: Merlot.02, Metric: default 10
      IP address: 192.168.10.1
    IP prefix: 192.168.1.1/32 metric 1000 up
    IP prefix: 192.168.10.0/24 metric 10 up
  No queued transmissions


user@Chardonnay> show route 192.168.1.1

inet.0: 12 destinations, 12 routes (12 active, 0 holddown, 0 hidden)
+ = Active Route, - = Last Active, * = Both

192.168.1.1/32     *[IS-IS/18] 00:08:20, metric 1030
                    > to 192.168.30.1 via so-0/1/1.0
```

Mesh Groups

In a full-mesh wide area network (WAN) environment, with routers connected across point-to-point interfaces, each IS-IS router forms an Up adjacency with each other router. When a new LSP is received by one of the routers, it is reflooded to each router it is currently adjacent with (except the router it received the LSP from). This might cause a waste of resources when multiple routers are connected in this fashion.

The Chianti, Merlot, Chablis, and Cabernet routers in Figure 3.22 are connected in a full mesh, with Up adjacencies formed with each other router:

```
user@Chianti> show isis adjacency
Interface          System      L State      Hold (secs) SNPA
so-0/1/0.600       Merlot      2 Up             21
so-0/1/1.600       Chablis     2 Up             26
so-0/1/1.700       Cabernet    2 Up             19
```

When the Chianti router generates a new LSP and floods it to all of its neighbors with a sequence number of 0x00001111, each neighbor receives the LSP, examines the contents of the link-state database, and finds that this is new information. It is then placed into the local link-state database and flooded to each adjacent neighbor, except the peer from which the LSP was received.

Figure 3.22 shows the complete process of reflooding in our sample network. Chianti sends its LSP to Merlot, Chablis, and Cabernet. Merlot then refloods the LSP to Chablis and Cabernet. Chablis refloods the copy it received from Chianti to Cabernet and Merlot. The Cabernet router also refloods the LSP received from Chianti to both Merlot and Chablis. With the exception of Chianti, who originated the LSP, each of the other routers in our sample network received three copies of the exact same LSP. Clearly, this repetitive transmission of identical information is not useful.

FIGURE 3.22 · LSP flooding without mesh groups

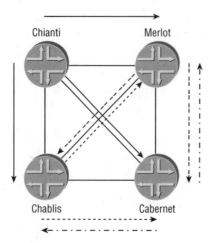

The JUNOS software provides a solution, called a *mesh group*, to mitigate the flooding of LSPs in a mesh-like environment. This works effectively on our full mesh of point-to-point links. Each interface is configured with a 32-bit mesh group value, which is local to the router. LSPs received on this interface are not reflooded to any other interface on the router, which is also configured with the same mesh group value. In our sample network, we configure each router with `mesh-group 101` at the interface hierarchy level in IS-IS:

```
user@Chianti> show configuration protocols isis
level 1 disable;
interface so-0/1/0.600 {
    mesh-group 101;
}
interface so-0/1/1.600 {
    mesh-group 101;
}
interface so-0/1/1.700 {
    mesh-group 101;
}
interface lo0.0;
```

 The JUNOS software allows the keyword *blocked* to be added to the `mesh-group` command, which prevents any LSP from being transmitted out the interface.

The addition of this configuration option doesn't affect the adjacency status or link-state database contents for any router in the network. As an example, the Merlot router currently appears as so:

```
user@Merlot> show isis adjacency
Interface          System         L State       Hold (secs) SNPA
so-0/1/0.600       Chianti        2 Up                    26
so-0/1/1.600       Cabernet       2 Up                    22
so-0/1/1.700       Chablis        2 Up                    25

user@Merlot> show isis database
IS-IS level 1 link-state database:
  0 LSPs

IS-IS level 2 link-state database:
LSP ID                  Sequence Checksum Lifetime Attributes
Chianti.00-00              0x43f   0x632b    1089 L1 L2
Merlot.00-00              0x439   0x5933    1194 L1 L2
```

```
Cabernet.00-00                    0x5    0xb069      835  L1 L2
Chablis.00-00                     0x5    0x678f      784  L1 L2
   4 LSPs
```

What we've accomplished by using the `mesh-group` command is a reduction in the flooding of identical LSPs across our point-to-point full-mesh environment. Figure 3.23 shows the improved result.

FIGURE 3.23   LSP flooding with mesh groups

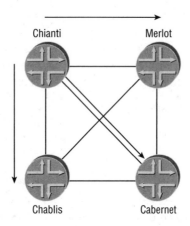

Overload Bit

The IS-IS specifications define a bit in the LSP header called the *overload bit*. When a router sets this bit to the value 1, other routers in the network remove the overloaded router from the forwarding topology. In essence it is no longer used to forward transit traffic through the network. Routes local to the overloaded router, however, are still reachable as stub links in the IS-IS forwarding topology. The original purpose for defining this bit was to provide a method for protecting the network against a router with memory problems that could result in a corrupted or incomplete link-state database. Modern implementations of the protocol, including the JUNOS software, do not suffer from such ailments as running out of memory space. Therefore, the setting of this bit is more useful for administrative purposes.

Two reasons are often cited for using the overload bit in a modern network. The first is a desire to perform some kind of maintenance on the router, which will affect user traffic. A network operator sets the bit on the appropriate router, and each other system in the network recalculates its SPF forwarding tree by removing the overloaded device. Provided the network contains enough redundant links, user data traffic is moved off the router so that the maintenance can be performed. After the router returns to service, the bit is cleared and the router is added to the SPF tree once again.

A second reason for setting the overload bit is to allow it time to form BGP neighbor relationships after a reload of the router. Suppose an IS-IS router is at the edge of your network where it has four peering relationships with other Autonomous Systems. Each external Border Gateway Protocol (EBGP) peer is sending the complete Internet routing table to the local router. The time it takes to form these sessions and receive these routes is much longer than the time is takes the router to form its IS-IS adjacencies and complete its link-state database. This time differential might cause user traffic to flow to the IS-IS router, where it is dropped due to incomplete routing information. The setting of the overload bit on this device for a short time period helps to avoid this potential issue.

The JUNOS software uses the `overload` command at the global IS-IS configuration hierarchy to set the overload bit. You can enable the bit value indefinitely or for a specified period of time. Let's explore each option in some further detail.

Permanent Overload

Using the sample network in Figure 3.21, we see that the Riesling router has a route to the loopback address of Merlot (192.168.2.2), Shiraz (192.168.3.3), and Chardonnay (192.168.4.4):

```
user@Riesling> show route protocol isis 192.168/16 terse

inet.0: 13 destinations, 13 routes (13 active, 0 holddown, 0 hidden)
Restart Complete
+ = Active Route, - = Last Active, * = Both

A Destination      P Prf  Metric 1  Metric 2  Next hop       AS path
* 192.168.2.2/32   I 18       10             >192.168.10.2
* 192.168.3.3/32   I 18       20             >192.168.10.2
* 192.168.4.4/32   I 18       30             >192.168.10.2
* 192.168.20.0/24  I 18       20             >192.168.10.2
* 192.168.30.0/24  I 18       30             >192.168.10.2
```

We set the overload bit on the Shiraz router. When no timer value is supplied, as in this case, the bit is set immediately in the LSP for Shiraz:

```
 [edit protocols isis]
user@Shiraz# show
overload;
level 1 disable;
interface so-0/1/0.0;
interface so-0/1/2.0;
interface lo0.0;

user@Shiraz> show isis database
IS-IS level 1 link-state database:
  0 LSPs
```

```
IS-IS level 2 link-state database:
LSP ID                     Sequence Checksum Lifetime Attributes
Riesling.00-00              0x177    0x8c3b      988 L1 L2
Merlot.00-00                0x189    0xaf78     1012 L1 L2
Merlot.02-00                  0x1    0xd922      990 L1 L2
Shiraz.00-00                0x176    0xba6a     1195 L1 L2 Overload
Chardonnay.00-00            0x167    0x249f     1035 L1 L2
  5 LSPs
```

The presence of this bit causes the Riesling router to recalculate its SPF tree without including Shiraz as a transit router. The result of the SPF calculation is the loss of connectivity to Chardonnay's loopback address of 192.168.4.4:

user@Riesling> **show route protocol isis 192.168/16 terse**

```
inet.0: 12 destinations, 12 routes (12 active, 0 holddown, 0 hidden)
Restart Complete
+ = Active Route, - = Last Active, * = Both

A Destination         P Prf   Metric 1   Metric 2  Next hop          AS path
* 192.168.2.2/32      I  18         10               >192.168.10.2
* 192.168.3.3/32      I  18         20               >192.168.10.2
* 192.168.20.0/24     I  18         20               >192.168.10.2
* 192.168.30.0/24     I  18         30               >192.168.10.2
```

We maintain reachability to the loopback of Shiraz (192.168.3.3) since the router is now a stub connection to the network and this address is reachable on Shiraz itself.

Our current configuration permanently sets the overload bit in Shiraz's LSP until the overload command is removed from the configuration. In other words, the bit will still be set after the routing process restarts or even after the router reboots.

Temporary Overload

The JUNOS software provides the ability to set the overload bit for a specific amount of time between 60 and 1800 seconds. We accomplish this by configuring the overload command and using the *timeout* option. After the routing process on the router starts, the timer begins and the overload bit is set in the local router's LSP. Once the timer expires, the bit is cleared and an updated LSP is advertised into the network. The configuration within [edit protocols isis] remains intact until a network administrator manually deletes it, which may cause the router to again return to an overload mode should the routing process restart.

After returning the routers in Figure 3.21 to a normal operational state, we configure the Shiraz router to set its overload bit for 60 seconds after a restart of its routing process. This configuration does not affect the current operation of the network because Shiraz doesn't yet set the overload bit in its LSP:

```
[edit protocols isis]
user@Shiraz# show
overload timeout 60;
level 1 disable;
interface so-0/1/0.0;
interface so-0/1/2.0;
interface lo0.0;
```

```
user@Shiraz> show isis database
IS-IS level 1 link-state database:
  0 LSPs
```

```
IS-IS level 2 link-state database:
LSP ID                    Sequence Checksum Lifetime Attributes
Riesling.00-00              0x178   0x8a3c      605 L1 L2
Merlot.00-00               0x18a   0xad79      734 L1 L2
Merlot.02-00                 0x2   0xd723      734 L1 L2
Shiraz.00-00               0x179   0xb075     1196 L1 L2
Chardonnay.00-00           0x168   0x22a0      717 L1 L2
  5 LSPs
```

We temporarily remove and reapply the IS-IS configuration on Shiraz using the deactivate and activate commands. This forces Shiraz to set the overload bit in its local LSP, which is visible using the show isis database command. After the 60-second timer expires, the overload bit is cleared and a new LSP is advertised to the network:

```
[edit]
user@Shiraz# deactivate protocols isis
```

```
[edit]
user@Shiraz# commit
commit complete
```

```
[edit]
user@Shiraz# activate protocols isis
```

```
[edit]
user@Shiraz# commit and-quit
commit complete
Exiting configuration mode

user@Shiraz> show system uptime
Current time:       2003-03-11 15:38:59 UTC
System booted:      2003-03-08 13:48:06 UTC (3d 01:50 ago)
Protocols started: 2003-03-11 15:35:25 UTC (00:03:34 ago)
Last configured:    2003-03-11 15:38:56 UTC (00:00:03 ago) by user
3:38PM UTC  up 3 days,  1:51, 1 user, load averages: 0.02, 0.03, 0.00

user@Shiraz> show isis database
IS-IS level 1 link-state database:
  0 LSPs

IS-IS level 2 link-state database:
LSP ID                     Sequence Checksum Lifetime Attributes
Shiraz.00-00                 0x1    0xd4fa      1194 L1 L2 Overload
  1 LSPs

user@Shiraz> show system uptime
Current time:       2003-03-11 15:39:54 UTC
System booted:      2003-03-08 13:48:06 UTC (3d 01:51 ago)
Protocols started: 2003-03-11 15:35:25 UTC (00:04:29 ago)
Last configured:    2003-03-11 15:38:56 UTC (00:00:58 ago) by user
3:39PM UTC  up 3 days,  1:52, 1 user, load averages: 0.01, 0.02, 0.00

user@Shiraz> show isis database
IS-IS level 1 link-state database:
  0 LSPs

IS-IS level 2 link-state database:
LSP ID                     Sequence Checksum Lifetime Attributes
Riesling.00-00               0x179  0x883d       847 L1 L2
Merlot.00-00                 0x18e  0xa57d      1185 L1 L2
Merlot.02-00                 0x3    0xd524      1077 L1 L2
Shiraz.00-00                 0x181  0x40d9      1187 L1 L2 Overload
Chardonnay.00-00             0x16d  0x18a5      1161 L1 L2
  5 LSPs
```

```
user@Shiraz> show system uptime
Current time:      2003-03-11 15:39:59 UTC
System booted:     2003-03-08 13:48:06 UTC (3d 01:52 ago)
Protocols started: 2003-03-11 15:35:25 UTC (00:04:34 ago)
Last configured:   2003-03-11 15:38:56 UTC (00:01:03 ago) by user
3:40PM UTC  up 3 days,  1:52, 1 user, load averages: 0.00, 0.02, 0.00

user@Shiraz> show isis database
IS-IS level 1 link-state database:
  0 LSPs

IS-IS level 2 link-state database:
LSP ID                   Sequence Checksum Lifetime Attributes
Riesling.00-00            0x179    0x883d       823 L1 L2
Merlot.00-00             0x18e    0xa57d      1161 L1 L2
Merlot.02-00               0x3    0xd524      1053 L1 L2
Shiraz.00-00             0x182    0x9e7e      1183 L1 L2
Chardonnay.00-00         0x16d    0x18a5      1137 L1 L2
  5 LSPs
```

By using the show system uptime command, we gain a sense of time to validate the 60-second overload timer. After starting the IS-IS process, the LSP for Shiraz has the overload bit set. After 58 seconds, the bit is still set in the LSP, but it is cleared by the time we check again after 63 seconds have elapsed.

Multilevel IS-IS

Thus far in the chapter, we've been touching on the issue of multiple levels of operation in IS-IS. We have yet to provide some background and details for how these levels interact with each other. We'll first examine the default operation of a multilevel IS-IS network and then look at how "extra" routing information is advertised across the boundary between levels.

Internal Route Default Operation

In the "IS-IS Areas and Levels" section earlier we discussed the flooding scope of LSPs in both a Level 1 and a Level 2 area. We stated that a Level 1 LSP is flooded only within its own Level 1 area. This allows each router in the area to have explicit routing knowledge of the prefixes included in that area. All other prefixes in the network are reached through a Level 2 router, which is also connected to the Level 1 area. This L1/L2 border router, in turn, is connected to the contiguous set of Level 2 areas composing the backbone of the network. The Level 1 routers forward user traffic based on a locally installed default route pointing to the closest L1/L2 router attached to the backbone. Each Level 1 router watches for an LSP with the Attached bit set to the value 1, which indicates that the originating L1/L2 router has knowledge of another Level 2 area. This knowledge is gained either through an adjacency with a Level 2 router in another area or through the receipt of an LSP from an IS-IS router in another Level 2 area.

As every Level 1 router in the network is forwarding traffic for unknown prefixes to a Level 2 router, it stands to reason that the Level 2 router has explicit knowledge of the unknown route. In fact, this is a sound assumption. Each L1/L2 border router announces its local Level 1 routes in its Level 2 LSP to the backbone. This allows all Level 2 routers to have explicit routing knowledge of all routes in the network.

FIGURE 3.24   Multilevel IS-IS network

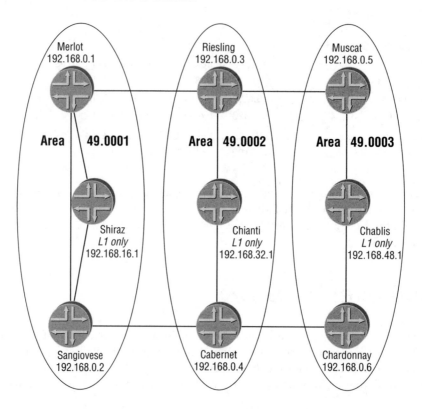

Figure 3.24 displays a multilevel IS-IS network with three areas defined. Each area contains a single Level 1 router and two Level 1/ Level 2 routers. The Level 1 LSP generated by the Shiraz router contains the 192.168.16.1 /32, 192.168.17.0 /24, and 192.168.18.0 /24 routes:

```
user@Shiraz> show isis database Shiraz.00-00 detail
IS-IS level 1 link-state database:

Shiraz.00-00  Sequence: 0x56, Checksum: 0x52a2, Lifetime: 780 secs
```

```
IS neighbor:                        Merlot.00  Metric:      10
IS neighbor:                     Sangiovese.00  Metric:      10
IP prefix:                   192.168.16.1/32 Metric:        0 Internal Up
IP prefix:                   192.168.17.0/24 Metric:        10 Internal Up
IP prefix:                   192.168.18.0/24 Metric:        10 Internal Up
```

This LSP is received by both the Merlot and Sangiovese routers, since each has a Level 1 adjacency with Shiraz. Each L1/L2 router runs the SPF algorithm against its Level 1 database and installs a route to the loopback address of Shiraz (192.168.16.1 /32):

```
user@Merlot> show route 192.168.16.1

inet.0: 21 destinations, 21 routes (21 active, 0 holddown, 0 hidden)
Restart Complete
+ = Active Route, - = Last Active, * = Both

192.168.16.1/32    *[IS-IS/15] 17:40:32, metric 10
                    > to 192.168.17.2 via so-0/1/0.0


user@Sangiovese> show route 192.168.16.1

inet.0: 21 destinations, 21 routes (21 active, 0 holddown, 0 hidden)
+ = Active Route, - = Last Active, * = Both

192.168.16.1/32    *[IS-IS/15] 17:40:16, metric 10, tag 1
                    > to 192.168.18.2 via so-0/1/1.0
```

Each L1/L2 router installed the route with a preference value of 15, which represents an IS-IS internal Level 1 route. This route is then advertised by both Merlot and Sangiovese to provide routing knowledge for the backbone. Using Merlot as a sample, we see the 192.168.16.1 /32 route in the Level 1 LSP from Shiraz and in the Level 2 LSP locally generated by Merlot:

```
user@Merlot> show isis database level 1 Shiraz.00-00 detail
IS-IS level 1 link-state database:

Shiraz.00-00  Sequence: 0x57, Checksum: 0x50a3, Lifetime: 748 secs
    IS neighbor:                      Merlot.00  Metric:      10
    IS neighbor:                   Sangiovese.00  Metric:      10
    IP prefix:                 192.168.16.1/32 Metric:        0 Internal Up
    IP prefix:                 192.168.17.0/24 Metric:        10 Internal Up
    IP prefix:                 192.168.18.0/24 Metric:        10 Internal Up


user@Merlot> show isis database level 2 Merlot.00-00 detail
```

```
IS-IS level 2 link-state database:

Merlot.00-00  Sequence: 0x59, Checksum: 0x111c, Lifetime: 829 secs
    IS neighbor:                   Merlot.02  Metric:     10
    IP prefix:            192.168.0.1/32 Metric:      0 Internal Up
    IP prefix:            192.168.0.2/32 Metric:     20 Internal Up
    IP prefix:            192.168.1.0/24 Metric:     10 Internal Up
    IP prefix:           192.168.16.1/32 Metric:     10 Internal Up
    IP prefix:           192.168.17.0/24 Metric:     10 Internal Up
    IP prefix:           192.168.18.0/24 Metric:     20 Internal Up
```

The router output clearly demonstrates the default behavior of a multilevel IS-IS network. The Level 1 router advertises prefixes using the IP internal reachability TLV (128) with the Up/Down bit set to the value 0 (Up). This allows the L1/L2 router to advertise the prefix from Level 1 up to Level 2. The prefix is again advertised in Level 2 using TLV 128 with the Up/Down bit cleared, which allows the protocol to announce the prefix across all Level 2 area boundaries. In addition, the prefix could be advertised up to another IS-IS level should one ever be defined in the future.

The Level 2 LSP generated by Merlot is flooded to all other Level 2 routers, including the Chardonnay router in area 49.0003. This allows Chardonnay to install an internal Level 2 route for 192.168.16.1 /32 in its local routing table:

```
user@Chardonnay> show isis database Merlot.00-00 detail
IS-IS level 1 link-state database:

IS-IS level 2 link-state database:

Merlot.00-00  Sequence: 0x5e, Checksum: 0x72aa, Lifetime: 1141 secs
    IS neighbor:                   Merlot.02  Metric:     10
    IS neighbor:               Sangiovese.03  Metric:     10
    IP prefix:            192.168.0.1/32 Metric:      0 Internal Up
    IP prefix:            192.168.0.2/32 Metric:     10 Internal Up
    IP prefix:            192.168.1.0/24 Metric:     10 Internal Up
    IP prefix:            192.168.5.0/24 Metric:     10 Internal Up
    IP prefix:           192.168.16.1/32 Metric:     10 Internal Up
    IP prefix:           192.168.17.0/24 Metric:     10 Internal Up
    IP prefix:           192.168.18.0/24 Metric:     20 Internal Up

user@Chardonnay> show route 192.168.16.1

inet.0: 24 destinations, 24 routes (24 active, 0 holddown, 0 hidden)
+ = Active Route, - = Last Active, * = Both
```

```
192.168.16.1/32    *[IS-IS/18] 17:38:22, metric 30
                   > to 192.168.4.1 via fe-0/0/2.0
```

With the Up/Down bit set to Up in Merlot's Level 2 LSP, Chardonnay doesn't include it in its Level 1 LSP for area 49.0003:

user@Chardonnay> **show isis database level 1 Chardonnay.00-00 detail**
IS-IS level 1 link-state database:

```
Chardonnay.00-00  Sequence: 0x54, Checksum: 0x6c8, Lifetime: 907 secs
   IS neighbor:            Chardonnay.03  Metric:      10
   IP prefix:            192.168.0.6/32 Metric:       0 Internal Up
   IP prefix:            192.168.50.0/24 Metric:      10 Internal Up
```

In a similar fashion, each L1/L2 router advertises its local Level 1 routes into the Level 2 flooding topology. This allows the loopback addresses of the Level 1 only routers (192.168.16.1, 192.168.32.1, and 192.168.48.1) to appear in the routing table of Sangiovese, a backbone router:

user@Sangiovese> **show route 192.168.16.1/32 terse**

```
inet.0: 25 destinations, 25 routes (25 active, 0 holddown, 0 hidden)
+ = Active Route, - = Last Active, * = Both
```

A	Destination	P	Prf	Metric 1	Metric 2	Next hop	AS path
*	192.168.16.1/32	I	15	10		>192.168.18.2	

user@Sangiovese> **show route 192.168.32.1/32 terse**

```
inet.0: 25 destinations, 25 routes (25 active, 0 holddown, 0 hidden)
+ = Active Route, - = Last Active, * = Both
```

A	Destination	P	Prf	Metric 1	Metric 2	Next hop	AS path
*	192.168.32.1/32	I	18	20		>192.168.3.2	

user@Sangiovese> **show route 192.168.48.1/32 terse**

```
inet.0: 25 destinations, 25 routes (25 active, 0 holddown, 0 hidden)
+ = Active Route, - = Last Active, * = Both
```

A	Destination	P	Prf	Metric 1	Metric 2	Next hop	AS path
*	192.168.48.1/32	I	18	30		>192.168.3.2	

Once a user data packet reaches the backbone, it is forwarded to the L1/L2 router connected to the destination. The L1/L2 router has explicit knowledge of its directly connected Level 1 forwarding topology. The router then forwards the data packet to the appropriate Level 1 router. Of course, the real "issue" in this scenario is getting the data packet to the backbone in the first place. This is accomplished with a default route on the Level 1 router.

Each L1/L2 router with knowledge of another Level 2 area sets the Attached bit in its Level 1 LSP. The Riesling router in Figure 3.24 is configured for area 49.0002 and has a Level 2 adjacency with both the Merlot and Muscat routers, each of which has a different area address:

```
user@Riesling> show configuration interfaces lo0
unit 0 {
    family inet {
        address 192.168.0.3/32;
    }
    family iso {
        address 49.0002.1921.6800.0003.00;
    }
}
```

```
user@Riesling> show isis adjacency
Interface          System        L State        Hold (secs) SNPA
fe-0/0/0.0         Muscat        2 Up                     7  0:90:69:68:54:1
fe-0/0/1.0         Merlot        2 Up                     6  0:90:69:67:b4:1
fe-0/0/2.0         Chianti       1 Up                     7  0:90:69:6e:fc:1
```

These two adjacencies allow Riesling to set the Attached bit in its Level 1 LSP:

```
user@Riesling> show isis database level 1
IS-IS level 1 link-state database:
LSP ID                     Sequence Checksum Lifetime Attributes
Riesling.00-00                0x55    0xb1f1      609 L1 L2 Attached
Cabernet.00-00                0x56    0xda17      809 L1 L2 Attached
Cabernet.03-00                0x55    0xe0f9      809 L1 L2
Chianti.00-00                 0x58    0xc74b     1003 L1
Chianti.02-00                 0x57    0xb10c      652 L1
   5 LSPs
```

We see that the Cabernet router has also set the Attached bit in its Level 1 LSP for area 49.0002. This bit value allows the Level 1 router of Chianti to install a local copy of the 0.0.0.0 /0 default route. The next hop for this route is the metrically closest attached Level 2 router:

```
user@Chianti> show route 0/0 exact
```

```
inet.0: 10 destinations, 10 routes (10 active, 0 holddown, 0 hidden)
+ = Active Route, - = Last Active, * = Both

0.0.0.0/0            *[IS-IS/15] 18:32:50, metric 10
                      to 192.168.34.1 via fe-0/0/0.0
                    > to 192.168.33.1 via fe-0/0/1.0
```

As each of the L1/L2 routers is a single hop away, the default route on Chianti has two next hops installed in the routing table.

> Unlike the operation of OSPF where the default route is advertised by the area border router, a Level 1 IS-IS router installs its own copy of the route. The L1/L2 router does not advertise it to the Level 1 area.

We have now established reachability to all portions of the network. The Chianti router can ping both Level 2 routers as well as Level 1 routers in other areas.

```
user@Chianti> ping 192.168.0.1 source 192.168.32.1 rapid
PING 192.168.0.1 (192.168.0.1): 56 data bytes
!!!!!
--- 192.168.0.1 ping statistics ---
5 packets transmitted, 5 packets received, 0% packet loss
round-trip min/avg/max/stddev = 0.852/2.349/7.807/2.733 ms

user@Chianti> ping 192.168.16.1 source 192.168.32.1 rapid
PING 192.168.16.1 (192.168.16.1): 56 data bytes
!!!!!
--- 192.168.16.1 ping statistics ---
5 packets transmitted, 5 packets received, 0% packet loss
round-trip min/avg/max/stddev = 0.867/0.946/1.226/0.140 ms

user@Chianti> ping 192.168.48.1 source 192.168.32.1 rapid
PING 192.168.48.1 (192.168.48.1): 56 data bytes
!!!!!
--- 192.168.48.1 ping statistics ---
5 packets transmitted, 5 packets received, 0% packet loss
round-trip min/avg/max/stddev = 0.897/0.985/1.289/0.152 ms

user@Chianti> ping 192.168.0.6 source 192.168.32.1 rapid
PING 192.168.0.6 (192.168.0.6): 56 data bytes
!!!!!
```

```
--- 192.168.0.6 ping statistics ---
5 packets transmitted, 5 packets received, 0% packet loss
round-trip min/avg/max/stddev = 0.888/0.989/1.287/0.150 ms
```

External Route Default Operation

The default use of external routes in a multilevel IS-IS network, those injected using a routing policy, is somewhat similar in nature to internal routes. There is one major exception, which we'll discover as we explore our sample network. Each of the Level 1 routers in Figure 3.24 is injecting four external static routes into the network. The routes for the Shiraz router are within the 172.16.16.0 /20 address space. Chianti is using the 172.16.32.0 /20 address space, while Chablis is using the range of 172.16.48.0 /20. In addition, the Chardonnay router is injecting routes in the 172.16.64.0 /20 address range into the Level 2 backbone.

The Level 1 LSP generated by Chianti now contains the external routes injected by the routing policy:

```
user@Chianti> show isis database Chianti.00-00 detail
IS-IS level 1 link-state database:

Chianti.00-00  Sequence: 0x5a, Checksum: 0x2d30, Lifetime: 1015 secs
    IS neighbor:                Cabernet.03  Metric:      10
    IS neighbor:                 Chianti.02  Metric:      10
    IP prefix:              172.16.32.0/24 Metric:       0 External Up
    IP prefix:              172.16.33.0/24 Metric:       0 External Up
    IP prefix:              172.16.34.0/24 Metric:       0 External Up
    IP prefix:              172.16.35.0/24 Metric:       0 External Up
    IP prefix:             192.168.32.1/32 Metric:       0 Internal Up
    IP prefix:             192.168.33.0/24 Metric:      10 Internal Up
    IP prefix:             192.168.34.0/24 Metric:      10 Internal Up
```

This LSP is received by both Riesling and Cabernet, each of which installs Level 1 routes in their routing tables for the external routes:

```
user@Riesling> show route 172.16.32/20 terse

inet.0: 34 destinations, 34 routes (34 active, 0 holddown, 0 hidden)
Restart Complete
+ = Active Route, - = Last Active, * = Both

A Destination        P Prf   Metric 1   Metric 2  Next hop        AS path
* 172.16.32.0/24     I 160        10                >192.168.33.2
* 172.16.33.0/24     I 160        10                >192.168.33.2
```

```
* 172.16.34.0/24    I 160       10           >192.168.33.2
* 172.16.35.0/24    I 160       10           >192.168.33.2
```

user@Cabernet> **show route 172.16.32/20 terse**

```
inet.0: 33 destinations, 33 routes (33 active, 0 holddown, 0 hidden)
+ = Active Route, - = Last Active, * = Both

A Destination       P Prf   Metric 1   Metric 2  Next hop         AS path
* 172.16.32.0/24    I 160       10               >192.168.34.2
* 172.16.33.0/24    I 160       10               >192.168.34.2
* 172.16.34.0/24    I 160       10               >192.168.34.2
* 172.16.35.0/24    I 160       10               >192.168.34.2
```

An examination of the Level 2 LSP generated by Cabernet reveals a unique behavior for these external routes:

user@Cabernet> **show isis database level 2 Cabernet.00-00 detail**
```
IS-IS level 2 link-state database:

Cabernet.00-00  Sequence: 0x5c, Checksum: 0x7064, Lifetime: 583 secs
    IS neighbor:                Cabernet.02  Metric:      10
    IS neighbor:                Cabernet.04  Metric:      10
    IP prefix:            192.168.0.3/32 Metric:      20 Internal Up
    IP prefix:            192.168.0.4/32 Metric:       0 Internal Up
    IP prefix:            192.168.3.0/24 Metric:      10 Internal Up
    IP prefix:            192.168.4.0/24 Metric:      10 Internal Up
    IP prefix:           192.168.32.1/32 Metric:      10 Internal Up
    IP prefix:           192.168.33.0/24 Metric:      20 Internal Up
    IP prefix:           192.168.34.0/24 Metric:      10 Internal Up
```

The router output shows that the routes in the 172.16.32.0 /20 address range aren't included in Cabernet's Level 2 LSP. This is in line with the default treatment of external routes in an IS-IS network. While at odds with the operation of internal routes, external routes are not advertised out of their level by default. This means that the other Level 2 routers, like Sangiovese, don't have routes in their routing table for that address space:

user@Sangiovese> **show route 172.16.32/20**

user@Sangiovese>

When we look at routes injected into a Level 2 router, we see a similar behavior. The external routes on the Chardonnay router are included in its Level 2 LSP and flooded into the backbone.

This provides explicit routing knowledge to the Level 2 routers in the network, allowing them to install external Level 2 routes in the routing table:

```
user@Merlot> show isis database Chardonnay.00-00 detail
IS-IS level 1 link-state database:

IS-IS level 2 link-state database:

Chardonnay.00-00  Sequence: 0x5d, Checksum: 0x4a9e, Lifetime: 356 secs
    IS neighbor:              Cabernet.02  Metric:      10
    IP prefix:               172.16.64.0/24 Metric:       0 External Up
    IP prefix:               172.16.65.0/24 Metric:       0 External Up
    IP prefix:               172.16.66.0/24 Metric:       0 External Up
    IP prefix:               172.16.67.0/24 Metric:       0 External Up
    IP prefix:               192.168.0.5/32 Metric:      20 Internal Up
    IP prefix:               192.168.0.6/32 Metric:       0 Internal Up
    IP prefix:               192.168.4.0/24 Metric:      10 Internal Up
    IP prefix:               192.168.48.1/32 Metric:      10 Internal Up
    IP prefix:               192.168.49.0/24 Metric:      20 Internal Up
    IP prefix:               192.168.50.0/24 Metric:      10 Internal Up

user@Merlot> show route 172.16.64/20

inet.0: 34 destinations, 34 routes (34 active, 0 holddown, 0 hidden)
Restart Complete
+ = Active Route, - = Last Active, * = Both

172.16.64.0/24      *[IS-IS/165] 00:45:00, metric 30
                     > to 192.168.5.2 via fe-0/0/0.0
172.16.65.0/24      *[IS-IS/165] 00:45:00, metric 30
                     > to 192.168.5.2 via fe-0/0/0.0
172.16.66.0/24      *[IS-IS/165] 00:45:00, metric 30
                     > to 192.168.5.2 via fe-0/0/0.0
172.16.67.0/24      *[IS-IS/165] 00:45:00, metric 30
                     > to 192.168.5.2 via fe-0/0/0.0
```

The setting of the Up/Down bit to an **Up** position in the Level 2 LSP of Chardonnay indicates that the routes are not advertised down into the Level 1 area. We verify this with an examination of the Level 1 LSP of Merlot:

```
user@Merlot> show isis database level 1 Merlot.00-00 detail
IS-IS level 1 link-state database:
```

```
Merlot.00-00  Sequence: 0x63, Checksum: 0x7bf5, Lifetime: 819 secs
     IS neighbor:            Sangiovese.03  Metric:      10
     IS neighbor:            Shiraz.00  Metric:          10
     IP prefix:          192.168.0.1/32 Metric:       0 Internal Up
     IP prefix:          192.168.5.0/24 Metric:      10 Internal Up
     IP prefix:          192.168.17.0/24 Metric:     10 Internal Up
```

 Real World Scenario

External Routes and Wide Metrics

The default behavior of the JUNOS software is the advertisement of IP routes using both the small metric TLVs (128 and 130) as well as the wide metric TLVs (135). The presence of TLVs 128 and 130 in the received LSP causes the router to "ignore" the settings located in the extended IP reachability TLV (135). We see this behavior on the Cabernet router in Figure 3.24 as it receives both sets of TLVs from the Level 1 router of Chianti:

```
user@Cabernet> show isis database Chianti.00-00 extensive | find TLV
  TLVs:
    Area address: 49.0002 (3)
    Speaks: IP
    Speaks: IPv6
    IP router id: 192.168.32.1
    IP address: 192.168.32.1
    Hostname: Chianti
    IS neighbor: Cabernet.03, Internal, Metric: default 10
    IS neighbor: Chianti.02, Internal, Metric: default 10
    IS neighbor: Cabernet.03, Metric: default 10
      IP address: 192.168.34.2
    IS neighbor: Chianti.02, Metric: default 10
      IP address: 192.168.33.2
    IP prefix: 192.168.32.1/32, Internal, Metric: default 0, Up
    IP prefix: 192.168.34.0/24, Internal, Metric: default 10, Up
    IP prefix: 192.168.33.0/24, Internal, Metric: default 10, Up
    IP prefix: 192.168.32.1/32 metric 0 up
    IP prefix: 192.168.34.0/24 metric 10 up
    IP prefix: 192.168.33.0/24 metric 10 up
    IP external prefix: 172.16.32.0/24, Internal, Metric: default 0, Up
    IP external prefix: 172.16.33.0/24, Internal, Metric: default 0, Up
```

```
      IP external prefix: 172.16.34.0/24, Internal, Metric: default 0, Up
      IP external prefix: 172.16.35.0/24, Internal, Metric: default 0, Up
      IP prefix: 172.16.32.0/24 metric 0 up
      IP prefix: 172.16.33.0/24 metric 0 up
      IP prefix: 172.16.34.0/24 metric 0 up
      IP prefix: 172.16.35.0/24 metric 0 up
   No queued transmissions
```

Using just the 172.16.32.0 /24 route as an example, we see both TLV 130 (`IP external prefix`) as well as TLV 135 (`IP prefix`) advertising the route. By default, external Level 1 routes are not advertised to the Level 2 database. We can verify that Cabernet is not advertising this route by examining its Level 2 LSP:

```
user@Cabernet> show isis database level 2 Cabernet.00-00 detail
IS-IS level 2 link-state database:

Cabernet.00-00  Sequence: 0xdb, Checksum: 0xc01, Lifetime: 1196 secs
    IS neighbor:                  Cabernet.02  Metric:       10
    IS neighbor:                  Cabernet.04  Metric:       10
    IP prefix:             192.168.0.4/32 Metric:       0 Internal Up
    IP prefix:             192.168.3.0/24 Metric:      10 Internal Up
    IP prefix:             192.168.4.0/24 Metric:      10 Internal Up
    IP prefix:            192.168.32.1/32 Metric:      10 Internal Up
    IP prefix:             192.168.33.0/24 Metric:     20 Internal Up
    IP prefix:             192.168.34.0/24 Metric:     10 Internal Up
```

We now configure the Chianti router to only use the wide metric TLVs by using the wide-metrics-only command. This causes the Level 1 LSP from that router to only advertise the 172.16.32.0 /24 route using TLV 135:

```
user@Cabernet> show isis database Chianti.00-00 extensive | find TLV
  TLVs:
    Area address: 49.0002 (3)
    Speaks: IP
    Speaks: IPv6
    IP router id: 192.168.32.1
    IP address: 192.168.32.1
    Hostname: Chianti
    IS neighbor: Cabernet.03, Metric: default 10
      IP address: 192.168.34.2
    IS neighbor: Chianti.02, Metric: default 10
```

```
      IP address: 192.168.33.2
    IP prefix: 192.168.32.1/32 metric 0 up
    IP prefix: 192.168.34.0/24 metric 10 up
    IP prefix: 192.168.33.0/24 metric 10 up
    IP prefix: 172.16.32.0/24 metric 0 up
    IP prefix: 172.16.33.0/24 metric 0 up
    IP prefix: 172.16.34.0/24 metric 0 up
    IP prefix: 172.16.35.0/24 metric 0 up
  No queued transmissions
```

Recall from the section "Extended IP Reachability TLV" earlier that TLV 135 does not contain an Internal/External bit. This means that all prefixes advertised using TLV 135 are seen as internal routes. All internal Level 1 routes are advertised to Level 2, by default, so the 172.16.32.0 /24 prefix is advertised by Cabernet into the Level 2 database:

```
user@Cabernet> show isis database level 2 Cabernet.00-00 detail
IS-IS level 2 link-state database:

Cabernet.00-00  Sequence: 0xdc, Checksum: 0x25ec, Lifetime: 1007 secs
    IS neighbor:            Cabernet.02  Metric:       10
    IS neighbor:            Cabernet.04  Metric:       10
    IP prefix:            172.16.32.0/24 Metric:       10 Internal Up
    IP prefix:            172.16.33.0/24 Metric:       10 Internal Up
    IP prefix:            172.16.34.0/24 Metric:       10 Internal Up
    IP prefix:            172.16.35.0/24 Metric:       10 Internal Up
    IP prefix:            192.168.0.4/32 Metric:        0 Internal Up
    IP prefix:            192.168.3.0/24 Metric:       10 Internal Up
    IP prefix:            192.168.4.0/24 Metric:       10 Internal Up
    IP prefix:            192.168.32.1/32 Metric:      10 Internal Up
    IP prefix:            192.168.33.0/24 Metric:       20 Internal Up
    IP prefix:            192.168.34.0/24 Metric:       10 Internal Up
```

Route Leaking

The JUNOS software provides you with the ability to override the default route advertisement rules in a multilevel IS-IS network. This concept, called *route leaking*, involves the use of a routing policy to identify routes eligible for announcement to another level. While route leaking is often associated with sending Level 2 routes down into a Level 1 area, it also applies to the announcement of external Level 1 routes up into the Level 2 backbone.

Using Figure 3.24 as a guide, we verify that the Muscat and Chardonnay routers are not advertising the loopback address of Shiraz (192.168.16.1) to the Level 1 database of area 49.0003:

```
user@Muscat> show isis database level 1 Muscat.00-00 detail
IS-IS level 1 link-state database:

Muscat.00-00  Sequence: 0x3, Checksum: 0x6d28, Lifetime: 1170 secs
   IP prefix:               192.168.0.5/32 Metric:        0 Internal Up
   IP prefix:               192.168.49.0/24 Metric:       10 Internal Up
```

```
user@Chardonnay> show isis database level 1 Chardonnay.00-00 detail
IS-IS level 1 link-state database:

Chardonnay.00-00  Sequence: 0x60, Checksum: 0x2869, Lifetime: 1140 secs
   IP prefix:               192.168.0.6/32 Metric:        0 Internal Up
   IP prefix:               192.168.50.0/24 Metric:       10 Internal Up
```

As an additional data point, the Chablis router in area 49.0003 has only learned the loopback addresses of its local L1/L2 routers:

```
user@Chablis> show route terse protocol isis

inet.0: 14 destinations, 14 routes (14 active, 0 holddown, 0 hidden)
+ = Active Route, - = Last Active, * = Both

A Destination        P Prf   Metric 1   Metric 2  Next hop          AS path
* 0.0.0.0/0          I  15       10                192.168.50.1
                                                  >192.168.49.1
* 192.168.0.5/32     I  15       10               >192.168.49.1
* 192.168.0.6/32     I  15       10               >192.168.50.1
```

We use a routing policy on the L1/L2 routers to advertise the Level 2 routes to the Level 1 area. The policy, *adv-L2-to-L1*, locates all IS-IS routes in the routing table learned by using the Level 2 database. We verify that these routes should only be advertised to the Level 1 LSP with the to level 1 syntax. This step is highly recommended since we can only apply our policy at the global IS-IS configuration hierarchy. Finally, we have the policy accept the routes for inclusion in the LSP. The policy is currently configured on the Muscat router as:

```
[edit]
user@Muscat# show policy-options
policy-statement adv-L2-to-L1 {
```

```
    term level-2-routes {
        from {
            protocol isis;
            level 2;
        }
        to level 1;
        then accept;
    }
}
```

We then apply the policy to the IS-IS configuration on Muscat. After committing our configuration, we check the Level 1 LSP generated by Muscat and look for the Level 2 routes:

user@Muscat> **show isis database level 1 Muscat.00-00 detail**
<u>IS-IS level 1 link-state database:</u>

```
Muscat.00-00  Sequence: 0x60, Checksum: 0x12be, Lifetime: 1191 secs
    IS neighbor:                 Muscat.03  Metric:       10
    IP prefix:            172.16.64.0/24 Metric:       50 External Down
    IP prefix:            172.16.65.0/24 Metric:       50 External Down
    IP prefix:            172.16.66.0/24 Metric:       50 External Down
    IP prefix:            172.16.67.0/24 Metric:       50 External Down
    IP prefix:           192.168.0.1/32 Metric:       20 Internal Down
    IP prefix:           192.168.0.2/32 Metric:       30 Internal Down
    IP prefix:           192.168.0.3/32 Metric:       10 Internal Down
    IP prefix:           192.168.0.4/32 Metric:       30 Internal Down
    IP prefix:           192.168.0.5/32 Metric:        0 Internal Up
    IP prefix:           192.168.1.0/24 Metric:       20 Internal Down
    IP prefix:           192.168.3.0/24 Metric:       40 Internal Down
    IP prefix:           192.168.4.0/24 Metric:       50 Internal Down
    IP prefix:           192.168.5.0/24 Metric:       30 Internal Down
    IP prefix:          192.168.16.1/32 Metric:       30 Internal Down
    IP prefix:          192.168.17.0/24 Metric:       30 Internal Down
    IP prefix:          192.168.18.0/24 Metric:       40 Internal Down
    IP prefix:          192.168.32.1/32 Metric:       20 Internal Down
    IP prefix:          192.168.33.0/24 Metric:       20 Internal Down
    IP prefix:          192.168.34.0/24 Metric:       30 Internal Down
    IP prefix:          192.168.49.0/24 Metric:       10 Internal Up
```

The larger number of routes present in Muscat's Level 1 LSP shows that the route leaking policy is working as expected. Specifically, the loopback address of the Shiraz router

(192.168.16.1) is included in the LSP. This allows the Level 1 router of Chablis to have an explicit route in its routing table for this address:

```
user@Chablis> show route 192.168.16.1

inet.0: 32 destinations, 32 routes (32 active, 0 holddown, 0 hidden)
+ = Active Route, - = Last Active, * = Both

192.168.16.1/32    *[IS-IS/18] 00:04:16, metric 40
                   > to 192.168.49.1 via fe-0/0/2.0
```

If we follow Muscat's Level 1 LSP through the area, it also arrives in the database of the Chardonnay router. It is at this point that we see the benefit of using the Up/Down bit in our TLVs. Under normal circumstances, an internal Level 1 IS-IS route is automatically injected into the Level 2 LSP of the L1/L2 router. Performing this default function while leaking routes might cause a routing loop in the network. The addition of the Up/Down bit prevents this from occurring. The leaked routes in Muscat's Level 1 LSP all have the Up/Down bit set to the value 1 (**Down**). This informs Chardonnay that these are leaked routes from Level 2 and that they should not be advertised back to the Level 2 database. We verify that the Level 2 LSP from Chardonnay doesn't contain the 192.168.16.1 route:

```
user@Chardonnay> show isis database level 2 Chardonnay.00-00 detail
IS-IS level 2 link-state database:

Chardonnay.00-00  Sequence: 0x64, Checksum: 0xffe1, Lifetime: 497 secs
   IS neighbor:              Cabernet.02  Metric:     10
   IP prefix:          172.16.64.0/24 Metric:      0 External Up
   IP prefix:          172.16.65.0/24 Metric:      0 External Up
   IP prefix:          172.16.66.0/24 Metric:      0 External Up
   IP prefix:          172.16.67.0/24 Metric:      0 External Up
   IP prefix:          192.168.0.5/32 Metric:     20 Internal Up
   IP prefix:          192.168.0.6/32 Metric:      0 Internal Up
   IP prefix:          192.168.4.0/24 Metric:     10 Internal Up
   IP prefix:          192.168.48.1/32 Metric:    10 Internal Up
   IP prefix:          192.168.49.0/24 Metric:     20 Internal Up
   IP prefix:          192.168.50.0/24 Metric:     10 Internal Up
```

As we expected, the route is not present in Chardonnay's Level 2 LSP. Some additional routing information is not included in this LSP as well—namely the 172.16.48.0 /20 external routes injected by the Chablis router. In fact, these Level 1 external routes are not present in any Level 2 LSP. We verify this on the Cabernet router where the 172.16.32.0 /20 routes should appear from area 49.0002:

```
user@Cabernet> show isis database level 2 Cabernet.00-00 detail
IS-IS level 2 link-state database:
```

```
Cabernet.00-00  Sequence: 0x64, Checksum: 0x9834, Lifetime: 939 secs
   IS neighbor:                 Cabernet.02  Metric:       10
   IS neighbor:                 Cabernet.04  Metric:       10
   IP prefix:          192.168.0.3/32 Metric:       20 Internal Up
   IP prefix:          192.168.0.4/32 Metric:        0 Internal Up
   IP prefix:          192.168.3.0/24 Metric:       10 Internal Up
   IP prefix:          192.168.4.0/24 Metric:       10 Internal Up
   IP prefix:          192.168.32.1/32 Metric:      10 Internal Up
   IP prefix:          192.168.33.0/24 Metric:      20 Internal Up
   IP prefix:          192.168.34.0/24 Metric:      10 Internal Up
```

These prefixes are in the Level 1 database as advertised by the Chianti router:

```
user@Cabernet> show isis database level 1 Chianti.00-00 detail
IS-IS level 1 link-state database:

Chianti.00-00  Sequence: 0x61, Checksum: 0x1f37, Lifetime: 878 secs
   IS neighbor:                 Cabernet.03  Metric:       10
   IS neighbor:                 Chianti.02   Metric:       10
   IP prefix:          172.16.32.0/24 Metric:        0 External Up
   IP prefix:          172.16.33.0/24 Metric:        0 External Up
   IP prefix:          172.16.34.0/24 Metric:        0 External Up
   IP prefix:          172.16.35.0/24 Metric:        0 External Up
   IP prefix:          192.168.32.1/32 Metric:       0 Internal Up
   IP prefix:          192.168.33.0/24 Metric:      10 Internal Up
   IP prefix:          192.168.34.0/24 Metric:      10 Internal Up
```

The Up/Down bit is set to Up for these routes, making them eligible for a route leaking policy. The **adv-L1-to-L2** policy is created on Cabernet to locate all Level 1 IS-IS routes and advertise them to Level 2. It currently is configured as:

```
[edit]
user@Cabernet# show policy-options
policy-statement adv-L1-to-L2 {
    term level-1-routes {
        from {
            protocol isis;
            level 1;
        }
        to level 2;
        then accept;
    }
}
```

We apply the policy to the global IS-IS hierarchy level on Cabernet and verify the advertisement of the routes in the Level 2 LSP:

```
user@Cabernet> show isis database level 2 Cabernet.00-00 detail
IS-IS level 2 link-state database:

Cabernet.00-00  Sequence: 0x66, Checksum: 0xfb7, Lifetime: 1188 secs
    IS neighbor:              Cabernet.02  Metric:       10
    IS neighbor:              Cabernet.04  Metric:       10
    IP prefix:            172.16.32.0/24 Metric:       10 External Up
    IP prefix:            172.16.33.0/24 Metric:       10 External Up
    IP prefix:            172.16.34.0/24 Metric:       10 External Up
    IP prefix:            172.16.35.0/24 Metric:       10 External Up
    IP prefix:            192.168.0.3/32 Metric:       20 Internal Up
    IP prefix:            192.168.0.4/32 Metric:        0 Internal Up
    IP prefix:            192.168.3.0/24 Metric:       10 Internal Up
    IP prefix:            192.168.4.0/24 Metric:       10 Internal Up
    IP prefix:           192.168.32.1/32 Metric:       10 Internal Up
    IP prefix:           192.168.33.0/24 Metric:       20 Internal Up
    IP prefix:           192.168.34.0/24 Metric:       10 Internal Up
```

The Level 2 routers in the network, like Merlot, now have explicit routes to the 172.16.32.0 /20 address space:

```
user@Merlot> show route 172.16.32/20

inet.0: 38 destinations, 38 routes (38 active, 0 holddown, 0 hidden)
Restart Complete
+ = Active Route, - = Last Active, * = Both

172.16.32.0/24      *[IS-IS/165] 00:02:39, metric 30
                     > to 192.168.5.2 via fe-0/0/0.0
172.16.33.0/24      *[IS-IS/165] 00:02:39, metric 30
                     > to 192.168.5.2 via fe-0/0/0.0
172.16.34.0/24      *[IS-IS/165] 00:02:39, metric 30
                     > to 192.168.5.2 via fe-0/0/0.0
172.16.35.0/24      *[IS-IS/165] 00:02:39, metric 30
                     > to 192.168.5.2 via fe-0/0/0.0
```

Also recall that we have a route leaking policy applied on the Muscat router in area 49.0003 that advertises Level 2 routes to Level 1. The routes in the 172.16.32.0 /20 address range are now being included in the Level 2 LSP of Cabernet. This means that they arrive in the Level 2 database of the Muscat router and are eligible for the route leaking policy configured there. In the end, the Level 1 router of Chablis installs explicit routes in its routing table for this address space:

```
user@Muscat> show isis database level 2 Cabernet.00-00 detail
IS-IS level 2 link-state database:

Cabernet.00-00  Sequence: 0x66, Checksum: 0xfb7, Lifetime: 870 secs
    IS neighbor:               Cabernet.02  Metric:      10
    IS neighbor:               Cabernet.04  Metric:      10
    IP prefix:            172.16.32.0/24 Metric:      10 External Up
    IP prefix:            172.16.33.0/24 Metric:      10 External Up
    IP prefix:            172.16.34.0/24 Metric:      10 External Up
    IP prefix:            172.16.35.0/24 Metric:      10 External Up
    IP prefix:            192.168.0.3/32 Metric:      20 Internal Up
    IP prefix:            192.168.0.4/32 Metric:       0 Internal Up
    IP prefix:            192.168.3.0/24 Metric:      10 Internal Up
    IP prefix:            192.168.4.0/24 Metric:      10 Internal Up
    IP prefix:          192.168.32.1/32 Metric:      10 Internal Up
    IP prefix:          192.168.33.0/24 Metric:      20 Internal Up
    IP prefix:          192.168.34.0/24 Metric:      10 Internal Up

user@Muscat> show isis database level 1 Muscat.00-00 detail
IS-IS level 1 link-state database:

Muscat.00-00  Sequence: 0x62, Checksum: 0x731c, Lifetime: 866 secs
    IS neighbor:               Muscat.03  Metric:      10
    IP prefix:            172.16.32.0/24 Metric:      50 External Down
    IP prefix:            172.16.33.0/24 Metric:      50 External Down
    IP prefix:            172.16.34.0/24 Metric:      50 External Down
    IP prefix:            172.16.35.0/24 Metric:      50 External Down
    IP prefix:            172.16.64.0/24 Metric:      50 External Down
    IP prefix:            172.16.65.0/24 Metric:      50 External Down
    IP prefix:            172.16.66.0/24 Metric:      50 External Down
    IP prefix:            172.16.67.0/24 Metric:      50 External Down
    IP prefix:            192.168.0.1/32 Metric:      20 Internal Down
    IP prefix:            192.168.0.2/32 Metric:      30 Internal Down
    IP prefix:            192.168.0.3/32 Metric:      10 Internal Down
    IP prefix:            192.168.0.4/32 Metric:      30 Internal Down
    IP prefix:            192.168.0.5/32 Metric:       0 Internal Up
    IP prefix:            192.168.1.0/24 Metric:      20 Internal Down
```

```
IP prefix:                  192.168.3.0/24 Metric:     40 Internal Down
IP prefix:                  192.168.4.0/24 Metric:     50 Internal Down
IP prefix:                  192.168.5.0/24 Metric:     30 Internal Down
IP prefix:                 192.168.16.1/32 Metric:     30 Internal Down
IP prefix:                 192.168.17.0/24 Metric:     30 Internal Down
IP prefix:                 192.168.18.0/24 Metric:     40 Internal Down
IP prefix:                 192.168.32.1/32 Metric:     20 Internal Down
IP prefix:                 192.168.33.0/24 Metric:     20 Internal Down
IP prefix:                 192.168.34.0/24 Metric:     30 Internal Down
IP prefix:                 192.168.49.0/24 Metric:     10 Internal Up
```

```
user@Chablis> show route 172.16.32/20

inet.0: 36 destinations, 36 routes (36 active, 0 holddown, 0 hidden)
+ = Active Route, - = Last Active, * = Both

172.16.32.0/24      *[IS-IS/165] 00:05:52, metric 60
                     > to 192.168.49.1 via fe-0/0/2.0
172.16.33.0/24      *[IS-IS/165] 00:05:52, metric 60
                     > to 192.168.49.1 via fe-0/0/2.0
172.16.34.0/24      *[IS-IS/165] 00:05:52, metric 60
                     > to 192.168.49.1 via fe-0/0/2.0
172.16.35.0/24      *[IS-IS/165] 00:05:52, metric 60
                     > to 192.168.49.1 via fe-0/0/2.0
```

Address Summarization

The summarization of addresses in a link-state protocol occurs only when information is moved from one database structure into another. In an IS-IS network, this location is the L1/L2 router. This natural boundary point is the logical location for summarizing routing information. The IS-IS protocol specifications do not reference an inherent method for summarization, which results in the lack of a syntax keyword similar to the OSPF area-range command. In its place, the JUNOS software uses routing policies to summarize routes and announce them across the level boundary point. In fact, much of our discussion in the "Multilevel IS-IS" section earlier contained an examination of the routing table and a view of how that information was advertised in an LSP. This reliance on the contents of the routing table dovetails nicely with the use of routing policies.

Three main categories of routes are available for summarization in an IS-IS network: internal Level 1 routes advertised to Level 2; external Level 1 routes advertised to Level 2; and Level 2 routes advertised to Level 1. While each category shares a similar configuration, let's explore each of these groups separately.

Internal Level 1 Routes

The effectiveness of summarizing internal Level 1 routes is greatly dependent on the method of allocating your internal address space. If portions of your address block are not contiguous within each level, you'll find it challenging to create a summarization scheme that greatly reduces the number of routes in the Level 2 backbone. Using our sample network in Figure 3.24, we see that the internal Level 1 routes in area 49.0001 fall into the address range of 192.168.16.0 /20:

```
user@Merlot> show isis database level 1 detail
IS-IS level 1 link-state database:

Merlot.00-00  Sequence: 0x71, Checksum: 0x806, Lifetime: 1195 secs
   IS neighbor:                 Shiraz.00  Metric:       10
   IP prefix:             192.168.17.0/24 Metric:       10 Internal Up


Sangiovese.00-00  Sequence: 0x6c, Checksum: 0x98cc, Lifetime: 1169 secs
   IS neighbor:                 Shiraz.00  Metric:       10
   IP prefix:             192.168.18.0/24 Metric:       10 Internal Up


Shiraz.00-00  Sequence: 0x6d, Checksum: 0x2b52, Lifetime: 528 secs
   IS neighbor:                 Merlot.00  Metric:       10
   IS neighbor:             Sangiovese.00  Metric:       10
   IP prefix:               172.16.3.0/24 Metric:        0 External Up
   IP prefix:              172.16.16.0/24 Metric:        0 External Up
   IP prefix:              172.16.17.0/24 Metric:        0 External Up
   IP prefix:              172.16.18.0/24 Metric:        0 External Up
   IP prefix:              172.16.19.0/24 Metric:        0 External Up
   IP prefix:             192.168.16.1/32 Metric:        0 Internal Up
   IP prefix:             192.168.17.0/24 Metric:       10 Internal Up
   IP prefix:             192.168.18.0/24 Metric:       10 Internal Up

user@Merlot> show route 192.168.16/20


inet.0: 38 destinations, 38 routes (38 active, 0 holddown, 0 hidden)
Restart Complete
+ = Active Route, - = Last Active, * = Both
```

```
192.168.16.1/32    *[IS-IS/15] 21:47:36, metric 10
                    > to 192.168.17.2 via so-0/1/0.0
192.168.17.0/24    *[Direct/0] 21:51:40
                    > via so-0/1/0.0
192.168.17.1/32    *[Local/0] 21:51:40
                      Local via so-0/1/0.0
192.168.18.0/24    *[IS-IS/15] 00:00:29, metric 20
                    > to 192.168.17.2 via so-0/1/0.0
```

We first create a policy, called *sum-int-L1-to-L2*, which prevents the L1/L2 routers from automatically advertising the internal Level 1 routes into the Level 2 backbone. This policy is currently configured on the Merlot router as:

```
[edit]
user@Merlot# show policy-options
policy-statement sum-int-L1-to-L2 {
    term suppress-specifics {
        from {
            route-filter 192.168.16.0/20 longer;
        }
        to level 2;
        then reject;
    }
}
```

After applying the policy to the global IS-IS hierarchy level on Merlot, we validate that its Level 2 LSP doesn't contain the internal Level 1 routes:

```
user@Merlot> show isis database level 2 Merlot.00-00 detail
IS-IS level 2 link-state database:

Merlot.00-00  Sequence: 0x77, Checksum: 0x5692, Lifetime: 1191 secs
    IS neighbor:              Merlot.02  Metric:      10
    IS neighbor:              Sangiovese.03  Metric:  10
    IP prefix:        192.168.0.1/32 Metric:      0 Internal Up
    IP prefix:        192.168.1.0/24 Metric:     10 Internal Up
    IP prefix:        192.168.5.0/24 Metric:     10 Internal Up
```

While the policy is operating as planned, we've only accomplished half the work. We now need to advertise the 192.168.16.0/20 summary route to the Level 2 backbone. The lack of a syntax command in IS-IS for summarization means that we have to manually create the summary route and use our routing policy to advertise it to IS-IS. Within the [edit routing-options] hierarchy, we create our summary route:

```
[edit routing-options]
user@Merlot# show
aggregate {
    route 192.168.16.0/20;
}
```

The ***sum-int-L1-to-L2*** policy is modified to advertise the newly created aggregate route to IS-IS. The policy now appears as so:

```
[edit]
user@Merlot# show policy-options
policy-statement sum-int-L1-to-L2 {
    term suppress-specifics {
        from {
            route-filter 192.168.16.0/20 longer;
        }
        to level 2;
        then reject;
    }
    term send-aggregate-route {
        from protocol aggregate;
        to level 2;
        then accept;
    }
}
```

Once we commit the configuration, we find the summary route advertised in the Level 2 LSP for the Merlot router:

```
user@Merlot> show isis database level 2 Merlot.00-00 detail
IS-IS level 2 link-state database:

Merlot.00-00  Sequence: 0x78, Checksum: 0x4dee, Lifetime: 1192 secs
    IS neighbor:              Merlot.02  Metric:       10
    IS neighbor:              Sangiovese.03  Metric:   10
    IP prefix:        192.168.0.1/32 Metric:        0 Internal Up
    IP prefix:        192.168.1.0/24 Metric:       10 Internal Up
    IP prefix:        192.168.5.0/24 Metric:       10 Internal Up
    IP prefix:        192.168.16.0/20 Metric:       10 External Up
```

After configuring a similar routing policy and aggregate route on Sangiovese, the other L1/L2 router in the area, we find that the rest of the Level 2 backbone routers only contain a single IS-IS route for the internal Level 1 routes from area 49.0001. We see this single route on the Riesling router:

```
user@Riesling> show route 192.168.16/20

inet.0: 28 destinations, 28 routes (28 active, 0 holddown, 0 hidden)
Restart Complete
+ = Active Route, - = Last Active, * = Both

192.168.16.0/20    *[IS-IS/165] 00:03:49, metric 20
                    > to 192.168.1.1 via fe-0/0/1.0
```

External Level 1 Routes

In the "Multilevel IS-IS" section earlier we used a routing policy to advertise external Level 1 routes to the Level 2 backbone because these routes are naturally bounded by the L1/L2 router. A similar configuration is used when we want to summarize the external Level 1 routes before advertising them. The external routes injected by the Chianti router in area 49.0002 fall within the 172.16.32.0 /20 address range:

```
user@Chianti> show isis database Chianti.00-00 detail
IS-IS level 1 link-state database:

Chianti.00-00  Sequence: 0x6a, Checksum: 0xd40, Lifetime: 1048 secs
    IS neighbor:                 Cabernet.03  Metric:      10
    IS neighbor:                 Chianti.02   Metric:      10
    IP prefix:           172.16.32.0/24 Metric:       0 External Up
    IP prefix:           172.16.33.0/24 Metric:       0 External Up
    IP prefix:           172.16.34.0/24 Metric:       0 External Up
    IP prefix:           172.16.35.0/24 Metric:       0 External Up
    IP prefix:         192.168.32.1/32 Metric:       0 Internal Up
    IP prefix:         192.168.33.0/24 Metric:      10 Internal Up
    IP prefix:         192.168.34.0/24 Metric:      10 Internal Up
```

A summary route is created on both the Riesling and Cabernet routers to represent the external Level 1 routes:

```
[edit]
user@Riesling# show routing-options
aggregate {
    route 172.16.32.0/20;
```

```
}

[edit]
user@Cabernet# show routing-options
aggregate {
    route 172.16.32.0/20;
}
```

A routing policy called ***sum-ext-L1-to-L2*** is created on both routers to advertise the locally configured aggregate route to just the Level 2 backbone. The policy appears on Riesling as:

```
[edit]
user@Riesling# show policy-options
policy-statement sum-ext-L1-to-L2 {
    term adv-aggregate {
        from protocol aggregate;
        to level 2;
        then accept;
    }
}
```

We apply the policy to IS-IS at the global configuration hierarchy level and commit the configuration. The summary route then appears in the Level 2 LSP advertised by Riesling to the backbone:

```
[edit]
user@Riesling# show protocols isis
export sum-ext-L1-to-L2;
interface fe-0/0/0.0 {
    level 1 disable;
}
interface fe-0/0/1.0 {
    level 1 disable;
}
interface fe-0/0/2.0 {
    level 2 disable;
}
interface lo0.0 {
    level 1 disable;
}

user@Riesling> show isis database level 2 Riesling.00-00 detail
IS-IS level 2 link-state database:
```

```
Riesling.00-00  Sequence: 0x6f, Checksum: 0xf115, Lifetime: 1190 secs
    IS neighbor:                    Merlot.02  Metric:      10
    IS neighbor:                    Muscat.02  Metric:      10
    IP prefix:             172.16.32.0/20 Metric:      10 External Up
    IP prefix:             192.168.0.3/32 Metric:       0 Internal Up
    IP prefix:             192.168.1.0/24 Metric:      10 Internal Up
    IP prefix:             192.168.2.0/24 Metric:      10 Internal Up
    IP prefix:            192.168.32.1/32 Metric:      10 Internal Up
    IP prefix:            192.168.33.0/24 Metric:      10 Internal Up
    IP prefix:            192.168.34.0/24 Metric:      20 Internal Up
```

We configure the Cabernet router in a similar fashion to avoid a single point of failure in the network. The remaining Level 2 routers in the network now have a single summary route of 172.16.32.0 /20 in their routing table, representing the external Level 1 routes injected by Chianti. We see this route on the Merlot router as:

```
user@Merlot> show route 172.16.32/20

inet.0: 32 destinations, 32 routes (32 active, 0 holddown, 0 hidden)
+ = Active Route, - = Last Active, * = Both

172.16.32.0/20      *[IS-IS/165] 00:03:58, metric 20
                     > to 192.168.1.2 via fe-0/0/1.0
```

Level 2 Route Summarization

As you might expect at this point, we use a routing policy to advertise a locally configured summary route to the Level 1 database to represent the native Level 2 backbone routes. The sample network in Figure 3.24 currently has Level 2 routes within the 192.168.0.0 /21 address space:

```
user@Merlot> show isis database level 2 detail
IS-IS level 2 link-state database:

Merlot.00-00  Sequence: 0x7a, Checksum: 0x49f0, Lifetime: 843 secs
    IS neighbor:                    Merlot.02  Metric:      10
    IS neighbor:                Sangiovese.03  Metric:      10
    IP prefix:             192.168.0.1/32 Metric:       0 Internal Up
    IP prefix:             192.168.1.0/24 Metric:      10 Internal Up
    IP prefix:             192.168.5.0/24 Metric:      10 Internal Up
    IP prefix:            192.168.16.0/20 Metric:      10 External Up
```

```
Sangiovese.00-00   Sequence: 0x78, Checksum: 0xbac4, Lifetime: 983 secs
    IS neighbor:                   Sangiovese.03  Metric:       10
    IS neighbor:                   Cabernet.04  Metric:         10
    IP prefix:                192.168.0.2/32 Metric:        0 Internal Up
    IP prefix:                192.168.3.0/24 Metric:       10 Internal Up
    IP prefix:                192.168.5.0/24 Metric:       10 Internal Up
    IP prefix:               192.168.16.0/20 Metric:       10 External Up

Riesling.00-00   Sequence: 0x71, Checksum: 0x39ad, Lifetime: 1134 secs
    IS neighbor:                     Merlot.02  Metric:        10
    IS neighbor:                     Muscat.02  Metric:        10
    IP prefix:                172.16.32.0/20 Metric:       10 External Up
    IP prefix:                192.168.0.3/32 Metric:        0 Internal Up
    IP prefix:                192.168.1.0/24 Metric:       10 Internal Up
    IP prefix:                192.168.2.0/24 Metric:       10 Internal Up
    IP prefix:               192.168.32.0/20 Metric:       10 External Up

Cabernet.00-00   Sequence: 0x74, Checksum: 0x8a59, Lifetime: 1141 secs
    IS neighbor:                   Cabernet.02  Metric:        10
    IS neighbor:                   Cabernet.04  Metric:        10
    IP prefix:                172.16.32.0/20 Metric:       10 External Up
    IP prefix:                192.168.0.4/32 Metric:        0 Internal Up
    IP prefix:                192.168.3.0/24 Metric:       10 Internal Up
    IP prefix:                192.168.4.0/24 Metric:       10 Internal Up
    IP prefix:               192.168.32.0/20 Metric:       10 External Up

Muscat.00-00   Sequence: 0x71, Checksum: 0x7d88, Lifetime: 1165 secs
    IS neighbor:                     Muscat.02  Metric:        10
    IP prefix:                192.168.0.5/32 Metric:        0 Internal Up
    IP prefix:                192.168.2.0/24 Metric:       10 Internal Up
    IP prefix:               192.168.48.0/20 Metric:       10 External Up

Chardonnay.00-00   Sequence: 0x73, Checksum: 0xff5b, Lifetime: 1178 secs
    IS neighbor:                   Cabernet.02  Metric:        10
    IP prefix:                192.168.0.6/32 Metric:        0 Internal Up
    IP prefix:                192.168.4.0/24 Metric:       10 Internal Up
    IP prefix:               192.168.48.0/20 Metric:       10 External Up
```

These routes are currently not advertised to the Level 1 database in area 49.0003. We see this by examining the LSP advertised by the Muscat router:

```
user@Muscat> show isis database level 1 Muscat.00-00 detail
IS-IS level 1 link-state database:
```

```
Muscat.00-00  Sequence: 0x6f, Checksum: 0xfdf2, Lifetime: 726 secs
   IS neighbor:                    Muscat.03  Metric:       10
   IP prefix:             192.168.49.0/24 Metric:      10 Internal Up
```

As before, an aggregate route is created on the L1/L2 router to represent the routes being summarized:

```
[edit]
user@Muscat# show routing-options
aggregate {
    route 192.168.48.0/20;
    route 192.168.0.0/21;
}
```

The **sum-L2-to-L1** routing policy is created on Muscat to advertise the appropriate aggregate route to just the Level 1 area. The policy is configured as so:

```
[edit]
user@Muscat# show policy-options policy-statement sum-L2-to-L1
term adv-aggregate {
    from {
        protocol aggregate;
        route-filter 192.168.0.0/21 exact;
    }
    to level 1;
    then accept;
}
```

We apply the policy to our IS-IS configuration and verify that the correct route appears in the Level 1 LSP advertised by Muscat:

```
user@Muscat> show isis database level 1 Muscat.00-00 detail
IS-IS level 1 link-state database:

Muscat.00-00  Sequence: 0x71, Checksum: 0x2931, Lifetime: 1192 secs
   IS neighbor:                    Muscat.03  Metric:       10
   IP prefix:              192.168.0.0/21 Metric:      10 External Up
   IP prefix:             192.168.49.0/24 Metric:      10 Internal Up
```

The Chablis router in area 49.0003 now has an explicit route for the Level 2 routes in its local routing table:

```
user@Chablis> show route 192.168.0/21
```

```
inet.0: 13 destinations, 13 routes (13 active, 0 holddown, 0 hidden)
+ = Active Route, - = Last Active, * = Both

192.168.0.0/21    *[IS-IS/160] 00:01:42, metric 20
                  > to 192.168.49.1 via fe-0/0/2.0
```

Summary

In this chapter, we examined the operation of the IS-IS routing protocol. We first discussed the various type, length, value (TLV) formats used to advertise information. We then explored the Shortest Path First (SPF) algorithm and saw how it calculates the path to each destination in the network.

We then discussed some configuration options available within the JUNOS software for use with IS-IS. We first saw how graceful restart can help mitigate churn in a network. A look at interface metrics and authentication options followed. We then explored how a mesh group operates by reducing the flooding of LSPs. This was followed by the use of the overload bit in the network.

We concluded the chapter with an exploration of how IS-IS operates in a multilevel configuration. We saw how reachability was attained for each router in the network and the default flooding rules for routes from different levels. We then discussed methods for altering the default flooding rules using routing policies to leak routes between levels. Finally, we learned how to summarize routes in an IS-IS network using locally configured aggregate routes and routing policies.

Exam Essentials

Be able to identify the uses of the various IS-IS PDUs.   IS-IS routers use Hello PDUs to form and maintain adjacencies with other routers in the network. Link-state PDUs contain information that populates the database. Each router generates an LSP for each operational level and floods that LSP into the network. Sequence number PDUs are used to request database information from a neighbor and to maintain the integrity of the database.

Be able to list the TLVs used by an IS-IS router.   An individual IS-IS uses several TLVs to describe portions of the network. Each PDU contains a separate, and somewhat different, set of TLVs. Some TLVs describe the local configuration of the router, while others advertise adjacencies. Still others include IP routing information advertised to the network by the local router.

Be able to describe the difference between an IS-IS area and an IS-IS level.   An IS-IS area only controls the adjacency formation process. A Level 1 router only forms an adjacency with another router in the same area, whereas a Level 2 router forms an adjacency with a router in any area. An IS-IS level controls the flooding of LSPs. Level 2 LSPs are flooded across a contiguous set of Level 2 areas; a Level 1 LSP is normally flooded within its own Level 1 area.

Know the authentication options available for use in the JUNOS software. The JUNOS software supports both plain-text (simple) and MD5 authentication within the confines of the IS-IS protocol. The configuration of authentication at the level hierarchy causes the authentication TLV to be placed into all PDUs generated by the router. The local router can also "secure" just the Hello PDUs transmitted on a specific interface to control which neighbors it forms an adjacency with.

Be able to describe the operation of a multilevel IS-IS network. Internal Level 1 routes are flooded throughout the area providing each router with knowledge of the Level 1 topology. These routes are advertised by an L1/L2 router into the Level 2 backbone, which provides the entire level with knowledge of all routes in the network. Routers in the Level 1 area reach unknown destinations through a locally installed default route pointing to the metrically closest attached Level 2 router. These Level 2 routers set the Attached bit in their Level 1 LSPs when they form a Level 2 adjacency across an area boundary.

Be able to configure address summarization within IS-IS. To effectively summarize addresses in IS-IS, you use a combination of locally configured aggregate routes and routing policies. Each aggregate route represents the addresses you wish to summarize. You then create and apply routing policies that locate the aggregate routes and advertise them into the specific level you desire.

Review Questions

1. Which IS-IS TLV reports adjacencies to neighboring systems in the network?

    A. IS reachability

    B. IS neighbors

    C. IP internal reachability

    D. IP external reachability

2. Which IS-IS TLV is used to support TE extensions that advertise information about available and reserved bandwidth in the network?

    A. IS reachability

    B. Extended IS reachability

    C. IP internal reachability

    D. Extended IP reachability

3. Which IS-IS TLV supports the use of wide metrics for connected IP subnets?

    A. IP internal reachability

    B. IP external reachability

    C. IP interface address

    D. Extended IP reachability

4. Which IS-IS software feature is supported through the use of TLV 10?

    A. Authentication

    B. Wide metrics

    C. Graceful restart

    D. Route leaking

5. What is the default lifetime given to all LSPs in the JUNOS software?

    A. 1200 seconds

    B. 2400 seconds

    C. 3600 seconds

    D. 4800 seconds

6. Which configuration statement configures a plain-text password of **test-password** for all PDUs transmitted by the router?

   A. `set protocols isis authentication-type simple authentication-key` **test-password**

   B. `set protocols isis authentication-type plain-text authentication-key` **test-password**

   C. `set protocols isis level 2 authentication-type simple authentication-key` **test-password**

   D. `set protocols isis level 2 authentication-type plain-text` `authentication-key` **test-password**

7. What is the largest metric able to be advertised in the IS-IS IP internal reachability TLV?

   A. 10

   B. 63

   C. 1023

   D. 16,777,215

8. What IS-IS software feature reduces the flooding of LSPs in the network?

   A. Attached bit

   B. Mesh groups

   C. Multi-level configuration

   D. Overload bit

9. How does an IS-IS Level 1 internal router reach IP prefixes native to the Level 2 backbone?

   A. It has an explicit route for each Level 2 prefix.

   B. It has a summary route representing all Level 2 prefixes.

   C. It receives a default route in the Level 1 LSP from an attached L1/L2 router.

   D. It installs a local default route based on the attached bit in the Level 1 LSP from an L1/L2 router.

10. Which term describes the advertisement of prefixes in an IS-IS network from a Level 2 area into a Level 1 area?

   A. Route summarization

   B. Route leaking

   C. Route announcements

   D. None of the above

Answers to Review Questions

1. A. Of the options given, only the IS reachability TLV reports an adjacency with a neighbor router. The IS neighbors TLV is used to report the MAC address of neighboring systems in a Hello PDU. Both the IP internal and IP external reachability TLVs report IP routing information, not adjacency status.

2. B. Information concerning available and reserved bandwidth in the network is carried in sub-TLVs encoded within the extended IS reachability TLV.

3. D. The extended IP reachability TLV uses a 32-bit address space to support interface metrics between 0 and 16,777,215.

4. A. TLV 10 is the authentication TLV, which is used to secure and verify the transmission and reception of PDUs in an IS-IS network.

5. A. Each new LSP created within the JUNOS software is given a lifetime value of 1200 seconds, which then counts down to 0. The local router refreshes its own LSPs when the lifetime reaches approximately 317 seconds.

6. C. Only option C correctly configures a plain-text (`simple`) password for all transmitted PDUs. The configuration must occur at the level portion of the configuration hierarchy, which eliminates options A and B. Option D uses the incorrect syntax of `plain-text` for the `authentication-type` command.

7. B. The IP internal reachability TLV uses 6 bits to represent the metric value. This means the maximum metric value is 63.

8. B. By default, an IS-IS router refloods a received LSP to all adjacent neighbors, except for the neighbor it received it from. In a fully meshed environment, this behavior can cause excess flooding. Using mesh groups reduces this excess by informing the local router which interfaces to not flood the LSP on.

9. D. When an L1/L2 router has knowledge of another Level 2 area, it sets the Attached bit in its Level 1 LSP. All Level 1 routers receiving this LSP install a local copy of the default route pointing to the L1/L2 router.

10. B. When a routing policy is used to advertise IS-IS prefixes from a Level 2 area to a Level 1 area, it is commonly called route leaking.

Chapter

4

Border Gateway Protocol (BGP)

JNCIS EXAM OBJECTIVES COVERED IN THIS CHAPTER:

- ✓ Describe the BGP route selection process and CLI commands used to verify its operation
- ✓ Define the functions of the following BGP parameters— passive; authentication; prefix limits; multipath; multihop
- ✓ Identify the functionality and alteration of the BGP attributes
- ✓ Define the capabilities and operation of graceful restart
- ✓ Define the configuration and consequences of BGP route flap damping

In this chapter, we explore the operation of the Border Gateway Protocol (BGP) at some depth. Before beginning this chapter, you should be familiar with how two BGP routers form a TCP relationship using port 179. This reliable transport mechanism ensures that messages are received by each peer, provides for flow control capabilities, and allows for the retransmission of data packets, if necessary. BGP was designed as a reachability protocol for the Internet. As such, it supports fine-grained policy controls to limit what routes are advertised to and/or received from a peer. BGP also supports a network environment of mesh-like connectivity by preventing routing loops in the Internet. BGP peering sessions can occur within an Autonomous System (AS) or between AS networks. A session between two AS networks is referred to as an external BGP (EBGP) session, while a peering session within an AS is referred to as internal BGP (IBGP). Established peers advertise routes to each other, which are placed in the Adjacency-RIB-In table specific to that peer. The best path to each destination from the inbound RIB tables is then moved into the Local-RIB table, where it is used to forward traffic. These best routes are further placed into an Adjacency-RIB-Out table for each peer, where they are advertised to that peer in an update message.

In this chapter, we first review the format of the BGP update message used to transport reachability information. We follow this with an exhaustive examination of the BGP attributes used to define various routes and provide a description and format of each attribute. We then explore the operation of the BGP route selection algorithm and discuss some router commands available to verify its operation. We conclude this chapter with an exploration of various configuration options available to BGP. These include graceful restart, authentication, the limiting of prefixes, and the damping of unstable routes.

The BGP Update Message

Routing information in BGP is sent and withdrawn between two peers using the Update message. If needed, each message contains information previously advertised by the local router that is no longer valid. This might include a route that is no longer available or a set of attributes that has been modified. The same Update message may also contain new route information advertised to the remote peer. When the message includes new information, a single set of BGP attributes is advertised along with all the route prefixes using those attributes. This format reduces the total number of packets BGP routers send between themselves when exchanging routing knowledge.

Figure 4.1 shows the format of the Update message, including the common BGP header. The fields include the following:

Marker (16 octets)   This field is set to all 1s to detect a loss of synchronization.

Length (2 octets)   The total length of the BGP message is encoded in this field. Possible values range from 19 to 4096.

Type (1 octet)   The type of BGP message is located in this field. Five type codes have been defined:

- 1 for an Open message
- 2 for an Update message
- 3 for a Notification message
- 4 for a Keepalive message
- 5 for a Route-Refresh message

Unfeasible Routes Length (2 octets)   This field specifies the length of the Withdrawn Routes field that follows. A value of 0 designates that no routes are being withdrawn with this Update message.

Withdrawn Routes (Variable)   This field lists the routes previously announced that are now being withdrawn. Each route is encoded as a (Length, Prefix) tuple. The 1-octet length field displays the number of bits in the subnet mask, whereas the variable-length prefix field displays the IPv4 route.

Total Path Attributes Length (2 octets)   This field specifies the length of the Path Attributes field that follows. A value of 0 designates that no routes are being advertised with this Update message.

Path Attributes (Variable)   The attributes of the path advertisement are contained in this field. Each attribute is encoded as a (Type, Length, Value), or TLV, triple.

Network Layer Reachability Information (Variable)   This field lists the routes advertised to the remote peer. Each route is encoded as a (Length, Prefix) tuple, where the length is the number of bits in the subnet mask and the prefix is the IPv4 route.

FIGURE 4.1   The BGP Update message

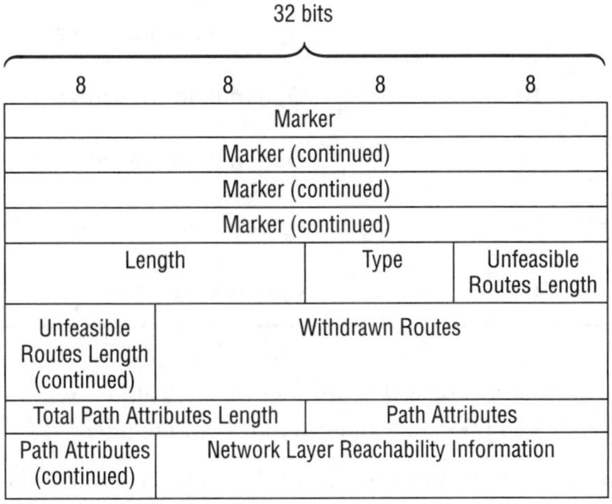

The BGP Update message

BGP Attributes

The attributes associated with each BGP route are very important to the operation of the protocol. They are used to select the single version of the route, which is placed into the local router's routing table. They can also be used to filter out unwanted announcements from a peer or be modified in an attempt to influence a routing decision for a peer. Table 4.1 displays some common BGP attributes.

TABLE 4.1   Common BGP Attributes

Attribute Name	Attribute Code	Attribute Type
Origin	1	Well-known mandatory
AS Path	2	Well-known mandatory
Next Hop	3	Well-known mandatory
Multiple Exit Discriminator	4	Optional nontransitive
Local Preference	5	Well-known discretionary
Atomic Aggregate	6	Well-known discretionary
Aggregator	7	Optional transitive
Community	8	Optional transitive
Originator ID	9	Optional nontransitive
Cluster List	10	Optional nontransitive
Multiprotocol Reachable NLRI	14	Optional nontransitive
Multiprotocol Unreachable NLRI	15	Optional nontransitive
Extended Community	16	Optional transitive

Each attribute in the Update message encodes the information in Table 4.1 within the 2-octet Attribute Type portion of its TLV. The possible values in that field include:

Optional Bit (Bit 0)   An attribute is either well known (a value of 0) or optional (a value of 1).

Transitive Bit (Bit 1)   Optional attributes can be either nontransitive (a value of 0) or transitive (a value of 1). Well-known attributes are always transitive.

Partial Bit (Bit 2) Only optional transitive attributes use this bit. A 0 value means each BGP router along the path recognized this attribute. A value of 1 means that at least one BGP router along the path did not recognize the attribute.

Extended Length Bit (Bit 3) This bit sets the size of the Attribute Length field in the TLV to 1 octet (a value of 0) or 2 octets (a value of 1).

Unused (Bits 4–7) These bit positions are not used and must be set to 0.

Type Code (Bits 8–15) The specific kind of attribute is encoded in this 1-octet field. The available type codes are found in Table 4.1.

The interaction of the BGP attributes is one main reason why network engineers feel that there is a steep learning curve associated with understanding BGP. Let's explore each of the commonly used attributes in further detail.

Origin

The *Origin* code, type code 1, is a well-known, mandatory attribute that must be supported by all BGP implementations and that is included in every BGP update.

The router that first injects the route into BGP attaches the Origin attribute as a measure of believability related to the origin of the particular route. The values available for the Origin attribute include IGP, EGP, or incomplete. The IGP (abbreviated I) origin is a tag designated for all routes learned through a traditional interior gateway protocol such as Open Shortest Path First (OSPF), Intermediate System to Intermediate System (IS-IS), or Routing Information Protocol (RIP). The EGP (abbreviated E) origin is a tag designated for routes learned through the original exterior gateway protocol, which is called Exterior Gateway Protocol (EGP). The last origin of incomplete (abbreviated ?) is a tag designated for all routes that do not fall into either the IGP or EGP categories.

Each of the tags is assigned a numerical value for use in transmitting the attribute to other BGP speakers. An origin of IGP has a value of 0, EGP is assigned a value of 1, and unknown origins (incomplete) are assigned a value of 2. When the attribute is used in the BGP route selection algorithm, a lower value is preferred, so routes learned from an IGP are selected over routes learned from an EGP. In turn, EGP routes are better than unknown, incomplete routes.

The format of the Origin attribute is shown in Figure 4.2. The fields of the attribute include:

Attribute Type (2 octets) This 2-octet field encodes information concerning the Origin attribute. The Optional bit is set to a value of 0 and the Transitive bit is set to a value of 1. These settings signify that this as a well-known attribute. The type code bits are set to a constant value of 0x01.

Attribute Length (Variable) This variable-length field is 1 octet long for the Origin attribute. Therefore, the Extended bit in the Attribute Type field is set to a value of 0.

The Origin attribute places a constant value of 1 in this field.

Origin (1 octet) This field contains the origin value assigned to the route. The possible values are 0 (IGP), 1 (EGP), and 2 (incomplete).

FIGURE 4.2 BGP Origin attribute

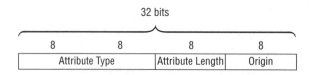

AS Path

All BGP implementations must support the *AS Path* attribute, type code 2. This well-known, mandatory attribute must be included in every BGP update.

The AS Path attribute contains the information required for a BGP router to perform route selection and install a usable route in the routing table to the destination. The attribute is modified across an EBGP peering session as a particular route exits the AS. At this point, the AS number of the system advertising the route is prepended to the beginning of the attribute. By default, each AS is viewed as a single hop from the perspective of a BGP router.

The attribute is used as a tiebreaker in the BGP route selection algorithm, with a shorter path length being preferred. For example, the AS Path 65111 65222 has a path length of 2. The path 65111 65222 65333 has a length of 3 and the path 65444 has a length of 1. Of the three examples, the shortest path length is 1, so the local router prefers the AS Path of 65444.

Figure 4.3 shows the fields of the AS Path attribute:

Attribute Type (2 octets)   This 2-octet field encodes information about the AS Path attribute. The Optional bit is set to a value of 0 and the Transitive bit is set to a value of 1. These settings signify that this as a well-known attribute. The type code bits are set to a constant value of 0x02.

Attribute Length (Variable)   This variable-length field can be either 1 or 2 octets long, depending on the number of AS values encoded in the path.

AS Path Segments (Variable)   This AS Path value can consist of multiple segments, with each segment representing either an ordered or an unordered list of values. Each of the segments is encoded using a TLV format as follows:

Segment Type (1 octet)   This field details whether the segment is an AS Set or an AS Sequence. A value of 1 in the type field represents an unordered set of AS values—an *AS Set*. A value of 2 represents an *AS Sequence*, or an ordered sequence of AS values. By default, all AS values are contained in an AS Sequence format.

Segment Length (1 octet)   This field displays the length of the Segment Value field that follows. Each AS number is encoded using 2 octets, so the total number of values in the path can be inferred from this field.

Segment Value (Variable)   This field contains the actual AS values being advertised. Each AS is encoded in its own 2-octet field.

 Additional segment types are defined for use in a BGP confederation, which we discuss in Chapter 5, "Advanced Border Gateway Protocol (BGP)."

FIGURE 4.3   BGP AS Path attribute

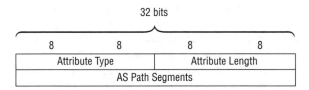

Next Hop

The *Next Hop* attribute, type code 3, is also a well-known mandatory attribute. As such, each BGP router must understand the attribute and include it in every BGP update.

The Next Hop attribute, often referred to as the *BGP Next Hop*, is the IP address of the next hop router along the path to the destination. Each BGP router performs a recursive lookup in its local routing table to locate an active route to the BGP Next Hop. The result of this recursive lookup becomes the physical next hop assigned to the BGP route. Reachability to the BGP Next Hop is critical to the operation of BGP. Without it, the advertised routes are not usable by the local router.

The attribute is only modified, by default, when a route is advertised across an EBGP peering session. This might cause reachability problems within an AS when the route is advertised to an IBGP peer. Possible solutions to this problem include setting the Next Hop address via a routing policy, using an IGP passive interface, using a routing policy to advertise connected interface routes, establishing an IGP adjacency across the AS boundary, or using static routes within your AS. For the remainder of the chapter, we alter the value of the Next Hop attribute with a routing policy.

The fields of the Next Hop attribute are shown in Figure 4.4:

Attribute Type (2 octets)   Information about the Next Hop attribute is included in this 2-octet field. As a well-known attribute, the Optional bit is set to a value of 0 and the Transitive bit is set to a value of 1. The type code bits are set to a constant value of 0x03.

Attribute Length (Variable)   This variable-length field is 1 octet long for the Next Hop attribute and contains a constant value of 4. This means that the Extended bit in the Attribute Type field is set to a value of 0.

Next Hop (4 octets)   This field contains the IP address of the BGP Next Hop for the advertised route.

FIGURE 4.4   BGP Next Hop attribute

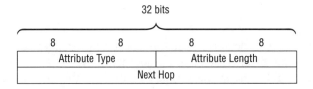

Multiple Exit Discriminator

The *Multiple Exit Discriminator (MED)* attribute, type code 4, is an optional, nontransitive attribute of BGP. As such, a BGP implementation doesn't have to understand or use this attribute at all. Those that do, however, retain it only within the borders of a particular AS. This means that a MED attribute received from an EBGP peer is advertised to all IBGP peers, who may use the encoded value. MED values received from IBGP peers, however, are not readvertised to an EBGP peer. In other words, the router on the edge of the AS removes the attribute prior to sending the route.

 The JUNOS software interprets the absence of the attribute as a MED value of 0.

The MED attribute is a form of a routing metric assigned to BGP routes. The function of the attribute is to assist a neighboring AS in selecting a network link to forward traffic across when sending traffic to the local AS. This assumes that multiple network links exist between the two neighboring systems.

Figure 4.5 displays the fields of the MED attribute:

Attribute Type (2 octets)   This 2-octet field encodes information relevant to the MED attribute. The Optional bit is set to a value of 1 and the Transitive bit is set to a value of 0, designating the MED attribute as optional and nontransitive. The type code bits are set to a constant value of 0x04.

Attribute Length (Variable)   This variable-length field is 1 octet long for the MED attribute; the Extended bit in the Attribute Type field is set to a value of 0. A constant value of 4 is placed in this field.

Multiple Exit Discriminator (4 octets)   This field contains the MED value currently assigned to the route. Possible values range from 0 to 4,294,967,295.

FIGURE 4.5   BGP MED attribute

Local Preference

The *Local Preference* attribute, type code 5, is a well-known discretionary attribute. All BGP implementations must understand the attribute, but it is not required to be present on every advertised route. In fact, the Local Preference value is only used within the confines of a single AS and is never advertised to an EBGP peer.

The attribute is typically used to set the preferred exit point out of the AS for a particular route. Two factors make the Local Preference attribute well suited for this task. First, each router within the AS has the attribute assigned to all routes. Second, the attribute is the first tiebreaker in the BGP route selection algorithm. This allows each BGP router in the network to make the same routing decision.

The Local Preference attribute is displayed in Figure 4.6. The fields of the attribute are:

Attribute Type (2 octets) The Local Preference attribute is well known, which requires that this field encode the Optional bit to the value 0 and the Transitive bit to the value 1. The type code bits are set to a constant value of 0x05.

Attribute Length (Variable) This variable-length field is 1 octet long for the Local Preference attribute. As such, the Extended bit in the Attribute Type field is set to a value of 0. A constant value of 4 is placed in this field.

Local Preference (4 octets) This field contains the Local Preference value currently assigned to the route. All routes receive a default value of 100, but possible values range from 0 to 4,294,967,295.

FIGURE 4.6 BGP Local Preference attribute

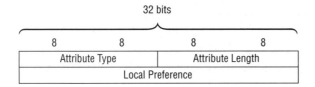

Atomic Aggregate

The *Atomic Aggregate* attribute, type code 6, is a well-known discretionary attribute. As with the Local Preference attribute, each BGP router must understand the attribute, but it is not required to be present in every BGP update. The Atomic Aggregate attribute is designed as a notification to other BGP routers in the Internet that an aggregate (less specific) route was selected over a more specific route. In addition, some of the BGP attributes of the more specific route are not included in the aggregate's advertisement.

As an example, suppose that a BGP router in AS 65000 receives the route 192.168.1.0 /24 from a peer in AS 65333 and the route 192.168.0.0 /16 from a peer in AS 65444. In essence, these two routes overlap each other since the /24 route is a subset of the /16 route. A BGP router then has a choice regarding which of the routes to install in its local routing table. If the less specific 192.168.0.0 /16 route is the only route installed, then the local router must attach the Atomic Aggregate attribute to the route before readvertising it. Routers that install this announcement see an AS Path of 65000 65444. The attribute, however, alerts those routers that packets sent to the 192.168.0.0 /16 address space might not traverse the included AS networks. In this particular case, packets to the 192.168.1.0 /24 network traverse AS 65333.

The JUNOS software installs every unique route in its local routing table. This means that a less specific route is never selected over a more specific route. Hence, the Atomic Aggregate attribute is not attached to any route, by default, on a Juniper Networks router.

The fields of the Atomic Aggregate attribute are shown in Figure 4.7. Because this attribute is only designed as a notification to other BGP routers, no value is included with the attribute.

Attribute Type (2 octets)   This 2-octet field contains information relevant to the Atomic Aggregate attribute. As a well-known attribute, the Optional bit is set to a value of 0 and the Transitive bit is set to a value of 1. The type code bits are set to a constant value of 0x06.

Attribute Length (Variable)   This variable-length field is 1 octet long for the Atomic Aggregate attribute and contains a constant value of 0.

FIGURE 4.7   BGP Atomic Aggregate attribute

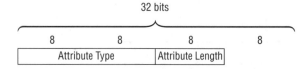

Aggregator

The *Aggregator* attribute, type code 7, is an optional transitive attribute of BGP. This means that an individual BGP implementation doesn't have to understand or use the attribute at all. However, the attribute must be advertised across all AS boundaries and remain attached to the BGP route.

The attribute is designed as a method of alerting other BGP routers where route aggregation occurred. The Aggregator attribute contains the AS number and the router ID of the router that performed the aggregation. Within the JUNOS software, this attribute is assigned to a route when a routing policy advertises an aggregate route into BGP. In addition, the aggregate route must have at least one contributing route learned from BGP.

Figure 4.8 displays the fields of the Aggregator attribute:

Attribute Type (2 octets)   This 2-octet field encodes information relevant to the Aggregator attribute as an optional transitive attribute. Both the Optional and Transitive bits are set to a value of 1. The type code bits are set to a constant value of 0x07.

Attribute Length (Variable)   This variable-length field is 1 octet long for the Aggregator attribute, which means that the Extended bit in the Attribute Type field is set to a value of 0. A constant value of 6 is placed in this field.

Aggregator (6 octets)   This field contains the Aggregator value currently assigned to the route. The first 2 octets encode the AS number of the aggregating router, whereas the last 4 octets represent its router ID.

FIGURE 4.8   BGP Aggregator attribute

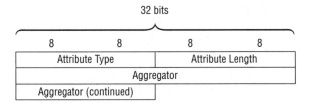

Community

The *Community* attribute, type code 8, is also an optional transitive attribute. As with the Aggregator attribute, an individual BGP implementation doesn't have to understand the Community attribute, but it must be advertised to all established peers. The attribute is encoded as a 4-octet value, where the first 2 octets represent an AS number and the remaining 2 octets represent a locally defined value. The JUNOS software always displays the Community attribute in the format 65001:1001.

One main role of the Community attribute is to be an administrative tag value used to associate routes together. Ideally these routes would share some common properties, but that is not required. Communities are a very flexible tool within BGP; an individual community value can be assigned to a single route or multiple routes. Conversely, a BGP route can be assigned a single community value or multiple values. The vast majority of networks use the Community attribute to assist in implementing their administrative routing policies. A route's assigned value can allow it to be accepted into the network, rejected from the network, or modify other BGP attributes.

> Chapter 1, "Routing Policy," contains details on creating, using, and modifying communities inside a routing policy.

The Community attribute, shown in Figure 4.9, includes the following fields:

Attribute Type (2 octets)   This 2-octet field encodes information about the Community attribute. As an optional transitive attribute, both the Optional and Transitive bits are set to the value 1. The type code bits are set to a constant value of 0x08.

Attribute Length (Variable)   This variable-length field can be either 1 or 2 octets long, depending on the number of community values assigned to the route. Because each value is encoded using 4 octets, the total number of assigned values can be inferred from this field.

Community (Variable)   This field contains the community values currently assigned to the route. Each value uses 4 octets of space to represent its value.

FIGURE 4.9   BGP Community attribute

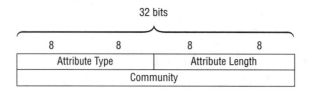

Well-Known Communities

Request for Comments (RFC) 1997, "BGP Communities Attribute," defines three community values that are considered well known and that should be understood by all BGP implementations. Each of these values uses 65535 (0xFFFF) in the AS portion of the community space. The three well-known communities are:

No-Export   The *No-Export* community allows routes to be advertised to the neighboring AS. The routers in the neighboring AS may not, however, advertise the routes to any other AS. This community value (0xFFFFFF01) is configured in the JUNOS software using the syntax no-export within the community definition.

No-Advertise   The *No-Advertise* community allows routes to be advertised to an immediate BGP peer, but these routes should not be advertised any further than that. This community value (0xFFFFFF02) is configured in the JUNOS software using the syntax no-advertise within the community definition.

No-Export-Subconfed   The *No-Export-Subconfed* community allows routes to be advertised to the neighboring sub-AS in a network using confederations. The advertised routes should not be advertised any further than that particular sub-AS. This community value (0xFFFFFF03) is configured in the JUNOS software using the syntax no-export-subconfed within the community definition.

FIGURE 4.10   Using the No-Export community

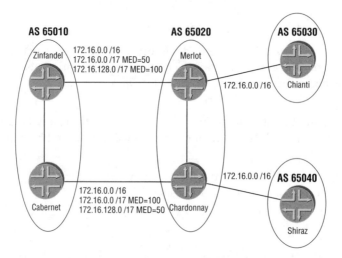

The Cabernet and Zinfandel routers in Figure 4.10 are assigned the 172.16.0.0 /16 address space in AS 65010. The administrators of AS 65010 have assigned their address space so that the 172.16.0.0 /17 subnet is closer to Zinfandel while the 172.16.128.0 /17 subnet is closer to Cabernet. They would like to advertise these two subnets, as well as their larger aggregate route, to their peers in AS 65020. The two subnets should be used by AS 65020 to forward user traffic based on the assigned MED values. In addition, the 172.16.0.0 /16 aggregate route should be readvertised for reachability from the Internet (represented by Chianti in AS 65030 and Shiraz in AS 65040). The Internet routers don't have a need to receive the subnet routes since they provide no useful purpose outside the boundary of AS 65020. While the administrators of AS 65020 could filter these subnets before advertising them, it is a perfect scenario for using the No-Export well-known community. The routes advertised out of AS 65010 by Cabernet include:

```
user@Cabernet> show route advertising-protocol bgp 10.222.6.2

inet.0: 13 destinations, 13 routes (13 active, 0 holddown, 0 hidden)
  Prefix                  Nexthop          MED     Lclpref    AS path
* 172.16.0.0/16           Self             0                  I
* 172.16.0.0/17           Self             100                I
* 172.16.128.0/17         Self             50                 I
```

Chardonnay, in AS 65020, is further advertising these same routes to Shiraz:

```
user@Chardonnay> show route advertising-protocol bgp 10.222.44.1

inet.0: 15 destinations, 17 routes (15 active, 0 holddown, 0 hidden)
  Prefix                  Nexthop          MED     Lclpref    AS path
* 172.16.0.0/16           Self                                65010 I
* 172.16.0.0/17           Self                                65010 I
* 172.16.128.0/17         Self                                65010 I
```

To implement the administrative policy, we first create the **only-to-AS65020** community on the Zinfandel and Cabernet routers. This community has a single member of no-export:

```
[edit policy-options]
user@Cabernet# show | match no-export
community only-to-AS65020 members no-export;
```

We then apply this community to the subnets in a routing policy. Because the BGP configuration already contains the **adv-routes** policy, we simply edit it to appear as:

```
[edit policy-options]
user@Cabernet# show policy-statement adv-routes
term aggregate {
    from {
        route-filter 172.16.0.0/16 exact;
    }
}
```

```
        then accept;
}
term subnets {
    from {
        route-filter 172.16.0.0/16 longer;
    }
    then {
        community add only-to-AS65020;
        accept;
    }
}
```

Using the *detail* option with the show route advertising-protocol bgp command reveals the No-Export community attached to the subnet routes:

user@Cabernet> **show route advertising-protocol bgp 10.222.6.2 detail**

```
inet.0: 13 destinations, 13 routes (13 active, 0 holddown, 0 hidden)
* 172.16.0.0/16 (1 entry, 1 announced)
 BGP group external-peers type External
     Nexthop: Self
     MED: 0
     AS path: I
 Communities:

* 172.16.0.0/17 (1 entry, 1 announced)
 BGP group external-peers type External
     Nexthop: Self
     MED: 100
     AS path: I
 Communities: no-export

* 172.16.128.0/17 (1 entry, 1 announced)
 BGP group external-peers type External
     Nexthop: Self
     MED: 50
     AS path: I
 Communities: no-export
```

The Chardonnay router in AS 65020 no longer advertises the subnet routes to its Internet peer:

user@Chardonnay> **show route advertising-protocol bgp 10.222.44.1**

```
inet.0: 15 destinations, 17 routes (15 active, 0 holddown, 0 hidden)
  Prefix                Nexthop           MED    Lclpref    AS path
* 172.16.0.0/16         Self                                 65010 I
```

These same principles can be used with the No-Advertise community when multiple links exist between EBGP peers. Figure 4.11 shows what might be a typical example.

FIGURE 4.11   Using the No-Advertise community

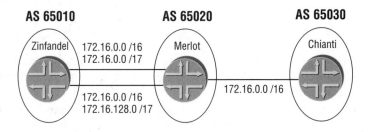

Originator ID

The *Originator ID* attribute, type code 9, is an optional, nontransitive attribute of BGP. As such, an individual BGP implementation doesn't have to understand or use this attribute at all. When used, however, the attribute must remain within the boundaries of its local AS.

The attribute is used as a method of loop prevention in a BGP network using route reflection. It contains the router ID of the router that announced the route to the first route reflector in the network. The attribute is attached to the route by that first route reflector.

 We discuss the operation of route reflection in greater detail in Chapter 5.

Figure 4.12 displays the fields of the Originator ID attribute:

Attribute Type (2 octets)   This field includes information relevant to the Originator ID attribute. The optional, nontransitive nature of the attribute requires that the Optional bit be set to a value of 1 and the Transitive bit be set to a value of 0. The type code bits are set to a constant value of 0x09.

Attribute Length (Variable)   This variable-length field is 1 octet long for the Originator ID attribute, which requires the Extended bit in the Attribute Type field be set to a value of 0. A constant value of 4 is placed in this field.

Originator ID (4 octets)   This field contains the router ID of the router that announced the route to the first route reflector in the network.

FIGURE 4.12 BGP Originator ID attribute

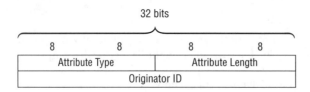

Cluster List

The *Cluster List* attribute, type code 10, is also an optional, nontransitive attribute. As with the Originator ID and MED attributes, BGP routers don't need to understand the attribute, but it must not be advertised outside the local AS.

The attribute is used in a route reflection network to prevent routing loops within the local AS. Individual routers in the network, the route reflectors, are assigned a unique 32-bit value that is similar to the local AS number. Each time a route reflector advertises a route, it prepends this value to the Cluster List attribute.

The Cluster List attribute, displayed in Figure 4.13, includes these fields:

Attribute Type (2 octets)   This field includes information relevant to the Cluster List attribute. The Optional bit is set to a value of 1 and the Transitive bit is set to a value of 0, designating the attribute as optional and nontransitive. The type code bits are set to a constant value of 0x0a.

Attribute Length (Variable)   This variable-length field can be either 1 or 2 octets long, depending on the number of unique values assigned to the route.

Cluster List (Variable)   This field contains the ordered list of unique identifiers through which the route has passed. Each identifier is encoded using its unique 32-bit value.

FIGURE 4.13 BGP Cluster List attribute

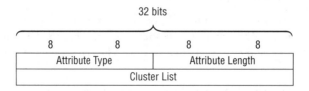

Multiprotocol Reachable NLRI

The *Multiprotocol Reachable NLRI (MP-Reach-NLRI)* attribute, type code 14, is an optional nontransitive BGP attribute. This classification allows routers to use the attribute if they desire and scopes the advertisement to two neighboring ASs.

The attribute is used by two BGP peers that wish to advertise routing knowledge other than IPv4 unicast routes. The peers negotiate their ability to use the MP-Reach-NLRI attribute during the establishment of the peering session. When the attribute is used in an Update message, the Origin and AS Path attributes are always included. In addition, the Local Preference attribute is added when the Update message is transmitted over an IBGP peering session. The MP-Reach-NLRI attribute is sometimes advertised in an Update message that contains no IPv4 unicast routes. In this scenario, the Next Hop attribute is not included. This omission of a well-known mandatory attribute is possible since the MP-Reach-NLRI attribute contains both routing and next-hop knowledge.

Figure 4.14 shows the Multiprotocol Reachable NLRI attribute, which includes the following fields:

Attribute Type (2 octets)   This field includes information concerning the nature of the Multiprotocol Reachable NLRI attribute. The Optional bit is set to a value of 1 and the Transitive bit is set to a value of 0, designating the attribute as optional and nontransitive. The type code bits are set to a constant value of 0x0e.

Attribute Length (Variable)   This variable-length field can be either 1 or 2 octets long, depending on the number of routes contained within the attribute.

Address Family Identifier (2 octets)   This field includes information about the type of Network Layer routing information carried within the attribute. Possible options include IPv4 (1), IPv6 (2), and Layer 2 VPN (196).

Subsequent Address Family Identifier (1 octet)   This field provides further detail about the type of routing information carried within the attribute. Each of these options is a subset within its specific Address Family Identifier (AFI). Possible options include unicast (1), multicast (2), and labeled VPN unicast (128).

Length of Next-Hop Address (1 octet)   This field displays the length of the Network Address field that follows.

Network Address of Next Hop (Variable)   The network layer Next Hop used for the advertised routes is included in this field. The usage of this parameter is similar in function to the BGP Next Hop attribute.

Number of SNPAs (1 octet)   This field displays the number of Layer 2 sub-network points of attachment (SNPA) contained in the following field. A value of 0 indicates that no SNPAs are included in the attribute.

Sub-Network Points of Attachment (Variable)   This variable-length field contains any advertised Layer 2 SNPAs. Each SNPA is encoded using a 1-octet length field followed by the SNPA value itself.

Network Layer Reachability Information (Variable)   The routing information included in the attribute is encoded in this field. Each NLRI is represented by a 1-octet length field followed by a variable-length prefix field.

FIGURE 4.14   BGP Multiprotocol Reachable NLRI attribute

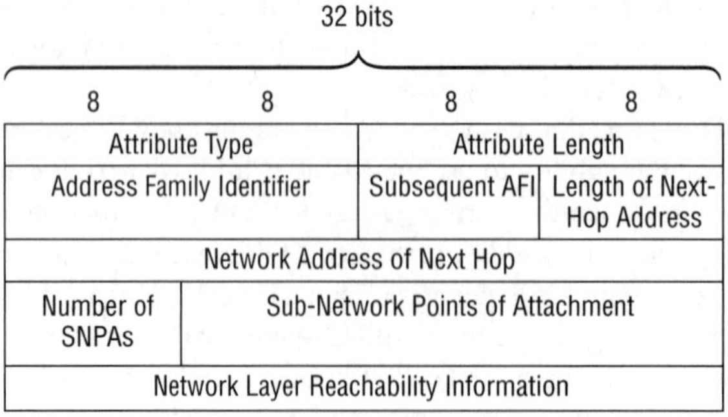

Multiprotocol Unreachable NLRI

The *Multiprotocol Unreachable NLRI (MP-Unreach-NLRI)* attribute, type code 15, is also an optional nontransitive BGP attribute. As with its MP-Reach-NLRI counterpart, individual routers may use the attribute if they desire. The use of the attribute, however, is limited to two neighboring ASs.

The attribute is used to withdraw routing knowledge that was previously advertised using the MP-Reach-NLRI. The attribute is shown in Figure 4.15 and includes the following fields:

Attribute Type (2 octets)   This field includes information concerning the Multiprotocol Unreachable NLRI attribute. Because this is an optional, nontransitive attribute, the Optional bit is set to a value of 1 and the Transitive bit is set to a value of 0. The type code bits are set to a constant value of 0x0f.

Attribute Length (Variable)   This variable-length field can be either 1 or 2 octets long, depending on the number of routes contained within the attribute.

Address Family Identifier (2 octets)   This field includes information about the type of Network Layer routing information carried within the attribute. Possible options include IPv4 (1), IPv6 (2), and Layer 2 VPN (196).

Subsequent Address Family Identifier (1 octet)   This field provides further detail about the type of routing information carried within the attribute. Each of these options is a subset within its specific AFI. Possible options include unicast (1), multicast (2), and labeled VPN unicast (128).

Withdrawn Routes (Variable)   This field contains the routing information being withdrawn by the local router. Each route is represented by a 1-octet length field followed by a variable-length prefix field.

Extended Community

The *Extended Community* attribute, type code 16, is an optional transitive attribute. As with the Community attribute, an individual BGP implementation doesn't have to understand this attribute, but it must be advertised to all established peers.

FIGURE 4.15   BGP Multiprotocol Unreachable NLRI attribute

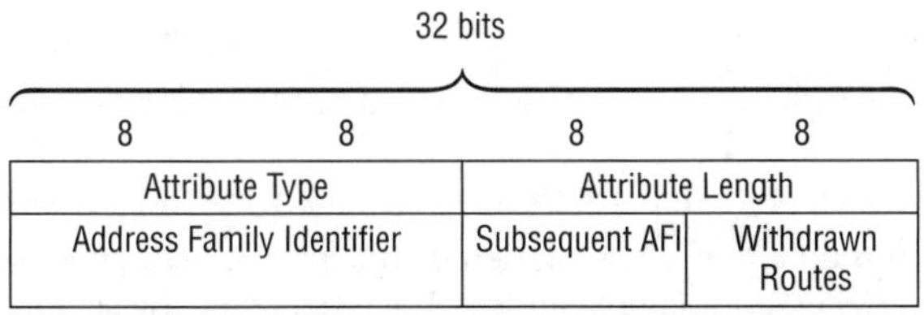

The Extended Community attribute is also used as an administrative tag value for grouping routes together. The format of the Extended Community provides network administrators with greater flexibility for use in routing policies. The attribute, shown in Figure 4.16, includes the following fields:

Attribute Type (2 octets)   This 2-octet field encodes information about the Extended Community attribute. Because this is an optional transitive attribute, both the Optional and Transitive bits are set to a value of 1. The type code bits are set to a constant value of 0x10.

Attribute Length (Variable)   This variable-length field can be either 1 or 2 octets long, depending on the number of community values assigned to the route. Since each value is encoded using 8 octets, the total number of assigned values can be inferred from this field.

Extended Community (Variable)   This field contains the community values currently assigned to the route. Each value uses 8 octets of space to represent its value.

The Extended Community attribute is encoded as an 8-octet value consisting of a type portion, an administrator value, and an assigned number. The first 2 octets of the community are used for the type portion, while the remaining 6 octets include both the administrator value and assigned number. The high-order byte within the type portion of the community determines the format of the remaining fields and has the following defined values:

- 0x00—The administrator field is 2 octets (AS number) and the assigned number field is 4 octets.

- 0x01—The administrator field is 4 octets (IPv4 address) and the assigned number field is 2 octets.

FIGURE 4.16   BGP Extended Community attribute

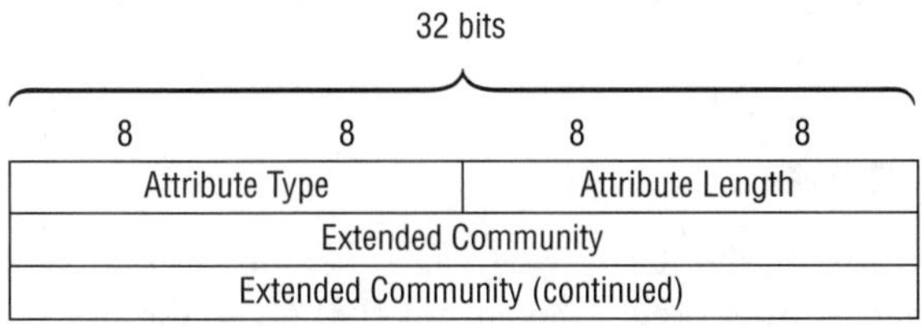

The low-order byte then determines the actual type of community being advertised. Some of the defined values are:

- 0x02—Route target that indicates the devices that will receive the routing information
- 0x03—Route origin indicating the devices that sourced the routing information

 Additional community types are defined by the Internet Assigned Numbers Authority (IANA) and equipment vendors, but are outside the scope of this book.

While it is important to understand the format and construction of the Extended Community attribute, the JUNOS software provides an easy method for configuring these communities on the router. Suppose you would like to create a community value that is a route target and uses your AS number in the administrator field. You would configure this information on the router as so:

```
[edit policy-options]
user@host# set community ext-comm members target:65010:1111
```

Note the use of the colon (:) to separate the three portions of the community. The JUNOS software uses this separation to automatically encode this community using a type field of 0x0002. In a similar fashion, an origin community using an IP address in the administrator field (0x0103) is configured as

```
[edit policy-options]
user@host# set community ext-comm members origin:192.168.1.1:2222
```

Selecting BGP Routes

When a BGP router receives multiple path advertisements for the exact same route destination, it can use only one of those advertisements to forward user data traffic. This single best advertisement is placed into the local routing and forwarding tables and is further advertised to other BGP peers. The process by which a router determines the advertisement to use is defined by the BGP route selection algorithm. In this section, we review the steps of the algorithm as well as provide some further details about its operation. We follow this with a look at some JUNOS software show commands used to see the results of the algorithm. Finally, we discuss a configuration option that allows some of the final algorithm steps to be skipped.

The Decision Algorithm

The *BGP route selection algorithm* in the JUNOS software uses a deterministic set of steps to select the active route for the routing table. This means that given the same set of route attributes, the algorithm makes the same selection every time. The steps of the algorithm are as follows:

1. The router first verifies that a current route exists in the `inet.0` routing table that provides reachability to the address specified by the Next Hop attribute. Should a valid route not exist, the path advertisement is not usable by the router and the route is marked as `hidden` in the routing table.

2. The router checks the Local Preference value and prefers all advertisements with the highest value. This is the only step in the algorithm that prefers a higher value over a lower value.

3. The router evaluates the length of the AS Path attribute. A shorter path length is preferred over a longer path length. When the attribute contains an AS Set segment, designated by the { and } braces, this set of values is considered to have a length of 1. For example, the AS Path of `65010 {65020 65030 65040}` has a path length of 2.

4. The router checks the value in the Origin attribute. A lower Origin value is preferred over a higher value.

5. The router checks the value of the MED attribute for routes advertised from the same neighboring AS. A lower MED value is preferred over a higher MED value.

6. The router checks the type of BGP peer the path advertisement was learned from. Advertisements from EBGP peers are preferred over advertisements from IBGP peers.

7. The router determines the IGP metric cost to each BGP peer it received a path advertisement from. Advertisements from the peer with the lowest IGP cost are preferred. For all IBGP advertisements, the router also selects a physical next hop (or multiple next hops) for the advertisements from the lowest-cost peer. These physical next hops are selected using the following criteria:

    a. The router examines both the `inet.0` and the `inet.3` routing tables for the address of the BGP Next Hop. The physical next hop(s) associated with the lowest JUNOS software route preference is preferred. This often means that the router uses the `inet.3` version of the next hop—a Multiprotocol Label Switching (MPLS)–label switched path.

    b. Should the preference values in the `inet.0` and the `inet.3` routing tables be equal, the router uses the physical next hop(s) of the instance in `inet.3`.

    c. Should the preference values be identical and the routes be in the same routing table, `inet.0` for example, the router evaluates the number of equal-cost paths of each route instance. The instance with the larger number of paths is preferred and its physical next hops are installed. This situation might occur when the default preference values are modified and the `traffic-engineering bgp-igp` MPLS configuration command is used.

8. The router determines the length of the Cluster List attribute. A shorter list length is preferred over a longer list length.

9. The router determines the router ID for each peer that advertised a path to the route destination. A lower router ID value is preferred over a higher router ID value.

10. The router determines the peer ID for each peer that advertised a path to the router destination. A lower peer ID value is preferred over a higher peer ID value. The peer ID is the IP address of the established BGP peering session.

When any step in the algorithm results in a single path advertisement, the router stops processing and installs that version of the route as the active route in the routing table.

Verifying the Algorithm Outcome

While the JUNOS software logically maintains separate BGP routing information bases (Adjacency-RIB-IN, Local-RIB, Adjacency-RIB-Out), all BGP routes are actually stored in the routing table on the Routing Engine. As such, these routes are visible using the show route command-line interface (CLI) command.

FIGURE 4.17   BGP sample network

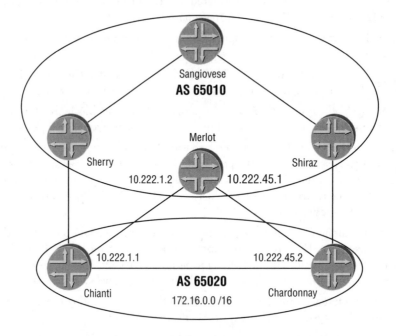

In Figure 4.17, the Chianti and Chardonnay routers in AS 65020 are advertising routes in the 172.16.0.0/16 address space to AS 65010. We can see these routes on the Sangiovese router as

user@Sangiovese> **show route protocol bgp terse**

```
inet.0: 12 destinations, 15 routes (12 active, 0 holddown, 0 hidden)
+ = Active Route, - = Last Active, * = Both
```

A Destination	P Prf	Metric 1	Metric 2	Next hop	AS path
* 172.16.1.0/24	B 170	100		>10.222.28.1	65020 I
	B 170	100		>10.222.4.2	65020 I
* 172.16.2.0/24	B 170	100		>10.222.28.1	65020 I

		B 170	100	>10.222.4.2	65020 I
*	172.16.3.0/24	B 170	100	>10.222.28.1	65020 I
		B 170	100	>10.222.4.2	65020 I

The router output shows two sets of information for each of the received BGP routes. This correlates to the two path advertisements received by Sangiovese from its IBGP peers Sherry and Shiraz. Looking specifically at the 172.16.3.0 /24 route, we see that the advertisement from Sherry (10.222.28.1) is marked active. This categorization informs you that the advertisement is installed in the forwarding table and is eligible for readvertisement to any established EBGP peers. The remaining advertisements not selected by the algorithm are listed in the routing table to allow for easier troubleshooting and network verification.

When you use the *detail* option of the show route command, the router output provides all the information necessary to verify the outcome of the BGP route selection algorithm. Let's see what information that includes:

```
user@Sangiovese> show route detail 172.16.1/24

inet.0: 12 destinations, 15 routes (12 active, 0 holddown, 0 hidden)
172.16.1.0/24 (2 entries, 1 announced)
        *BGP    Preference: 170/-101
                Source: 192.168.16.1
                Next hop: 10.222.28.1 via fe-0/0/0.0, selected
                Protocol next hop: 192.168.16.1 Indirect next hop: 84cfbd0 58
                State: <Active Int Ext>
                Local AS: 65010 Peer AS: 65010
                Age: 11:14     Metric: 0        Metric2: 10
                Task: BGP_65010.192.168.16.1+3518
                Announcement bits (2): 0-KRT 4-Resolve inet.0
                AS path: 65020 I
                Localpref: 100
                Router ID: 192.168.16.1
         BGP    Preference: 170/-101
                Source: 192.168.36.1
                Next hop: 10.222.4.2 via fe-0/0/1.0, selected
                Protocol next hop: 192.168.36.1 Indirect next hop: 84cfc78 59
                State: <NotBest Int Ext>
                Inactive reason: Router ID
                Local AS: 65010 Peer AS: 65010
                Age: 4:10      Metric: 0        Metric2: 10
                Task: BGP_65010.192.168.36.1+2631
                AS path: 65020 I
                Localpref: 100
                Router ID: 192.168.36.1
```

Using the selection algorithm as a guide, let's correlate the router output for the active advertisement to the algorithm steps:

- BGP Next Hop—`Protocol next hop: 192.168.16.1`
- Local Preference—`Localpref: 100`
- AS Path—`AS path: 65020 I`
- Origin—`AS path: 65020 I`
- Multiple Exit Discriminator—`Metric: 0`
- EBGP vs. IBGP—`Local AS: 65010 Peer AS: 65010`
- Cost to IGP peer—`Metric2: 10`
- Cluster List—Not present in this output but appears as `Cluster list:`
- Router ID—`Router ID: 192.168.16.1`
- Peer ID—`Source: 192.168.16.1`

Using the output of this CLI command, you can manually calculate the route selection algorithm to verify that the correct route was chosen. Of course, this requires that you memorize the steps of the algorithm (not a bad thing in the long run). The JUNOS software, however, provides information as to why the inactive path advertisements were not selected. Each unused advertisement contains an `Inactive reason:` tag in the `show route detail` output. For the 172.16.1.0 /24 route, the router ID selection step was used to select the active path advertisement. Not all of the inactive reason descriptions are quite so obvious, so we detail them here:

- Local Preference—`Local Preference`
- AS Path—`AS path`
- Origin—`Origin`
- Multiple Exit Discriminator—`Not best in its group`. This statement reflects the default use of deterministic MEDs.
- EBGP vs. IBGP—`Interior > Exterior > Exterior via Interior`. This statement represents the fact that IGP-learned routes (`Interior`) are preferred over EBGP-learned routes (`Exterior`). Both categories are preferred over IBGP-learned routes (`Exterior via Interior`).
- Cost to IGP peer—`IGP metric`
- Cluster List—`Cluster list length`
- Router ID—`Router ID`
- Peer ID—`Update source`

Skipping Algorithm Steps

At first this might sound counterintuitive. How can a deterministic selection be made when you allow certain steps to be skipped? The answer to that question lies in the operation of the `multipath` command. This command allows next hops from multiple path advertisements (sent from the same neighboring AS) to be installed in the routing table. These physical next hops are associated with the advertisement that normally would be selected by the algorithm. When `multipath` is configured and the router arrives at the router ID selection step, all of the next hops from the remaining path advertisements are used for forwarding user data traffic. In essence, the router ID and peer ID decision steps are skipped.

NOTE   No more than 16 path advertisements can be used by the `multipath` command.

The Merlot router in Figure 4.17 has two EBGP peering sessions to AS 65020. Each of the AS 65020 routers is advertising routes in the 172.16.0.0 /16 address range. These routes appear on Merlot as:

```
user@Merlot> show route protocol bgp terse

inet.0: 12 destinations, 15 routes (12 active, 0 holddown, 0 hidden)
+ = Active Route, - = Last Active, * = Both

A Destination      P Prf   Metric 1   Metric 2  Next hop      AS path
* 172.16.1.0/24    B 170      100                >10.222.1.1   65020 I
                   B 170      100                >10.222.45.2  65020 I
* 172.16.2.0/24    B 170      100                >10.222.1.1   65020 I
                   B 170      100                >10.222.45.2  65020 I
* 172.16.3.0/24    B 170      100                >10.222.1.1   65020 I
                   B 170      100                >10.222.45.2  65020 I
```

All of the path advertisements from Chianti (10.222.1.1) are preferred over the advertisements from Chardonnay (10.222.45.2), and each lists a single physical next hop in the routing table. Using the `show bgp summary` command, we see the active and received routes from Merlot's EBGP peers:

```
user@Merlot> show bgp summary
Groups: 1 Peers: 2 Down peers: 0
Table          Tot Paths  Act Paths Suppressed    History Damp State    Pending
inet.0              6          3          0            0         0            0
Peer              AS    InPkt    OutPkt   OutQ   Flaps Last Up/Dwn State
10.222.1.1      65020      31        33      0       0      14:53 3/3/0
10.222.45.2     65020      33        34      0       0      15:03 0/3/0
```

In this scenario, Merlot will forward all user traffic for the 172.16.0.0 /16 address space to Chianti, leaving the link to Chardonnay idle. We can utilize the advertisements from Chardonnay by configuring the external peer group on Merlot with the `multipath` command:

```
[edit]
user@Merlot# show protocols bgp
```

```
group external-peers {
    type external;
    multipath;
    neighbor 10.222.1.1 {
        peer-as 65020;
    }
    neighbor 10.222.45.2 {
        peer-as 65020;
    }
}
```

Once this configuration is committed, we see a change in the output of the show bgp summary command:

```
user@Merlot> show bgp summary
Groups: 1 Peers: 2 Down peers: 0
Table          Tot Paths  Act Paths Suppressed    History Damp State    Pending
inet.0                 6          6          0          0          0          0
Peer              AS     InPkt    OutPkt    OutQ   Flaps Last Up/Dwn State
10.222.1.1     65020         2         4        0       0          6 3/3/0
10.222.45.2    65020         2         3        0       0          2 3/3/0
```

Merlot has received and is using three path advertisements from both Chianti and Chardonnay. A quick look at the routing table shows that the active advertisement contains multiple physical next hops while the inactive path advertisements retain their single next hop values:

```
user@Merlot> show route protocol bgp 172.16.1/24

inet.0: 12 destinations, 15 routes (12 active, 0 holddown, 0 hidden)
+ = Active Route, - = Last Active, * = Both

172.16.1.0/24        *[BGP/170] 00:01:55, MED 0, localpref 100, from 10.222.1.1
                        AS path: 65020 I
                        to 10.222.1.1 via so-0/3/0.0
                      > to 10.222.45.2 via so-0/3/1.0
                      [BGP/170] 00:01:51, MED 0, localpref 100
                        AS path: 65020 I
                      > to 10.222.45.2 via so-0/3/1.0
```

The end result of using the multipath command is that the physical next hops from the inactive advertisements are copied and installed with the active path. This allows the router to randomly select a physical next hop to install in the forwarding table for each route.

Configuration Options

The JUNOS software contains a multitude of BGP configuration options at the global, group, or neighbor level. In this section, we focus our attention on a few key items. The first option discussed is how to configure multihop EBGP, which leads us into an examination of how the JUNOS software load-balances BGP routes. Following that, we look at using graceful restart to maintain stability in the network as well as securing your BGP connections using authentication. After exploring some peer-specific options for controlling connections and the number of received routes, we conclude this section with a discussion on damping BGP route advertisements.

Multihop BGP

External BGP peering sessions, by default, are established across a single physical hop. This type of connection is not always convenient in certain operating environments. Some of these include an AS operating a confederation network, certain types of provider-provisioned virtual private networks (VPNs), and multiple physical connections between two BGP peers. It is the multiple physical link scenario that we concentrate on here.

FIGURE 4.18   BGP multihop example

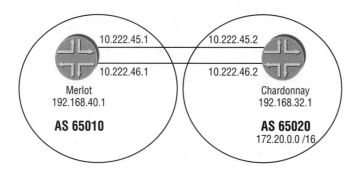

Figure 4.18 shows the Merlot and Chardonnay routers connected across two logical circuits. The network administrators would like to forward BGP traffic across both links while also allowing for redundancy should a circuit fail. Let's walk through the possibilities for configuring BGP in this environment. First, we have the default restriction of the EBGP peers being physically connected. This leads us to configuring two separate BGP sessions between the peers. While this certainly provides for redundancy, it leaves BGP traffic flowing across a single link. Remember that when the same route is received from multiple BGP peers, the route selection algorithm selects one advertisement for forwarding user traffic. In our example, it will be the 10.222.45.0 /24 link since the peer ID is lower on this session than across the other physical link. Clearly, this doesn't solve our administrative goal.

Our second option is to add the `multipath` command to our configuration. This allows us to have two peering sessions for redundancy while also allowing the active path advertisement to contain both physical next hops from the peering sessions. The downside to this environment is the configuration and maintenance of these two peering sessions. The routing process must account for each peer and process all incoming Update packets from both sessions. This is closer to a better solution, but we're not quite there yet.

The final option of using *multihop* between the peers provides the best of all worlds. Simply put, EBGP multihop allows the peering routers to not be directly connected. In our scenario, this allows us to maintain a single peering session between the loopback addresses of the peers. This leads to a single route advertisement across the AS boundary and less overhead for the routing process. Network reachability between the loopback addresses is typically provided by a static route that uses the two physical connections as next-hop values. When the BGP Next Hop recursive lookup is performed, the two physical next hops are located and installed with each active route. In the end, our routing table looks identical to the multipath scenario, but we have only a single peering session.

The Merlot router has a static route configured for reachability to the loopback address of Chardonnay:

```
user@Merlot> show route 192.168.32.1

inet.0: 12 destinations, 12 routes (12 active, 0 holddown, 0 hidden)
+ = Active Route, - = Last Active, * = Both

192.168.32.1/32     *[Static/5] 00:01:29
                    > to 10.222.45.2 via so-0/3/1.0
                      to 10.222.46.2 via so-0/3/1.1
```

The configuration for Merlot currently appears as so:

```
user@Merlot> show configuration protocols bgp
group external-peers {
    type external;
    multihop;
    local-address 192.168.40.1;
    peer-as 65020;
    neighbor 192.168.32.1;
}
```

Although peering to the loopback address of the EBGP peer provides us with a single session, it also requires a bit more configuration work. For example, we've included the `local-address` command to allow each peer to recognize the incoming BGP packets, similar to an IBGP peering session. Of course, we've included the loopback address of the peer within the `neighbor` statement. Finally, the `multihop` command is configured to allow the EBGP peering session to form between the peers.

The two EBGP routers now have a single peering session established between themselves and Chardonnay is advertising three routes into AS 65010:

```
user@Merlot> show bgp summary
Groups: 1 Peers: 1 Down peers: 0
Table          Tot Paths  Act Paths Suppressed   History Damp State   Pending
inet.0                3          3          0         0      0      0         0
Peer              AS     InPkt    OutPkt    OutQ   Flaps Last Up/Dwn State
192.168.32.1    65020    2117      2123       0       1   17:23:45 3/3/0
```

```
user@Merlot> show route protocol bgp

inet.0: 15 destinations, 15 routes (15 active, 0 holddown, 0 hidden)
+ = Active Route, - = Last Active, * = Both

172.20.1.0/24       *[BGP/170] 17:25:54, MED 0, localpref 100, from 192.168.32.1
                       AS path: 65020 I
                       to 10.222.45.2 via so-0/3/1.0
                     > to 10.222.46.2 via so-0/3/1.1
172.20.2.0/24       *[BGP/170] 17:25:54, MED 0, localpref 100, from 192.168.32.1
                       AS path: 65020 I
                       to 10.222.45.2 via so-0/3/1.0
                     > to 10.222.46.2 via so-0/3/1.1
172.20.3.0/24       *[BGP/170] 17:25:54, MED 0, localpref 100, from 192.168.32.1
                       AS path: 65020 I
                       to 10.222.45.2 via so-0/3/1.0
                     > to 10.222.46.2 via so-0/3/1.1
```

The router output shows a single path advertisement for each destination. Each route has two physical next hops listed, which represent the separate logical circuits between the peers. This environment provides redundancy and the use of the multiple circuits that we originally desired.

BGP Load Balancing

When a Juniper Networks router receives multiple routes from an IBGP peer and multiple equal-cost paths exist between those peers, user traffic is forwarded using a process called *per-prefix load balancing*. This means that each BGP route contains multiple physical next hops in the routing table and each route makes its own separate next hop decision. This allows the total amount of traffic forwarded across the network to be spread across the multiple equal-cost paths.

FIGURE 4.19 BGP load balancing example

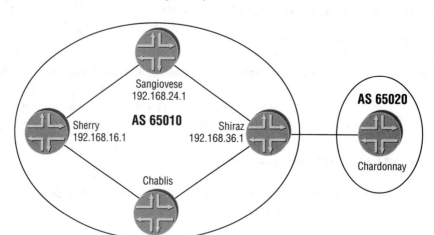

Figure 4.19 shows the Sherry, Sangiovese, Chablis, and Shiraz routers in AS 65010 and the Chardonnay router in AS 65020. Chardonnay is advertising Internet routes to AS 65010; these routes have been simplified in our sample network to:

```
user@Shiraz> show route receive-protocol bgp 10.222.44.2
```

```
inet.0: 16 destinations, 16 routes (16 active, 0 holddown, 0 hidden)
  Prefix                 Nexthop            MED     Lclpref    AS path
* 10.10.10.0/24          10.222.44.2        0                  65020 64777 I
* 172.16.1.0/24          10.222.44.2        0                  65020 64888 I
* 192.168.100.0/24       10.222.44.2        0                  65020 64999 I
```

The Sherry router has multiple equal-cost IS-IS paths for 192.168.36.1, the loopback address of Shiraz:

```
user@Sherry> show route 192.168.36.1
```

```
inet.0: 18 destinations, 18 routes (18 active, 0 holddown, 0 hidden)
+ = Active Route, - = Last Active, * = Both

192.168.36.1/32     *[IS-IS/18] 00:56:07, metric 20
                     > to 10.222.28.2 via fe-0/0/0.0
                       to 10.222.30.2 via fe-0/0/0.1
```

Shiraz is advertising the routes received from Chardonnay with its loopback address as the BGP Next Hop. Sherry receives these routes and performs a recursive lookup in inet.0 for the BGP Next Hop value. It finds that two next hops exist for 192.168.36.1—10.222.28.2

and 10.222.30.2. All of the routes received from Shiraz are then placed into the routing table with these two next hops installed:

user@Sherry> **show route protocol bgp**

```
inet.0: 18 destinations, 18 routes (18 active, 0 holddown, 0 hidden)
+ = Active Route, - = Last Active, * = Both

10.10.10.0/24     *[BGP/170] 00:00:07, MED 0, localpref 100, from 192.168.36.1
                    AS path: 65020 64777 I
                  > to 10.222.28.2 via fe-0/0/0.0
                    to 10.222.30.2 via fe-0/0/0.1
172.16.1.0/24     *[BGP/170] 00:00:07, MED 0, localpref 100, from 192.168.36.1
                    AS path: 65020 64888 I
                    to 10.222.28.2 via fe-0/0/0.0
                  > to 10.222.30.2 via fe-0/0/0.1
192.168.100.0/24  *[BGP/170] 00:00:07, MED 0, localpref 100, from 192.168.36.1
                    AS path: 65020 64999 I
                  > to 10.222.28.2 via fe-0/0/0.0
                    to 10.222.30.2 via fe-0/0/0.1
```

The router output shows that each BGP route has selected a next hop to actually forward traffic across. In our small example, two of the received routes are forwarding traffic on interface fe-0/0/0.0 while the third route is using fe-0/0/0.1. This randomized selection process is repeated by the router for each received BGP route, which allows for load balancing across the network on a per-prefix basis.

To forward user traffic across both interfaces you need to configure per-packet load balancing. This topic is discussed in the *JNCIA Study Guide* (Sybex, 2003).

Graceful Restart

One large cause of instability in the Internet is the restart of a BGP session. This restart might be due to a router failure, a circuit failure, the restarting of the routing process, or an administrative reset of the session. When one of these events occurs, the remote peer either receives a Notification message from the local router or stops receiving Keepalive messages. In either case, the peering session is dropped. This causes the remote router to remove any routes advertised by the restarting router from its routing table. In addition, the remote peer also sends Update messages to other BGP peers withdrawing those routes. Finally, it selects new path advertisements, if possible, which might also have to be announced to its peers in an Update message. When the local router returns to service and reestablishes the peering session, it once again advertises its routes to the remote peer, where they are reinstalled in the routing table. This causes another flood of Update messages from the remote peer, withdrawing and installing new routing information.

When the number of affected routes is quite large—for example, the Internet routing table—this process is quite disruptive to the operation of BGP. In certain cases, this disruption can either be mitigated or eliminated by the operation of *graceful restart*. Graceful restart is the common name for allowing a routing process or peering session to restart without stopping the forwarding of user data traffic through the router. The JUNOS software supports this functionality within BGP, as well as the other major routing processes. Let's explore the operation of graceful restart in a BGP network and discuss the use of the End-of-RIB marker. In addition, we look at configuring graceful restart on the router.

Restart Operation

The high-level operation of the BGP graceful restart mechanism is quite simple. During the establishment of the peering session, each of the routers negotiates its ability to utilize graceful restart. This is accomplished using a special capability announcement, which details the address families that are supported for graceful restart. Only when both peers agree to support graceful restart does it actually get used for the session. Once the session is established, the routing and forwarding state between the peers remains usable when one of the peers restarts. After the restarting router returns to service, it attempts to reestablish the session. During this process, the capability announcement for graceful restart has the *restart state bit* set, indicating that it is in a restart event. In addition, the capability announcement might have the *forwarding state bit* set for each of the supported address families. This indicates that the restarting router can still forward user traffic while completing its restart. The remote router marks all routes it previously received from the restarting router as stale and completes the session establishment. Once fully reestablished, the remote router sends all routing knowledge to the restarting router to fully populate the Adjacency-RIB-In table. When finished, a special announcement known as the End-of-RIB marker is sent to notify the restarting router that the routing updates are complete. This allows the restarting router to perform BGP route selection and advertise information to its peers in a normal operational mode. The restarting router then sends the special marker to indicate that it has completed its routing updates. This concludes the restart event, and both peers return to their normal operational modes.

End-of-RIB Marker

After two restart-capable BGP routers exchange their full routing tables with each other, a special Update message, called the *End-of-RIB marker,* is exchanged. This message contains no withdrawn routes and no advertised routes; it is an empty Update message. The End-of-RIB marker is exchanged between peers after every set of routing updates are advertised to help speed convergence times.

The Sangiovese and Shiraz routers are IBGP peers in AS 65010 and have been configured to support graceful restart. We see the variables supported for the current session using the show bgp neighbor *neighbor-address* command:

```
user@Sangiovese> show bgp neighbor 192.168.36.1
```

```
Peer: 192.168.36.1+3098 AS 65010 Local: 192.168.24.1+179 AS 65010
  Type: Internal    State: Established    Flags: <>
  Last State: OpenConfirm   Last Event: RecvKeepAlive
  Last Error: None
  Options: <Preference LocalAddress HoldTime GracefulRestart Refresh>
  Local Address: 192.168.24.1 Holdtime: 90 Preference: 170
  Number of flaps: 2
  Error: 'Cease' Sent: 2 Recv: 0
  Peer ID: 192.168.36.1    Local ID: 192.168.24.1    Active Holdtime: 90
  Keepalive Interval: 30
  NLRI for restart configured on peer: inet-unicast
  NLRI advertised by peer: inet-unicast
  NLRI for this session: inet-unicast
  Peer supports Refresh capability (2)
  Restart time configured on the peer: 120
  Stale routes from peer are kept for: 300
  Restart time requested by this peer: 120
  NLRI that peer supports restart for: inet-unicast
  NLRI peer can save forwarding state: inet-unicast
  NLRI that peer saved forwarding for: inet-unicast
  NLRI that restart is negotiated for: inet-unicast
  NLRI of received end-of-rib markers: inet-unicast
  NLRI of all end-of-rib markers sent: inet-unicast
  Table inet.0 Bit: 10000
    RIB State: BGP restart is complete
    Send state: in sync
    Active prefixes:            3
    Received prefixes:          3
    Suppressed due to damping:  0
  Last traffic (seconds): Received 30    Sent 28    Checked 28
  Input messages:  Total 15    Updates 5      Refreshes 0    Octets 687
  Output messages: Total 13    Updates 0      Refreshes 0    Octets 306
  Output Queue[0]: 0
```

In the Options field we see that GracefulRestart has been advertised in the capabilities announcement. During the session establishment, each peer advertises a restart time in the Open message. We see that the peer requested a time of 120 seconds (Restart time requested) and the local router did the same (Restart time configured). In addition, the router output shows the address families that the peers are supporting. For this particular BGP session, only the inet-unicast (IPv4) routes are capable of graceful restart operations.

When the Sangiovese router encounters a restart event, we see the following information received by Shiraz in the BGP Open message:

```
user@Shiraz> monitor traffic interface fe-0/0/0 size 4096 detail
Listening on fe-0/0/0, capture size 4096 bytes

11:00:44.643978  In IP (tos 0xc0, ttl 64, id 37564, len 107)
    192.168.24.1.bgp > 192.168.36.1.3760: P 1:56(55) ack 56 win 16445
    <nop,nop,timestamp 50721382 50710953>: BGP, length: 55
        Open Message (1), length: 55
            Version 4, my AS 65010, Holdtime 90s, ID 192.168.24.1
            Optional parameters, length: 26
              Option Capabilities Advertisement (2), length: 6
                Multiprotocol Extensions, length: 4
                  AFI IPv4 (1), SAFI Unicast (1)
              Option Capabilities Advertisement (2), length: 2
                Route Refresh (Cisco), length: 0
              Option Capabilities Advertisement (2), length: 2
                Route Refresh, length: 0
              Option Capabilities Advertisement (2), length: 8
                Graceful Restart, length: 6
                  Restart Flags: [R], Restart Time 120s
                    AFI IPv4 (1), SAFI Unicast (1), Forwarding state preserved: yes
```

Shiraz marks the routes previously advertised by Sangiovese as stale and advertises its local routing knowledge to its peer:

```
user@Shiraz> monitor traffic interface fe-0/0/0 size 4096 detail
Listening on fe-0/0/0, capture size 4096 bytes

11:00:44.645835 Out VID [0: 100] IP (tos 0xc0, ttl 64, id 54671, len 119)
    192.168.36.1.3760 > 192.168.24.1.bgp: P 75:142(67) ack 75 win 16426
    <nop,nop,timestamp 50710953 50721382>: BGP, length: 67
            Update Message (2), length: 67
              Origin (1), length: 1, flags [T]: IGP
              AS Path (2), length: 4, flags [T]: 65020
              Next Hop (3), length: 4, flags [T]: 192.168.36.1
              Multi Exit Discriminator (4), length: 4, flags [O]: 0
              Local Preference (5), length: 4, flags [T]: 100
              Updated routes:
                172.16.1.0/24
                172.16.2.0/24
                172.16.3.0/24
```

Shiraz then transmits the End-of-RIB marker for the IPv4 routes (an empty Update message) to inform Sangiovese that it can run the route selection algorithm and return to normal operation:

```
user@Shiraz> monitor traffic interface fe-0/0/0 size 4096 detail
Listening on fe-0/0/0, capture size 4096 bytes

11:00:44.646716 Out VID [0: 100] IP (tos 0xc0, ttl 64, id 54672, len 75)
    192.168.36.1.3760 > 192.168.24.1.bgp: P 142:165(23) ack 94 win 16407
    <nop,nop,timestamp 50710953 50721382>: BGP, length: 23
        Update Message (2), length: 23
```

The End-of-RIB marker contains just the required fields in an Update message. This includes the Marker (16 octets), Length (2 octets), Type (1 octet), Unfeasible Routes Length (2 octets), and Path Attribute Length (2 octets) fields. These fields result in the marker having a length of 23 octets.

Restart Configuration

The JUNOS software supports graceful restart for all of the major routing protocols. As such, the configuration of this feature occurs within the [edit routing-options] configuration hierarchy. In addition, the BGP process has the ability to disable graceful restart within the protocol itself as well as configure other restart timers. The Sangiovese router in our restart example is configured to support graceful restart as so:

```
user@Sangiovese> show configuration routing-options
graceful-restart;
autonomous-system 65010;
```

Within either the global, group, or neighbor level of the BGP configuration, the following graceful restart options exist:

```
[edit protocols bgp]
user@Sangiovese# set graceful-restart ?
Possible completions:
  disable             Disable graceful restart
  restart-time        Restart time used when negotiating with a peer (1..600)
  stale-routes-time   Maximum time for which stale routes are kept (1..600)
```

The individual options alter the graceful restart process in specific ways, which include:

disable The disable option prevents the local router from performing any graceful restart functions within BGP.

restart-time   The restart-time option allows the local router to advertise a restart timer other than the default 120 seconds in its Open messages. Both the local and remote routers negotiate this value and select the smaller advertised timer. The possible values for this timer range from 1 to 600 seconds.

stale-routes-time   The stale-routes-time timer begins running as soon as the restart event occurs. It is the amount of time that the routes advertised by the restarting peer are used for forwarding before being deleted. This timer is locally significant and isn't negotiated with the remote router. The default value for this timer is 300 seconds, with possible values between 1 and 600 seconds.

Authentication

BGP uses the Transmission Control Protocol (TCP) as its underlying transport mechanism. This exposes the protocol to potential security hazards related to attacking TCP. One main protection against these vulnerabilities is the use of authentication on all BGP sessions. The JUNOS software supports MD5 authentication at the global, group, and neighbor levels of the configuration. Once enabled, each TCP segment transmitted by the router includes a 16-octet MD5 digest, or hash, based on the configured password and the included TCP data. Receiving routers use the same algorithm to calculate a digest value and compare it against the received value. Only when the two digest values match does the packet get processed by the receiving router.

The Shiraz and Chardonnay routers are EBGP peers in Figure 4.19. Each peer configures MD5 authentication on the peering session using the authentication-key *value* command. The current configuration of Shiraz appears as so:

```
[edit protocols bgp group external-peers]
user@Shiraz> show
type external;
authentication-key "$9$mPz69Cu1EytuNb2aiHtuOBIc"; # SECRET-DATA
peer-as 65020;
neighbor 10.222.44.2;
```

We verify that the peering session is authenticated by examining the output of the show bgp neighbor *neighbor-address* command:

```
user@Shiraz> show bgp neighbor 10.222.44.2
Peer: 10.222.44.2+179 AS 65020 Local: 10.222.44.1+2609 AS 65010
  Type: External    State: Established    Flags: <>
  Last State: OpenConfirm    Last Event: RecvKeepAlive
  Last Error: None
  Options: <Preference HoldTime AuthKey GracefulRestart PeerAS Refresh>
  Authentication key is configured
  Holdtime: 90 Preference: 170
  Number of flaps: 1
```

```
Error: 'Cease' Sent: 1 Recv: 0
Peer ID: 192.168.32.1    Local ID: 192.168.36.1    Active Holdtime: 90
Keepalive Interval: 30
Local Interface: fe-0/0/1.0
---(more)---
```

We see the current state of the session is Established and that the AuthKey option was included during the setup stage. Finally, the Authentication key is configured message is proof positive that the MD5 digest is included for all BGP packets advertised over this session. As an added data point, we can view the Chardonnay router receiving and transmitting BGP Keepalive packets with the digest included:

```
user@Chardonnay> monitor traffic interface fe-0/0/0 size 4096 detail
Listening on fe-0/0/0, capture size 4096 bytes

12:28:13.685271  In IP (tos 0xc0, ttl 1, id 55707, len 91)
    10.222.44.1.2609 > 10.222.44.2.bgp: P 56:75(19) ack 56 win 17321
    <nop,nop,timestamp 51241247 51217521,nop,nop,
    md5 34472a073f95469b558925bb7d3bd5da>: BGP, length: 19
        Keepalive Message (4), length: 19

12:28:13.685369 Out IP (tos 0xc0, ttl 1, id 49999, len 91)
    10.222.44.2.bgp > 10.222.44.1.2609: P 56:75(19) ack 75 win 17302
    <nop,nop,timestamp 51217521 51241247,nop,nop,
    md5 5d9bb07d24ec5fe36ace9b6667f389b9>: BGP, length: 19
        Keepalive Message (4), length: 19
```

Avoiding Connection Collisions

When two BGP routers establish a peering relationship, each router forms a TCP connection with its peer. The peers then begin transmitting Open messages to each other in an attempt to form the BGP peering session. These parallel connections, called *connection collision*, are not needed by BGP and one must be closed down. By default, the session initiated by the peer with the higher router ID is used and the other session is closed. The JUNOS software contains two configuration options that affect this connection collision process. In short, they force one of the peers to initiate the peering session while the other router accepts the session.

Using *passive*

You can stop the initiation of a BGP session by configuring the *passive* option at the global, group, or neighbor level of the BGP configuration hierarchy. This command forces the local router to wait for the establishment of the TCP and BGP connections from its remote peer.

The Sherry, Sangiovese, and Shiraz routers are IBGP peers in AS 65010. Under normal circumstances, the session between Sherry (192.168.16.1) and Sangiovese (192.168.24.1) is initiated by Sangiovese based on their current router ID values. We see that this holds true for the currently established session:

```
user@Sangiovese> show bgp neighbor 192.168.16.1
Peer: 192.168.16.1+179 AS 65010 Local: 192.168.24.1+2912 AS 65010
  Type: Internal    State: Established    Flags: <>
  Last State: OpenConfirm   Last Event: RecvKeepAlive
  Last Error: None
  Options: <Preference LocalAddress HoldTime Passive Refresh>
  Local Address: 192.168.24.1 Holdtime: 90 Preference: 170
  Number of flaps: 0
  Peer ID: 192.168.16.1    Local ID: 192.168.24.1    Active Holdtime: 90
  Keepalive Interval: 30
  NLRI advertised by peer: inet-unicast
  NLRI for this session: inet-unicast
  Peer supports Refresh capability (2)
  Table inet.0 Bit: 10000
    RIB State: BGP restart is complete
    Send state: in sync
    Active prefixes:           0
    Received prefixes:         0
    Suppressed due to damping: 0
  Last traffic (seconds): Received 3    Sent 3    Checked 3
  Input messages:  Total 14   Updates 0    Refreshes 0   Octets 266
  Output messages: Total 16   Updates 0    Refreshes 0   Octets 330
  Output Queue[0]: 0
```

The router output shows that the remote peer of Sherry is using TCP port 179 (+179) while the local router is using TCP port 2912 (+2912) for the peering session. This indicates that the peering session was established from Sangiovese to Sherry. To alter this scenario, we configure the passive command on Sangiovese for the peering session to Sherry:

```
user@Sangiovese> show configuration protocols bgp
group internal-peers {
    type internal;
    local-address 192.168.24.1;
    neighbor 192.168.16.1 {
        passive;
    }
    neighbor 192.168.36.1;
}
```

After closing the BGP session, we see that it was reestablished from Sherry to Sangiovese using the output from show bgp neighbor ***neighbor-address***:

```
user@Sangiovese> show bgp neighbor 192.168.16.1
Peer: 192.168.16.1+3173 AS 65010 Local: 192.168.24.1+179 AS 65010
  Type: Internal     State: Established     Flags: <>
  Last State: OpenConfirm    Last Event: RecvKeepAlive
  Last Error: None
  Options: <Preference LocalAddress HoldTime Passive Refresh>
  Local Address: 192.168.24.1 Holdtime: 90 Preference: 170
  Number of flaps: 1
  Error: 'Cease' Sent: 0 Recv: 1
  Peer ID: 192.168.16.1     Local ID: 192.168.24.1     Active Holdtime: 90
  Keepalive Interval: 30
  NLRI advertised by peer: inet-unicast
  NLRI for this session: inet-unicast
  Peer supports Refresh capability (2)
  Table inet.0 Bit: 10000
    RIB State: BGP restart is complete
    Send state: in sync
    Active prefixes:            0
    Received prefixes:          0
    Suppressed due to damping:  0
  Last traffic (seconds): Received 4     Sent 4     Checked 4
  Input messages:  Total 9      Updates 0     Refreshes 0     Octets 197
  Output messages: Total 10     Updates 0     Refreshes 0     Octets 216
  Output Queue[0]: 0
```

Using *allow*

The JUNOS software configuration of *allow* takes the passive concept one step further. Not only does the local router not send any BGP Open messages for its peers, you don't even need to configure the peers. The allow command uses a configured subnet range to verify incoming requests against. For example, a configuration of allow 10.10.0.0/16 permits any BGP router with a peering address in the 10.10.0.0 /16 subnet range to initiate a session with the local router. While this is not recommended for a production environment, it works extremely well in a lab or classroom network.

The Sangiovese router in AS 65010 alters its BGP configuration to appear as

```
user@Sangiovese> show configuration protocols bgp
group internal-peers {
    type internal;
```

```
local-address 192.168.24.1;
allow 192.168.0.0/16;
}
```

This allows incoming IBGP peering sessions from Sherry (192.168.16.1) and Shiraz (192.168.36.1). After restarting the BGP process on Sangiovese, we see the sessions reestablished with the IBGP peers. In addition, the peering sessions are established by the remote peers:

```
user@Sangiovese> show bgp neighbor | match peer
Peer: 192.168.16.1+2435 AS 65010 Local: 192.168.24.1+179 AS 65010
  Peer ID: 192.168.16.1    Local ID: 192.168.24.1    Active Holdtime: 90
  NLRI advertised by peer: inet-unicast
  Peer supports Refresh capability (2)

Peer: 192.168.36.1+2961 AS 65010 Local: 192.168.24.1+179 AS 65010
  Peer ID: 192.168.36.1    Local ID: 192.168.24.1    Active Holdtime: 90
  NLRI advertised by peer: inet-unicast
  Peer supports Refresh capability (2)
```

> **WARNING**   Using the allow command disables the default refresh capability for inbound and outbound route advertisements. Therefore, any change to a routing policy requires a manual soft clearing of the BGP session to correctly implement the policy.

Establishing Prefix Limits

By default, a BGP router accepts all advertised routes from a peer. In certain circumstances, this default behavior is not desirable. Perhaps there are memory limitations on your router, or you have an administrative or contractual requirement for your network. Often, this second rationale drives the need to limit advertised routes from a peer. Within the JUNOS software, this is accomplished with the prefix-limit command. This configuration option is applied within the family inet unicast portion of the BGP configuration for IPv4 routes and allows for the setting of a maximum number of routes to receive. In addition, you can program the router to respond to this maximum value in multiple ways.

The Shiraz and Chardonnay routers in Figure 4.19 are EBGP peers. The administrators of AS 65010 have contracted a peering agreement with AS 65020 to accept no more than 10 routes across the peering session. This administrative requirement is configured on the Shiraz router as so:

```
user@Shiraz> show configuration protocols bgp group external-peers
type external;
family inet {
    unicast {
        prefix-limit {
```

```
        maximum 10;
      }
    }
}
peer-as 65020;
neighbor 10.222.44.2;
```

This sets the maximum number of IPv4 unicast routes allowed from Chardonnay as 10. When the maximum value is reached, a message is written to the messages file on the router's hard drive:

```
user@Shiraz> show log messages | match prefix-limit
Apr  3 13:53:02 Shiraz rpd[2637]: 10.222.44.2 (External AS 65020):
    Configured maximum prefix-limit(10) exceeded for inet-unicast nlri: 11
```

The BGP peering session remains established and the received routes are placed into the local routing table:

```
user@Shiraz> show bgp summary
Groups: 2 Peers: 3 Down peers: 0
```

Table	Tot Paths	Act Paths	Suppressed	History	Damp State	Pending
inet.0	11	11	0	0	0	0

Peer	AS	InPkt	OutPkt	OutQ	Flaps	Last Up/Dwn	State
192.168.16.1	65010	44	54	0	0	21:50	0/0/0
192.168.24.1	65010	44	53	0	0	21:46	0/0/0
10.222.44.2	65020	23	24	0	0	9:10	11/11/0

```
user@Shiraz> show route protocol bgp terse

inet.0: 24 destinations, 24 routes (24 active, 0 holddown, 0 hidden)
+ = Active Route, - = Last Active, * = Both
```

A Destination	P	Prf	Metric 1	Metric 2	Next hop	AS path
* 172.16.1.0/24	B	170	100	0	>10.222.44.2	65020 I
* 172.16.2.0/24	B	170	100	0	>10.222.44.2	65020 I
* 172.16.3.0/24	B	170	100	0	>10.222.44.2	65020 I
* 172.16.4.0/24	B	170	100	0	>10.222.44.2	65020 I
* 172.16.5.0/24	B	170	100	0	>10.222.44.2	65020 I
* 172.16.6.0/24	B	170	100	0	>10.222.44.2	65020 I
* 172.16.7.0/24	B	170	100	0	>10.222.44.2	65020 I
* 172.16.8.0/24	B	170	100	0	>10.222.44.2	65020 I
* 172.16.9.0/24	B	170	100	0	>10.222.44.2	65020 I
* 172.16.10.0/24	B	170	100	0	>10.222.44.2	65020 I
* 172.16.11.0/24	B	170	100	0	>10.222.44.2	65020 I

When used by itself, the prefix-limit maximum command doesn't actually accomplish much. After all, you've contracted with your peer to only accept 10 routes and they've sent more than that. Thus far, you've only given them a slap on the wrist by writing the message to the log file. The JUNOS software provides you with more control than that, however. For example, you can apply the *teardown* option to the prefix-limit command, which allows the local router to terminate the BGP peering session immediately in addition to writing a message to the log file. Let's now update Shiraz's configuration with this option:

```
user@Shiraz> show configuration protocols bgp group external-peers
type external;
family inet {
    unicast {
        prefix-limit {
            maximum 10;
            teardown;
        }
    }
}
peer-as 65020;
neighbor 10.222.44.2;
```

When Chardonnay advertises the eleventh route to Shiraz in this situation, the BGP peering session is torn down:

```
user@Shiraz> show bgp summary
Groups: 2 Peers: 3 Down peers: 0
```

Table	Tot Paths	Act Paths	Suppressed	History	Damp State	Pending
inet.0	10	10	0	0	0	0

Peer	AS	InPkt	OutPkt	OutQ	Flaps	Last Up/Dwn	State
192.168.16.1	65010	58	69	0	0	28:56	0/0/0
192.168.24.1	65010	58	68	0	0	28:52	0/0/0
10.222.44.2	65020	38	39	0	0	16:16	10/10/0

```
user@Shiraz> show bgp summary
Groups: 2 Peers: 3 Down peers: 1
```

Table	Tot Paths	Act Paths	Suppressed	History	Damp State	Pending
inet.0	0	0	0	0	0	0

Peer	AS	InPkt	OutPkt	OutQ	Flaps	Last Up/Dwn	State
192.168.16.1	65010	59	70	0	0	29:11	0/0/0
192.168.24.1	65010	59	69	0	0	29:07	0/0/0
10.222.44.2	65020	39	39	0	1	4	Active

The *teardown* option also allows for a percentage value to be applied:

```
user@Shiraz> show configuration protocols bgp group external-peers
type external;
family inet {
    unicast {
        prefix-limit {
            maximum 10;
            teardown 80;
        }
    }
}
peer-as 65020;
neighbor 10.222.44.2;
```

This allows the local router to begin logging messages to the syslog daemon when the number of received routes exceeds 80 percent of the configured maximum value. When you have network management systems in place to monitor this activity, you are then alerted that the maximum value is approaching. This might enable you to take some corrective measures before the session is torn down.

The main issue with the configuration we've completed thus far is that we end up in a vicious cycle. The peering session is torn down, but both peers immediately attempt to reestablish it. By default, the session once again returns to service and routes are advertised between the peers. Most likely, the remote peer is still advertising too many prefixes and the maximum value is quickly reached. The session is again torn down and the cycle repeats itself until the remote peer no longer sends more routes than allowed. This pattern can be broken with the inclusion of the *idle-timeout value* option as part of the *teardown* option. When configured, the local router refuses any incoming setup requests from the remote peer for the configured time. Possible time values range from 1 to 2400 minutes (40 hours). Let's now configure Shiraz to reject session setup requests for a period of 2 minutes:

```
user@Shiraz> show configuration protocols bgp group external-peers
type external;
family inet {
    unicast {
        prefix-limit {
            maximum 10;
            teardown 80 idle-timeout 2;
        }
    }
}
peer-as 65020;
neighbor 10.222.44.2;
```

When Chardonnay advertises its eleventh route using this configuration, the session remains down for at least 2 minutes. During this downtime, the administrators of AS 65020 are alerted to the problem and stop advertising more routes than they are supposed to. This allows the session to reestablish:

```
user@Shiraz> show system uptime
Current time:      2003-04-03 14:24:13 UTC
System booted:     2003-03-28 14:08:47 UTC (6d 00:15 ago)
Protocols started: 2003-03-28 14:09:43 UTC (6d 00:14 ago)
Last configured:   2003-04-03 14:17:07 UTC (00:07:06 ago) by user
2:24PM UTC  up 6 days, 15 mins, 1 user, load averages: 0.04, 0.05, 0.01
```

```
user@Shiraz> show bgp summary
Groups: 2 Peers: 3 Down peers: 1
```

Table	Tot Paths	Act Paths	Suppressed	History	Damp State	Pending
inet.0	0	0	0	0	0	0

Peer	AS	InPkt	OutPkt	OutQ	Flaps	Last Up/Dwn	State
192.168.16.1	65010	102	113	0	0	50:44	0/0/0
192.168.24.1	65010	102	112	0	0	50:40	0/0/0
10.222.44.2	65020	103	132	0	30	1:57	Idle

```
user@Shiraz> show system uptime
Current time:      2003-04-03 14:24:18 UTC
System booted:     2003-03-28 14:08:47 UTC (6d 00:15 ago)
Protocols started: 2003-03-28 14:09:43 UTC (6d 00:14 ago)
Last configured:   2003-04-03 14:17:07 UTC (00:07:11 ago) by user
2:24PM UTC  up 6 days, 16 mins, 1 user, load averages: 0.03, 0.05, 0.01
```

```
user@Shiraz> show bgp summary
Groups: 2 Peers: 3 Down peers: 0
```

Table	Tot Paths	Act Paths	Suppressed	History	Damp State	Pending
inet.0	10	10	0	0	0	0

Peer	AS	InPkt	OutPkt	OutQ	Flaps	Last Up/Dwn	State
192.168.16.1	65010	102	115	0	0	50:49	0/0/0
192.168.24.1	65010	102	114	0	0	50:45	0/0/0
10.222.44.2	65020	105	136	0	30	1	10/10/0

One final administrative control involves the replacement of a configured minute value with the keyword forever within the *idle-timeout* option. This configuration tears down the peering session and keeps it down indefinitely. The session is only allowed to reestablish when an administrator uses the clear bgp neighbor **neighbor-address** command from the CLI. This configuration option appears in the configuration of Shiraz as so:

```
user@Shiraz> show configuration protocols bgp group external-peers
type external;
```

```
family inet {
    unicast {
        prefix-limit {
            maximum 10;
            teardown 80 idle-timeout forever;
        }
    }
}
peer-as 65020;
neighbor 10.222.44.2;
```

Route Damping

In the "Graceful Restart" section earlier, we discussed the effects that a restarting router might have in a BGP network with the rapid addition and withdrawal of routing information. In general terms, these flapping routes can quickly cause a cascade of messages to propagate throughout the Internet, wasting valuable processing power and bandwidth. The "cure" for containing link flapping is the use of *route damping* at the edges of your network. Route damping monitors just the behavior of EBGP-received routes and determines whether those routes are installed locally and are further sent to any IBGP peers. When routes are stable, not being withdrawn and readvertised, the routes are propagated. However, when a route begins to flap excessively, it is no longer sent into the IBGP full-mesh. This limits the processing of a flapping route not only within your AS, but also within your peer networks and the Internet at large.

 The JUNOS software does not perform route damping on IBGP-learned routes.

Figure of Merit

The determination of excessive flapping is made by a value called the *figure of merit*. Each new route received from an EBGP peer is assigned a default value of 0 when damping is enabled on that peering session. The merit value is increased when one of the following events occurs: 1000 points are added when a route is withdrawn; 1000 points are added when a route is readvertised; 500 points are added when the path attributes of a route change. The figure of merit decreases exponentially based on a time variable, which we discuss next.

The figure of merit interacts with individual routes using a combination of factors:

Suppression threshold   An individual route is suppressed, not readvertised, when its figure of merit increases beyond a defined *suppress* value. The JUNOS software uses a default value of 3000 for the `suppress` keyword, with possible ranges between 1 and 20,000.

Reuse threshold   After being suppressed, a route is once again advertised to IBGP peers when its figure of merit decreases below a defined *reuse* value. The JUNOS software uses a default value of 750 for the `reuse` keyword, with possible ranges between 1 and 20,000.

Figure of Merit Maximum Value

The damping figure of merit has an implicit maximum value, which is calculated using the following formula:

```
ceiling = reuse × exp(max-suppress ÷ half-life) × log(2)
```

When calculated with the default damping values, the figure of merit ceiling is $750 \times 54.598 \times .301$ = 12326.76. While you don't need to keep this figure handy on a regular basis, it useful to know when you're altering the suppress value to a large number. This is because a configured suppression value larger than the figure of merit ceiling results in no damping of received routes.

Decay timer   The current figure of merit value for a route is reduced in an exponential fashion using a defined *half-life* value. This allows the figure of merit to decrease gradually to half its current value by the expiration of the timer. This exponential decay process means that routes are reusable individually as they cross the `reuse` value instead of as a large group when the timer expires. The JUNOS software uses a default value of 15 minutes for the `half-life` keyword, with possible ranges between 1 and 45 minutes.

Maximum suppression time   Regardless of its current figure of merit value, a route may only be suppressed for a maximum amount of time known as the *max-suppress* value. The JUNOS software uses a default value of 60 minutes for the `max-suppress` keyword, with possible ranges between 1 and 720 minutes (6 hours).

Suppose that we have an EBGP-speaking router, which has damping enabled. When a new route is received by the router, it is assigned a figure of merit value equaling 0. At some point in the future, the route is withdrawn by the remote peer and the local router increments the figure of merit to 1000. During the time that the route is withdrawn, the local router retains a memory of that route and decays the figure of merit exponentially based on the default 15-minute `half-life`. As soon as the remote router readvertises the route, the local router receives it and increments its figure of merit by another 1000. As before, the local router begins to decay the current figure of merit value. After a short period of time, the remote router withdraws and quickly readvertises the route to the local router. The figure of merit is increased by 2000, which places it above the `suppress` default value of 3000. The local router removes the route from its local routing table and withdraws the route from any IBGP peers that it had previously advertised the route to. This particular route is now *damped* and remains unusable by the local router.

At this point, the route's figure of merit is somewhere around 3800 due to small decayed reductions. The source of the flapping in the remote AS is resolved and the route becomes stable. In other words, it is no longer withdrawn from and readvertised to the local router. After 15 minutes, the local router reduces the figure of merit to 1900, and after 30 minutes it is reduced to 950. Since the figure of merit is still higher than the `reuse` value of 750, the route remains suppressed. After another 15 minutes have passed (45 minutes total), the figure of merit is reduced to a value of 375. This value is below the `reuse` limit, which makes the route usable by the local router. In reality, the exponential decay allows the route to be advertised to all IBGP peers between 30 and 45 minutes after it was suppressed by the local router.

The JUNOS software updates the figure of merit values approximately every 20 seconds.

Damping Configuration

The application of the default figure of merit values to all received EBGP routes in the JUNOS software is quite simple. You only need to apply the damping command at either the global, group, or neighbor level of the BGP hierarchy. When you use this command at the global level, it only applies to EBGP peers. All IBGP peering sessions ignore this particular configuration option.

The Shiraz router in Figure 4.19 has damping configured within the **external-peers** peer group as so:

```
user@Shiraz> show configuration protocols bgp group external-peers
type external;
damping;
peer-as 65020;
neighbor 10.222.44.2;
```

This allows Shiraz to assign and manipulate the figure of merit for routes it receives from Chardonnay. These advertised routes are currently:

```
user@Shiraz> show route protocol bgp terse

inet.0: 15 destinations, 15 routes (15 active, 0 holddown, 0 hidden)
+ = Active Route, - = Last Active, * = Both

A Destination        P Prf   Metric 1   Metric 2  Next hop        AS path
* 172.16.1.0/24      B 170      100                >10.222.44.2    65020 I
* 172.16.2.0/24      B 170      100                >10.222.44.2    65020 I
* 172.16.3.0/24      B 170      100                >10.222.44.2    65020 I
```

Due to a network link problem in AS 65020, the 172.16.3.0 /24 route is withdrawn by Chardonnay:

```
user@Shiraz> show route protocol bgp terse

inet.0: 15 destinations, 15 routes (14 active, 0 holddown, 1 hidden)
+ = Active Route, - = Last Active, * = Both

* 172.16.1.0/24      B 170      100                >10.222.44.2    65020 I
* 172.16.2.0/24      B 170      100                >10.222.44.2    65020 I
```

The Shiraz router maintains a memory of this route, currently marked as `hidden`, and calculates its current figure of merit as 940. We can see the details of any withdrawn routes that have a figure of merit above 0 by using the `show route damping history detail` command:

```
user@Shiraz> show route damping history detail

inet.0: 15 destinations, 15 routes (14 active, 0 holddown, 1 hidden)
172.16.3.0/24 (1 entry, 0 announced)
        BGP                     /-101
                Source: 10.222.44.2
                Next hop: 10.222.44.2 via fe-0/0/1.0, selected
                State: <Hidden Ext>
                Local AS: 65010 Peer AS: 65020
                Age: 1:26:03   Metric: 0
                Task: BGP_65020.10.222.44.2+179
                AS path: 65020 I
                Localpref: 100
                Router ID: 192.168.32.1
                Merit (last update/now): 1000/940
                Default damping parameters used
                Last update:       00:01:28 First update:       00:01:28
                Flaps: 1
                History entry. Expires in:       00:33:40
```

The router output shows that the default damping parameters are in use, and displays the current figure of merit and its value when the last increment occurred. Because this was the first withdrawal of the 172.16.3.0/24 route, its value was set to 1000. In the intervening minute and 28 seconds, the local router decayed the figure of merit to its current value of 940. The last line of the output tells us that the local router will remove this route entry in 33 minutes and 40 seconds, provided no other events occur with this route. The timer doesn't get a chance to completely decrement since the route is once again advertised by Chardonnay to Shiraz:

```
user@Shiraz> show route protocol bgp terse

inet.0: 15 destinations, 15 routes (15 active, 0 holddown, 0 hidden)
+ = Active Route, - = Last Active, * = Both
```

A Destination	P Prf	Metric 1	Metric 2	Next hop	AS path
* 172.16.1.0/24	B 170	100		>10.222.44.2	65020 I
* 172.16.2.0/24	B 170	100		>10.222.44.2	65020 I
* 172.16.3.0/24	B 170	100		>10.222.44.2	65020 I

Since the route is active in the inet.0 routing table, its figure of merit must still be below the 3000 suppress value. However, the local router is still maintaining a non-zero figure of merit and decaying it based on the 15-minute half-life. These types of routes are visible with the show route damping decayed detail command:

```
user@Shiraz> show route damping decayed detail

inet.0: 15 destinations, 15 routes (15 active, 0 holddown, 0 hidden)
172.16.3.0/24 (1 entry, 1 announced)
        *BGP    Preference: 170/-101
                Source: 10.222.44.2
                Next hop: 10.222.44.2 via fe-0/0/1.0, selected
                State: <Active Ext>
                Local AS: 65010 Peer AS: 65020
                Age: 22      Metric: 0
                Task: BGP_65020.10.222.44.2+179
                Announcement bits (3): 0-KRT 3-BGP.0.0.0.0+179 4-Resolve inet.0
                AS path: 65020 I
                Localpref: 100
                Router ID: 192.168.32.1
                Merit (last update/now): 1662/1636
                Default damping parameters used
                Last update:      00:00:22 First update:      00:04:28
                Flaps: 2
```

From the output we can tell that the figure of merit was at 662 when the route was readvertised. This caused the local router to increment the figure of merit by 1000 to arrive at the 1662 Merit last update value. In the 22 seconds since this route was installed in the routing table, the router decayed the figure of merit to its current value of 1636.

The 172.16.3.0/24 route now flaps (both withdrawn and readvertised) twice from within AS 65020. These route flaps cause the local router to increment the figure of merit by 4000, which means it is higher than the default suppress value of 3000. The local router then suppresses the route and marks it as hidden in the local routing table. In addition, we can see that one route has been damped by examining the output of the show bgp summary command:

```
user@Shiraz> show route protocol bgp terse

inet.0: 15 destinations, 15 routes (14 active, 0 holddown, 1 hidden)
+ = Active Route, - = Last Active, * = Both

A Destination       P Prf   Metric 1   Metric 2  Next hop        AS path
* 172.16.1.0/24     B 170     100                >10.222.44.2    65020 I
* 172.16.2.0/24     B 170     100                >10.222.44.2    65020 I
```

```
user@Shiraz> show bgp summary
Groups: 2 Peers: 3 Down peers: 0
Table          Tot Paths  Act Paths Suppressed    History Damp State    Pending
inet.0                 3          2          1           0         1           0
Peer              AS    InPkt    OutPkt    OutQ    Flaps Last Up/Dwn State
192.168.16.1   65010      319       335       0        0   2:39:29 0/0/0
192.168.24.1   65010      319       334       0        0   2:39:25 0/0/0
10.222.44.2    65020      326       356       0       30   1:48:41 2/3/1
```

The details of the suppressed routes are visible by using the show route damping suppressed detail command. We currently find the 172.16.3.0 /24 route in the output from Shiraz:

```
user@Shiraz> show route damping suppressed detail

inet.0: 15 destinations, 15 routes (14 active, 0 holddown, 1 hidden)
172.16.3.0/24 (1 entry, 0 announced)
        BGP                    /-101
                Source: 10.222.44.2
                Next hop: 10.222.44.2 via fe-0/0/1.0, selected
                State: <Hidden Ext>
                Local AS: 65010 Peer AS: 65020
                Age: 3:21        Metric: 0
                Task: BGP_65020.10.222.44.2+179
                AS path: 65020 I
                Localpref: 100
                Router ID: 192.168.32.1
                Merit (last update/now): 4404/3775
                Default damping parameters used
                Last update:        00:03:21 First update:        00:21:40
                Flaps: 6
                Suppressed. Reusable in:        00:35:00
                Preference will be: 170
```

The current figure of merit for the 172.16.3.0 /24 route is 3775, and it is reusable by the local router in approximately 35 minutes. You have the option of manually clearing the figure of merit value and reusing the route immediately with the clear bgp damping command. This is a useful tool for situations when the network administrators of AS 65020 resolve the problem with the flapping route. They then contact you and ask for the 172.16.3.0 /24 route to be readvertised. We can see the effect of this command on the Shiraz router:

```
user@Shiraz> show route damping suppressed

inet.0: 15 destinations, 15 routes (14 active, 0 holddown, 1 hidden)
```

```
+ = Active Route, - = Last Active, * = Both

172.16.3.0/24        [BGP ] 00:22:23, MED 0, localpref 100
                        AS path: 65020 I
                     > to 10.222.44.2 via fe-0/0/1.0

user@Shiraz> clear bgp damping

user@Shiraz> show route damping suppressed

inet.0: 15 destinations, 15 routes (15 active, 0 holddown, 0 hidden)

user@Shiraz> show route protocol bgp terse

inet.0: 15 destinations, 15 routes (15 active, 0 holddown, 0 hidden)
+ = Active Route, - = Last Active, * = Both

A Destination        P Prf   Metric 1  Metric 2  Next hop      AS path
* 172.16.1.0/24      B 170       100             >10.222.44.2  65020 I
* 172.16.2.0/24      B 170       100             >10.222.44.2  65020 I
* 172.16.3.0/24      B 170       100             >10.222.44.2  65020 I
```

Damping Using a Routing Policy

At this point in the chapter, you shouldn't be surprised that the JUNOS software provides multiple methods for applying route damping in a network. The configuration of the damping command not only enables the functionality, but also applies the default parameters to all received EBGP routes. When you have an environment where you'd like to selectively damp routes, you configure and use a routing policy on the router.

Within the [edit policy-options] configuration hierarchy, you can build a damping profile using the damping *name* command. Within the profile, you assign values to the various damping variables to meet your particular goals. For example, the *easy-damp* profile on the Shiraz router in Figure 4.19 is currently configured as

```
user@Shiraz> show configuration policy-options | find damping
damping easy-damp {
    half-life 5;
    reuse 6000;
    suppress 8000;
    max-suppress 30;
}
```

This profile allows a longer time before a route is suppressed by Shiraz using the **suppress** 8000 value. Once suppressed, the route is readvertised more quickly than the default values by a combination of the **reuse**, **half-life**, and **max-suppress** values. A configured profile is then eligible to be used in a routing policy as an action. For example, the Shiraz router would like to apply damping more leniently to the 172.16.3.0 /24 route when it's received from Chardonnay. This administrative desire is represented by the ***inbound-damping*** policy:

```
user@Shiraz> show configuration policy-options | find damping
policy-statement inbound-damping {
    term easy-damp {
        from {
            route-filter 172.16.3.0/24 exact;
        }
        then damping easy-damp;
    }
}
damping easy-damp {
    half-life 5;
    reuse 6000;
    suppress 8000;
    max-suppress 30;
}
```

In addition to changing what damping values are applied to a route, you can instruct the router to not perform any damping for particular routes. This is also defined within a damping profile by configuring the **disable** keyword. What you end up with in this scenario is a sort of reverse logic, where the default action of the **damping** command is to damp and you're applying a configuration to turn this functionality off for certain routes. As an example, the Shiraz router wants to exempt the 172.16.2.0 /24 route from being damped when it is received from Chardonnay. We configure a new damping profile called ***do-not-damp*** as so:

```
user@Shiraz> show configuration policy-options | find do-not-damp
damping do-not-damp {
    disable;
}
```

We then modify the ***inbound-damping*** routing policy to apply the new profile to the appropriate route:

```
user@Shiraz> show configuration policy-options | find damping
policy-statement inbound-damping {
    term easy-damp {
```

```
        from {
            route-filter 172.16.3.0/24 exact;
        }
        then damping easy-damp;
    }
    term no-damping {
        from {
            route-filter 172.16.2.0/24 exact;
        }
        then damping do-not-damp;
    }
}
damping easy-damp {
    half-life 5;
    reuse 6000;
    suppress 8000;
    max-suppress 30;
}
damping do-not-damp {
    disable;
}
```

At some point in the future, the routes advertised from Chardonnay are withdrawn and then readvertised twice in quick succession. A quick look at the show bgp summary output tells us that some damping has occurred:

```
user@Shiraz> show bgp summary
Groups: 2 Peers: 3 Down peers: 0
Table          Tot Paths  Act Paths  Suppressed    History  Damp State    Pending
inet.0                 3          2           1          0           2          0
Peer             AS      InPkt     OutPkt    OutQ  Flaps Last Up/Dwn State
192.168.16.1   65010      2472       2492       0      0   20:36:07 0/0/0
192.168.24.1   65010      2472       2491       0      0   20:36:03 0/0/0
10.222.44.2    65020      2482       2513       0     30   19:45:19 2/3/1
```

As we've seen previously, the 2/3/1 notation for the Chardonnay router means that one route is actively being suppressed by Shiraz. In addition, the Damp State reading in the output's header field informs us that two routes in the inet.0 routing table have a non-zero figure of merit value. Let's first examine what route is currently suppressed:

```
user@Shiraz> show route damping suppressed detail
```

```
inet.0: 15 destinations, 15 routes (14 active, 0 holddown, 1 hidden)
172.16.1.0/24 (1 entry, 0 announced)
           BGP                    /-101
                     Source: 10.222.44.2
                     Next hop: 10.222.44.2 via fe-0/0/1.0, selected
                     State: <Hidden Ext>
                     Local AS: 65010 Peer AS: 65020
                     Age: 3:20      Metric: 0
                     Task: BGP_65020.10.222.44.2+179
                     AS path: 65020 I
                     Localpref: 100
                     Router ID: 192.168.32.1
                     Merit (last update/now): 4000/3428
                     Default damping parameters used
                     Last update:       00:03:20 First update:       00:03:41
                     Flaps: 4
                     Suppressed. Reusable in:        00:33:00
                     Preference will be: 170
```

Interestingly, the suppressed route is 172.16.1.0 /24, which wasn't accounted for in the
inbound-damping policy. This means that the route was accepted by the default BGP import
policy and subjected to the values applied by the damping command. In fact, the router is telling
us this is the case by displaying the Default damping parameters used output. Let's see what
BGP routes are active in the routing table at this point:

user@Shiraz> **show route protocol bgp terse**

```
inet.0: 15 destinations, 15 routes (14 active, 0 holddown, 1 hidden)
+ = Active Route, - = Last Active, * = Both

A Destination       P Prf   Metric 1   Metric 2  Next hop       AS path
* 172.16.2.0/24     B 170      100               >10.222.44.2   65020 I
* 172.16.3.0/24     B 170      100               >10.222.44.2   65020 I
```

Both the 172.16.2.0 /24 and the 172.16.3.0 /24 routes are active and were configured in our
damping policy. Let's see which route has a non-zero figure or merit value:

user@Shiraz> **show route damping decayed detail**

```
inet.0: 15 destinations, 15 routes (14 active, 0 holddown, 1 hidden)
172.16.3.0/24 (1 entry, 1 announced)
         *BGP    Preference: 170/-101
                 Source: 10.222.44.2
```

```
Next hop: 10.222.44.2 via fe-0/0/1.0, selected
State: <Active Ext>
Local AS: 65010 Peer AS: 65020
Age: 3:34      Metric: 0
Task: BGP_65020.10.222.44.2+179
Announcement bits (3): 0-KRT 3-BGP.0.0.0.0+179 4-Resolve inet.0
AS path: 65020 I
Localpref: 100
Router ID: 192.168.32.1
Merit (last update/now): 4000/2462
damping-parameters: easy-damp
Last update:      00:03:34 First update:      00:03:55
Flaps: 4
```

As per our administrative desire, the 172.16.3.0 /24 route continues to be active in the routing table after a number of route flaps. In fact, we can see that the ***easy-damp*** profile has been applied to the route. The 172.16.2.0 /24 route was intended not to have any damping parameters applied to it. This configuration is also successful by the lack of damping information seen in the output of the show route detail command:

```
user@Shiraz> show route 172.16.2/24 detail

inet.0: 15 destinations, 15 routes (14 active, 0 holddown, 1 hidden)
172.16.2.0/24 (1 entry, 1 announced)
       *BGP    Preference: 170/-101
               Source: 10.222.44.2
               Next hop: 10.222.44.2 via fe-0/0/1.0, selected
               State: <Active Ext>
               Local AS: 65010 Peer AS: 65020
               Age: 3:55      Metric: 0
               Task: BGP_65020.10.222.44.2+179
               Announcement bits (3): 0-KRT 3-BGP.0.0.0.0+179 4-Resolve inet.0
               AS path: 65020 I
               Localpref: 100
               Router ID: 192.168.32.1
```

Summary

In this chapter, we examined the operation of the Border Gateway Protocol within the JUNOS software. We first examined the BGP Update message used to advertise and withdraw routes from a peer. We followed this with a look at each of the defined BGP attributes used in today's network environments. The format of each attribute was displayed and an explanation was supplied for each defined variable. The route attributes are instrumental in the selection of an active BGP route, so our discussion moved to the operation of the route selection algorithm. We talked about each step of the process in depth and then saw some CLI commands available to verify the operation of the selection process.

We concluded the chapter with an exploration of some BGP configuration options available on a Juniper Networks router. We began with methods of supplying multiple physical next hops to a single BGP route using either multipath or multihop. This led us into a short examination of how BGP load-balances multiple routes received from an IBGP peer. The next configuration option discussed was graceful restart and its effect on the forwarding of traffic as well as the stability of the network. Peer options were examined next, including MD5 authentication as well as the `passive` and `allow` commands. After looking at methods for limiting the number of prefixes received from a peer, we saw the effectiveness of BGP route damping. This included a look at the default damping parameters and the selective alteration of its operation using a routing policy.

Exam Essentials

Be able to describe the format of the common route attributes.   The most common attributes assigned to an IPv4 unicast route are Local Preference, AS Path, Origin, Next Hop, and the Multiple Exit Discriminator. Each attribute is defined using a TLV encoding paradigm where the attribute value contains the specific BGP information used for route selection.

Understand the steps of the route selection algorithm.   The JUNOS software uses a defined 10-step algorithm for selecting the active BGP route. After examining some BGP attributes, the selection process then looks at where the route was received from and the cost to exit the local AS before relying on properties of the advertising router.

Be able to describe the CLI command used to verify the operation of the selection algorithm. All received IPv4 unicast BGP routes are stored in the `inet.0` routing table. By using the `show route detail` command, you can view each of the attributes used by the selection algorithm. In addition, you can view the step that caused a particular path advertisement to not be used. This information is displayed by the `Inactive reason:` field in the router's output.

Know the methods used to assign multiple physical next hops to a single BGP route.   Both the `multipath` and `multihop` commands allow a single BGP route to contain multiple physical next-hop values. The concept of multipath affects the route selection algorithm in that the router ID and peer ID tie-breaking steps are not performed. The next hops available from the remaining routes are assigned to the route that would have been selected and placed into the routing table.

For EBGP sessions over multiple logical circuits, multihop allows a single route advertisement between the peers. During the recursive lookup of the BGP Next Hop value, the multiple physical next hops to the EBGP peer are assigned to the received routes.

Understand the operation graceful restart.   A new BGP capability was defined to support graceful restart. This allows two peers to negotiate their ability to support this function. In addition, the capability announcement contains flags that inform the peer if a restart event is in progress and if the forwarding state has been maintained. Additionally, a special form of an Update message, called the End-of-RIB marker, is defined to signal the end of routing updates to each peer. This marker is simply an Update message with no withdrawn or advertised routes included.

Be able to configure route damping for received BGP routes.   BGP route damping is the suppression of routing knowledge based on a current figure of merit value. This value is incremented each time information about a route changes and is decreased exponentially over time. The functionality is configured using the `damping` command and can selectively be applied to routes through a routing policy using damping profiles.

Review Questions

1. How long is the AS Path of 65010 65020 {64666 64777 64888}?

   A. 2

   B. 3

   C. 4

   D. 5

2. Which Origin value does the JUNOS software most prefer when performing the BGP route selection algorithm?

   A. IGP

   B. EGP

   C. Incomplete

   D. Unknown

3. Which two BGP attribute properties accurately describe the Local Preference attribute?

   A. Well-known

   B. Optional

   C. Transitive

   D. Non-Transitive

4. Which two BGP attributes are used when two peers advertise routes that are not IPv4 unicast routes?

   A. Originator ID

   B. Cluster List

   C. MP-Reach-NLRI

   D. MP-Unreach-NLRI

5. Which BGP route selection criterion is skipped when the `multipath` command is configured?

   A. MED

   B. IGP Cost

   C. Cluster List length

   D. Router ID

6. You're examining the output of the `show route detail` command and see a BGP path advertisement with an inactive reason of `Not best in group`. What selection criterion caused this route to not be selected?

   A. MED

   B. EBGP vs. IBGP

   C. IGP Cost

   D. Peer ID

7. How do two BGP peers know that they each support graceful restart?

   A. They begin transmitting End-of-RIB markers.

   B. They negotiate their support during the establishment of the session.

   C. They set the Restart State bit in the End-of-RIB marker.

   D. Graceful restart is a well-known and mandatory function of BGP.

8. What defines a BGP Update message as an End-of-RIB marker?

   A. It contains only updated routes.

   B. It contains only withdrawn routes.

   C. It contains both withdrawn and updated routes.

   D. It contains neither withdrawn nor updated routes.

9. Which BGP neighbor configuration option prevents the local router from sending an Open message to a configured peer?

   A. `allow`

   B. `passive`

   C. `multihop`

   D. `multipath`

10. When a BGP route is withdrawn from the local router, how much is the figure of merit increased?

    A. 0

    B. 500

    C. 1000

    D. 2000

Answers to Review Questions

1. B. An AS Set, designated by the curly braces, always represents a path length of 1. When combined with the AS Sequence length of 2, the total path length becomes 3.

2. A. The JUNOS software always prefers an Origin code of IGP when performing the route selection algorithm.

3. A, C. The Local Preference attribute is a well-known discretionary attribute. All well-known attributes are transitive in nature.

4. C, D. In situations where non-IPv4 unicast routes are advertised between peers, the MP-Reach-NLRI and MP-Unreach-NLRI attributes are used. These attributes advertise and withdraw information between the peers.

5. D. The `multipath` command skips both the router ID and peer ID route selection criteria. The physical next hops of the remaining routes are installed with the active route in the routing table.

6. A. The JUNOS software groups routes from the same neighboring AS together based on the operation of deterministic MEDs. When the MED value of a grouped route causes it to be eliminated from contention, the `Not best in group` inactive reason is displayed.

7. B. Graceful restart support is negotiated during the session establishment using a capability announcement. Only when both peers support this functionality is it used for the session.

8. D. An End-of-RIB marker is an Update message with no routing information present. This includes both withdrawn and updated routes.

9. B. The `passive` command prevents the router from sending an Open message to its peers and establishing a BGP session. You must continue to explicitly configure peers when using this command.

10. C. The withdrawal or update of a BGP route increases the figure of merit by a value of 1000. When the attributes of an announced route change, the figure of merit is increased by 500.

Chapter

5

Advanced Border Gateway Protocol (BGP)

JNCIS EXAM OBJECTIVES COVERED IN THIS CHAPTER:

- ✓ Identify the functionality and alteration of the BGP attributes
- ✓ Describe the operation and configuration of a route reflection BGP network
- ✓ Describe the operation and configuration of a confederation BGP network
- ✓ Identify the characteristics of multiprotocol BGP and list the reasons for enabling it

In this chapter, we examine the methods available within the JUNOS software to manipulate and alter some of the BGP attributes, including Origin, AS Path, Multiple Exit Discriminator, and Local Preference. Following this, we explore methods for scaling an IBGP full mesh using route reflection and confederations. We see how each method operates, how each modifies a route's attributes, and how each is configured on the router. We conclude the chapter with a discussion on Multiprotocol BGP, including when to use it and how it operates.

Modifying BGP Attributes

The JUNOS software provides methods for altering and modifying most of the BGP attributes. This allows you to control which routes are accepted or rejected by a peering session. Additionally, you have the ability to alter the selection of the active BGP route when you modify certain attributes. Some of the attributes are changeable through a configuration, a routing policy action, or both. Let's examine each attribute in some detail.

Origin

The Origin attribute provides a BGP router with information about the original source of the route. The attribute is included in every routing update and is a selection criterion in the route selection algorithm. After discussing the default setting of the attribute, we see how to modify its value with a routing policy.

Default Origin Operation

A Juniper Networks router, by default, forwards all active BGP routes in the `inet.0` routing table to the appropriate established peers. The injection of new routing knowledge into BGP occurs when you apply a routing policy to the protocol. This policy matches some set of routes in the routing table and accepts them. This action causes each newly injected route to receive an Origin value of IGP (`I`).

Figure 5.1 shows three IBGP peers within AS 65010: Cabernet, Merlot, and Zinfandel. The Cabernet router has locally configured static routes in the 172.16.1.0 /24 address range and the Zinfandel router has customer static routes in the 172.16.2.0 /24 address space. We've configured a policy on each router to match the static routes and accept them. When applied as an export policy, the Merlot router receives the following routes:

```
user@Merlot> show route protocol bgp terse

inet.0: 20 destinations, 20 routes (20 active, 0 holddown, 0 hidden)
```

```
+ = Active Route, - = Last Active, * = Both

A Destination        P Prf   Metric 1   Metric 2  Next hop        AS path
* 172.16.1.4/30      B 170       100           0 >10.222.1.1      I
* 172.16.1.8/30      B 170       100           0 >10.222.1.1      I
* 172.16.2.4/30      B 170       100           0 >10.222.3.1      I
* 172.16.2.8/30      B 170       100           0 >10.222.3.1      I
```

The JUNOS software always displays the Origin attribute in conjunction with the AS Path attribute. In the output from Merlot, we see that the AS path column contains no AS values (native IBGP routes) but has the Origin listed as I, for IGP routes. This default behavior is also exhibited when the Zinfandel router exports its IS-IS learned routes into BGP:

```
user@Zinfandel> show route protocol isis

inet.0: 20 destinations, 20 routes (20 active, 0 holddown, 0 hidden)
+ = Active Route, - = Last Active, * = Both

10.222.1.0/24      *[IS-IS/18] 15:56:32, metric 20
                      to 10.222.2.1 via at-0/1/0.0
                    > to 10.222.3.2 via at-0/1/1.0
192.168.20.1/32    *[IS-IS/18] 15:56:32, metric 10
                    > to 10.222.2.1 via at-0/1/0.0
192.168.40.1/32    *[IS-IS/18] 15:57:02, metric 10
                    > to 10.222.3.2 via at-0/1/1.0

user@Zinfandel> show route advertising-protocol bgp 192.168.40.1

inet.0: 20 destinations, 20 routes (20 active, 0 holddown, 0 hidden)
  Prefix              Nexthop          MED    Lclpref   AS path
* 10.222.1.0/24       10.222.3.2       20     100       I
* 172.16.2.4/30       Self             0      100       I
* 172.16.2.8/30       Self             0      100       I
* 192.168.20.1/32     10.222.2.1       10     100       I
* 192.168.40.1/32     10.222.3.2       10     100       I
```

 The JUNOS software uses the existing next-hop value for routes redistributed from an IGP. This avoids potential suboptimal routing in the network.

FIGURE 5.1 Origin sample network

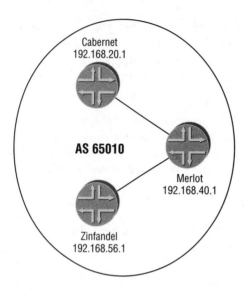

Altering the Origin Attribute

You have the option of setting the Origin attribute to any of the three possible values in a routing policy. This is accomplished with the `then origin value` policy action. All of the possible Origin values are represented within the policy action as `egp`, `igp`, and `incomplete`. The current policy used on the Zinfandel router in Figure 5.1 is as follows:

```
user@Zinfandel> show configuration policy-options
policy-statement advertise-routes {
    term statics {
        from protocol static;
        then accept;
    }
    term isis {
        from protocol isis;
        then accept;
    }
}
```

To mirror the operation of another router vendor, the administrators of AS 65010 would like the IS-IS routes to be advertised with an incomplete Origin value. After modifying the routing policy, we can verify its operation:

```
[edit policy-options policy-statement advertise-routes]
user@Zinfandel# show
```

```
term statics {
    from protocol static;
    then accept;
}
term isis {
    from protocol isis;
    then {
        origin incomplete;
        accept;
    }
}
```

```
user@Zinfandel> show route advertising-protocol bgp 192.168.40.1
```

```
inet.0: 20 destinations, 20 routes (20 active, 0 holddown, 0 hidden)
  Prefix              Nexthop          MED    Lclpref    AS path
* 10.222.1.0/24       10.222.3.2       20     100        ?
* 172.16.2.4/30       Self             0      100        I
* 172.16.2.8/30       Self             0      100        I
* 192.168.20.1/32     10.222.2.1       10     100        ?
* 192.168.40.1/32     10.222.3.2       10     100        ?
```

In a similar fashion, we can again alter the **advertise-routes** policy to modify the Origin for the static routes. For the sake of completeness, we advertise these routes with a value of EGP (E):

```
[edit policy-options policy-statement advertise-routes]
user@Zinfandel# show
term statics {
    from protocol static;
    then {
        origin egp;
        accept;
    }
}
term isis {
    from protocol isis;
    then {
        origin incomplete;
        accept;
    }
}
```

```
user@Zinfandel> show route advertising-protocol bgp 192.168.40.1

inet.0: 20 destinations, 20 routes (20 active, 0 holddown, 0 hidden)
  Prefix                Nexthop           MED    Lclpref   AS path
* 10.222.1.0/24         10.222.3.2        20     100       ?
* 172.16.2.4/30         Self              0      100       E
* 172.16.2.8/30         Self              0      100       E
* 192.168.20.1/32       10.222.2.1        10     100       ?
* 192.168.40.1/32       10.222.3.2        10     100       ?
```

AS Path

The AS Path attribute is also included in every BGP routing update. It supplies information about the AS networks a particular route has transited, and this information is used to select the active BGP route. Additionally, the AS Path provides a routing loop avoidance mechanism as all received routes are dropped when any local AS value appears in the path. The JUNOS software provides multiple methods for altering this attribute, including both configuration options and routing policy actions. Each requires some explanation before providing the details of its usage.

Modifying the AS Path: Configuration Statements

According to the BGP specifications, an implementation should not remove any information from the AS Path attribute. Only additional information should be added to the beginning of the path using a prepend action. While this is nice in theory, real-world problems have required vendors to bend the letter of the specification while trying to maintain its spirit. To this end, the JUNOS software provides four different methods for altering the default operation of the AS Path attribute using configuration statements. Let's explore each of these in further detail.

Removing Private AS Values

The Internet Assigned Numbers Authority (IANA) has set aside several AS values for private use in networks. These AS numbers begin at 64512 and continue to 65534, with 65535 as a reserved value. Much like the private IP address ranges, these private AS numbers should not be attached to routes advertised to the Internet.

Figure 5.2 shows a service provider with an assigned AS of 1111. This provider has customers who would like to connect using BGP but who don't have an assigned AS number. These customers would like to have multiple links available to the provider for load balancing and fail-over redundancy. To facilitate the needs of the customer, the provider assigns each customer a private AS number and configures BGP between the networks. The result of this configuration is the leaking of the private AS number to the Internet, as seen on the Zinfandel router in AS 2222:

```
user@Zinfandel> show route protocol bgp terse

inet.0: 15 destinations, 15 routes (15 active, 0 holddown, 0 hidden)
```

```
+ = Active Route, - = Last Active, * = Both

A Destination          P Prf   Metric 1   Metric 2  Next hop        AS path
* 172.16.1.0/24        B 170      100                >10.222.3.2     1111 65010 I
* 172.20.4.0/24        B 170      100                >10.222.3.2     1111 65020 I
```

One possible solution to this problem is the re-generation of the customer routes within AS 1111. This requires configuring local static routes and advertising them into BGP with a routing policy. While quite effective in preventing the advertisement of the private AS numbers to the Internet, this solution is not very scalable since each possible customer route needs to be duplicated within AS 1111. A more dynamic solution can be found through the use of the `remove-private` configuration option in the JUNOS software. This command is applied to any EBGP peering session where the removal of private AS numbers is needed. Before the default prepend action occurs during the outbound route advertisement, the router checks the current AS Path attribute looking for private AS values. This check starts with the most recent AS value in the path and continues until a globally unique AS is located. During this check, all private AS values are removed from the attribute. The router then adds its local AS value to the path and advertises the route to the EBGP peer.

Private AS values buried within the AS Path attribute are not affected by the `remove-private` command. For example, AS 65333 is not removed from the AS Path of 64888 64999 1111 65333 2222.

FIGURE 5.2   Removing private AS numbers

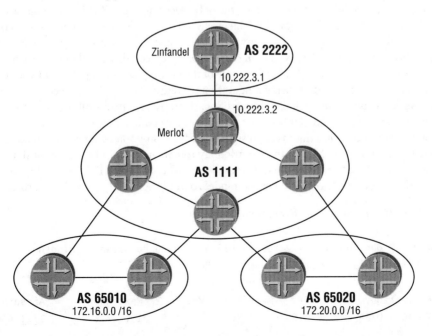

The Merlot router in Figure 5.2 applies the `remove-private` option to its EBGP peering session with Zinfandel:

```
[edit protocols bgp]
user@Merlot# show group external-peers
type external;
remove-private;
peer-as 2222;
neighbor 10.222.3.1;
```

When we check the routing table on the Zinfandel router, we see that the AS values of 65010 and 65020 are no longer visible within AS 2222:

```
user@Zinfandel> show route protocol bgp terse

inet.0: 15 destinations, 15 routes (15 active, 0 holddown, 0 hidden)
+ = Active Route, - = Last Active, * = Both


A Destination        P Prf   Metric 1   Metric 2   Next hop        AS path
* 172.16.1.0/24      B 170      100                 >10.222.3.2     1111 I
* 172.20.4.0/24      B 170      100                 >10.222.3.2     1111 I
```

Migrating to a New Global AS Number

A second method for altering the information in the AS Path attribute is best explained in the context of migrating from one globally assigned AS to another. At first, this might not seem like a good reason for altering the path information. After all, the only place you need to make a configuration change is within the [edit routing-options] hierarchy. This simple change can be easily accomplished in a maintenance window. Of course, any administrator of a large network (hundreds of routers) knows this type of task is easier said than done. Even if you could swap all of your router's configurations in a few hours, this only alters one side of the peering relationship. Each of your customers and peers also needs to update their configurations to reflect the new AS number—which is a much harder task. To assist with making this transition, the JUNOS software allows you to form a BGP peering session using an AS number other than the value configured within the `routing-options` hierarchy. You accomplish this task by using the `local-as` option within your configuration.

Figure 5.3 shows the Merlot and Chardonnay routers using AS 1111 to establish peering connections with AS 2222 and AS 4444. Routes in the address range of 172.16.0.0/16 are advertised by the Shiraz router in AS 4444. The Zinfandel router in AS 2222 currently sees these routes as

```
user@Zinfandel> show route protocol bgp terse

inet.0: 12 destinations, 12 routes (12 active, 0 holddown, 0 hidden)
+ = Active Route, - = Last Active, * = Both


A Destination        P Prf   Metric 1   Metric 2   Next hop        AS path
* 172.16.1.0/24      B 170      100                 >10.222.3.2     1111 4444 I
```

FIGURE 5.3   Migrating to a new AS number

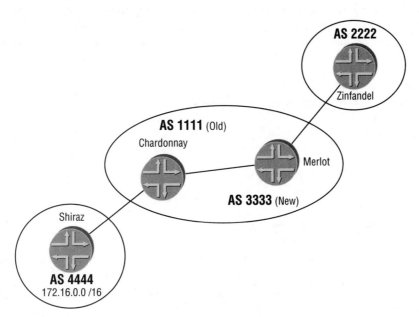

The AS 1111 network now merges with another network, which is currently using AS 3333 as its AS number. The newly combined entity decides to use AS 3333 as the AS value on all of its routers and configures this within the routing-options hierarchy. Additionally, the configuration within AS 2222 is altered to reflect the new AS number. This allows the peering session between Merlot and Zinfandel to reestablish. The session between Shiraz and Chardonnay is currently not operational:

```
user@Merlot> show bgp summary
Groups: 2 Peers: 2 Down peers: 0
Table          Tot Paths  Act Paths Suppressed    History Damp State    Pending
inet.0                 0          0          0          0         0          0
Peer              AS     InPkt    OutPkt   OutQ   Flaps Last Up/Dwn State
192.168.32.1    3333         8         9      0       0      3:11 0/0/0
10.222.3.1      2222         5         6      0       0      1:52 0/0/0

user@Chardonnay> show bgp summary
Groups: 2 Peers: 2 Down peers: 1
Table          Tot Paths  Act Paths Suppressed    History Damp State    Pending
inet.0                 0          0          0          0         0          0
Peer              AS     InPkt    OutPkt   OutQ   Flaps Last Up/Dwn State
192.168.40.1    3333        10        14      0       0      4:37 0/0/0
10.222.44.1     4444         1         2      0       0      5:29 Active
```

Since the administrators of the Shiraz router in AS 4444 are not able to update their side of the peering session, we can reestablish the session by adding some configuration to Chardonnay. We apply the local-as command to the peering session with Shiraz, which uses AS 1111 as our AS number during the session setup. After committing our configuration, the session is once again operational:

```
[edit protocols bgp]
user@Chardonnay# show group external-peers
type external;
peer-as 4444;
local-as 1111;
neighbor 10.222.44.1;
```

```
user@Chardonnay> show bgp summary
Groups: 2 Peers: 2 Down peers: 0
Table          Tot Paths  Act Paths Suppressed    History Damp State     Pending
inet.0                 3          3          0          0         0           0
Peer             AS      InPkt     OutPkt     OutQ   Flaps Last Up/Dwn State
192.168.40.1    3333       20         25        0       0    10:00 0/0/0
10.222.44.1     4444        5          6        0       0     1:08 3/3/0
```

The routes advertised by the Shiraz router are once again visible on Zinfandel in AS 2222:

```
user@Zinfandel> show route protocol bgp terse

inet.0: 12 destinations, 12 routes (12 active, 0 holddown, 0 hidden)
+ = Active Route, - = Last Active, * = Both

A Destination       P Prf   Metric 1   Metric 2  Next hop      AS path
* 172.16.1.0/24     B 170        100             >10.222.3.2   3333 1111 4444 I
```

A closer examination of the AS Path in Zinfandel's output reveals some interesting information; both AS 1111 and AS 3333 appear in the path. The addition of the peer-specific AS number in the path output is the default behavior of the local-as command. To users in the Internet, it appears as if AS 1111 is still a viable network. Additionally, Chardonnay performs the function of an EBGP peer for its IBGP session with Merlot—it updates the path. The routes are visible on Merlot as:

```
user@Merlot> show route protocol bgp terse

inet.0: 16 destinations, 16 routes (16 active, 0 holddown, 0 hidden)
+ = Active Route, - = Last Active, * = Both

A Destination       P Prf   Metric 1   Metric 2  Next hop      AS path
* 172.16.1.0/24     B 170        100         100 >10.222.45.2  1111 4444 I
```

Should you wish to completely remove the old AS information from the AS Path attribute, the JUNOS software provides the *private* option to the local-as command. This allows Chardonnay to keep knowledge of AS 1111 to itself and not update the AS Path attribute before advertising the routes to Merlot:

```
[edit protocols bgp]
user@Chardonnay# show group external-peers
type external;
peer-as 4444;
local-as 1111 private;
neighbor 10.222.44.1;
```

We can now verify that AS 1111 no longer appears in the path information on both Merlot and Zinfandel:

```
user@Merlot> show route protocol bgp terse

inet.0: 16 destinations, 16 routes (16 active, 0 holddown, 0 hidden)
+ = Active Route, - = Last Active, * = Both

A Destination       P Prf   Metric 1   Metric 2  Next hop        AS path
* 172.16.1.0/24     B 170       100        100 >10.222.45.2      4444 I


user@Zinfandel> show route protocol bgp terse

inet.0: 12 destinations, 12 routes (12 active, 0 holddown, 0 hidden)
+ = Active Route, - = Last Active, * = Both

A Destination       P Prf   Metric 1   Metric 2  Next hop        AS path
* 172.16.1.0/24     B 170       100            >10.222.3.2       3333 4444 I
```

WARNING   The local-as command should only be used in this specific circumstance. Its configuration within a normal BGP configuration could cause unexpected results in your network.

Providing Backbone Service for BGP Peers

The final two methods for altering AS Path information within the JUNOS software are explained through the use of an unusual network configuration.

The sample network in Figure 5.4 provides the backdrop for our discussion. The Chardonnay and Merlot routers in AS 64888 are providing a backbone service to the BGP routers in AS 65010. Both the Shiraz and Zinfandel routers are advertising a portion of the 172.16.0.0/16 address space assigned to that AS, but no internal network connectivity is provided between them. Instead, AS 64888 is providing the backbone and network reachability for the different sections of AS 65010.

FIGURE 5.4 Backbone service for BGP peers

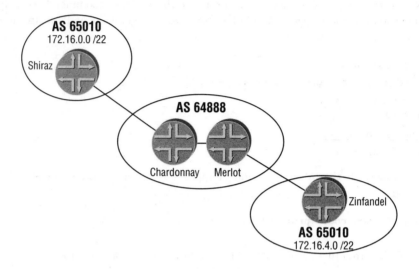

This configuration is similar in nature to a Layer 3 VPN, which we discuss in Chapter 9, "Layer 2 and Layer 3 Virtual Private Networks."

The problem with our configuration is the successful advertisement of the 172.16.0.0 /16 routes to both portions of AS 65010. Let's begin by examining the routes advertised by the Shiraz router. These routes are received by its EBGP peer of Chardonnay and are transmitted across AS 64888 to Merlot:

```
user@Merlot> show route protocol bgp terse

inet.0: 19 destinations, 19 routes (19 active, 0 holddown, 0 hidden)
+ = Active Route, - = Last Active, * = Both

A Destination        P Prf   Metric 1   Metric 2  Next hop        AS path
* 172.16.1.0/24      B 170       100         100 >10.222.45.2     65010 I
* 172.16.5.0/24      B 170       100           0 >10.222.3.1      65010 I
```

These active BGP routes are then readvertised by Merlot to Zinfandel. While Merlot claims to have sent the routes, however, the Zinfandel router doesn't appear to receive them. They don't even appear as hidden routes on Zinfandel:

```
user@Merlot> show route advertising-protocol bgp 10.222.3.1 172.16.0/22

inet.0: 19 destinations, 19 routes (19 active, 0 holddown, 0 hidden)
```

```
   Prefix                   Nexthop            MED     Lclpref     AS path
 * 172.16.1.0/24            Self                                   65010 I
```

```
user@Zinfandel> show route receive-protocol bgp 10.222.3.2
```

```
inet.0: 12 destinations, 12 routes (12 active, 0 holddown, 0 hidden)
```

```
user@Zinfandel>
```

Some of you may already see the issue here, but let's explain what's occurring. An examination of the AS Path attribute in the output from Merlot states that the current path is 65010. The only AS Path information not seen on Merlot is the default AS prepend accomplished as the packets leave the router. This means that Zinfandel receives a path of 64888 65010. When a BGP router receives an announced route, it first examines the path to determine if a loop exists. In our case, Zinfandel sees its own AS in the path of the received route. Believing this to be a routing loop, the routes are dropped and are not visible by any JUNOS software show command. Administratively, we know that this is not a routing loop and would like Zinfandel to receive the advertised routes. This desire is accomplished through the use of the as-override command.

This configuration option is applied to an EBGP peering session and works in a similar fashion to the remove-private command. The main difference between the two options is that the AS number of the EBGP peer is located in the path and not all private AS numbers. When the local router finds the peer's AS, it replaces that AS with its own local AS number. This allows the receiving router to not see its own AS in the path and therefore accept the route. We now configure the Merlot router with the as-override command:

```
[edit protocols bgp]
user@Merlot# show group external-peers
type external;
peer-as 65010;
as-override;
neighbor 10.222.3.1;
```

The routes are now received by the Zinfandel router with an AS Path of 64888 64888:

```
user@Zinfandel> show route receive-protocol bgp 10.222.3.2
```

```
inet.0: 15 destinations, 18 routes (15 active, 0 holddown, 3 hidden)
   Prefix                   Nexthop            MED     Lclpref     AS path
 * 172.16.1.0/24            10.222.3.2                             64888 64888 I
```

Let's now focus on the 172.16.4.0 /22 routes advertised by Zinfandel. We see that they are advertised by Chardonnay to Shiraz, which claims not to have received them:

```
user@Chardonnay> show route advertising-protocol bgp 10.222.44.1 172.16.4/22
```

```
inet.0: 20 destinations, 20 routes (20 active, 0 holddown, 0 hidden)
  Prefix                  Nexthop             MED     Lclpref   AS path
* 172.16.5.0/24           Self                                  65010 I
```

```
user@Shiraz> show route receive-protocol bgp 10.222.44.2
```

```
inet.0: 10 destinations, 10 routes (10 active, 0 holddown, 0 hidden)
```

```
user@Shiraz>
```

We have the same issue on this side of the network—an AS Path loop. This provides us with the opportunity to use the final JUNOS software configuration option for altering the AS Path information. This involves the *loops* option as part of the autonomous-system command. When you use this configuration option, you are allowing the local AS number to appear in the path more than once. In fact, the AS number can appear as many as 10 times, though just twice is enough in our case. We configure this on the receiving router of Shiraz and check our results:

```
[edit]
user@Shiraz# show routing-options
static {
    route 172.16.1.0/24 reject;
}
autonomous-system 65010 loops 2;
```

```
user@Shiraz> show route receive-protocol bgp 10.222.44.2
```

```
inet.0: 10 destinations, 10 routes (10 active, 0 holddown, 0 hidden)
```

```
user@Shiraz>
```

We haven't received any routes from Chardonnay, so it might appear that we have a problem with our configuration—but in fact we don't. While the JUNOS software default behavior for BGP peering sessions is effectively a soft inbound reconfiguration, this applies only to routes that are present in the Adjacency-RIB-In table. Since these routes were seen as a routing loop, they were immediately discarded and not retained in that table. This simply means that we need to manually ask Chardonnay to send the routes again:

```
user@Shiraz> clear bgp neighbor soft-inbound
```

```
user@Shiraz> show route protocol bgp terse
```

```
inet.0: 13 destinations, 16 routes (13 active, 0 holddown, 3 hidden)
+ = Active Route, - = Last Active, * = Both
```

```
A Destination          P Prf  Metric 1  Metric 2  Next hop      AS path
* 172.16.5.0/24        B 170     100               >10.222.44.2  64888 65010 I
```

The routes now appear in the routing table of Shiraz with an AS Path of 64888 65010.

> **WARNING** Extreme care should be taken when you use the as-override and *loops* commands. Improper use could result in routing loops in your network.

Modifying the AS Path: Routing Policy

Most network administrators alter the AS Path attribute by using a routing policy to add information to the path. This artificially increases the path length, potentially making the advertised route less desirable to receiving routers. The longer path lengths could therefore affect inbound user traffic flows into the local AS. The JUNOS software provides the ability to prepend your local AS or a customer AS to the path. Let's see how these two options work.

Prepending Your Own AS Number

The most common method of adding information to the AS Path attribute is including more than one instance of your own AS number before advertising the route. This is accomplished with a routing policy applied as routes are sent to an EBGP peer. The policy action of as-path-prepend *value* adds the supplied AS numbers to the AS Path attribute after the default prepend occurs.

FIGURE 5.5   AS Path prepend example

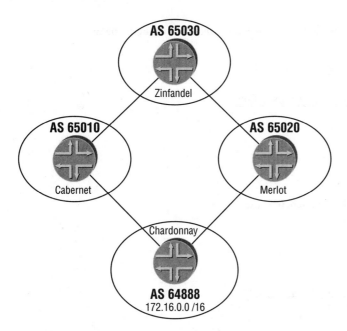

Figure 5.5 provides an example of how prepending your local AS onto the path affects the route decisions of other networks. The Chardonnay router in AS 64888 has peering sessions with both the Cabernet and Merlot routers. Each of these routers, in turn, has a peering session with the Zinfandel router in AS 65030. The administrators of AS 64888 would like user traffic from AS 65030 to transit through Cabernet on its way to the 172.16.0.0/16 address space. The current BGP routes on Zinfandel include

```
user@Zinfandel> show route protocol bgp

inet.0: 10 destinations, 11 routes (10 active, 0 holddown, 0 hidden)
+ = Active Route, - = Last Active, * = Both

172.16.0.0/16        *[BGP/170] 00:01:04, localpref 100
                        AS path: 65020 64888 I
                     > to 10.222.3.2 via at-0/1/1.0
                      [BGP/170] 00:01:00, localpref 100
                        AS path: 65010 64888 I
                     > to 10.222.61.2 via so-0/3/0.0
```

Zinfandel has received the 172.16.0.0/16 route from both AS 65020 and AS 65010. Each of the route announcements has a path length of 2, which prevents Zinfandel from using this attribute to select the best BGP route. To accomplish our administrative goal, we configure the **prepend-to-aggregate** policy on the Chardonnay router. This policy is applied to AS 65020 and the Merlot router:

```
[edit policy-options]
user@Chardonnay# show policy-statement prepend-to-aggregate
term prepend {
    from protocol aggregate;
    then {
        as-path-prepend "64888 64888";
        accept;
    }
}


[edit]
user@Chardonnay# show protocols bgp
group external-peers {
    type external;
    export adv-routes;
    neighbor 10.222.45.1 {
        export prepend-to-aggregate;
        peer-as 65020;
```

```
        }
    neighbor 10.222.6.1 {
        peer-as 65010;
    }
}
```

After committing our configuration, we can check to see what information Chardonnay thinks it is sending to its peers:

```
user@Chardonnay> show route advertising-protocol bgp 10.222.6.1

inet.0: 11 destinations, 11 routes (11 active, 0 holddown, 0 hidden)
  Prefix              Nexthop         MED     Lclpref    AS path
* 172.16.0.0/16       Self                               I

user@Chardonnay> show route advertising-protocol bgp 10.222.45.1

inet.0: 11 destinations, 11 routes (11 active, 0 holddown, 0 hidden)
  Prefix              Nexthop         MED     Lclpref    AS path
* 172.16.0.0/16       Self                               64888 64888 [64888] I
```

It would appear that we've succeeded in our goal. The 172.16.0.0/16 route is advertised to both peers, but the version sent to Merlot has AS 64888 prepended twice onto the path. The [64888] notation in the router output reminds us that the default prepend action is still occurring as the routes are advertised. In essence, we've included three instances of our AS with that route advertisement. Similar results are seen from the perspective of the Zinfandel router in AS 65030:

```
user@Zinfandel> show route protocol bgp

inet.0: 10 destinations, 11 routes (10 active, 0 holddown, 0 hidden)
+ = Active Route, - = Last Active, * = Both

172.16.0.0/16       *[BGP/170] 00:06:15, localpref 100
                      AS path: 65010 64888 I
                    > to 10.222.61.2 via so-0/3/0.0
                     [BGP/170] 00:06:27, localpref 100
                      AS path: 65020 64888 64888 64888 I
                    > to 10.222.3.2 via at-0/1/1.0
```

Prepending a Customer AS Number

Certain network topologies lend themselves to the prepending of a customer AS number to the path. This often occurs when a service provider has a customer attached via BGP across multiple peering points. The routes advertised by that customer into the provider's network are not prepended to allow for potential load balancing of traffic into the customer network. However, the customer would like the majority of its traffic from the Internet to arrive via a particular upstream AS. Figure 5.6 provides such an example.

The service provider network (AS 65010) consists of the Merlot, Chardonnay, and Sangiovese routers. It has two connections to the customer AS of 64888. In addition, two upstream peers are connected to the provider network: Cabernet in AS 65020 and Zinfandel in AS 65030. The customer routes are within the address space of 172.16.0.0 /22 and are visible on the Merlot router:

```
user@Merlot> show route protocol bgp terse

inet.0: 13 destinations, 13 routes (13 active, 0 holddown, 0 hidden)
+ = Active Route, - = Last Active, * = Both

A Destination        P Prf   Metric 1   Metric 2  Next hop        AS path
* 172.16.1.0/24      B 170        100           0 >10.222.45.2    64888 I
```

Merlot then advertises the routes to its upstream peers of Cabernet and Zinfandel:

```
user@Cabernet> show route protocol bgp terse

inet.0: 12 destinations, 12 routes (12 active, 0 holddown, 0 hidden)
+ = Active Route, - = Last Active, * = Both

A Destination        P Prf   Metric 1   Metric 2  Next hop        AS path
* 172.16.1.0/24      B 170        100             >10.222.1.2     65010 64888 I
```

```
user@Zinfandel> show route protocol bgp terse

inet.0: 12 destinations, 12 routes (12 active, 0 holddown, 0 hidden)
+ = Active Route, - = Last Active, * = Both

A Destination        P Prf   Metric 1   Metric 2  Next hop        AS path
* 172.16.1.0/24      B 170        100             >10.222.3.2     65010 64888 I
```

The customer in AS 64888 would like traffic forwarded from the Internet to traverse the Zinfandel router in AS 65030. They have requested that the provider enforce this requirement by prepending the AS Path length. One option available to the administrators of AS 65010 is to prepend the AS of their customer using the as-path-expand last-as count *value* policy action. When applied to an EBGP peering session, this policy action examines the AS Path attribute before the default prepend action takes place. The first AS number located, which is also the last value added to the path, is prepended as specified in the *value* area (up to 32 times). The router then performs its default prepend action and advertises the routes.

FIGURE 5.6   Customer AS prepend example

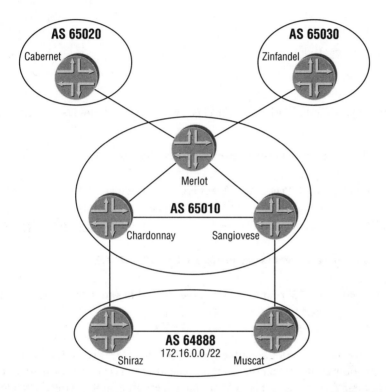

For our example, we create the ***prepend-customer-as*** policy on the Merlot router and apply it to the peering session with Cabernet. The policy locates any routes with AS 64888 in the path and prepends it three additional times onto the path:

```
[edit]
user@Merlot# show policy-options
policy-statement prepend-customer-as {
    term prepend {
        from as-path AS64888;
        then {
            as-path-expand last-as count 3;
        }
    }
}
as-path AS64888 ".* 64888 .*";
```

```
[edit]
user@Merlot# show protocols bgp group external-peers
type external;
neighbor 10.222.3.1 {
    peer-as 65030;
}
neighbor 10.222.1.1 {
    export prepend-customer-as;
    peer-as 65020;
}
```

After committing our configuration, we can check what routes Merlot is sending to Cabernet and Zinfandel:

```
user@Merlot> show route advertising-protocol bgp 10.222.1.1

inet.0: 13 destinations, 13 routes (13 active, 0 holddown, 0 hidden)
  Prefix              Nexthop        MED    Lclpref    AS path
* 172.16.1.0/24       Self                             64888 64888 64888 64888 I


user@Merlot> show route advertising-protocol bgp 10.222.3.1

inet.0: 13 destinations, 13 routes (13 active, 0 holddown, 0 hidden)
  Prefix              Nexthop        MED    Lclpref    AS path
* 172.16.1.0/24       Self                             64888 I
```

The routes advertised by Merlot are adhering to our administrative policy. A closer examination of the route output shows that the default prepend action is not represented, but remember that it still occurs. We can check this by examining the routing table on the Zinfandel router:

```
user@Zinfandel> show route protocol bgp

inet.0: 12 destinations, 12 routes (12 active, 0 holddown, 0 hidden)
+ = Active Route, - = Last Active, * = Both

172.16.1.0/24       *[BGP/170] 00:30:21, localpref 100
                      AS path: 65010 64888 I
                    > to 10.222.3.2 via at-0/1/1.0
```

Multiple Exit Discriminator

The Multiple Exit Discriminator (MED) attribute is optional and doesn't need to be included in each routing update. Its use is valuable when two ASs have multiple physical links between themselves. A MED value is set by the administrators of one AS for all routes advertised into its peer. This allows the peer AS to make routing decisions based on the advertised MEDs and potentially load-balance traffic across the multiple physical links. We first discuss how the JUNOS software evaluates the MED attribute and some ways to alter that selection process. We then see how to modify the attribute value using both configuration options as well as routing policy actions.

MED Selection Mechanisms

By default, a BGP router only compares the MED values of two path advertisements when they arrive from the same neighboring AS. The JUNOS software automatically groups advertisements from the same AS together to compare their MED values. The best value from each group is then compared with each other using other route attributes. This evaluation process is known as *deterministic MED*. To better appreciate how the deterministic MED process works, suppose that the 192.168.1.0 /24 route is received from three different peers. The possible path advertisements are

- Path 1—via EBGP; AS Path of 65010; MED of 200
- Path 2—via IBGP; AS Path of 65020; MED of 150; IGP cost of 5
- Path 3—via IBGP; AS Path of 65010; MED of 100; IGP cost of 10

Using the deterministic MED scheme, the router groups paths 1 and 3 together since they were both received from AS 65010. Between these two advertisements, path 3 has a better (lower) MED value. The router then eliminates path 1 from the selection process and evaluates path 3 against path 2. These two paths were received from different AS networks, so the router doesn't evaluate the MEDs. Instead, it uses other route attributes to select the active path—in this case, the IGP metric cost to the IBGP peer. The IGP cost of path 2 is better (lower) than the IGP cost of path 3. This allows the router to install path 2 as the active path for the 192.168.1.0 /24 route.

You have two options for altering this default method of operation within the JUNOS software. Let's discuss each of them separately.

Always Comparing MED Values

The first method for altering the MED behavior allows the router to always use the MED values to compare routes. This occurs regardless of the neighboring AS the path advertisement was received from. You enable this feature by using the `path-selection always-compare-med` command at the BGP global hierarchy level. Let's assume that the same three paths are received for the 192.168.1.0 /24 route:

- Path 1—via EBGP; AS Path of 65010; MED of 200
- Path 2—via IBGP; AS Path of 65020; MED of 150; IGP cost of 5
- Path 3—via IBGP; AS Path of 65010; MED of 100; IGP cost of 10

After enabling the `always-compare-med` function, the router begins to group all received advertisements into a single group. The MED values of each route are then compared against each other. Because a lower MED value is preferred, the router chooses path 3 as the active path to the destination. This is installed in the local routing table and user data packets are forwarded using the attributes of this path.

Exercise care when using this configuration option. Not all network operators agree on what a good MED value is. One AS might use 50 as a good value, while another might choose 5. Worse yet, some operators might not set a MED at all, which is interpreted as a 0 value.

Emulating the Cisco Systems Default Behavior

The second MED evaluation method allows you to emulate the default behavior of a Cisco Systems router. This operational mode evaluates routes in the order that they are received and doesn't group them according to their neighboring AS. In essence, this is the opposite of the deterministic MED process. This feature is also configured at the global BGP hierarchy level with the `path-selection cisco-non-deterministic` command. To accurately determine the effect of this feature, let's use the same three path advertisements for the 192.168.1.0 /24 route:

- Path 1—via EBGP; AS Path of 65010; MED of 200
- Path 2—via IBGP; AS Path of 65020; MED of 150; IGP cost of 5
- Path 3—via IBGP; AS Path of 65010; MED of 100; IGP cost of 10

These advertisements are received in quick succession, within a second, in the order listed. Path 3 was received most recently so the router compares it against path 2, the next most recent advertisement. The cost to the IBGP peer is better for path 2, so the router eliminates path 3 from contention. When comparing paths 1 and 2 together, the router prefers path 1 since it was received from an EBGP peer. This allows the router to install path 1 as the active path for the route.

 We do not recommend using this configuration option in your network. It is provided solely for interoperability to allow all routers in the network to make consistent route selections.

Altering the MED: Configuration Statements

Routes advertised by a Juniper Networks router may be assigned a MED value using one of several configuration options. You have the ability to use each option at either the global, group, or peer level of the configuration. When you use these options, the router applies the configured MED value to all routes advertised to a peer. In addition to setting a manual value, you may associate the IGP metric used within the AS to the advertised BGP route. Let's see how each of these categories works.

Manually Setting the MED

Network administrators might wish to manually set a MED value on all advertised routes when their AS is connected to only one BGP peer AS.

FIGURE 5.7   MED attribute sample network

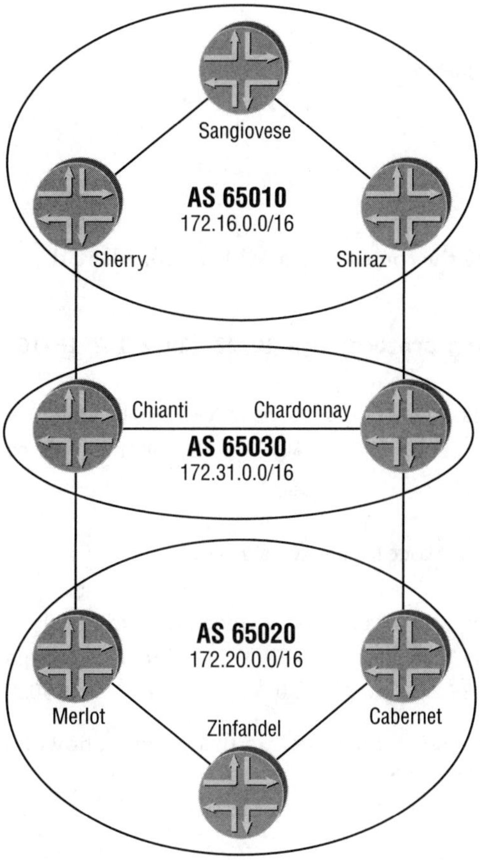

We see that AS 65010 in Figure 5.7 contains the Sherry, Sangiovese, and Shiraz routers. The address range of 172.16.0.0 /16 is assigned to that network, and the Sangiovese router is advertising routes to its IBGP peers:

```
user@Sangiovese> show route advertising-protocol bgp 192.168.16.1

inet.0: 15 destinations, 18 routes (15 active, 0 holddown, 0 hidden)
  Prefix                  Nexthop              MED    Lclpref    AS path
* 172.16.1.0/24           Self                 0      100        I
```

The administrators of AS 65010 would like their inbound user traffic to arrive on the Sherry router. Therefore, the routes advertised by Sherry should have a lower MED than the routes advertised by Shiraz. We accomplish this administrative goal by using the metric-out command at the BGP peer group level for the EBGP peers. This option allows the routes to receive a static MED value between 0 and 4,294,967,295. The configuration of the Sherry router now appears as so:

```
[edit protocols bgp]
user@Sherry# show group external-peers
type external;
metric-out 20;
peer-as 65030;
neighbor 10.222.29.2;
```

The Sherry router is now advertising the routes with a MED of 20, where they are received by the Chianti router in AS 65030:

```
user@Sherry> show route advertising-protocol bgp 10.222.29.2 172.16/16

inet.0: 18 destinations, 21 routes (18 active, 0 holddown, 0 hidden)
  Prefix              Nexthop         MED     Lclpref    AS path
* 172.16.1.0/24       Self            20                 I


user@Chianti> show route receive-protocol bgp 10.222.29.1

inet.0: 18 destinations, 24 routes (18 active, 0 holddown, 0 hidden)
  Prefix              Nexthop         MED     Lclpref    AS path
  172.16.1.0/24       10.222.29.1     20                 65010 I
```

A similar configuration is applied to the Shiraz router. In this instance, however, a MED value of 50 is applied to the advertised routes:

```
[edit protocols bgp]
user@Shiraz# show group external-peers
type external;
metric-out 50;
peer-as 65030;
neighbor 10.222.44.2;


user@Shiraz> show route advertising-protocol bgp 10.222.44.2 172.16/16

inet.0: 16 destinations, 19 routes (16 active, 0 holddown, 0 hidden)
  Prefix              Nexthop         MED     Lclpref    AS path
* 172.16.1.0/24       Self            50                 I
```

The advertised MED values allow the routers in AS 65030 to forward traffic to AS 65010 through the Sherry router:

```
user@Chianti> show route 172.16/16

inet.0: 18 destinations, 21 routes (18 active, 0 holddown, 0 hidden)
+ = Active Route, - = Last Active, * = Both

172.16.1.0/24      *[BGP/170] 00:04:29, MED 20, localpref 100
                      AS path: 65010 I
                    > to 10.222.29.1 via ge-0/3/0.0
```

The router output from the Chianti router shows the active BGP route using the ge-0/3/0.0 interface connected to Sherry in AS 65010. The Chardonnay router, on the other hand, is using the routes advertised by Chianti (192.168.20.1) over its so-0/3/0.600 interface. This occurs even as Chardonnay receives the same routes directly from Shiraz on its fe-0/0/0.0 interface:

```
user@Chardonnay> show route 172.16/16

inet.0: 18 destinations, 24 routes (18 active, 0 holddown, 0 hidden)
+ = Active Route, - = Last Active, * = Both

172.16.1.0/24      *[BGP/170] 00:01:59, MED 20, localpref 100, from 192.168.20.1
                      AS path: 65010 I
                    > to 10.222.100.1 via so-0/3/0.600
                     [BGP/170] 00:01:59, MED 50, localpref 100
                      AS path: 65010 I
                    > to 10.222.44.1 via fe-0/0/0.0
```

Associating the MED to the IGP Metric

Some network administrators correlate their internal IGP metrics to a single standard. This might be a representation of the various link bandwidths in the network, or it might represent the physical distance between the network devices (fiber route miles). Regardless of the details, the correlation allows internal routing to follow the shortest path according to the administrative setup. Should your IGP be configured in such a manner, it would be ideal to have a way to communicate this knowledge to BGP routers in a neighboring AS. This would allow those peers to forward traffic into your AS with the knowledge that it would be using the shortest paths possible.

Referring back to Figure 5.7, we see that the Merlot, Zinfandel, and Cabernet routers in AS 65020 have been assigned the 172.20.0.0 /16 address space. The administrators of AS 65020 would like to assign MED values to these routes that represent their internal IGP metrics. The JUNOS software provides two configuration options to assist AS 65020 in reaching its goal. These are the metric-out igp and metric-out minimum-igp configuration commands. While both options advertise the current IGP metric associated with the IBGP peer that advertised the route, they perform this function in slightly different manners. The igp feature directly tracks the IGP cost to the IBGP peer. When the IGP cost goes down, so does the advertised MED value. Conversely, when the IGP cost goes up the MED value goes up as well.

The Merlot router has a current IGP cost of 20 to Zinfandel, who is advertising the 172.20.0.0 /16 routes to BGP:

```
user@Merlot> show route 192.168.56.1

inet.0: 18 destinations, 21 routes (18 active, 0 holddown, 0 hidden)
+ = Active Route, - = Last Active, * = Both

192.168.56.1/32    *[IS-IS/18] 00:05:50, metric 20
                    > to 10.222.3.1 via at-0/2/0.0

user@Merlot> show route 172.20/16

inet.0: 18 destinations, 21 routes (18 active, 0 holddown, 0 hidden)
+ = Active Route, - = Last Active, * = Both

172.20.1.0/24      *[BGP/170] 23:45:25, MED 0, localpref 100, from 192.168.56.1
                    AS path: I
                    > to 10.222.3.1 via at-0/2/0.0
```

Merlot currently advertises these routes to AS 65030 with no MED value attached:

```
user@Merlot> show route advertising-protocol bgp 10.222.1.1 172.20/16

inet.0: 18 destinations, 21 routes (18 active, 0 holddown, 0 hidden)
  Prefix            Nexthop          MED    Lclpref    AS path
* 172.20.1.0/24     Self                               I
```

The metric-out igp command is now applied to the EBGP peer group on the Merlot router. This allows the router to assign a MED of 20, the current IGP cost to 192.168.56.1, to the BGP routes:

```
[edit protocols bgp]
user@Merlot# show group external-peers
type external;
metric-out igp;
peer-as 65030;
neighbor 10.222.1.1;

user@Merlot> show route advertising-protocol bgp 10.222.1.1 172.20/16
```

```
inet.0: 18 destinations, 21 routes (18 active, 0 holddown, 0 hidden)
  Prefix                Nexthop          MED    Lclpref    AS path
* 172.20.1.0/24         Self             20                I
```

When the IGP cost from Merlot to Zinfandel rises to 50, the advertised MED value to Chianti also changes to 50:

```
user@Merlot> show route 192.168.56.1

inet.0: 18 destinations, 21 routes (18 active, 0 holddown, 0 hidden)
+ = Active Route, - = Last Active, * = Both

192.168.56.1/32     *[IS-IS/18] 00:00:05, metric 50
                    > to 10.222.3.1 via at-0/2/0.0

user@Merlot> show route advertising-protocol bgp 10.222.1.1 172.20/16

inet.0: 18 destinations, 21 routes (18 active, 0 holddown, 0 hidden)
  Prefix                Nexthop          MED    Lclpref    AS path
* 172.20.1.0/24         Self             50                I
```

As we would expect, a reduction in the IGP cost to 10 also changes the advertised MED value:

```
user@Merlot> show route 192.168.56.1

inet.0: 18 destinations, 21 routes (18 active, 0 holddown, 0 hidden)
+ = Active Route, - = Last Active, * = Both

192.168.56.1/32     *[IS-IS/18] 00:00:03, metric 10
                    > to 10.222.3.1 via at-0/2/0.0

user@Merlot> show route advertising-protocol bgp 10.222.1.1 172.20/16

inet.0: 18 destinations, 21 routes (18 active, 0 holddown, 0 hidden)
  Prefix                Nexthop          MED    Lclpref    AS path
* 172.20.1.0/24         Self             10                I
```

On the Cabernet router across the AS, we configure the metric-out minimum-igp option. As the name suggests, the advertised MED value only changes when the IGP cost to the IBGP peer goes down. A rise in the IGP cost doesn't affect the MED values at all. The router monitors and remembers the lowest IGP cost until the routing process is restarted. The current cost from Cabernet to Zinfandel is 30, which matches the advertised MED values to Chardonnay in AS 65030:

```
[edit protocols bgp]
user@Cabernet# show group external-peers
```

```
type external;
metric-out minimum-igp;
peer-as 65030;
neighbor 10.222.6.2;
```

user@Cabernet> **show route 192.168.56.1**

```
inet.0: 18 destinations, 21 routes (18 active, 0 holddown, 0 hidden)
+ = Active Route, - = Last Active, * = Both

192.168.56.1/32    *[IS-IS/18] 00:02:18, metric 30
                    > to 10.222.61.1 via so-0/3/0.0
```

user@Cabernet> **show route advertising-protocol bgp 10.222.6.2 172.20/16**

```
inet.0: 18 destinations, 21 routes (18 active, 0 holddown, 0 hidden)
  Prefix              Nexthop           MED    Lclpref    AS path
* 172.20.1.0/24       Self              30                I
```

The advertised MED value decreases to 20 when the IGP cost also decreases:

user@Cabernet> **show route 192.168.56.1**

```
inet.0: 18 destinations, 21 routes (18 active, 0 holddown, 0 hidden)
+ = Active Route, - = Last Active, * = Both

192.168.56.1/32    *[IS-IS/18] 00:00:04, metric 20
                    > to 10.222.61.1 via so-0/3/0.0
```

user@Cabernet> **show route advertising-protocol bgp 10.222.6.2 172.20/16**

```
inet.0: 18 destinations, 21 routes (18 active, 0 holddown, 0 hidden)
  Prefix              Nexthop           MED    Lclpref    AS path
* 172.20.1.0/24       Self              20                I
```

When the IGP cost to Zinfandel rises to 50, however, the advertised MED value remains at 20:

user@Cabernet> **show route 192.168.56.1**

```
inet.0: 18 destinations, 21 routes (18 active, 0 holddown, 0 hidden)
+ = Active Route, - = Last Active, * = Both
```

```
192.168.56.1/32    *[IS-IS/18] 00:00:04, metric 50
                    > to 10.222.61.1 via so-0/3/0.0
```

```
user@Cabernet> show route advertising-protocol bgp 10.222.6.2 172.20/16
```

```
inet.0: 18 destinations, 21 routes (18 active, 0 holddown, 0 hidden)
  Prefix              Nexthop          MED    Lclpref    AS path
* 172.20.1.0/24       Self             20                I
```

Altering the MED: Routing Policy

When you use the configuration options to set the MED value on advertised BGP routes, all possible routes are affected. In fact, this is a common theme in the JUNOS software BGP configuration. To apply the MED values only to specific routes, use a routing policy to locate those routes and then set your desired value. The options for setting the MED in a routing policy are identical to those available with configuration knobs. You can set the value manually or via a routing policy.

Manually Setting the MED

Using Figure 5.7 as a guide, the network administrators of AS 65010 would like to set the MED only for routes originating in their AS. A routing policy called **set-med** is configured that locates these routes using an AS Path regular expression and sets the advertised MED value to 10. The policy is currently configured as so:

```
user@Sherry> show configuration policy-options | find set-med
policy-statement set-med {
    term only-AS65010-routes {
        from as-path local-to-AS65010;
        then {
            metric 10;
        }
    }
}
as-path local-to-AS65010 "()";
```

We apply the policy to the EBGP peer group, and the 172.16.0.0 /16 routes are advertised with a MED value of 10:

```
[edit protocols bgp]
user@Sherry# show group external-peers
type external;
export set-med;
peer-as 65030;
```

```
neighbor 10.222.29.2;
```

```
user@Sherry> show route advertising-protocol bgp 10.222.29.2 172.16/16
```

```
inet.0: 18 destinations, 21 routes (18 active, 0 holddown, 0 hidden)
  Prefix                 Nexthop            MED     Lclpref    AS path
* 172.16.1.0/24          Self               10                 I
```

A similar configuration on the Shiraz router in AS 65010 advertises the 172.16.0.0/16 routes with a MED value of 40. This ensures that all inbound traffic from AS 65030 uses the Sherry-Chianti EBGP peering session:

```
[edit policy-options]
user@Shiraz# show | find set-med
policy-statement set-med {
    term only-AS65010-routes {
        from as-path local-to-AS65010;
        then {
            metric 40;
        }
    }
}
as-path local-to-AS65010 "()";
```

```
[edit protocols bgp]
user@Shiraz# show group external-peers
type external;
export set-med;
peer-as 65030;
neighbor 10.222.44.2;
```

```
user@Shiraz> show route advertising-protocol bgp 10.222.44.2 172.16/16
```

```
inet.0: 16 destinations, 19 routes (16 active, 0 holddown, 0 hidden)
  Prefix                 Nexthop            MED     Lclpref    AS path
* 172.16.1.0/24          Self               40                 I
```

Associating the MED to the IGP Metric

The administrators of AS 65020 in Figure 5.7 would also like to advertise MED values for just their assigned address space of 172.20.0.0/16 and not all BGP routes. Appropriate routing policies are

configured on the Merlot and Cabernet routers using the `igp` and `minimum-igp` MED options. The
set-med policy on the Merlot router appears as so:

```
user@Merlot> show configuration policy-options | find set-med
policy-statement set-med {
    term only-AS65020-routes {
        from {
            route-filter 172.20.0.0/16 orlonger;
        }
        then {
            metric igp;
        }
    }
}
```

As before, the advertised MED value directly tracks the IGP cost to the Zinfandel router:

```
user@Merlot> show route 192.168.56.1

inet.0: 18 destinations, 21 routes (18 active, 0 holddown, 0 hidden)
+ = Active Route, - = Last Active, * = Both

192.168.56.1/32     *[IS-IS/18] 00:01:53, metric 15
                     > to 10.222.3.1 via at-0/2/0.0

user@Merlot> show route advertising-protocol bgp 10.222.1.1 172.20/16

inet.0: 18 destinations, 21 routes (18 active, 0 holddown, 0 hidden)
  Prefix                 Nexthop          MED     Lclpref     AS path
* 172.20.1.0/24          Self             15                  I
```

A lower IGP results in a lower MED value:

```
user@Merlot> show route 192.168.56.1

inet.0: 18 destinations, 21 routes (18 active, 0 holddown, 0 hidden)
+ = Active Route, - = Last Active, * = Both

192.168.56.1/32     *[IS-IS/18] 00:00:02, metric 10
                     > to 10.222.3.1 via at-0/2/0.0

user@Merlot> show route advertising-protocol bgp 10.222.1.1 172.20/16
```

```
inet.0: 18 destinations, 21 routes (18 active, 0 holddown, 0 hidden)
  Prefix                    Nexthop         MED     Lclpref    AS path
* 172.20.1.0/24             Self            10                 I
```

As expected, a higher MED value results from an IGP cost increase:

```
user@Merlot> show route 192.168.56.1

inet.0: 18 destinations, 21 routes (18 active, 0 holddown, 0 hidden)
+ = Active Route, - = Last Active, * = Both

192.168.56.1/32    *[IS-IS/18] 00:00:03, metric 20
                    > to 10.222.3.1 via at-0/2/0.0

user@Merlot> show route advertising-protocol bgp 10.222.1.1 172.20/16

inet.0: 18 destinations, 21 routes (18 active, 0 holddown, 0 hidden)
  Prefix                    Nexthop         MED     Lclpref    AS path
* 172.20.1.0/24             Self            20                 I
```

The Cabernet router in AS 65030 also has a ***set-med*** policy configured, but this version uses the `minimum-igp` action to set the MED value:

```
[edit policy-options]
user@Cabernet# show | find set-med
policy-statement set-med {
    term only-AS65020-routes {
        from {
            route-filter 172.20.0.0/16 orlonger;
        }
        then {
            metric minimum-igp;
        }
    }
}


[edit protocols bgp]
user@Cabernet# show group external-peers
type external;
export set-med;
peer-as 65030;
neighbor 10.222.6.2;
```

The MED values advertised to Chardonnay in AS 65030 now represent the smallest known IGP cost to the Zinfandel router:

```
user@Cabernet> show route 192.168.56.1

inet.0: 18 destinations, 21 routes (18 active, 0 holddown, 0 hidden)
+ = Active Route, - = Last Active, * = Both

192.168.56.1/32    *[IS-IS/18] 00:02:39, metric 15
                    > to 10.222.61.1 via so-0/3/0.0

user@Cabernet> show route advertising-protocol bgp 10.222.6.2 172.20/16

inet.0: 18 destinations, 21 routes (18 active, 0 holddown, 0 hidden)
  Prefix              Nexthop           MED    Lclpref    AS path
* 172.20.1.0/24       Self              15                I

user@Cabernet> show route 192.168.56.1

inet.0: 18 destinations, 21 routes (18 active, 0 holddown, 0 hidden)
+ = Active Route, - = Last Active, * = Both

192.168.56.1/32    *[IS-IS/18] 00:00:02, metric 30
                    > to 10.222.61.1 via so-0/3/0.0

user@Cabernet> show route advertising-protocol bgp 10.222.6.2 172.20/16

inet.0: 18 destinations, 21 routes (18 active, 0 holddown, 0 hidden)
  Prefix              Nexthop           MED    Lclpref    AS path
* 172.20.1.0/24       Self              15                I
```

Local Preference

The Local Preference attribute is the first value compared between two BGP routes in the route selection process. It is often used to set the exit point out of the local AS for a particular route. The JUNOS software allows you to modify this attribute with a routing policy action as well as a configuration option. As you might expect, the configuration option affects all advertised BGP routes while the routing policy allows you to be more selective.

The Chianti and Chardonnay routers in Figure 5.7 are located in AS 65030 and are advertising the 172.31.0.0 /16 aggregate route into AS 65010:

```
user@Chianti> show route advertising-protocol bgp 10.222.29.1 172.31/16
```

```
inet.0: 20 destinations, 24 routes (20 active, 0 holddown, 0 hidden)
  Prefix                  Nexthop              MED     Lclpref    AS path
* 172.31.0.0/16           Self                                    I
```

```
user@Chardonnay> show route advertising-protocol bgp 10.222.44.1 172.31/16
```

```
inet.0: 20 destinations, 24 routes (20 active, 0 holddown, 0 hidden)
  Prefix                  Nexthop              MED     Lclpref    AS path
* 172.31.0.0/16           Self                                    I
```

By default, all received EBGP routes are assigned a Local Preference value of 100. We see this on the Sangiovese router:

```
user@Sangiovese> show route 172.31/16
```

```
inet.0: 16 destinations, 20 routes (16 active, 0 holddown, 0 hidden)
+ = Active Route, - = Last Active, * = Both
```

```
172.31.0.0/16        *[BGP/170] 00:00:49, localpref 100, from 192.168.16.1
                        AS path: 65030 I
                     > to 10.222.28.1 via fe-0/0/0.0
                      [BGP/170] 00:00:06, localpref 100, from 192.168.36.1
                        AS path: 65030 I
                     > to 10.222.4.2 via fe-0/0/1.0
```

The AS 65010 administrators would like to affect the routing decision made by the Sangiovese router for forwarding data packets to the 172.31.0.0 /16 route. The Shiraz router should be used as the exit point out of AS 65010. The first step in accomplishing this goal is reducing the Local Preference value advertised by the Sherry router to 50. We accomplish this by using the local-preference configuration command at the BGP neighbor level:

```
[edit protocols bgp group internal-peers]
user@Sherry# show
type internal;
local-address 192.168.16.1;
export nhs;
neighbor 192.168.24.1 {
    local-preference 50;
}
neighbor 192.168.36.1;
```

This change only alters the route as it's advertised to Sangiovese. The local version of the route is not affected, and its Local Preference remains at 100:

```
user@Sherry> show route 172.31/16

inet.0: 19 destinations, 23 routes (19 active, 0 holddown, 0 hidden)
+ = Active Route, - = Last Active, * = Both

172.31.0.0/16      *[BGP/170] 00:30:47, localpref 100
                      AS path: 65030 I
                    > to 10.222.29.2 via ge-0/1/0.0
                     [BGP/170] 00:01:09, localpref 100, from 192.168.36.1
                      AS path: 65030 I
                    > to 10.222.28.2 via fe-0/0/0.0

user@Sherry> show route advertising-protocol bgp 192.168.24.1 172.31/16

inet.0: 19 destinations, 23 routes (19 active, 0 holddown, 0 hidden)
  Prefix                 Nexthop          MED    Lclpref    AS path
* 172.31.0.0/16          Self                       50      65030 I
```

On the opposite side of the AS, the Shiraz router uses a routing policy to alter the Local Preference to 150 for just the 172.31.0.0 /16 route. All other routes sent to Sangiovese don't have the attribute value changed from the default of 100. The routing policy appears as so:

```
user@Shiraz> show configuration policy-options | find set-local-preference
policy-statement set-local-preference {
    term only-AS65030-routes {
        from {
            route-filter 172.31.0.0/16 exact;
        }
        then {
            local-preference 150;
            accept;
        }
    }
}
as-path local-to-AS65010 "()";
```

The policy is applied to the BGP neighbor level configuration so that the Sangiovese router is the only router affected. As we saw with the Sherry router, the local version of the 172.31.0.0 / 16 route maintains a Local Preference value of 100 while the advertised route has a value of 150:

```
[edit protocols bgp]
user@Shiraz# show group internal-peers
```

```
type internal;
local-address 192.168.36.1;
export nhs;
neighbor 192.168.16.1;
neighbor 192.168.24.1 {
    export [ nhs set-local-preference ];
}
```

user@Shiraz> **show route 172.31/16**

```
inet.0: 17 destinations, 21 routes (17 active, 0 holddown, 0 hidden)
+ = Active Route, - = Last Active, * = Both

172.31.0.0/16       *[BGP/170] 00:44:33, localpref 100
                      AS path: 65030 I
                    > to 10.222.44.2 via fe-0/0/1.0
                     [BGP/170] 00:15:38, localpref 100, from 192.168.16.1
                      AS path: 65030 I
                    > to 10.222.4.1 via fe-0/0/0.0
```

user@Shiraz> **show route advertising-protocol bgp 192.168.24.1 172.31/16**

```
inet.0: 17 destinations, 21 routes (17 active, 0 holddown, 0 hidden)
  Prefix              Nexthop         MED    Lclpref    AS path
* 172.31.0.0/16       Self                     150       65030 I
```

 Don't forget to copy any applied group level policies to the neighbor level in this type of configuration. For example, the *nhs* policy is also applied to the 192.168.24.1 peer to ensure the BGP Next Hop of the route is reachable.

When we examine the routing table of the Sangiovese router, we see that the 172.31.0.0 /16 route is received with different Local Preference values. The higher value from the Shiraz router (192.168.36.1) is preferred over the lower value advertised from the Sherry router (192.168.16.1):

user@Sangiovese> **show route 172.31/16**

```
inet.0: 16 destinations, 20 routes (16 active, 0 holddown, 0 hidden)
+ = Active Route, - = Last Active, * = Both

172.31.0.0/16       *[BGP/170] 00:06:18, localpref 150, from 192.168.36.1
```

```
    AS path: 65030 I
 > to 10.222.4.2 via fe-0/0/1.0
 [BGP/170] 00:21:57, localpref 50, from 192.168.16.1
    AS path: 65030 I
 > to 10.222.28.1 via fe-0/0/0.0
```

WARNING   The examples used in this section are effective for highlighting the operation of the configuration options available to you. They are not recommended as a best practice in your network. Generally speaking, the Local Preference attribute is assigned to all received EBGP routes using an inbound routing policy. This ensures that all routers in the network make consistent routing decisions.

IBGP Scaling Methods

When you ask a network engineer why you need a full mesh of IBGP peering sessions, you often times get a response similar to "Because an IBGP-learned route can't be readvertised to another IBGP peer." While this is certainly a valid response, it is also not a complete answer. The reason for preventing the readvertisement of IBGP routes and requiring the full mesh is to avoid routing loops within an AS. Recall that the AS Path attribute is the means by which BGP routers avoid loops. The path information is examined for the local AS number only when the route is received from an EBGP peer. Since the attribute is only modified across AS boundaries, this system works extremely well. Unfortunately, the fact that the attribute is only modified across AS boundaries leaves us with problems internally. As a quick example, suppose that routers A, B, and C are all in the same AS. Router A receives a route from an EBGP peer and sends the route to B, who installs it as the active route. The route is then sent to router C, who installs it locally and sends it back to router A. Should router A install the route, we've formed a loop within our AS. We couldn't detect the loop since the AS Path attribute wasn't modified during these advertisements. Therefore, the protocol designers decided that the only assurance of never forming a routing loop was to prevent an IBGP peer from advertising an IBGP-learned route within the AS. For route reachability, the IBGP peers are then fully meshed.

    Full-mesh networks have inherent scalability issues. For protocols that utilize a neighbor-discovery mechanism, the issues surround database and routing table sizes as well as performance during a network outage. For a BGP network, one additional issue is the explicit configuration of each BGP peer. Let's assume that an AS has five operational IBGP peers and needs to add a sixth. In addition to the new router configuring its five other peers, each of the current routers must update its configuration to include the sixth router. In addition, the network protocol state grows exponentially as more peers are added. In our six-router network, a total of 15 IBGP peering sessions must be maintained ($n \times (n-1)) \div 2$. Things only worsen as the number of IBGP peers grows. Imagine having to reconfigure 99 existing routers to add a new peer to the cloud. This 100-router IBGP full mesh also requires the maintenance of 4950 peering sessions.

We have two main methods for alleviating these issues and scaling an AS to thousands of routers—route reflection and confederations. Each of these approaches replaces the full mesh of IBGP peering sessions and ensures a loop-free BGP network. These common goals are achieved using different methods and procedures, which we discuss in some depth throughout this section.

Route Reflection

The approach taken in a *route reflection* network to solving the full-mesh problem is allowing an IBGP-learned route to be readvertised, or reflected, to an IBGP peer. This is allowed to occur only on special routers called *route reflectors* (RR), which utilize some BGP attributes defined specifically for a route reflection network. Each RR is assigned certain peers, known as *clients*, for which it reflects IBGP routes. Together, the route reflector and its clients are considered a *cluster* in the network. The route reflector sends and receives BGP routes for all other nonclient peers according to the rules set forth in the original BGP specification.

To prevent routing loops in the network, two new BGP attributes and a new identifier value are defined by the route reflection specification. These items are:

Cluster ID   The *cluster ID* is similar in nature to the AS number defined for each router. A unique 32-bit value is assigned to each cluster in the network that identifies and separates it from other network clusters.

Cluster List   The *Cluster List* is a BGP attribute that operates like the AS Path attribute. It contains a list of sequential cluster IDs for each cluster a particular route has transited. It is used as the main loop avoidance mechanism and is never transmitted outside the local AS.

Originator ID   The *Originator ID* is also a BGP attribute defined for use by route reflectors. It identifies the router that first advertised the route to the route reflector in the network. Route reflectors use the Originator ID as a second check against routing loops within the AS. Like the Cluster List attribute, the Originator ID is local to the AS and is never transmitted across an EBGP peering session.

Operational Theory

Now that we've touched on the basics of what a route reflection network is and the terms used to describe it, let's discuss how routes are propagated. In addition, we'll touch on some design issues related to route reflection.

Figure 5.8 shows the Zinfandel, Chablis, and Cabernet routers in a route reflection cluster. The Zinfandel router is the route reflector for the cluster, assigned an identifier of 1.1.1.1, while Chablis and Cabernet are the clients. Each of the clients forms an IBGP peering session with just the RR and not with each other. This reduction in peering sessions pays large dividends as the network size grows and greatly reduces the number of overall peering sessions in the AS. The route reflector forwards active BGP routes based on how they were received using the following rules:

From an EBGP peer   When an RR receives an active BGP route from an EBGP peer, it forwards the route to all clients in its cluster as well as to all other IBGP nonclient peers. The Cluster List and Originator attributes are added only to routes advertised to clients within the cluster.

From an IBGP client peer   When an RR receives an active BGP route from an IBGP peer that belongs to its cluster, it forwards the route to all other clients in its cluster as well as all other IBGP nonclient peers. These IBGP advertisements contain the Originator ID attribute and a modified Cluster List. The route reflector also advertises the route to all of its EBGP peers without adding the route reflection attributes.

From an IBGP nonclient peer   When an RR receives an active BGP route from an IBGP peer that is not within a cluster, it forwards the route to all clients in its cluster with the appropriate attributes attached. The route reflector also advertises the routes to its EBGP peers without the route reflection attributes.

Even though the RR is readvertising routes, it is important to remember that it is still a BGP router. This means that route selection is performed on all path advertisements, a single route is selected and placed in the routing table, and that single route is advertised to its peers.

FIGURE 5.8   Basic route reflection network

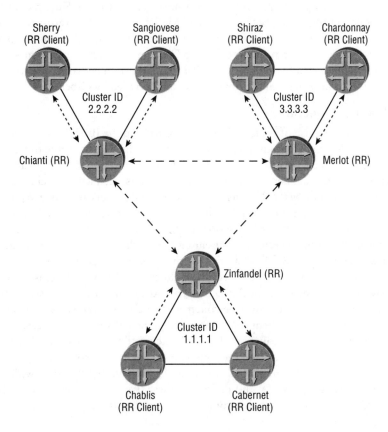

Suppose that the Cabernet router receives a path advertisement from an EBGP peer. The advertisement is selected as the active route and is readvertised to its IBGP peers. In our case, Cabernet has only a single peer—Zinfandel. The advertisement is received by Zinfandel, accepted, and placed into the routing table. Since the route was learned from an IBGP peer in its cluster, Zinfandel reflects the route inside the cluster and advertises it to Chablis. During the reflection process, Zinfandel attaches both the Originator ID and Cluster List attributes to the route. The router ID of Cabernet becomes the Originator ID for the route, and the cluster ID of 1.1.1.1 is placed into the Cluster List. None of the other attributes attached to the route are altered by default; they continue to represent the values set by Cabernet. Of course, the Zinfandel router also has additional IBGP peers in the network, so let's see what happens across those peering sessions.

The Chianti router is the RR for cluster 2.2.2.2 and Merlot is the RR for cluster 3.3.3.3, each with two clients in its cluster. These two route reflectors have nonclient peering sessions with each other in addition to the Zinfandel router. In the end, we have an IBGP full mesh established between Zinfandel, Chianti, and Merlot. These nonclient peers of Zinfandel must also receive a copy of the EBGP-learned route from the Cabernet router. This version of the route also includes the Cluster List and Originator ID attributes.

At this point, Zinfandel's participation in route reflection is complete. Both Chianti and Merlot, themselves route reflectors, receive the route and examine the Cluster List attribute for their local cluster ID. Neither of the routers finds a routing loop and installs the route. Since the route was received from a nonclient IBGP peer, both Chianti and Merlot may only readvertise the route to clients in their local cluster. This allows the Sherry, Sangiovese, Shiraz, and Chardonnay routers to receive the route that originally entered the local AS via Cabernet. In the end, each of these four routers sees no difference between a full-mesh IBGP and a route reflection network. The route was received internally with the exact same attribute values as advertised by Cabernet.

Hierarchical Route Reflection

In very large networks, the use of route reflection helps to keep the IBGP peering sessions and protocol reconfiguration to a minimum. However, the possibility exists for the full mesh of sessions between the route reflectors to grow too large. Figure 5.9 represents this exact scenario.

Our sample network now contains five route reflection clusters, each with two clients. There are now 10 IBGP sessions supporting the RR full mesh. As additional clusters are added to the network, we find ourselves facing the same problem that route reflection was designed to solve: large configurations and protocol state. This type of scenario is mitigated through the use of *hierarchical route reflection*, which allows a route reflector for one cluster to be a client in a separate cluster. The end result is the replacement of the RR full mesh with another cluster, as seen in Figure 5.10.

A new router is installed as the route reflector for cluster 6.6.6.6 with the existing reflectors as its clients. The readvertising rules for this new RR are identical to the rules used by the other reflectors. At a high level, let's see how each router in the network receives a route advertised by a client in cluster 1.1.1.1. The client sends the route to the RR for cluster 1.1.1.1, router A, who reflects it inside the cluster. Router A also sends the route to its nonclient IBGP peers, which is only router F in this case. From the viewpoint of router F, a route was just received from an RR client in cluster 6.6.6.6. This allows router F to readvertise the route within its cluster, which sends it to routers B, C, D, and E. Each of these five routers sees a route advertised by a nonclient IBGP peer and reflects that route into its particular cluster.

FIGURE 5.9 Large full mesh of RR peerings

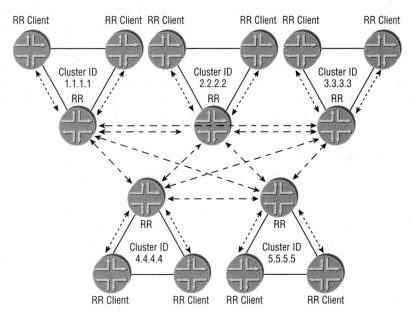

FIGURE 5.10 Hierarchical route reflection

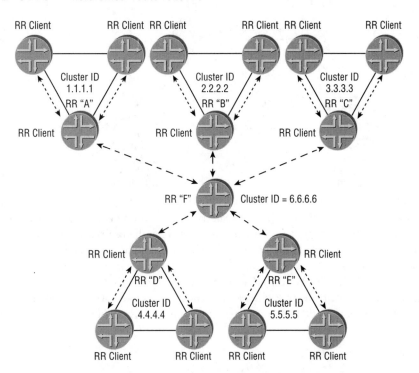

The success of a hierarchical route reflection network relies on the careful establishment of clients and route reflectors. When you assign these roles, always place yourself in the router's position and think about where routes are received from and which peers you can readvertise those routes to.

Hierarchical route reflection has no limit to the number of levels or layers used. Provided that reachability is maintained and no routing loops are introduced, you can build your network in any fashion you desire.

Designing for Redundancy

In the examples we've examined thus far, you may have noticed the potential for disaster to strike. Specifically, the way in which we've used our route reflectors leaves us exposed to a single point of failure—the route reflector itself. When a client establishes an IBGP peering session to a single RR, it becomes reliant on that peer for all network reachability. Should the route reflector stop operating, the client no longer has the ability to forward and receive traffic from the core of the AS. This vulnerability leads many network administrators to use two route reflectors in each cluster.

FIGURE 5.11 Using two route reflectors in a cluster

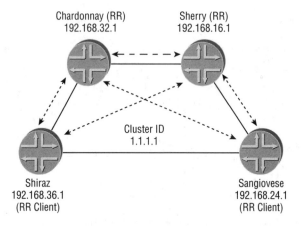

Figure 5.11 shows a cluster with both Sherry and Chardonnay as route reflectors in cluster 1.1.1.1. Both of the reflectors establish a session between themselves as well as sessions within the cluster to the Shiraz and Sangiovese routers. In our example, the RR peering is accomplished outside the cluster, but this is not required. This configuration doesn't alter the operation of the route reflectors with regard to the advertisement of routing information. When the Sangiovese router receives a route from an EBGP peer, it sends it to its two IBGP peers of Sherry and Chardonnay. Both reflectors add the Originator ID and Cluster List attributes to the route and reflect

it within the cluster to Shiraz. Additionally, both Sherry and Chardonnay forward the route to their nonclient IBGP peers (which are each other). If we look at this last piece of the flooding, we gain an interesting insight into the operation of route reflection. Because both Sherry and Chardonnay are configured as route reflectors, each router examines the incoming routes for the Cluster List attribute. If the attribute is attached, the router further looks for their local cluster ID in the Cluster List. In our example, both routers see the ID of 1.1.1.1 in the Cluster List and drop the route. This process occurs even if the route reflectors are peering within the cluster as clients of one another.

Configuring the Network

Configuring route reflection within the JUNOS software is a very simple and straightforward process. After establishing the appropriate peering sessions, you only need to configure the route reflector using the `cluster` *value* command within an appropriate peer group. This command treats each IBGP peer in the peer group as a route reflection client. All other configured peers on the router are treated as nonclient peers. The *value* portion of the command contains the 32-bit unique cluster identifier for your network.

Choosing the Cluster ID

From a technical standpoint, the specific value you assign as the cluster ID is insignificant as long as it is unique throughout your network. It appears within the Cluster List attribute only on internally advertised routes and is used for routing loop avoidance. From a troubleshooting perspective, however, the choice of the cluster ID values may have great importance. Let's talk about two main scenarios.

The first possibility is a route reflection cluster with a single route reflector. In this instance, many network administrators find it helpful to use the router ID of the route reflector as the cluster ID value. When you use this system, you can view the Cluster List of any route in your network and immediately know which route reflectors have readvertised the route.

The second possibility is a cluster with multiple route reflectors, often two routers. Using the router ID from one of the route reflectors is not as helpful in this case, but some networks do use this system. This is especially true when the cluster represents a point of presence (POP) in the network. Seeing the router ID in the Cluster List at least provides you with the POPs the route has traversed. More often than not, the cluster ID for a dual-route reflector cluster is an arbitrary value that makes sense to the network administrators. Many networks use a system similar to the one we've employed in this chapter; 1.1.1.1, followed by 2.2.2.2, followed by 3.3.3.3, etc. As long as the system is consistent and straightforward, it will be easily understood when troubleshooting must occur.

FIGURE 5.12 Basic route reflection sample network

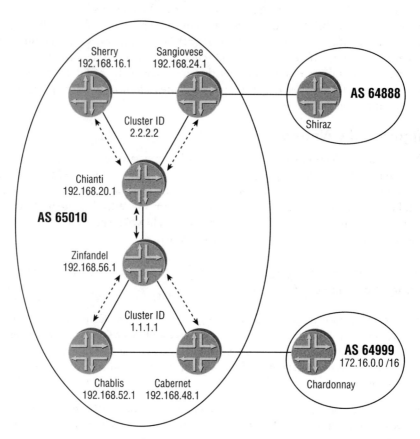

AS 65010 in Figure 5.12 contains six routers running a route reflection network. The Chianti router is a reflector for cluster 2.2.2.2 and the Zinfandel router is a reflector for cluster 1.1.1.1, with each cluster containing two clients. The Cabernet router has an EBGP peering session with Chardonnay in AS 64999 and is receiving routes in the 172.16.0.0 /16 address space. These routes appear on Cabernet as

```
user@Cabernet> show route protocol bgp

inet.0: 20 destinations, 20 routes (20 active, 0 holddown, 0 hidden)
+ = Active Route, - = Last Active, * = Both

172.16.1.0/24      *[BGP/170] 00:33:23, MED 0, localpref 100
                      AS path: 64999 I
                    > to 10.222.6.2 via fe-0/0/1.0
```

The configuration of Cabernet shows only a single peering session to its local route reflector of Zinfandel (192.168.56.1):

```
user@Cabernet> show configuration protocols bgp
group internal-peers {
    type internal;
    local-address 192.168.48.1;
    export nhs;
    neighbor 192.168.56.1;
}
group external-peers {
    type external;
    neighbor 10.222.6.2 {
        peer-as 64999;
    }
}
```

We can now examine the routing table on the Zinfandel router and see the 172.16.0.0 /16 routes:

```
user@Zinfandel> show route protocol bgp

inet.0: 20 destinations, 20 routes (20 active, 0 holddown, 0 hidden)
+ = Active Route, - = Last Active, * = Both

172.16.1.0/24      *[BGP/170] 00:36:08, MED 0, localpref 100, from 192.168.48.1
                      AS path: 64999 I
                    > to 10.222.61.2 via so-0/3/0.0
```

When we look at the configuration of Zinfandel, we see two peer groups configured. The *internal-peers* group contains the address of Chianti, its nonclient IBGP peer. The *cluster-1* group contains both the Chablis and Cabernet routers. The cluster 1.1.1.1 command in the *cluster-1* group defines these peers as route reflection clients:

```
user@Zinfandel> show configuration protocols bgp
group internal-peers {
    type internal;
    local-address 192.168.56.1;
    neighbor 192.168.20.1;
}
group cluster-1 {
    type internal;
    local-address 192.168.56.1;
    cluster 1.1.1.1;
```

```
    neighbor 192.168.48.1;
    neighbor 192.168.52.1;
}
```

Applying what we know about the operation of Zinfandel as a route reflector, we assume that the 172.16.0.0 /16 routes are advertised to both Chablis and Chianti. The output of the show route advertising-protocol bgp *neighbor-address* command proves this to be a correct assumption:

```
user@Zinfandel> show route advertising-protocol bgp 192.168.52.1

inet.0: 20 destinations, 20 routes (20 active, 0 holddown, 0 hidden)
  Prefix                Nexthop           MED     Lclpref    AS path
* 172.16.1.0/24         192.168.48.1      0       100        64999 I


user@Zinfandel> show route advertising-protocol bgp 192.168.20.1

inet.0: 20 destinations, 20 routes (20 active, 0 holddown, 0 hidden)
  Prefix                Nexthop           MED     Lclpref    AS path
* 172.16.1.0/24         192.168.48.1      0       100        64999 I
```

When we use the *detail* option, we see the Originator ID attached to the routes. The router ID of Cabernet (192.168.48.1) is used as the Originator ID since it was the router that first advertised the route to a route reflector in the network. In addition, we see the local cluster ID value that the router prepends into the Cluster List attribute. The Cluster List itself is not displayed since Zinfandel adds the attribute during the prepend operation:

```
user@Zinfandel> show route advertising-protocol bgp 192.168.52.1 detail

inet.0: 20 destinations, 20 routes (20 active, 0 holddown, 0 hidden)
* 172.16.1.0/24 (1 entry, 1 announced)
 BGP group cluster-1 type Internal
     Nexthop: 192.168.48.1
     MED: 0
     Localpref: 100
     AS path: 64999 I
 Communities:
     Cluster ID: 1.1.1.1
     Originator ID: 192.168.48.1
```

Remember that the output of the show route advertising-protocol bgp *neighbor-address* command displays the effect of all outgoing policies with the exception of the default AS Path prepend action for EBGP peers. This same concept holds true for the Cluster List attribute.

Once the routes are installed on the other client in cluster 1.1.1.1 (Chablis), we can see all of the route reflection attributes applied to the route:

```
user@Chablis> show route 172.16.1/24 detail

inet.0: 19 destinations, 19 routes (19 active, 0 holddown, 0 hidden)
172.16.1.0/24 (1 entry, 1 announced)
        *BGP    Preference: 170/-101
                Source: 192.168.56.1
                Next hop: 10.222.60.2 via fe-0/0/0.0, selected
                Protocol next hop: 192.168.48.1 Indirect next hop: 84cfbd0 57
                State: <Active Int Ext>
                Local AS: 65010 Peer AS: 65010
                Age: 51:40     Metric: 0      Metric2: 10
                Task: BGP_65010.192.168.56.1+179
                Announcement bits (2): 0-KRT 4-Resolve inet.0
                AS path: 64999 I (Originator) Cluster list:  1.1.1.1
                AS path:  Originator ID: 192.168.48.1
                Localpref: 100
                Router ID: 192.168.56.1
```

The Chianti router is advertising the route within its cluster since it was received from a non-client IBGP peer (Zinfandel):

```
user@Chianti> show route advertising-protocol bgp 192.168.16.1

inet.0: 22 destinations, 22 routes (22 active, 0 holddown, 0 hidden)
  Prefix                 Nexthop          MED    Lclpref    AS path
* 172.16.1.0/24          192.168.48.1     0      100        64999 I

user@Chianti> show route advertising-protocol bgp 192.168.24.1

inet.0: 22 destinations, 22 routes (22 active, 0 holddown, 0 hidden)
  Prefix                 Nexthop          MED    Lclpref    AS path
* 172.16.1.0/24          192.168.48.1     0      100        64999 I
```

The 172.16.1.0 /24 route is visible on the Sangiovese router as

```
user@Sangiovese> show route 172.16.1/24 detail

inet.0: 23 destinations, 23 routes (23 active, 0 holddown, 0 hidden)
172.16.1.0/24 (1 entry, 1 announced)
        *BGP    Preference: 170/-101
```

```
Source: 192.168.20.1
Next hop: 10.222.28.1 via fe-0/0/0.0, selected
Protocol next hop: 192.168.48.1 Indirect next hop: 84cfbd0 68
State: <Active Int Ext>
Local AS: 65010 Peer AS: 65010
Age: 54:43      Metric: 0      Metric2: 40
Task: BGP_65010.192.168.20.1+4330
Announcement bits (3): 0-KRT 3-BGP.0.0.0.0+179 4-Resolve inet.0
AS path: 64999 I (Originator) Cluster list:  2.2.2.2 1.1.1.1
AS path:  Originator ID: 192.168.48.1
Localpref: 100
Router ID: 192.168.20.1
```

As we should expect, the Originator ID value is still set to 192.168.48.1, the router ID of Cabernet. This attribute remains constant throughout the route reflection network and is stripped from the route when it is advertised across an AS boundary. In addition, the Cluster List attribute shows us that the route transited cluster 1.1.1.1 followed by cluster 2.2.2.2. This second ID value was prepended onto the list by Chianti when it reflected the route. When the routes are received by the Shiraz router in AS 64888, we see that the route reflection attributes are removed and that the Sangiovese router added the local AS of 65010 to the AS Path attribute:

user@Shiraz> **show route receive-protocol bgp 10.222.4.1 detail**

```
inet.0: 12 destinations, 12 routes (12 active, 0 holddown, 0 hidden)
* 172.16.1.0/24 (1 entry, 1 announced)
      Nexthop: 10.222.4.1
      AS path: 65010 64999 I
```

In accordance with the general theory of BGP, Shiraz has no knowledge of the internal connectivity of AS 65010. It only knows that the active path transits this AS.

Hierarchical Route Reflection

As we discussed in the "Operational Theory" section earlier, the operation of a network using hierarchical route reflection is no different than a simple route reflection network. It should come as no surprise, then, that the configuration of hierarchical route reflection is no different.

Figure 5.13 shows seven routers in AS 65010 arrayed in a hierarchical route reflection design. The configuration of Zinfandel, the route reflector for Cluster 1.1.1.1, appears as so:

user@Zinfandel> **show configuration protocols bgp**
```
group internal-peers {
    type internal;
    local-address 192.168.56.1;
    neighbor 192.168.20.1;
}
```

```
group cluster-1 {
    type internal;
    local-address 192.168.56.1;
    cluster 1.1.1.1;
    neighbor 192.168.48.1;
    neighbor 192.168.52.1;
}
```

This is very similar to the route reflector configuration for cluster 2.2.2.2 on the Merlot router:

```
user@Merlot> show configuration protocols bgp
group internal-peers {
    type internal;
    local-address 192.168.40.1;
    neighbor 192.168.20.1;
}
group cluster-2 {
    type internal;
    local-address 192.168.40.1;
    cluster 2.2.2.2;
    neighbor 192.168.32.1;
    neighbor 192.168.36.1;
}
```

FIGURE 5.13   Hierarchical route reflection sample network

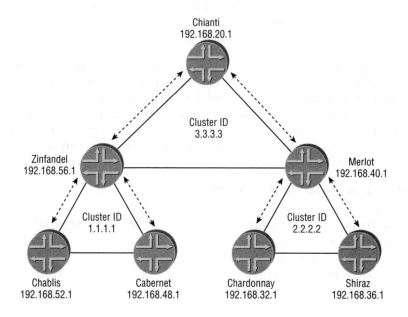

In fact, if you were just shown the configurations of these two route reflectors you might not know that hierarchical route reflection was being used. From the viewpoint of these routers, they are each responsible for a single cluster and have an additional IBGP peer. You do have one clue available to you and it lies in the ***internal-peers*** peer group of each router. In a simple route reflection network, each reflector peers with all of the other route reflectors. This particular peer group contains only a single neighbor statement for 192.168.20.1, which is not a peer route reflector but the same third router. The configuration of this router, Chianti, shows a cluster ID of 3.3.3.3 and route reflector clients of Zinfandel and Merlot:

```
user@Chianti> show configuration protocols bgp
group cluster-3 {
    type internal;
    local-address 192.168.20.1;
    cluster 3.3.3.3;
    neighbor 192.168.40.1;
    neighbor 192.168.56.1;
}
```

Suppose that the Shiraz router receives routes in the 172.16.0.0 /16 address range from an EBGP peer in AS 64999. These routes include the following:

```
user@Shiraz> show route protocol bgp

inet.0: 25 destinations, 25 routes (25 active, 0 holddown, 0 hidden)
+ = Active Route, - = Last Active, * = Both

172.16.1.0/24       *[BGP/170] 12:32:56, MED 0, localpref 100
                      AS path: 64999 I
                    > to 10.222.4.1 via fe-0/0/0.0
```

Based on the configurations of the route reflectors, we can assume that each router in the network has received these same routes and installed them in their local routing table. If we examine the details of the route attributes on the Chablis router, for example, we should find that the Originator ID is set to the router ID of Shiraz (192.168.36.1). Additionally, the Cluster List attribute should appear as 1.1.1.1 3.3.3.3 2.2.2.2 since the route was reflected first by Merlot, then by Chianti, and finally by Zinfandel. Let's verify our assumptions by viewing the 172.16.1.0 /24 route on Chablis:

```
user@Chablis> show route 172.16.1/24 detail

inet.0: 23 destinations, 23 routes (23 active, 0 holddown, 0 hidden)
172.16.1.0/24 (1 entry, 1 announced)
    *BGP  Preference: 170/-101
          Source: 192.168.56.1
```

```
Next hop: 10.222.60.2 via fe-0/0/0.0, selected
Protocol next hop: 192.168.36.1 Indirect next hop: 84cfbd0 57
State: <Active Int Ext>
Local AS: 65010 Peer AS: 65010
Age: 12:24:08   Metric: 0      Metric2: 30
Task: BGP_65010.192.168.56.1+179
Announcement bits (2): 0-KRT 4-Resolve inet.0
AS path: 64999 I (Originator) Cluster list:  1.1.1.1 3.3.3.3 2.2.2.2
AS path:  Originator ID: 192.168.36.1
Localpref: 100
Router ID: 192.168.56.1
```

Using Two Route Reflectors

For completeness, let's take a quick moment to examine the configuration and operation of a route reflection cluster containing two reflectors. Using Figure 5.11 as a guide, we see that the configuration of the clients, Sangiovese and Shiraz, appear as normal BGP configurations. The main difference, in this case, is the inclusion of two internal peers as opposed to a single peer in our simple route reflection examples:

```
user@Sangiovese> show configuration protocols bgp
group internal-peers {
    type internal;
    local-address 192.168.24.1;
    neighbor 192.168.16.1;
    neighbor 192.168.32.1;
}

user@Shiraz> show configuration protocols bgp
group internal-peers {
    type internal;
    local-address 192.168.36.1;
    neighbor 192.168.16.1;
    neighbor 192.168.32.1;
}
```

In fact, the configurations of the two route reflectors, Sherry and Chardonnay, also appear very similar to a simple route reflection network. The exception is the configuration of the cluster 1.1.1.1 command on both routers:

```
user@Sherry> show configuration protocols bgp
group internal-peers {
```

```
    type internal;
    local-address 192.168.16.1;
    neighbor 192.168.32.1;
}
group cluster-1 {
    type internal;
    local-address 192.168.16.1;
    cluster 1.1.1.1;
    neighbor 192.168.24.1;
    neighbor 192.168.36.1;
}
```

```
user@Chardonnay> show configuration protocols bgp
group internal-peers {
    type internal;
    local-address 192.168.32.1;
    neighbor 192.168.16.1;
}
group cluster-1 {
    type internal;
    local-address 192.168.32.1;
    cluster 1.1.1.1;
    neighbor 192.168.24.1;
    neighbor 192.168.36.1;
}
```

Once the IBGP peering sessions are established, the Sangiovese router advertises its received EBGP routes to both route reflectors:

```
user@Sangiovese> show route advertising-protocol bgp 192.168.16.1

inet.0: 15 destinations, 15 routes (15 active, 0 holddown, 0 hidden)
  Prefix              Nexthop          MED      Lclpref    AS path
* 172.16.1.0/24       Self             0        100        64999 I


user@Sangiovese> show route advertising-protocol bgp 192.168.32.1

inet.0: 15 destinations, 15 routes (15 active, 0 holddown, 0 hidden)
  Prefix              Nexthop          MED      Lclpref    AS path
* 172.16.1.0/24       Self             0        100        64999 I
```

Both Sherry and Chardonnay reflect the routes within the cluster to the Shiraz router, providing two path advertisements for the same set of routes. The BGP route selection algorithm is run against these multiple paths and an active route is selected. In this case, the router ID of Sherry (192.168.16.1) is better than the router ID of Chardonnay (192.168.32.1). The show route detail output for the 172.16.1.0 /24 routes also shows the correct route reflection attributes attached to the routes:

```
user@Shiraz> show route 172.16.1/24 detail

inet.0: 15 destinations, 18 routes (15 active, 0 holddown, 0 hidden)
172.16.1.0/24 (2 entries, 1 announced)
        *BGP    Preference: 170/-101
                Source: 192.168.16.1
                Next hop: 10.222.4.1 via fe-0/0/0.0, selected
                Protocol next hop: 192.168.24.1 Indirect next hop: 84cfbd0 52
                State: <Active Int Ext>
                Local AS: 65010 Peer AS: 65010
                Age: 19:15      Metric: 0       Metric2: 10
                Task: BGP_65010.192.168.16.1+179
                Announcement bits (2): 0-KRT 4-Resolve inet.0
                AS path: 64999 I (Originator) Cluster list: 1.1.1.1
                AS path:  Originator ID: 192.168.24.1
                Localpref: 100
                Router ID: 192.168.16.1
         BGP    Preference: 170/-101
                Source: 192.168.32.1
                Next hop: 10.222.4.1 via fe-0/0/0.0, selected
                Protocol next hop: 192.168.24.1 Indirect next hop: 84cfbd0 52
                State: <NotBest Int Ext>
                Inactive reason: Router ID
                Local AS: 65010 Peer AS: 65010
                Age: 13:11      Metric: 0       Metric2: 10
                Task: BGP_65010.192.168.32.1+1801
                AS path: 64999 I (Originator) Cluster list: 1.1.1.1
                AS path:  Originator ID: 192.168.24.1
                Localpref: 100
                Router ID: 192.168.32.1
```

Both Sherry and Chardonnay also reflect the routes to their nonclient IBGP peers—each other. If we just examine the routes sent from Sherry to Chardonnay, we see the following advertisement:

```
user@Sherry> show route advertising-protocol bgp 192.168.32.1 detail

inet.0: 19 destinations, 19 routes (19 active, 0 holddown, 0 hidden)
```

```
* 172.16.1.0/24 (1 entry, 1 announced)
 BGP group internal-peers type Internal
      Nexthop: 192.168.24.1
      MED: 0
      Localpref: 100
      AS path: 64999 I
 Communities:
      Cluster ID: 1.1.1.1
      Originator ID: 192.168.24.1
```

It appears as if the appropriate attributes are attached to the route as they are advertised. However, Chardonnay reports that it hasn't received any routes from Sherry:

```
user@Chardonnay> show route receive-protocol bgp 192.168.16.1

inet.0: 23 destinations, 23 routes (23 active, 0 holddown, 0 hidden)

user@Chardonnay>
```

This is a similar symptom to an AS Path routing loop. One EBGP peer states that it advertised routes, but the other peer states that it didn't receive them. In fact, that's exactly the case we have here except the routing loop is a function of the Cluster List attribute. Because both of the route reflectors are configured with `cluster 1.1.1.1`, the receipt of routes with that value in the Cluster List signals a routing loop. As such, the routes are immediately dropped and not shown via any CLI command. To verify this theory, we can view the received Update packet from Sherry using the `monitor traffic interface` command:

```
user@Chardonnay> monitor traffic interface fe-0/0/0.1 size 4096 detail
Listening on fe-0/0/0.1, capture size 4096 bytes

06:33:34.424251  In IP (tos 0xc0, ttl 64, id 24353, len 133)
    192.168.16.1.bgp > 192.168.32.1.3210: P 19:100(81) ack 20 win 16384
    <nop,nop,timestamp 75053260 75008652>: BGP, length: 81
        Update Message (2), length: 81
          Origin (1), length: 1, flags [T]: IGP
          AS Path (2), length: 4, flags [T]: 64999
          Next Hop (3), length: 4, flags [T]: 192.168.24.1
          Multi Exit Discriminator (4), length: 4, flags [O]: 0
          Local Preference (5), length: 4, flags [T]: 100
          Originator ID (9), length: 4, flags [O]: 192.168.24.1
          Cluster List (10), length: 4, flags [O]: 1.1.1.1
          Updated routes:
            172.16.1.0/24
            172.16.2.0/24
            172.16.3.0/24
```

Confederations

A network operating with a *confederation* paradigm approaches the full-mesh problem by breaking the network up into smaller pieces. Each piece is considered to be a *sub-AS*, or *member AS*, of the larger global confederation that is your network. Each sub-AS is assigned its own unique AS number, and the normal rules of BGP still apply within that sub-AS. This means that a full mesh of IBGP peering sessions is required and no router may readvertise an IBGP-learned route to another IBGP peer. Connectivity between the sub-AS networks is maintained using a modified form of EBGP often called *confederation BGP* (CBGP). CBGP peers add their sub-AS number to the AS Path attribute as routes are exchanged, which allows the AS Path to still be used for preventing routing loops. When routes are further advertised out of the confederation, your global AS, the details of the sub-AS networks are removed from the AS Path and replaced with your global AS number. This keeps the details of your internal network invisible to other systems in the spirit of the original BGP specifications.

Throughout our discussion, we use various terms specific to operating and configuring a confederation network. In fact, we've already mentioned a few; these terms include the following:

AS Confederation   The *AS confederation* is technically the collection of the sub-AS networks you create. Generally speaking, it is your globally assigned AS number, and it is how other systems in the Internet view you.

AS Confederation ID   Your *AS confederation ID* is the value that identifies your AS confederation as a whole to the Internet. In other words, it is your globally unique AS number.

Member AS   *Member AS* is the formal name for each sub-AS you create in your network. In essence, each small network is a member of the larger confederation that makes up your global AS.

Member AS Number   Each member AS in your confederation receives its own *member AS number*. This unique value is placed into the AS Path attribute and is used for loop prevention.

Operational Theory

Each sub-AS in a confederation network uses BGP in a way that looks and acts like a "real" AS. It's assigned its own unique identifier from the private AS range, all of the peers form IBGP peering relationships, and routes are not readvertised among the internal routers.

A typical confederation network is displayed in Figure 5.14 within the global AS 1111. Sub-AS 64555 contains the Sherry, Sangiovese, and Chianti routers, which have formed an IBGP full mesh within the member AS. The Shiraz, Chardonnay, and Merlot routers in sub-AS 64777 have done the same. Routes advertised into either of the member AS networks are advertised to each of the peer routers in the sub-AS to maintain reachability. The real "power" of a confederation network is the ability to connect the member AS networks together using CBGP peering sessions.

Confederation BGP sessions are very similar to EBGP peering sessions. The two routers share a common physical subnet, they belong to two different sub-AS networks, and they modify the AS Path attribute when advertising routes to each other. The main difference between the two peering types is how the rest of the BGP attributes are treated. For a CBGP peering session, these attributes are not modified or deleted by default. As an example, this action allows the Local Preference value to be seen by all routers in the confederation. In turn, all routers in the global

AS can now make consistent routing and forwarding decisions for all routes. The information added to the AS Path by a CBGP router is contained in one of two newly defined AS Path segments. The *AS Confederation Sequence*, segment type code 3, is an ordered list of the member AS networks through which the route has passed. It is operationally identical to an AS Sequence segment and is the default segment type used by the JUNOS software. The second new path segment is an *AS Confederation Set*, segment type code 4. Much like the AS Set, this new segment contains an unordered list of member AS numbers and is typically generated due to route aggregation within the global AS network.

 The AS Confederation Sequence and AS Confederation Set path segments are not used when the router calculates the length of the AS path for route selection purposes. Only global AS values count toward the overall path length.

FIGURE 5.14   BGP confederation network

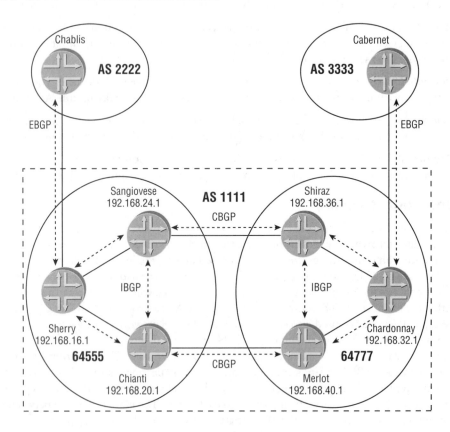

Real World Scenario

IBGP Scaling in a Sub-AS

Depending on the exact design of your confederation network, it is entirely possible that a single sub-AS portion may grow quite large. Since each sub-AS must maintain an IBGP full mesh of peering sessions, we might end up with the same situation our confederation was supposed to solve. One solution to this issue is segmenting the large sub-AS into smaller sub-AS networks. Another option uses route reflection within the sub-AS for scalability.

Routes received from an EBGP or CBGP peer are advertised to all IBGP peers within the sub-AS. These routes are not readvertised to other IBGP peers due to the full-mesh requirement. Route reflection clusters can effectively operate within a sub-AS since they replace the concept of a full mesh. Let's see how this might work.

Suppose that routers A, B, and C are all within a single sub-AS. Router A has an EBGP peer from which it is receiving routes, and router C has a CBGP peer to advertise routes to. In a normal sub-AS, router A receives routes from its EBGP peer and advertises them directly to router C, where they are sent to the CBGP peer. We now make these three routers a route reflection cluster with router B as the reflector. When router A receives the EBGP routes, it now only sends them to router B, where they are reflected to router C. Router C accepts these routes and then readvertises them to its CBGP peer. In the end, the routes take an "extra hop" as they are advertised across the sub-AS, but the end result is the same. When a large number of routers exist in the sub-AS, the benefit of the route reflection cluster outweighs the liability of the "extra hop."

The confederation as a whole connects to other global AS networks using EBGP peering sessions. Routes advertised across this connection abide by all of the normal BGP rules regarding attributes. Local Preference is removed from the routes, the AS Path is updated with your globally assigned AS, and other nontransitive attributes are removed from the routes.

Within our example confederation network we can see all of the peering types used for connectivity. The two sub-AS networks of 64555 and 64777 are connected using CBGP peering sessions on the Sangiovese-Shiraz link as well as the Chianti-Merlot link. The confederation is assigned the globally unique AS value of 1111 and connects to the Chablis router in AS 2222 as well as the Cabernet router in AS 3333. Let's see how these peering sessions affect the advertisement of routes in the confederation.

Suppose that the Cabernet router in AS 3333 advertises routes to its EBGP peer of Chardonnay. The routes are selected as active, placed in the local routing table, and readvertised by Chardonnay to any additional EBGP peers, all CBGP peers, and all IBGP peers. The only routers fitting any of these descriptions are Merlot and Shiraz, which are IBGP peers of Chardonnay. Each of these routers selects the routes as active and places them in the local routing table. Since the routes were received over an IBGP session, Merlot and Shiraz can only advertise them to EBGP and CBGP peers. As such, Merlot sends the routes to Chianti and Shiraz sends the routes to Sangiovese. During this announcement, both routers add the member AS value of 64777 as an AS Confederation Sequence within the AS Path attribute.

The routes are now received in member AS 64555 by Sangiovese and Chianti, which each check the AS Path attribute for their local member AS number. Not finding it in the attribute, they assume that a routing loop is not forming and accept the routes. Because the routes were received from a CBGP peer, these routers can advertise them to any EBGP, CBGP, or IBGP peers with established sessions. In our case, the IBGP full mesh means that each router sends the routes to each other as well as to Sherry. At this point, Sherry accepts the routes, installs them, and advertises them to any CBGP or EBGP peers. The Sherry router has only a single EBGP peering session to Chablis, so the routes are advertised into AS 2222. During this announcement, Sherry removes all AS Confederation Sequence and AS Confederation Set path segments from the AS Path attribute. In their place, the global AS value of 1111 is added to the path using the BGP default prepend action.

The removal of the member AS numbers, which are usually private AS values, is completed automatically by the configuration of the confederation. Using the remove-private command for this purpose does not accomplish this goal. In fact, the command interferes with reachability within your confederation. For a further explanation of this negative characteristic, please see the *JNCIP Study Guide*.

Configuring the Network

The configuration of a confederation network within the JUNOS software occurs entirely within the [edit routing-options] configuration hierarchy. You first assign the local member AS value to the router using the autonomous-system *value* command, where the global AS value is normally configured. You then inform your router that it is participating in a confederation network by using the confederation *value* members [*member-AS-numbers*] command. The *value* portion of this command is the confederation identifier assigned to your network—your globally assigned AS number. Each of the member AS values you've assigned within your confederation, including your local member AS, are included in the *member-AS-numbers* portion of the command. The confederation command allows the router to know if the external session you've established should operate as a CBGP session or an EBGP session.

Using Figure 5.14 as a guide, we can see that the BGP configuration of the Chardonnay router is quite ordinary. It has a peer group for its EBGP peer and a peer group for its internal sub-AS peers:

```
user@Chardonnay> show configuration protocols bgp
group EBGP-Peers {
    type external;
    peer-as 3333;
    neighbor 10.222.6.1;
}
group sub-AS-Peers {
    type internal;
    local-address 192.168.32.1;
    export nhs;
    neighbor 192.168.36.1;
    neighbor 192.168.40.1;
}
```

Choosing the Member AS Values

Technically speaking, the values you assign to your member AS networks are completely contained within your confederation network, assuming you've configured everything correctly. This means that the values can be any AS number that is different from your globally unique AS value. However, it is considered a best practice by most network administrators that the member AS values be assigned from the private AS range. This is helpful for several reasons.

First, the member AS values are placed into the AS Path attribute within the confederation. When private AS numbers are used, you can easily spot these values in the output of the show route command to view the path taken by the route or troubleshoot why a particular route is not being used to forward traffic. Second, using private AS numbers allows for easier readability of your configuration. You'll see that CBGP and EBGP peer configurations look very similar, even identical. Without you constantly referring to a network map or consulting the [edit routing-options] hierarchy, the private AS numbers clearly show which peers are CBGP and which are EBGP.

Besides, if you use a nonprivate AS value within your confederation you might still receive a BGP route with that nonprivate AS value in the AS Path. In this situation, you'll drop that route since the local router believes that a routing loop is forming.

The details of the confederation configuration are within the routing-options configuration hierarchy. When we examine this portion of the configuration, we see that Chardonnay has configured its sub-AS value using the autonomous-system command:

```
user@Chardonnay> show configuration routing-options
autonomous-system 64777;
confederation 1111 members [ 64555 64777 ];
```

The confederation command contains the globally unique AS number assigned to this network. In addition, each member AS in the confederation is listed. When taken together, these commands allow the routers to form peering relationships using the proper AS information. For example, the output of the show bgp neighbor command on the Cabernet router shows that the remote AS is 1111:

```
user@Cabernet> show bgp neighbor
Peer: 10.222.6.2+3801 AS 1111  Local: 10.222.6.1+179  AS 3333
  Type: External    State: Established    Flags: <>
  Last State: OpenConfirm   Last Event: RecvKeepAlive
  Last Error: Open Message Error
  Export: [ adv-routes ]
  Options: <Preference HoldTime PeerAS Refresh>
  Holdtime: 90 Preference: 170
  Number of flaps: 0
```

```
Error: 'Open Message Error' Sent: 4 Recv: 0
Peer ID: 192.168.32.1    Local ID: 192.168.48.1    Active Holdtime: 90
Keepalive Interval: 30
Local Interface: fe-0/0/1.0
---(more)---
```

The CBGP peering configurations in the network are very similar, so let's just examine the session between Chianti and Merlot. As with each other router in the confederation, both Chianti and Merlot have their member AS number and the confederation information configured within the `routing-options` hierarchy:

```
user@Chianti> show configuration routing-options
autonomous-system 64555;
confederation 1111 members [ 64555 64777 ];
```

```
user@Merlot> show configuration routing-options
autonomous-system 64777;
confederation 1111 members [ 64555 64777 ];
```

When we look at the BGP configuration of Chianti, we see two peer groups configured. The **sub-AS-Peers** group contains the addresses of Sherry and Sangiovese, its member AS IBGP peers. The **CBGP-Peers** group contains information on the Merlot router:

```
user@Chianti> show configuration protocols bgp
group sub-AS-Peers {
    type internal;
    local-address 192.168.20.1;
    neighbor 192.168.16.1;
    neighbor 192.168.24.1;
}
group CBGP-Peers {
    type external;
    multihop;
    local-address 192.168.20.1;
    peer-as 64777;
    neighbor 192.168.40.1;
}
```

While the CBGP peer group looks similar to a typical EBGP configuration, there are some differences. In following a confederation best practice, the CBGP sessions are configured to use the loopback address of the peer. Because the session is external in nature, the `multihop` command is required before the session is established. Reachability to the peer's loopback address is provided by the network's IGP, which is operational throughout the entire AS. You might also notice that no time-to-live (TTL) was specified in this configuration as we normally see for an EBGP peering session. This is an appropriate option for a typical EBGP peering since we want the session to fail when a physical link failure occurs between the two routers. This core belief is not valid when considering a CBGP peering session. In fact, should the physical link between two peers fail, we want the session to remain active using whatever network links are available. This ensures that routes are still advertised to all routers in the confederation.

NOTE   The omission of the TTL allows the router to use the default value of 64.

At this point, all of the peering sessions are established and Cabernet begins advertising routes to Chardonnay. These routes represent the 172.16.0.0 /16 address space and appear as so:

```
user@Chardonnay> show route protocol bgp terse

inet.0: 27 destinations, 27 routes (27 active, 0 holddown, 0 hidden)
+ = Active Route, - = Last Active, * = Both

A Destination        P Prf   Metric 1   Metric 2  Next hop       AS path
* 172.16.1.0/24      B 170        100          0 >10.222.6.1     3333 I
```

These EBGP-learned routes are then advertised by Chardonnay to its IBGP peers of Shiraz and Merlot:

```
user@Chardonnay> show route advertising-protocol bgp 192.168.36.1

inet.0: 27 destinations, 27 routes (27 active, 0 holddown, 0 hidden)
  Prefix               Nexthop          MED    Lclpref    AS path
* 172.16.1.0/24        Self             0      100        3333 I


user@Chardonnay> show route advertising-protocol bgp 192.168.40.1

inet.0: 27 destinations, 27 routes (27 active, 0 holddown, 0 hidden)
  Prefix               Nexthop          MED    Lclpref    AS path
* 172.16.1.0/24        Self             0      100        3333 I
```

When we examine details of the 172.16.1.0 /24 route on Merlot, we see no information about our confederation network. This is not surprising since the routes have only been advertised within a single sub-AS at this point:

```
user@Merlot> show route 172.16.1/24 detail

inet.0: 23 destinations, 23 routes (23 active, 0 holddown, 0 hidden)
172.16.1.0/24 (1 entry, 1 announced)
        *BGP    Preference: 170/-101
                Source: 192.168.32.1
                Next hop: 10.222.45.2 via so-0/3/1.0, selected
```

```
              Protocol next hop: 192.168.32.1 Indirect next hop: 84cfbd0 49
              State: <Active Int Ext>
              Local AS: 64777 Peer AS: 64777
              Age: 1d 6:37:44          Metric: 0          Metric2: 10
              Task: BGP_64777.192.168.32.1+179
              Announcement bits (3): 0-KRT 3-BGP.0.0.0.0+179 4-Resolve inet.0
              AS path: 3333 I
              Localpref: 100
              Router ID: 192.168.32.1
```

The Merlot router now advertises the 172.16.0.0 /16 routes to just its CBGP peer of Chianti and not its IBGP peer of Shiraz:

```
user@Merlot> show route advertising-protocol bgp 192.168.36.1


user@Merlot> show route advertising-protocol bgp 192.168.20.1

inet.0: 23 destinations, 23 routes (23 active, 0 holddown, 0 hidden)
  Prefix              Nexthop         MED    Lclpref   AS path
* 172.16.1.0/24       192.168.32.1    0      100       3333 I
```

Remember that the output of the show route advertising-protocol bgp *neighbor-address* command doesn't display the default AS Path prepend action. This affects our ability to verify the addition of the AS Confederation Sequence with this output.

Once the routes are installed on Chianti, we can see sub-AS 64777 appear within the AS Path attribute for each route:

```
user@Chianti> show route protocol bgp terse

inet.0: 23 destinations, 23 routes (23 active, 0 holddown, 0 hidden)
+ = Active Route, - = Last Active, * = Both

A Destination      P Prf   Metric 1   Metric 2  Next hop      AS path
* 172.16.1.0/24    B 170      100            0 >10.222.1.2    (64777) 3333 I
```

Since Chianti learned these routes from a CBGP peer, it may advertise them to all of its IBGP peers, including Sherry. A quick look at the routing table of Sherry shows these routes:

```
user@Sherry> show route protocol bgp


inet.0: 23 destinations, 23 routes (23 active, 0 holddown, 0 hidden)
```

+ = Active Route, - = Last Active, * = Both

```
172.16.1.0/24      *[BGP/170] 00:09:44, MED 0, localpref 100, from 192.168.20.1
                      AS path: (64777) 3333 I
                      to 10.222.29.2 via ge-0/1/0.0
                    > to 10.222.28.2 via fe-0/0/0.0
```

As a final step, the routes are advertised to Sherry's EBGP peer of Chablis in AS 2222:

```
user@Sherry> show route advertising-protocol bgp 10.222.5.2

inet.0: 23 destinations, 23 routes (23 active, 0 holddown, 0 hidden)
  Prefix                  Nexthop           MED     Lclpref    AS path
* 172.16.1.0/24           Self                                 (64777) 3333 I
```

While we don't see the removal of the AS Confederation Sequence with this command, a look at the actual packet transmission shows AS 1111 correctly prepended to the AS Path:

```
user@Sherry> monitor traffic interface fe-0/0/2.0 size 4096 detail
Listening on fe-0/0/2.0, capture size 4096 bytes

05:30:17.678882 Out IP (tos 0xc0, ttl 1, id 57922, len 107)
    10.222.5.1.4813 > 10.222.5.2.bgp: P 19:74(55) ack 100 win 16384
    <nop,nop,timestamp 92018522 91989155>: BGP, length: 55
        Update Message (2), length: 55
          Origin (1), length: 1, flags [T]: IGP
          AS Path (2), length: 6, flags [T]: 1111 3333
          Next Hop (3), length: 4, flags [T]: 10.222.5.1
          Updated routes:
            172.16.1.0/24
            172.16.2.0/24
            172.16.3.0/24
```

Of course, the correct AS Path information is also visible when we examine the routing table of Chablis:

```
user@Chablis> show route protocol bgp

inet.0: 10 destinations, 10 routes (10 active, 0 holddown, 0 hidden)
+ = Active Route, - = Last Active, * = Both

172.16.1.0/24      *[BGP/170] 00:02:08, localpref 100
                      AS path: 1111 3333 I
                    > to 10.222.5.1 via fe-0/0/1.0
```

Using Multiprotocol BGP

The maturity of BGP and its widespread use across the Internet make it a unique platform for advertising information both between ASs as well as inside them. This information might include IPv6 routes for forwarding user data traffic or IPv4 routes used in a multicast network for reverse path forwarding checks. Recently, information associated with virtual private networks (VPN) and Multiprotocol Label Switching (MPLS) has also been transmitted across BGP peering sessions. The ability of BGP to transmit this information is generally referred to as *Multiprotocol BGP* (MBGP). More specifically, MBGP is a capability negotiated between two peers during the establishment of the peering session. Each peer describes its ability to support different reachability information by sending a Capability option in the BGP Open message. Figure 5.15 shows the format of the Capability option, whose fields include the following:

Capability Type   This field displays the actual capability being negotiated between the peers. For MBGP, this field is set to a constant value of 1, which signifies multiprotocol extensions.

Capability Length   This field displays the length of the remaining fields in the Capability option. A constant value of 4 is used for all MBGP negotiations.

Address Family Identifier   The *Address Family Identifier* (AFI) field encodes the type of network layer information that the peer would like to use during the session. Possible AFI values used by the JUNOS software include

- 1—IPv4
- 2—IPv6
- 196—Layer 2 VPN

Reserved   This field is not used and is set to a constant value of 0x00.

Subsequent Address Family Identifier   The *Subsequent Address Family Identifier* (SAFI) field provides further information about the routing knowledge transmitted between the peers. The possible SAFI values used by the JUNOS software include the following:

- 1—Unicast
- 2—Multicast
- 4—Labeled unicast
- 128—Labeled VPN unicast
- 129—Labeled VPN multicast

FIGURE 5.15   MBGP capability negotiation format

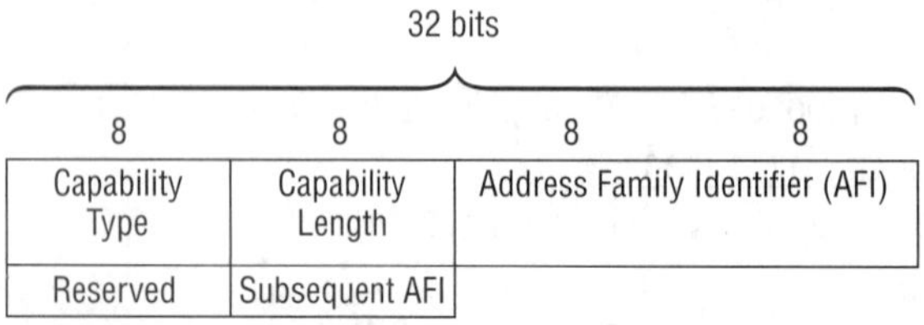

8	8	8	8
Capability Type	Capability Length	Address Family Identifier (AFI)	
Reserved	Subsequent AFI		

Each set of routing information used by the router is uniquely described by both its AFI and SAFI codes. With the exception of IPv4 unicast routes, all other *Network Layer Reachability Information* (NLRI) is advertised and withdrawn using the MP-Reach-NLRI and MP-Unreach-NLRI BGP attributes. (We discuss the format of these attributes in Chapter 4, "Border Gateway Protocol (BGP).") Let's examine the possible advertised NLRI by seeing how each attribute is configured, negotiated, and stored by the router.

Internet Protocol Version 4

Routing knowledge transmitted using an AFI of 1 represent IPv4 routes. The NLRI sent in routing updates is a 32-bit value represented by a prefix and subnet mask. Depending on the SAFI value associated with the NLRI, it may contain special attributes or be used for a particular function.

IPv4 Unicast Routes

The SAFI of 1 implies that the IPv4 NLRI is a unicast route. Routes received with this SAFI are placed into the `inet.0` routing table and are used for forwarding user data traffic to the advertised NLRI. There is nothing really new or special about IPv4 unicast routes since they are the default set of knowledge advertised by the JUNOS software.

FIGURE 5.16   MBGP sample network

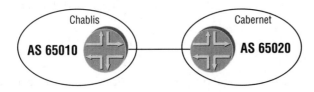

Figure 5.16 shows the Chablis router in AS 65010 and the Cabernet router in AS 65020. Chablis is configured for an EBGP peering session as so:

```
user@Chablis> show configuration protocols bgp
group external-peers {
    type external;
    neighbor 10.222.60.2 {
        peer-as 65020;
    }
}
```

We see the unicast IPv4 capability negotiation in the BGP Open messages sent by Chablis:

```
user@Chablis> monitor traffic interface fe-0/0/0 size 4096 detail
Listening on fe-0/0/0, capture size 4096 bytes

17:08:47.888135 Out IP (tos 0xc0, ttl 1, id 24676, len 97)
```

```
10.222.60.1.1147 > 10.222.60.2.bgp: P 1:46(45) ack 1 win 17376
<nop,nop,timestamp 110857412 110848025>: BGP, length: 45
     Open Message (1), length: 45
       Version 4, my AS 65010, Holdtime 90s, ID 192.168.52.1
       Optional parameters, length: 16
         Option Capabilities Advertisement (2), length: 6
           Multiprotocol Extensions, length: 4
             AFI IPv4 (1), SAFI Unicast (1)
         Option Capabilities Advertisement (2), length: 2
           Route Refresh (Cisco), length: 0
         Option Capabilities Advertisement (2), length: 2
           Route Refresh, length: 0
```

Once the session is established between the routers, we can see that any received NLRI for the session is placed into the inet.0 routing table:

```
user@Chablis> show bgp summary
Groups: 1 Peers: 1 Down peers: 0
Table         Tot Paths  Act Paths Suppressed    History Damp State    Pending
inet.0              0          0          0            0         0            0
Peer            AS      InPkt     OutPkt    OutQ   Flaps Last Up/Dwn State
10.222.60.2   65020        5         10       0       2        13 0/0/0
```

IPv4 Multicast Routes

Within the context of MBGP, we often talk about sending multicast routes to a peer. Unfortunately, this name is a bit of a misnomer and can be misleading. In reality, what we are sending to the peer are IPv4 unicast routes to be used for a different purpose. MBGP multicast routes are used to perform reverse path forwarding (RPF) checks for received multicast data streams. The establishment of the forwarding tree and the sending of multicast traffic are handled by the Protocol Independent Multicast (PIM) configuration of the network. Within the JUNOS software, IPv4 routes received with a SAFI value of 2 (representing multicast) are placed into the inet.2 routing table.

At the global, group, or neighbor level of the BGP configuration, the family inet multicast command allows the router to negotiate support for IPv4 routes with a SAFI of 2. Both the Chablis and Cabernet routers in Figure 5.16 have altered their configuration to only advertise multicast routes over their MBGP session. The configuration of the Chablis router now appears as so:

```
user@Chablis> show configuration protocols bgp
family inet {
    multicast;
}
```

```
group external-peers {
    type external;
    neighbor 10.222.60.2 {
        peer-as 65020;
    }
}
```

The appropriate AFI and SAFI values are transmitted in the Open messages sent by Chablis:

```
user@Chablis> monitor traffic interface fe-0/0/0 size 4096 detail
Listening on fe-0/0/0, capture size 4096 bytes

13:23:11.991401 Out IP (tos 0xc0, ttl 1, id 24357, len 97)
   10.222.60.1.3805 > 10.222.60.2.bgp: P 1:46(45) ack 1 win 17376
   <nop,nop,timestamp 92224007 92215022>: BGP, length: 45
        Open Message (1), length: 45
         Version 4, my AS 65010, Holdtime 90s, ID 192.168.52.1
         Optional parameters, length: 16
          Option Capabilities Advertisement (2), length: 6
           Multiprotocol Extensions, length: 4
            AFI IPv4 (1), SAFI Multicast (2)
          Option Capabilities Advertisement (2), length: 2
           Route Refresh (Cisco), length: 0
          Option Capabilities Advertisement (2), length: 2
           Route Refresh, length: 0
```

The inet.2 routing table is now used to store the NLRI received from Cabernet across the peering session:

```
user@Chablis> show bgp summary
Groups: 1 Peers: 1 Down peers: 0
Table          Tot Paths  Act Paths Suppressed    History Damp State     Pending
inet.2              0          0          0            0         0             0
Peer             AS      InPkt     OutPkt     OutQ    Flaps Last Up/Dwn State
   |#Active/Received/Damped...
10.222.60.2    65020         7          9        0        1      1:25 0/0/0
                   0/0/0
```

NOTE   The default output of the show bgp summary command extends beyond the limit of an 80-character terminal screen. The second set of 0/0/0 routing information represents the inet.2 routing table. When IPv4 multicast routes are sent in addition to other MBGP routes, the output of this command is altered for clarity. You can see this new format in the next section, "IPv4 Labeled Unicast Routes."

We can view the `inet.2` information without wrapping the output by using the `| trim` *value* option. This option removes the number of columns specified in the *value* portion from the left side of the router output:

```
user@Chablis> show bgp summary | trim 25
eers: 0
 Act Paths Suppressed    History Damp State    Pending
        0         0          0       0            0
   InPkt    OutPkt    OutQ   Flaps Last Up/Dwn State|#Active/Received/Damped...
       7         9       0       0     3:10 0/0/0              0/0/0
```

IPv4 Labeled Unicast Routes

Suppose you have an environment where two separate ASs are providing VPN services to their customers. At some point, one of these customers would like to set up a single VPN with multiple locations within each of the different AS networks. Several methods are available for configuring this type of setup, one of which includes the advertisement of IPv4 routes that are assigned an MPLS label. These routes represent the internally reachable addresses of each AS and allow for the establishment of a label-switched path across both domains.

 The exact configuration and operation of this type of network is outside the scope of this book.

IPv4 labeled unicast routes are transmitted once you configure the peer routers with the `family inet labeled-unicast` command. Referring back to Figure 5.16, we see the configuration of the Chablis router is altered to support this NLRI:

```
user@Chablis> show configuration protocols bgp
family inet {
    labeled-unicast;
}
group external-peers {
    type external;
    neighbor 10.222.60.2 {
        peer-as 65020;
    }
}
```

IPv4 labeled unicast routes use a SAFI value of 4. We see this on Open messages sent by Cabernet and received on the Chablis router:

```
user@Chablis> monitor traffic interface fe-0/0/0 size 4096 detail
Listening on fe-0/0/0, capture size 4096 bytes
```

```
13:56:43.444993  In IP (tos 0xc0, ttl 1, id 18265, len 97)
    10.222.60.2.bgp > 10.222.60.1.2093: P 1:46(45) ack 46 win 17331
    <nop,nop,timestamp 92416161 92425150>: BGP, length: 45
        Open Message (1), length: 45
            Version 4, my AS 65020, Holdtime 90s, ID 192.168.48.1
            Optional parameters, length: 16
              Option Capabilities Advertisement (2), length: 6
                Multiprotocol Extensions, length: 4
                AFI IPv4 (1), SAFI labeled Unicast (4)
              Option Capabilities Advertisement (2), length: 2
                Route Refresh (Cisco), length: 0
              Option Capabilities Advertisement (2), length: 2
                Route Refresh, length: 0
```

The output of the show bgp summary command displays the inet.0 routing table as the recipient of the labeled unicast NLRI. Since the routes are truly MBGP routes, the exact configuration of the output is modified. The State column now shows the Established state as Establ and the negotiated MBGP NLRI appears as separate routing tables below each peer's address:

```
user@Chablis> show bgp summary
Groups: 1 Peers: 1 Down peers: 0
Table           Tot Paths  Act Paths Suppressed    History Damp State    Pending
inet.0                  0          0          0          0        0            0
Peer              AS      InPkt     OutPkt     OutQ   Flaps Last Up/Dwn State
10.222.60.2    65020        10         12        0       1          20 Establ
   inet.0: 0/0/0
```

IPv4 Labeled VPN Unicast Routes

When an Internet Service Provider (ISP) is providing a Layer 3 VPN service to its customers, it is actively participating in the routing domain of each customer. The active routes from one customer site are received on the near-end router, where they are advertised to the far end of the ISP network using MBGP. The far-end router then advertises these routes to the second customer site. For complete connectivity, the same process happens in reverse.

 We discuss Layer 3 VPNs in further detail in Chapter 9.

The routes advertised between the near-end and far-end ISP routers contain attributes that provide separation between the ISP's customers. These attributes include BGP extended communities and MPLS labels. The peering session between these routers is established with the family inet-vpn unicast command and uses a SAFI value of 128. While the Chablis and

Cabernet routers in Figure 5.16 aren't within the same AS, we can use them to view the negotiation of the labeled VPN unicast routes. The configuration of the Chablis router is now

```
user@Chablis> show configuration protocols bgp
family inet-vpn {
    unicast;
}
group external-peers {
    type external;
    neighbor 10.222.60.2 {
        peer-as 65020;
    }
}
```

The BGP Open messages sent by Chablis show an AFI of 1 for IPv4 and a SAFI of 128 for labeled VPN unicast routes:

```
user@Chablis> monitor traffic interface fe-0/0/0 size 4096 detail
Listening on fe-0/0/0, capture size 4096 bytes

13:27:22.784757 Out IP (tos 0xc0, ttl 1, id 24386, len 97)
    10.222.60.1.2759 > 10.222.60.2.bgp: P 1:46(45) ack 1 win 17376
    <nop,nop,timestamp 92249086 92240100>: BGP, length: 45
        Open Message (1), length: 45
            Version 4, my AS 65010, Holdtime 90s, ID 192.168.52.1
            Optional parameters, length: 16
              Option Capabilities Advertisement (2), length: 6
                Multiprotocol Extensions, length: 4
                  AFI IPv4 (1), SAFI labeled VPN Unicast (128)
              Option Capabilities Advertisement (2), length: 2
                Route Refresh (Cisco), length: 0
              Option Capabilities Advertisement (2), length: 2
                Route Refresh, length: 0
```

All received NLRI from Cabernet over this peering session is placed into the bgp.13vpn.0 routing table:

```
user@Chablis> show bgp summary
Groups: 1 Peers: 1 Down peers: 0
Table          Tot Paths  Act Paths Suppressed    History Damp State    Pending
bgp.13vpn.0            0          0          0          0          0          0
Peer             AS      InPkt    OutPkt    OutQ  Flaps Last Up/Dwn State
10.222.60.2   65020          5         7       0      1         11 Establ
  bgp.13vpn.0: 0/0/0
```

IPv4 Labeled VPN Multicast Routes

Labeled VPN multicast routes are related to labeled VPN unicast routes in a manner similar to how IPv4 multicast and unicast routes are related. The labeled VPN multicast routes are actually IPv4 NLRI with extended communities and MPLS labels attached to associate them with a specific customer VPN. They are placed into a separate routing table, where they are used to perform multicast RPF checks. This NLRI uses a SAFI value of 129 and is configured with the `family inet-vpn multicast` command at the global, group, or neighbor level of the BGP hierarchy.

We can once again modify the configuration of the routers in Figure 5.16 to view the negotiation of this NLRI. The Chablis router is now configured to support labeled VPN multicast routes:

```
user@Chablis> show configuration protocols bgp
family inet-vpn {
    multicast;
}
group external-peers {
    type external;
    neighbor 10.222.60.2 {
        peer-as 65020;
    }
}
```

Chablis advertises this capability in the Open messages sent to Cabernet:

```
user@Chablis> monitor traffic interface fe-0/0/0 size 4096 detail
Listening on fe-0/0/0, capture size 4096 bytes

13:31:52.446070 Out IP (tos 0xc0, ttl 1, id 24420, len 97)
   10.222.60.1.2077 > 10.222.60.2.bgp: P 1:46(45) ack 1 win 17376
   <nop,nop,timestamp 92276052 92267066>: BGP, length: 45
        Open Message (1), length: 45
          Version 4, my AS 65010, Holdtime 90s, ID 192.168.52.1
          Optional parameters, length: 16
            Option Capabilities Advertisement (2), length: 6
              Multiprotocol Extensions, length: 4
                AFI IPv4 (1), SAFI labeled VPN Multicast (129)
            Option Capabilities Advertisement (2), length: 2
              Route Refresh (Cisco), length: 0
            Option Capabilities Advertisement (2), length: 2
              Route Refresh, length: 0
```

As you would expect, the JUNOS software maintains a separate routing table for all received labeled VPN multicast routes. The output of the show bgp summary command on Chablis reveals that the bgp.13vpn.2 routing table is used for this purpose:

```
user@Chablis> show bgp summary
Groups: 1 Peers: 1 Down peers: 0
Table          Tot Paths  Act Paths Suppressed    History Damp State    Pending
bgp.13vpn.2           0          0          0          0         0            0
Peer              AS       InPkt     OutPkt     OutQ   Flaps Last Up/Dwn State
10.222.60.2    65020          8         10        0       1          24 Establ
  bgp.13vpn.2: 0/0/0
```

Layer 2 Virtual Private Networks

The AFI of 196 represents reachability knowledge used in a Layer 2 VPN environment. Unlike its counterparts in IPv4 and IPv6, the NLRI for the Layer 2 VPN AFI is not an actual route used for forwarding. In fact, it isn't even an IP route at all. Instead, it is information concerning the Layer 2 logical circuit information used to connect the customer to the ISP network. While this sounds a bit strange at first, it makes a little more sense when we describe it in some context.

We saw in the "IPv4 Labeled VPN Unicast Routes" section earlier that an ISP providing a Layer 3 VPN service actively participates in the routing domain of the customer. This active participation does not occur in a Layer 2 VPN environment. The ISP in this configuration is simply providing a logical circuit between the customer end points. This circuit, in turn, is used by the customer to route its own traffic across the ISP network. The routers at the edge of the ISP network simply transmit circuit information and MPLS label information to each other. The peering session between the ISP edge routers is established using the family l2vpn unicast command using a SAFI value of 128.

NOTE   We also discuss Layer 2 VPNs in further detail in Chapter 9.

Using Figure 5.16 as a guide, we once again update the configuration of the Chablis and Cabernet routers to view the establishment of their BGP session. In this scenario, the configuration of the Chablis now appears as so:

```
user@Chablis> show configuration protocols bgp
family l2vpn {
    unicast;
}
group external-peers {
    type external;
    neighbor 10.222.60.2 {
        peer-as 65020;
    }
}
```

Real World Scenario

Advertising Multiple Address Families

Throughout this section we've been configuring our BGP peers to advertise reachability information for a specific AFI/SAFI. While this is good for learning purposes, it's not exactly realistic for the real world. A very common application of MBGP is two IBGP peers in an AS supporting transit service, Layer 3 VPNs, and Layer 2 VPNs. Let's see how this configuration and session negotiation works.

Our sample routers of Chablis and Cabernet are now configured as IBGP peers within AS 65010. We've updated their peering session to advertise multiple NLRI using the following configuration:

```
user@Chablis> show configuration protocols bgp
group internal-peers {
    type internal;
    local-address 192.168.52.1;
    family inet {
        unicast;
    }
    family inet-vpn {
        unicast;
    }
    family l2vpn {
        unicast;
    }
    neighbor 192.168.48.1;
}
```

Each of the configured AFI/SAFI combinations is advertised separately in the BGP Open message sent by the Chablis router to its IBGP peer:

```
user@Chablis> monitor traffic interface fe-0/0/0 size 4096 detail
Listening on fe-0/0/0, capture size 4096 bytes

01:38:23.542234 Out IP (tos 0xc0, ttl 64, id 26978, len 113)
    192.168.52.1.3774 > 192.168.48.1.bgp: P 1:62(61) ack 1 win 16500
    <nop,nop,timestamp 113914947 113905494>: BGP, length: 61
        Open Message (1), length: 61
        Version 4, my AS 65010, Holdtime 90s, ID 192.168.52.1
        Optional parameters, length: 32
          Option Capabilities Advertisement (2), length: 6
            Multiprotocol Extensions, length: 4
              AFI IPv4 (1), SAFI Unicast (1)
```

```
          Option Capabilities Advertisement (2), length: 6
            Multiprotocol Extensions, length: 4
              AFI IPv4 (1), SAFI labeled VPN Unicast (128)
          Option Capabilities Advertisement (2), length: 6
            Multiprotocol Extensions, length: 4
              AFI Layer-2 VPN (196), SAFI labeled VPN Unicast (128)
          Option Capabilities Advertisement (2), length: 2
            Route Refresh (Cisco), length: 0
          Option Capabilities Advertisement (2), length: 2
            Route Refresh, length: 0
```

After the peering session reaches the Established state, we see the various routing tables used to store received NLRI from the remote peer:

```
user@Chablis> show bgp summary
Groups: 1 Peers: 1 Down peers: 0
Table          Tot Paths  Act Paths Suppressed    History Damp State    Pending
inet.0                 0          0          0          0          0          0
bgp.l3vpn.0            0          0          0          0          0          0
bgp.l2vpn.0            0          0          0          0          0          0
Peer               AS      InPkt      OutPkt    OutQ   Flaps Last Up/Dwn State
192.168.48.1    65010         19          21       0       1       3:33 Establ
   inet.0: 0/0/0
   bgp.l3vpn.0: 0/0/0
   bgp.l2vpn.0: 0/0/0
```

When we view the BGP Open messages sent by Chablis to Cabernet, we see an AFI of 196 representing the Layer 2 VPN and a SAFI of 128 for labeled VPN unicast routes:

```
user@Chablis> monitor traffic interface fe-0/0/0 size 4096 detail
Listening on fe-0/0/0, capture size 4096 bytes

13:51:10.408862 Out IP (tos 0xc0, ttl 1, id 24577, len 97)
   10.222.60.1.4034 > 10.222.60.2.bgp: P 1:46(45) ack 1 win 17376
   <nop,nop,timestamp 92391847 92382858>: BGP, length: 45
        Open Message (1), length: 45
          Version 4, my AS 65010, Holdtime 90s, ID 192.168.52.1
          Optional parameters, length: 16
            Option Capabilities Advertisement (2), length: 6
```

```
            Multiprotocol Extensions, length: 4
               AFI Layer-2 VPN (196), SAFI labeled VPN Unicast (128)
        Option Capabilities Advertisement (2), length: 2
          Route Refresh (Cisco), length: 0
        Option Capabilities Advertisement (2), length: 2
          Route Refresh, length: 0
```

The NLRI received by Chablis across this peering session is placed into the bgp.l2vpn.0 routing table:

```
user@Chablis> show bgp summary
Groups: 1 Peers: 1 Down peers: 0
Table           Tot Paths  Act Paths Suppressed    History Damp State    Pending
bgp.l2vpn.0            0          0          0          0         0          0
Peer             AS       InPkt     OutPkt     OutQ   Flaps Last Up/Dwn State
10.222.60.2    65020        7          9         0       1          15 Establ
  bgp.l2vpn.0: 0/0/0
```

Summary

In this chapter, we saw the various methods available within the JUNOS software for modifying the BGP attributes. The Origin attribute was altered using a routing policy as routes were advertised to a peer. We then saw how both configuration options and routing policies affected the AS Path attribute. The AS Path was prepended using our local as well as our customer's AS value. The attribute also had values removed or modified using configuration options such as remove-private and as-override. We then discussed the Multiple Exit Discriminator and how to set the MED value using a policy and a configuration knob. We also saw two different methods for associating the advertised MED to the internal IGP metric in our AS. Finally, methods for altering how the JUNOS software evaluates and uses the MED attribute were discussed. We concluded our attribute discussion by using a routing policy and a configuration option to change the Local Preference attribute before advertising a route to a peer.

We then explored two different methods for scaling a large IBGP full mesh of routers. The first option was route reflection, which allows an IBGP-learned route to be readvertised to another IBGP peer. The router responsible for this was the route reflector within a cluster. The second method of scaling an IBGP network is confederations. A BGP confederation network breaks the AS into smaller member AS networks, or sub-AS networks. Within each sub-AS an IBGP full mesh was still required, but each sub-AS was connected using an EBGP-like connection known as confederation BGP.

We concluded the chapter with a discussion on Multiprotocol BGP (MBGP). We examined some reasons for using MBGP inside a local AS or between multiple ASs. The configuration and verification of each unique AFI/SAFI set was explored.

Exam Essentials

Be able to list the configuration options available for modifying the AS Path attribute.   The JUNOS software provides four different configuration options related to the AS Path attribute. The remove-private command selectively removes private AS values in the path before advertising a route. The local-as command allows a BGP router to establish a session using an AS value other than the value configured within the [edit routing-options hierarchy]. The as-override command removes instances in the AS Path of an EBGP peer and replaces them with the local AS value. This is used when a network is providing a VPN-like service to a customer. The final configuration option, loops, also assists in a VPN-like service offering. This command, however, allows multiple instances of the local AS to appear in the path.

Be familiar methods available for using the MED attribute in path selections.   The default behavior of the JUNOS software is to group routes received from the same AS together and compare their attached MED values. This is known as deterministic MED evaluation. You have the option of allowing the router to always compare the MED values, regardless of the neighboring AS that advertised the route. In addition, you can mimic the default behavior of the Cisco Systems MED operation, which evaluates routes based on when the local router received them from a peer.

Be able to describe the two methods for altering the Local Preference attribute.   The JUNOS software provides the local-preference configuration option to set the attribute value on all advertised BGP routes. In addition, the local-preference keyword is used as a routing policy action to change the Local Preference value. The policy action can be used as routes are advertised to a peer in an export policy. More commonly, the attribute value is changed by an import routing policy.

Be able to describe the operation of a BGP route reflection network.   The use of route reflection within an AS allows a router called the route reflector to send IBGP-learned routes to other IBGP peers. Each route reflector is assigned clients within a cluster that it is responsible for. Routing loops are avoided through the addition of two new BGP attributes: the Originator ID and the Cluster List. Each route readvertised by the route reflector has the Cluster List attribute modified with the local cluster ID value. Any received route that already contains the local cluster ID is dropped.

Be able to describe the operation of a BGP confederation network.   A BGP network using confederations reduces the problem of the IBGP full mesh into smaller, more manageable groups of routers. Each group of routers is called a sub-AS and receives its own unique sub-AS number from the private AS range. Within each sub-AS, the IBGP full mesh is maintained. Each sub-AS is connected through a CBGP peering session that modifies the AS Path attribute for loop prevention. The information included in the AS Path is either an AS Confederation Sequence or an AS Confederation Set.

Be able to configure Multiprotocol BGP.   The configuration of MBGP occurs at the global, group, or neighbor level when the family command is used. This command requires the addition of various keywords to uniquely describe the AFI/SAFI being negotiated. For example, family inet multicast enables the advertisement and receipt of IPv4 multicast routes.

Review Questions

1. Which routing policy action sets the Origin attribute to its worst possible value?

   A. `then origin igp`

   B. `then origin egp`

   C. `then origin incomplete`

   D. `then origin unknown`

2. Your local AS value is 1234. Instead of sending your EBGP peer an AS Path of 1234 64678 4321, you want to send a path of 1234 4321. What JUNOS software command accomplishes this?

   A. `as-override`

   B. `as-loops`

   C. `local-as`

   D. `remove-private`

3. Which statement best describes the default operation of the JUNOS software in relation to using the MED value on a BGP route?

   A. The routes are grouped by neighboring AS, and the MED is compared against routes in each group.

   B. The routes are combined together regardless of the neighboring AS, and the MED is compared against all routes.

   C. The MED values of the routes are compared as they were received in an oldest-to youngest fashion.

   D. The MED values of the routes are compared as they were received in a youngest-to-oldest fashion.

4. The AS value assigned to your AS is 5432. Which routing policy action results in an advertised AS Path of 5432 5432 5432 1234 6789?

   A. `then as-path-prepend 2`

   B. `then as-path-prepend 3`

   C. `then as-path-prepend "5432 5432"`

   D. `then as-path-prepend "5432 5432 5432"`

5. What value identifies a grouping of a BGP route reflector(s) and its clients within an AS?

   A. Cluster ID

   B. Originator ID

   C. Router ID

   D. Peer ID

6. Which BGP attribute is modified by a route reflector to signify that the route has been readvertised within the IBGP network?

   A. Cluster ID

   B. Cluster List

   C. Originator ID

   D. Router ID

7. What type of route reflection design is used when the route reflector full mesh grows excessively large?

   A. Basic route reflection

   B. Hierarchical route reflection

   C. Two route reflectors in a single cluster

   D. Fully meshed route reflection clients

8. In a BGP confederation network, what type of peering session is used between each sub-AS?

   A. IBGP

   B. CBGP

   C. EBGP

   D. MBGP

9. What BGP attribute is modified, by default, when a route is advertised between sub-AS networks?

   A. Next Hop

   B. Local Preference

   C. AS Path

   D. Multiple Exit Discriminator

10. Which form of BGP allows for the use of reachability information that is not an IPv4 unicast route?

   A. IBGP

   B. CBGP

   C. EBGP

   D. MBGP

Answers to Review Questions

1. C. The valid completions for the Origin policy action are `igp`, `egp`, and `incomplete`. Of those three, the `incomplete` action sets the attribute to a value of 2, its worst possible value.

2. D. The `remove-private` command removes private AS values, such as 64678, from the beginning of the AS Path. It stops operating when it reaches the first globally assigned AS value. The local router then prepends its local AS onto the path.

3. A. Option A correctly describes the operation of deterministic MEDs, which is the JUNOS software default operational mode.

4. C. Since the default AS Path prepend action always takes place before a route is advertised, you only need to additionally prepend your local AS twice. This is accomplished only by option C.

5. A. A route reflector and its clients are uniquely identified in a BGP network by its cluster ID.

6. B. When a route reflector readvertises a route, either within or outside of the cluster, it adds its local cluster ID to the Cluster List.

7. B. An individual router can be a route reflector for one cluster while being a client in another cluster. This is the basic principle of a hierarchical route reflection design. This replaces the route reflector full mesh with a separate cluster.

8. B. Within a confederation network, each sub-AS is connected using an EBGP-like session called a confederation BGP (CBGP).

9. C. By default, only the AS Path attribute is modified when a route is advertised between sub-AS networks. The advertising CBGP peer adds its sub-AS value to the path within an AS Confederation Sequence.

10. D. MBGP allows two BGP peers to advertise and receive reachability information for multiple address families.

Multicast

JNCIS EXAM OBJECTIVES COVERED IN THIS CHAPTER:

- ✓ Identify the PIM-SM rendezvous point election mechanisms
- ✓ Describe the operation of a multicast network using each of the RP election mechanisms
- ✓ Define the methods available to scope multicast traffic
- ✓ Describe the use and configuration of MSDP within a single PIM domain
- ✓ Describe the use and operation of MSDP across multiple PIM domains
- ✓ Describe methods for maintaining separate unicast and multicast forwarding topologies

In this chapter, we explore the operation of multicast within the JUNOS software. Before reading this chapter, you should be familiar with how multicast group addresses are used in a network as well as how multicast data packets are forwarded in a network.

We begin by examining the three methods of electing a Protocol Independent Multicast (PIM) rendezvous point (RP) in a network and discuss the packet formats used in the election process. Our exploration includes a verification of the current multicast group to RP mapping in the network as well as the establishment of the rendezvous point tree (RPT). We then explain how multicast packets are forwarded through the RP to the interested clients and how PIM routers form the shortest path tree (SPT). We conclude this chapter by discussing how the Multicast Source Discovery Protocol (MSDP) is used in conjunction with PIM RPs to advertise active multicast sources both inside a single domain as well as across multiple domains. This allows us to explore some methods for creating and maintaining separate unicast and multicast forwarding topologies.

PIM Rendezvous Points

A sparse-mode PIM domain requires the selection of a *rendezvous point* (RP) for each multicast group. The JUNOS software supports three methods for selecting an RP. In addition to statically configuring the group-to-RP mapping, you can use the dynamic methods of Auto-RP and bootstrap routing. Let's explore the operation of each method in further detail.

Static Configuration

From a configuration and operational standpoint, perhaps the easiest method for electing a PIM rendezvous point is a *static RP* assignment. You first select a router in the network to be the RP and then inform every other router what its IP address is. Unfortunately, the one glaring problem with statically mapping the PIM RP address is that it becomes a single point of failure in the network. If the original RP stops operating, a new router must be selected and configured. In addition, every other router in the network must be informed of the RP's new address. This negative aspect of static RP addressing is similar to using static routing to replace your Interior Gateway Protocol (IGP).

FIGURE 6.1 Static RP sample network

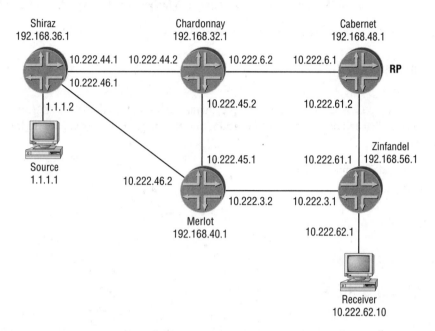

Figure 6.1 shows a PIM sparse-mode network with five routers: Shiraz, Chardonnay, Cabernet, Merlot, and Zinfandel. A multicast source, 1.1.1.1 /32, is connected to the Shiraz router while an interested listener is connected to Zinfandel. The network administrators have decided that the Cabernet router is the RP for the domain. The configuration of Cabernet as a local RP is:

```
user@Cabernet> show configuration protocols pim rp
local {
    address 192.168.48.1;
}
```

This allows Cabernet to view its loopback address as a valid RP in the output of the show pim rps command:

```
user@Cabernet> show pim rps
Instance: PIM.master

Family: INET
RP address        Type      Holdtime Timeout Active groups Group prefixes
192.168.48.1      static           0  None                0 224.0.0.0/4
```

As we would expect, the local configuration of the RP appears as a statically learned RP on Cabernet. Additionally, the lack of a specific multicast group address range allows Cabernet to service all possible multicast groups as seen by the `Group prefixes` output. The configuration of the other PIM routers is similar to that of Zinfandel, which is connected to the interested listener:

```
user@Zinfandel> show configuration protocols pim rp
static {
    address 192.168.48.1;
}
```

As we saw on Cabernet, the output of `show pim rps` lists 192.168.48.1 as the address of the RP. This was learned by a static configuration, and this single RP is serving all multicast group addresses:

```
user@Zinfandel> show pim rps
Instance: PIM.master

Family: INET
RP address      Type      Holdtime Timeout Active groups Group prefixes
192.168.48.1    static        0    None                0 224.0.0.0/4
```

Establishing the RPT

Once the PIM routers in the network learn the address of the RP, they can send Join and Prune messages to that router. Within the context of our network in Figure 6.1, the Zinfandel router generates a PIM Join message for traffic from the 224.6.6.6 group address. Because this traffic may arrive from any valid source in the network, Zinfandel installs a (*,G) state on the router. The Join message is forwarded hop by hop through the network to the RP, which is a single hop away in our example. Once it reaches the RP, the RPT is established in the network. Using a `traceoptions` file on the Cabernet router, we see the Join message received by the RP:

```
Apr 27 08:39:15 PIM fe-0/0/0.0 RECV 10.222.61.1 -> 224.0.0.13 V2
Apr 27 08:39:15    JoinPrune to 10.222.61.2 holdtime 210 groups 1
                      sum 0xb354 len 34
Apr 27 08:39:15    group 224.6.6.6 joins 1 prunes 0
Apr 27 08:39:15      join list:
Apr 27 08:39:15        source 192.168.48.1 flags sparse,rptree,wildcard
```

The Join message is addressed to the 224.0.0.13 address for all PIM routers and includes a single join request for the 224.6.6.6 group address. While at first it may appear unusual to list the address of the RP (192.168.48.1) as the source for the group, an examination of the message flags reveals some interesting information. First, the `wildcard` flag tells us that the actual source of the traffic is not known and that this Join message is headed to the RP. Second, the `rptree` flag informs us that this message is forming a branch of the RPT, with the interface address of 10.222.61.1 as a downstream node. Finally, the listing of the RP as the source for the group allows each PIM router to forward the message along the appropriate network links to the RP itself.

We can verify the current PIM state in the network by examining the output of the `show pim join extensive` command on Zinfandel, the last-hop router:

```
user@Zinfandel> show pim join extensive
Instance: PIM.master Family: INET

Group: 224.6.6.6
    Source: *
    RP: 192.168.48.1
    Flags: sparse,rptree,wildcard
    Upstream interface: fe-0/0/0.0
    Upstream State: Join to RP
    Downstream Neighbors:
        Interface: fe-0/0/2.0
            10.222.62.1 State: Join    Flags: SRW  Timeout: Infinity
```

We can see that Zinfandel has joined the RPT for the 224.6.6.6 group address as the `Upstream State:` reports a `Join to RP` output. When user data traffic for the group begins to flow, Zinfandel expects to receive it on the `fe-0/0/0.0` interface. The traffic is then sent further downstream to the 10.222.62.1 neighbor on its `fe-0/0/2.0` interface. The output of this command on the RP itself reveals similar information:

```
user@Cabernet> show pim join extensive
Instance: PIM.master Family: INET

Group: 224.6.6.6
    Source: *
    RP: 192.168.48.1
    Flags: sparse,rptree,wildcard
    Upstream interface: local
    Upstream State: Local RP
    Downstream Neighbors:
        Interface: fe-0/0/0.0
            10.222.61.1 State: Join    Flags: SRW  Timeout: 157
```

The main difference in this output is the listing of a `local` upstream interface. This occurs as the RP itself expects to receive the multicast traffic stream encapsulated in a PIM Register message from the first-hop router. In addition, the `Upstream State` displays that this router is the `Local RP`.

Establishing the SPT

When the multicast source begins sending data packets onto its connected local area network (LAN), the first-hop router of Shiraz receives them on its `fe-0/0/3.0` interface. Shiraz encapsulates these packets in a PIM Register message and unicasts them to the RP for the domain. The output of the show pim rps extensive command shows this Register state:

```
user@Shiraz> show pim rps extensive
Instance: PIM.master

Family: INET
RP: 192.168.48.1
Learned via: static configuration
Time Active: 1d 04:44:15
Holdtime: 0
Device Index: 144
Subunit: 32769
Interface: pe-0/2/0.32769
Group Ranges:
        224.0.0.0/4
Register State for RP:
Group           Source       FirstHop       RP Address      State     Timeout
224.6.6.6       1.1.1.1      192.168.36.1    192.168.48.1    Send
```

Additionally, we see the Register message itself appear on Cabernet as so:

```
Apr 27 12:29:34 PIM fe-0/0/2.0 RECV 10.250.0.123 -> 192.168.48.1 V1
Apr 27 12:29:34   Register Source 1.1.1.1 Group 224.6.6.6 sum 0xdbfe len 292
```

Remember that the first-hop router and the RP require special hardware to encapsulate and de-encapsulate the Register message.

The receipt of the Register message by Cabernet triggers two separate events. First, Cabernet de-encapsulates the native multicast packets and forwards them along the RPT towards the last-hop router of Zinfandel. Second, Cabernet begins counting the number of multicast packets received via the Register messages. When the number increases past a preset threshold, the RP generates PIM Join messages and forwards them towards the first-hop router. This allows the RP to receive the multicast traffic natively without the overhead of de-encapsulating the Register messages. The JUNOS software uses a nonconfigurable value of 0 packets for this threshold, which prompts the RP to immediately generate a PIM Join message. This message appears in a traceoptions file as:

```
Apr 27 12:29:45 PIM fe-0/0/2.0 SENT 10.222.6.1 -> 224.0.0.13 V2
Apr 27 12:29:45   JoinPrune to 10.222.6.2 holdtime 210 groups 1
                    sum 0xdbfc len 34
Apr 27 12:29:45   group 224.6.6.6 joins 1 prunes 0
Apr 27 12:29:45     join list:
Apr 27 12:29:45       source 1.1.1.1 flags sparse
```

The only flag set in this Join message is the sparse flag, which allows each PIM router to forward the join request hop-by-hop directly towards the source of the traffic—1.1.1.1. After sending this message, the RP no longer requires the encapsulated traffic from Shiraz. A Register-Stop message is generated and sent to the first-hop router. This allows the RP to use the native multicast traffic it receives from Shiraz. The details of the Register-Stop message include:

```
Apr 27 12:29:46 PIM SENT 192.168.48.1 -> 10.250.0.123 V1
Apr 27 12:29:46   RegisterStop Source 1.1.1.1 Group 224.6.6.6 sum 0xf3ee len 16
```

At this point, the last-hop router of Zinfandel is receiving multicast traffic for the 224.6.6.6 group address along the RPT. These packets are forwarded out its fe-0/0/2.0 interface toward the interested listener. Zinfandel then examines the source address of the packets and generates a PIM Join message. This message is sent toward the source of the traffic using interface so-0/1/1.0:

```
Apr 27 12:29:48 PIM so-0/1/1.0 SENT 10.222.3.1 -> 224.0.0.13 V2
Apr 27 12:29:48   JoinPrune to 10.222.3.2 holdtime 210 groups 1
                   sum 0xdefc len 34
Apr 27 12:29:48   group 224.6.6.6 joins 1 prunes 0
Apr 27 12:29:48    join list:
Apr 27 12:29:48     source 1.1.1.1 flags sparse
```

 The process of transferring from the RPT to the SPT happens immediately after the last-hop router receives the first multicast packet.

As we saw with the Join message from the RP, only the sparse flag is set for the 1.1.1.1 source. This allows each router between Zinfandel and Shiraz to establish (S,G) PIM state in the network for forwarding these data packets. This establishes the SPT in the network, which we can view on the Merlot router:

```
user@Merlot> show pim join extensive
Instance: PIM.master Family: INET

Group: 224.6.6.6
    Source: 1.1.1.1
    Flags: sparse
    Upstream interface: so-0/1/3.0
    Upstream State: Join to Source
    Keepalive timeout: 155
    Downstream Neighbors:
        Interface: so-0/1/1.0
            10.222.3.1 State: Join   Flags: S   Timeout: 169
```

After Zinfandel begins receiving the traffic via the SPT, it generates a Prune message and forwards it towards the RP. This removes the (S,G) state in the network along the RPT. This message from Zinfandel appears as so:

```
Apr 27 12:29:49 PIM fe-0/0/0.0 SENT 10.222.61.1 -> 224.0.0.13 V2
Apr 27 12:29:49    JoinPrune to 10.222.61.2 holdtime 210 groups 1
                       sum 0xa3fc len 34
Apr 27 12:29:49    group 224.6.6.6 joins 0 prunes 1
Apr 27 12:29:49      prune list:
Apr 27 12:29:49        source 1.1.1.1 flags sparse,rptree
```

The rptree flag allows the network routers to forward the message to the RP, eliminating the current PIM state related to the 1.1.1.1 source. This Prune message does not, however, remove the (*,G) state in the network for the RPT. This remains intact should a new multicast source appear in the network that is closer to the last-hop router than 1.1.1.1 currently is. The receipt of the Prune message by Cabernet prompts it to generate its own Prune message and forward it towards Shiraz. This message removes any (S,G) state from the network between the RP and the first-hop router. The output of a traceoptions file shows the receipt of the message from Zinfandel on the fe-0/0/0.0 interface and the advertisement of the local Prune message using the fe-0/0/2.0 interface:

```
Apr 27 12:29:46 PIM fe-0/0/0.0 RECV 10.222.61.1 -> 224.0.0.13 V2
Apr 27 12:29:46    JoinPrune to 10.222.61.2 holdtime 210 groups 1
                       sum 0xa3fc len 34
Apr 27 12:29:46    group 224.6.6.6 joins 0 prunes 1
Apr 27 12:29:46      prune list:
Apr 27 12:29:46        source 1.1.1.1 flags sparse,rptree

Apr 27 12:29:46 PIM fe-0/0/2.0 SENT 10.222.6.1 -> 224.0.0.13 V2
Apr 27 12:29:46    JoinPrune to 10.222.6.2 holdtime 210 groups 1
                       sum 0xdbfc len 34
Apr 27 12:29:46    group 224.6.6.6 joins 0 prunes 1
Apr 27 12:29:46      prune list:
Apr 27 12:29:46        source 1.1.1.1 flags sparse
```

Steady State Operation of the Network

The flurry of PIM protocol messages that establishes the SPT allows native multicast traffic to flow from Shiraz to Zinfandel. This SPT remains in place as long as the source is active and the interested client replies to Internet Group Management Protocol (IGMP) messages from Zinfandel. It is maintained through the periodic transmission of Join messages between the SPT routers. One such set of messages appears in the output of a traceoptions file on Merlot:

```
Apr 27 12:31:50 PIM so-0/1/1.0 RECV 10.222.3.1 -> 224.0.0.13 V2
Apr 27 12:31:50    JoinPrune to 10.222.3.2 holdtime 210 groups 1
                       sum 0xdefc len 34
```

```
Apr 27 12:31:50   group 224.6.6.6 joins 1 prunes 0
Apr 27 12:31:50      join list:
Apr 27 12:31:50         source 1.1.1.1 flags sparse


Apr 27 12:32:42 PIM so-0/1/3.0 SENT 10.222.46.2 -> 224.0.0.13 V2
Apr 27 12:32:42      JoinPrune to 10.222.46.1 holdtime 210 groups 1
                         sum 0xb3fd len 34
Apr 27 12:32:42      group 224.6.6.6 joins 1 prunes 0
Apr 27 12:32:42      join list:
Apr 27 12:32:42         source 1.1.1.1 flags sparse
```

The Join message received on Merlot's so-0/1/1.0 interface from 10.222.3.1 is generated by Zinfandel, the last-hop router. Zinfandel also generates PIM messages during this operational phase to maintain the RPT between itself and the RP. Here's an example of this message:

```
Apr 27 12:31:22 PIM fe-0/0/0.0 SENT 10.222.61.1 -> 224.0.0.13 V2
Apr 27 12:31:22      JoinPrune to 10.222.61.2 holdtime 210 groups 1
                         sum 0xab31 len 42
Apr 27 12:31:22      group 224.6.6.6 joins 1 prunes 1
Apr 27 12:31:22      join list:
Apr 27 12:31:22         source 192.168.48.1 flags sparse,rptree,wildcard
Apr 27 12:31:22      prune list:
Apr 27 12:31:22         source 1.1.1.1 flags sparse,rptree
```

This PIM message contains both a join and a prune request. The join portion maintains the state of the RPT. The address of the RP (192.168.48.1) is listed as the source of the traffic in addition to setting both the rptree and wildcard flags. To ensure that the RP doesn't send data packets from the 1.1.1.1 source, a prune is also included. This explicitly lists the multicast source address and includes the rptree flag to allow the network routers to forward the message to the RP. This operational mode keeps the RP aware that Zinfandel would still like traffic for the 224.6.6.6 group address but not from the 1.1.1.1 source. If a new source of traffic appears in the network, the RP forwards these packets along the RPT and allows Zinfandel to choose between the two sources of traffic.

The RP requires this explicit Prune message for the 1.1.1.1 source since it still receives messages from Shiraz informing it that the source is active. This notification comes in the format of a Null Register message containing just the source and group addresses for the traffic. Cabernet responds to these messages by transmitting a Register-Stop message back to Shiraz. This polling process continues as long as the traffic source is operational and Shiraz is receiving packets on its LAN interface. These Register messages appear in a traceoptions file on Cabernet as:

```
Apr 27 12:33:36 PIM fe-0/0/2.0 RECV 10.250.0.123 -> 192.168.48.1 V1
Apr 27 12:33:36      Register Source 1.1.1.1 Group 224.6.6.6 sum 0xdbfe len 292

Apr 27 12:33:36 PIM SENT 192.168.48.1 -> 10.250.0.123 V1
Apr 27 12:33:36      RegisterStop Source 1.1.1.1 Group 224.6.6.6 sum 0xf3ee len 16
```

Auto-RP

The second method available for selecting the RP in a PIM domain is *Auto-RP*. This is a proprietary system developed by Cisco Systems that is supported within the JUNOS software. Unlike the static configuration of the RP address, Auto-RP provides a dynamic method of selecting and learning the address of the RP routers. In addition, Auto-RP allows the network to failover from an operational RP to a backup RP.

Each router configured as an Auto-RP RP generates messages announcing its capabilities to the network. These *Cisco-RP-Announce* packets are flooded in a dense-mode fashion to the 224.0.1.39 /32 multicast group address. The current Auto-RP mapping agent in the domain collects these messages and selects the RP for each group address range. The router advertising the most specific range is selected as the RP for that set of addresses. When multiple routers advertise the same address range, like the default 224.0.0.0 /4, then the router with the highest IP address is selected as the RP. Once the group-to-RP mappings have been made, the mapping agent advertises this decision to the network in a *Cisco-RP-Discovery* message. This packet is also forwarded in a dense-mode fashion to the 224.0.1.40 /32 group address.

Both the Cisco-RP-Announce and Cisco-RP-Discovery messages share the same packet format, which is shown in Figure 6.2. The message fields include the following:

Version (4 bits) This field displays the current version of Auto-RP used in the network. The JUNOS software sets this field to a constant value of 1.

Type (4 bits) This field contains the type of Auto-RP message encoded in the packet. A value of 1 represents a Cisco-RP-Announce message, and a value of 2 represents a Cisco-RP-Discovery message.

RP Count (1 octet) This field displays the total number of RPs contained in the message. For each router in the total count, the RP Address, RP Version, Group Count, and Encoded Group Address fields are repeated.

Hold Time (2 octets) This field contains the amount of time, in seconds, that the particular message is valid for. This allows for the dynamic failover of RP information in the domain. The value 0 in this field means that the current RP is always valid, provided it's operational.

Reserved (4 octets) This field is not used and is set to a constant value of 0x00000000.

RP Address (4 octets) The IP address of the RP is encoded in this field as a 32-bit value. The remaining fields of the Auto-RP message pertain to the unique address displayed here.

RP Version (1 octet) The first 6 bits of this field are reserved and each must be set to a value of 0. The final 2 bits in the field represent the current version of PIM supported by the RP. Four possible bit combinations have been defined:

- 00—PIM version is unknown.
- 01—Only PIM version 1 is supported.
- 10—Only PIM version 2 is supported.
- 11—Both versions 1 and 2 are supported.

Group Count (1 octet) This field displays the total number of group address ranges associated with the particular RP. The following field is repeated for each unique address range.

Encoded Group Address (6 octets)   This field uses three separate subfields to describe the multicast group address range associated with the RP. These subfields include the following:

N Bit (1 octet)   The first 7 bits of this field are reserved and each must be set to a value of 0. The final bit position, the N bit, represents how user data traffic for the address range should be forwarded. A value of 0 informs all Auto-RP routers to forward traffic in a sparse-mode fashion. A value of 1 informs the domain that the address range should be treated in a negative fashion. In other words, routers should use dense-mode forwarding for user data packets.

Mask Length (1 octet)   This field displays the length of the group address range encoded in the following field.

Group Address (4 octets)   This field displays the 32-bit multicast group address associated with the RP.

FIGURE 6.2   Auto-RP packet format

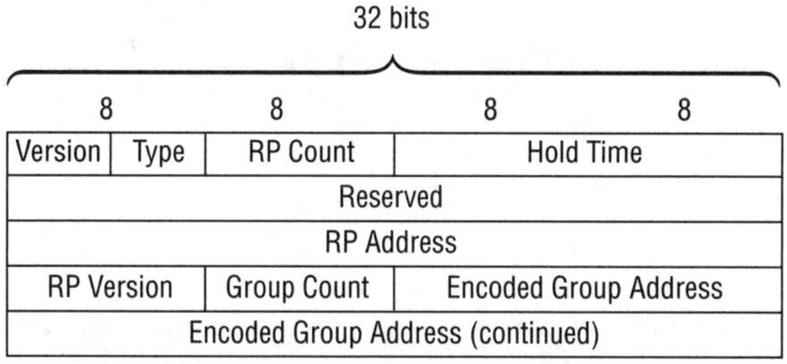

```
                         32 bits
          ┌─────────────────┴─────────────────┐
      8           8           8           8
  ┌─────────┬──────┬────────────┬──────────────────────┐
  │ Version │ Type │  RP Count  │      Hold Time        │
  ├─────────┴──────┴────────────┴──────────────────────┤
  │                    Reserved                         │
  ├─────────────────────────────────────────────────────┤
  │                   RP Address                        │
  ├──────────────┬──────────────┬───────────────────────┤
  │  RP Version  │ Group Count  │ Encoded Group Address  │
  ├──────────────┴──────────────┴───────────────────────┤
  │        Encoded Group Address (continued)            │
  └─────────────────────────────────────────────────────┘
```

FIGURE 6.3   Auto-RP sample network

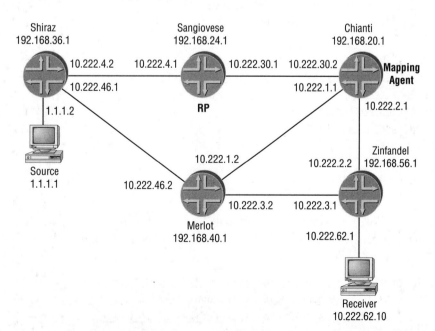

Figure 6.3 shows a network consisting of five routers: Shiraz, Sangiovese, Chianti, Merlot, and Zinfandel. The PIM domain is using Auto-RP for the selection and advertisement of the RP, which requires each router to configure some Auto-RP properties. The Zinfandel router, as well as Shiraz and Merlot, is set to discovery mode:

```
user@Zinfandel> show configuration protocols pim rp
auto-rp discovery;
```

The Chianti router is the mapping agent for the domain. It is responsible for receiving the Cisco-RP-Announce messages advertised by the candidate RPs in the network and advertising the RP-to-group mappings. It requires the mapping option to be set:

```
user@Chianti> show configuration protocols pim rp
auto-rp mapping;
```

Finally, the candidate RP for the domain (Sangiovese) requires both a local RP configuration and an announce Auto-RP option. The configuration of PIM on Sangiovese is currently:

```
user@Sangiovese> show configuration protocols pim rp
local {
    address 192.168.24.1;
}
auto-rp announce;
```

After each router commits its configuration, Sangiovese begins generating Cisco-RP-Announce messages. These messages are flooded in a dense-mode fashion throughout the network. We can view this PIM state with the show pim join extensive command on Sangiovese:

```
user@Sangiovese> show pim join extensive
Instance: PIM.master Family: INET


Group: 224.0.1.39
    Source: 192.168.24.1
    Flags: dense
    Upstream interface: local
    Downstream interfaces:
        local
        lo0.0
        at-0/1/0.0
        fe-0/0/2.0
```

The output of a traceoptions file on Sangiovese also displays this announcement to the network. We see the RP address of 192.168.24.1 advertising support for the entire multicast group address range—224.0.0.0 /4:

```
Apr 27 14:54:45 PIM SENT 192.168.24.1 -> 224.0.1.39+496 AutoRP v1
Apr 27 14:54:45   announce hold 150 rpcount 1 len 20 rp 192.168.24.1
Apr 27 14:54:45   version 2 groups 1 prefixes 224.0.0.0/4
```

The mapping agent for the domain, Chianti, receives the announce message and performs the RP-to-group address mapping. Since we've only used a single RP for all group addresses, the Cisco-RP-Discovery message includes this same information. These two messages are seen in a `traceoptions` file on the Chianti router:

```
Apr 27 14:54:53  PIM at-0/2/0.0 RECV 192.168.24.1+496 -> 224.0.1.39 AutoRP v1
Apr 27 14:54:53    announce hold 150 rpcount 1 len 20 rp 192.168.24.1
Apr 27 14:54:53    version 2 groups 1 prefixes 224.0.0.0/4


Apr 27 14:55:10  PIM SENT 192.168.20.1 -> 224.0.1.40+496 AutoRP v1
Apr 27 14:55:10    mapping hold 150 rpcount 1 len 20 rp 192.168.24.1
Apr 27 14:55:10    version 2 groups 1 prefixes 224.0.0.0/4
```

Once the network routers receive the discovery messages, they install 192.168.24.1 as the RP for the domain. We see the last-hop router of Zinfandel with PIM state for both Auto-RP groups. In addition, the active RP for the domain is visible:

```
user@Zinfandel> show pim join extensive
Instance: PIM.master Family: INET

Group: 224.0.1.39
    Source: 192.168.24.1
    Flags: dense
    Upstream interface: fe-0/0/1.0
    Downstream interfaces:
        local
        lo0.0
        so-0/1/1.0

Group: 224.0.1.40
    Source: 192.168.20.1
    Flags: dense
    Upstream interface: fe-0/0/1.0
    Downstream interfaces:
        local
        lo0.0
        so-0/1/1.0 (Pruned timeout 3)


user@Zinfandel> show pim rps extensive
Instance: PIM.master
```

```
Family: INET
RP address      Type        Holdtime Timeout Active groups Group prefixes
192.168.24.1    auto-rp       150     150                 1 224.0.0.0/4
```

The RPT from Zinfandel to Sangiovese is then built for the 224.6.6.6 group address. We verify this with the output of the show pim join extensive command:

```
user@Sangiovese> show pim join extensive
Instance: PIM.master Family: INET

Group: 224.0.1.39
    Source: 192.168.24.1
    Flags: dense
    Upstream interface: local
    Downstream interfaces:
        local
        lo0.0
        at-0/1/0.0
        fe-0/0/2.0

Group: 224.0.1.40
    Source: 192.168.20.1
    Flags: dense
    Upstream interface: at-0/1/0.0
    Downstream interfaces:
        local
        lo0.0
        fe-0/0/2.0

Group: 224.6.6.6
    Source: *
    RP: 192.168.24.1
    Flags: sparse,rptree,wildcard
    Upstream interface: local
    Upstream State: Local RP
    Downstream Neighbors:
        Interface: at-0/1/0.0
            10.222.30.2 State: Join    Flags: SRW  Timeout: 177
```

The presence of the RP in the domain allows traffic to flow from the multicast source to the interested listeners. This process is identical to the operation we saw in the "Establishing the SPT" section earlier in the chapter.

Bootstrap Routing

The third RP selection method available in a PIM-SM network is *bootstrap routing*. This is a standardized method for electing an RP using version 2 of the PIM specification. Like Auto-RP, the RP address is learned dynamically throughout the network with support for redundancy and failover. In addition, bootstrap routing allows a form of load balancing when multiple RP routers support identical group address ranges. However, each individual multicast group can still have only a single operational RP at any one time.

Electing the Bootstrap Router

A PIM domain supporting bootstrap routing selects a single device to act as a collection and distribution point for RP information. This device is known as the *bootstrap router* (BSR). Each candidate bootstrap router (C-BSR) in the domain sets a local priority value and advertises its ability in a *bootstrap message*. This message is advertised hop by hop to each PIM router in the domain, where the router with the highest priority is elected as the BSR. If multiple routers advertise identical priority values, the device with the highest IP address becomes the BSR for the domain. Figure 6.4 displays the format of the bootstrap message, which is also used to advertise RP information into the network. For the purposes of electing the BSR, only the first eight fields (through the BSR Address) are used. The various fields of the bootstrap message include the following:

Version (4 bits)   This field displays the current version of PIM used for the bootstrap message. It is set to a constant value of 2.

Type (4 bits)   This field contains the type of PIM message encoded in the packet. Bootstrap messages use a value of 4 in this field and are addressed to the 224.0.0.13 /32 multicast group address.

Reserved (1 octet)   This field is not used and is set to a constant value of 0x00.

Checksum (2 octets)   This field displays a standard IP checksum for the entire PIM packet contents.

Fragment Tag (2 octets)   If an individual bootstrap message is too large for transmission on a network link, it is fragmented into smaller packets. When this occurs, the router generates a random number and places it in all of the fragmented packets. This allows the receiving routers to correlate the received fragments and combine them into a single message.

Hash Mask Length (1 octet)   This field displays the length, in bits, that each router should use for the BSR hash algorithm. For an IPv4 multicast network, a value of 30 is used for this length.

BSR Priority (1 octet)   The priority value of the current BSR is placed in this field. During the BSR election time, each candidate router places its local value in this field and transmits the message into the network. When a bootstrap message with a higher priority value is received, the local router stops transmitting its own messages into the network.

BSR Address (6 octets)   This field contains the address of the BSR for the domain. It is formatted using the PIM encoded unicast address format.

Group Address (8 octets)   This field contains a multicast group address in the encoded group address format. This field may be repeated multiple times throughout the message to advertise multiple address ranges. Each remaining field in the message refers only to the group address that precedes it.

RP Count (1 octet) This field displays the total number of RPs in the message. Each is able to service the advertised group address range.

Fragment RP Count (1 octet) When a bootstrap message is fragmented, this field displays the total of RP addresses present in this fragment for the advertised group address range.

Reserved (2 octets) This field is not used and is set to a constant value of 0x0000.

RP Address (6 octets) This field is repeated based on the value in the RP count field. It contains the address of the RP using the encoded unicast address format. The following fields are associated specifically with this advertised RP address: RP Hold Time, RP Priority, and Reserved.

RP Hold Time (2 octets) The field displays the amount if time, in seconds, that the associated RP address is valid. Each received bootstrap message refreshes this timer value. If the value reaches 0, the RP is not used for any PIM-SM operations.

RP Priority (1 octet) This field displays the priority of the associated RP address. It is used by PIM routers in deciding which advertised RP to use for its multicast traffic. Possible values range between 0 and 255, with the value 0 representing the best priority.

Reserved (1 octet) This field is not used and is set to a constant value of 0x00.

The formats of the encoded unicast and group addresses can be found in the *JNCIA Study Guide*.

FIGURE 6.4 Bootstrap message format

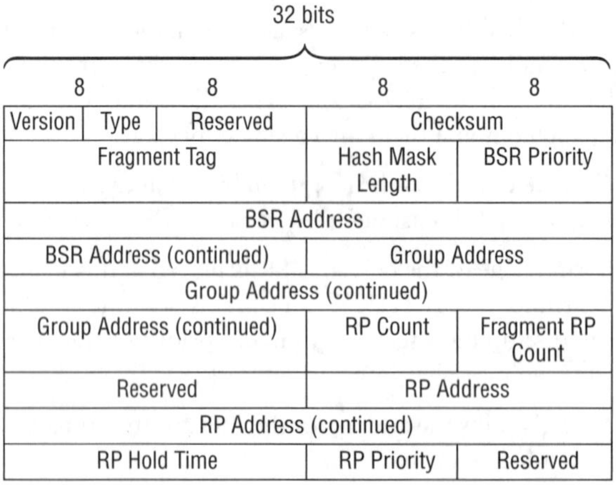

32 bits

Version	Type	Reserved	Checksum	
Fragment Tag			Hash Mask Length	BSR Priority
BSR Address				
BSR Address (continued)		Group Address		
Group Address (continued)				
Group Address (continued)		RP Count	Fragment RP Count	
Reserved		RP Address		
RP Address (continued)				
RP Hold Time		RP Priority	Reserved	

FIGURE 6.5   BSR sample network

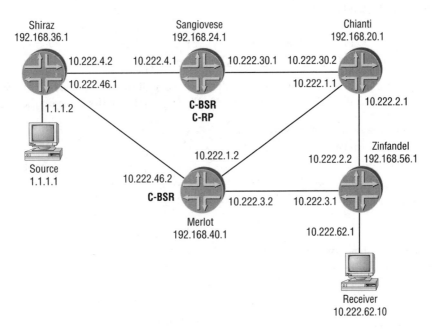

Figure 6.5 again shows a PIM-SM domain containing five routers: Shiraz, Sangiovese, Chianti, Merlot, and Zinfandel. The network is using bootstrap routing to collect and advertise RP information to the domain's routers. Both the Sangiovese and Merlot routers are configured as candidate bootstrap routers for the domain. Their PIM configuration appears as so:

```
user@Merlot> show configuration protocols pim rp
bootstrap-priority 100;
```

```
user@Sangiovese> show configuration protocols pim rp
bootstrap-priority 200;
```

Each C-BSR lists itself as a Candidate in the output of the show pim bootstrap command and sends bootstrap messages into the domain:

```
user@Merlot> show pim bootstrap
Instance: PIM.master

BSR            Pri Local address   Pri State     Timeout
None             0 192.168.40.1    100 Candidate      46
```

```
user@Sangiovese> show pim bootstrap
Instance: PIM.master


BSR              Pri Local address   Pri State      Timeout
None               0 192.168.24.1    200 Candidate       49
```

After each candidate views the priority value encoded in the bootstrap message, the Sangiovese router is elected as the BSR for the PIM domain. Both candidate BSRs agree on the selection:

```
user@Sangiovese> show pim bootstrap
Instance: PIM.master


BSR              Pri Local address   Pri State      Timeout
192.168.24.1     200 192.168.24.1    200 Elected         57



user@Merlot> show pim bootstrap
Instance: PIM.master


BSR              Pri Local address   Pri State      Timeout
192.168.24.1     200 192.168.40.1    100 Candidate      119
```

Advertising RP Capabilities

Each router in a bootstrap PIM domain with a local RP configuration advertises its capabilities in a *Candidate-RP Advertisement* (C-RP-Adv) message. These messages are unicast to the address of the BSR for the domain. The various fields of the C-RP-Adv message are shown in Figure 6.6 and include:

Version (4 bits)   This field displays the current version of PIM used for the message. It is set to a constant value of 2.

Type (4 bits)   This field contains the type of PIM message encoded in the packet. A Candidate-RP Advertisement message uses a value of 8 in this field and are unicast to the address of the domain's BSR.

Reserved (1 octet)   This field is not used and is set to a constant value of 0x00.

Checksum (2 octets)   This field displays a standard IP checksum for the entire PIM packet contents.

Prefix Count (1 octet)   This field displays the number of distinct multicast group address ranges the candidate RP supports. A value of 0 in this field means that the candidate supports the entire 224.0.0.0 /4 address range.

Priority (1 octet)   This field displays the priority of the candidate RP address for its advertised group addresses. Lower numerical values are preferred over higher values. The JUNOS software places a default value of 0, the highest priority, in this field.

Hold Time (2 octets)   This field displays the amount of time, in seconds, that the network BSR should retain knowledge of the candidate RP and its advertised group address ranges.

RP Address (6 octets)   This field contains the address of the candidate RP using the encoded unicast address format.

Group Address (8 octets)   This field is repeated based on the value displayed in the Prefix Count field. It contains an advertised multicast group address range in the encoded group address format.

Within the PIM domain shown in Figure 6.5, the Sangiovese router is configured as a local RP. This configuration appears as

```
user@Sangiovese> show configuration protocols pim rp
bootstrap-priority 200;
local {
    address 192.168.24.1;
}
```

> The selection of Sangiovese as a candidate RP and a candidate BSR is not a coincidence. It is currently a best practice to make each C-RP a C-BSR as well. This aids in network troubleshooting as well as the timely advertisement of the RP information from the BSR in the domain.

The C-RP-Adv messages advertised by each candidate RP in the domain are collected by the BSR. They are then combined into a single bootstrap message called the *RP-Set*. The RP-Set contains the address of the RP, its priority, and its advertised group addresses. Information from each candidate RP is included in the RP-Set, which is advertised by the BSR in a standard bootstrap message utilizing all of the possible message fields.

FIGURE 6.6   Candidate-RP Advertisement message format

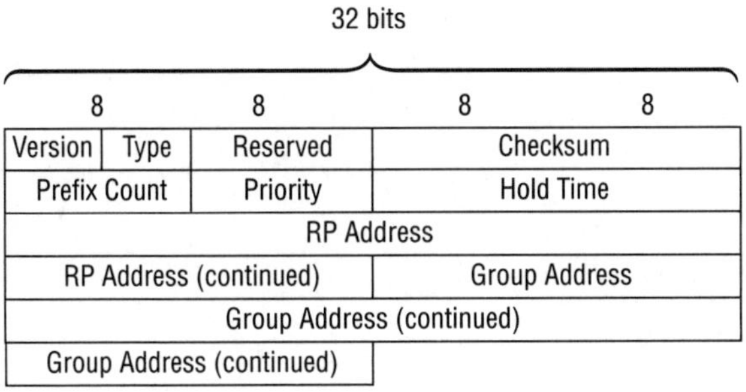

32 bits

8	8	8	8
Version	Type	Reserved	Checksum
Prefix Count	Priority	Hold Time
RP Address
RP Address (continued)	Group Address
Group Address (continued)
Group Address (continued)

Once Sangiovese commits its local RP configuration, each router in the network learns the address of each available RP. The Sangiovese router views itself as both a static and a bootstrap RP in the output of the show pim rps command:

```
user@Sangiovese> show pim rps
Instance: PIM.master


Family: INET
RP address       Type       Holdtime Timeout Active groups Group prefixes
192.168.24.1     bootstrap     150    None              0 224.0.0.0/4
192.168.24.1     static          0    None              0 224.0.0.0/4
```

The JUNOS software prefers RPs learned through bootstrap routing over those learned through Auto-RP. Both dynamic options are preferred over a statically configured RP.

Each router in the domain also views Sangiovese as the RP, including the last-hop router of Zinfandel:

```
user@Zinfandel> show pim rps
Instance: PIM.master


Family: INET
RP address       Type       Holdtime Timeout Active groups Group prefixes
192.168.24.1     bootstrap     150    150               1 224.0.0.0/4
```

Zinfandel now has the ability to build an RPT from itself to Sangiovese for the 224.6.6.6 group address. We can verify this with the output of the show pim rps extensive command:

```
user@Zinfandel> show pim rps extensive
Instance: PIM.master


Family: INET
RP: 192.168.24.1
Learned from 10.222.2.1 via:
Time Active: 00:00:29
Holdtime: 150 with 121 remaining
Device Index: 0
Subunit: 0
Interface: None
Group Ranges:
        224.0.0.0/4
```

Active groups using RP:
        224.6.6.6

        total 1 groups active

Once the multicast source at 1.1.1.1 begins sending data packets into the network, the RP sends the traffic along the RPT. This allows Zinfandel to locate the source of the traffic and build an SPT between itself and the first-hop router of Shiraz. This operation of the network during this time is explained in the "Establishing the SPT" section earlier.

The Multicast Source Discovery Protocol

The core tenet of operating a sparse-mode PIM network is that the multicast source and its interested receivers connect at a single RP router. This presents an interesting problem for scaling a multicast network, particularly when separate ASs are involved. Selecting a single RP device in this environment is not a viable solution, so network designers developed a separate protocol for advertising active multicast sources from one RP to another. This is the job of the *Multicast Source Discovery Protocol (MSDP)*. MSDP allows an RP in one PIM domain to advertise knowledge of traffic sources to RP routers in the same or different domains. Before discussing the use of MSDP within a single network or between AS networks, let's explore the operation of the protocol itself.

Operational Theory

Two routers that wish to communicate using MSDP first establish a TCP peering session between themselves using the well-known port number 639. Each peer is configured with the address of its local end of the connection as well as the address of its remote peer. The peer with the higher of the two IP addresses then waits for the other peer to establish the session. This avoids the connection collision problem seen in a BGP peering session. The TCP connection is maintained by the transmission of keepalive messages or source active messages within the 75-second peer hold timer.

Once an MSDP router learns of a new multicast source in its domain, it generates a *source active message* and forwards it to all established peers. The MSDP router learns of traffic sources in the network since it normally is also the RP for the domain. The source active (SA) message contains the address of the originating RP, the multicast group address, and the source of the multicast traffic. The specific format of the SA message is displayed in Figure 6.7; the fields are as follows:

Type (1 octet)   This field displays the type of MSDP message contained in the packet. An SA message uses a constant value of 1.

Length (2 octets)   This field contains the total length of the message.

Entry Count (1 octet)   This field displays the number of distinct source address and group address pairings contained in the message.

RP Address (4 octets)   This field contains the IPv4 address of the RP that originated the SA message.

Reserved (3 octets)   This field is not used and is set to a constant value of 0x000000.

Source Prefix Length (1 octet)   This field displays the length of the subnet mask for the Source Address field that follows. For a host address, this field must be set to a constant value of 32.

Group Address (4 octets)   This field displays the address of the multicast group being sent to the network.

Source Address (4 octets)   This field displays the source address of the multicast traffic stream.

Encapsulated Data Packet (Variable)   This variable-length field contains the multicast data packet received by the originating RP router. This field is not required to be contained in an SA message.

The originating RP floods the SA message to its MSDP peers, which further flood the message to their peers. This system of flooding messages provides a simple method for propagating information about the multicast source to multiple routers. Each MSDP peer accepts or rejects the flooded SA messages based on a set of rules discussed in the "Peer-RPF Flooding" section later in this chapter. If any of the receiving MSDP routers have a local (*,G) state for the advertised group address, they generate a PIM Join message addressed to the multicast source. This message is forwarded to the first-hop router in the originating domain, establishing an SPT between that router and the MSDP peer. The MSDP router then forwards the native multicast traffic down its local RPT towards the interested listeners. As the traffic reaches the last-hop router, a Join message is created and a separate SPT is formed between the local router and the first-hop router.

More precisely, the (S,G) Join message from the last-hop router travels only as far as the first router with an existing (S,G) state, which adds an interface to its outgoing interface list. In practice, the (S,G) Join rarely leaves the AS in which it was created.

FIGURE 6.7   MSDP source active message format

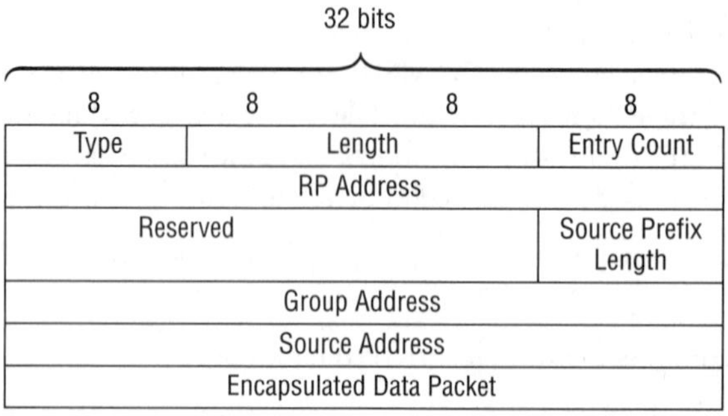

32 bits

8	8	8	8
Type	Length		Entry Count
RP Address			
Reserved			Source Prefix Length
Group Address			
Source Address			
Encapsulated Data Packet			

Mesh Groups

It is possible, in certain network configurations, for the default flooding of MSDP SA messages to cause multiple copies of the same message to arrive on a single router. Suppose that four routers (Shiraz, Chianti, Merlot, and Zinfandel) are connected in a full-mesh topology with point-to-point interfaces between them. When Shiraz receives an SA message from some remote peer, it refloods the message to all of its other MSDP peers—Chianti, Merlot, and Zinfandel in this case. In addition, the Merlot and Chianti routers also forward the same SA message to the Zinfandel router. The end result is that Zinfandel receives three separate messages, each containing the same information. This can potentially lead to a waste of network bandwidth and router resources, which is avoided through the use of mesh groups.

An MSDP *mesh group* is a set of routers that have peering sessions established so that a router can receive multiple copies of the SA message. The mesh group members are configured as a peer group within the [edit protocols msdp] configuration hierarchy. You use the mode mesh-group command within the group to prevent an SA message from being reflooded from one group member to another. The mesh group configuration of the Zinfandel router looks like this:

```
user@Zinfandel> show configuration protocols msdp
group set-as-mesh {
    mode mesh-group;
    local-address 192.168.56.1;
    peer 192.168.40.1;
    peer 192.168.20.1;
    peer 192.168.24.1;
}
group remaining-peers {
    local-address 192.168.56.1;
    peer 192.168.52.1;
}
```

Peer-RPF Flooding

To ensure that the flooding of SA messages is performed in a logical manner, each MSDP router makes an individual decision whether or not to accept an advertised message. Only messages that are accepted by the local router are reflooded to its MSDP peers. The following *peer-RPF flooding* rules dictate which received SA messages are accepted by the local router:

1. If the peer advertising the SA message belongs to a configured mesh group, accept the message.

2. If the peer advertising the SA message is configured as a default peer, accept the message.

3. If the peer advertising the SA message is the originating RP listed in the message contents, accept the message.

4. When the MSDP peer is not the originating RP of the message, perform a route lookup for the IP address of the originating RP and follow these rules:

    a. If the result of the route lookup returns a BGP route, determine if the IP address of the advertising MSDP peer equals the IP address listed in the BGP Next Hop attribute. If the IP addresses are identical, accept the message.

    b. If the result of the route lookup returns a BGP route, examine the AS Path of the route to determine if the AS of the advertising peer is along the path to the originator. If the active path contains the AS of the advertising router, accept the message.

    c. If the result of the route lookup returns an IGP route, compare the physical next-hop address of the originating RP to the physical next-hop of the advertising peer. If the next-hop values are identical, accept the message.

5. Reject the received SA message.

These peer-RPF rules do not locate the single "best" received SA message, in the same way as the BGP route selection algorithm. Instead, they allow multiple messages containing the same originating RP, source, and group information to be accepted. They are designed to ensure that SA messages are received only from peers that are closest to the originating RP. This prevents the endless flooding of SA messages between MSDP peers and keeps a flooding loop from forming.

Anycast RP

Each of the PIM RP election and selection mechanisms (static, Auto-RP, and bootstrap routing) require that a single physical router serve as the connection point between the source and the interested clients. This single point of failure in the network is mitigated somewhat by Auto-RP and BSR through their dynamic processes. The main disadvantage, however, is the time involved in noticing the failure and electing a new RP for that group address range. The use of MSDP within a single PIM domain drastically alters and enhances this paradigm by allowing multiple physical routers to share knowledge about multicast sources. This creates a virtual RP for the domain and is commonly called *anycast RP*. Let's examine how this works.

Operational Theory

Each router participating in an anycast RP network configures itself as a local RP using a common shared IP address, known as the *anycast address*. This address is then advertised by the IGP to allow non-RP routers reachability to this address. Each non-RP router views the anycast address as the RP for all possible multicast addresses and forwards all PIM protocol traffic to the metrically closest RP. The non-RP routers in the domain continue to use one of the three RP election mechanisms to learn the anycast RP address, but a static RP configuration is most common.

Figure 6.8 shows a sample network utilizing an anycast RP configuration. Both the Sangiovese and Cabernet routers are configured as local RPs and are advertising the shared anycast address using the IGP for the domain. When the interested client at 10.222.62.10 generates an IGMP packet for a multicast group, the Zinfandel router sends a PIM Join message to the closest physical RP router. Assuming that the default IGP metric values are used, this message is sent to Cabernet and an RPT is established between the RP and Zinfandel. As the multicast source at 1.1.1.1 sends its data traffic into the network, the first-hop router of Shiraz encapsulates the traffic into a Register message and sends it to Sangiovese—its closest RP router.

FIGURE 6.8   MSDP anycast RP sample network

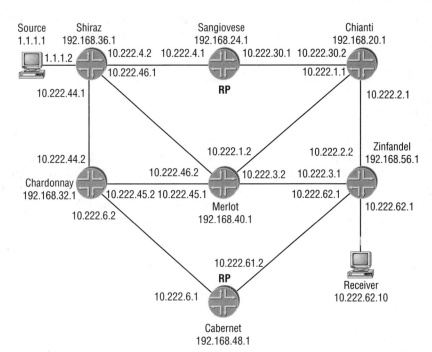

This situation poses a problem for a traditional PIM-SM network since the multicast traffic and the client request have arrived at two different routers that can't connect them. In an anycast RP environment, however, the use of MSDP resolves our dilemma. When the Sangiovese router receives the Register message from Shiraz, it examines its local PIM state to locate any (*,G) state related to the advertised group address. In addition, it generates an SA message and forwards it to its MSDP peer of Cabernet, which does have a local (*,G) state for the advertised group. Cabernet de-encapsulates the multicast data packet contained in the SA message and forwards it along the RPT toward Zinfandel while also generating a PIM Join message. This message is forwarded toward the first-hop router of Shiraz and builds an SPT between Shiraz and Cabernet for the specific (S,G) state representing the traffic flow. Native multicast traffic now flows from Shiraz through Chardonnay to Cabernet over an SPT and further to Zinfandel over an RPT.

As we would expect in a PIM-SM network, the receipt of multicast data packets by the last-hop router of Zinfandel prompts the generation of a PIM Join message, which is forwarded towards Shiraz. This message installs a final SPT between Shiraz and Zinfandel for traffic flowing from the source to the interested listener.

Anycast RP Configuration

The configuration of the anycast RP network represented in Figure 6.8 shows the non-RP routers using a static RP configuration to learn the shared anycast address of 192.168.200.1. We see an example of this on the Zinfandel router:

```
user@Zinfandel> show configuration protocols pim rp
static {
    address 192.168.200.1;
}
```

The configuration of the anycast RP routers themselves (Sangiovese and Cabernet) requires three separate steps. First, the shared anycast address of 192.168.200.1 /32 is configured on the lo0.0 interface. This allows the address to be advertised in the IGP of the domain. The inclusion of the primary keyword on the unique loopback address ensures that the automatic selection of a router ID returns the unique value and not the shared anycast value. The interface configuration of the RP routers looks like this:

```
user@Sangiovese> show configuration interfaces lo0
unit 0 {
    family inet {
        address 192.168.24.1/32 {
            primary;
        }
        address 192.168.200.1/32;
    }
}
```

```
user@Cabernet> show configuration interfaces lo0
unit 0 {
    family inet {
        address 192.168.48.1/32 {
            primary;
        }
        address 192.168.200.1/32;
    }
}
```

A quick examination of the routing table on Merlot shows the 192.168.200.1 /32 address as a reachable OSPF route for the domain:

```
user@Merlot> show route 192.168.200.1

inet.0: 27 destinations, 31 routes (27 active, 0 holddown, 0 hidden)
```

```
+ = Active Route, - = Last Active, * = Both

192.168.200.1/32   *[OSPF/10] 00:07:45, metric 2
                        via so-0/1/0.0
                    > via so-0/1/1.0
                        via so-0/1/2.0
                        via so-0/1/3.0
```

The second step in configuring the anycast RP routers is the definition of the shared address as the local RP address. This is accomplished within the [edit protocols pim rp] configuration hierarchy:

```
user@Sangiovese> show configuration protocols pim rp
local {
    address 192.168.200.1;
}


user@Cabernet> show configuration protocols pim rp
local {
    address 192.168.200.1;
}
```

Finally, each of the anycast RP routers is connected together in an MSDP full mesh using the unique loopback addresses for the session establishment. This allows each router to generate and receive SA messages for communicating multicast sources in the network. The MSDP configuration requires the specific inclusion of both the peer's address and the local router's address. We see this configuration on our anycast RP routers:

```
user@Sangiovese> show configuration protocols msdp
group anycast-rp {
    local-address 192.168.24.1;
    peer 192.168.48.1;
}


user@Cabernet> show configuration protocols msdp
group anycast-rp {
    local-address 192.168.48.1;
    peer 192.168.24.1;
}
```

Verifying the Status of the Network

Once the configuration of the PIM domain is complete, we can verify the operation of the network from two distinct perspectives. First, we ensure that the anycast RP routers are communicating over their MSDP peering session. The output of the **show msdp** command reveals each configured peer and its current status. We use this command on the Cabernet router and receive the following:

```
user@Cabernet> show msdp
Peer address    Local address   State         Last up/down Peer-Group
192.168.24.1    192.168.48.1    Established      00:14:34 anycast-rp
```

The possible MSDP peering states include Disabled, Inactive, Listen, and Established. In our case, the Established state tells us that the peering session is fully operational. When active multicast sources are announced over the peering session, we can view the resulting SA cache with the **show msdp source-active** command. We have no current traffic in the network, so this command returns no output on the Cabernet router:

```
user@Cabernet> show msdp source-active

user@Cabernet>
```

The other major network verification to perform is the knowledge of the shared anycast address as the RP for the domain. A quick examination of the **show pim rps** output from the Shiraz and Zinfandel routers shows that 192.168.200.1 is the current RP address, as expected:

```
user@Shiraz> show pim rps
Instance: PIM.master

Family: INET
RP address      Type     Holdtime Timeout Active groups Group prefixes
192.168.200.1   static          0   None              0 224.0.0.0/4

user@Zinfandel> show pim rps
Instance: PIM.master

Family: INET
RP address      Type     Holdtime Timeout Active groups Group prefixes
192.168.200.1   static          0   None              0 224.0.0.0/4
```

Monitoring Traffic Flows

Now that the PIM domain has determined that the 192.168.200.1 anycast RP routers should be used for multicast traffic, we can monitor the formation of the RPT from Cabernet to Zinfandel. The interested client connected to Zinfandel generates an IGMP message for the 224.6.6.6 multicast group. As a result, a PIM Join message is sent by Zinfandel toward Cabernet out its so-0/1/2.0 interface (10.222.61.1):

```
May  6 12:47:11 PIM so-0/1/2.0 SENT 10.222.61.1 -> 224.0.0.13 V2
May  6 12:47:11   JoinPrune to 10.222.61.2 holdtime 210 groups 1 sum 0x1b54 len 34
```

```
May  6 12:47:11    group 224.6.6.6 joins 1 prunes 0
May  6 12:47:11      join list:
May  6 12:47:11         source 192.168.200.1 flags sparse,rptree,wildcard
```

Zinfandel also reports an active group (224.6.6.6) utilizing the RP address of 192.168.200.1:

```
user@Zinfandel> show pim rps extensive
Instance: PIM.master

Family: INET
RP: 192.168.200.1
Learned via: static configuration
Time Active: 00:05:51
Holdtime: 0
Device Index: 0
Subunit: 0
Interface: None
Group Ranges:
        224.0.0.0/4
Active groups using RP:
        224.6.6.6

        total 1 groups active
```

From the perspective of the Cabernet router, we see an established (*,G) PIM state representing the RPT to Zinfandel:

```
user@Cabernet> show pim join extensive
Instance: PIM.master Family: INET

Group: 224.6.6.6
    Source: *
    RP: 192.168.200.1
    Flags: sparse,rptree,wildcard
    Upstream interface: local
    Upstream State: Local RP
    Downstream Neighbors:
        Interface: so-0/1/0.0
            10.222.61.1 State: Join   Flags: SRW  Timeout: 171
```

When the multicast source at 1.1.1.1 begins transmitting data packets toward Shiraz, these packets are encapsulated in Register messages and forwarded to Sangiovese, where an MSDP

SA message is generated. We can see that the MSDP peers have installed the SA message in their local cache:

```
user@Sangiovese> show msdp source-active
Group address    Source address  Peer address   Originator       Flags
224.6.6.6        1.1.1.1         local          192.168.200.1    Accept

user@Cabernet> show msdp source-active
Group address    Source address  Peer address   Originator       Flags
224.6.6.6        1.1.1.1         192.168.24.1    192.168.24.1     Accept
```

The receipt of the SA message by Cabernet allows the multicast traffic to flow along the RPT towards Zinfandel and to the interested client. After receiving the traffic, Zinfandel examines its local RPF table to locate the source of the traffic and sends a (S,G) Join toward the first-hop router of Shiraz. This results in an SPT rooted at Shiraz and flowing through Merlot and Zinfandel, as seen in the output of the show pim join extensive command:

```
user@Shiraz> show pim join extensive
Instance: PIM.master Family: INET

Group: 224.6.6.6
    Source: 1.1.1.1
    Flags: sparse
    Upstream interface: fe-0/0/3.0
    Upstream State: Local Source
    Keepalive timeout: 181
    Downstream Neighbors:
        Interface: so-0/1/1.0
            10.222.46.2 State: Join   Flags: S    Timeout: 172

user@Merlot> show pim join extensive
Instance: PIM.master Family: INET

Group: 224.6.6.6
    Source: 1.1.1.1
    Flags: sparse
    Upstream interface: so-0/1/3.0
    Upstream State: Join to Source
    Keepalive timeout: 183
    Downstream Neighbors:
        Interface: so-0/1/1.0
            10.222.3.1 State: Join   Flags: S    Timeout: 163
```

```
user@Zinfandel> show pim join extensive
Instance: PIM.master Family: INET

Group: 224.6.6.6
    Source: *
    RP: 192.168.200.1
    Flags: sparse,rptree,wildcard
    Upstream interface: so-0/1/2.0
    Upstream State: Join to RP
    Downstream Neighbors:
        Interface: fe-0/0/3.0
            10.222.62.1 State: Join   Flags: SRW  Timeout: Infinity

Group: 224.6.6.6
    Source: 1.1.1.1
    Flags: sparse,spt
    Upstream interface: so-0/1/1.0
    Upstream State: Join to RP, Join to Source
    Keepalive timeout: 196
    Downstream Neighbors:
        Interface: fe-0/0/3.0
            10.222.62.1 State: Join   Flags: S     Timeout: Infinity
```

Inter-Domain MSDP

The use of MSDP to connect RP routers in different PIM domains is one of the original design goals of the protocol. The configuration and operation of MSDP in this environment is quite similar to that of an anycast RP network. The main difference between the two is that the domains under each administrator's control each elect their own RP using one of the three possible election methods. These RP routers are then connected across the AS boundaries using MSDP.

Operational Theory

Each PIM domain elects its own RP routers for servicing PIM protocol traffic. These routers are then configured as MSDP peers to advertise active sources between the PIM domains. Most times, these peering sessions follow the external BGP peerings between the ASs. In other words, it is rare to find an MSDP peering session from a local router to a remote peer that is in an AS more than one hop away.

FIGURE 6.9 MSDP inter-domain sample network

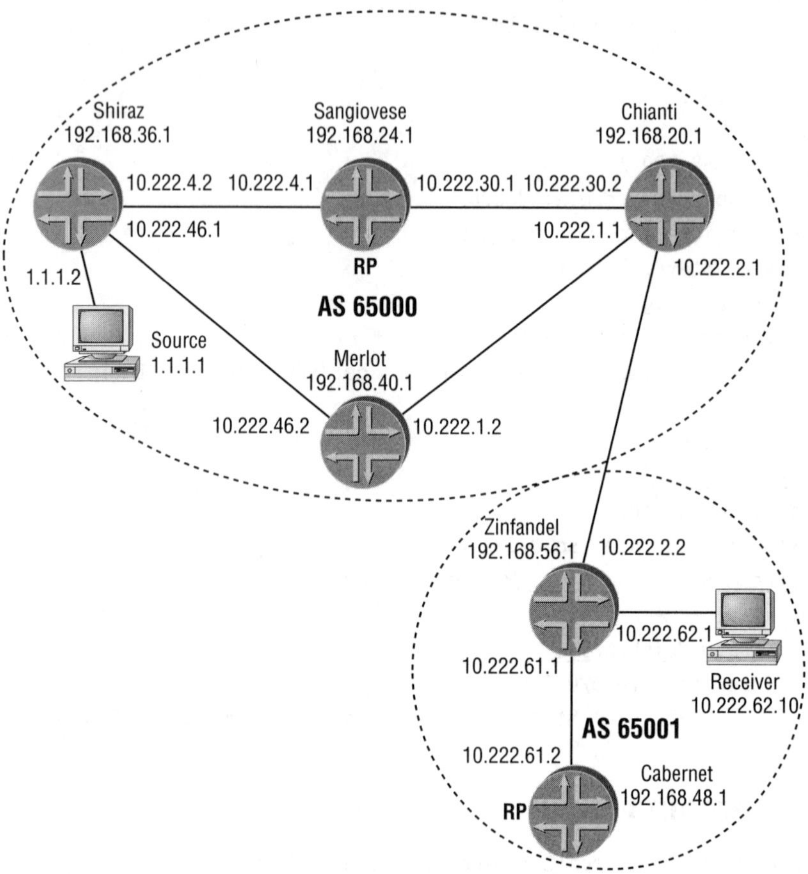

The sample network shown in Figure 6.9 shows AS 65000 and AS 65001 connected by the Chianti and Zinfandel routers. Each AS represents a separate PIM domain, and each has elected its own RP using a static configuration. When the interested client in AS 65001 generates an IGMP message, it sends it to the Zinfandel router, where a PIM Join message is created and advertised to the local RP of Cabernet. As a source in AS 65000 begins to send multicast data traffic into the network, the packets are forwarded to the local RP for its domain—Sangiovese.

Upon the receipt of the PIM Register message from Shiraz, Sangiovese generates an MSDP SA message and forwards it to its MSDP peer in AS 65001. This peer, Cabernet, already has an existing (*,G) state for the advertised multicast group and sends a PIM Join toward the source of the traffic. In addition, Cabernet extracts the multicast data packets from the SA message and forwards them along the RPT towards Zinfandel. Once the Zinfandel router learns the source of the traffic stream, it creates a local (S,G) PIM state for the group address and sends Join messages toward the source as well. In our specific example, the Zinfandel router is already along the SPT created between Shiraz and its local RP of Cabernet. This allows Zinfandel to simply add its client interface to the downstream interfaces associated with the (S,G) state created by Cabernet's earlier Join message.

Configuring and Verifying MSDP

The configuration of the MSDP peers in Figure 6.9 is very straightforward. Each of the routers configures its local peering address and the address of its remote peer:

```
user@Sangiovese> show configuration protocols msdp
group inter-domain-mcast {
    local-address 192.168.24.1;
    peer 192.168.48.1;
}

user@Cabernet> show configuration protocols msdp
group inter-domain-mcast {
    local-address 192.168.48.1;
    peer 192.168.24.1;
}
```

The output of the show msdp command reveals each configured peer and its current status. We use this command on the Sangiovese and Cabernet routers and receive the following information:

```
user@Sangiovese> show msdp
Peer address    Local address    State        Last up/down Peer-Group
192.168.48.1    192.168.24.1     Established      00:17:32 inter-domain-mcast

user@Cabernet> show msdp
Peer address    Local address    State        Last up/down Peer-Group
192.168.24.1    192.168.48.1     Established      00:18:42 inter-domain-mcast
```

Once the multicast source at 1.1.1.1 begins forwarding packets to Shiraz, we can view the SA cache on each of the MSDP peers:

```
user@Sangiovese> show msdp source-active
Group address   Source address  Peer address    Originator       Flags
224.6.6.6       1.1.1.1         local           192.168.24.1     Accept

user@Cabernet> show msdp source-active
Group address   Source address  Peer address    Originator       Flags
224.6.6.6       1.1.1.1         192.168.24.1    192.168.24.1     Accept
```

As we expected, the PIM SPT is built from Shiraz, through Merlot, to Chianti, and finally to Zinfandel. The output of the show pim join extensive command provides the proof of its formation:

```
user@Shiraz> show pim join extensive
Instance: PIM.master Family: INET

Group: 224.6.6.6
    Source: 1.1.1.1
    Flags: sparse
    Upstream interface: fe-0/0/3.0
    Upstream State: Local Source
    Keepalive timeout: 208
    Downstream Neighbors:
        Interface: so-0/1/1.0
            10.222.46.2 State: Join    Flags: S    Timeout: 201


user@Merlot> show pim join extensive
Instance: PIM.master Family: INET

Group: 224.6.6.6
    Source: 1.1.1.1
    Flags: sparse
    Upstream interface: so-0/1/3.0
    Upstream State: Join to Source
    Keepalive timeout: 207
    Downstream Neighbors:
        Interface: so-0/1/0.0
            10.222.1.1 State: Join    Flags: S    Timeout: 193


user@Chianti> show pim join extensive
Instance: PIM.master Family: INET

Group: 224.6.6.6
    Source: 1.1.1.1
    Flags: sparse
    Upstream interface: so-0/1/0.0
    Upstream State: Join to Source
    Keepalive timeout: 170
    Downstream Neighbors:
        Interface: so-0/1/1.0
            10.222.2.2 State: Join    Flags: S    Timeout: 186
```

```
user@Zinfandel> show pim join extensive
Instance: PIM.master Family: INET

Group: 224.6.6.6
    Source: *
    RP: 192.168.48.1
    Flags: sparse,rptree,wildcard
    Upstream interface: so-0/1/2.0
    Upstream State: Join to RP
    Downstream Neighbors:
        Interface: fe-0/0/3.0
            10.222.62.1 State: Join    Flags: SRW  Timeout: Infinity

Group: 224.6.6.6
    Source: 1.1.1.1
    Flags: sparse,spt
    Upstream interface: so-0/1/0.0
    Upstream State: Join to RP, Join to Source
    Keepalive timeout: 156
    Downstream Neighbors:
        Interface: fe-0/0/3.0
            10.222.62.1 State: Join    Flags: S    Timeout: Infinity
```

Reverse Path Forwarding

Multicast data packets and PIM protocol packets are forwarded through the network using the information in the *reverse path forwarding* (RPF) table. Multicast traffic flows use the RPF table to prevent forwarding loops, while PIM uses it to forward packets upstream towards the RP or traffic source. By default, the JUNOS software uses the inet.0 routing table as the RPF table. We can verify this by examining the output of the show multicast rpf command:

```
user@Sherry> show multicast rpf inet summary
Multicast RPF table: inet.0, 20 entries
```

This routing table, of course, is automatically populated with information by the routing protocols and easily provides the required knowledge. This makes managing the RPF table quite simple. The main disadvantage of using inet.0 is the fact that both unicast and multicast traffic use the same set of links for all packet flows. Some network administrators would like to separate these types of traffic onto different links in the network for control over how resources are used. The JUNOS software provides a method for establishing this type of multicast network. Let's see how this works in some further detail.

Creating a New RPF Table

A Juniper Networks router has the ability to use any operational routing table as the multicast RPF table. The only real requirement is that the selected table contain IP unicast routing information. However, the JUNOS software has set aside the inet.2 routing table for RPF usage, and most administrators use this table in place of inet.0. To this end, we'll focus our examples and configurations in this section on populating and using the inet.2 table for RPF checks.

The inet.2 routing table already exists on the router, so we only need to populate it with routing knowledge for it to appear in the output of the show route command. One convenient method for accomplishing this task in the JUNOS software is through a rib-group. A *rib-group* is a listing of routing tables that is applied to a particular source of routing knowledge. The rib-group specifies into which tables the particular routing source should place its information. It is created within the [edit routing-options] hierarchy and is applied to a particular protocol or route source. Let's examine how to use rib-groups to add routes to the inet.2 RPF table.

Adding Local Routes to *inet.2*

The transmission of PIM protocol packets in a multicast network occurs in a hop-by-hop fashion. As such, each PIM router requires knowledge of its directly connected interfaces and subnets. This information is represented as Local and Direct routes within the JUNOS software and should be included in the RPF table.

Figure 6.10 shows a network containing two ASs, which are forwarding multicast traffic between themselves. The administrators of these two AS networks have decided to use the inet.2 routing table for RPF checks. The first step in this process is copying the local routes into this table by using a rib-group. Much like a routing policy, the rib-group is given a name in the configuration and is supplied the tables into which the routes should be placed. The Chianti router currently has a rib-group called ***populate-inet2***, which contains an import-rib statement. The rib-group lists both inet.0 and inet.2 as tables where it can place routing information. The configuration currently appears as so:

```
user@Chianti> show configuration routing-options rib-groups
populate-inet2 {
    import-rib [ inet.0 inet.2 ];
}
```

The first table listed in the import-rib statement must be the primary routing table for the protocol that uses the rib-group. The primary routing table is the location in which routes are placed by default. In the majority of cases, this is the inet.0 routing table.

All locally connected interfaces and subnets on the router are represented by the `interface-routes` hierarchy within the [`edit routing-options`] portion of the configuration. We apply the ***populate-inet2*** rib-group on Chianti to place these routes into the new RPF table:

```
user@Chianti> show configuration routing-options
interface-routes {
    rib-group inet populate-inet2;
}
rib-groups {
    populate-inet2 {
        import-rib [ inet.0 inet.2 ];
    }
}
autonomous-system 65000;
```

FIGURE 6.10   RPF sample network

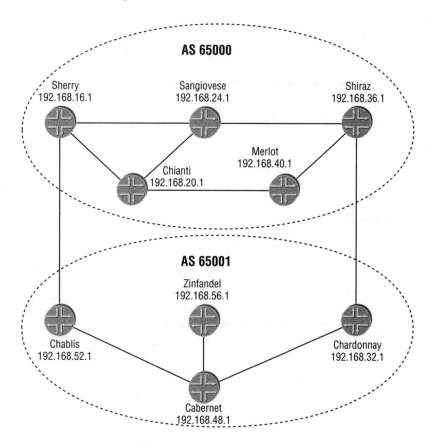

We verify our configuration with the output of the show route command. Each of the connected subnets in the 10.222.0.0 /16 address space now appears in the inet.2 routing table:

```
user@Chianti> show route 10.222/16 terse table inet.2

inet.2: 11 destinations, 11 routes (11 active, 0 holddown, 0 hidden)
+ = Active Route, - = Last Active, * = Both

A Destination         P Prf   Metric 1   Metric 2  Next hop        AS path
* 10.222.1.0/24       D   0                         >so-0/1/0.0
* 10.222.1.1/32       L   0                         Local
* 10.222.2.0/24       D   0                         >so-0/1/1.0
* 10.222.2.1/32       L   0                         Local
* 10.222.29.0/24      D   0                         >ge-0/2/0.0
* 10.222.29.2/32      L   0                         Local
* 10.222.30.0/24      D   0                         >so-0/1/2.0
* 10.222.30.2/32      L   0                         Local
```

The Zinfandel router in AS 65001 has a similar rib-group configuration applied to its interface routes. This configuration and the resulting routing table look like this:

```
user@Zinfandel> show configuration routing-options
interface-routes {
    rib-group inet populate-inet2;
}
static {
    route 192.168.57.0/24 next-hop 10.222.62.3;
}
rib-groups {
    populate-inet2 {
        import-rib [ inet.0 inet.2 ];
    }
}
autonomous-system 65001;

user@Zinfandel> show route 10.222/16 terse table inet.2

inet.2: 11 destinations, 11 routes (11 active, 0 holddown, 0 hidden)
+ = Active Route, - = Last Active, * = Both

A Destination         P Prf   Metric 1   Metric 2  Next hop        AS path
* 10.222.2.0/24       D   0                         >so-0/1/0.0
* 10.222.2.2/32       L   0                         Local
```

```
*  10.222.3.0/24      D   0                      >so-0/1/1.0
*  10.222.3.1/32      L   0                      Local
*  10.222.61.0/24     D   0                      >so-0/1/2.0
*  10.222.61.1/32     L   0                      Local
*  10.222.62.0/24     D   0                      >so-0/1/3.0
*  10.222.62.1/32     L   0                      Local
```

In addition, the 192.168.57.0/24 route is configured as a static route on Zinfandel. This type of knowledge is also useful in the multicast RPF table and is placed there with a rib-group. We use the same ***populate-inet2*** group that we've previously defined and simply apply it at the [edit routing-options static] hierarchy level. This allows all configured static routes on the router to be placed in both routing tables. The configuration of Zinfandel is altered to reflect this desire:

```
user@Zinfandel> show configuration routing-options
interface-routes {
    rib-group inet populate-inet2;
}
static {
    rib-group populate-inet2;
    route 192.168.57.0/24 next-hop 10.222.62.3;
}
rib-groups {
    populate-inet2 {
        import-rib [ inet.0 inet.2 ];
    }
}
autonomous-system 65001;
```

Again, the result is clearly visible in the output of the show route command:

```
user@Zinfandel> show route protocol static

inet.0: 26 destinations, 33 routes (26 active, 0 holddown, 0 hidden)
+ = Active Route, - = Last Active, * = Both

192.168.57.0/24    *[Static/5] 00:01:15
                    > to 10.222.62.3 via so-0/1/3.0

inet.2: 12 destinations, 12 routes (12 active, 0 holddown, 0 hidden)
+ = Active Route, - = Last Active, * = Both

192.168.57.0/24    *[Static/5] 00:01:15
                    > to 10.222.62.3 via so-0/1/3.0
```

Adding OSPF Routes to *inet.2*

The routers in AS 65001 currently have all locally configured routing knowledge in the `inet.2` routing table. While this ensures reachability to directly connected PIM neighbors, it doesn't provide knowledge of the domain's RP—192.168.48.1 /32. This routing information is supplied by OSPF within the boundaries of the network. As such, it is critical that OSPF routes be placed into the new RPF table. After all, if the PIM routers can't reach the RP, then the network isn't able to forward sparse-mode traffic.

Conveniently, the same ***populate-inet2*** rib-group used for the local routes can be used to place OSPF routes into the new RPF table. The rib-group is applied at the global OSPF level, as we see on the Chardonnay router:

```
user@Chardonnay> show configuration protocols ospf
rib-group populate-inet2;
area 0.0.0.0 {
    interface lo0.0;
    interface so-0/1/2.0;
}
```

As we would expect, the OSPF routes calculated by Chardonnay's Shortest Path First (SPF) process are placed into both routing tables defined by the rib-group:

```
user@Chardonnay> show route protocol ospf terse table inet.2
```

`inet.2`: 15 destinations, 16 routes (15 active, 0 holddown, 0 hidden)
+ = Active Route, - = Last Active, * = Both

A	Destination	P	Prf	Metric 1	Metric 2	Next hop	AS path
	10.222.6.0/24	O	10	1		>so-0/1/2.0	
*	10.222.60.0/24	O	10	2		>so-0/1/2.0	
*	10.222.61.0/24	O	10	2		>so-0/1/2.0	
*	10.222.62.0/24	O	10	3		>so-0/1/2.0	
*	192.168.48.1/32	O	10	1		>so-0/1/2.0	
*	192.168.52.1/32	O	10	2		>so-0/1/2.0	
*	192.168.56.1/32	O	10	2		>so-0/1/2.0	

This routing knowledge provides Chardonnay with the ability to forward PIM packets to the RP address of 192.168.48.1.

Adding IS-IS Routes to *inet.2*

The JUNOS software provides two separate methods for placing IS-IS routes into the `inet.2` routing table. The first option uses a rib-group applied at the global IS-IS configuration hierarchy. This places identical routing knowledge into all tables defined by the rib-group. The second option involves the use of the multi-topology TLVs defined within the IS-IS protocol itself. The

JUNOS software uses these TLVs to support multicast traffic forwarding by calculating a separate SPF tree and placing the results into the inet.2 routing table automatically. The use of these TLVs allows you to define separate IS-IS metrics for unicast and multicast traffic and enforce separate forwarding topologies within your PIM domain.

You enable the use of the multi-topology TLVs with the multicast-topology command at the global IS-IS hierarchy level. This allows the router to scan the inet.2 routing table for operational IS-IS interfaces and advertise them in the local router's LSP. Of course, you'll need to use a rib-group to place the router's connected interfaces into inet.2 in the first place.

The routers in AS 65000 are using IS-IS as their domain's IGP. Each router is configured with the ***populate-inet2*** rib-group, which is applied to the locally configured interface routes on the Merlot router:

```
user@Merlot> show configuration routing-options
interface-routes {
    rib-group inet populate-inet2;
}
rib-groups {
    populate-inet2 {
        import-rib [ inet.0 inet.2 ];
    }
}
autonomous-system 65000;
```

We then configure the multicast-topology command on each router in AS 65000. This allows IS-IS to natively populate the inet.2 routing table using information contained in the multi-topology TLVs. The IS-IS configuration of Merlot is shown here in addition to the output of the show route protocol isis command:

```
user@Merlot> show configuration protocols isis
multicast-topology;
level 1 disable;
interface so-0/1/0.0;
interface so-0/1/3.0;
interface lo0.0;
```

```
user@Merlot> show route protocol isis terse

inet.0: 27 destinations, 32 routes (27 active, 0 holddown, 0 hidden)
+ = Active Route, - = Last Active, * = Both

A Destination        P Prf   Metric 1   Metric 2  Next hop        AS path
* 1.1.1.0/24         I  18        20               >10.222.46.1
```

*	10.222.4.0/24	I	18	20	>10.222.46.1
*	10.222.28.0/24	I	18	30	>10.222.1.1
					10.222.46.1
*	10.222.29.0/24	I	18	20	>10.222.1.1
*	10.222.30.0/24	I	18	20	>10.222.1.1
*	192.168.16.1/32	I	18	20	>10.222.1.1
*	192.168.20.1/32	I	18	10	>10.222.1.1
*	192.168.24.1/32	I	18	20	>10.222.1.1
					10.222.46.1
*	192.168.36.1/32	I	18	10	>10.222.46.1

inet.2: 20 destinations, 20 routes (20 active, 0 holddown, 0 hidden)
+ = Active Route, - = Last Active, * = Both

A	Destination	P	Prf	Metric 1	Metric 2	Next hop	AS path
*	1.1.1.0/24	I	18	20		>10.222.46.1	
*	10.222.4.0/24	I	18	20		>10.222.46.1	
*	10.222.28.0/24	I	18	30		>10.222.1.1	
						10.222.46.1	
*	10.222.29.0/24	I	18	20		>10.222.1.1	
*	10.222.30.0/24	I	18	20		>10.222.1.1	
*	192.168.16.1/32	I	18	20		>10.222.1.1	
*	192.168.20.1/32	I	18	10		>10.222.1.1	
*	192.168.24.1/32	I	18	20		>10.222.1.1	
						10.222.46.1	
*	192.168.36.1/32	I	18	10		>10.222.46.1	

We can view the newly created TLVs advertised by Merlot in its local link-state PDU:

```
user@Merlot> show isis database Merlot.00-00 extensive | find TLV
  TLVs:
    Area address: 49.1111 (3)
    Speaks: IP
    Speaks: IPv6
    Topology: unicast
    Topology: ipv4 multicast
    IP router id: 192.168.40.1
    IP address: 192.168.40.1
    Hostname: Merlot
    IS neighbor: Shiraz.00, Internal, Metric: default 10
    IS neighbor: Chianti.00, Internal, Metric: default 10
```

```
   IS extended neighbor: Shiraz.00, Metric: default 10
     IP address: 10.222.46.2
     Neighbor's IP address: 10.222.46.1
   IS extended neighbor: Chianti.00, Metric: default 10
     IP address: 10.222.1.2
     Neighbor's IP address: 10.222.1.1
   IP prefix: 192.168.40.1/32, Internal, Metric: default 0, Up
   IP prefix: 10.222.1.0/24, Internal, Metric: default 10, Up
   IP prefix: 10.222.46.0/24, Internal, Metric: default 10, Up
   IP extended prefix: 192.168.40.1/32 metric 0 up
   IP extended prefix: 10.222.1.0/24 metric 10 up
   IP extended prefix: 10.222.46.0/24 metric 10 up
   Multicast IP prefix: 10.222.46.0/24 metric 10 up
   Multicast IP prefix: 10.222.1.0/24 metric 10 up
   Multicast IP prefix: 192.168.40.1/32 metric 0 up
   Multicast IS neighbor: Shiraz.00, Metric: default 10
   Multicast IS neighbor: Chianti.00, Metric: default 10
 No queued transmissions
```

Currently, the Merlot router has multicast IS-IS adjacencies with the Shiraz and Chianti routers. By default, the same metric values are used for both the unicast and multicast TLVs. This results in identical SPF trees and concurrent traffic flows. The usefulness of the multi-topology TLVs, however, comes from the ability to alter the metric values used by the local router for multicast traffic.

From the perspective of the Sherry router in Figure 6.10, two possible networks paths exist to reach the Shiraz router. The first path uses Sangiovese as a transit node, while the alternate path uses both Chianti and Merlot as transit nodes. By virtue of the default IS-IS metric of 10 being used in both TLVs, the path via Sangiovese has a total cost of 20 and is active in both `inet.0` and `inet.2`:

```
user@Sherry> show route 192.168.36.1

inet.0: 25 destinations, 30 routes (25 active, 0 holddown, 0 hidden)
+ = Active Route, - = Last Active, * = Both

192.168.36.1/32     *[IS-IS/18] 2d 12:43:11, metric 20
                     > to 10.222.28.2 via at-0/1/0.0


inet.2: 18 destinations, 18 routes (18 active, 0 holddown, 0 hidden)
+ = Active Route, - = Last Active, * = Both


192.168.36.1/32     *[IS-IS/18] 00:27:36, metric 20
                     > to 10.222.28.2 via at-0/1/0.0
```

The administrators of AS 65000 would like to forward multicast traffic between Sherry and Shiraz through the alternate Chianti/Merlot path. This is accomplished by configuring smaller multicast-only metrics on the IS-IS interfaces by using the `ipv4-multicast-metric` command. Each router along the path alters its configuration to advertise a metric of 5 for each interface instead of the default value of 10. The configuration of the Sherry router now appears as so:

```
user@Sherry> show configuration protocols isis
multicast-topology;
level 1 disable;
interface at-0/1/0.0;
interface ge-0/2/0.0 {
    level 2 ipv4-multicast-metric 5;
}
interface lo0.0;
```

This alters the information advertised by Sherry in its IS-IS TLV for just the multicast adjacency to Chianti, which is represented by the designated IS (DIS) notation of `Sherry.02`. The advertised unicast metric remains at its default value of 10:

```
user@Sherry> show isis database extensive Sherry.00-00 | find TLV
  TLVs:
    Area address: 49.1111 (3)
    Speaks: IP
    Speaks: IPv6
    Topology: unicast
    Topology: ipv4 multicast
    IP router id: 192.168.16.1
    IP address: 192.168.16.1
    Hostname: Sherry
    IS neighbor: Sangiovese.00, Internal, Metric: default 10
    IS neighbor: Sherry.02, Internal, Metric: default 10
    IS extended neighbor: Sangiovese.00, Metric: default 10
      IP address: 10.222.28.1
      Neighbor's IP address: 10.222.28.2
    IS extended neighbor: Sherry.02, Metric: default 10
      IP address: 10.222.29.1
    Multicast IS neighbor: Sangiovese.00, Metric: default 10
    Multicast IS neighbor: Sherry.02, Metric: default 5
    IP prefix: 10.222.28.0/24, Internal, Metric: default 10, Up
    IP prefix: 10.222.29.0/24, Internal, Metric: default 10, Up
    IP prefix: 192.168.16.1/32, Internal, Metric: default 0, Up
    IP extended prefix: 10.222.28.0/24 metric 10 up
    IP extended prefix: 10.222.29.0/24 metric 10 up
```

```
    IP extended prefix: 192.168.16.1/32 metric 0 up
    Multicast IP prefix: 192.168.16.1/32 metric 0 up
    Multicast IP prefix: 10.222.29.0/24 metric 5 up
    Multicast IP prefix: 10.222.28.0/24 metric 10 up
  No queued transmissions
```

Once the routers along the alternate path complete their configurations, we find the metric of the 192.168.36.1/32 route in inet.2 to be 15. Additionally, the next-hop interface for the route is altered from at-0/1/0.0 to ge-0/2/0.0:

```
user@Sherry> show route 192.168.36.1

inet.0: 25 destinations, 30 routes (25 active, 0 holddown, 0 hidden)
+ = Active Route, - = Last Active, * = Both

192.168.36.1/32    *[IS-IS/18] 2d 12:57:13, metric 20
                   > to 10.222.28.2 via at-0/1/0.0

inet.2: 18 destinations, 18 routes (18 active, 0 holddown, 0 hidden)
+ = Active Route, - = Last Active, * = Both

192.168.36.1/32    *[IS-IS/18] 00:06:52, metric 15
                   > to 10.222.29.2 via ge-0/2/0.0
```

Adding BGP Routes to *inet.2*

To transmit multicast traffic successfully between the two AS networks shown in Figure 6.10, each network requires knowledge of possible multicast sources in the RPF table. In our multi-AS example, this type of routing knowledge is provided by BGP.

As we saw with IS-IS, the JUNOS software provides two separate methods for placing BGP routes into the inet.2 routing table. You should not be surprised at this point that the first option uses a rib-group for this purpose. Of course, this option doesn't enforce a separate unicast and multicast forwarding topology. To achieve this administrative goal, we configure the BGP routers to support multiprotocol BGP (MBGP). This option allows us to advertise routes from and place routes into the inet.2 routing table. It uses the MP-Reachable-NLRI BGP attribute for announcing information and is enabled through the family inet command in BGP. This command requires one of three options to be enabled—unicast, multicast, or any. The unicast option advertises just IPv4 routes found in inet.0 to an established peer with a Subsequent Address Family Identifier (SAFI) value of 1. The multicast option advertises just routes from inet.2 with a SAFI value of 2. Finally, the any option advertises both inet.0 and inet.2 routes along with their respective SAFI values.

NOTE   MBGP (and its associated SAFI values) is discussed in greater detail in Chapter 5, "Advanced Border Gateway Protocol (BGP)."

The administrators of AS 65000 and AS 65001 would like to forward both unicast and multicast traffic between their respective networks. To this end, every router in Figure 6.10 applies the `family inet any` command to all possible BGP peers. The configurations of the Sherry and Chablis routers now look like this:

```
user@Sherry> show configuration protocols bgp
group internal {
    type internal;
    local-address 192.168.16.1;
    family inet {
        any;
    }
    export nhs;
    neighbor 192.168.20.1;
    neighbor 192.168.24.1;
    neighbor 192.168.36.1;
    neighbor 192.168.40.1;
}
group external {
    type external;
    family inet {
        any;
    }
    export local-loopbacks;
    peer-as 65001;
    neighbor 10.222.5.2;
}

user@Chablis> show configuration protocols bgp
group internal {
    type internal;
    local-address 192.168.52.1;
    family inet {
        any;
    }
    export nhs;
    neighbor 192.168.32.1;
    neighbor 192.168.48.1;
    neighbor 192.168.56.1;
}
group external {
```

```
    type external;
    family inet {
        any;
    }
    export local-loopbacks;
    peer-as 65000;
    neighbor 10.222.5.1;
}
```

We can verify that the peers have negotiated the ability to use both the unicast and multicast SAFIs by examining the output of the show bgp neighbor command:

```
user@Chablis> show bgp neighbor 10.222.5.1
Peer: 10.222.5.1+179  AS 65000 Local: 10.222.5.2+2807 AS 65001
  Type: External    State: Established    Flags: <>
  Last State: OpenConfirm   Last Event: RecvKeepAlive
  Last Error: None
  Export: [ local-loopbacks ]
  Options: <Preference HoldTime AddressFamily PeerAS Refresh>
  Address families configured: inet-unicast inet-multicast
  Holdtime: 90 Preference: 170
  Number of flaps: 0
  Peer ID: 192.168.16.1    Local ID: 192.168.52.1    Active Holdtime: 90
  Keepalive Interval: 30
  Local Interface: at-0/2/0.0
  NLRI advertised by peer: inet-unicast inet-multicast
  NLRI for this session: inet-unicast inet-multicast
  Peer supports Refresh capability (2)
  Table inet.0 Bit: 10001
    RIB State: BGP restart is complete
    Send state: in sync
    Active prefixes:          6
    Received prefixes:        6
    Suppressed due to damping: 0
  Table inet.2 Bit: 20001
    RIB State: BGP restart is complete
    Send state: in sync
    Active prefixes:          6
    Received prefixes:        6
    Suppressed due to damping: 0
  Last traffic (seconds): Received 21   Sent 22   Checked 22
```

```
Input messages:   Total 32    Updates 18    Refreshes 0    Octets 1278
Output messages:  Total 26    Updates 10    Refreshes 0    Octets 940
Output Queue[0]: 0
Output Queue[1]: 0
```

The established BGP session is using both inet-unicast and inet-multicast as NLRI for the session. We can see that the local router of Chablis configured both address families (Address families configured) and that the remote router of Sherry advertised this capability as well (NLRI advertised by peer). In addition, both routing tables currently contain six active BGP prefixes. These are the loopback address of the five routers in AS 65000 in addition to the multicast source subnet of 1.1.1.0 /24:

```
user@Chablis> show route protocol bgp terse
```

```
inet.0: 24 destinations, 31 routes (24 active, 0 holddown, 0 hidden)
+ = Active Route, - = Last Active, * = Both
```

A Destination	P Prf	Metric 1	Metric 2	Next hop	AS path
* 1.1.1.0/24	B 170	100	0	>10.222.5.1	65000 I
	B 170	100	0	>so-0/1/0.0	65000 I
* 192.168.16.1/32	B 170	100	0	>10.222.5.1	65000 I
	B 170	100	0	>so-0/1/0.0	65000 I
* 192.168.20.1/32	B 170	100	0	>10.222.5.1	65000 I
	B 170	100	0	>so-0/1/0.0	65000 I
* 192.168.24.1/32	B 170	100	0	>10.222.5.1	65000 I
	B 170	100	0	>so-0/1/0.0	65000 I
* 192.168.36.1/32	B 170	100	0	>10.222.5.1	65000 I
	B 170	100	0	>so-0/1/0.0	65000 I
* 192.168.40.1/32	B 170	100	0	>10.222.5.1	65000 I
	B 170	100	0	>so-0/1/0.0	65000 I
* 192.168.57.0/24	B 170	100		>so-0/1/0.0	I

```
inet.2: 21 destinations, 28 routes (21 active, 0 holddown, 0 hidden)
+ = Active Route, - = Last Active, * = Both
```

A Destination	P Prf	Metric 1	Metric 2	Next hop	AS path
* 1.1.1.0/24	B 170	100	0	>10.222.5.1	65000 I
	B 170	100	0	>so-0/1/0.0	65000 I
* 192.168.16.1/32	B 170	100	0	>10.222.5.1	65000 I
	B 170	100	0	>so-0/1/0.0	65000 I
* 192.168.20.1/32	B 170	100	0	>10.222.5.1	65000 I
	B 170	100	0	>so-0/1/0.0	65000 I

* 192.168.24.1/32	B 170	100	0 >10.222.5.1	65000	I
	B 170	100	0 >so-0/1/0.0	65000	I
* 192.168.36.1/32	B 170	100	0 >10.222.5.1	65000	I
	B 170	100	0 >so-0/1/0.0	65000	I
* 192.168.40.1/32	B 170	100	0 >10.222.5.1	65000	I
	B 170	100	0 >so-0/1/0.0	65000	I
* 192.168.57.0/24	B 170	100	>so-0/1/0.0		I

The same route selection algorithm used to select the best BGP route in inet.0 is also used for all BGP routes in inet.2. Provided the BGP attribute values are identical in both tables, the router selects the same path for data forwarding, which results in congruent unicast and multicast forwarding. For example, the Cabernet router receives a BGP path advertisement for the 1.1.1.0/24 network from both Chardonnay and Chablis. The path from Chardonnay is selected in both routing tables based on the router ID of the IBGP peer:

```
user@Cabernet> show route 1.1.1/24

inet.0: 23 destinations, 32 routes (23 active, 0 holddown, 0 hidden)
+ = Active Route, - = Last Active, * = Both

1.1.1.0/24         *[BGP/170] 00:12:12, MED 0, localpref 100, from 192.168.32.1
                      AS path: 65000 I
                   > via so-0/1/1.0
                    [BGP/170] 00:12:36, MED 0, localpref 100, from 192.168.52.1
                      AS path: 65000 I
                   > via so-0/1/2.0

inet.2: 20 destinations, 29 routes (20 active, 0 holddown, 0 hidden)
+ = Active Route, - = Last Active, * = Both

1.1.1.0/24         *[BGP/170] 00:12:12, MED 0, localpref 100, from 192.168.32.1
                      AS path: 65000 I
                   > via so-0/1/1.0
                    [BGP/170] 00:12:36, MED 0, localpref 100, from 192.168.52.1
                      AS path: 65000 I
                   > via so-0/1/2.0
```

The administrators of AS 65001 would prefer to forward multicast traffic across the Sherry-Chablis link instead of the Shiraz-Chardonnay link. Although this is easily accomplished by configuring the Chardonnay router to filter the 1.1.1.0/24 route, that is not a desirable approach because this link should be used in the event of a failure of the primary link. Therefore, the administrators of AS 65001 instead modify the Local Preference value of all routes received from the Sherry router. The new value of 200 for these routes allows Chablis to be the preferred exit point for multicast traffic. To accomplish this goal, a routing policy called *alter-inet2-localpref* is created on Chablis:

```
user@Chablis> show configuration policy-options | find alter-inet2-localpref
policy-statement alter-inet2-localpref {
    term set-to-200 {
        to rib inet.2;
        then {
            local-preference 200;
        }
    }
}
```

The to rib inet.2 portion of the policy affects only received BGP routes with a SAFI value of 2. These routes have the Local Preference value set to 200 before being installed in the local routing table. The policy is applied as an import policy for the BGP peering session with Sherry:

```
user@Chablis> show configuration protocols bgp group external
type external;
import alter-inet2-localpref;
family inet {
    any;
}
export local-loopbacks;
peer-as 65000;
neighbor 10.222.5.1;
```

As a result of this routing policy, the Cabernet router now prefers the path advertised by Chablis in the inet.2 routing table. Within inet.0, however, the route attributes remain unchanged and the path advertised from Chardonnay is preferred:

```
user@Cabernet> show route 1.1.1/24

inet.0: 23 destinations, 32 routes (23 active, 0 holddown, 0 hidden)
+ = Active Route, - = Last Active, * = Both

1.1.1.0/24         *[BGP/170] 00:31:15, MED 0, localpref 100, from 192.168.32.1
                      AS path: 65000 I
                    > via so-0/1/1.0
                    [BGP/170] 00:31:39, MED 0, localpref 100, from 192.168.52.1
                      AS path: 65000 I
                    > via so-0/1/2.0
```

inet.2: 20 destinations, 23 routes (20 active, 0 holddown, 0 hidden)
+ = Active Route, - = Last Active, * = Both

1.1.1.0/24   *[BGP/170] 00:07:58, MED 0, localpref 200, from 192.168.52.1
                      AS path: 65000 I
                    > via so-0/1/2.0

Using an Alternate RPF Table

Once a new RPF table is created and populated with routing information, the multicast proto-cols themselves need to be informed of its existence. Until this occurs, RPF checks continue to be performed against the contents of the inet.0 routing table. You notify both PIM and MSDP of a different RPF table by applying a rib-group within their portions of the configuration. Using the sample network in Figure 6.10, let's see how this is accomplished.

The network administrators in AS 65000 and AS 65001 have created and populated the inet.2 routing table with complete knowledge of the network. They have additionally altered the forward-ing topology for the multicast traffic flows by altering information only within the inet.2 table. Unfortunately, the PIM process on the routers is still using the inet.0 table for RPF checks. We can verify this with the show multicast rpf command on the Cabernet router:

```
user@Cabernet> show multicast rpf inet summary
Multicast RPF table: inet.0, 23 entries
```

To begin using inet.2 as the RPF table, we first create a rib-group within the [edit routing-options] configuration hierarchy. Unlike the rib-group definitions we used in pre-vious sections, this configuration simply lists inet.2 as the sole table in the import-rib state-ment. This rib-group appears on Cabernet as:

```
user@Cabernet> show configuration routing-options
interface-routes {
    rib-group inet populate-inet2;
}
rib-groups {
    populate-inet2 {
        import-rib [ inet.0 inet.2 ];
    }
    use-inet2-for-rpf {
        import-rib inet.2;
    }
}
autonomous-system 65001;
```

While you might be surprised that the ***use-inet2-for-rpf*** rib-group contains a listing only for inet.2, keep in mind that PIM and MSDP don't actually place routes into this routing table. The purpose of the rib-group is simply to inform them that inet.2 is the new RPF table. This allows the protocols to refer to this routing table when performing RPF checks or verifying upstream interfaces.

We then apply the ***use-inet2-for-rpf*** rib-group to the PIM process on each router in the network. In addition, the MSDP peers of Cabernet and Shiraz receive a similar rib-group application. The configuration of Cabernet now appears as:

```
user@Cabernet> show configuration protocols msdp
rib-group use-inet2-for-rpf;

user@Cabernet> show configuration protocols pim
rib-group inet use-inet2-for-rpf;
rp {
    local {
        address 192.168.48.1;
    }
}
interface all;
interface fxp0.0 {
    disable;
}
```

Finally, we verify that the inet.2 routing table is the new RPF table:

```
user@Cabernet> show multicast rpf inet summary
Multicast RPF table: inet.2, 20 entries
```

Summary

In this chapter, we saw how the JUNOS software uses each of the three RP election mechanisms to construct a rendezvous point tree (RPT) and a shortest path tree (SPT) in a PIM sparse-mode network. The simplest RP election mechanism to configure was static assignment of the RP address. However, this method doesn't provide capabilities for dynamic failover and redundancy, so we explored both Auto-RP and Bootstrap routing. We discussed the various configuration options and operation of Auto-RP and BSR within the context of a single PIM domain. Each RP election method displayed the ability to assign roles to certain routers in the network and dynamically select and learn the address of the RP for each multicast group address range.

We concluded the chapter with a discussion of the Multicast Source Discovery Protocol (MSDP) and explained how it exchanges knowledge of active multicast sources between peer routers. We explored the use of MSDP within a single PIM domain for creating a virtual RP. This use of MSDP is commonly referred to as anycast RP since multiple physical routers share a common RP address. All non-RP routers use this anycast address as the RP address for all possible multicast groups and transmit their protocol packets to the metrically closest anycast router. This is not the only use for MSDP, however, since it was originally designed for communications between RP routers in different PIM domains. Each individual domain elects an RP using one of the three defined methods, and these routers are then peered together using MSDP. Routers create an RPT between themselves and the RP in their respective domain. Active multicast sources are transmitted between peers using SA messages. When a peer router receives a message for a group that belongs to an established RPT, that peer creates an SPT between itself and the source of the traffic. In this method, data traffic flows across multiple PIM domains.

Exam Essentials

Be able to describe the operation of Auto-RP.   The Auto-RP process allows a PIM-SM domain to dynamically select and advertise RP routers in the network. Each configured RP sends Cisco-RP-Announce messages into the network in a dense-mode fashion using the 224.0.1.39 /32 group address. These are collected by the domain mapping agent, which selects a single RP for each multicast group address range. The RP selections are then advertised by the mapping agent in a Cisco-RP-Discovery message. This message is also densely flooded throughout the domain using the 224.0.1.40 /32 group address.

Be familiar with the process of electing a bootstrap router and selecting an RP in a BSR domain.   Every candidate bootstrap router in the domain generates and floods bootstrap messages that contain its locally configured BSR priority. The router with the highest priority value, or highest IP address in the event of a tie, becomes the BSR for the domain. After this election process occurs, each local RP generates a Candidate-RP-Advertisement and unicasts it to the BSR. These messages are collected by the BSR and combined into an RP-Set, which the BSR then advertises into the domain. Each PIM router then uses the information in the RP-Set to determine the RP for each possible multicast group address.

Be able to describe the operation of MSDP within a single PIM domain.   Multiple physical routers may share the responsibilities of the RP router for the same multicast group range when each is peered together using MSDP. This concept, called anycast RP, allows the multiple physical routers to become a virtual RP router for the domain. Each non-RP router communicates directly with the metrically closest RP as dictated by the IGP routing to the common anycast address.

Be able to describe the operation of a MSDP in a multidomain environment.   When multiple PIM domains desire to transmit multicast traffic to each other across their boundaries, each domain elects its own RP. These RP routers are then peered together using MSDP, which allows any individual RP to announce active sources to its peers. The advertisement of the multicast source to each RP provides the information necessary to establish an SPT from the interested client in one domain to the source of the traffic in another domain.

Understand and be able to identify methods for populating a new RPF table. The most common method in the JUNOS software for placing routing knowledge into more than one table is a rib-group. A group definition allows you to define multiple routing tables into which a routing source may place information. The rib-group is then applied to interface routes, static routes, OSPF routes, and so forth.

Be able to describe methods available for advertising multicast-specific information. Both IS-IS and BGP contain native methods for populating the inet.2 routing table with multicast-specific information. IS-IS uses multi-topology TLVs to advertise data to the network, while BGP utilizes the capabilities of multiprotocol BGP to advertise multicast information between peers.

Review Questions

1. Which Auto-RP configuration option allows a router to advertise its local RP configuration but not select the RP for each group address range?

   A. `discovery`

   B. `announce`

   C. `mapping`

   D. `local`

2. Which Auto-RP configuration option allows a router to perform the group-to-RP mapping in the network?

   A. `discovery`

   B. `announce`

   C. `mapping`

   D. `local`

3. What is the first criterion used to elect a bootstrap router in a PIM domain?

   A. Lowest configured priority value

   B. Highest configured priority value

   C. Lowest router ID

   D. Highest router ID

4. What type of message is generated by a router in a PIM Auto-RP domain to inform the network of its desire to be an RP?

   A. Cisco-RP-Announce

   B. Cisco-RP-Discovery

   C. Candidate-RP-Advertisement

   D. Source active message

5. What type of message is generated by a local RP and unicast to the bootstrap router in a PIM domain?

   A. Cisco-RP-Announce

   B. Cisco-RP-Discovery

   C. Candidate-RP-Advertisement

   D. Source active message

6. What type of message contains the RP-to-group assignments in a PIM Auto-RP domain?

A. Cisco-RP-Announce

B. Cisco-RP-Discovery

C. Candidate-RP-Advertisement

D. Source active message

7. What type of configuration is often used when a set of MSDP peers have a full mesh of connections between themselves?

A. local-address *address*

B. peer *address*

C. mode standard

D. mode mesh-group

8. Based on the following configuration information, what is the anycast address used in this PIM domain?

```
protocols {
    msdp {
        local-address 192.168.1.1;
        peer 192.168.2.2;
        peer 192.168.3.3;
    }
    pim {
        rp {
            local {
                address 192.168.4.4;
            }
        }
        interface all;
    }
}
```

A. 192.168.1.1

B. 192.168.2.2

C. 192.168.3.3

D. 192.168.4.4

9. A multicast client in PIM domain A would like to connect to a group address that has an active source in PIM domain B. The RP routers in each domain have an established MSDP peering session between them. What type of forwarding tree is built before any source active messages are transmitted?

  A. An RPT from the DR to the RP in domain A.

  B. An RPT from the DR to the RP in domain B.

  C. An SPT from the RP in domain A to the first-hop router.

  D. An SPT from the RP in domain B to the first-hop router.

  E. An SPT from the DR to the first-hop router.

10. Which JUNOS software routing table is used by default for reverse path forwarding checks?

  A. `inet.0`

  B. `inet.1`

  C. `inet.2`

  D. `inet.3`

Answers to Review Questions

1. B. The announce option for Auto-RP allows a router to generate Cisco-RP-Announce messages and flood them into the network. It does not, however, allow the local router to perform any mapping functions in the network.

2. C. The mapping option for Auto-RP allows a router to generate Cisco-RP-Announce messages when it is a local RP. It also allows the router to perform the RP-to-group mapping and advertise that selection in a Cisco-RP-Discovery message.

3. B. The primary election criterion for a bootstrap router is the highest configured priority value in the domain. The value can range from 0 to 255, with a value of 0 meaning that the local router can never become the BSR for the domain.

4. A. When an Auto-RP router is configured with either the announce or mapping option and has a local RP address configured, it generates a Cisco-RP-Announce message. This message is flooded to the 224.0.1.39 /32 group address and informs the network it would like to be an RP for the domain.

5. C. After learning of the domain's BSR, each local RP generates a Candidate-RP-Advertisement and forwards it via unicast routing to the BSR.

6. B. When an Auto-RP router is configured with the mapping option, it can select an RP for each multicast group address range. This information is then flooded to the network using the 224.0.1.40 /32 group address in a Cisco-RP-Discovery message.

7. D. When multiple MSDP routers have a full mesh of peering sessions between themselves, excessive flooding of source active messages can occur. To alleviate this situation, each of the peers can be placed into a mesh group on each router using the mode mesh-group command.

8. D. The anycast address in an anycast RP network is always used as the local RP address. Based on the configuration in the question, the local RP address is 192.168.4.4. Hence, this is the anycast address.

9. A. When a PIM router receives an IGMP Report message from a client, it automatically builds an RPT from itself to the RP within its own PIM domain. In our example, this is the RP in domain A.

10. A. By default, the JUNOS software uses the inet.0 routing table for all RPF checks.

Chapter
7

Multiprotocol Label Switching (MPLS)

JNCIS EXAM OBJECTIVES COVERED IN THIS CHAPTER:

- ✓ Define the functions and characteristics of RSVP
- ✓ Define the functions and characteristics of LDP

In this chapter, we explore how the JUNOS software uses Multiprotocol Label Switching (MPLS) to forward user data traffic across a network. Before beginning this chapter, you should be familiar with the basic concepts of MPLS. You should know that a label-switched path (LSP) allows traffic forwarding based on label values encoded in a 4-octet shim header placed between the Layer 2 and Layer 3 headers. The routers along the path of an LSP fall into one of four categories—ingress, transit, penultimate, and egress. Each router performs a specific operation when user traffic is forwarded through the LSP. You should be familiar with the basic configuration and establishment of an LSP using the Resource Reservation Protocol (RSVP). Each interface requires support for MPLS packets, and the routing protocol daemon is informed of which operational interfaces support RSVP and MPLS. The LSP itself uses RSVP Path and Resv messages to establish the LSP. You can control the actual network links used by the LSP when you configure a named path, which supplies loose and strict hops. Finally, you should know that only BGP routes, by default, are allowed to use established LSPs but that specific IPv4 destinations can be associated with a particular LSP.

In this chapter, we examine the two signaling protocols used to establish LSPs—RSVP and the Label Distribution Protocol (LDP). In addition, we investigate how each protocol operates in an MPLS network, exchanges label information, and establishes label-switched paths.

Signaling Protocols

The JUNOS software supports two protocols for the dynamic signaling and setup of an LSP: RSVP and LDP. Each signaling option effectively establishes an LSP and forwards user data traffic using MPLS labels. However, each of the protocols accomplishes this in different ways. Let's see how each of the signaling mechanisms works.

Resource Reservation Protocol

The *Resource Reservation Protocol* (RSVP) was originally designed to provide end-user hosts with the ability to reserve network resources for data traffic flows. While this concept makes theoretical sense for a single enterprise network, it was never widely implemented for the Internet at large. In essence, the ISPs that make up the Internet didn't want individual customers altering the operation of their networks.

One of the basic concepts of RSVP is that a traffic flow consists of an identifiable session between two endpoints. Traditionally, these endpoints were the hosts in the network. The concept of a session ties neatly into the concept of an LSP, which transports a traffic flow between two individual routers in the network. This led network designers to extend the RSVP protocol specification to support traffic-engineering capabilities. This extended specification (RSVP-TE) allows an RSVP session to be established between two routers (or endpoints) in the network for the purpose of transporting a specific traffic flow.

Many of the original RSVP components are still used in an MPLS network, including the basic packet format of an RSVP message. Figure 7.1 displays the format of an RSVP message, which includes the following:

Version (4 bits)   The version field displays the current version of RSVP represented by the message. A constant value of 0x1 is placed in this field.

Flags (4 bits)   The Flags field is used to signal support for protocol extensions to neighboring RSVP routers. Currently only a single flag is defined for use in an MPLS network. The flag definitions are:

Bit 3   This flag bit is currently not defined and is set to a constant value of 0.

Bit 2   This flag bit is currently not defined and is set to a constant value of 0.

Bit 1   This flag bit is currently not defined and is set to a constant value of 0.

Bit 0   This flag bit signals support for the reduction of refresh overhead messages. This extension allows multiple RSVP messages to be bundled together into a single message format. When the bit is set to a value of 1, the local router supports the extensions. When the extensions are not supported, the flag is set to a value of 0.

Message Type (1 octet)   This field displays the type of RSVP message encoded in the packet. The possible type codes are:

- 1—Path
- 2—Resv
- 3—PathErr
- 4—ResvErr
- 5—PathTear
- 6—ResvTear
- 7—ResvConf
- 12—Bundle
- 13—Ack
- 15—Srefresh
- 20—Hello
- 25—Integrity Challenge
- 26—Integrity Response

RSVP Checksum (2 octets)   This field displays a standard IP checksum for the entire RSVP message. When the checksum is computed, the local router assumes this field contains all zeros.

FIGURE 7.1 RSVP message format

32 bits

8		8	8	8
Version	Flags	Message Type	RSVP Checksum	
Send TTL		Reserved	RSVP Length	
Objects				

Send TTL (1 octet) This field contains the identical value used in the Time-to-Live (TTL) field of the IP header. It is used to detect a non-RSVP capable router along the path of an LSP.

Reserved (1 octet) This field is not used and must be set to a constant value of 0x00.

RSVP Length (2 octets) This field displays the length of the entire RSVP packet, including any optional objects that are attached to the message.

Objects (Variable) This variable-length field contains one or more RSVP objects. Each object is represented by a fixed-length header and a variable-length data field.

The information required to set up and maintain an RSVP session is encoded in multiple *objects* used in the various message types. Table 7.1 displays some RSVP objects and the messages that use them. The common reference for each object is a combination of its RSVP class name in addition to its specific object title. For example, IPv4/UDP is an object within the Session class. When you reference this object as a singular entity, it is called the IPv4/UDP Session object.

TABLE 7.1 RSVP Objects

Class Name	Class #	Object Name	C-Type #	Message Usage
Session	1	IPv4/UDP	1	`Path`
				`Resv`
				`PathErr`
				`ResvErr`
				`PathTear`
				`ResvTear`
		IPv6/UDP	2	`Path`
				`Resv`
				`PathErr`

TABLE 7.1 RSVP Objects *(continued)*

Class Name	Class #	Object Name	C-Type #	Message Usage
				ResvErr
				PathTear
				ResvTear
		LSP-Tunnel-IPv4	7	Path
				Resv
				PathErr
				ResvErr
				PathTear
				ResvTear
		LSP-Tunnel-IPv6	8	Path
				Resv
				PathErr
				ResvErr
				PathTear
				ResvTear
RSVP-Hop	3	IPv4	1	Path
				Resv
		IPv6	2	Path
				Resv
Integrity	4	Integrity	1	All types
Time-Values	5	Time-Values	1	Path
				Resv

TABLE 7.1 RSVP Objects *(continued)*

Class Name	Class #	Object Name	C-Type #	Message Usage
Error-Spec	6	IPv4	1	PathErr
				ResvErr
		IPv6	2	PathErr
				ResvErr
Scope	7	IPv4	1	Resv
		IPv6	2	Resv
Style	8	Style	1	Resv
Flowspec	9	Reserved	1	Resv
		Integrated Services	2	Resv
Filter-Spec	10	IPv4	1	Resv
		IPv6	2	Resv
		LSP-Tunnel-IPv4	7	Resv
		LSP-Tunnel-IPv6	8	Resv
Sender-Template	11	IPv4	1	Path
		IPv6	2	Path
		IPv6 Flow-Label	3	Path
		LSP-Tunnel-IPv4	7	Path
		LSP-Tunnel-IPv6	8	Path
Sender-Tspec	12	Integrated Services	2	Path
Adspec	13	Integrated Services	2	Path
Policy-Data	14	Type 1 Policy-Data	1	Path

TABLE 7.1   RSVP Objects *(continued)*

Class Name	Class #	Object Name	C-Type #	Message Usage
				Resv
Resv-Confirm	15	IPv4	1	Resv
		IPv6	2	Resv
Label	16	Label	1	Resv
		Generalized Label	2	Resv
		Waveband Switching	3	Resv
Label Request	19	Label Request (no label range)	1	Path
		Label Request (ATM label range)	2	Path
		Label Request (Frame Relay label range)	3	Path
		Generalized Label Request	4	Path
		Juniper Networks Extension	11	Path
Explicit Route	20	Explicit Route	1	Path
Record Route	21	Record Route	1	Path
				Resv
Hello	22	Hello Request	1	Hello
		Hello Acknowledgement	2	Hello
Message-ID	23	Message-ID	1	Path
				Resv

TABLE 7.1   RSVP Objects *(continued)*

Class Name	Class #	Object Name	C-Type #	Message Usage
Message-ID-Ack	24	Message-ID-Ack	1	Path
				Resv
		Message-ID-Nack	2	Path
Message-ID-List	25	Message-ID-List	1	Path
				Resv
		IPv4/Message-ID Src-List	2	Path
		IPv6/Message-ID Src-List	3	Path
		IPv4/Message-ID Mcast-List	4	Path
		IPv6/Message-ID Mcast-List	5	Path
Detour	63	Detour	7	Path
Challenge	64	Challenge	1	Integrity Challenge
				Integrity Response
Restart-Cap	131	Restart-Cap	1	Hello
Properties	204	Object-Type	1	Path
				Resv
Fast Reroute	205	Fast Reroute	1	Path
		Fast Reroute (existing implementations)	7	Path
Session Attribute	207	LSP-Tunnel-RA	1	Path
		LSP-Tunnel	7	Path

A detailed explanation of every RSVP object listed is outside the scope of this book. Within this chapter, we'll focus only on the objects used to establish label-switched paths in an MPLS network.

Before we explore the format and use of RSVP objects, let's discuss the RSVP messages used in an MPLS network.

The *Path* Message

When an MPLS-capable router sets up an LSP, it generates a `Path` message and forwards it downstream to the egress router. The destination address of the message is the IP address of the egress router, but each device along the path examines the contents of the `Path` message. This hop-by-hop examination occurs since the ingress router sets the IP Router-Alert option in the message's IP header. The `Path` message may contain some of the following RSVP objects: Session, RSVP-Hop, Time-Values, Session Attribute, Sender Template, Sender-Tspec, Adspec, Explicit Route, Label Request, Properties, Record Route, Integrity, Fast Reroute, and Detour.

FIGURE 7.2   Sample MPLS network

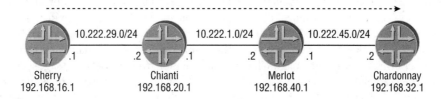

Figure 7.2 shows a simple MPLS network consisting of four routers; Sherry, Chianti, Merlot, and Chardonnay. An MPLS LSP is established from Sherry to Chardonnay using RSVP. We use the `show mpls lsp ingress` command on the Sherry router to verify that the LSP is operational:

```
user@Sherry> show mpls lsp ingress
Ingress LSP: 1 sessions
To              From            State Rt ActivePath       P       LSPname
192.168.32.1    192.168.16.1    Up    0                   *       Sherry-to-Char
Total 1 displayed, Up 1, Down 0
```

The configuration on Sherry that created the **Sherry-to-Char** LSP looks like this:

```
user@Sherry> show configuration protocols mpls
label-switched-path Sherry-to-Char {
    to 192.168.32.1;
}
interface all;
```

When the configuration was committed, Sherry generated an RSVP `Path` message addressed to the egress address of 192.168.36.1 and sent it downstream. After some processing at the Chianti router, the `Path` message is advertised further downstream to Merlot. We see the message arrive at Merlot and appear in the output of a `traceoptions` file, which is collecting RSVP information:

```
Apr 24 10:56:24 RSVP recv Path 192.168.16.1->192.168.32.1 Len=228 so-0/1/0.0
Apr 24 10:56:24   Session7 Len 16 192.168.32.1(port/tunnel ID 44214) Proto 0
Apr 24 10:56:24   Hop      Len 12 10.222.1.1/0x084ec198
Apr 24 10:56:24   Time     Len  8 30000 ms
Apr 24 10:56:24   SessionAttribute Len 28 Prio (7,0) flag 0x0 "Sherry-to-Char"
Apr 24 10:56:24   Sender7  Len 12 192.168.16.1(port/lsp ID  1)
Apr 24 10:56:24   Tspec    Len 36 rate 0bps size 0bps peak Infbps m 20 M 1500
Apr 24 10:56:24   ADspec   Len 48
Apr 24 10:56:24   SrcRoute Len 20  10.222.1.2 S 10.222.45.2 S
Apr 24 10:56:24   LabelRequest Len  8 EtherType 0x800
Apr 24 10:56:24   Properties Len 12 Primary path
Apr 24 10:56:24   RecRoute Len 20  10.222.1.1 10.222.29.1
```

When Merlot receives this particular `Path` message, it examines the information in the `Session7` and `Sender7` objects to determine if this unique combination was already seen in a previous `Path` message. Because this is a new LSP, we know that the message has not been seen by Merlot. This "newness" means that Merlot creates a new RSVP soft-state set of information known as a *Path State Block*. This soft-state information includes information from the `Path` message such as the Session, Sender Template, and Sender-Tspec objects. Additionally, the interface address of the previous hop along the LSP (10.222.1.1) is stored, which allows the router to send a `Resv` message to the appropriate upstream device.

Because Merlot is not the egress router, it then prepares to send the `Path` message further downstream. Before doing so, it adds the outgoing interface address (10.222.45.1) to the Record Route object and places it in the RSVP-Hop object. We can see the message sent to Chardonnay in the `traceoptions` file as

```
Apr 24 10:56:24 RSVP send Path 192.168.16.1->192.168.32.1 Len=228 so-0/1/2.0
Apr 24 10:56:24   Session7 Len 16 192.168.32.1(port/tunnel ID 44214) Proto 0
Apr 24 10:56:24   Hop      Len 12 10.222.45.1/0x08550264
Apr 24 10:56:24   Time     Len  8 30000 ms
Apr 24 10:56:24   SessionAttribute Len 28 Prio (7,0) flag 0x0 "Sherry-to-Char"
Apr 24 10:56:24   Sender7  Len 12 192.168.16.1(port/lsp ID  1)
Apr 24 10:56:24   Tspec    Len 36 rate 0bps size 0bps peak Infbps m 20 M 1500
Apr 24 10:56:24   ADspec   Len 48
Apr 24 10:56:24   SrcRoute Len 12  10.222.45.2 S
Apr 24 10:56:24   LabelRequest Len  8 EtherType 0x800
Apr 24 10:56:24   Properties Len 12 Primary path
Apr 24 10:56:24   RecRoute Len 28  10.222.45.1 10.222.1.1 10.222.29.1
```

After the `Path` message reaches the egress router of Chardonnay, the resources of the LSP are established in the network by `Resv` messages.

The *Resv* Message

The Chardonnay router, our LSP egress router, generates a `Resv` message and forwards it upstream to Merlot. The destination address of the `Resv` message is the interface address of the Merlot router. This information is gleaned from the RSVP-Hop object in the `Path` message received by Chardonnay. An individual `Resv` message may contain some of the following RSVP objects: Session, RSVP-Hop, Time-Values, Style, Flowspec, Filter-Spec, Label, Record Route, and Integrity.

The first `Resv` message received on Merlot is from the Chardonnay router. We see the details of this message in the output of our `traceoptions` file:

```
Apr 24 10:56:24 RSVP recv Resv 10.222.45.2->10.222.45.1 Len=120 so-0/1/2.0
Apr 24 10:56:24   Session7 Len 16 192.168.32.1(port/tunnel ID 44214) Proto 0
Apr 24 10:56:24   Hop      Len 12 10.222.45.2/0x08550264
Apr 24 10:56:24   Time     Len  8 30000 ms
Apr 24 10:56:24   Style    Len  8 FF
Apr 24 10:56:24   Flow     Len 36 rate 0bps size 0bps peak Infbps m 20 M 1500
Apr 24 10:56:24   Filter7  Len 12 192.168.16.1(port/lsp ID  1)
Apr 24 10:56:24   Label    Len  8  3
Apr 24 10:56:24   RecRoute Len 12  10.222.45.2
```

When Merlot receives this first `Resv` message, it creates an additional set of RSVP soft state information known as a *Resv State Block*. This state information is uniquely identified by the data in the Session, RSVP-Hop, and Flowspec objects. The Resv State Block stores these data fields as well as the outgoing interface for the traffic flow and the style of the particular reservation request. Merlot then consults the Path State Block information previously stored and locates the next upstream router. This lookup is keyed against the information stored in the Session and Filter-Spec objects.

When a matching Path State Block is found, Merlot records the label advertised from the downstream router. In our particular example, Chardonnay advertised a label value of 3, signaling Merlot to perform penultimate hop popping (PHP). Because Merlot is not the ingress router, a new `Resv` message is formulated for advertisement upstream to Chianti. Before sending the message, Merlot adds its outgoing interface address (10.222.1.2) to the Record Route object and places it in the RSVP-Hop object. Additionally, a label value of 100,001 is allocated and included in the Label object of the `Resv` message. We can see these message details in the `traceoptions` file on Merlot:

```
Apr 24 10:56:24 RSVP send Resv 10.222.1.2->10.222.1.1 Len=128 so-0/1/0.0
Apr 24 10:56:24   Session7 Len 16 192.168.32.1(port/tunnel ID 44214) Proto 0
Apr 24 10:56:24   Hop      Len 12 10.222.1.2/0x084ec198
Apr 24 10:56:24   Time     Len  8 30000 ms
Apr 24 10:56:24   Style    Len  8 FF
```

```
Apr 24 10:56:24   Flow     Len 36 rate 0bps size 0bps peak Infbps m 20 M 1500
Apr 24 10:56:24   Filter7  Len 12 192.168.16.1(port/lsp ID  1)
Apr 24 10:56:24   Label    Len  8  100001
Apr 24 10:56:24   RecRoute Len 20  10.222.1.2 10.222.45.2
```

When the flow of Resv messages reaches the Sherry router, the LSP is successful established.

The *PathErr* Message

An RSVP PathErr message is sent hop by hop to the ingress router from the device noticing the error. PathErr messages do not destroy any established soft state in the network, but are used simply to signal error information, often a processing problem with a Path message, to the ingress router. These messages are sent in a hop-by-hop fashion upstream and are addressed to the interface address of the previous hop. A PathErr message may contain some of the following RSVP objects: Session, Error-Spec, Sender-Template, and Sender-Tspec.

Using Figure 7.2 as a guide, we once again build an LSP from Sherry to Chardonnay. The LSP is provided an explicit route through the network using a named path of *strict-hops*, which is applied to the LSP as so:

```
user@Sherry> show configuration protocols mpls
label-switched-path Sherry-to-Chardonnay {
    to 192.168.32.1;
    bandwidth 15m;
    no-cspf;
    primary strict-hops;
}
path strict-hops {
    10.222.29.2 strict;
    10.222.1.2 strict;
    10.222.111.2 strict;
}
interface all;
```

The final address listed in the *strict-hops* path is 10.222.111.2, which does not correspond to the address of the Chardonnay router. This causes the Path message processing to fail at Merlot, since the next hop in the explicit route is not reachable. Merlot generates a PathErr message address to 10.222.1.1, the interface address of Chianti, to signal the ingress router of the problem. The message details are visible in the traceoptions file:

```
Apr 25 07:06:00 RSVP recv Path 192.168.16.1->192.168.32.1 Len=228 so-0/1/0.0
Apr 25 07:06:00   Session7 Len 16 192.168.32.1(port/tunnel ID 44222) Proto 0
Apr 25 07:06:00   Hop      Len 12 10.222.1.1/0x084ec198
Apr 25 07:06:00   Time     Len  8 30000 ms
Apr 25 07:06:00   SessionAttribute Len 28 Prio (7,0) flag 0x0 "Sherry-to-Char"
Apr 25 07:06:00   Sender7  Len 12 192.168.16.1(port/lsp ID  1)
```

```
Apr 25 07:06:00   Tspec    Len 36 rate 0bps size 0bps peak Infbps m 20 M 1500
Apr 25 07:06:00   ADspec   Len 48
Apr 25 07:06:00   SrcRoute Len 20   10.222.1.2 S 10.222.111.2 S
Apr 25 07:06:00   LabelRequest Len  8 EtherType 0x800
Apr 25 07:06:00   Properties Len 12 Primary path
Apr 25 07:06:00   RecRoute Len 20   10.222.1.1 10.222.29.1


Apr 25 07:06:00 RSVP originate PathErr 10.222.1.2->10.222.1.1
Apr 25 07:06:00   Explicit Route: bad strict route LSP Sherry-to-Char(1/44222)
Apr 25 07:06:00 RSVP send PathErr 10.222.1.2->10.222.1.1 Len=84 so-0/1/0.0
Apr 25 07:06:00   Session7 Len 16 192.168.32.1(port/tunnel ID 44222) Proto 0
Apr 25 07:06:00   Error    Len 12 code 24 value 2 flag 0 by 10.222.1.2
Apr 25 07:06:00   Sender7  Len 12 192.168.16.1(port/lsp ID  1)
Apr 25 07:06:00   Tspec    Len 36 rate 15Mbps size 15Mbps peak Infbps m 20 M 1500
```

From Merlot's perspective, we see the arrival of the Path message from Sherry, which contains an explicit route shown as SrcRoute Len 20 10.222.1.2 S 10.222.111.2 S. As Merlot is not capable of forwarding the Path message to 10.222.111.2, it generates a PathErr message containing the error information of Explicit Route: bad source route. This message travels upstream to the Sherry router, where the status of the LSP is listed as nonoperational. We can gather valuable information as to why the LSP is not working from the output of the show mpls lsp ingress extensive command:

```
user@Sherry> show mpls lsp ingress extensive
Ingress LSP: 1 sessions

192.168.32.1
  From: 192.168.16.1, State: Dn, ActiveRoute: 0, LSPname: Sherry-to-Char
  ActivePath: (none)
  LoadBalance: Random
  Encoding type: Packet, Switching type: Packet, GPID: IPv4
  Primary    strict-hops       State: Dn
    Bandwidth: 15Mbps
    2 Apr 25 07:06:33  10.222.1.2: Explicit Route: bad strict route[3 times]
    1 Apr 25 07:05:53  Originate Call
  Created: Fri Arp 25 07:05:47 2003
Total 1 displayed, Up 0, Down 1
```

The *ResvErr* Message

An RSVP ResvErr message is also used to alert routers in the network to potential problems. The message is sent hop by hop to the egress router from the device noticing the error. Like the PathErr message, ResvErr messages do not destroy any established soft state in the network.

The messages are addressed to the IP interface address of the next downstream hop along the path. A `ResvErr` message may contain some of the following RSVP objects: Session, RSVP-Hop, Error-Spec, Style, Flowspec, and Filter-Spec.

Once the ***Sherry-to-Char*** LSP is established in Figure 7.2, the interface address of the Chianti router is changed from 10.222.29.2 /24 to 10.222.29.100 /24. This address change causes Chianti to include 10.222.29.100 in the RSVP-Hop object in its next `Resv` refresh message to Sherry. We see this message in the `traceoptions` output on Chianti:

```
Apr 25 10:35:37 RSVP send Resv 10.222.29.100->10.222.29.1 Len=136 ge-0/2/0.0
Apr 25 10:35:37     Session7 Len 16 192.168.32.1(port/tunnel ID 44234) Proto 0
Apr 25 10:35:37     Hop       Len 12 10.222.29.100/0x084fb0cc
Apr 25 10:35:37     Time      Len  8 30000 ms
Apr 25 10:35:37     Style     Len  8 FF
Apr 25 10:35:37     Flow      Len 36 rate 0bps size 0bps peak Infbps m 20 M 1500
Apr 25 10:35:37     Filter7   Len 12 192.168.61.1(port/lsp ID  1)
Apr 25 10:35:37     Label     Len  8  100007
Apr 25 10:35:37     RecRoute  Len 28  10.222.29.100 10.222.1.2 10.222.45.2
```

When Sherry receives this `Resv` message, it compares its contents against the current Resv State Block and finds that the interface address has been changed. Sherry then generates a `ResvErr` message and forwards it downstream to the egress router. This message is received by Chianti, which then forwards it along to Merlot:

```
Apr 25 10:35:37 RSVP recv ResvErr 10.222.29.1->10.222.29.100 Len=104 ge-0/2/0.0
Apr 25 10:35:37     Session7 Len 16 192.168.32.1(port/tunnel ID 44234) Proto 0
Apr 25 10:35:37     Hop       Len 12 10.222.29.1/0x084fb0cc
Apr 25 10:35:37     Error     Len 12 code 4 value 0 flag 0 by 10.222.29.1
Apr 25 10:35:37     Style     Len  8 FF
Apr 25 10:35:37     Flow      Len 36 rate 0bps size 0bps peak Infbps m 20 M 1500
Apr 25 10:35:37     Filter7   Len 12 192.168.16.1(port/lsp ID  1)

Apr 25 10:35:37 RSVP send ResvErr 10.222.1.1->10.222.1.2 Len=104 so-0/1/0.0
Apr 25 10:35:37     Session7 Len 16 192.168.32.1(port/tunnel ID 44234) Proto 0
Apr 25 10:35:37     Hop       Len 12 10.222.1.1/0x084ec198
Apr 25 10:35:37     Error     Len 12 code 4 value 0 flag 0 by 10.222.29.1
Apr 25 10:35:37     Style     Len  8 FF
Apr 25 10:35:37     Flow      Len 36 rate 0bps size 0bps peak Infbps m 20 M 1500
Apr 25 10:35:37     Filter7   Len 12 192.168.16.1(port/lsp ID  1)
```

The *PathTear* Message

Once an LSP is established in the network, RSVP maintains its soft-state data structures as long as the LSP is operational. Once the LSP is no longer needed, the state information is removed from the router's memory. This removal of state information is the function of the `PathTear` message. The message travels downstream to the egress router, removing the Path State Block and Resv State Block information along the way. The destination address of the `PathTear` message is the IP address of the egress router, but the IP Router-Alert option is set to allow each device along the path to examine the message contents. The `PathTear` message may contain some of the following RSVP objects: Session, RSVP-Hop, Sender-Template, and Sender-Tspec.

The **Sherry-to-Char** LSP from Figure 7.2 is operational in the network. We verify its status on the ingress router of Sherry:

```
user@Sherry> show mpls lsp
Ingress LSP: 1 sessions
To              From           State Rt ActivePath      P      LSPname
192.168.32.1    192.168.16.1   Up    0                  *      Sherry-to-Char
Total 1 displayed, Up 1, Down 0

Egress LSP: 0 sessions
Total 0 displayed, Up 0, Down 0

Transit LSP: 0 sessions
Total 0 displayed, Up 0, Down 0
```

Suppose the network link between the Chianti and Merlot routers now fails. This link failure causes Merlot to generate a `PathTear` message addressed to the egress address of 192.168.32.1. The message replicates the information originally found in the `Path` message that established the LSP. This allows Merlot and Chardonnay to remove all RSVP state information associated with the **Sherry-to-Char** LSP. We can view the contents of the message in the output of the `traceoptions` file on Merlot:

```
Apr 25 09:56:54 RSVP send PathTear 192.168.16.1->192.168.32.1 Len=84 so-0/1/2.0
Apr 25 09:56:54    Session7 Len 16 192.168.32.1(port/tunnel ID 44230) Proto 0
Apr 25 09:56:54    Hop      Len 12 10.222.45.1/0x08550264
Apr 25 09:56:54    Sender7  Len 12 192.168.16.1(port/lsp ID  1)
Apr 25 09:56:54    Tspec    Len 36 rate 0bps size 0bps peak Infbps m 20 M 1500
```

The *ResvTear* Message

In a similar fashion to the `PathTear` message, a `ResvTear` message also removes RSVP state information in the network. The `ResvTear` message travels upstream to the ingress router in a hop-by-hop fashion. The destination address of the message is the IP interface address of the previous hop along the path. The `ResvTear` message may contain some of the following RSVP objects: Session, RSVP-Hop, Style, and Filter-Spec.

When the network link between the Chianti and Merlot routers fails, the state information on Chianti and Sherry is no longer needed. The Chianti router generates a `ResvTear` message addressed to the interface address of Sherry—10.222.29.1. The message replicates the information originally found in the Resv message that established the LSP. We can view the output of the traceoptions file on Chianti and see the ResvTear message sent upstream:

```
Apr 25 09:54:57 RSVP send ResvTear 10.222.29.2->10.222.29.1 Len=56 ge-0/2/0.0
Apr 25 09:54:57    Session7 Len 16 192.168.32.1(port/tunnel ID 44230) Proto 0
Apr 25 09:54:57    Hop      Len 12 10.222.29.2/0x084fb0cc
Apr 25 09:54:57    Style    Len  8 FF
Apr 25 09:54:57    Filter7  Len 12 192.168.16.1(port/lsp ID  1)
```

RSVP Objects

Now that we have some understanding of how RSVP uses its messages to establish and withdraw its soft-state information, we can focus on the details of the objects used in those messages. It should be clear at this point in the chapter that the information carried in each message is the key to understanding the operation of an RSVP-based MPLS network.

The LSP-Tunnel-IPv4 Session Object

The *LSP-Tunnel-IPv4 Session object* is perhaps the most widely seen object in an MPLS network. Not only is the object required in every RSVP message type, but it's also the key to uniquely identifying an LSP and its soft-state information. Figure 7.3 shows the format of the Session object, which includes the following fields:

Object Length (2 octets)   This field displays the total length of the RSVP object. For the LSP-Tunnel-IPv4 Session object, a constant value of 16 is placed in this field.

Class Number (1 octet)   The value that represents the object's class is placed into this field. The Session object falls within the Session class, which uses a value of 1.

The values assigned to the RSVP classes are encoded using one of three bit patterns. These patterns are used when the received class value is not recognized, or unknown. The bit patterns (where b is a 0 or 1) are:

  0bbbbbbb   The receipt of an unknown class value using this bit pattern causes the local router to reject the message and return an error to the originating node.

  10bbbbbb   The receipt of an unknown class value using this bit pattern causes the local router to ignore the object. It is not forwarded to any RSVP neighbors, and no error messages are generated.

  11bbbbbb   The receipt of an unknown class value using this bit pattern causes the local router to also ignore the object. In this case, however, the router forwards the object to its neighbors without examining or modifying it in any way.

C-Type Value (1 octet)   The specific type of object within its overall class is displayed in this field. The LSP-Tunnel-IPv4 Session object uses a value of 7 for its C-Type.

IPv4 Tunnel Endpoint Address (4 octets)   This field displays the IPv4 address of the LSP egress router.

Reserved (2 octets)   This field is not used and must be set to a constant value of 0x0000.

FIGURE 7.3   The LSP-Tunnel-IPv4 Session object

```
                              32 bits
                    ┌───────────────────────┐
        8        8        8        8
  ┌──────────────────────┬──────────────┬─────────────┐
  │   Object Length      │ Class Number │ C-Type Value│
  ├──────────────────────┴──────────────┴─────────────┤
  │           IPv4 Tunnel Endpoint Address            │
  ├──────────────────────┬────────────────────────────┤
  │      Reserved        │        Tunnel ID           │
  ├──────────────────────┴────────────────────────────┤
  │              Extended Tunnel ID                   │
  └───────────────────────────────────────────────────┘
```

Tunnel ID (2 octets)   This field contains a unique value generated by the ingress router of the LSP. This helps to distinguish the particular LSP from other paths originating at the same ingress router. The selected value remains constant throughout the life of the LSP.

Extended Tunnel ID (4 octets)   An ingress router places its IPv4 address in this field to further identify the session. This allows the LSP to be uniquely identified by the ingress-egress router addresses. Although the use of this field is not required, the JUNOS software places the ingress address here by default.

We see the Session object appear in a `Path` message received by the Merlot router in Figure 7.2:

```
Apr 24 10:56:24 RSVP recv Path 192.168.16.1->192.168.32.1 Len=228 so-0/1/0.0
Apr 24 10:56:24   Session7 Len 16 192.168.32.1(port/tunnel ID 44214) Proto 0
Apr 24 10:56:24   Hop       Len 12 10.222.1.1/0x084ec198
Apr 24 10:56:24   Time      Len  8 30000 ms
Apr 24 10:56:24   SessionAttribute Len 28 Prio (7,0) flag 0x0 "Sherry-to-Char"
Apr 24 10:56:24   Sender7   Len 12 192.168.16.1(port/lsp ID  1)
Apr 24 10:56:24   Tspec     Len 36 rate 0bps size 0bps peak Infbps m 20 M 1500
Apr 24 10:56:24   ADspec    Len 48
Apr 24 10:56:24   SrcRoute Len 20  10.222.1.2 S 10.222.45.2 S
Apr 24 10:56:24   LabelRequest Len  8 EtherType 0x800
Apr 24 10:56:24   Properties Len 12 Primary path
Apr 24 10:56:24   RecRoute Len 20  10.222.1.1 10.222.29.1
```

The C-Type value of 7 and the Session class of the object appears in the output as `Session7`. Within the object itself, we see the egress router address of 192.168.32.1 displayed along with the tunnel ID value of 44214.

The IPv4 RSVP-Hop Object

The *IPv4 RSVP-Hop object* is used to identify the IP interface address of the neighboring RSVP router. It allows each device in the network to store information in both the Path and Resv State Blocks. In addition, it is instrumental in properly routing RSVP messages in the network. Figure 7.4 shows the format of the RSVP-Hop object, which contains the following fields:

Object Length (2 octets)   This field displays the total length of the RSVP object. For the IPv4 RSVP-Hop object, a constant value of 12 is placed in this field.

FIGURE 7.4   The IPv4 RSVP-Hop object

```
                              32 bits
                       _____︵_____
                      /                                  \
          8           8              8              8
        ┌────────────────────────────┬──────────────┬────────────┐
        │      Object Length          │ Class Number │ C-Type Value│
        ├─────────────────────────────┴──────────────┴────────────┤
        │            IPv4 Next/Previous Hop Address                │
        ├──────────────────────────────────────────────────────────┤
        │              Logical Interface Handle                    │
        └──────────────────────────────────────────────────────────┘
```

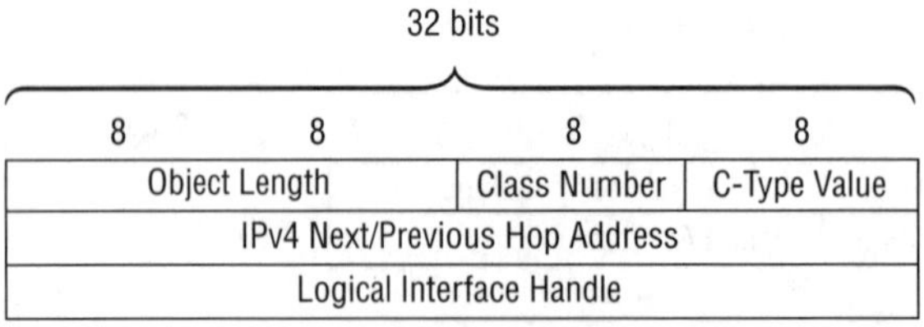

Class Number (1 octet)   The value that represents the object's class is placed into this field. The RSVP-Hop object falls within the RSVP-Hop class, which uses a value of 3.

C-Type Value (1 octet)   The specific type of object within its overall class is displayed in this field. The IPv4 RSVP-Hop object uses a value of 1 for its C-Type.

IPv4 Next/Previous Hop Address (4 octets)   This field displays the IPv4 address of the neighboring RSVP router.

Logical Interface Handle (4 octets)   Each interface that transmits and receives RSVP messages is assigned a unique 32-bit value known as the *logical interface handle*. The sending router populates this field, which contains the unique ID value. This value allows the router receiving the message to associate it with the appropriate logical interface.

The RSVP-Hop object also appears in `Path` messages received by the Merlot router for the **Sherry-to-Char** LSP:

```
Apr 24 10:56:24 RSVP recv Path 192.168.16.1->192.168.32.1 Len=228 so-0/1/0.0
Apr 24 10:56:24    Session7 Len 16 192.168.32.1(port/tunnel ID 44214) Proto 0
Apr 24 10:56:24    Hop       Len 12 10.222.1.1/0x084ec198
Apr 24 10:56:24    Time      Len  8 30000 ms
Apr 24 10:56:24    SessionAttribute Len 28 Prio (7,0) flag 0x0 "Sherry-to-Char"
Apr 24 10:56:24    Sender7   Len 12 192.168.16.1(port/lsp ID  1)
Apr 24 10:56:24    Tspec     Len 36 rate 0bps size 0bps peak Infbps m 20 M 1500
Apr 24 10:56:24    ADspec    Len 48
Apr 24 10:56:24    SrcRoute Len 20   10.222.1.2 S 10.222.45.2 S
Apr 24 10:56:24    LabelRequest Len  8 EtherType 0x800
Apr 24 10:56:24    Properties Len 12 Primary path
Apr 24 10:56:24    RecRoute Len 20   10.222.1.1 10.222.29.1
```

When Merlot receives the `Path` message, it associates the 10.222.1.1 address as the interface address of the next upstream router. The logical interface handle of 0x084ec198 is stored in the Path State Block for this session. As `Resv` messages arrive from the downstream router, Merlot uses the information in the RSVP-Hop object to forward its own `Resv` message upstream, with the address retrieved from the object encoded as the destination address. Additionally, Merlot places the logical interface handle it received in the `Path` message into the RSVP-Hop object it places in its own Resv message. The inclusion of the logical handle allows the upstream router to correlate the received Resv message with the correct interface.

The Time-Values Object

The *Time-Values object* is included in all Path and Resv messages used in the MPLS network. It contains a refresh value that is used by the receiving router to calculate the lifetime of the RSVP soft-state information. The value advertised in the Time-Values object is used by the local router to regenerate the appropriate message and send it to its RSVP neighbor. Figure 7.5 displays the format of the Time-Values object, which includes these fields:

Object Length (2 octets)   This field displays the total length of the RSVP object. For the Time-Values object, a constant value of 8 is placed in this field.

Class Number (1 octet)   The value that represents the object's class is placed into this field. The Time-Values object falls within the Time-Values class, which uses a value of 5.

C-Type Value (1 octet)   The specific type of object within its overall class is displayed in this field. The Time-Values object uses a value of 1 for its C-Type.

Refresh Period (4 octets)   This field displays the refresh time, in milliseconds, of the particular RSVP message. The JUNOS software uses a default value of 30,000 (30 seconds) for the refresh period.

The Merlot router in Figure 7.2 is receiving Resv messages for the ***Sherry-to-Char*** LSP from its downstream neighbor. The output of a traceoptions file shows the details of that Resv message:

```
Apr 24 10:56:24 RSVP recv Resv 10.222.45.2->10.222.45.1 Len=120 so-0/1/2.0
Apr 24 10:56:24    Session7 Len 16 192.168.32.1(port/tunnel ID 44214) Proto 0
Apr 24 10:56:24    Hop      Len 12 10.222.45.2/0x08550264
Apr 24 10:56:24    Time     Len  8 30000 ms
Apr 24 10:56:24    Style    Len  8 FF
Apr 24 10:56:24    Flow     Len 36 rate 0bps size 0bps peak Infbps m 20 M 1500
Apr 24 10:56:24    Filter7  Len 12 192.168.16.1(port/lsp ID  1)
Apr 24 10:56:24    Label    Len  8  3
Apr 24 10:56:24    RecRoute Len 12  10.222.45.2
```

The 30000 ms refresh time advertised in the Resv message informs Merlot that it should expect a refresh of this RSVP state every 30 seconds. In addition, the advertised value also allows Merlot to calculate the timeout value for the state information.

FIGURE 7.5   The Time-Values object

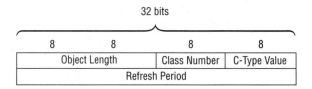

The IPv4 Error-Spec Object

The *IPv4 Error-Spec object* appears in either a PathErr or ResvErr message to provide a root cause for the error message. The object includes the IP address of the router that first discovered the error, which allows all devices in the network to locate the failure point. The fields of the IPv4 Error-Spec object, shown in Figure 7.6, include:

Object Length (2 octets) This field displays the total length of the RSVP object. For the IPv4 Error-Spec object, a constant value of 12 is placed in this field.

Class Number (1 octet) The value that represents the object's class is placed into this field. The Error-Spec object falls within the Error-Spec class, which uses a value of 6.

C-Type Value (1 octet) The specific type of object within its overall class is displayed in this field. The IPv4 Error-Spec object uses a value of 1 for its C-Type.

IPv4 Error Node Address (4 octets) This field displays the IPv4 address of the RSVP router that detected an error condition.

Flags (1 octet) This field contains flags that allow certain information to be carried in the Error-Spec object. Currently, two flags are defined for use within RSVP. Bit 0 (0x01) is used only when the object is contained in a ResvErr message. It signifies that an active reservation was in place and remains in place on the router detecting the device. Bit 1 (0x02) is also used only when the object is contained in a ResvErr message. It signifies that a reservation failure occurred that required more resources than the recipient of the message requested.

Error Code (1 octet) This field displays the major error encountered by the RSVP router.

Error Value (2 octets) This field displays additional specific information pertaining to the reported error code.

For a complete list of error codes and values, please refer to Request for Comments (RFC) 2205, "Resource Reservation Protocol—Version 1 Functional Specification."

FIGURE 7.6 The IPv4 Error-Spec object

32 bits

8	8	8	8
Object Length		Class Number	C-Type Value
IPv4 Error Node Address			
Flags	Error Code	Error Value	

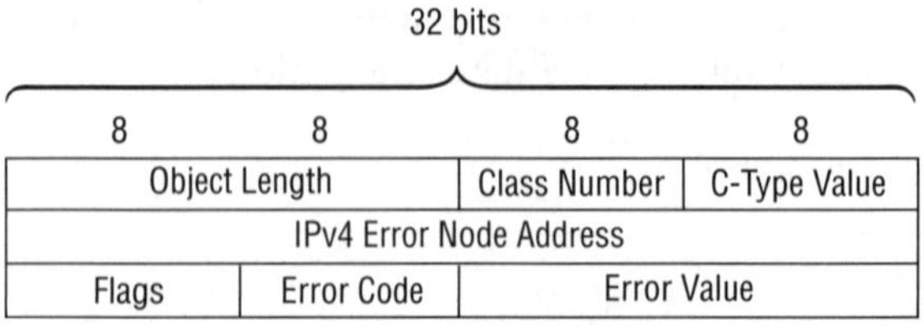

After the ***Sherry-to-Char*** LSP is established in Figure 7.2, the IP interface address of the Chianti router is changed. This causes Sherry (10.222.29.1) to generate a `ResvErr` message containing the IPv4 Error-Spec object. The contents of this message are seen on the Merlot router:

```
Apr 25 10:35:19 RSVP recv ResvErr 10.222.1.1->10.222.1.2 Len=104 so-0/1/0.0
Apr 25 10:35:19   Session7 Len 16 192.168.32.1(port/tunnel ID 44234) Proto 0
Apr 25 10:35:19   Hop      Len 12 10.222.1.1/0x084ec198
Apr 25 10:35:19   Error    Len 12 code 4 value 0 flag 0 by 10.222.29.1
Apr 25 10:35:19   Style    Len  8 FF
Apr 25 10:35:19   Flow     Len 36 rate 100Mbps size 100Mbps peak Infbps m 20 M
1500
Apr 25 10:35:19   Filter7  Len 12 192.168.61.1(port/lsp ID  1)
```

The Style Object

The *Style object* is used in a `Resv` message to determine how reservations are made in the network. By default, the JUNOS software creates a unique reservation for each RSVP session and sender. This means that every new combination of Session and Sender-Template objects requires a new reservation of resources. This reservation style is known as *fixed filter* (FF). A second reservation style called *shared explicit* (SE) allows a single set of reserved resources for a session to be shared among multiple senders. In other words, multiple Sender-Template objects that share a common Session object are allowed to use the same resources. Finally, RSVP devices may use a reservation style known as *wildcard filter* (WF). This allows for a set of resources to be shared among all possible senders. The wildcard filter reservation style is not supported by the JUNOS software.

Figure 7.7 shows the format of the Style object, which includes the following fields:

Object Length (2 octets)   This field displays the total length of the RSVP object. For the Style object, a constant value of 8 is placed in this field.

Class Number (1 octet)   The value that represents the object's class is placed into this field. The Style object falls within the Style class, which uses a value of 8.

C-Type Value (1 octet)   The specific type of object within its overall class is displayed in this field. The Style object uses a value of 1 for its C-Type.

Flags (1 octet)   This field contains bit flags used to relay information to RSVP routers. No flags are currently defined.

Option Vector (3 octets)   This field displays the type of reservation being established by the object. The field is divided into three distinct portions. The first portion of the field uses the 19 most significant bits and is a reserved value with all of the bits set to 0.

The second portion of the field uses the next two most significant bits (3 and 4) to specify whether the reservation is shared. A value of 01 is a distinct reservation and is used by the FF style. A value of 10 represents a shared reservation and is used by the WF and SE styles.

The final 3 bits of the field (0, 1, and 2) determines which senders may use the reservation. A value of 001 is a wildcard notation that allows any possible sender to utilize the resources. This is used by the WF reservation style. A value of 010 denotes an explicit use of resources by only known senders. This explicit notation is used by the FF and SE reservation styles.

The final two portions of the field (5 total bits) are combined to yield the three distinct reservation styles as follows:

- 01010—Fixed filter (FF)
- 10001—Wildcard filter (WF)
- 10010—Shared explicit (SE)

FIGURE 7.7 The Style object

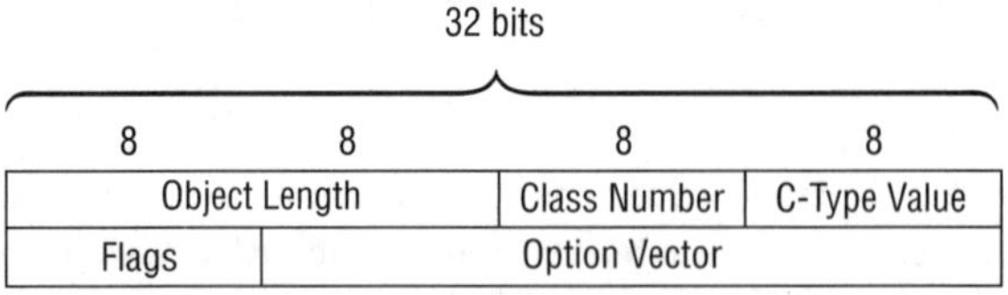

32 bits

8	8	8	8
Object Length		Class Number	C-Type Value
Flags		Option Vector	

Refer back to Figure 7.2 and the LSP established between Sherry and Chardonnay. When the Merlot router transmits a Resv message upstream for that session, it details the specific style for the reservation in the Style object:

```
Apr 24 10:56:24 RSVP send Resv 10.222.1.2->10.222.1.1 Len=128 so-0/1/0.0
Apr 24 10:56:24    Session7 Len 16 192.168.32.1(port/tunnel ID 44214) Proto 0
Apr 24 10:56:24    Hop      Len 12 10.222.1.2/0x084ec198
Apr 24 10:56:24    Time     Len  8 30000 ms
Apr 24 10:56:24    Style    Len  8 FF
Apr 24 10:56:24    Flow     Len 36 rate 0bps size 0bps peak Infbps m 20 M 1500
Apr 24 10:56:24    Filter7  Len 12 192.168.16.1(port/lsp ID  1)
Apr 24 10:56:24    Label    Len  8  100001
Apr 24 10:56:24    RecRoute Len 20  10.222.1.2 10.222.45.2
```

Using the output from the traceoptions file on Merlot, we see that the ***Sherry-to-Char*** LSP is using the default JUNOS software reservation style of fixed filter.

The Integrated Services Flowspec Object

The *Integrated Services Flowspec object* appears in Resv messages and contains information pertaining to the bandwidth request of the LSP, if any. The format and use of the object fields was designed for a controlled load environment where average and peak data rates could be defined. Modern implementations, including the JUNOS software, don't use these fields as they were originally intended. Instead, the bandwidth reservation for the LSP is placed there. Figure 7.8 details the format of the Integrated Services (IntServ) Flowspec object, which includes the following fields:

Object Length (2 octets) This field displays the total length of the RSVP object. For the Intserv Flowspec object, a constant value of 36 is placed in this field.

Class Number (1 octet)   The value that represents the object's class is placed into this field. The Intserv Flowspec object falls within the Flowspec class, which uses a value of 9.

C-Type Value (1 octet)   The specific type of object within its overall class is displayed in this field. The Intserv Flowspec object uses a value of 2 for its C-Type.

Version Number (2 octets)   This 2-octet field uses the first 4 bits to encode the version of the object message format. A constant value of 0 is placed in this portion of the field. The remaining 20 bits of the field are reserved and must be set to a constant value of 0x00000.

Flowspec Length (2 octets)   This field displays the total number of 32-bit words that make up the Service portion of the object. When used in an MPLS environment, this includes all of the remaining fields in the figure. A constant value of 7 is placed in this field.

Service Number (1 octet)   This field displays the type of Integrated Service this Flowspec object supports. A constant value of 5 is placed in this field to represent a controlled load session.

Reserved (1 octet)   This field is not used and is set to a constant value of 0x00.

Data Length (2 octets)   This field displays the total number of 32-bit words that make up the data portion of the object. As with the Flowspec length field, this includes all of the remaining fields in the figure. A constant value of 6 is placed in this field.

Parameter ID (1 octet)   This field displays the ID value associated with the controlled load data. For the IntServ Flowspec object, a value of 127 is placed in this field.

Parameter Flags (1 octet)   This field contains bit flags used to advertise information to other routers concerning the object. No flag values are currently defined, and this field is set to a constant value of 0x00.

Parameter Length (2 octets)   This field displays the total number of 32-bit words that make up the parameter portion of the object. As before, this includes all of the remaining fields in the figure. A constant value of 5 is placed in this field.

Token Bucket Rate (4 octets)   This field displays the bandwidth reservation request for the LSP, if one was configured. A value of 0x00000000 in this field represents a reservation with no bandwidth requirement.

Token Bucket Size (4 octets)   This field also displays the bandwidth reservation request for the LSP. Again, a value of 0x00000000 means that no bandwidth was requested.

Peak Data Rate (4 octets)   This field was originally designed to display the maximum load of data able to be sent through the reservation. This field is not used by the JUNOS software, and a constant value of 0x7f800000 is placed in this field, which represents an infinite peak bandwidth limit.

Minimum Policed Unit (4 octets)   This field displays the smallest packet size supported through the LSP. The router treats all packets smaller than 20 bytes as if they were 20 bytes in length.

Maximum Packet Size (4 octets)   This field displays the largest packet size supported through the LSP. The router treats all packets larger than 1500 bytes as if they were 1500 bytes in length.

FIGURE 7.8 The Integrated Services Flowspec object

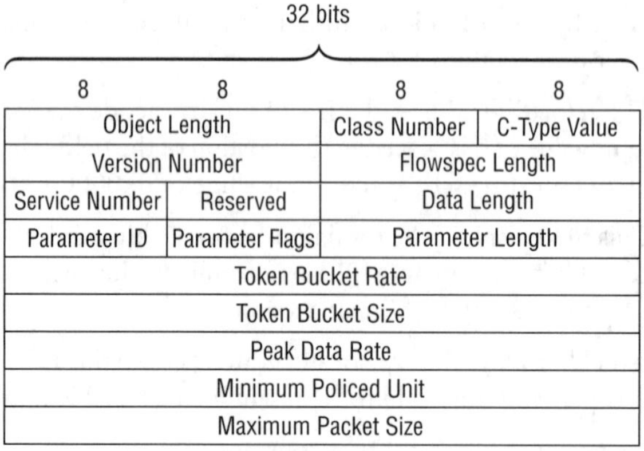

32 bits

8	8	8	8
Object Length		Class Number	C-Type Value
Version Number		Flowspec Length	
Service Number	Reserved	Data Length	
Parameter ID	Parameter Flags	Parameter Length	
Token Bucket Rate			
Token Bucket Size			
Peak Data Rate			
Minimum Policed Unit			
Maximum Packet Size			

Using the **Sherry-to-Char** LSP in Figure 7.2 as a guide, the IntServ Flowspec object is carried in the Resv messages that sets up and maintains the LSP. The Merlot router is sending a Resv message upstream to Chianti, whose contents are visible in a `traceoptions` file:

```
Apr 24 10:56:24 RSVP send Resv 10.222.1.2->10.222.1.1 Len=128 so-0/1/0.0
Apr 24 10:56:24   Session7 Len 16 192.168.32.1(port/tunnel ID 44214) Proto 0
Apr 24 10:56:24   Hop      Len 12 10.222.1.2/0x084ec198
Apr 24 10:56:24   Time     Len  8 30000 ms
Apr 24 10:56:24   Style    Len  8 FF
Apr 24 10:56:24   Flow     Len 36 rate 0bps size 0bps peak Infbps m 20 M 1500
Apr 24 10:56:24   Filter7  Len 12 192.168.16.1(port/lsp ID  1)
Apr 24 10:56:24   Label    Len  8  100001
Apr 24 10:56:24   RecRoute Len 20  10.222.1.2 10.222.45.2
```

Within the object, we see that no bandwidth requests are configured for this LSP. This is evident by the `rate 0bps` and `size 0bps` output on the router. The infinite peak data rate associated with the LSP is represented as `peak Infbps`, while the minimum (m) and maximum (M) packet sizes are also displayed.

The LSP-Tunnel-IPv4 Filter-Spec Object

The *LSP-Tunnel-IPv4 Filter-Spec object* is contained in a Resv message and is used to uniquely identify the sender for the LSP. This information is useful for sharing resources in the network for a single RSVP session with multiple senders. The shared explicit reservation style requires this information in the Resv State Block to adequately allocate the network resources. Figure 7.9 shows the format of the Filter-Spec object, which includes the following fields:

Object Length (2 octets)   This field displays the total length of the RSVP object. For the LSP-Tunnel-IPv4 Filter-Spec object, a constant value of 12 is placed in this field.

Class Number (1 octet)   The value that represents the object's class is placed into this field. The Filter-Spec object falls within the Filter-Spec class, which uses a value of 10.

FIGURE 7.9   The LSP-Tunnel-IPv4 Filter-Spec object

32 bits

8	8	8	8
· Object Length		Class Number	C-Type Value
IPv4 Tunnel Sender Address			
Reserved		LSP ID	

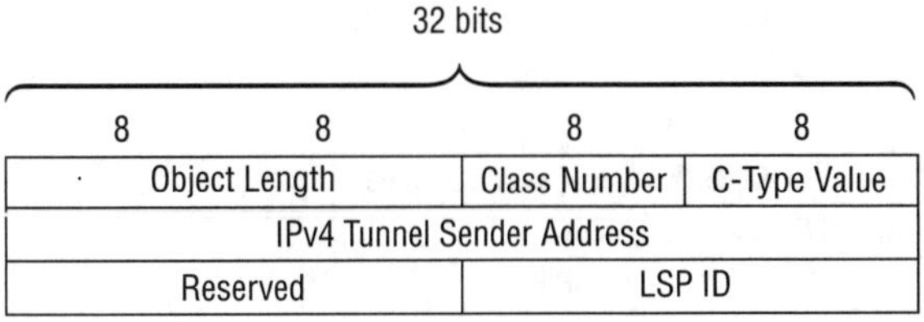

C-Type Value (1 octet)   The specific type of object within its overall class is displayed in this field. The LSP-Tunnel-IPv4 Filter-Spec object uses a value of 7 for its C-Type.

IPv4 Tunnel Sender Address (4 octets)   This field displays the IPv4 address of the LSP ingress router.

Reserved (2 octets)   This field is not used and must be set to a constant value of 0x0000.

LSP ID (2 octets)   This field contains a unique value generated by the ingress router of the LSP. This helps to distinguish the particular sender and its resources from other paths originating at the same ingress router for the same RSVP session.

We can see the Filter-Spec object in a Resv message received by the Merlot router in Figure 7.2:

```
Apr 24 10:56:24 RSVP recv Resv 10.222.45.2->10.222.45.1 Len=120 so-0/1/2.0
Apr 24 10:56:24   Session7 Len 16 192.168.32.1(port/tunnel ID 44214) Proto 0
Apr 24 10:56:24   Hop      Len 12 10.222.45.2/0x08550264
Apr 24 10:56:24   Time     Len  8 30000 ms
Apr 24 10:56:24   Style    Len  8 FF
Apr 24 10:56:24   Flow     Len 36 rate 0bps size 0bps peak Infbps m 20 M 1500
Apr 24 10:56:24   Filter7  Len 12 192.168.16.1(port/lsp ID  1)
Apr 24 10:56:24   Label    Len  8 3
Apr 24 10:56:24   RecRoute Len 12  10.222.45.2
```

The C-Type value of 7 and the Filter-Spec class of the object appear in the output as Filter7. Within the object itself, we see the ingress router address of 192.168.16.1 displayed along with the LSP ID value of 1.

The LSP-Tunnel-IPv4 Sender Template Object

The *LSP-Tunnel-IPv4 Sender Template object* is contained in a Path message and is used to uniquely identify the sender for the LSP. This information contained in this object is identical to that found in the LSP-Tunnel-IPv4 Filter-Spec object. As such, it is useful for differentiating among sending sources, or LSP IDs, within a single RSVP session. This information is stored in the Path State Block for each router along the path of the LSP. Figure 7.10 displays the format of the Sender Template object, which includes these fields:

Object Length (2 octets)   This field displays the total length of the RSVP object. For the LSP-Tunnel-IPv4 Sender Template object, a constant value of 12 is placed in this field.

FIGURE 7.10   The LSP-Tunnel-IPv4 Sender Template object

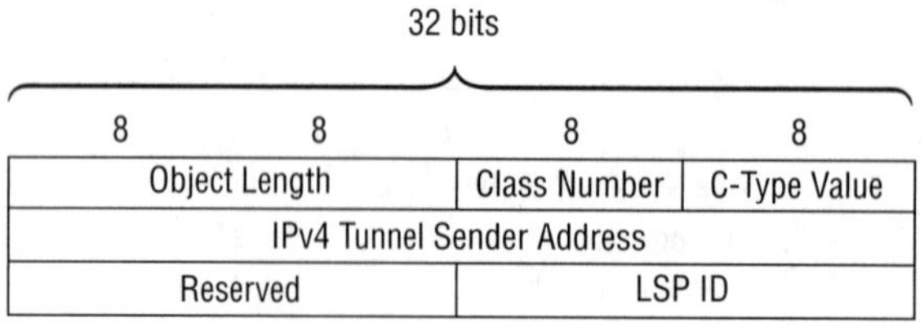

Class Number (1 octet)   The value that represents the object's class is placed into this field. The Sender Template object falls within the Sender Template class, which uses a value of 11.

C-Type Value (1 octet)   The specific type of object within its overall class is displayed in this field. The LSP-Tunnel-IPv4 Sender Template object uses a value of 7 for its C-Type.

IPv4 Tunnel Sender Address (4 octets)   This field displays the IPv4 address of the LSP ingress router.

Reserved (2 octets)   This field is not used and must be set to a constant value of 0x0000.

LSP ID (2 octets)   This field contains a unique value generated by the ingress router of the LSP. This helps to distinguish the particular sender and its resources from other paths originating at the same ingress router for the same RSVP session.

Using Figure 7.2 as a guide, we can view a `Path` message arriving on the Merlot router for the ***Sherry-to-Char*** LSP:

```
Apr 24 10:56:24 RSVP recv Path 192.168.16.1->192.168.32.1 Len=228 so-0/1/0.0
Apr 24 10:56:24    Session7 Len 16 192.168.32.1(port/tunnel ID 44214) Proto 0
Apr 24 10:56:24    Hop      Len 12 10.222.1.1/0x084ec198
Apr 24 10:56:24    Time     Len  8 30000 ms
Apr 24 10:56:24    SessionAttribute Len 28 Prio (7,0) flag 0x0 "Sherry-to-Char"
Apr 24 10:56:24    Sender7  Len 12 192.168.16.1(port/lsp ID  1)
Apr 24 10:56:24    Tspec    Len 36 rate 0bps size 0bps peak Infbps m 20 M 1500
Apr 24 10:56:24    ADspec   Len 48
Apr 24 10:56:24    SrcRoute Len 20  10.222.1.2 S 10.222.45.2 S
Apr 24 10:56:24    LabelRequest Len  8 EtherType 0x800
Apr 24 10:56:24    Properties Len 12 Primary path
Apr 24 10:56:24    RecRoute Len 20  10.222.1.1 10.222.29.1
```

The C-Type value of 7 and the Sender Template class of the object appear in the output as `Sender7`. Within the object itself, we see the ingress router address of 192.168.16.1 displayed along with the LSP ID value of 1.

The Integrated Services Sender-Tspec Object

The *Integrated Services Sender-Tspec object* appears in `Path` messages and contains information pertaining to the bandwidth request of the LSP, if any. Like the IntServ Flowspec object, the format and use of the object fields was designed for a controlled load environment where average and peak data rates could be defined. Modern implementations, including the JUNOS software, place the bandwidth reservation for the LSP in these fields. Figure 7.11 details the format of the Integrated Services (IntServ) Sender-Tspec object, which includes the following:

Object Length (2 octets)   This field displays the total length of the RSVP object. For the Intserv Sender-Tspec object, a constant value of 36 is placed in this field.

Class Number (1 octet)   The value that represents the object's class is placed into this field. The Intserv Sender-Tspec object falls within the Sendter-Tspec class, which uses a value of 12.

C-Type Value (1 octet)   The specific type of object within its overall class is displayed in this field. The Intserv Sender-Tspec object uses a value of 2 for its C-Type.

Version Number (2 octets)   This 2-octet field uses the first 4 bits to encode the version of the object message format. A constant value of 0 is placed in this portion of the field. The remaining 20 bits of the field are reserved and must be set to a constant value of 0x00000.

Tspec Length (2 octets)   This field displays the total number of 32-bit words that make up the Service portion of the object. When used in an MPLS environment, this includes all of the remaining fields in the figure. A constant value of 7 is placed in this field.

Service Number (1 octet)   This field displays the type of Integrated Service this Sender-Tspec Object supports. A constant value of 1 is placed in this field to represent a default controlled load session.

Reserved (1 octet)   This field is not used and is set to a constant value of 0x00.

Data Length (2 octets)   This field displays the total number of 32-bit words that make up the data portion of the object. As with the Tspec Length field, this includes all of the remaining fields in the figure. A constant value of 6 is placed in this field.

Parameter ID (1 octet)   This field displays the ID value associated with the controlled load data. For the IntServ Sender-Tspec object, a value of 127 is placed in this field.

Parameter Flags (1 octet)   This field contains bit flags used to advertise information to other routers concerning the object. No flag values are currently defined, and this field is set to a constant value of 0x00.

Parameter Length (2 octets)   This field displays the total number of 32-bit words that make up the parameter portion of the object. As before, this includes all of the remaining fields in the figure. A constant value of 5 is placed in this field.

Token Bucket Rate (4 octets)   This field displays the bandwidth reservation request for the LSP, if one was configured. A value of 0x00000000 in this field represents a reservation with no bandwidth requirement.

Token Bucket Size (4 octets)   This field also displays the bandwidth reservation request for the LSP. Again, a value of 0x00000000 means that no bandwidth was requested.

Peak Data Rate (4 octets)   This field was originally designed to display the maximum load of data able to be sent through the reservation. This field is not used by the JUNOS software, and a constant value of 0x7f800000 is placed in this field, which represents an infinite peak bandwidth limit.

FIGURE 7.11   The Integrated Services Sender-Tspec object

32 bits

8	8	8	8
Object Length		Class Number	C-Type Value
Version Number		Tspec Length	
Service Number	Reserved	Data Length	
Parameter ID	Parameter Flags	Parameter Length	
Token Bucket Rate			
Token Bucket Size			
Peak Data Rate			
Minimum Policed Unit			
Maximum Packet Size			

Minimum Policed Unit (4 octets)   This field displays the smallest packet size supported through the LSP. The router treats all packets smaller than 20 bytes as if they were 20 bytes in length.

Maximum Packet Size (4 octets)   This field displays the largest packet size supported through the LSP. The router treats all packets larger than 1500 bytes as if they were 1500 bytes in length.

Path messages for the ***Sherry-to-Char*** LSP in Figure 7.2 are received by the Merlot router. We can view the contents of these messages in the output of a `traceoptions` file:

```
Apr 24 10:56:24 RSVP recv Path 192.168.16.1->192.168.32.1 Len=228 so-0/1/0.0
Apr 24 10:56:24    Session7 Len 16 192.168.32.1(port/tunnel ID 44214) Proto 0
Apr 24 10:56:24    Hop      Len 12 10.222.1.1/0x084ec198
Apr 24 10:56:24    Time     Len  8 30000 ms
Apr 24 10:56:24    SessionAttribute Len 28 Prio (7,0) flag 0x0 "Sherry-to-Char"
Apr 24 10:56:24    Sender7  Len 12 192.168.16.1(port/lsp ID  1)
Apr 24 10:56:24    Tspec    Len 36 rate 0bps size 0bps peak Infbps m 20 M 1500
Apr 24 10:56:24    ADspec   Len 48
Apr 24 10:56:24    SrcRoute Len 20  10.222.1.2 S 10.222.45.2 S
Apr 24 10:56:24    LabelRequest Len  8 EtherType 0x800
Apr 24 10:56:24    Properties Len 12 Primary path
Apr 24 10:56:24    RecRoute Len 20  10.222.1.1 10.222.29.1
```

Within the object, we see that no bandwidth requests are configured for this LSP. This is evident by the `rate 0bps` and `size 0bps` output on the router. The infinite peak data rate associated with the LSP is represented as `peak Infbps`, while the minimum (`m`) and maximum (`M`) packet sizes are also displayed.

The Label Object

The *Label object* is contained in `Resv` messages and advertises an MPLS label value upstream to the neighboring router. The label is used by that upstream router to forward packets within the LSP to the advertising router. The allocation of a label value for inclusion in this object must be prompted by a request for label in the `Path` message for this LSP. Figure 7.12 displays for fields for the Label object:

Object Length (2 octets)   This field displays the total length of the RSVP object. For the Label object, a constant value of 8 is placed in this field.

Class Number (1 octet)   The value that represents the object's class is placed into this field. The Label object falls within the Label class, which uses a value of 16.

C-Type Value (1 octet)   The specific type of object within its overall class is displayed in this field. The Label object uses a value of 1 for its C-Type.

Label Value (4 octets)   This field contains the label value advertised by the downstream router. The value is right-justified within the 32-bit field and occupies bits 0 through 19.

FIGURE 7.12   The Label object

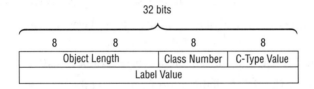

We can see the Label object in a `Resv` message received by the Merlot router in Figure 7.2:

```
Apr 24 10:56:24 RSVP recv Resv 10.222.45.2->10.222.45.1 Len=120 so-0/1/2.0
Apr 24 10:56:24   Session7 Len 16 192.168.32.1(port/tunnel ID 44214) Proto 0
Apr 24 10:56:24   Hop      Len 12 10.222.45.2/0x08550264
Apr 24 10:56:24   Time     Len  8 30000 ms
Apr 24 10:56:24   Style    Len  8 FF
Apr 24 10:56:24   Flow     Len 36 rate 0bps size 0bps peak Infbps m 20 M 1500
Apr 24 10:56:24   Filter7  Len 12 192.168.16.1(port/lsp ID  1)
Apr 24 10:56:24   Label    Len  8 3
Apr 24 10:56:24   RecRoute Len 12  10.222.45.2
```

The egress router of Chardonnay (10.222.45.2) advertises a label value of 3 to Merlot, which requests that PHP be performed for this LSP. Merlot stores this information in its RSVP soft state, allocates its own label value, and advertises a new `Resv` message upstream to Chianti:

```
Apr 24 10:56:24 RSVP send Resv 10.222.1.2->10.222.1.1 Len=128 so-0/1/0.0
Apr 24 10:56:24   Session7 Len 16 192.168.32.1(port/tunnel ID 44214) Proto 0
Apr 24 10:56:24   Hop      Len 12 10.222.1.2/0x084ec198
Apr 24 10:56:24   Time     Len  8 30000 ms
```

```
Apr 24 10:56:24   Style    Len  8 FF
Apr 24 10:56:24   Flow     Len 36 rate 0bps size 0bps peak Infbps m 20 M 1500
Apr 24 10:56:24   Filter7  Len 12 192.168.16.1(port/lsp ID  1)
Apr 24 10:56:24   Label    Len  8  100001
Apr 24 10:56:24   RecRoute Len 20  10.222.1.2 10.222.45.2
```

The Label Request Object

The *Label Request object* is contained in `Path` messages and prompts the advertisement of label values upstream in `Resv` messages. You can use three different forms of Label Request objects in an MPLS network. The first request type doesn't specify a specific range of labels, which allows the downstream routers to allocate any possible value. This request type is the only form used by the JUNOS software. The other two label request types allow for an allocation from either an ATM or Frame Relay label range. Figure 7.13 shows the format of the Label Request object, which includes the following fields:

Object Length (2 octets) This field displays the total length of the RSVP object. For the Label Request object, a constant value of 8 is placed in this field.

Class Number (1 octet) The value that represents the object's class is placed into this field. The Label Request object falls within the Label Request class, which uses a value of 19.

C-Type Value (1 octet) The specific type of object within its overall class is displayed in this field. The Label Request object uses a value of 1 for its C-Type.

Reserved (2 octets) This field is not used and is set to a constant value of 0x0000.

Layer 3 Protocol ID (2 octets) This field contains information about the Layer 3 protocol carried in the LSP. The standard EtherType value of 0x0800 is used in this field to represent IPv4.

FIGURE 7.13   The Label Request object

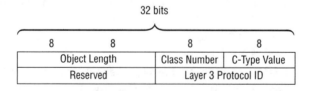

Referring back to the LSP created in Figure 7.2, we can view the Label Request object in the Path message received by Merlot:

```
Apr 24 10:56:24 RSVP recv Path 192.168.16.1->192.168.32.1 Len=228 so-0/1/0.0
Apr 24 10:56:24   Session7 Len 16 192.168.32.1(port/tunnel ID 44214) Proto 0
Apr 24 10:56:24   Hop      Len 12 10.222.1.1/0x084ec198
Apr 24 10:56:24   Time     Len  8 30000 ms
Apr 24 10:56:24   SessionAttribute Len 28 Prio (7,0) flag 0x0 "Sherry-to-Char"
Apr 24 10:56:24   Sender7  Len 12 192.168.16.1(port/lsp ID  1)
Apr 24 10:56:24   Tspec    Len 36 rate 0bps size 0bps peak Infbps m 20 M 1500
Apr 24 10:56:24   ADspec   Len 48
```

```
Apr 24 10:56:24   SrcRoute Len 20  10.222.1.2 S 10.222.45.2 S
Apr 24 10:56:24   LabelRequest Len  8 EtherType 0x800
Apr 24 10:56:24   Properties Len 12 Primary path
Apr 24 10:56:24   RecRoute Len 20  10.222.1.1 10.222.29.1
```

The upstream router of Chianti (10.222.1.1) has requested that a label be allocated for the **Sherry-to-Char** LSP being established by this message. The `EtherType 0x800` notation informs the Merlot router that IPv4 data traffic will be using this LSP once it is operational.

The Explicit Route Object

The *Explicit Route object* (ERO) is contained in `Path` messages and allows the ingress router to specify the path of the LSP through the network by containing a list of nodes, defined as a sub-object, through which the RSVP messages must pass. These nodes are in the form of an IPv4 prefix, an IPv6 prefix, or an Autonomous System number, with the JUNOS software supporting just IPv4 prefixes. When the `Path` message is received by a router, the ERO is examined to first determine if the first node is strictly or loosely defined. The local router then determines whether the first node address in the ERO equals the local router's address. At this point, one of two possible scenarios exists. If the first node in the ERO is loosely defined and the local address is not equal to the address listed in the ERO, the local router processes the `Path` message and forwards it to the address listed in the ERO.

The second scenario occurs when the first ERO address is strictly defined, in which case the local address must match the ERO address in order for the local router to process the `Path` message. If the address values do not match, the local router does not process the message and instead generates a `PathErr` message and forwards the error message back to the ingress router. Assuming that the strict hop is correctly defined, the local router creates its local Path State Block and prepares to forward the message further downstream. Before doing so, however, the first address in the ERO is removed to allow the next downstream router to perform the same sanity checks we've discussed here.

Figure 7.14 displays the fields of the Explicit Route object when it contains IPv4 prefixes. The various fields are as follows:

Object Length (2 octets)   This field displays the total length of the RSVP object.

Class Number (1 octet)   The value that represents the object's class is placed into this field. The Explicit Route Object falls within the Explicit Route class, which uses a value of 20.

C-Type Value (1 octet)   The specific type of object within its overall class is displayed in this field. The Explicit Route object uses a value of 1 for its C-Type.

L bit and Type (1 octet)   The most significant bit in this 1-octet field is called the L bit and is used to denote if the included address is loosely or strictly defined. When the bit is set to a value of 1, the address is a loose node. Strict node addresses are defined by a value of 0 for this bit.

The remaining 7 bits in the field encode the type of address contained in the subobject. For an IPv4 address, a constant value of 0x01 is used in this field.

Length (1 octet)   This field displays the length of the subobject, including the type and length fields. For an IPv4 address, a constant value of 0x08 is used in this field.

IPv4 Address (4 octets) This field contains the IPv4 address listed as a node along the path.

Prefix Length (1 octet) This field displays the prefix length of the preceding IPv4 address. For a host address, the default configuration, a constant value of 32 is placed in this field.

Reserved (1 octet) This field is not used and is set to a constant value of 0x00.

FIGURE 7.14 The Explicit Route object

32 bits

8	8	8	8
Object Length		Class Number	C-Type Value
L Bit and Type	Length	IPv4 Address	
IPv4 Address (continued)		Prefix Length	Reserved

The Sherry router in Figure 7.2 generates a `Path` message for the ***Sherry-to-Char*** LSP, which contains the strict-hop address in the ERO. We can view this information in the output of a `traceoptions` file on Sherry:

```
May 12 12:09:17 RSVP send Path 192.168.16.1->192.168.32.1 Len=224 ge-0/2/0.0
May 12 12:09:17    Session7 Len 16 192.168.32.1(port/tunnel ID 24025) Proto 0
May 12 12:09:17    Hop      Len 12 10.222.29.1/0x08528264
May 12 12:09:17    Time     Len  8 30000 ms
May 12 12:09:17    SessionAttribute Len 24 Prio (7,0) flag 0x0 "Sherry-to-Char"
May 12 12:09:17    Sender7  Len 12 192.168.16.1(port/lsp ID  1)
May 12 12:09:17    Tspec    Len 36 rate 0bps size 0bps peak Infbps m 20 M 1500
May 12 12:09:17    ADspec   Len 48
May 12 12:09:17    SrcRoute Len 28  10.222.29.2 S 10.222.1.2 S 10.222.45.2 S
May 12 12:09:17    LabelRequest Len  8 EtherType 0x800
May 12 12:09:17    Properties Len 12 Primary path
May 12 12:09:17    RecRoute Len 12  10.222.29.1
```

The `SrcRoute` output contains the ERO information within the `Path` message. Each of the three downstream routers is specified as a strict-hop node along the path. The LSP should first traverse the router whose address is 10.222.29.2 (Chianti); it will then be sent to 10.222.1.2 (Merlot) before reaching the final address of 10.222.45.2 (Chardonnay). Because the final address in the ERO equals the address of the egress router, 192.168.36.1, Chardonnay stops processing the `Path` message and generates a corresponding `Resv` message for transmission upstream.

The Record Route Object

The *Record Route object* (RRO) may be contained in either a `Path` or a `Resv` message. The RRO contains subobjects that describe the nodes through which the message has passed. These node addresses are in the form of an IPv4 prefix or an IPv6 prefix. In addition, a label value for the RSVP session may be recorded in a subobject within the RRO. Currently, the JUNOS software supports only an IPv4 prefix address in the Record Route object.

The object is useful for troubleshooting the operation of an LSP, but it mainly allows routers in the network to detect loops during the setup of an LSP. When an RSVP router receives a message that contains a Record Route object, the contents of that object are examined. If the local router finds one of its local addresses in the object fields, a loop has formed and the message is not processed any further. In addition, the local router generates an error message (either a PathErr or a ResvErr) and sends it to the router from which it received the original message. The fields used for IPv4 addresses in the Record Route object are displayed in Figure 7.15 and include the following:

Object Length (2 octets)   This field displays the total length of the RSVP object.

Class Number (1 octet)   The value that represents the object's class is placed into this field. The Record Route object falls within the Record Route class, which uses a value of 21.

C-Type Value (1 octet)   The specific type of object within its overall class is displayed in this field. The Record Route object uses a value of 1 for its C-Type.

Type (1 octet)   This field encodes the type of address contained in the sub-object. For an IPv4 address, a constant value of 0x01 is used in this field.

Length (1 octet)   This field displays the length of the subobject, including the type and length fields. For an IPv4 address, a constant value of 0x08 is used in this field.

IPv4 Address (4 octets)   This field contains a 32-bit host address that represents the router processing the RSVP message. While any valid network-accessible address is allowed here, the JUNOS software places the address of the router's outgoing interface in this field.

Prefix Length (1 octet)   This field displays the prefix length of the preceding IPv4 address. A constant value of 32 is placed in this field.

Flags (1 octet)   This field contains flags that alert other routers in the network about the capabilities or conditions of the local node. Currently, four flag values are defined:

Bit 0   This flag bit, 0x01, is set to indicate that the next downstream link from the router is protected by a local repair mechanism, such as fast reroute link protection. The flag is set only when the Session Attribute object requests that link protection be enabled for the LSP.

Bit 1   This flag bit, 0x02, is set to indicate that the local router is actively using a repair mechanism to maintain the LSP due to some outage condition.

Bit 2   This flag bit, 0x04, is set to indicate that the local router has a backup path enabled that provides the same bandwidth reservation guarantees as established for an LSP protected through a local protection scheme.

Bit 3   This flag bit, 0x08, is set to indicate that the next downstream node as well as the downstream link is protected by a local repair mechanism, such as fast reroute node protection. This flag is set only when the next downstream node is protected against failure and the Session Attribute object requests that node protection be enabled for the LSP.

FIGURE 7.15 The Record Route object

32 bits

8	8	8	8
Object Length		Class Number	C-Type Value
Type	Length	IPv4 Address	
IPv4 Address (continued)		Prefix Length	Flags

The Merlot router is receiving both `Path` and `Resv` messages for the **Sherry-to-Char** LSP in Figure 7.2. A Record Route object is present in both types of messages:

```
May 12 14:04:12 RSVP recv Path 192.168.16.1->192.168.32.1 Len=224 so-0/1/0.0
May 12 14:04:12    Session7 Len 16 192.168.32.1(port/tunnel ID 24025) Proto 0
May 12 14:04:12    Hop      Len 12 10.222.1.1/0x085280cc
May 12 14:04:12    Time     Len  8 30000 ms
May 12 14:04:12    SessionAttribute Len 24 Prio (7,0) flag 0x0 "Sherry-to-Char"
May 12 14:04:12    Sender7  Len 12 192.168.16.1(port/lsp ID  1)
May 12 14:04:12    Tspec    Len 36 rate 0bps size 0bps peak Infbps m 20 M 1500
May 12 14:04:12    ADspec   Len 48
May 12 14:04:12    SrcRoute Len 20  10.222.1.2 S 10.222.45.2 S
May 12 14:04:12    LabelRequest Len  8 EtherType 0x800
May 12 14:04:12    Properties Len 12 Primary path
May 12 14:04:12    RecRoute Len 20  10.222.1.1 10.222.29.1

May 12 14:04:12 RSVP recv Resv 10.222.45.2->10.222.45.1 Len=120 so-0/1/2.0
May 12 14:04:12    Session7 Len 16 192.168.32.1(port/tunnel ID 24025) Proto 0
May 12 14:04:12    Hop      Len 12 10.222.45.2/0x08572264
May 12 14:04:12    Time     Len  8 30000 ms
May 12 14:04:12    Style    Len  8 FF
May 12 14:04:12    Flow     Len 36 rate 0bps size 0bps peak Infbps m 20 M 1500
May 12 14:04:12    Filter7  Len 12 192.168.16.1(port/lsp ID  1)
May 12 14:04:12    Label    Len  8 3
May 12 14:04:12    RecRoute Len 12  10.222.45.2
```

Within each message type, the `RecRoute` output contains the information encoded within the RRO. When we examine the `Path` message, which is first in the output, we find that the 10.222.29.1 router (Sherry) processed the message first followed by the 10.222.1.1 router (Chianti). Because none of Merlot's local interfaces appear in the RRO, the `Path` message is processed locally and Merlot adds its own downstream interface address (10.22.45.1) to the RRO before sending the message to Chardonnay.

When Merlot receives a `Resv` message for the LSP from Chardonnay, the RRO contains just the address of the egress router, 10.222.45.2. As with the `Path` message, Merlot examines the object in the `Resv` message to ensure that one of its local addresses doesn't appear. After performing this check, Merlot processes the message and sends a corresponding `Resv` message upstream to Chianti after adding its outgoing interface address of 10.222.1.2 to the object.

The Detour Object

The *Detour object* is contained in a `Path` message, which establishes a fast reroute detour in the network. This `Path` message inherits the Session, Sender-Template, and Session Attribute objects from the established LSP. This allows the detour path to be associated with the main RSVP session on all possible routers. The Detour object itself lists the originating node of the `Path` message, the point of local repair, and the address of the downstream node being protected against failures. These ID values may be repeated in a single Detour object when an RSVP router merges multiple detour paths as they head toward the egress router.

 We discuss the functionality of an LSP supporting fast reroute in greater detail in Chapter 8, "Advanced MPLS."

Figure 7.16 displays the fields of the Detour object, which include the following:

Object Length (2 octets)   This field displays the total length of the RSVP object.

Class Number (1 octet)   The value that represents the object's class is placed into this field. The Detour object falls within the Detour class, which uses a value of 63.

C-Type Value (1 octet)   The specific type of object within its overall class is displayed in this field. The Detour object uses a value of 7 for its C-Type.

Local Repair Node ID (4 octets)   This field encodes the address of the router creating the detour path through the network. While any possible address on the local router may be used, the JUNOS software places the address of the outgoing interface in this field.

Avoid Node ID (4 octets)   This field encodes the router ID of the downstream node that is being protected against failures.

FIGURE 7.16   The Detour object

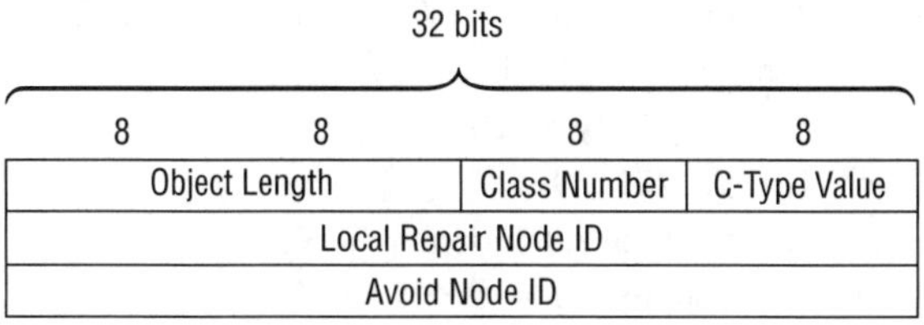

32 bits

8	8	8	8
Object Length		Class Number	C-Type Value
Local Repair Node ID			
Avoid Node ID			

FIGURE 7.17 Fast reroute LSP establishment

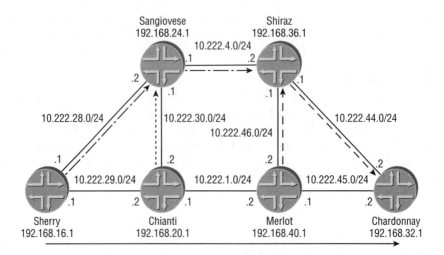

Figure 7.17 shows the ***Sherry-to-Char*** LSP now configured to support fast reroute. Once the LSP becomes established through the Chianti, Merlot, and Chardonnay routers, the ingress router and all transit routers create detour paths through the network to protect against link and node failures. Sherry, the ingress router, creates a detour through the Sangiovese and Shiraz routers before reaching the egress router of Chardonnay. In the output of a `traceoptions` file on Sherry, we first see the `Path` message establishing the LSP followed by the generation of a second `Path` message establishing the detour path:

```
May 12 17:41:01 RSVP send Path 192.168.16.1->192.168.32.1 Len=244 ge-0/2/0.0
May 12 17:41:01    Session7 Len 16 192.168.32.1(port/tunnel ID 24027) Proto 0
May 12 17:41:01    Hop     Len 12 10.222.29.1/0x08528264
May 12 17:41:01    Time    Len  8 30000 ms
May 12 17:41:01    SessionAttribute Len 24 Prio (7,0) flag 0x0 "Sherry-to-Char"
May 12 17:41:01    Sender7  Len 12 192.168.16.1(port/lsp ID  1)
May 12 17:41:01    Tspec   Len 36 rate 0bps size 0bps peak Infbps m 20 M 1500
May 12 17:41:01    ADspec   Len 48
May 12 17:41:01    SrcRoute Len 28  10.222.29.2 S 10.222.1.2 S 10.222.45.2 S
May 12 17:41:01    LabelRequest Len  8 EtherType 0x800
May 12 17:41:01    Properties Len 12 Primary path
May 12 17:41:01    RecRoute Len 12  10.222.29.1
May 12 17:41:01    FastReroute Len 20 Prio(7,0) Hop 6 BW 0bps
May 12 17:41:01       Include 0x00000000 Exclude 0x00000000

May 12 17:41:04 RSVP send Path 192.168.16.1->192.168.32.1 Len=236 at-0/1/0.0
May 12 17:41:04    Session7 Len 16 192.168.32.1(port/tunnel ID 24027) Proto 0
```

```
May 12 17:41:04    Hop      Len 12 10.222.28.1/0x085280cc
May 12 17:41:04    Time     Len  8 30000 ms
May 12 17:41:04    SessionAttribute Len 24 Prio (7,0) flag 0x0 "Sherry-to-Char"
May 12 17:41:04    Sender7  Len 12 192.168.16.1(port/lsp ID  1)
May 12 17:41:04    Tspec    Len 36 rate 0bps size 0bps peak Infbps m 20 M 1500
May 12 17:41:04    ADspec   Len 48
May 12 17:41:04    SrcRoute Len 28  10.222.28.2 S 10.222.4.2 S 10.222.44.2 S
May 12 17:41:04    LabelRequest Len  8 EtherType 0x800
May 12 17:41:04    Properties Len 12 Primary path
May 12 17:41:04    RecRoute Len 12  10.222.28.1
May 12 17:41:04    Detour   Len 12  Branch from 10.222.28.1 to avoid 192.168.20.1
```

Within the detour Path message type, we see the same information in the Session7,
SessionAttribute, and Sender7 objects. The configured ERO (SrcRoute) details the
path through the network for the detour, whereas the Detour object itself lists the outgoing
interface on the Sherry router (10.222.28.1) and the protected downstream node of Chianti
(192.168.20.1).

Chianti, the first transit router, also creates a detour path to the egress router to protect the
LSP against failures associated with the Merlot router. This detour also uses Sangiovese, Shiraz,
and Chardonnay as its network path. When the Sangiovese router receives the detour Path messages from both Sherry and Chianti, it finds that they belong to the same RSVP session. This
allows Sangiovese to merge the detour paths together and send a single Path message downstream to Shiraz. During this merge process, the Detour object lists both Sherry (10.222.28.1)
and Chianti (10.222.30.2) as local repair nodes. The output of a traceoptions file on Sangiovese shows the receipt of these two Path messages and the generation of the merged Path message sent downstream:

```
May 12 17:43:55 RSVP recv Path 192.168.16.1->192.168.32.1 Len=236 at-0/1/0.0
May 12 17:43:55    Session7 Len 16 192.168.32.1(port/tunnel ID 24027) Proto 0
May 12 17:43:55    Hop      Len 12 10.222.28.1/0x085280cc
May 12 17:43:55    Time     Len  8 30000 ms
May 12 17:43:55    SessionAttribute Len 24 Prio (7,0) flag 0x0 "Sherry-to-Char"
May 12 17:43:55    Sender7  Len 12 192.168.16.1(port/lsp ID  1)
May 12 17:43:55    Tspec    Len 36 rate 0bps size 0bps peak Infbps m 20 M 1500
May 12 17:43:55    ADspec   Len 48
May 12 17:43:55    SrcRoute Len 28  10.222.28.2 S 10.222.4.2 S 10.222.44.2 S
May 12 17:43:55    LabelRequest Len  8 EtherType 0x800
May 12 17:43:55    Properties Len 12 Primary path
May 12 17:43:55    RecRoute Len 12  10.222.28.1
May 12 17:43:55    Detour   Len 12  Branch from 10.222.28.1 to avoid 192.168.20.1

May 12 17:43:55 RSVP recv Path 192.168.16.1->192.168.32.1 Len=244 so-0/2/0.0
May 12 17:43:55    Session7 Len 16 192.168.32.1(port/tunnel ID 24027) Proto 0
May 12 17:43:55    Hop      Len 12 10.222.30.2/0x08528330
```

```
May 12 17:43:55    Time      Len  8 30000 ms
May 12 17:43:55    SessionAttribute Len 24 Prio (7,0) flag 0x0 "Sherry-to-Char"
May 12 17:43:55    Sender7  Len 12 192.168.16.1(port/lsp ID  1)
May 12 17:43:55    Tspec     Len 36 rate 0bps size 0bps peak Infbps m 20 M 1500
May 12 17:43:55    ADspec    Len 48
May 12 17:43:55    SrcRoute Len 28  10.222.30.1 S 10.222.4.2 S 10.222.44.2 S
May 12 17:43:55    LabelRequest Len  8 EtherType 0x800
May 12 17:43:55    Properties Len 12 Primary path
May 12 17:43:55    RecRoute Len 20  10.222.30.2 10.222.29.1
May 12 17:43:55    Detour   Len 12  Branch from 10.222.30.2 to avoid 192.168.40.1


May 12 17:43:55 RSVP send Path 192.168.16.1->192.168.32.1 Len=244 fe-0/0/2.0
May 12 17:43:55    Session7 Len 16 192.168.32.1(port/tunnel ID 24027) Proto 0
May 12 17:43:55    Hop       Len 12 10.222.4.1/0x085650cc
May 12 17:43:55    Time      Len  8 30000 ms
May 12 17:43:55    SessionAttribute Len 24 Prio (7,0) flag 0x0 "Sherry-to-Char"
May 12 17:43:55    Sender7  Len 12 192.168.16.1(port/lsp ID  1)
May 12 17:43:55    Tspec     Len 36 rate 0bps size 0bps peak Infbps m 20 M 1500
May 12 17:43:55    ADspec    Len 48
May 12 17:43:55    SrcRoute Len 20  10.222.4.2 S 10.222.44.2 S
May 12 17:43:55    LabelRequest Len  8 EtherType 0x800
May 12 17:43:55    Properties Len 12 Primary path
May 12 17:43:55    RecRoute Len 20  10.222.4.1 10.222.28.1
May 12 17:43:55    Detour   Len 20  Branch from 10.222.28.1 to avoid 192.168.20.1
May 12 17:43:55        Branch from 10.222.30.2 to avoid 192.168.40.1
```

Finally, the Shiraz router also performs a merge of detour paths in our sample network. The first detour arrives from the Sangiovese router, and the second arrives from Merlot. We see the merged Detour object in the Path message sent by Shiraz to Chardonnay:

```
May 12 17:41:01 RSVP send Path 192.168.16.1->192.168.32.1 Len=260 so-0/1/0.0
May 12 17:41:01    Session7 Len 16 192.168.32.1(port/tunnel ID 24027) Proto 0
May 12 17:41:01    Hop       Len 12 10.222.44.1/0x085a7198
May 12 17:41:01    Time      Len  8 30000 ms
May 12 17:41:01    SessionAttribute Len 24 Prio (7,0) flag 0x0 "Sherry-to-Char"
May 12 17:41:01    Sender7  Len 12 192.168.16.1(port/lsp ID  1)
May 12 17:41:01    Tspec     Len 36 rate 0bps size 0bps peak Infbps m 20 M 1500
May 12 17:41:01    ADspec    Len 48
May 12 17:41:01    SrcRoute Len 12  10.222.44.2 S
May 12 17:41:01    LabelRequest Len  8 EtherType 0x800
May 12 17:41:01    Properties Len 12 Primary path
May 12 17:41:01    RecRoute Len 36 10.222.44.1 10.222.46.2 10.222.1.1 10.222.29.1
```

```
May 12 17:41:01   Detour   Len 28   Branch from 10.222.46.2 to avoid 192.168.32.1
May 12 17:41:01         Branch from 10.222.28.1 to avoid 192.168.20.1
May 12 17:41:01         Branch from 10.222.30.2 to avoid 192.168.40.1
```

The Fast Reroute Object

The *Fast Reroute object* is contained in Path messages sent along the path of an established LSP. It alerts all downstream routers that the ingress router desires protection along the LSP's path. Each router along the LSP, with the exception of the egress, then creates a detour path around the next downstream node using the Detour object. Information within the Fast Reroute object allows each of the routers to consult a local traffic engineering database for calculating a path to the egress router. This information includes a bandwidth reservation, a hop count, LSP priority values, and administrative group knowledge. We discuss the mechanics of fast reroute in greater depth in Chapter 8.

The format of the Fast Reroute object is displayed in Figure 7.18. The field definitions include the following:

Object Length (2 octets)   This field displays the total length of the RSVP object. A constant value of 20 is placed in this field.

Class Number (1 octet)   The value that represents the object's class is placed into this field. The Fast Reroute object falls within the Fast Reroute class, which uses a value of 205.

C-Type Value (1 octet)   The specific type of object within its overall class is displayed in this field. The Fast Reroute object uses a value of 1 for its C-Type.

Setup Priority (1 octet)   This field contains the priority of the LSP used for assigning resources during its establishment in the network. Possible values range from 0 through 7, with 0 representing the strongest priority value and 7 the weakest priority value. The JUNOS software uses a setup priority value of 7 by default.

Hold Priority (1 octet)   This field contains the priority of the LSP used for maintaining resources after becoming established in the network. Possible values range from 0 through 7, with 0 representing the strongest priority value and 7 the weakest priority value. The JUNOS software uses a hold priority value of 0 by default.

Hop Limit (1 octet)   This field displays the total number of transit hops a detour path may take through the network, excluding the local repair node and any router performing a detour merge operation. For example, a hop limit value of 2 means that the detour can leave the local repair node and transit two other routers before being merged or reaching the egress router.

Reserved (1 octet)   This field is not used and is set to a constant value of 0x00.

Bandwidth (4 octets)   When populated, this field displays the bandwidth reservation (in bytes per second) that should be performed for all detour paths. By default, the JUNOS software places a value of 0 in this field. You may alter this default by configuring a bandwidth within the `fast-reroute` definition of the LSP.

Include Any (4 octets)   This field contains information pertaining to network links that are assigned a particular administrative group. When a group value is placed in this field, each network link along the detour path must be assigned to that group. A value of 0 in this field means that no group values are required and that all network links may be used.

Exclude Any (4 octets)   This field contains information pertaining to network links that are assigned a particular administrative group. When a group value is placed in this field, each network link along the detour path must *not* be assigned to that group. A value of 0 in this field means that any network link may be used.

FIGURE 7.18   The Fast Reroute object

32 bits

8	8	8	8
Object Length		Class Number	C-Type Value
Setup Priority	Hold Priority	Hop Limit	Reserved
Bandwidth			
Include Any			
Exclude Any			

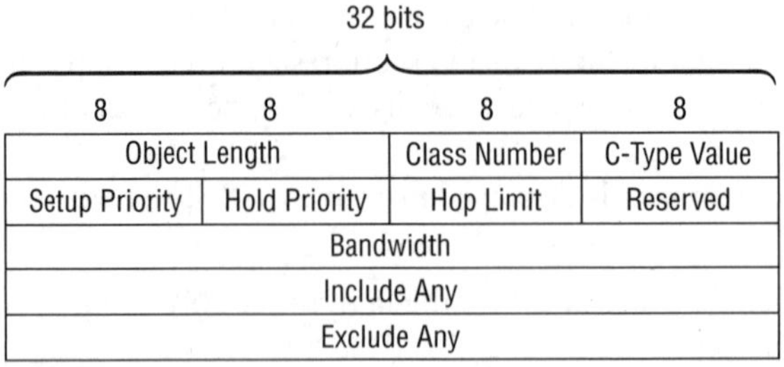

Using the sample network shown in Figure 7.17 as a guide, we examine the Path message generated by the Sherry router for the ***Sherry-to-Char*** LSP:

```
May 12 17:41:01 RSVP send Path 192.168.16.1->192.168.32.1 Len=244 ge-0/2/0.0
May 12 17:41:01   Session7 Len 16 192.168.32.1(port/tunnel ID 24027) Proto 0
May 12 17:41:01   Hop     Len 12 10.222.29.1/0x08528264
May 12 17:41:01   Time    Len  8 30000 ms
May 12 17:41:01   SessionAttribute Len 24 Prio (7,0) flag 0x0 "Sherry-to-Char"
May 12 17:41:01   Sender7  Len 12 192.168.16.1(port/lsp ID  1)
May 12 17:41:01   Tspec    Len 36 rate 0bps size 0bps peak Infbps m 20 M 1500
May 12 17:41:01   ADspec   Len 48
May 12 17:41:01   SrcRoute Len 28  10.222.29.2 S 10.222.1.2 S 10.222.45.2 S
May 12 17:41:01   LabelRequest Len  8 EtherType 0x800
May 12 17:41:01   Properties Len 12 Primary path
May 12 17:41:01   RecRoute Len 12  10.222.29.1
May 12 17:41:01   FastReroute Len 20 Prio(7,0) Hop 6 BW 0bps
May 12 17:41:01    Include 0x00000000 Exclude 0x00000000
```

The FastReroute output displays the information contained in the Fast Reroute object. The default setup (7) and hold (0) priority values are requested, and the hop limit is set to 6 hops. No bandwidth reservation is assigned to the detour paths, and all possible links in the network are usable by the detours. This is revealed by examining the Include and Exclude fields and finding all zero values.

The LSP-Tunnel Session Attribute Object

The *LSP-Tunnel Session Attribute object* is contained in a Path message and is used by the ingress router to advertise the priority values associated with the LSP. In addition, the name of the RSVP session is included in the object, which allows for easier troubleshooting on transit and egress routers. Finally, information concerning the operation of the LSP and its resource reservations is contained here as well. Figure 7.19 displays the format of the Session Attribute object, which includes the following fields:

Object Length (2 octets)   This field displays the total length of the RSVP object.

Class Number (1 octet)   The value that represents the object's class is placed into this field. The LSP-Tunnel Session Attribute object falls within the Session Attribute class, which uses a value of 207.

C-Type Value (1 octet)   The specific type of object within its overall class is displayed in this field. The LSP-Tunnel Session Attribute object uses a value of 7 for its C-Type.

Setup Priority (1 octet)   This field contains the priority of the LSP used for assigning resources during its establishment in the network. Possible values range from 0 through 7, with 0 representing the strongest priority value and 7 the weakest priority value. The JUNOS software uses a setup priority value of 7 by default.

Hold Priority (1 octet)   This field contains the priority of the LSP used for maintaining resources after becoming established in the network. Possible values range from 0 through 7, with 0 representing the strongest priority value and 7 the weakest priority value. The JUNOS software uses a hold priority value of 0 by default.

Flags (1 octet)   This field contains flags that alert other routers in the network about the capabilities of the LSP and its resource reservations. Currently, five flag values are defined:

Bit 0   This flag bit, 0x01, is set to permit downstream routers to use a local repair mechanism, such as fast reroute link protection, allowing transit routers to alter the explicit route of the LSP.

Bit 1   This flag bit, 0x02, is set to request that label recording be performed along the LSP path. This means that each downstream node should place its assigned label into the Record Route object in the Resv message.

Bit 2   This flag bit, 0x04, is set to indicate that the egress router should use the Shared Explicit reservation style for the LSP. This allows the ingress router to reroute the primary path of the LSP without first releasing the LSP's resources.

Bit 3   This flag bit, 0x08, is set to indicate that each router along the LSP should reserve bandwidth for its fast reroute detour path. The detour paths in the network use this bit value only when the Fast Reroute object is omitted from the Path message created by the ingress router.

Bit 4   This flag bit, 0x10, is set to permit downstream routers to use a node repair mechanism, such as fast reroute node protection. Each router should then calculate a detour path that protects the LSP from a failure of the next downstream node.

Name Length (1 octet) This field displays the length of the Session Name field that follows.

Session Name (Variable) This variable-length field contains the configured ASCII name of the LSP. Its inclusion in a `Path` message allows each router along the path to display the LSP name in relevant `show` commands.

FIGURE 7.19 The LSP-Tunnel Session Attribute object

32 bits

8	8	8	8
Object Length		Class Number	C-Type Value
Setup Priority	Hold Priority	Flags	Name Length
Session Name			

The Merlot router is receiving `Path` messages from Chianti for the ***Sherry-to-Char*** LSP in Figure 7.17. The Session Attribute object appears within the message as so:

```
May 12 17:40:51 RSVP recv Path 192.168.16.1->192.168.32.1 Len=244 so-0/1/0.0
May 12 17:40:51   Session7 Len 16 192.168.32.1(port/tunnel ID 24027) Proto 0
May 12 17:40:51   Hop      Len 12 10.222.1.1/0x085280cc
May 12 17:40:51   Time     Len  8 30000 ms
May 12 17:40:51   SessionAttribute Len 24 Prio (7,0) flag 0x0 "Sherry-to-Char"
May 12 17:40:51   Sender7  Len 12 192.168.16.1(port/lsp ID  1)
May 12 17:40:51   Tspec    Len 36 rate 0bps size 0bps peak Infbps m 20 M 1500
May 12 17:40:51   ADspec   Len 48
May 12 17:40:51   SrcRoute Len 20  10.222.1.2 S 10.222.45.2 S
May 12 17:40:51   LabelRequest Len  8 EtherType 0x800
May 12 17:40:51   Properties Len 12 Primary path
May 12 17:40:51   RecRoute Len 20  10.222.1.1 10.222.29.1
May 12 17:40:51   FastReroute Len 20 Prio(7,0) Hop 6 BW 0bps
May 12 17:40:51     Include 0x00000000 Exclude 0x00000000
```

The information within the object informs us that the default JUNOS software setup (7) and hold (0) priority values are used for this LSP and that no flags have been set. In addition, the inclusion of the LSP name allows Merlot to display the string in the output of the `show mpls lsp` command:

```
user@Merlot> show mpls lsp
Ingress LSP: 0 sessions
Total 0 displayed, Up 0, Down 0

Egress LSP: 0 sessions
```

```
Total 0 displayed, Up 0, Down 0


Transit LSP: 1 sessions
To              From            State Rt Style Labelin Labelout LSPname
192.168.32.1    192.168.16.1    Up    1  1 FF   100112         3 Sherry-to-Char
Total 1 displayed, Up 1, Down 0
```

RSVP Sessions

When an LSP is established in the network, it is assigned certain resources, including a label value and a bandwidth reservation when it's requested. In addition, the use of fast reroute for the LSP means that each detour path created in the network needs to be associated with the protected LSP. All of this information is connected by a common set of data referred to as an *RSVP session*. Specifically, a session is identified by the unique combination of information in Path and Resv message objects. Within a Path message, the Session, Sender-Template, and Session Attribute objects define a session, while the Session and Filter-Spec objects are used in a Resv message.

The Sherry router is currently the ingress router for an LSP in an MPLS network. It generates the following Path message and forwards it to the first transit router in the path:

```
May 13 13:20:30 RSVP send Path 192.168.16.1->192.168.32.1 Len=244 ge-0/2/0.0
May 13 13:20:30   Session7 Len 16 192.168.32.1(port/tunnel ID 24039) Proto 0
May 13 13:20:30   Hop       Len 12 10.222.29.1/0x08528264
May 13 13:20:30   Time      Len 8 30000 ms
May 13 13:20:30   SessionAttribute Len 24 Prio (7,0) flag 0x0 "Sherry-to-Char"
May 13 13:20:30   Sender7  Len 12 192.168.16.1(port/lsp ID  1)
May 13 13:20:30   Tspec     Len 36 rate 0bps size 0bps peak Infbps m 20 M 1500
May 13 13:20:30   ADspec    Len 48
May 13 13:20:30   SrcRoute Len 28  10.222.29.2 S 10.222.1.2 S 10.222.45.2 S
May 13 13:20:30   LabelRequest Len  8 EtherType 0x800
May 13 13:20:30   Properties Len 12 Primary path
May 13 13:20:30   RecRoute Len 12  10.222.29.1
May 13 13:20:30   FastReroute Len 20 Prio(7,0) Hop 6 BW 0bps
May 13 13:20:30     Include 0x00000000 Exclude 0x00000000
```

The Session7 object defines the egress router address as 192.168.32.1 and assigns a tunnel ID value of 24039 to the LSP. The ingress router information is displayed in the Sender7 object, where we see the 192.168.16.1 address and an LSP ID value of 1. The LSP itself is assigned the name **Sherry-to-Char**, which is contained in the SessionAttribute object. This same information is contained in the Resv message Sherry receives from the next downstream node:

```
May 13 13:20:30 RSVP recv Resv 10.222.29.2->10.222.29.1 Len=136 ge-0/2/0.0
May 13 13:20:30   Session7 Len 16 192.168.32.1(port/tunnel ID 24039) Proto 0
May 13 13:20:30   Hop       Len 12 10.222.29.2/0x08528264
May 13 13:20:30   Time      Len 8 30000 ms
```

```
May 13 13:20:30    Style    Len  8 FF
May 13 13:20:30    Flow     Len 36 rate 0bps size 0bps peak Infbps m 20 M 1500
May 13 13:20:30    Filter7  Len 12 192.168.16.1(port/lsp ID  1)
May 13 13:20:30    Label    Len  8  100144
May 13 13:20:30    RecRoute Len 28  10.222.29.2(flag=0x9)
May 13 13:20:30        10.222.1.2(flag=0x1) 10.222.45.2
```

The egress router address and tunnel ID value are once again contained in the Session7 object. This is the same object data used in the Path message. Information concerning the ingress router is now placed into the Filter7 object. Here we see the LSP ID value of 1 associated with the router address of 192.168.16.1.

The receipt of the Resv message by Sherry completes the establishment of the LSP. We can view the RSVP session details in the output of the show rsvp session detail ingress command as so:

```
user@Sherry> show rsvp session detail ingress
Ingress RSVP: 1 sessions

192.168.32.1
  From: 192.168.16.1, LSPstate: Up, ActiveRoute: 0
  LSPname: Sherry-to-Char, LSPpath: Primary
  Suggested label received: -, Suggested label sent: -
  Recovery label received: -, Recovery label sent: 100144
  Resv style: 1 FF, Label in: -, Label out: 100144
  Time left:     -,  Since: Tue May 13 13:20:18 2003
  Tspec: rate 0bps size 0bps peak Infbps m 20 M 1500
  Port number: sender 1 receiver 24039 protocol 0
  FastReroute desired
  PATH rcvfrom: localclient
  PATH sentto: 10.222.29.2 (ge-0/2/0.0) 18 pkts
  RESV rcvfrom: 10.222.29.2  (ge-0/2/0.0) 20 pkts
  Explct route: 10.222.29.2 10.222.1.2 10.222.45.2
  Record route: <self>  10.222.29.2  10.222.1.2  10.222.45.2
    Detour is Up
    Detour PATH sentto: 10.222.28.2 (at-0/1/0.0) 17 pkts
    Detour RESV rcvfrom: 10.222.28.2  (at-0/1/0.0) 17 pkts
    Detour Explct route: 10.222.28.2 10.222.4.2 10.222.44.2
    Detour Record route: <self>  10.222.28.2  10.222.4.2  10.222.44.2
    Detour Label out: 100192
Total 1 displayed, Up 1, Down 0
```

The addresses of the ingress and egress routers are clearly visible in the router output, as is the name of the LSP. The command also displays, however, the ID numbers assigned by Sherry for this session within the `Port number` section. The tunnel ID value of 24039 appears as the `receiver`, while the LSP ID value 1 appears as the `sender`. Finally, the ingress router has requested that the LSP be protected through a fast reroute mechanism, as shown by the `FastReroute` desired output. This means that Sherry generates a `Path` message for the creation of the detour path. When the detour is established, Sherry receives a `Resv` message from the first downstream node along the detour. Both of these messages are associated with the original RSVP session through the inclusion of the appropriate objects:

```
May 13 13:20:30 RSVP send Path 192.168.16.1->192.168.32.1 Len=236 at-0/1/0.0
May 13 13:20:30   Session7 Len 16 192.168.32.1(port/tunnel ID 24039) Proto 0
May 13 13:20:30   Hop      Len 12 10.222.28.1/0x085280cc
May 13 13:20:30   Time     Len  8 30000 ms
May 13 13:20:30   SessionAttribute Len 24 Prio (7,0) flag 0x0 "Sherry-to-Char"
May 13 13:20:30   Sender7  Len 12 192.168.16.1(port/lsp ID   1)
May 13 13:20:30   Tspec    Len 36 rate 0bps size 0bps peak Infbps m 20 M 1500
May 13 13:20:30   ADspec   Len 48
May 13 13:20:30   SrcRoute Len 28  10.222.28.2 S 10.222.4.2 S 10.222.44.2 S
May 13 13:20:30   LabelRequest Len  8 EtherType 0x800
May 13 13:20:30   Properties Len 12 Primary path
May 13 13:20:30   RecRoute Len 12  10.222.28.1
May 13 13:20:30   Detour   Len 12  Branch from 10.222.28.1 to avoid 192.168.20.1

May 13 13:20:39 RSVP recv Resv 10.222.28.2->10.222.28.1 Len=136 at-0/1/0.0
May 13 13:20:39   Session7 Len 16 192.168.32.1(port/tunnel ID 24039) Proto 0
May 13 13:20:39   Hop      Len 12 10.222.28.2/0x085280cc
May 13 13:20:39   Time     Len  8 30000 ms
May 13 13:20:39   Style    Len  8 FF
May 13 13:20:39   Flow     Len 36 rate 0bps size 0bps peak Infbps m 20 M 1500
May 13 13:20:39   Filter7  Len 12 192.168.16.1(port/lsp ID   1)
May 13 13:20:39   Label    Len  8  100192
May 13 13:20:39   RecRoute Len 28  10.222.28.2 10.222.4.2 10.222.44.2
```

The Label Distribution Protocol

The second dynamic method of establishing an LSP within the JUNOS software is the *Label Distribution Protocol* (LDP). Unlike the extended version of RSVP, no traffic engineering capabilities are available with LDP, and each label-switched path follows the Interior Gateway Protocol (IGP) shortest path through the network. Each LDP-speaking router advertises an address reachable via an MPLS label into the LDP domain. This label information is exchanged by neighbors in a hop-by-hop fashion so that every router in the network becomes an ingress router to every other router in the network. The end result of this process is a full mesh of LSPs in the domain. Before this can occur, however, each set of adjacent routers forms an LDP neighbor relationship.

Becoming LDP Neighbors

After the protocol is enabled on a local router, it begins sending *LDP Hello messages* on all of its operational interfaces. These messages are addressed to the 224.0.0.2 /32 well-known destination address and are sent using UDP port 646. The Hello message, as well as all other LDP messages, is encoded using a type, length, value (TLV) paradigm. Each message contains a common LDP header, which is followed by a set of fields describing the message itself. The body of the message contains multiple TLVs, some of which are mandatory, whereas others are optional. Figure 7.20 displays the format of the LDP Hello message, which includes a single mandatory TLV, the hello parameters TLV. The JUNOS software uses two optional TLVs in the Hello message to describe the local router and its properties. The message's fields are as follows:

LDP Version (2 octets)   This field displays the current version of LDP being used by the sending router. It is set to a constant value of 1.

PDU Length (2 octets)   This field displays the total length, in bytes, of the remaining fields contained in the PDU.

LDP ID (6 octets)   This field contains a unique LDP ID, which describes the label space used by the local router. The first 4 octets of the ID value represent the advertising node as a unique device in the network. The router ID of the node is placed in this portion of the ID. The final 2 octets of the ID are used to describe the method of label allocation used by the local router. When a per-router allocation system is in use, as is the JUNOS software default, these octets are set to a value of 0. The LDP ID is displayed in a format of 192.168.1.1:0.

Message Type (2 octets)   The first bit in this field is defined as the U, or unknown, bit. It is designed as a method for telling routers how to handle a message that is unknown to the local router. When the bit is clear (set to 0), the router must return an error message to the sender if the message type is not recognized. If the bit is set to a value of 1, the local router may ignore the unknown TLV message silently while continuing to process the remainder of the message. For an LDP Hello message, the U bit is set to a value of 0.

The remaining bits in this field represent the type of message contained in the packet. Hello messages place a constant value of 0x0100 in this field.

Message Length (2 octets)   This field displays the total length, in bytes, of the remaining fields contained in the message.

Message ID (4 octets)   This field contains a 32-bit value generated by the advertising router, which uniquely identifies this particular message.

Hello TLV Type (2 octets)   The first bit in this field is also defined as a U bit. As before, it defines how a receiving router handles an unknown TLV. The hello parameters TLV uses a value of 0 for this bit, requiring all routers to return an error message to the source. The second bit in the field is the F, or forward, bit. It is used only when the U bit is set to a value of 1 and the LDP message is forwarded beyond the receiving router. When the F bit is cleared, the receiving router doesn't forward the unknown TLV along with the message. When the F bit is set to a value of 1, the unknown TLV is readvertised along with the LDP message. This bit is not used by the hello parameters TLV and is set to a value of 0.

The remaining bits in this field represent the type code of the TLV. The hello parameters TLV uses a constant value of 0x0400 in this field.

Hello TLV Length (2 octets) This field displays the length, in bytes, of the remaining fields in the TLV. The hello parameters TLV uses a constant value of 4 in this field.

Hold Time (2 octets) This field displays the hold time, in seconds, requested by the advertising router. Each set of LDP neighbors negotiates a hold time for their relationship based on the lower value proposed by either neighbor. The JUNOS software uses a hold time of 15 seconds, by default, for all Hello messages.

Flags and Reserved (2 octets) The first 2 bits in this field, the T and R bits, are designated as flags and are discussed next. The remaining bits in the field are reserved and are set to a constant value of 0.

> **T Bit** The first flag bit, the T bit, encodes the form of hello that the message represents. When the bit is set to a value of 1, the Hello message is a *targeted Hello*. This means that the two LDP neighbors are not directly connected across a network link. A value of 0 for this flag bit means that the Hello message is a *link Hello* and that the neighbors are directly connected.

> **R Bit** This second flag bit, the R bit, is used when the Hello message is a targeted Hello. When it is set to a value of 1, the local router is requesting that its neighbor respond with its own targeted Hello message. A value of 0 for the flag makes no such request.

Optional TLV Type (2 octets) This field contains the type code for any optional TLV used in the message. The JUNOS software uses both an IPv4 transport address TLV (type code of 0x0401) and a configuration sequence number TLV (type code of 0x0402). Both of these TLVs set the U and F flag bits to 0 values.

The use of two TLVs means that the optional type, length, and value fields are repeated multiple times in a single Hello message. The transport address TLV informs the receiving router which address to use when establishing its LDP session with the local router. The configuration sequence number TLV is used by the sending router to alert any receiving routers that configuration changes have been made to the local router.

Optional TLV Length (2 octets) This field displays the length, in bytes, of the remaining optional TLV fields. Both the IPv4 transport address and configuration sequence number TLVs place a constant value of 4 in this field.

Optional TLV Value (Variable) This variable-length field contains the data carried by each optional TLV. The IPv4 transport address TLV places a 32-bit IP address in this field. By default, the JUNOS software uses the loopback address of the advertising router as the transport address.

The configuration sequence number TLV places a value of 1 in this field when LDP is first enabled on the local router. Each committed configuration change prompts the local router to increment this value by 1.

FIGURE 7.20   The LDP Hello message

```
                                  32 bits
                        ┌────────────────────────┴────────────────────────┐
          8             8             8             8

  ┌─────────────────────────────┬─────────────────────────────┐
  │         LDP Version          │          PDU Length          │
  ├─────────────────────────────┴─────────────────────────────┤
  │                           LDP ID                            │
  ├─────────────────────────────┬─────────────────────────────┤
  │      LDP ID (continued)      │         Message Type         │
  ├─────────────────────────────┼─────────────────────────────┤
  │        Message Length        │          Message ID          │
  ├─────────────────────────────┼─────────────────────────────┤
  │    Message ID (continued)    │        Hello TLV Type        │
  ├─────────────────────────────┼─────────────────────────────┤
  │       Hello TLV Length       │          Hold Time           │
  ├─────────────────────────────┼─────────────────────────────┤
  │      Flags and Reserved      │       Optional TLV Type      │
  ├─────────────────────────────┼─────────────────────────────┤
  │      Optional TLV Length     │      Optional TLV Value      │
  └─────────────────────────────┴─────────────────────────────┘
```

Figure 7.21 shows a sample network using LDP for advertising labels and establishing LSPs. Each of the six routers uses OSPF as the IGP, and each has enabled LDP on all of its operational interfaces. On the Chablis router, we see the advertisement of Hello messages to both Zinfandel and Cabernet in the output of a `traceoptions` file:

```
May 13 13:53:19 LDP sent UDP PDU 10.222.60.1 -> 224.0.0.2 (so-0/1/0.0)
May 13 13:53:19 ver 1, pkt len 42, PDU len 38, ID 192.168.52.1:0
May 13 13:53:19   Msg Hello (0x100), len 28, ID 1
May 13 13:53:19     TLV HelloParms (0x400), len 4
May 13 13:53:19       Hold time 15, flags <> (0x0)
May 13 13:53:19     TLV XportAddr (0x401), len 4
May 13 13:53:19       Address 192.168.52.1
May 13 13:53:19     TLV ConfSeq (0x402), len 4
May 13 13:53:19       Sequence 1

May 13 13:53:19 LDP sent UDP PDU 10.222.62.2 -> 224.0.0.2 (so-0/1/1.0)
May 13 13:53:19 ver 1, pkt len 42, PDU len 38, ID 192.168.52.1:0
May 13 13:53:19   Msg Hello (0x100), len 28, ID 2
May 13 13:53:19     TLV HelloParms (0x400), len 4
May 13 13:53:19       Hold time 15, flags <> (0x0)
May 13 13:53:19     TLV XportAddr (0x401), len 4
May 13 13:53:19       Address 192.168.52.1
May 13 13:53:19     TLV ConfSeq (0x402), len 4
May 13 13:53:19       Sequence 1
```

FIGURE 7.21 LDP sample network

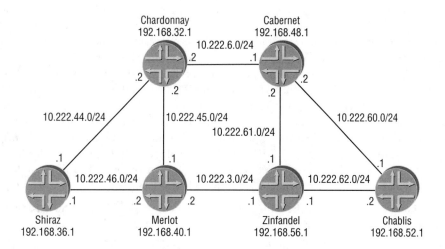

The first critical piece of information we notice in the Hello message is contained in the LDP header—the LDP ID. This ID value defines the *label space* used by the local router as a combination of a unique identifier and the label allocation method used. The ID 192.168.52.1:0 router output tells us that Chablis is using its router ID of 192.168.52.1 as its unique identifier. The zero notation at the end of the LDP ID means that Chablis is allocating labels in a per-node fashion, as opposed to a per-interface fashion, which is the JUNOS software default allocation method. This notion of a label space is used when the LDP neighbors form a protocol session between themselves. Only a single session is established for each label space, regardless of the number of neighbor relationships. A second important piece of information is needed for forming the protocol session, and it is also contained in the Hello message. The IPv4 transport address TLV informs the receiving LDP router of the address to be used for the session establishment.

The absence of the IPv4 transport address TLV in a Hello message means that the source address of the message should be used as the transport address.

After each neighbor receives Hello messages from one another, a neighbor relationship is formed between those routers. The show ldp neighbor output on the Chablis router shows both the Zinfandel (10.222.62.1) and Cabernet (10.222.60.2) routers as active neighbors:

```
user@Chablis> show ldp neighbor
Address             Interface          Label space ID        Hold time
10.222.60.2         so-0/1/0.0         192.168.48.1:0        12
10.222.62.1         so-0/1/1.0         192.168.56.1:0        12
```

Establishing LDP Sessions

Once two neighboring LDP routers know each other's label space and transport address via the Hello messages, an *LDP session* is established between those neighbors. This session is used for the advertisement of IPv4 interface addresses, labels, and reachable prefixes across an LSP. For reliable transport of this information, the session is established across a TCP connection between the routers. This TCP connection also uses the LDP well-known port number of 646 and is initiated by the router with the higher router ID, also known as the *active node*. Once the neighboring routers can communicate over the TCP transport connection, the active node generates and sends an *LDP initialization message* to its peer, the *passive node*. This initialization message contains basic information required to establish an LDP session between the neighbors, such as keepalive times and the LDP ID the session is connecting to. The JUNOS software also includes an optional TLV for support of graceful restart capabilities. The format of the LDP initialization message is shown in Figure 7.22; the fields are as follows:

LDP Version (2 octets)   This field displays the current version of LDP being used by the sending router. It is set to constant value of 1.

PDU Length (2 octets)   This field displays the total length, in bytes, of the remaining fields contained in the PDU.

LDP ID (6 octets)   This field contains the LDP ID of the sending router.

Message Type (2 octets)   The U bit is set to a value of 0 for all initialization messages. The remaining bits in this field represent the type of message contained in the packet. Initialization messages place a constant value of 0x0200 in this field.

Message Length (2 octets)   This field displays the total length, in bytes, of the remaining fields contained in the message.

Message ID (4 octets)   This field contains a 32-bit value generated by the advertising router that uniquely identifies this particular message.

Session TLV Type (2 octets)   Both the U and F bits are set to 0 within the session parameters TLV. The remaining bits in this field represent the type code of the TLV, which is set to a constant value of 0x0500 for the session parameters TLV.

Session TLV Length (2 octets)   This field displays the length, in bytes, of the remaining fields in the TLV. The session parameters TLV places a constant value of 14 in this field.

Protocol Version (2 octets)   This field displays the current version of LDP being used by the sending router. It is set to constant value of 1.

Hold Time (2 octets)   This field displays the amount of time, in seconds, requested by the advertising router as a hold time. Each set of LDP neighbors negotiates a hold time for their relationship based on the lower value proposed by either neighbor. The JUNOS software uses a hold time of 30 seconds, by default. However, the loss of a valid neighbor (using a 15-second hold time) results in the loss of the LDP session as well.

Flags and Reserved (1 octet)   The first 2 bits in this field, the A and D bits, are designated as flags and are discussed next. The remaining bits in the field are reserved and are set to a constant value of 0.

A Bit   The first flag bit, the A bit, encodes the method by which the local router advertises MPLS labels to peers. When the bit is cleared and set to 0, the sending router is using *Downstream Unsolicited* for advertising labels to peers. This means that the local router may send a label value upstream at any time after the LDP session is established. Setting the A bit to a value of 1 designates that the sending router is using *Downstream on Demand* for label advertisement. This requires the upstream router to explicitly request a label mapping before a label is advertised. The JUNOS software uses Downstream Unsolicited, by default, for all LDP sessions.

D Bit   This second flag bit, the D bit, is used when loop detection is being used based on advertised path vector TLVs encoded in all LDP messages. A value of 0 signals that loop detection is not enabled on the sending router. A value of 1, on the other hand, means that loop detection is enabled on the sending router. The JUNOS software sets this flag to a 0 value because loop prevention is accomplished through means outside of LDP.

Path Vector Limit (1 octet)   This field is used to set a limit on the number of hops a message may traverse before a loop is assumed. When loop detection is not used in the network, this field is not used and is set to a constant value of 0x00.

Maximum PDU Length (2 octets)   This field allows the LDP neighbors to negotiate the maximum PDU length each may transmit across the network link connecting them. This value is a negotiable item, and both neighbors use the lower advertised value. The JUNOS software places a value of 4096 in this field by default.

Receiver LDP ID (6 octets)   This field contains the LDP ID of the router that is receiving the initialization message. When combined with the LDP ID of the sending router, in the PDU header, this value allows the receiving router to associate the LDP session establishment with an active LDP neighbor.

Fault Tolerant TLV Type (2 octets)   The JUNOS software places the Fault Tolerant TLV in all initialization messages, by default, for support of graceful restart. The U bit is set to a value of 1, while the F bit is left clear. This allows receiving routers to silently ignore the TLV but not forward it along to any other LDP neighbors.

The remaining bits in this field display the type code of the TLV—0x0503. When combined with the settings of the U and F flags, the final TLV type appears as 0x8503.

Fault Tolerant TLV Length (2 octets)   This field displays the length, in bytes, of the remaining TLV fields. A constant value of 12 is placed in this field.

Fault Tolerant Flags (2 octets)   This field contains numerous flags that describe the state of the fault-tolerant restart session. For a full explanation of each flag, please refer to RFC 3479, "Fault Tolerance for the Label Distribution Protocol."

Reserved (2 octets)   This field is not used and is set to a constant value of 0x0000.

Fault Tolerant Reconnect Time (4 octets)   This field displays the amount of time, in milliseconds, that the sending router maintains control state associated with the restarting router.

Fault Tolerant Recovery Time (4 octets)   This field displays the maximum amount of time, in milliseconds, that the sending router uses for a restart timer. A value of 0 indicates that the sending router did not maintain the forwarding state throughout the restart event.

FIGURE 7.22   The LDP initialization message

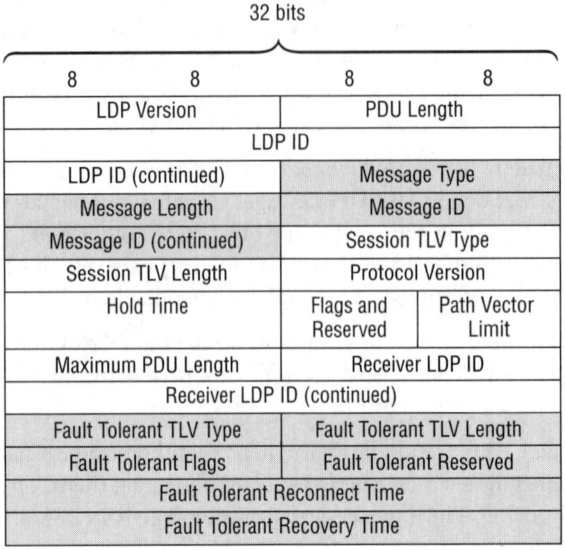

We've seen that the Chablis router in Figure 7.21 has active neighbor relationships with both the Zinfandel and Cabernet routers. When we focus our attention on just the session establishment between Chablis and Cabernet, we find that the Chablis router is the active node for the session because its router ID is higher than Cabernet's. As such, Chablis generates an LDP initialization message and forwards it to Cabernet:

```
May 13 13:53:34 LDP sent TCP PDU 192.168.52.1 -> 192.168.48.1 (none)
May 13 13:53:34 ver 1, pkt len 52, PDU len 48, ID 192.168.52.1:0
May 13 13:53:34   Msg Initialization (0x200), len 38, ID 8
May 13 13:53:34     TLV SesParms (0x500), len 14
May 13 13:53:34       Ver 1, holdtime 30, flags <> (0x0)
May 13 13:53:34       vect_lim 0, max_pdu 4096, id 192.168.48.1:0
May 13 13:53:34     TLV GracefulRestartParms (0x8503), len 12
May 13 13:53:34       Reconnect time 0 ms, recovery time 0 ms
```

In addition to the negotiable values of hold time and maximum PDU, Chablis includes the LDP ID of Cabernet (192.168.48.1:0) in the message. This allows Cabernet to locate the appropriate neighbor relationship to associate the session with. Once it is located, Cabernet responds to Chablis with its own initialization message:

```
May 13 13:53:34 LDP rcvd TCP PDU 192.168.48.1 -> 192.168.52.1 (none)
May 13 13:53:34 ver 1, pkt len 52, PDU len 48, ID 192.168.48.1:0
```

```
May 13 13:53:34    Msg Initialization (0x200), len 38, ID 55
May 13 13:53:34     TLV SesParms (0x500), len 14
May 13 13:53:34      Ver 1, holdtime 30, flags <> (0x0)
May 13 13:53:34      vect_lim 0, max_pdu 4096, id 192.168.52.1:0
May 13 13:53:34     TLV GracefulRestartParms (0x8503), len 12
May 13 13:53:34      Reconnect time 0 ms, recovery time 0 ms
```

This exchange of messages allows the LDP session between the peers to fully establish itself. Cabernet now appears in the output of the show ldp session command:

```
user@Chablis> show ldp session
  Address           State         Connection    Hold time
192.168.48.1        Operational   Open              20
192.168.56.1        Operational   Open              28
```

The addition of the *detail* option allows us to view additional information pertaining to the established session:

```
user@Chablis> show ldp session detail 192.168.48.1
Address: 192.168.48.1, State: Operational, Connection: Open, Hold time: 27
  Session ID: 192.168.52.1:0--192.168.48.1:0
  Next keepalive in 7 seconds
  Active, Maximum PDU: 4096, Hold time: 30, Neighbor count: 1
  Keepalive interval: 10, Connect retry interval: 1
  Local address: 192.168.52.1, Remote address: 192.168.48.1
  Up for 22:45:00
  Local - Restart: disabled, Helper mode: enabled
  Remote - Restart: disabled, Helper mode: enabled
  Local maximum recovery time: 120000 msec
  Next-hop addresses received:
    so-0/1/0.0
    10.222.6.1
    192.168.48.1
    10.222.60.2
    10.222.61.2
```

The session between Chablis and Cabernet is currently Operational with a hold time of 30 seconds. Each router then calculates the timer used to send keepalive messages between the peers to maintain the session. The negotiated hold time of 30 seconds is divided by three, which results in a 10-second keepalive timer. The receipt of any LDP message within this timer window resets it to the maximum value. When no other messages have been transmitted within the keepalive time, the local router generates an *LDP keepalive message* and sends it to the remote peer. Figure 7.23 shows the format of the keepalive message, which includes the following fields:

LDP Version (2 octets)   This field displays the current version of LDP being used by the sending router. It is set to a constant value of 1.

PDU Length (2 octets) This field displays the total length, in bytes, of the remaining fields contained in the PDU. It is set to a constant value of 14.

LDP ID (6 octets) This field contains the LDP ID of the sending router.

Message Type (2 octets) The U bit is set to a value of 0 for all keepalive messages. The remaining bits in this field represent the type of message contained in the packet. Keepalive messages place a constant value of 0x0201 in this field.

Message Length (2 octets) This field displays the total length, in bytes, of the remaining fields contained in the message. It is set to a constant value of 4.

Message ID (4 octets) This field contains a 32-bit value generated by the advertising router that uniquely identifies this particular message.

FIGURE 7.23 The LDP keepalive message

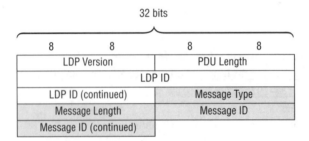

Exchanging Information Across a Session

Once two LDP peers establish a session between themselves, they begin advertising network knowledge across that session. This information consists of local interface addresses for each peer as well as label values for forwarding MPLS packets through the network. Each set of information uses its own message formats and contains unique information. Let's examine each in further detail.

Advertising Interface Addresses

The first set of information transmitted between two LDP peers is the IPv4 interface address for all LDP operational interfaces on the local router. This allows the receiving router to associate future label advertisements with a physical next-hop address for the local router. These addresses are advertised in an *LDP address message*, which is displayed in Figure 7.24. The fields of the message include:

LDP Version (2 octets) This field displays the current version of LDP being used by the sending router. It is set to a constant value of 1.

PDU Length (2 octets) This field displays the total length, in bytes, of the remaining fields contained in the PDU.

LDP ID (6 octets)   This field contains the LDP ID of the sending router.

Message Type (2 octets)   The U bit is set to a value of 0 for all address messages. The remaining bits in this field represent the type of message contained in the packet. Address messages place a constant value of 0x0300 in this field.

Message Length (2 octets)   This field displays the total length, in bytes, of the remaining fields contained in the message.

Message ID (4 octets)   This field contains a 32-bit value generated by the advertising router that uniquely identifies this particular message.

Address TLV Type (2 octets)   Both the U and F bits are set to 0 within the address list TLV. The remaining bits in this field represent the type code of the TLV, which is set to a constant value of 0x0101 for the address list TLV.

Address TLV Length (2 octets)   This field displays the length, in bytes, of the remaining fields in the TLV.

Address Family (2 octets)   This field displays the type of addresses contained in the TLV. For IPv4 interface addresses, a constant value of 1 is placed in this field.

Address Values (Variable)   This variable-length field displays the interface addresses being advertised by the local router. Each address is encoded as a 32-bit value.

FIGURE 7.24   LDP address message

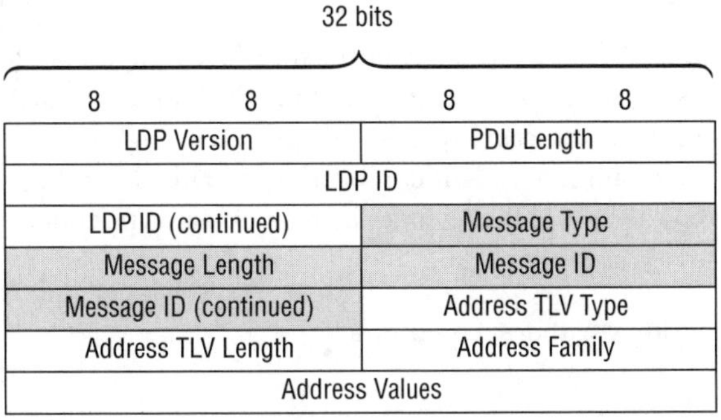

The LDP session between the Chablis and Cabernet routers in Figure 7.21 can be used to examine the advertisement of addresses associated with those peers. Chablis currently has three addresses that are associated with LDP interfaces. We see those address values transmitted in an address message to Cabernet:

```
May 13 13:53:34 LDP sent TCP PDU 192.168.52.1 -> 192.168.48.1 (none)
May 13 13:53:34 ver 1, pkt len 36, PDU len 32, ID 192.168.52.1:0
May 13 13:53:34   Msg Address (0x300), len 22, ID 10
May 13 13:53:34     TLV AddrList (0x101), len 14
```

```
May 13 13:53:34        Address list, family 1
May 13 13:53:34          192.168.52.1
May 13 13:53:34          10.222.60.1
May 13 13:53:34          10.222.62.2
```

These address values represent the loopback interface of Chablis as well as its connections to Zinfandel and Cabernet. If Chablis has a requirement for advertising additional interface addresses in the future, it simply generates a new address message containing the new address and sends it to its peers.

From the perspective of the Cabernet router, there are four interface addresses that it needs to send to Chablis. These include the physical network links to Chardonnay, Zinfandel, and Chablis as well as its own local loopback interface. The address message containing this information looks like this:

```
May 13 13:53:34 LDP rcvd TCP PDU 192.168.48.1 -> 192.168.52.1 (none)
May 13 13:53:34 ver 1, pkt len 40, PDU len 36, ID 192.168.48.1:0
May 13 13:53:34   Msg Address (0x300), len 26, ID 57
May 13 13:53:34     TLV AddrList (0x101), len 18
May 13 13:53:34       Address list, family 1
May 13 13:53:34          10.222.6.1
May 13 13:53:34          192.168.48.1
May 13 13:53:34          10.222.60.2
May 13 13:53:34          10.222.61.2
```

If either of these peers disables LDP on an interface, or the interface is no longer operational, the previously advertised address must be removed from the peer's database. This is accomplished with an LDP address withdraw message, which is displayed in Figure 7.25. The fields of this message, as well as their meanings, are identical to those described for the address message. The only difference between the two LDP messages is the message type code value, which is set to 0x0301 for an address withdraw message.

FIGURE 7.25   The LDP address withdraw message

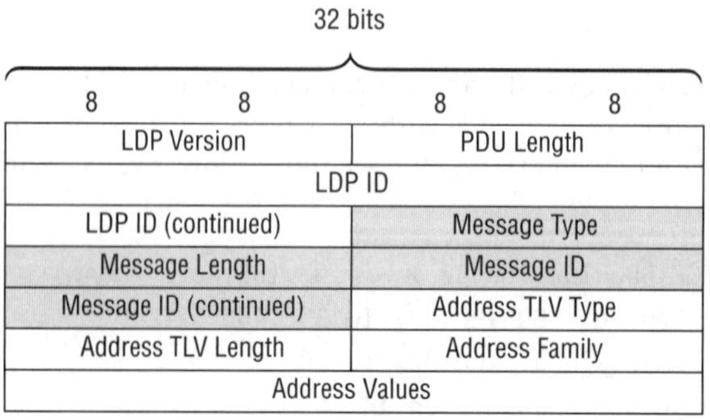

Advertising Label Values

The main purpose for using LDP in a network is the establishment of LSPs for forwarding data traffic using MPLS labels. As such, it is critical that we understand how LDP advertises label values to each router in the network. Before discussing this advertisement in detail, however, we first need to examine a concept known as a *forwarding equivalence class* (FEC). In simple terms, a FEC is a prefix that is mapped by an egress router to an LSP. More specifically, a FEC represents a flow of IP packets through an MPLS network where each packet in the flow is processed identically and forward across the same physical path. For the purposes of our discussion, we'll assume that a FEC represents an IP prefix reachable through the egress router by means of an IP routing table lookup. The egress router then advertises this information upstream to all LDP peers with a specific label value assigned to it. These peers become an ingress router for an LSP that terminates at the egress router. In addition, these peers readvertise the FEC further upstream with a label value allocated locally, making them a transit router in the network. The peers that receive this readvertisement of the FEC then become ingress routers themselves. In this manner, each router in the entire LDP network has a method of forwarding MPLS packets to the FEC advertised by the single egress router. Figure 7.26 shows a FEC advertised by the Chardonnay router and the MPLS forwarding path used by each other router in the network to reach this advertised prefix.

FIGURE 7.26   Forwarding equivalence class example

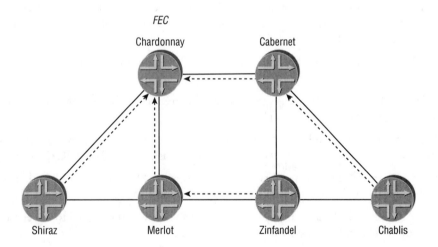

A Juniper Networks router, by default, advertises only its 32-bit loopback address as a FEC. This allows all LDP routers in the network to establish an LSP to the loopback address of every other router in the network, creating a full mesh of LSPs. These MPLS-reachable addresses are placed into the inet.3 routing table, where the Border Gateway Protocol (BGP) recursive lookup may locate them. The end result is the forwarding of BGP transit traffic across the network using label-switched paths established by LDP.

Every prefix advertised as a FEC is associated with a label value allocated by each router along the path of the LSP. This allows label advertisements to proceed in an upstream manner from the egress router to each ingress router without an explicit request for a label. The advertisement of a FEC and its label is accomplished with an *LDP label mapping message*. An individual message may contain a single label and FEC pair or multiple pairs. Figure 7.27 shows the format of the label mapping message, which includes the following fields:

LDP Version (2 octets)   This field displays the current version of LDP being used by the sending router. It is set to a constant value of 1.

PDU Length (2 octets)   This field displays the total length, in bytes, of the remaining fields contained in the PDU.

LDP ID (6 octets)   This field contains the LDP ID of the sending router.

Message Type (2 octets)   The U bit is set to a value of 0 for all label mapping messages. The remaining bits in this field represent the type of message contained in the packet. Label mapping messages place a constant value of 0x0400 in this field.

Message Length (2 octets)   This field displays the total length, in bytes, of the remaining fields contained in the message.

Message ID (4 octets)   This field contains a 32-bit value generated by the advertising router that uniquely identifies this particular message.

FEC TLV Type (2 octets)   Both the U and F bits are set to 0 within the FEC TLV. The remaining bits in this field represent the type code of the TLV, which is set to a constant value of 0x0100 for the FEC TLV.

FEC TLV Length (2 octets)   This field displays the length, in bytes, of the remaining fields in the TLV.

FEC Element Type (1 octet)   This field displays the specific form of the information contained in the FEC TLV. The three defined element types are

Wildcard   The wildcard FEC element, type code 0x01, is used only to remove previously advertised FEC and label values. It contains no information beyond the FEC element type field.

Prefix   The prefix FEC element, type code 0x02, is used by default for all addresses advertised by the JUNOS software. It is used to advertise and remove FEC prefixes in the network.

Host Address   The host address FEC element, type code 0x03, is used to advertise a complete and individual host address into the network.

Address Family (2 octets)   This field displays the type of address contained in the FEC TLV. For IPv4 prefixes, a constant value of 1 is placed in this field.

Prefix Length (1 octet)   This field displays the length of the prefix advertised in the FEC.

FEC Prefix (Variable)   This variable-length field contains the address advertised by the egress router as a FEC.

Label TLV Type (2 octets)   Both the U and F bits are set to 0 within the label TLV. The remaining bits in this field represent the type code of the TLV, which is set to a constant value of 0x0200 for the label TLV.

Label TLV Length (2 octets)   This field displays the length, in bytes, of the remaining fields in the TLV. A constant value of 4 is placed in this field.

Label (4 octets)   This field contains the label value associated with the FEC contained in the FEC TLV.

FIGURE 7.27   The LDP label mapping message

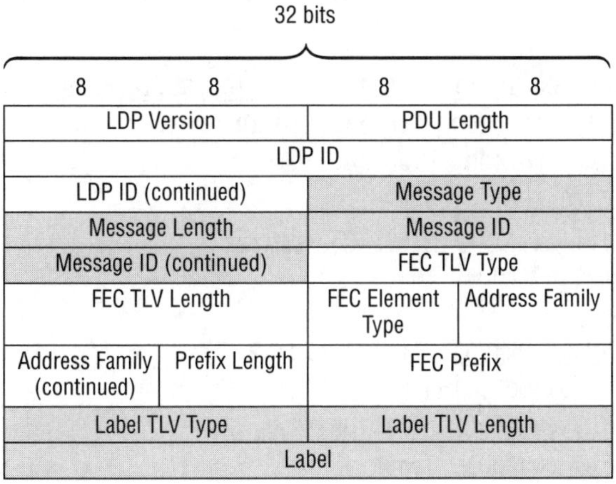

32 bits

8	8	8	8
LDP Version		PDU Length	
LDP ID			
LDP ID (continued)		Message Type	
Message Length		Message ID	
Message ID (continued)		FEC TLV Type	
FEC TLV Length		FEC Element Type	Address Family
Address Family (continued)	Prefix Length	FEC Prefix	
Label TLV Type		Label TLV Length	
Label			

Using the LDP session between Chablis and Cabernet in Figure 7.21 as a guide, we see that the Chablis router advertises its loopback address of 192.168.52.1 /32 as a FEC to Cabernet. The label value associated with this prefix is 3, which signals Cabernet to perform PHP when forwarding traffic to this address. The label mapping message containing this information is seen in the output of a `traceoptions` file on the Chablis router:

```
May 13 13:53:34 LDP sent TCP PDU 192.168.52.1 -> 192.168.48.1 (none)
May 13 13:53:34 ver 1, pkt len 38, PDU len 34, ID 192.168.52.1:0
May 13 13:53:34   Msg LabelMap (0x400), len 24, ID 11
May 13 13:53:34    TLV FEC (0x100), len 8
May 13 13:53:34     Prefix, family 1, 192.168.52.1/32
May 13 13:53:34    TLV Label (0x200), len 4
May 13 13:53:34     Label 3
```

The Cabernet router receives this label mapping message and places it into a local database structure where it is associated with the LDP session it arrived on. Cabernet then allocates a label value from its local set of available labels and readvertises the 192.168.52.1 /32 FEC to all of its LDP peers. This includes the Chablis router, as we see in this router output:

```
May 13 13:53:34 LDP rcvd TCP PDU 192.168.48.1 -> 192.168.52.1 (none)
May 13 13:53:34 ver 1, pkt len 38, PDU len 34, ID 192.168.48.1:0
May 13 13:53:34   Msg LabelMap (0x400), len 24, ID 64
May 13 13:53:34    TLV FEC (0x100), len 8
```

```
May 13 13:53:34        Prefix, family 1, 192.168.52.1/32
May 13 13:53:34        TLV Label (0x200), len 4
May 13 13:53:34        Label 104352
```

In addition to its local FEC of 192.168.48.1/32, the Cabernet router has received FEC advertisements for each of the other routers in the network—Zinfandel, Merlot, Shiraz, and Chardonnay. After allocating labels for each of the FECs, Cabernet advertises these prefixes to Chablis. Each individual FEC and label pair is encoded in a separate label mapping message contained in a single LDP PDU:

```
May 13 13:53:34 LDP rcvd TCP PDU 192.168.48.1 -> 192.168.52.1 (none)
May 13 13:53:34 ver 1, pkt len 150, PDU len 146, ID 192.168.48.1:0
May 13 13:53:34   Msg LabelMap (0x400), len 24, ID 58
May 13 13:53:34    TLV FEC (0x100), len 8
May 13 13:53:34      Prefix, family 1, 192.168.48.1/32
May 13 13:53:34    TLV Label (0x200), len 4
May 13 13:53:34      Label 3
May 13 13:53:34   Msg LabelMap (0x400), len 24, ID 59
May 13 13:53:34    TLV FEC (0x100), len 8
May 13 13:53:34      Prefix, family 1, 192.168.32.1/32
May 13 13:53:34    TLV Label (0x200), len 4
May 13 13:53:34      Label 104288
May 13 13:53:34   Msg LabelMap (0x400), len 24, ID 60
May 13 13:53:34    TLV FEC (0x100), len 8
May 13 13:53:34      Prefix, family 1, 192.168.36.1/32
May 13 13:53:34    TLV Label (0x200), len 4
May 13 13:53:34      Label 104304
May 13 13:53:34   Msg LabelMap (0x400), len 24, ID 61
May 13 13:53:34    TLV FEC (0x100), len 8
May 13 13:53:34      Prefix, family 1, 192.168.40.1/32
May 13 13:53:34    TLV Label (0x200), len 4
May 13 13:53:34      Label 104320
May 13 13:53:34   Msg LabelMap (0x400), len 24, ID 62
May 13 13:53:34    TLV FEC (0x100), len 8
May 13 13:53:34      Prefix, family 1, 192.168.56.1/32
May 13 13:53:34    TLV Label (0x200), len 4
May 13 13:53:34      Label 104336
```

As we saw earlier, Chablis receives these messages and stores them locally in a database. It then allocates labels for each of the FECs and advertises them to all LDP peers, including Cabernet:

```
May 13 13:53:34 LDP sent TCP PDU 192.168.52.1 -> 192.168.48.1 (none)
May 13 13:53:34 ver 1, pkt len 150, PDU len 146, ID 192.168.52.1:0
```

```
May 13 13:53:34   Msg LabelMap (0x400), len 24, ID 12
May 13 13:53:34     TLV FEC (0x100), len 8
May 13 13:53:34       Prefix, family 1, 192.168.48.1/32
May 13 13:53:34     TLV Label (0x200), len 4
May 13 13:53:34       Label 100000
May 13 13:53:34   Msg LabelMap (0x400), len 24, ID 13
May 13 13:53:34     TLV FEC (0x100), len 8
May 13 13:53:34       Prefix, family 1, 192.168.32.1/32
May 13 13:53:34     TLV Label (0x200), len 4
May 13 13:53:34       Label 100016
May 13 13:53:34   Msg LabelMap (0x400), len 24, ID 14
May 13 13:53:34     TLV FEC (0x100), len 8
May 13 13:53:34       Prefix, family 1, 192.168.36.1/32
May 13 13:53:34     TLV Label (0x200), len 4
May 13 13:53:34       Label 100032
May 13 13:53:34   Msg LabelMap (0x400), len 24, ID 15
May 13 13:53:34     TLV FEC (0x100), len 8
May 13 13:53:34       Prefix, family 1, 192.168.40.1/32
May 13 13:53:34     TLV Label (0x200), len 4
May 13 13:53:34       Label 100048
May 13 13:53:34   Msg LabelMap (0x400), len 24, ID 16
May 13 13:53:34     TLV FEC (0x100), len 8
May 13 13:53:34       Prefix, family 1, 192.168.56.1/32
May 13 13:53:34     TLV Label (0x200), len 4
May 13 13:53:34       Label 100064
```

The end result of this flooding is that each LDP router in the network receives a label from each LDP peer for every possible advertised FEC. This information is stored locally on each router within an *LDP database* associated with each peering session. The database displays the label-to-FEC mappings it has received from that peer, as well as the label-to-FEC mappings it advertised to the peer. For the Chablis-Cabernet peering session, we find the following output on the Chablis router:

```
user@Chablis> show ldp database session 192.168.48.1
Input label database, 192.168.52.1:0--192.168.48.1:0
  Label     Prefix
  104288    192.168.32.1/32
  104304    192.168.36.1/32
  104320    192.168.40.1/32
       3    192.168.48.1/32
  104352    192.168.52.1/32
  104336    192.168.56.1/32
```

```
Output label database, 192.168.52.1:0--192.168.48.1:0
   Label      Prefix
   100016     192.168.32.1/32
   100032     192.168.36.1/32
   100048     192.168.40.1/32
   100000     192.168.48.1/32
        3     192.168.52.1/32
   100064     192.168.56.1/32
```

At this point in our discussion, you might be worried about forwarding loops in the network. After all, if every router is going to advertise a label for every possible FEC, what prevents Chablis from forwarding a packet to Cabernet, which would forward it to Zinfandel, which would send it back to Chablis? The answer is quite simple really: LDP relies on the loop-prevention mechanisms of the network's IGP. The address of each received FEC is compared against the routing table of the router to verify that it currently has a valid physical next hop. This next-hop interface is then correlated to an LDP peering session based on the interface addresses received in the LDP address messages. Once the appropriate peering session is located, the local router takes the label value advertised over that session and places it, along with the FEC, in the inet.3 routing table. The end result of this process is that the LSP from each ingress router to each egress router follows the IGP shortest path through the network.

This method of loop prevention requires that each address advertised in a FEC be reachable via the IGP before being readvertised across other LDP sessions.

We can verify this process by examining information on the Chablis router a bit closer. The current set of loopback addresses contained in the routing table looks like this:

user@Chablis> **show route 192.168/16 terse protocol ospf**

```
inet.0: 21 destinations, 23 routes (21 active, 0 holddown, 0 hidden)
+ = Active Route, - = Last Active, * = Both
```

A	Destination	P	Prf	Metric 1	Metric 2	Next hop	AS path
*	192.168.32.1/32	O	10	2		>so-0/1/0.0	
*	192.168.36.1/32	O	10	3		>so-0/1/0.0	
						so-0/1/1.0	
*	192.168.40.1/32	O	10	2		>so-0/1/1.0	
*	192.168.48.1/32	O	10	1		>so-0/1/0.0	
*	192.168.56.1/32	O	10	1		>so-0/1/1.0	

When we compare this output to the information contained in the inet.3 routing table, we see that Chablis uses the same outgoing interface to reach each of the advertised FECs:

```
user@Chablis> show route table inet.3 terse

inet.3: 5 destinations, 5 routes (5 active, 0 holddown, 0 hidden)
+ = Active Route, - = Last Active, * = Both

A Destination        P Prf   Metric 1   Metric 2  Next hop        AS path
* 192.168.32.1/32    L   9          1             >so-0/1/0.0
* 192.168.36.1/32    L   9          1              so-0/1/0.0
                                                  >so-0/1/1.0
* 192.168.40.1/32    L   9          1             >so-0/1/1.0
* 192.168.48.1/32    L   9          1             >so-0/1/0.0
* 192.168.56.1/32    L   9          1             >so-0/1/1.0
```

The exception in this example is the 192.168.36.1 /32 route. This route has two equal-cost loop-free paths through the network. This allows each routing table to make its own selection for placement in the forwarding table. In our sample output, each table has selected a separate interface.

When an LDP router needs to remove a label and FEC that it had previously announced to a peer, it sends an *LDP label withdraw message* to that peer. This message is displayed in Figure 7.28, and it uses the same fields as the label mapping message. The main difference between the two messages is the type code used for the label withdraw message—0x0402.

FIGURE 7.28   The LDP label withdraw message

32 bits

8	8	8	8
LDP Version		PDU Length	
LDP ID			
LDP ID (continued)		Message Type	
Message Length		Message ID	
Message ID (continued)		FEC TLV Type	
FEC TLV Length		FEC Element Type	Address Family
Address Family (continued)	Prefix Length	FEC Prefix	
Label TLV Type		Label TLV Length	
Label			

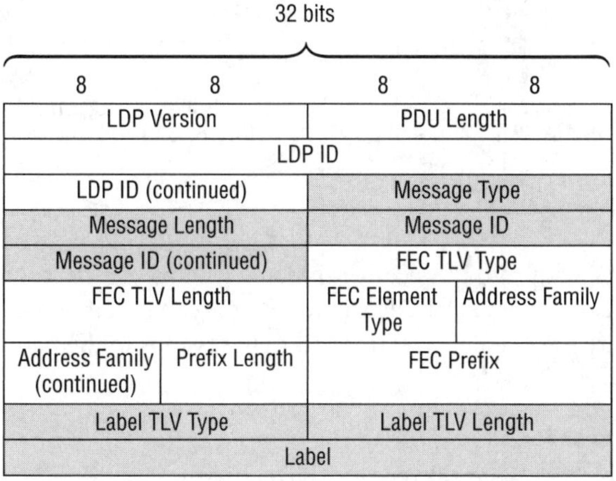

Using LDP through an RSVP Network

Some network administrators prefer using LDP for the establishment of LSPs but sometimes find a requirement to traffic-engineer their MPLS traffic. To address this situation, the JUNOS software permits the establishment of an LDP session across an RSVP network by tunneling the LDP traffic within RSVP-based LSPs. This type of network design is referred to as *LDP tunneling* and requires two RSVP signaled label-switched paths to exist between the LDP neighbors—one in each direction.

FIGURE 7.29   LDP tunneling

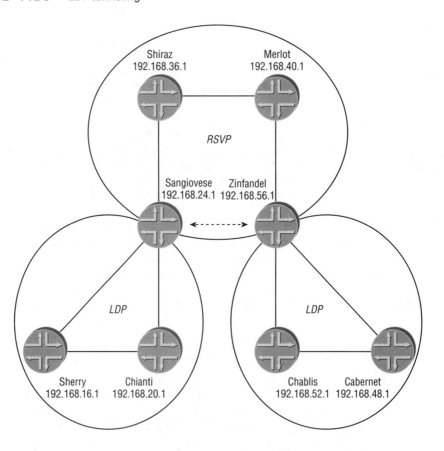

Figure 7.29 shows a network with two physically separated groups of LDP routers. The Sherry, Chianti, and Sangiovese routers are all LDP neighbors, as are the Chablis, Cabernet, and Zinfandel routers. We can verify the currently established LDP sessions in the network on the Sangiovese and Zinfandel routers:

```
user@Sangiovese> show ldp session
  Address           State         Connection      Hold time
```

```
192.168.16.1        Operational  Open           26
192.168.20.1        Operational  Open           26


user@Zinfandel> show ldp session
  Address           State        Connection     Hold time
192.168.48.1        Operational  Open           25
192.168.52.1        Operational  Open           29
```

The administrators of the network would like to forward user traffic from Cabernet to Sherry using MPLS labels. While this is easily accomplished by enabling LDP on the Shiraz and Merlot routers, the network requirement also calls for the engineering of traffic flows across the portion of the network already running RSVP. The solution to this administrative decision is to establish an LDP session between Sangiovese and Zinfandel using LDP tunneling. The first step in enabling this session is the creation of RSVP-based LSPs between the two remote LDP routers. These LSPs are currently operational across the RSVP core of the network:

```
user@Zinfandel> show mpls lsp
Ingress LSP: 1 sessions
To              From            State Rt ActivePath      P     LSPname
192.168.24.1    192.168.56.1    Up    0                 *     from-Zinfandel
Total 1 displayed, Up 1, Down 0

Egress LSP: 1 sessions
To              From            State Rt Style Labelin Labelout LSPname
192.168.56.1    192.168.24.1    Up    0  1 FF     3        - from-Sangiovese
Total 1 displayed, Up 1, Down 0

Transit LSP: 0 sessions
Total 0 displayed, Up 0, Down 0
```

The second step in forming an LDP session between the two remote routers is the application of the ldp-tunneling command to the RSVP-based LSPs:

```
[edit protocols mpls]
user@Zinfandel# set label-switched-path from-Zinfandel ldp-tunneling



[edit protocols mpls]
user@Sangiovese# set label-switched-path from-Sangiovese ldp-tunneling
```

Once we commit our configurations, both Sangiovese and Zinfandel begin sending LDP targeted Hello messages to each other through the LSPs. These messages are sent to the address of the RSVP egress router, as seen on the Sangiovese router:

```
May 15 10:54:55 LDP sent UDP PDU 192.168.24.1 -> 192.168.56.1 (lo0.0)
May 15 10:54:55 ver 1, pkt len 42, PDU len 38, ID 192.168.24.1:0
May 15 10:54:55   Msg Hello (0x100), len 28, ID 768
May 15 10:54:55     TLV HelloParms (0x400), len 4
May 15 10:54:55       Hold time 15, flags <Targ ReqTarg> (0xc000)
May 15 10:54:55     TLV XportAddr (0x401), len 4
May 15 10:54:55       Address 192.168.24.1
May 15 10:54:55     TLV ConfSeq (0x402), len 4
May 15 10:54:55       Sequence 5
```

The flags set in the Hello message mark this as a targeted Hello and request that the receiving router respond with its own targeted Hello message. Since Zinfandel has an established RSVP LSP that egresses at Sangiovese and the LSP is configured for ldp-tunneling, a targeted Hello is returned by Zinfandel:

```
May 15 10:54:57 LDP rcvd UDP PDU 192.168.56.1 -> 192.168.24.1 (lo0.0)
May 15 10:54:57 ver 1, pkt len 42, PDU len 38, ID 192.168.56.1:0
May 15 10:54:57   Msg Hello (0x100), len 28, ID 166073
May 15 10:54:57     TLV HelloParms (0x400), len 4
May 15 10:54:57       Hold time 15, flags <Targ ReqTarg> (0xc000)
May 15 10:54:57     TLV XportAddr (0x401), len 4
May 15 10:54:57       Address 192.168.56.1
May 15 10:54:57     TLV ConfSeq (0x402), len 4
May 15 10:54:57       Sequence 5
```

At this point, the LDP neighbor relationship is formed and the routers exchange LDP initialization messages. The end result of the process is an LDP session between the routers and the exchange of label information:

```
user@Sangiovese> show ldp session
  Address         State        Connection    Hold time
  192.168.16.1    Operational  Open             25
  192.168.20.1    Operational  Open             25
  192.168.56.1    Operational  Open             24


user@Sangiovese> show ldp neighbor
Address              Interface        Label space ID        Hold time
192.168.56.1         lo0.0            192.168.56.1:0            13
10.222.28.1          at-0/1/0.0       192.168.16.1:0            12
```

```
10.222.30.2        so-0/2/0.0        192.168.20.1:0            11
```

```
user@Sangiovese> show ldp database session 192.168.56.1
Input label database, 192.168.24.1:0--192.168.56.1:0
  Label        Prefix
  108480       192.168.16.1/32
  108496       192.168.20.1/32
  108464       192.168.24.1/32
  108432       192.168.48.1/32
  108448       192.168.52.1/32
      3        192.168.56.1/32

Output label database, 192.168.24.1:0--192.168.56.1:0
  Label        Prefix
  100352       192.168.16.1/32
  100368       192.168.20.1/32
      3        192.168.24.1/32
  100384       192.168.48.1/32
  100400       192.168.52.1/32
  100416       192.168.56.1/32
```

NOTE The use of the lo0.0 interface for the neighbor relationship across the RSVP LSP requires running LDP on the loopback interface of the peering routers.

Once the session between Sangiovese and Zinfandel is established, the Cabernet router receives a FEC for the loopback address of Sherry. This address, as well as the label mapping information from Zinfandel, is placed into the inet.3 routing table:

```
user@Cabernet> show route table inet.3 192.168.16.1

inet.3: 5 destinations, 5 routes (5 active, 0 holddown, 0 hidden)
+ = Active Route, - = Last Active, * = Both

192.168.16.1/32     *[LDP/9] 00:31:52, metric 1
                    > via so-0/1/0.0, Push 108480
```

This table entry allows Cabernet to push a label value of 108,480 onto a packet and forward it out its so-0.1.0.0 interface to the Zinfandel router. Zinfandel should, in turn, forward the packet to its LDP peer of Sangiovese that advertised a label value of 100,352 for that FEC:

```
user@Zinfandel> show ldp database session 192.168.24.1
Input label database, 192.168.56.1:0--192.168.24.1:0
```

```
Label       Prefix
100352      192.168.16.1/32
100368      192.168.20.1/32
     3      192.168.24.1/32
100384      192.168.48.1/32
100400      192.168.52.1/32
100416      192.168.56.1/32

Output label database, 192.168.56.1:0--192.168.24.1:0
Label       Prefix
108480      192.168.16.1/32
108496      192.168.20.1/32
108464      192.168.24.1/32
108432      192.168.48.1/32
108448      192.168.52.1/32
     3      192.168.56.1/32
```

Under normal circumstances, Zinfandel would swap label 108,480 with 100,352 and forward the packet directly to Sangiovese. In this particular case, however, Sangiovese is reachable only across an RSVP LSP. This means that along with performing the swap operation so that Sangiovese receives the label it advertised for the FEC, the Zinfandel router must push an additional label value onto the stack. This second label value (100,304) was advertised by Merlot for the RSVP LSP that egresses at Sangiovese. This information is contained in the output of the show rsvp session ingress command on Zinfandel:

```
user@Zinfandel> show rsvp session ingress
Ingress RSVP: 1 sessions
To              From           State Rt Style Labelin Labelout LSPname
192.168.24.1    192.168.56.1   Up     0  1 FF      -    100304 from-Zinfandel
Total 1 displayed, Up 1, Down 0
```

This simultaneous swap and push operation on Zinfandel is visible by examining the mpls.0 switching table using the *detail* option:

```
user@Zinfandel> show route table mpls.0 detail | find 108480
108480 (1 entry, 1 announced)
       *LDP    Preference: 9
               Next hop: via so-0/1/1.0 weight 1, selected
               Label-switched-path from-Zinfandel
               Label operation: Swap 100352, Push 100304(top)
               State: <Active Int>
               Age: 2  Metric: 1
               Task: LDP
```

```
            Announcement bits (1): 0-KRT
            AS path: I
            Prefixes bound to route: 192.168.16.1/32

108496 (1 entry, 1 announced)
        *LDP    Preference: 9
                Next hop: via so-0/1/1.0 weight 1, selected
                Label-switched-path from-Zinfandel
                Label operation: Swap 100368, Push 100304(top)
                State: <Active Int>
                Age: 2  Metric: 1
                Task: LDP
                Announcement bits (1): 0-KRT
                AS path: I
                Prefixes bound to route: 192.168.20.1/32
---(more)---[abort]
```

The top MPLS label in the stack is swapped by Merlot when it receives the data packet. It is then forwarded to the Shiraz router, which performs a label pop operation and forwards the remaining data to Sangiovese. The packet received by Sangiovese has an MPLS label assigned that Sangiovese advertised as a FEC to Zinfandel. This allows the Sangiovese router to recognize the label and perform a label operation on the received packet. In our example, this label operation is a pop because the next-hop router, Sherry, is the egress router and requested that Sangiovese perform PHP.

Summary

In this chapter, we examined the Resource Reservation Protocol (RSVP) and how to use it to establish label-switched paths. After a discussion of the various RSVP message types, we explored the RSVP objects themselves at great depth. Finally, we discussed the concept of an RSVP session and used show commands to prove the network was operating normally.

We concluded the chapter with a discussion of the Label Distribution Protocol (LDP). After examining how two routers become LDP neighbors, we described the establishment of an LDP session between those peers. Once the session was established, we saw the advertisement of interface addresses, forwarding equivalence classes, and labels between those peers. Finally, we established a session between two physically remote neighbors by tunneling LDP through an RSVP-based LSP.

Exam Essentials

Be able to explain how an RSVP-based path is established in an MPLS network.   An MPLS network using RSVP for signaling label-switched paths uses Path and Resv messages for the establishment of the LSP. Path messages are transmitted downstream, whereas Resv messages are transmitted upstream. Each message enables routers to allocate and maintain protocol state associated with the path.

Know the RSVP message types used in an MPLS network for removing protocol state.   RSVP routers remove protocol state from the network by transmitting PathTear and ResvTear messages. These messages traverse the LSP path in the same direction of their counterparts. PathTear messages are transmitted downstream, whereas ResvTear messages are sent upstream.

Be able to describe the RSVP objects used to route an LSP through the network and allocate label information.   An RSVP-based LSP uses the Explicit Route object to formulate a path through an MPLS network. This allows the LSP to utilize links other than that specified by the IGP shortest path. The actual path used by the LSP is detailed in the Record Route object, which is also used for loop prevention during the LSP establishment phase. Finally, the MPLS labels used to forward traffic through the LSP are assigned using the Label Request and Label objects.

Be able to describe how RSVP sessions are identified in an MPLS network.   Each established label-switched path belongs to a specific RSVP session in the network. This session is uniquely identified by information contained in the Sender-Template, Session, and Session Attribute objects. Specifically, the address of the egress router, the tunnel ID, and the LSP ID are used to identify the session.

Be able to describe how LDP forms a session between two peers.   Two neighboring LDP routers first begin exchanging Hello messages with each other. These messages contain the label space advertised by the local router as well as the transport address to be used for the establishment of the session. Once each router determines the neighbor on its interface, the peer with the higher transport address becomes the active node. This active node sends initialization messages to the passive node to begin the session setup phase. Once the passive peer returns its own initialization message, the session becomes fully established.

Understand how address and label information is propagated in an LDP network.   After two LDP routers form a session between themselves, they begin advertising their local interface addresses to the peer with address messages. This allows the receiving peer to associate a physical next hop with the established session. Once this exchange is completed, the peers advertise reachable prefixes and labels in a label mapping message. The prefixes advertised by each LDP router compose a FEC, which is readvertised throughout the LDP network.

Review Questions

1. Which RSVP object appears in both a `Path` and a `Resv` message?

   A. Label

   B. Label Request

   C. Explicit Route

   D. Record Route

2. Which RSVP object is used to signal all routers along the LSP to protect against downstream link and node failures?

   A. Detour

   B. Fast Reroute

   C. Session Attribute

   D. Sender-Template

3. Which RSVP reservation style is used by default within the JUNOS software?

   A. Fixed filter

   B. Wildcard filter

   C. Shared explicit

   D. Shared wildcard

4. Which RSVP message removes existing reservation state from routers along the path of an LSP?

   A. `PathTear` sent to the ingress router

   B. `ResvTear` sent to the ingress router

   C. `PathTear` sent to the egress router

   D. `ResvTear` sent to the egress router

5. What three RSVP objects are used to uniquely identify an RSVP session in the network?

   A. Sender-Template

   B. Sender-Tspec

   C. Session

   D. Session Attribute

6. What prompts each MPLS router to examine the contents of an RSVP `Path` message?

   A. The destination address is the local router's interface address.

   B. The Router Alert option is set in the IP packet header.

   C. It is sent to a well-known TCP port number.

   D. None of the above.

7. What RSVP object is used to avoid a forwarding loop along the path of an LSP?

A. Explicit Route

B. Record Route

C. Session Attribute

D. Session

8. What is the destination address and protocol information for an LDP Hello message?

A. Destined to 224.0.0.2 and UDP port 646

B. Destined to 224.0.0.2 and TCP port 646

C. Destined to 224.0.0.1 and UDP port 646

D. Destined to 224.0.0.1 and TCP port 646

9. What information does the JUNOS software include by default in the FEC advertised by each router?

A. All IP prefixes located on the local router

B. All interface addresses for the local router

C. Only subnets through which an LDP neighbor is located

D. Only the local router's loopback address

10. How does an LDP network prevent routing and forwarding loops?

A. Label information is advertised only between specific peers.

B. LDP routers perform a reverse path forwarding check for all packets.

C. The shortest-path first calculation is performed against the contents of the LDP database.

D. LDP routers use the IGP shortest-path information contained in the routing table.

Answers to Review Questions

1. D. Of the listed RSVP objects, only the Record Route object may appear in both a Path and a Resv message. The Explicit Route and Label Request objects appear only in Path messages, whereas the Label object appears only in Resv messages.

2. B. When included in a Path message, the Fast Reroute object informs each LSP of the ingress router's desire to protect the LSP against downstream failures. Each node along the LSP path then creates a detour around the downstream resource using a Path message with the Detour object.

3. A. The fixed filter (FF) reservation style is used by default on all RSVP LSPs created by the JUNOS software.

4. B. Existing reservation state is removed from the network through the use of the ResvTear message. This message type is always advertised in a hop-by-hop fashion to the ingress router.

5. A, C, D. The unique set of information contained in the Sender-Template, Session, and Session Attribute objects uniquely identifies an RSVP session in the network.

6. B. Within the IP packet header of the RSVP Path message, the Router Alert option is enabled. This allows each router along the path to examine the contents even though the destination address of the packet is the egress router's address.

7. B. When each RSVP router receives either a Path or a Resv message, it examines the Record Route object looking for one of its interface addresses. If it finds one, that means a forwarding loop is in place within the network and the LSP is not established.

8. A. All LDP Hello messages are transmitted to the well-known UDP port number of 646. In addition, all link Hellos are sent to the 224.0.0.2 multicast group address representing all routers on the subnet.

9. D. By default, only the loopback address of the local router is advertised as part of the FEC for that router.

10. D. Routing and forwarding loops are prevented in an LDP network by consulting the shortest-path information in the local routing table. The outgoing interface for a particular route is mapped to the label received from the LDP peer associated with that interface.

Chapter

8

Advanced MPLS

JNCIS EXAM OBJECTIVES COVERED IN THIS CHAPTER:

✓ Identify the operational steps of the constrained shortest path first algorithm

✓ Describe the extensions to OSPF that support traffic engineering

✓ Describe the extensions to IS-IS that support traffic engineering

✓ Define the reason(s) for configuring the following LSP attributes: primary; secondary; administrative groups; adaptive settings; priority/preemption; optimization; forwarding adjacencies into IGPs; fast reroute; metric; time-to-live options; auto-bandwidth; explicit null

In this chapter, we construct a link-state database specifically designed for engineering label-switched path (LSP) traffic flows. The JUNOS software uses this traffic engineering database (TED) to generate a Resource Reservation Protocol (RSVP) path through the network based on constraints you provide. We discuss the contents of the database and the algorithm used on those contents. We then examine some methods for protecting traffic flows in the Multiprotocol Label Switching (MPLS) network. This discussion centers on providing secondary backup paths across the domain as well as using fast reroute to protect traffic already using the LSP. We conclude the chapter with an exploration of various attributes that affect individual LSPs. We discuss some bandwidth reservation options as well as some methods for hiding the physical connectivity of your MPLS network. Finally, we investigate how user data traffic not associated with Border Gateway Protocol (BGP) can use an LSP for forwarding packets across the network.

Constrained Shortest Path First

The ability to engineer LSP traffic flows using RSVP is greatly enhanced through the use of an algorithm known as *Constrained Shortest Path First* (CSPF). This algorithm is a modified version of the SPF algorithm used within the link-state databases of Open Shortest Path First (OSPF) and Intermediate System to Intermediate System (IS-IS). It operates within a special database, the TED, constructed through extensions to the link-state protocols themselves. We discuss the basic use of the TED by RSVP, the extensions defined for the interior gateway protocols (IGPs), and the steps of the CSPF algorithm itself.

Using the Traffic Engineering Database

The topology of an RSVP network is populated into the TED by the link-state protocols. This basic network topology includes the devices capable of running MPLS as well as information on bandwidth availability, available priority values, and administrative controls—to name a few. When you define an LSP within the JUNOS software, you have the ability to supply constraints to the ingress router. These user-defined criteria are passed to the CSPF algorithm before it consults the information in the TED. The algorithm removes all network links from consideration that don't meet the constraints. It then places the remaining topology data into a temporary data structure. The shortest path between the ingress and egress routers is calculated by the algorithm using this subset of information. The result of the CSPF algorithm is formed into a strict-hop Explicit Route object (ERO) detailing each hop along the calculated path. The ERO is passed to the RSVP protocol process, where it is used for signaling and establishing the LSP in the network.

The creation of this ERO does not, however, prevent you from creating your own explicit route via a named path in the JUNOS software. All user-defined path information is passed to the CSPF algorithm as a requested constraint. After creating the subset of network links within the TED, the algorithm consults the information in the user-defined named path. The router runs a separate CSPF calculation to locate the path from the ingress router to the first node listed in the user's ERO. A second CSPF calculation is performed to find a path from the first node to the second node in the user's ERO. The router repeats this pattern of CSPF calculations until the egress router is reached. The results of the multiple computations are then combined into a single strict-hop ERO from the ingress to the egress.

The ability of CSPF to locate a viable network path for an LSP is greatly affected by the information in the TED, so let's investigate how the IGPs propagate this data.

OSPF Traffic Engineering Extensions

The OSPF protocol makes use of a *Type 10 Opaque LSA* for advertising traffic engineering information in a network. This LSA type has an area flooding scope, which limits the creation of the TED to a single OSPF area. This means that a large OSPF network with multiple areas will have multiple TEDs, one for each operational area.

Figure 8.1 displays the format of the Opaque LSA used by OSPF for advertising traffic engineering information. The fields of the LSA include the following:

Link-State Age (2 octets)   The Link-State Age field displays the time, in seconds, since the LSA was first originated into the network. The age begins at the value 0 and increments to a value of 3600 (1 hour).

Options (1 octet)   The local router advertises its capabilities in this field, which also appears in other OSPF packets. The router sets bit 6 in this field, indicating its support for traffic engineering.

Link-State Type (1 octet)   This field displays the type of link-state advertisement (LSA). Opaque LSAs set this field to a constant value of 10.

Opaque Type (1 octet)   The Opaque LSA specification defines the first octet of the link-state ID field as the Opaque Type field. When used to support traffic engineering, a constant value of 1 is placed in this field.

Reserved (1 octet)   This field is not used and is set to a constant value of 0x00.

Instance (2 octets)   The Instance field of a traffic engineering Opaque LSA is used by the local router to support multiple, separate LSAs. By default, the JUNOS software generates one LSA for the router itself as well as a separate LSA for each operational interface.

Advertising Router (4 octets)   This field displays the router ID of the OSPF device that originated the LSA.

Link-State Sequence Number (4 octets)   The sequence number field is a signed 32-bit value used to guarantee that each router in the area has the most recent version of the Opaque LSA.

Link-State Checksum (2 octets)   This field displays a standard IP checksum for the entire LSA, excluding the Link-State Age field.

Length (2 octets)   This field displays the length of the entire LSA, including the header fields.

FIGURE 8.1 Traffic engineering Opaque LSA format

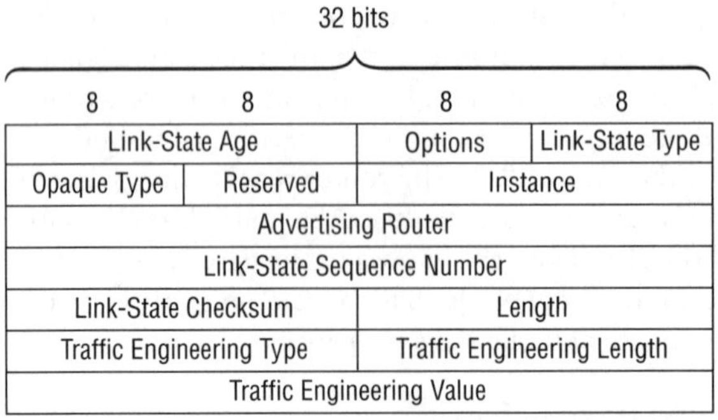

```
                          32 bits
        ┌────────────────────────────────────────────┐
          8         8          8            8
   ┌──────────────────────┬──────────┬─────────────────┐
   │    Link-State Age     │ Options  │ Link-State Type │
   ├───────────┬──────────┼──────────┴─────────────────┤
   │Opaque Type│ Reserved │         Instance            │
   ├───────────┴──────────┴─────────────────────────────┤
   │               Advertising Router                    │
   ├─────────────────────────────────────────────────────┤
   │            Link-State Sequence Number               │
   ├──────────────────────────┬──────────────────────────┤
   │   Link-State Checksum     │         Length           │
   ├──────────────────────────┼──────────────────────────┤
   │ Traffic Engineering Type  │ Traffic Engineering Length│
   ├──────────────────────────┴──────────────────────────┤
   │            Traffic Engineering Value                 │
   └─────────────────────────────────────────────────────┘
```

Traffic Engineering Type (2 octets) The traffic engineering data is encoded within the Opaque LSA using a type, length, value (TLV) paradigm. Currently two TLV type values are defined. The Router Address TLV uses a type code of 1, whereas the Link TLV uses a type code of 2.

Traffic Engineering Length (2 octets) This field displays the length, in bytes, of the value portion of the TLV.

Traffic Engineering Value (Variable) This field displays the specific information contained within the TLV being advertised.

The Sherry router is running OSPF and has enabled the traffic engineering extensions by applying the `traffic-engineering` command at the global OSPF level. The configuration of Sherry currently looks like this:

```
user@Sherry> show configuration protocols ospf
traffic-engineering;
area 0.0.0.0 {
    interface all;
    interface fxp0.0 {
        disable;
    }
}
```

This allows the Sherry router to generate traffic engineering Opaque LSAs, which it places into the local link-state database and floods to all its neighbors:

```
user@Sherry> show ospf database advertising-router 192.168.16.1
```

```
    OSPF link state database, area 0.0.0.0
 Type        ID              Adv Rtr          Seq        Age  Opt  Cksum  Len
 Router   *192.168.16.1     192.168.16.1    0x80000370    55  0x2  0xbad8  72
 Network  *10.0.15.2        192.168.16.1    0x80000365   201  0x2  0xbcb3  32
```

```
Network *10.0.16.1          192.168.16.1      0x80000364    801   0x2   0x5524   32
OpaqArea*1.0.0.1            192.168.16.1      0x80000001     55   0x2   0xb0a9   28
OpaqArea*1.0.0.2            192.168.16.1      0x80000001     50   0x2   0x94ce  124
OpaqArea*1.0.0.3            192.168.16.1      0x80000001     50   0x2   0x7bf1  124
OpaqArea*1.0.0.4            192.168.16.1      0x80000001     50   0x2   0x1246  124
```

The LSA whose link-state ID is currently 1.0.0.1 contains the *Router Address TLV* representing the router itself. The TLV uses a type code value of 1 and has a constant length of 4 octets. The value contained in the Router Address TLV includes an IP address that is consistently reachable on the local router. The loopback address of the local router is used for this value, 192.168.16.1 in the case of the Sherry router:

```
user@Sherry> show ospf database lsa-id 1.0.0.1 detail

   OSPF link state database, area 0.0.0.0
 Type       ID               Adv Rtr          Seq       Age  Opt  Cksum  Len
OpaqArea*1.0.0.1            192.168.16.1      0x80000001     58  0x2  0xb0a9  28
   Area-opaque TE LSA
   RtrAddr (1), length 4:  192.168.16.1
```

Each of the remaining TLVs advertised by Sherry represents the operational links on the router, and each contains a single *Link TLV*. The value portion of the TLV contains multiple sub-TLVs to describe the traffic engineering capabilities of the interface. The type codes of the defined sub-TLVs are

Link Type   The Link Type sub-TLV has a type code of 1 and a sub-TLV length of 1 octet. The value portion of the sub-TLV describes whether the link is a point-to-point or broadcast interface. Point-to-point interfaces use a value of 1 in the sub-TLV, whereas broadcast interfaces place a 2 in the value portion of the sub-TLV.

Link ID   The Link ID sub-TLV uses a type code of 2 and describes the opposite end of the link. The sub-TLV has a length of 4 octets and contains an IP address in the value portion of the sub-TLV. For a point-to-point link, the router ID of the remote neighbor is encoded in the sub-TLV. The interface address of the designated router is placed in the sub-TLV for all broadcast interfaces.

Local Interface IP Address   The use of the Local Interface IP Address sub-TLV is fairly straightforward—it contains the interface address of the local router for the link being described by the Opaque LSA. The sub-TLV uses a type code of 3 and has a length of 4 octets.

Remote Interface IP Address   The Remote Interface IP Address sub-TLV contains the interface address of the remote router for the link being described by the Opaque LSA. The sub-TLV uses a type code of 4 and has a length of 4 octets. Point-to-point interfaces use the remote router's address in this field, whereas broadcast links use a value of 0.0.0.0. When the link is configured as an unnumbered interface, the first 2 octets of the value portion contain all zeros. The remaining 2 octets contain a unique interface index value.

Traffic Engineering Metric The Traffic Engineering Metric sub-TLV has a type code of 5 and a sub-TLV length of 4 octets. It contains the metric value of the interface that should be used by the CSPF algorithm. The JUNOS software places the same value in this sub-TLV as it places in the Router LSA of the local router.

Maximum Bandwidth The Maximum Bandwidth sub-TLV contains the true bandwidth of the local interface in bytes per second. It uses a type code of 6 and has a constant length of 4 octets.

Maximum Reservable Bandwidth The Maximum Reservable Bandwidth sub-TLV displays the total amount of bandwidth, in bytes per second, available for reservations by the RSVP process. This value may be larger than the actual bandwidth of the interface to account for oversubscription of the interface. The sub-TLV has a type code of 7 and a constant length of 4 octets.

Unreserved Bandwidth The type code of the Unreserved Bandwidth sub-TLV is 8. It displays the amount of bandwidth, in bytes per second, that is currently available for reservations on the local interface. This value is calculated for each of the eight priority levels used by the extensions to the RSVP specification. Each unreserved bandwidth value has a length of 4 octets, which results in the entire sub-TLV having a length of 32 octets.

Resource Class/Color The Resource Class/Color sub-TLV has a type code of 9 and a sub-TLV length of 4 octets. The value portion of the sub-TLV contains a 32-bit vector used to encode membership in various administrative groups. An individual interface may belong to multiple groups, in which case multiple bits are set within the bit vector.

The Sherry router is generating three Opaque LSAs to represent its three operational links in the traffic engineering domain. Here are the contents of one of the LSAs:

```
user@Sherry> show ospf database lsa-id 1.0.0.2 detail

    OSPF link state database, area 0.0.0.0
  Type       ID               Adv Rtr          Seq        Age  Opt  Cksum  Len
OpaqArea*1.0.0.2              192.168.16.1     0x80000001  53   0x2  0x94ce 124
    Area-opaque TE LSA
    Link (2), length 100:
      Linktype (1), length 1:
        2
      LinkID (2), length 4:
        10.222.28.2
      LocIfAdr (3), length 4:
        10.222.28.1
      RemIfAdr (4), length 4:
        0.0.0.0
      TEMetric (5), length 4:
        1
      MaxBW (6), length 4:
        100Mbps
      MaxRsvBW (7), length 4:
```

```
      100Mbps
    UnRsvBW (8), length 32:
        Priority 0, 100Mbps
        Priority 1, 100Mbps
        Priority 2, 100Mbps
        Priority 3, 100Mbps
        Priority 4, 100Mbps
        Priority 5, 100Mbps
        Priority 6, 100Mbps
        Priority 7, 100Mbps
    Color (9), length 4:
      0
```

The Opaque LSA describes a Fast Ethernet interface because the Link Type sub-TLV has a value of 2 and the maximum bandwidth displayed in sub-TLV 6 (MaxBW) shows 100Mbps. The Maximum Reservable Bandwidth (MaxRsvBW) and the Unreserved Bandwidth (UnRsvBW) sub-TLVs each are each reporting 100Mbps in their value portions, which means that the interface is not oversubscribed and no current bandwidth reservations are in place across the interface. The local IP address of the interface is 10.222.28.1, which is connected to the designated router address of 10.222.28.2. The connection to the designated router (DR) prompts the remote interface address to be set to all zeros. Finally, the Resource Class/Color sub-TLV displays a value of 0, which represents no current administrative group memberships.

IS-IS Traffic Engineering Extensions

IS-IS advertises traffic engineering information in the *Extended IS Reachability TLV*, whose type code is 22. The JUNOS software advertises this TLV by default for all operational IS-IS interfaces in a specific level. Its use within this context, as well as the format of the TLV, is discussed in Chapter 3, "Intermediate System to Intermediate System (IS-IS)." When a particular interface is also configured to support RSVP, the traffic engineering information is included in the Extended IS Reachability TLV in the form of sub-TLVs. The specific information contained in the sub-TLVs is as follows:

Administrative Group   The Administrative Group sub-TLV has a type code of 3 and a length of 4 octets. The value portion of the sub-TLV contains a 32-bit vector used to encode membership in various administrative groups. An individual interface may belong to multiple groups, in which case multiple bits are set within the bit vector.

IPv4 Interface Address   The IP address of the local router's interface is contained in the IPv4 Interface Address sub-TLV. It uses a type code of 6 and has a constant length of 4 octets.

IPv4 Neighbor Address   The IP address of the remote router's interface is contained in the IPv4 Neighbor Address sub-TLV. It uses a type code of 8 and has a constant length of 4 octets. When the interface is operating in an unnumbered fashion, the neighbor's router ID is placed in this field.

Maximum Link Bandwidth   The true bandwidth, in bytes per second, of the local router's interface is contained in the Maximum Link Bandwidth sub-TLV. It uses a type code of 9 and has a constant length of 4 octets.

Maximum Reservable Link Bandwidth   The Maximum Reservable Bandwidth sub-TLV displays the total amount of bandwidth, in bytes per second, available for reservations by the RSVP process. This value may be larger than the actual bandwidth of the interface to account for over-subscription of the interface. The sub-TLV has a type code of 10 and a constant length of 4 octets.

Unreserved Bandwidth   The Unreserved Bandwidth sub-TLV uses a type code of 11 and has a constant length of 32 octets. It displays the amount of bandwidth, in bytes per second, that is currently available for reservations on the local interface. This value is calculated for each of the eight priority levels used by the RSVP traffic engineering process. Each unreserved bandwidth value is reported in a 4-octet field.

Traffic Engineering Default Metric   The Traffic Engineering Default Metric sub-TLV has a type code of 18 and a length of 3 octets. It is advertised only when the interface metric to be used for traffic engineering purposes differs from the interface metric used by the normal IS-IS routing process. The use of the `te-metric` command in the JUNOS software allows you to administratively set this metric value.

The Sherry router is running IS-IS and has enabled RSVP to support traffic engineering within the network. The configuration of the router currently looks like this:

```
user@Sherry> show configuration protocols
rsvp {
    interface all;
}
mpls {
    interface all;
}
isis {
    level 1 disable;
    level 2 wide-metrics-only;
    interface ge-0/2/0.0 {
        level 2 te-metric 30;
    }
    interface all;
    interface fxp0.0 {
        disable;
    }
}
```

This configuration allows Sherry to include traffic engineering information within the Extended IS Reachability TLV. We can view this data by examining the details of the link-state PDU generated by Sherry:

```
user@Sherry> show isis database Sherry.00-00 extensive | find TLV
  TLVs:
```

```
Area address: 49.1111 (3)
Speaks: IP
Speaks: IPv6
IP router id: 192.168.16.1
IP address: 192.168.16.1
Hostname: Sherry
IS extended neighbor: Sangiovese.00, Metric: default 10
  IP address: 10.222.28.1
  Neighbor's IP address: 10.222.28.2
  Current reservable bandwidth:
    Priority 0 : 155.52Mbps
    Priority 1 : 155.52Mbps
    Priority 2 : 155.52Mbps
    Priority 3 : 155.52Mbps
    Priority 4 : 155.52Mbps
    Priority 5 : 155.52Mbps
    Priority 6 : 155.52Mbps
    Priority 7 : 155.52Mbps
  Maximum reservable bandwidth: 155.52Mbps
  Maximum bandwidth: 155.52Mbps
  Administrative groups:  0  <none>
IS extended neighbor: Chablis.00, Metric: default 10
  IP address: 10.222.5.1
  Neighbor's IP address: 10.222.5.2
  Current reservable bandwidth:
    Priority 0 : 155.52Mbps
    Priority 1 : 155.52Mbps
    Priority 2 : 155.52Mbps
    Priority 3 : 155.52Mbps
    Priority 4 : 155.52Mbps
    Priority 5 : 155.52Mbps
    Priority 6 : 155.52Mbps
    Priority 7 : 155.52Mbps
  Maximum reservable bandwidth: 155.52Mbps
  Maximum bandwidth: 155.52Mbps
  Administrative groups:  0  <none>
IS extended neighbor: Chianti.02, Metric: default 10
  IP address: 10.222.29.1
  Traffic engineering metric: 30
  Current reservable bandwidth:
```

```
        Priority 0 : 1000Mbps
        Priority 1 : 1000Mbps
        Priority 2 : 1000Mbps
        Priority 3 : 1000Mbps
        Priority 4 : 1000Mbps
        Priority 5 : 1000Mbps
        Priority 6 : 1000Mbps
        Priority 7 : 1000Mbps
    Maximum reservable bandwidth: 1000Mbps
    Maximum bandwidth: 1000Mbps
    Administrative groups:  0  <none>
  IP extended prefix: 10.222.28.0/24 metric 10 up
  IP extended prefix: 10.222.5.0/24 metric 10 up
  IP extended prefix: 10.222.29.0/24 metric 10 up
  IP extended prefix: 192.168.16.1/32 metric 0 up
No queued transmissions
```

We see that Sherry is adjacent with three other IS-IS routers in the network: Sangiovese, Chianti, and Chablis. Each of these adjacencies prompts Sherry to advertise a TLV into the network that contains the neighbor ID of the peer, the IS-IS metric used to reach that neighbor, and the interface addresses for both the local and remote routers. Each TLV also includes traffic engineering information pertinent to the type of physical interface being used. For example, the adjacency with the Sangiovese router is formed over an OC-3c interface because the `Maximum bandwidth` is reported to be 155.52Mbps. This bandwidth is also reported for both the `Current reservable bandwidth` and the `Maximum reservable bandwidth`, which tells us that the interface is not oversubscribed and that no current reservations are in place. This particular interface, as well as the other two, doesn't currently belong to any administrative groups. We see this in the `Administrative groups: 0` display output. Finally, the `ge-0/2/0.0` interface connected to the Chianti router has the `te-metric` set to 30 in the router's configuration. This prompts the TLV representing this adjacency to include the Traffic Engineering Default Metric sub-TLV. This special metric value is seen in the router output as `Traffic engineering metric: 30`. The other two router interfaces do not include this sub-TLV and use the default IS-IS metric value of 10 for the traffic engineering calculations.

CSPF Algorithm Steps

Once the TED is populated by the IGPs, RSVP consults it when a new LSP is configured on the ingress router. The router uses any defined constraints supplied by the user when running the CSPF algorithm. These constraints include bandwidth reservations, administrative groups, and priority values. The algorithm creates a logical copy of the TED and performs the following steps to locate a path through the network meeting the constraints of the LSP:

1. When a bandwidth reservation is requested for the LSP, the algorithm removes all links from the database that don't have enough unreserved bandwidth available at the setup priority level of the LSP.

2. When the LSP requires a network path that includes links belonging to an administrative group, the algorithm removes all links that don't contain the requested group value.

3. When the LSP requires a network path that excludes links belonging to an administrative group, the algorithm removes all links that currently contain the requested group value.

4. The algorithm calculates the shortest path from the ingress to the egress router using the remaining information in the database. When an explicit route is requested by the user, separate shortest-path calculations are performed. The first is run from the ingress router to the first hop in the route. The next is calculated from the first hop of the route to the next hop in the route, if one is defined. This step-by-step process is performed for each node defined in the route until the egress router is encountered.

5. When multiple equal-cost paths exist from the ingress to egress router, the path whose last-hop interface address matches the egress router address is selected. This algorithm step is helpful when the egress router address is not a loopback address.

6. If multiple equal-cost paths still exist, the algorithm selects the path with the fewest number of physical hops.

7. In the event that multiple equal-cost paths continue to exist, the algorithm selects one of the paths based on the load-balancing configuration of the LSP: random, most-fill, or least-fill.

8. The algorithm generates an ERO containing the physical interface address of each node along the path from ingress to egress router. This ERO is used by the RSVP process to signal and establish the LSP.

If multiple LSPs are committed at the same time, the CSPF algorithm calculates paths for the LSP with the highest setup priority, followed by LSPs with lower priority values. We discuss priority values in the section "LSP Priority and Preemption," later in the chapter.

Let's examine some of the user constraints used by CSPF in greater detail.

Administrative Groups

One aspect of traffic engineering is the ability to control what types of traffic use certain network links. One method for reaching this administrative goal is the use of *administrative groups*. The group values are used to control which LSPs are established across the specific network links. Once the LSPs are set up, you then control what types of traffic use those network connections.

Each network interface is configured with one or more group values, which are propagated via the IGPs and placed into the TED. These advertisements are encoded as individual bit positions using a bit vector system, as shown in Figure 8.2.

FIGURE 8.2   Administrative groups bit vector

| 1 | 1 | 0 | 0 | 0 | 0 | 0 | 0 | 0 | 0 | 0 | 0 | 0 | 0 | 0 | 0 | 0 | 0 | 0 | 0 | 0 | 0 | 0 | 0 | 0 | 0 | 0 | 0 | 1 | 1 | 1 | 0 |

FIGURE 8.3 Administrative groups sample network

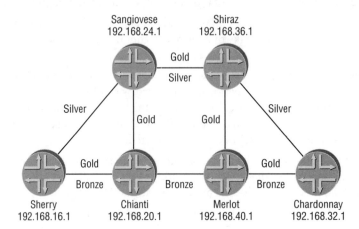

 NOTE A bit vector works in a fairly straightforward manner. Each group value is encoded as an individual bit. For example, a group value of 5 sets bit number 5 to a value of 1 in the vector. In a similar manner, a group value of 25 sets bit number 25 to a value of 1.

For ease of configuration and administration, the JUNOS software uses human-friendly names to locally represent the group values. These names are locally significant to the router because only the bit value is transmitted by the IGPs. Figure 8.3 shows a sample network with six routers running IS-IS and traffic engineering. The network administrators have defined certain links as Gold (a value of 2), others as Silver (a value of 15), and others as Bronze (a value of 28). The configuration of the Sherry router is currently set to

```
user@Sherry> show configuration protocols mpls
admin-groups {
    Gold 2;
    Silver 15;
    Bronze 28;
}
interface all;
interface at-0/1/0.0 {
    admin-group Silver;
}
interface ge-0/2/0.0 {
    admin-group [ Gold Bronze ];
}
```

This prompts Sherry to advertise the following traffic engineering information:

```
user@Sherry> show isis database Sherry.00-00 extensive | find TLV
  TLVs:
    Area address: 49.1111 (3)
    Speaks: IP
    Speaks: IPv6
    IP router id: 192.168.16.1
    IP address: 192.168.16.1
    Hostname: Sherry
    IS extended neighbor: Sangiovese.00, Metric: default 10
      IP address: 10.222.28.1
      Neighbor's IP address: 10.222.28.2
      Current reservable bandwidth:
        Priority 0 : 155.52Mbps
        Priority 1 : 155.52Mbps
        Priority 2 : 155.52Mbps
        Priority 3 : 155.52Mbps
        Priority 4 : 155.52Mbps
        Priority 5 : 155.52Mbps
        Priority 6 : 155.52Mbps
        Priority 7 : 155.52Mbps
      Maximum reservable bandwidth: 155.52Mbps
      Maximum bandwidth: 155.52Mbps
      Administrative groups:  0x8000  Silver
    IS extended neighbor: Chianti.02, Metric: default 10
      IP address: 10.222.29.1
      Traffic engineering metric: 30
      Current reservable bandwidth:
        Priority 0 : 1000Mbps
        Priority 1 : 1000Mbps
        Priority 2 : 1000Mbps
        Priority 3 : 1000Mbps
        Priority 4 : 1000Mbps
        Priority 5 : 1000Mbps
        Priority 6 : 1000Mbps
        Priority 7 : 1000Mbps
      Maximum reservable bandwidth: 1000Mbps
      Maximum bandwidth: 1000Mbps
      Administrative groups:  0x10000004  Bronze Gold
    IP extended prefix: 10.222.28.0/24 metric 10 up
```

```
    IP extended prefix: 10.222.29.0/24 metric 10 up
    IP extended prefix: 192.168.16.1/32 metric 0 up
  No queued transmissions
```

We examine the information in the TED directly through the show ted database command:

```
user@Sherry> show ted database Sherry.00 extensive
TED database: 8 ISIS nodes 6 INET nodes
NodeID: Sherry.00(192.168.16.1)
  Type: Rtr, Age: 284 secs, LinkIn: 2, LinkOut: 2
  Protocol: IS-IS(2)
    To: Sangiovese.00(192.168.24.1), Local: 10.222.28.1, Remote: 10.222.28.2
      Color: 0x8000 Silver
      Metric: 10
      Static BW: 155.52Mbps
      Reservable BW: 155.52Mbps
      Available BW [priority] bps:
        [0] 155.52Mbps    [1] 155.52Mbps    [2] 155.52Mbps    [3] 155.52Mbps
        [4] 155.52Mbps    [5] 155.52Mbps    [6] 155.52Mbps    [7] 155.52Mbps
      Interface Switching Capability Descriptor(1):
        Switching type: Packet
        Encoding type: Packet
        Maximum LSP BW [priority] bps:
          [0] 155.52Mbps    [1] 155.52Mbps    [2] 155.52Mbps    [3] 155.52Mbps
          [4] 155.52Mbps    [5] 155.52Mbps    [6] 155.52Mbps    [7] 155.52Mbps
    To: Chianti.02, Local: 10.222.29.1, Remote: 0.0.0.0
      Color: 0x10000004 Bronze Gold
      Metric: 30
      Static BW: 1000Mbps
      Reservable BW: 1000Mbps
      Available BW [priority] bps:
        [0] 1000Mbps    [1] 1000Mbps    [2] 1000Mbps    [3] 1000Mbps
        [4] 1000Mbps    [5] 1000Mbps    [6] 1000Mbps    [7] 1000Mbps
      Interface Switching Capability Descriptor(1):
        Switching type: Packet
        Encoding type: Packet
        Maximum LSP BW [priority] bps:
          [0] 1000Mbps    [1] 1000Mbps    [2] 1000Mbps    [3] 1000Mbps
          [4] 1000Mbps    [5] 1000Mbps    [6] 1000Mbps    [7] 1000Mbps
```

Both outputs report that the interface connected to the Sangiovese router is set with the group name of Silver. This administrative group is assigned to the 15th bit in the group vector, which results in the hexadecimal output of 0x8000.

> Remember that the least significant bit in the administrative group vector is bit position 0 and the most significant bit is position number 31.

The interface connecting Sherry to Chianti is currently assigned two administrative groups—Gold and Bronze. Both group values are present in the group vector by using the 0x10000004 notation to represent bit positions 28 and 2, respectively.

Once the network links have been assigned the appropriate groups values, we constrain the setup of an LSP by referencing the group names. The JUNOS software keyword of include means that the LSP may only use links that contain any one of the specified groups. For example, the **Sherry-to-Char** LSP is established from Sherry to Chardonnay using only links that belong to the Silver administrative group:

```
[edit protocols mpls]
user@Sherry# show label-switched-path Sherry-to-Char
to 192.168.32.1;
admin-group {
    include Silver;
}
```

The LSP transits the Sangiovese and Shiraz routers before terminating on Chardonnay. We can examine the received Record Route object (RRO) for the LSP and verify that these addresses belong to the appropriate routers:

```
user@Sherry> show mpls lsp detail ingress
Ingress LSP: 1 sessions

192.168.32.1
  From: 192.168.16.1, State: Up, ActiveRoute: 0, LSPname: Sherry-to-Char
  ActivePath:  (primary)
  LoadBalance: Random
  Encoding type: Packet, Switching type: Packet, GPID: IPv4
 *Primary                   State: Up
    Include: Silver
    Computed ERO (S [L] denotes strict [loose] hops): (CSPF metric: 30)
          10.222.28.2 S 10.222.4.2 S 10.222.44.2 S
    Received RRO:
          10.222.28.2 10.222.4.2 10.222.44.2
Total 1 displayed, Up 1, Down 0

user@Sangiovese> show route 10.222.28.2/32 terse
```

```
inet.0: 23 destinations, 23 routes (23 active, 0 holddown, 0 hidden)
+ = Active Route, - = Last Active, * = Both

A Destination        P Prf   Metric 1   Metric 2  Next hop       AS path
* 10.222.28.2/32     L   0                         Local

user@Shiraz> show route 10.222.4.2/32 terse

inet.0: 23 destinations, 23 routes (23 active, 0 holddown, 0 hidden)
+ = Active Route, - = Last Active, * = Both

A Destination        P Prf   Metric 1   Metric 2  Next hop       AS path
* 10.222.4.2/32      L   0                         Local

user@Chardonnay> show route 10.222.44.2/32 terse

inet.0: 24 destinations, 24 routes (24 active, 0 holddown, 0 hidden)
+ = Active Route, - = Last Active, * = Both

A Destination        P Prf   Metric 1   Metric 2  Next hop       AS path
* 10.222.44.2/32     L   0                         Local
```

In a similar manner, the ***Char-to-Sherry*** LSP is configured on the Chardonnay router to only use links belonging to the Gold administrative group. This LSP establishes across five separate links in the network:

```
[edit protocols mpls]
user@Chardonnay# show label-switched-path Char-to-Sherry
to 192.168.16.1;
admin-group {
    include Gold;
}


[edit protocols mpls]
user@Chardonnay# run show mpls lsp detail ingress
Ingress LSP: 1 sessions

192.168.16.1
  From: 192.168.32.1, State: Up, ActiveRoute: 0, LSPname: Char-to-Sherry
  ActivePath:  (primary)
  LoadBalance: Random
  Encoding type: Packet, Switching type: Packet, GPID: IPv4
 *Primary                   State: Up
```

```
Include: Gold
Computed ERO (S [L] denotes strict [loose] hops): (CSPF metric: 50)
      10.222.45.1 S 10.222.46.2 S 10.222.4.1 S 10.222.30.2 S 10.222.29.1 S
Received RRO:
      10.222.45.1 10.222.46.2 10.222.4.1 10.222.30.2 10.222.29.1
Total 1 displayed, Up 1, Down 0
```

An interesting problem occurs when we add the JUNOS keyword `exclude` to the ***Sherry-to-Char*** LSP on the Sherry router. The `exclude` command requires that the LSP not use any links that contain the specified group value. In this particular case, we inform the LSP to avoid the Gold links in the network. The configuration is updated to:

```
[edit protocols mpls]
user@Sherry# show label-switched-path Sherry-to-Char
to 192.168.32.1;
admin-group {
    include Silver;
    exclude Gold;
}
```

A quick look at the output of the `show mpls lsp ingress` command informs us that the LSP is no longer operational:

```
user@Sherry> show mpls lsp ingress
Ingress LSP: 1 sessions
To              From          State Rt ActivePath        P      LSPname
192.168.32.1    192.168.16.1  Dn    0 -                         Sherry-to-Char
Total 1 displayed, Up 0, Down 1
```

When we add the *extensive* option to the command, we can see the history log for the LSP:

```
user@Sherry> show mpls lsp ingress extensive
Ingress LSP: 1 sessions

192.168.32.1
  From: 192.168.16.1, State: Dn, ActiveRoute: 0, LSPname: Sherry-to-Char
  ActivePath: (none)
  LoadBalance: Random
  Encoding type: Packet, Switching type: Packet, GPID: IPv4
  Primary                     State: Dn
    Include: Silver    Exclude: Gold
    Will be enqueued for recomputation in 9 second(s).
    1 Jun  4 16:24:53  CSPF failed: no route toward 192.168.32.1[6 times]
  Created: Wed Jun  4 16:19:41 2003
Total 1 displayed, Up 0, Down 1
```

FIGURE 8.4 CSPF network pruning for include groups

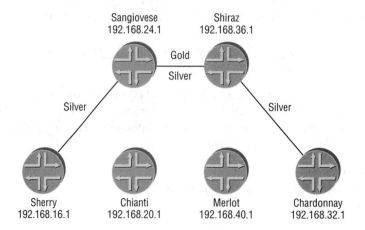

The CSPF failed: no route toward 192.168.32.1 output simply tells us that CSPF can't find a route from the ingress to egress routers, which also meets the constraints we provided. In this particular case we know that we've only asked for administrative group constraints, so we can consult the TED and examine the information each router is advertising to see why the LSP didn't set up. Instead of doing that here, let's take a graphical look at how CSPF operates.

Since we haven't requested any bandwidth reservations for the LSP, the algorithm first removes all network links that do not include the administrative group of Silver. The result of this database pruning is seen in Figure 8.4.

FIGURE 8.5 CSPF network pruning for exclude groups

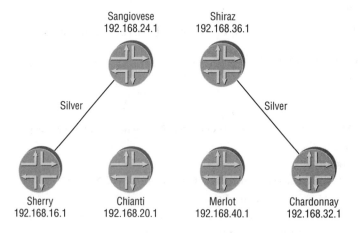

The algorithm then removes all links from the database that currently contain the excluded administrative group of Gold. The remaining links that meet the constraints are seen in Figure 8.5. At this point, CSPF then attempts to find a shortest path from the ingress to the egress router. Clearly, there is no connectivity between these two routers using the constraints, so the LSP is not established in the network.

LSP Priority and Preemption

During our discussion of the steps performed by the CSPF algorithm, we referred to the priority of the LSP. In reality, each LSP has two distinct values it uses: a setup and a hold priority. The *setup priority* value is used to determine if enough bandwidth is available at that priority level (between 0 and 7) to establish the LSP. The *hold priority* value is used by an established LSP to retain its bandwidth reservations in the network. As a backdrop for discussing these priority values, let's examine the information injected into the TED by the Sherry router in Figure 8.3:

```
user@Sherry> show ted database Sherry.00 extensive | find Chianti
    To: Chianti.02, Local: 10.222.29.1, Remote: 0.0.0.0
      Color: 0 <none>
      Metric: 10
      Static BW: 1000Mbps
      Reservable BW: 1000Mbps
      Available BW [priority] bps:
        [0] 1000Mbps     [1] 1000Mbps     [2] 1000Mbps     [3] 1000Mbps
        [4] 1000Mbps     [5] 1000Mbps     [6] 1000Mbps     [7] 1000Mbps
      Interface Switching Capability Descriptor(1):
        Switching type: Packet
        Encoding type: Packet
        Maximum LSP BW [priority] bps:
          [0] 1000Mbps     [1] 1000Mbps     [2] 1000Mbps     [3] 1000Mbps
          [4] 1000Mbps     [5] 1000Mbps     [6] 1000Mbps     [7] 1000Mbps
```

Each of the router interfaces is reporting available bandwidth values at each of the eight priority levels, with priority level 0 being the best and level 7 the worst. When you configure an LSP for a bandwidth reservation, the CSPF algorithm consults the bandwidth availability at the priority level corresponding to the LSP's setup priority value. By default, all LSPs created by the JUNOS software receive a setup priority value of 7, so the bandwidth at the lowest level is consulted. This default setting ensures that a newly establishing LSP doesn't consume bandwidth from an established LSP. Once CSPF finds a path through the network and creates the strict-hop ERO, the RSVP signaling process establishes the path. As the Resv message travels upstream to the ingress, the actual bandwidth on each interface is reserved at the LSP's hold priority value, which is 0 by default, as well as all of the lower priority values. This ensures that an established LSP can't have its bandwidth reservations taken away by a new LSP in the network. Once the bandwidth reservation has been accounted for on each router, updated TED information is generated and propagated throughout the network.

By default, the JUNOS software advertises TED information after a change of 10 percent of the interface's available bandwidth. You can alter this percentage between 1 and 20 percent with the update-threshold command. This is applied to individual interfaces within the [edit protocols rsvp] configuration hierarchy.

Using Figure 8.3 as a guide, we configure an LSP on the Sherry router to reserve 100Mbps of bandwidth along the network path through Chianti. The configuration of the LSP looks like this:

```
user@Sherry> show configuration protocols mpls
label-switched-path Sherry-to-Char {
    to 192.168.32.1;
    bandwidth 100m;
    primary via-Chianti;
}
path via-Chianti {
    192.168.20.1 loose;
}
interface all;
```

After verifying that the LSP is operational, we examine the TED information advertised by Sherry to the network:

```
user@Sherry> show mpls lsp ingress
Ingress LSP: 1 sessions
To              From            State Rt ActivePath      P     LSPname
192.168.32.1    192.168.16.1    Up      0 via-Chianti    *     Sherry-to-Char
Total 1 displayed, Up 1, Down 0

user@Sherry> show ted database Sherry.00 extensive | find Chianti
    To: Chianti.02, Local: 10.222.29.1, Remote: 0.0.0.0
      Color: 0 <none>
      Metric: 10
      Static BW: 1000Mbps
      Reservable BW: 1000Mbps
      Available BW [priority] bps:
       [0] 900Mbps      [1] 900Mbps      [2] 900Mbps      [3] 900Mbps
       [4] 900Mbps      [5] 900Mbps      [6] 900Mbps      [7] 900Mbps
      Interface Switching Capability Descriptor(1):
       Switching type: Packet
       Encoding type: Packet
       Maximum LSP BW [priority] bps:
        [0] 900Mbps      [1] 900Mbps      [2] 900Mbps      [3] 900Mbps
        [4] 900Mbps      [5] 900Mbps      [6] 900Mbps      [7] 900Mbps
```

LSP Priority Values

When you have a requirement to alter the default setup and hold priority values, it is a recommended good practice to configure them to the same value. This makes troubleshooting easier for operations personnel and provides an easy method for evaluating which LSP is more important than a second LSP. For example, an LSP with a priority setting of 1 1 will clearly preempt an LSP with a priority setting of 5 5.

Technically speaking, the priority values may be different, but the setup value must always be equal to or less than the hold priority. To illustrate why this restriction is in place, suppose that both LSP-1 and LSP-2 have their priority values set to 2 5. This means that the setup priority is 2 while the hold priority is 5. When LSP-1 is established in the network, it examines the bandwidth reservations at priority level 2 but only places a reservation at level 5 and below. The ingress router now attempts to establish LSP-2 and examines the bandwidth reservations at priority level 2. Since enough bandwidth is available in the network, the LSP is established and preempts LSP-1 from the network. However, the bandwidth reservation for LSP-2 is also only made at level 5 and below. LSP-1 now reattempts to establish itself and sees available bandwidth at priority level 2 and preempts LSP-2 from the network. This vicious cycle continues repeating itself, with one LSP preempting the other over and over again. To prevent this situation from ever occurring, the setup priority must be equal to or less than the hold priority.

The TED information reports that 100Mbps of bandwidth was reserved at all eight priority levels along the link between Sherry and Chianti. This correlates to the default setup and hold values of 7 and 0, respectively.

The JUNOS software provides you with the ability to designate some LSPs as being more important than others by manually configuring the priority values via the `priority` command. This means that you could have a new LSP *preempt* an established LSP from the network when there is contention for bandwidth resources. For example, suppose that all of the network links are Fast Ethernet connections and that an LSP is established with a bandwidth reservation of 90Mbps. When the default priority values are used, any new LSP requesting a bandwidth value greater than 10Mbps won't be established in the network. Now suppose that the 90Mbps established LSP has a hold priority of 3. Any new LSP with a setup priority value of 2 or better, regardless of its requested bandwidth amount, will be able to set up in the network. In this situation, the 90Mbps LSP is said to be preempted from the network by a higher priority LSP. See the sidebar "LSP Priority Values" to learn how this works in further detail.

The Sherry router now configures an LSP called *low-pri-LSP* along the network path through Sangiovese. This LSP is requesting a bandwidth reservation of 80Mbps and has its setup and hold priority values both set to 3. Its configuration looks like this:

```
user@Sherry> show configuration protocols mpls
label-switched-path Sherry-to-Char {
    to 192.168.32.1;
    bandwidth 100m;
```

```
        primary via-Chianti;
}
label-switched-path low-pri-LSP {
    to 192.168.32.1;
    bandwidth 80m;
    priority 3 3;
    primary via-Sangiovese;
}
path via-Chianti {
    192.168.20.1 loose;
}
path via-Sangiovese {
    192.168.24.1 loose;
}
interface all;
```

In addition to establishing the LSP, the 80Mbps of bandwidth reservation is removed from the links along the LSP's path. Specifically, the link between Sherry and Sangiovese now reports only 75.52Mbps of available bandwidth at the lower priority levels:

```
user@Sherry> show mpls lsp ingress name low-pri-LSP
Ingress LSP: 2 sessions
To              From            State Rt ActivePath        P    LSPname
192.168.32.1    192.168.16.1    Up     0 via-Sangiovese    *    low-pri-LSP
Total 1 displayed, Up 1, Down 0


user@Sherry> show ted database Sherry.00 extensive
TED database: 11 ISIS nodes 9 INET nodes
NodeID: Sherry.00(192.168.16.1)
  Type: Rtr, Age: 225 secs, LinkIn: 2, LinkOut: 2
  Protocol: IS-IS(2)
    To: Sangiovese.00(192.168.24.1), Local: 10.222.28.1, Remote: 10.222.28.2
      Color: 0 <none>
      Metric: 10
      Static BW: 155.52Mbps
      Reservable BW: 155.52Mbps
      Available BW [priority] bps:
        [0] 155.52Mbps    [1] 155.52Mbps    [2] 155.52Mbps    [3] 75.52Mbps
        [4] 75.52Mbps     [5] 75.52Mbps     [6] 75.52Mbps     [7] 75.52Mbps
      Interface Switching Capability Descriptor(1):
        Switching type: Packet
        Encoding type: Packet
```

```
            Maximum LSP BW [priority] bps:
              [0] 155.52Mbps    [1] 155.52Mbps    [2] 155.52Mbps    [3] 75.52Mbps
              [4] 75.52Mbps     [5] 75.52Mbps     [6] 75.52Mbps     [7] 75.52Mbps
       To: Chianti.02, Local: 10.222.29.1, Remote: 0.0.0.0
         Color: 0 <none>
         Metric: 10
         Static BW: 1000Mbps
         Reservable BW: 1000Mbps
         Available BW [priority] bps:
           [0] 900Mbps        [1] 900Mbps        [2] 900Mbps        [3] 900Mbps
           [4] 900Mbps        [5] 900Mbps        [6] 900Mbps        [7] 900Mbps
         Interface Switching Capability Descriptor(1):
           Switching type: Packet
           Encoding type: Packet
           Maximum LSP BW [priority] bps:
             [0] 900Mbps        [1] 900Mbps        [2] 900Mbps        [3] 900Mbps
             [4] 900Mbps        [5] 900Mbps        [6] 900Mbps        [7] 900Mbps
```

A new LSP, called *high-pri-LSP*, is now created on the Sherry router. While it is requesting 90Mbps of bandwidth, it is also using the default priority values:

```
user@Sherry> show configuration protocols mpls
label-switched-path Sherry-to-Char {
    to 192.168.32.1;
    bandwidth 100m;
    primary via-Chianti;
}
label-switched-path low-pri-LSP {
    to 192.168.32.1;
    bandwidth 80m;
    priority 3 3;
    primary via-Sangiovese;
}
label-switched-path high-pri-LSP {
    to 192.168.32.1;
    bandwidth 90m;
    primary via-Sangiovese;
}
path via-Chianti {
    192.168.20.1 loose;
}
```

```
path via-Sangiovese {
    192.168.24.1 loose;
}
interface all;
```

Because the new LSP is using a setup priority value of 7, only the available bandwidth at that level is evaluated in the TED. This means that not enough capacity is available for the new LSP to establish itself and that it is currently in a Down state:

```
user@Sherry> show mpls lsp ingress name high-pri-LSP
Ingress LSP: 3 sessions
To              From            State Rt ActivePath      P      LSPname
192.168.32.1    0.0.0.0         Dn    0 -                      high-pri-LSP
Total 1 displayed, Up 0, Down 1
```

The network administrators have decided that the **high-pri-LSP** LSP should have better access to the network's resources, so they have assigned it a setup and hold priority value of 1:

```
user@Sherry> show configuration protocols mpls | find high-pri-LSP
label-switched-path high-pri-LSP {
    to 192.168.32.1;
    bandwidth 90m;
    priority 1 1;
    primary via-Sangiovese;
}
path via-Chianti {
    192.168.20.1 loose;
}
path via-Sangiovese {
    192.168.24.1 loose;
}
interface all;
```

The LSP is now fully established in the network and the Sherry router has altered its TED information to reflect the new bandwidth reservation:

```
user@Sherry> show mpls lsp ingress name high-pri-LSP
Ingress LSP: 3 sessions
To              From            State Rt ActivePath      P      LSPname
192.168.32.1    192.168.16.1    Up    0 via-Sangiovese   *      high-pri-LSP
Total 1 displayed, Up 1, Down 0


user@Sherry> show ted database Sherry.00 extensive
TED database: 11 ISIS nodes 9 INET nodes
```

```
NodeID: Sherry.00(192.168.16.1)
  Type: Rtr, Age: 108 secs, LinkIn: 2, LinkOut: 2
  Protocol: IS-IS(2)
    To: Sangiovese.00(192.168.24.1), Local: 10.222.28.1, Remote: 10.222.28.2
      Color: 0 <none>
      Metric: 10
      Static BW: 155.52Mbps
      Reservable BW: 155.52Mbps
      Available BW [priority] bps:
        [0] 155.52Mbps    [1] 65.52Mbps    [2] 65.52Mbps    [3] 65.52Mbps
        [4] 65.52Mbps     [5] 65.52Mbps    [6] 65.52Mbps    [7] 65.52Mbps
      Interface Switching Capability Descriptor(1):
        Switching type: Packet
        Encoding type: Packet
        Maximum LSP BW [priority] bps:
          [0] 155.52Mbps   [1] 65.52Mbps   [2] 65.52Mbps   [3] 65.52Mbps
          [4] 65.52Mbps    [5] 65.52Mbps   [6] 65.52Mbps   [7] 65.52Mbps
    To: Chianti.02, Local: 10.222.29.1, Remote: 0.0.0.0
      Color: 0 <none>
      Metric: 10
      Static BW: 1000Mbps
      Reservable BW: 1000Mbps
      Available BW [priority] bps:
        [0] 900Mbps      [1] 900Mbps      [2] 900Mbps      [3] 900Mbps
        [4] 900Mbps      [5] 900Mbps      [6] 900Mbps      [7] 900Mbps
      Interface Switching Capability Descriptor(1):
        Switching type: Packet
        Encoding type: Packet
        Maximum LSP BW [priority] bps:
          [0] 900Mbps      [1] 900Mbps      [2] 900Mbps      [3] 900Mbps
          [4] 900Mbps      [5] 900Mbps      [6] 900Mbps      [7] 900Mbps
```

In addition to seeing that the *low-pri-LSP* is in a Down state, we can locate further information by examining the output of the show mpls lsp extensive command. Within the LSP history portion, we see that the LSP was preempted from the network with the Session preempted output:

```
user@Sherry> show mpls lsp ingress
Ingress LSP: 3 sessions
To             From           State Rt ActivePath      P    LSPname
192.168.32.1   192.168.16.1   Dn    0  -                    low-pri-LSP
192.168.32.1   192.168.16.1   Up    0  via-Sangiovese   *   high-pri-LSP
192.168.32.1   192.168.16.1   Up    0  via-Chianti      *   Sherry-to-Char
```

Total 3 displayed, Up 2, Down 1

```
user@Sherry> show mpls lsp extensive ingress name low-pri-LSP
Ingress LSP: 3 sessions

192.168.32.1
  From: 192.168.16.1, State: Dn, ActiveRoute: 0, LSPname: low-pri-LSP
  ActivePath: (none)
  LoadBalance: Random
  Encoding type: Packet, Switching type: Packet, GPID: IPv4
  Primary   via-Sangiovese   State: Dn
    Priorities: 3 3
    Bandwidth: 80Mbps
    Will be enqueued for recomputation in 28 second(s).
   15 Jun  4 23:48:20  CSPF failed: no route toward 192.168.32.1[21 times]
   14 Jun  4 23:38:46  Clear Call
   13 Jun  4 23:38:46  Deselected as active
   12 Jun  4 23:38:46  10.222.28.2: Requested bandwidth unavailable
   11 Jun  4 23:38:46  ResvTear received
   10 Jun  4 23:38:46  Down
    9 Jun  4 23:38:46  Change in active path
    8 Jun  4 23:38:46  10.222.4.2: Requested bandwidth unavailable
    7 Jun  4 23:38:46  CSPF failed: no route toward 192.168.32.1
    6 Jun  4 23:38:46  10.222.4.2: Session preempted
    5 Jun  4 23:25:29  Selected as active path
    4 Jun  4 23:25:29  Record Route:   10.222.28.2 10.222.4.2 10.222.44.2
    3 Jun  4 23:25:29  Up
    2 Jun  4 23:25:29  Originate Call
    1 Jun  4 23:25:29  CSPF: computation result accepted
  Created: Wed Jun  4 23:22:27 2003
Total 1 displayed, Up 0, Down 1
```

LSP Traffic Protection

When an established LSP experiences a failure and is torn down, the traffic that was transiting the LSP begins to be forwarded using native IPv4 lookups in the network. While this may not sound catastrophic, many network administrators prefer to always use an LSP for forwarding traffic. The reasons for this desire range from collecting accurate statistics for billing to guaranteeing levels of service to meet contractual arrangements. Within the JUNOS software, there are three methods for protecting traffic in the network. These include the use of primary paths, secondary paths, and fast reroute. Let's examine each in some detail.

Primary LSP Paths

As this point in your JUNOS software education, you're already aware of primary paths and have configured them on an LSP. After all, this is the method for assigning a user-defined ERO to an LSP. However, much more goes along with a primary path than this. This path definition may contain multiple user constraints, such as bandwidth reservations, priority values, user-defined EROs, and administrative groups. When the CSPF algorithm evaluates the TED, it uses the constraints provided within the primary path to locate a usable path.

An individual LSP can have zero or one *primary path* applied. When it is configured, the path must be used if it's available in the network. This means that the primary path carries with it a *revertive* capability. To better explain what this means, assume that an LSP is established in the network using a primary path. At some point, one of the path's links fails and the LSP is moved to a backup network path. When the primary path once again becomes usable, the LSP will reestablish along that path.

The revertive capability of the primary path is controlled by two configuration variables. The `retry-timer` controls the length of time that the ingress router waits between attempts to reestablish the primary path, and the `retry-limit` controls how many times the ingress attempts this reestablishment. The default value for the `retry-timer` is 30 seconds and can be set between 1 and 600 seconds (10 minutes). Once the primary path is reestablished, the ingress router waits for two instances of the timer to expire before actually using the primary path. This prevents potential thrashing in the network by ensuring that the new path is stable for a period of time before its use. By default, the JUNOS software sets the `retry-limit` to a value of 0, which means that the ingress router continually attempts to reestablish the primary path. You can set the limit to as high as 10,000, at which point the ingress router stops attempting to reestablish the path. If a viable network path becomes available after the limit is reached, you must manually clear the LSP on the ingress router to once again use the primary path.

FIGURE 8.6 Primary/secondary paths sample network

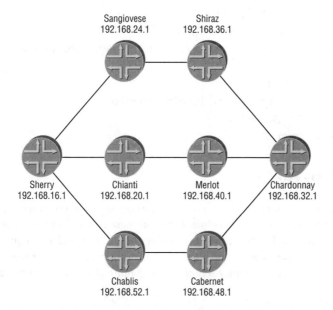

Figure 8.6 shows a network consisting of eight routers in an MPLS network. The ***Sherry-to-Char*** LSP is configured on the Sherry router with a primary path defined that reserves 20Mbps of bandwidth. The path definition also applies a user-defined ERO called ***via-Chablis***, which lists the loopback address of the Chablis router as a loose hop. Here is the configuration of the LSP:

```
[edit protocols mpls]
user@Sherry# show label-switched-path Sherry-to-Char
to 192.168.32.1;
primary via-Chablis {
    bandwidth 20m;
}
```

The LSP is operational and is using Chablis as a transit router:

```
user@Sherry> show mpls lsp extensive ingress
Ingress LSP: 1 sessions

192.168.32.1
  From: 192.168.16.1, State: Up, ActiveRoute: 0, LSPname: Sherry-to-Char
  ActivePath: via-Chablis (primary)
  LoadBalance: Random
  Encoding type: Packet, Switching type: Packet, GPID: IPv4
 *Primary    via-Chablis       State: Up
    Bandwidth: 20Mbps
    Computed ERO (S [L] denotes strict [loose] hops): (CSPF metric: 30)
          10.222.5.2 S 10.222.60.2 S 10.222.6.2 S
    Received RRO:
          10.222.5.2 10.222.60.2 10.222.6.2
    5 Jun  6 14:35:50  Selected as active path
    4 Jun  6 14:35:50  Record Route:  10.222.5.2 10.222.60.2 10.222.6.2
    3 Jun  6 14:35:50  Up
    2 Jun  6 14:35:50  Originate Call
    1 Jun  6 14:35:50  CSPF: computation result accepted
  Created: Fri Jun  6 14:34:19 2003
Total 1 displayed, Up 1, Down 0
```

Secondary LSP Paths

An individual LSP may define one or more secondary paths to provide for the continual forwarding of traffic should the primary path experience a failure. Each configured *secondary path* may contain multiple user constraints for use by the CSPF algorithm, and each path is treated in an equal manner by the LSP. This means that the path definitions don't carry with them any inherent priority for being established first. When the ingress router is notified of a failure along the primary path, it attempts to establish the first secondary path it locates in the configuration. Once this secondary path is established, user traffic again uses the LSP for forwarding across the network.

The **Sherry-to-Char** LSP is now configured with a secondary path named **via-Chianti**. This path definition requests a bandwidth reservation of 10Mbps from the network and assigns an ERO, which prompts the path to use Chianti as a transit router:

```
[edit protocols mpls]
user@Sherry# show label-switched-path Sherry-to-Char
to 192.168.32.1;
primary via-Chablis {
    bandwidth 20m;
}
secondary via-Chianti {
    bandwidth 10m;
}
```

Once the configuration is committed, the secondary path is known to the LSP. We can see this information in the output of the show mpls lsp extensive ingress command, where the secondary path appears after the primary path:

```
user@Sherry> show mpls lsp extensive ingress
Ingress LSP: 1 sessions

192.168.32.1
  From: 192.168.16.1, State: Up, ActiveRoute: 0, LSPname: Sherry-to-Char
  ActivePath: via-Chablis (primary)
  LoadBalance: Random
  Encoding type: Packet, Switching type: Packet, GPID: IPv4
 *Primary   via-Chablis     State: Up
    Bandwidth: 20Mbps
    Computed ERO (S [L] denotes strict [loose] hops): (CSPF metric: 30)
          10.222.5.2 S 10.222.60.2 S 10.222.6.2 S
    Received RRO:
          10.222.5.2 10.222.60.2 10.222.6.2
   5 Jun  6 14:51:54  Selected as active path
   4 Jun  6 14:51:54  Record Route:   10.222.5.2 10.222.60.2 10.222.6.2
   3 Jun  6 14:51:54  Up
   2 Jun  6 14:51:54  Originate Call
   1 Jun  6 14:51:54  CSPF: computation result accepted
  Secondary via-Chianti       State: Dn
    Bandwidth: 10Mbps
        No computed ERO.
  Created: Fri Jun  6 14:50:03 2003
Total 1 displayed, Up 1, Down 0
```

The secondary path is currently not operational, as reported by the State: Dn output. This is the normal operating state for a secondary path when the primary path is functioning. The ActivePath: portion of the router output provides a clue as to which path the LSP is using to forward traffic across the network. In a similar manner to the routing table, the presence of the asterisk (*) next to the path definition tells us that the primary path is the active path.

When the network link between Chianti and Cabernet in Figure 8.6 fails, the primary path of the LSP is torn down. This prompts the ingress router to establish the secondary path through the Chianti router:

```
user@Sherry> show mpls lsp extensive ingress
Ingress LSP: 1 sessions

192.168.32.1
  From: 192.168.16.1, State: Up, ActiveRoute: 0, LSPname: Sherry-to-Char
  ActivePath: via-Chianti (secondary)
  LoadBalance: Random
  Encoding type: Packet, Switching type: Packet, GPID: IPv4
  Primary   via-Chablis       State: Dn
    Bandwidth: 20Mbps
    Will be enqueued for recomputation in 6 second(s).
   14 Jun  6 14:59:40  CSPF failed: no route toward 192.168.32.1[2 times]
   13 Jun  6 14:59:37  Clear Call
   12 Jun  6 14:59:37  CSPF: link down/deleted 10.222.60.1(Chablis.00/
  192.168.52.1)->10.222.60.2(Cabernet.00/192.168.48.1)
   11 Jun  6 14:59:37  Deselected as active
   10 Jun  6 14:59:37  ResvTear received
    9 Jun  6 14:59:37  Down
    8 Jun  6 14:59:37  Change in active path
    7 Jun  6 14:59:37  CSPF failed: no route toward 192.168.32.1
    6 Jun  6 14:59:37  10.222.5.2: No Route toward dest
    5 Jun  6 14:51:54  Selected as active path
    4 Jun  6 14:51:54  Record Route:   10.222.5.2 10.222.60.2 10.222.6.2
    3 Jun  6 14:51:54  Up
    2 Jun  6 14:51:54  Originate Call
    1 Jun  6 14:51:54  CSPF: computation result accepted
 *Secondary via-Chianti       State: Up
    Bandwidth: 10Mbps
    Computed ERO (S [L] denotes strict [loose] hops): (CSPF metric: 30)
          10.222.29.2 S 10.222.1.2 S 10.222.45.2 S
    Received RRO:
          10.222.29.2 10.222.1.2 10.222.45.2
```

```
 5 Jun  6 14:59:37  Selected as active path
 4 Jun  6 14:59:37  Record Route:   10.222.29.2 10.222.1.2 10.222.45.2
 3 Jun  6 14:59:37  Up
 2 Jun  6 14:59:37  Originate Call
 1 Jun  6 14:59:37  CSPF: computation result accepted
   Created: Fri Jun  6 14:51:44 2003
Total 1 displayed, Up 1, Down 0
```

NOTE The output of the CSPF: link down/deleted history entry exceeds the 80-character limit of most terminal windows. It is included here in its entirety for completeness. Future router output will truncate the entry for readability.

The router output tells us that the primary path is currently down and the secondary path is in an Up state. When the ingress router received the `ResvTear` message from its neighbor, it cleared the primary path from the network. It then ran the CSPF algorithm using the constraints provided by the secondary path and found a usable set of links that met the constraints. The resulting ERO from the CSPF calculation was passed to the RSVP process and the secondary path was signaled. Once it became established, the router once again used it for forwarding user traffic across the network.

After clearing the primary path, the ingress router begins the 30-second retry timer for the path. When it expires, the CSPF algorithm is run in an attempt to locate a new path for the primary to use. After two unsuccessful attempts, the Sherry router finds the Chablis-Cabernet link restored and the primary path is re-signaled:

```
user@Sherry> show mpls lsp extensive ingress
Ingress LSP: 1 sessions

192.168.32.1
  From: 192.168.16.1, State: Up, ActiveRoute: 0, LSPname: Sherry-to-Char
  ActivePath: via-Chianti (secondary)
  LoadBalance: Random
  Encoding type: Packet, Switching type: Packet, GPID: IPv4
  Primary   via-Chablis     State: Up
    Bandwidth: 20Mbps
    Computed ERO (S [L] denotes strict [loose] hops): (CSPF metric: 30)
         10.222.5.2 S 10.222.60.2 S 10.222.6.2 S
    Received RRO:
         10.222.5.2 10.222.60.2 10.222.6.2
   18 Jun  6 15:00:09  Record Route:   10.222.5.2 10.222.60.2 10.222.6.2
   17 Jun  6 15:00:09  Up
   16 Jun  6 15:00:09  Originate Call
```

```
15  Jun   6 15:00:09   CSPF: computation result accepted
14  Jun   6 14:59:40   CSPF failed: no route toward 192.168.32.1[2 times]
13  Jun   6 14:59:37   Clear Call
12  Jun   6 14:59:37   CSPF: link down/deleted 10.222.60.1(Chablis.00/
11  Jun   6 14:59:37   Deselected as active
10  Jun   6 14:59:37   ResvTear received
 9  Jun   6 14:59:37   Down
 8  Jun   6 14:59:37   Change in active path
 7  Jun   6 14:59:37   CSPF failed: no route toward 192.168.32.1
 6  Jun   6 14:59:37   10.222.5.2: No Route toward dest
 5  Jun   6 14:51:54   Selected as active path
 4  Jun   6 14:51:54   Record Route:   10.222.5.2 10.222.60.2 10.222.6.2
 3  Jun   6 14:51:54   Up
 2  Jun   6 14:51:54   Originate Call
 1  Jun   6 14:51:54   CSPF: computation result accepted
*Secondary via-Chianti        State: Up
   Bandwidth: 10Mbps
   Computed ERO (S [L] denotes strict [loose] hops): (CSPF metric: 30)
         10.222.29.2 S 10.222.1.2 S 10.222.45.2 S
   Received RRO:
         10.222.29.2 10.222.1.2 10.222.45.2
 5  Jun   6 14:59:37   Selected as active path
 4  Jun   6 14:59:37   Record Route:   10.222.29.2 10.222.1.2 10.222.45.2
 3  Jun   6 14:59:37   Up
 2  Jun   6 14:59:37   Originate Call
 1  Jun   6 14:59:37   CSPF: computation result accepted
   Created: Fri Jun  6 14:51:34 2003
Total 1 displayed, Up 1, Down 0
```

Even though the primary path is now in an Up state, the secondary path is still the active path for the LSP. This is due to the waiting period imposed by the JUNOS software before using a newly established primary path. This period is defined as two iterations of the `retry-timer` setting, set to 30 seconds in our case. In reality, you might not always see the router wait for exactly 60 seconds. This has to do with the randomization of the timers within the router as well as when the LSP references the timer value. In this particular example, it appears as if the ingress router waited 29 seconds before selecting the primary path as the active path for the LSP:

```
user@Sherry> show mpls lsp extensive ingress
Ingress LSP: 1 sessions

192.168.32.1
  From: 192.168.16.1, State: Up, ActiveRoute: 0, LSPname: Sherry-to-Char
  ActivePath: via-Chablis (primary)
```

```
LoadBalance: Random
Encoding type: Packet, Switching type: Packet, GPID: IPv4
*Primary   via-Chablis      State: Up
   Bandwidth: 20Mbps
   Computed ERO (S [L] denotes strict [loose] hops): (CSPF metric: 30)
        10.222.5.2 S 10.222.60.2 S 10.222.6.2 S
   Received RRO:
        10.222.5.2 10.222.60.2 10.222.6.2
   19 Jun  6 15:00:38  Selected as active path
   18 Jun  6 15:00:09  Record Route:  10.222.5.2 10.222.60.2 10.222.6.2
   17 Jun  6 15:00:09  Up
   16 Jun  6 15:00:09  Originate Call
   15 Jun  6 15:00:09  CSPF: computation result accepted
   14 Jun  6 14:59:40  CSPF failed: no route toward 192.168.32.1[2 times]
   13 Jun  6 14:59:37  Clear Call
   12 Jun  6 14:59:37  CSPF: link down/deleted 10.222.60.1(Chablis.00/
   11 Jun  6 14:59:37  Deselected as active
   10 Jun  6 14:59:37  ResvTear received
    9 Jun  6 14:59:37  Down
    8 Jun  6 14:59:37  Change in active path
    7 Jun  6 14:59:37  CSPF failed: no route toward 192.168.32.1
    6 Jun  6 14:59:37  10.222.5.2: No Route toward dest
    5 Jun  6 14:51:54  Selected as active path
    4 Jun  6 14:51:54  Record Route:  10.222.5.2 10.222.60.2 10.222.6.2
    3 Jun  6 14:51:54  Up
    2 Jun  6 14:51:54  Originate Call
    1 Jun  6 14:51:54  CSPF: computation result accepted
 Secondary via-Chianti      State: Up
   Bandwidth: 10Mbps
   Computed ERO (S [L] denotes strict [loose] hops): (CSPF metric: 30)
        10.222.29.2 S 10.222.1.2 S 10.222.45.2 S
   Received RRO:
        10.222.29.2 10.222.1.2 10.222.45.2
    6 Jun  6 15:00:38  Deselected as active
    5 Jun  6 14:59:37  Selected as active path
    4 Jun  6 14:59:37  Record Route:  10.222.29.2 10.222.1.2 10.222.45.2
    3 Jun  6 14:59:37  Up
    2 Jun  6 14:59:37  Originate Call
    1 Jun  6 14:59:37  CSPF: computation result accepted
   Created: Fri Jun  6 14:51:08 2003
Total 1 displayed, Up 1, Down 0
```

It is interesting to note that the secondary path is still in an **Up** state. In fact, the router uses the same waiting period for clearing the secondary path as it used for activating the primary path. This helps to ensure a quicker recovery time in case the primary path rapidly fails after being selected as active. In our example, it appears as if the router waits for 1 minute and 29 seconds before removing the secondary path from the network:

```
user@Sherry> show mpls lsp extensive ingress
Ingress LSP: 1 sessions

192.168.32.1
  From: 192.168.16.1, State: Up, ActiveRoute: 0, LSPname: Sherry-to-Char
  ActivePath: via-Chablis (primary)
  LoadBalance: Random
  Encoding type: Packet, Switching type: Packet, GPID: IPv4
 *Primary   via-Chablis      State: Up
    Bandwidth: 20Mbps
    Computed ERO (S [L] denotes strict [loose] hops): (CSPF metric: 30)
          10.222.5.2 S 10.222.60.2 S 10.222.6.2 S
    Received RRO:
          10.222.5.2 10.222.60.2 10.222.6.2
   19 Jun  6 15:00:38  Selected as active path
   18 Jun  6 15:00:09  Record Route:   10.222.5.2 10.222.60.2 10.222.6.2
   17 Jun  6 15:00:09  Up
   16 Jun  6 15:00:09  Originate Call
   15 Jun  6 15:00:09  CSPF: computation result accepted
   14 Jun  6 14:59:40  CSPF failed: no route toward 192.168.32.1[2 times]
   13 Jun  6 14:59:37  Clear Call
   12 Jun  6 14:59:37  CSPF: link down/deleted 10.222.60.1(Chablis.00/
   11 Jun  6 14:59:37  Deselected as active
   10 Jun  6 14:59:37  ResvTear received
    9 Jun  6 14:59:37  Down
    8 Jun  6 14:59:37  Change in active path
    7 Jun  6 14:59:37  CSPF failed: no route toward 192.168.32.1
    6 Jun  6 14:59:37  10.222.5.2: No Route toward dest
    5 Jun  6 14:51:54  Selected as active path
    4 Jun  6 14:51:54  Record Route:   10.222.5.2 10.222.60.2 10.222.6.2
    3 Jun  6 14:51:54  Up
    2 Jun  6 14:51:54  Originate Call
    1 Jun  6 14:51:54  CSPF: computation result accepted
  Secondary via-Chianti      State: Dn
    Bandwidth: 10Mbps
```

```
      No computed ERO.
  7 Jun  6 15:02:07  Clear Call
  6 Jun  6 15:00:38  Deselected as active
  5 Jun  6 14:59:37  Selected as active path
  4 Jun  6 14:59:37  Record Route:  10.222.29.2 10.222.1.2 10.222.45.2
  3 Jun  6 14:59:37  Up
  2 Jun  6 14:59:37  Originate Call
  1 Jun  6 14:59:37  CSPF: computation result accepted
 Created: Fri Jun  6 14:49:21 2003
Total 1 displayed, Up 1, Down 0
```

Unfortunately, the granularity of the timestamps in the command output makes it appear as if the primary path was torn down and the secondary path was established instantaneously. In fact, this is not the case, and for some period of time, the ingress router was forwarding traffic using the IPv4 next hops in its routing table. This delay in the setup of the secondary path can be eliminated by establishing the secondary path before the primary path fails. Let's see how this works.

Standby Secondary Paths

Any or all of the secondary paths defined for an LSP can be signaled and established in the network once the primary path is operational. This is accomplished through the use of the standby command within the path definition. When applied, the ingress router waits for the primary path to fully become established in the network and be selected as the active path. It then consults the TED to locate a path that meets the constraints of the secondary path. If it locates a viable set of links, the ERO is passed to RSVP and the path is established and placed into the Up state.

The Sherry router in Figure 8.6 adds the standby option to the secondary path of *via-Chianti*:

```
[edit protocols mpls]
user@Sherry# show label-switched-path Sherry-to-Char
to 192.168.32.1;
primary via-Chablis {
    bandwidth 20m;
}
secondary via-Chianti {
    bandwidth 10m;
    standby;
}
```

This prompts the Sherry router to establish both the primary and secondary paths in the network:

```
user@Sherry> show mpls lsp ingress extensive
Ingress LSP: 1 sessions

192.168.32.1
```

```
From: 192.168.16.1, State: Up, ActiveRoute: 0, LSPname: Sherry-to-Char
ActivePath: via-Chablis (primary)
LoadBalance: Random
Encoding type: Packet, Switching type: Packet, GPID: IPv4
*Primary   via-Chablis       State: Up
   Bandwidth: 20Mbps
   Computed ERO (S [L] denotes strict [loose] hops): (CSPF metric: 30)
         10.222.5.2 S 10.222.60.2 S 10.222.6.2 S
   Received RRO:
         10.222.5.2 10.222.60.2 10.222.6.2
   6 Jun  6 15:41:25  Selected as active path
   5 Jun  6 15:41:25  Record Route:  10.222.5.2 10.222.60.2 10.222.6.2
   4 Jun  6 15:41:25  Up
   3 Jun  6 15:41:25  Originate Call
   2 Jun  6 15:41:25  CSPF: computation result accepted
   1 Jun  6 15:40:55  CSPF failed: no route toward 192.168.52.1
 Standby   via-Chianti       State: Up
   Bandwidth: 10Mbps
   Computed ERO (S [L] denotes strict [loose] hops): (CSPF metric: 30)
         10.222.29.2 S 10.222.1.2 S 10.222.45.2 S
   Received RRO:
         10.222.29.2 10.222.1.2 10.222.45.2
   4 Jun  6 15:41:25  Record Route:  10.222.29.2 10.222.1.2 10.222.45.2
   3 Jun  6 15:41:25  Up
   2 Jun  6 15:41:25  Originate Call
   1 Jun  6 15:41:25  CSPF: computation result accepted
   Created: Fri Jun  6 15:39:25 2003
Total 1 displayed, Up 1, Down 0
```

The history buffers were cleared for ease of readability. This was accomplished by deactivating and then reactivating the MPLS configuration on the Sherry router.

Once again the Chablis-Cabernet network link in Figure 8.6 fails and causes the primary path of the LSP to be torn down. Because the secondary path is already in an Up state, the ingress router simply installs it as the active path for the LSP:

```
user@Sherry> show mpls lsp ingress extensive
Ingress LSP: 1 sessions

192.168.32.1
```

```
     From: 192.168.16.1, State: Up, ActiveRoute: 0, LSPname: Sherry-to-Char
     ActivePath: via-Chianti (secondary)
     LoadBalance: Random
     Encoding type: Packet, Switching type: Packet, GPID: IPv4
     Primary   via-Chablis       State: Dn
       Bandwidth: 20Mbps
       Will be enqueued for recomputation in 18 second(s).
      14 Jun  6 15:46:17  CSPF failed: no route toward 192.168.32.1[2 times]
      13 Jun  6 15:46:17  Clear Call
      12 Jun  6 15:46:17  CSPF: link down/deleted 10.222.60.1(Chablis.00/
      11 Jun  6 15:46:17  ResvTear received
      10 Jun  6 15:46:17  Down
       9 Jun  6 15:46:17  Deselected as active
       8 Jun  6 15:46:17  CSPF failed: no route toward 192.168.32.1
       7 Jun  6 15:46:17  10.222.5.2: No Route toward dest
       6 Jun  6 15:41:25  Selected as active path
       5 Jun  6 15:41:25  Record Route:  10.222.5.2 10.222.60.2 10.222.6.2
       4 Jun  6 15:41:25  Up
       3 Jun  6 15:41:25  Originate Call
       2 Jun  6 15:41:25  CSPF: computation result accepted
       1 Jun  6 15:40:55  CSPF failed: no route toward 192.168.52.1
    *Standby   via-Chianti       State: Up
       Bandwidth: 10Mbps
       Computed ERO (S [L] denotes strict [loose] hops): (CSPF metric: 30)
             10.222.29.2 S 10.222.1.2 S 10.222.45.2 S
       Received RRO:
             10.222.29.2 10.222.1.2 10.222.45.2
       5 Jun  6 15:46:17  Selected as active path
       4 Jun  6 15:41:25  Record Route:  10.222.29.2 10.222.1.2 10.222.45.2
       3 Jun  6 15:41:25  Up
       2 Jun  6 15:41:25  Originate Call
       1 Jun  6 15:41:25  CSPF: computation result accepted
     Created: Fri Jun  6 15:40:45 2003
  Total 1 displayed, Up 1, Down 0
```

After the link returns to service, the primary path is signaled and established but is not selected as the active path for the LSP. After waiting for the primary path to remain stable, the ingress router once again selects it as the active path. The secondary path is deselected but remains operational due to its standby configuration:

```
user@Sherry> show mpls lsp ingress extensive
Ingress LSP: 1 sessions
```

```
192.168.32.1
  From: 192.168.16.1, State: Up, ActiveRoute: 0, LSPname: Sherry-to-Char
  ActivePath: via-Chablis (primary)
  LoadBalance: Random
  Encoding type: Packet, Switching type: Packet, GPID: IPv4
 *Primary   via-Chablis       State: Up
    Bandwidth: 20Mbps
    Computed ERO (S [L] denotes strict [loose] hops): (CSPF metric: 30)
          10.222.5.2 S 10.222.60.2 S 10.222.6.2 S
    Received RRO:
          10.222.5.2 10.222.60.2 10.222.6.2
   19 Jun  6 15:47:44  Selected as active path
   18 Jun  6 15:46:46  Record Route:  10.222.5.2 10.222.60.2 10.222.6.2
   17 Jun  6 15:46:46  Up
   16 Jun  6 15:46:46  Originate Call
   15 Jun  6 15:46:46  CSPF: computation result accepted
   14 Jun  6 15:46:17  CSPF failed: no route toward 192.168.32.1[2 times]
   13 Jun  6 15:46:17  Clear Call
   12 Jun  6 15:46:17  CSPF: link down/deleted 10.222.60.1(Chablis.00/
   11 Jun  6 15:46:17  ResvTear received
   10 Jun  6 15:46:17  Down
    9 Jun  6 15:46:17  Deselected as active
    8 Jun  6 15:46:17  CSPF failed: no route toward 192.168.32.1
    7 Jun  6 15:46:17  10.222.5.2: No Route toward dest
    6 Jun  6 15:41:25  Selected as active path
    5 Jun  6 15:41:25  Record Route:  10.222.5.2 10.222.60.2 10.222.6.2
    4 Jun  6 15:41:25  Up
    3 Jun  6 15:41:25  Originate Call
    2 Jun  6 15:41:25  CSPF: computation result accepted
    1 Jun  6 15:40:55  CSPF failed: no route toward 192.168.52.1
  Standby   via-Chianti       State: Up
    Bandwidth: 10Mbps
    Computed ERO (S [L] denotes strict [loose] hops): (CSPF metric: 30)
          10.222.29.2 S 10.222.1.2 S 10.222.45.2 S
    Received RRO:
          10.222.29.2 10.222.1.2 10.222.45.2
    6 Jun  6 15:47:44  Deselected as active
    5 Jun  6 15:46:17  Selected as active path
    4 Jun  6 15:41:25  Record Route:  10.222.29.2 10.222.1.2 10.222.45.2
```

```
     3 Jun  6 15:41:25  Up
     2 Jun  6 15:41:25  Originate Call
     1 Jun  6 15:41:25  CSPF: computation result accepted
   Created: Fri Jun  6 15:38:24 2003
Total 1 displayed, Up 1, Down 0
```

Using Only Secondary Paths

The use of a standby secondary path in conjunction with a primary path eases the failover of traffic between the paths. The revertive nature of the primary path, however, means that the ingress will move traffic back to the primary after it is available again. Some network administrators do not wish to incur the "extra" network churn that results from the revert action. They would prefer that the failure of the primary path cause traffic to use the secondary path and remain there indefinitely. While there is no mechanism to keep a primary path from reverting to active status, the JUNOS software allows you to configure multiple secondary paths on an LSP without defining a primary path. The ingress router uses these multiple secondary paths in the order they appear in the configuration.

Within the network displayed in Figure 8.6, the **Sherry-to-Char** LSP is reconfigured to contain two secondary paths—**via-Chablis** and **via-Chianti**:

```
[edit protocols mpls]
user@Sherry# show label-switched-path Sherry-to-Char
to 192.168.32.1;
secondary via-Chablis;
secondary via-Chianti;
```

The Sherry router runs the CSPF algorithm against the contents of the TED for the first secondary path listed, **via-Chablis**, in an attempt to locate a viable set of links that meet the constraints. The output of the show mpls lsp extensive command tells us that this path setup was successful:

```
user@Sherry> show mpls lsp extensive ingress
Ingress LSP: 1 sessions

192.168.32.1
  From: 192.168.16.1, State: Up, ActiveRoute: 0, LSPname: Sherry-to-Char
  ActivePath: via-Chablis (secondary)
  LoadBalance: Random
  Encoding type: Packet, Switching type: Packet, GPID: IPv4
 *Secondary via-Chablis       State: Up
    Computed ERO (S [L] denotes strict [loose] hops): (CSPF metric: 30)
         10.222.5.2 S 10.222.60.2 S 10.222.6.2 S
    Received RRO:
         10.222.5.2 10.222.60.2 10.222.6.2
```

```
 5 Jun  6 16:45:30  Selected as active path
 4 Jun  6 16:45:30  Record Route:  10.222.5.2 10.222.60.2 10.222.6.2
 3 Jun  6 16:45:30  Up
 2 Jun  6 16:45:30  Originate Call
 1 Jun  6 16:45:30  CSPF: computation result accepted
 Secondary via-Chianti      State: Dn
        No computed ERO.
  Created: Fri Jun  6 16:43:54 2003
Total 1 displayed, Up 1, Down 0
```

When the Chablis-Cabernet link once again fails, the ***via-Chianti*** secondary path is signaled and established in the network. This then becomes the active path for the LSP:

```
user@Sherry> show mpls lsp extensive ingress
Ingress LSP: 1 sessions

192.168.32.1
  From: 192.168.16.1, State: Up, ActiveRoute: 0, LSPname: Sherry-to-Char
  ActivePath: via-Chianti (secondary)
  LoadBalance: Random
  Encoding type: Packet, Switching type: Packet, GPID: IPv4
  Secondary via-Chablis      State: Dn
    Will be enqueued for recomputation in 6 second(s).
   13 Jun  6 16:49:39  CSPF failed: no route toward 192.168.32.1
   12 Jun  6 16:49:39  Clear Call
   11 Jun  6 16:49:39  CSPF: link down/deleted 10.222.60.1(Chablis.00
   10 Jun  6 16:49:39  Deselected as active
    9 Jun  6 16:49:39  ResvTear received
    8 Jun  6 16:49:39  Down
    7 Jun  6 16:49:39  CSPF failed: no route toward 192.168.32.1
    6 Jun  6 16:49:39  10.222.5.2: No Route toward dest
    5 Jun  6 16:45:30  Selected as active path
    4 Jun  6 16:45:30  Record Route:  10.222.5.2 10.222.60.2 10.222.6.2
    3 Jun  6 16:45:30  Up
    2 Jun  6 16:45:30  Originate Call
    1 Jun  6 16:45:30  CSPF: computation result accepted
 *Secondary via-Chianti      State: Up
    Computed ERO (S [L] denotes strict [loose] hops): (CSPF metric: 30)
        10.222.29.2 S 10.222.1.2 S 10.222.45.2 S
    Received RRO:
        10.222.29.2 10.222.1.2 10.222.45.2
```

```
 5  Jun  6 16:49:39  Selected as active path
 4  Jun  6 16:49:39  Record Route:  10.222.29.2 10.222.1.2 10.222.45.2
 3  Jun  6 16:49:39  Up
 2  Jun  6 16:49:39  Originate Call
 1  Jun  6 16:49:39  CSPF: computation result accepted
  Created: Fri Jun  6 16:45:22 2003
Total 1 displayed, Up 1, Down 0
```

After the link returns to service, the ingress router reestablishes the ***via-Chablis*** path since it was previously the active path for the LSP. The current active path for the LSP doesn't change, however, and remains ***via-Chianti***:

```
user@Sherry> show mpls lsp extensive ingress
Ingress LSP: 1 sessions

192.168.32.1
  From: 192.168.16.1, State: Up, ActiveRoute: 0, LSPname: Sherry-to-Char
  ActivePath: via-Chianti (secondary)
  LoadBalance: Random
  Encoding type: Packet, Switching type: Packet, GPID: IPv4
  Secondary via-Chablis       State: Up
    Computed ERO (S [L] denotes strict [loose] hops): (CSPF metric: 30)
          10.222.5.2 S 10.222.60.2 S 10.222.6.2 S
    Received RRO:
          10.222.5.2 10.222.60.2 10.222.6.2
 17  Jun  6 16:49:54  Record Route:  10.222.5.2 10.222.60.2 10.222.6.2
 16  Jun  6 16:49:54  Up
 15  Jun  6 16:49:54  Originate Call
 14  Jun  6 16:49:54  CSPF: computation result accepted
 13  Jun  6 16:49:39  CSPF failed: no route toward 192.168.32.1
 12  Jun  6 16:49:39  Clear Call
 11  Jun  6 16:49:39  CSPF: link down/deleted 10.222.60.1(Chablis.00/
 10  Jun  6 16:49:39  Deselected as active
  9  Jun  6 16:49:39  ResvTear received
  8  Jun  6 16:49:39  Down
  7  Jun  6 16:49:39  CSPF failed: no route toward 192.168.32.1
  6  Jun  6 16:49:39  10.222.5.2: No Route toward dest
  5  Jun  6 16:45:30  Selected as active path
  4  Jun  6 16:45:30  Record Route:  10.222.5.2 10.222.60.2 10.222.6.2
  3  Jun  6 16:45:30  Up
  2  Jun  6 16:45:30  Originate Call
  1  Jun  6 16:45:30  CSPF: computation result accepted
```

```
    *Secondary via-Chianti        State: Up
        Computed ERO (S [L] denotes strict [loose] hops): (CSPF metric: 30)
            10.222.29.2 S 10.222.1.2 S 10.222.45.2 S
        Received RRO:
            10.222.29.2 10.222.1.2 10.222.45.2
      5 Jun  6 16:49:39  Selected as active path
      4 Jun  6 16:49:39  Record Route:   10.222.29.2 10.222.1.2 10.222.45.2
      3 Jun  6 16:49:39  Up
      2 Jun  6 16:49:39  Originate Call
      1 Jun  6 16:49:39  CSPF: computation result accepted
     Created: Fri Jun  6 16:45:20 2003
   Total 1 displayed, Up 1, Down 0
```

Once the retry waiting period expires, the ingress router determines that the **via-Chablis** secondary path is not needed and it is cleared from the network. The active path for the LSP remains the **via-Chianti** secondary path, and we've successfully created a non-revertive LSP:

```
user@Sherry> show mpls lsp extensive ingress
Ingress LSP: 1 sessions

192.168.32.1
   From: 192.168.16.1, State: Up, ActiveRoute: 0, LSPname: Sherry-to-Char
   ActivePath: via-Chianti (secondary)
   LoadBalance: Random
   Encoding type: Packet, Switching type: Packet, GPID: IPv4
   Secondary via-Chablis        State: Dn
        No computed ERO.
    18 Jun  6 16:50:52  Clear Call
    17 Jun  6 16:49:54  Record Route:   10.222.5.2 10.222.60.2 10.222.6.2
    16 Jun  6 16:49:54  Up
    15 Jun  6 16:49:54  Originate Call
    14 Jun  6 16:49:54  CSPF: computation result accepted
    13 Jun  6 16:49:39  CSPF failed: no route toward 192.168.32.1
    12 Jun  6 16:49:39  Clear Call
    11 Jun  6 16:49:39  CSPF: link down/deleted 10.222.60.1(Chablis.00/
    10 Jun  6 16:49:39  Deselected as active
     9 Jun  6 16:49:39  ResvTear received
     8 Jun  6 16:49:39  Down
     7 Jun  6 16:49:39  CSPF failed: no route toward 192.168.32.1
     6 Jun  6 16:49:39  10.222.5.2: No Route toward dest
     5 Jun  6 16:45:30  Selected as active path
     4 Jun  6 16:45:30  Record Route:   10.222.5.2 10.222.60.2 10.222.6.2
```

```
   3 Jun  6 16:45:30  Up
   2 Jun  6 16:45:30  Originate Call
   1 Jun  6 16:45:30  CSPF: computation result accepted
*Secondary via-Chianti      State: Up
   Computed ERO (S [L] denotes strict [loose] hops): (CSPF metric: 30)
         10.222.29.2 S 10.222.1.2 S 10.222.45.2 S
   Received RRO:
         10.222.29.2 10.222.1.2 10.222.45.2
   5 Jun  6 16:49:39  Selected as active path
   4 Jun  6 16:49:39  Record Route:  10.222.29.2 10.222.1.2 10.222.45.2
   3 Jun  6 16:49:39  Up
   2 Jun  6 16:49:39  Originate Call
   1 Jun  6 16:49:39  CSPF: computation result accepted
  Created: Fri Jun  6 16:44:05 2003
Total 1 displayed, Up 1, Down 0
```

Fast Reroute

At this point in the chapter, we've talked about protecting traffic using secondary paths as well as paths in the standby state. These options work very well as long-term solutions in the network, but each has the potential for dropping packets in a failure mode. Specifically, these are the packets injected into the LSP by the ingress router between the time the failure occurs and the time the ingress is notified of the failure via a `ResvTear` message. For critical applications, this short failure time and its packet drops are unacceptable. The resolution to this situation is the use of *fast reroute* on an LSP. The basic operation of fast reroute involves the establishment of detour paths through the network that are associated with the RSVP session of the main LSP. Each router along the LSP's path creates a detour to protect against the failure of its next downstream neighbor or the next downstream link.

During a failure mode, the next upstream router from the point of failure immediately forwards traffic for the LSP along the detour path. This quick decision allows for minimal packet loss, if any occurs at all. This node also generates a `PathErr` message and forwards it to the ingress router. The error message is designed to alert the ingress that a failure occurred along the path and that the detour is being used to forward traffic.

The action taken by the ingress router then depends on its configuration and the state of the network. If a standby secondary path is established, the ingress router begins using it to forward traffic. The primary path, along with the detours, are torn down and the ingress attempts to locate another primary path through the network matching the LSP constraints. This same process occurs when a secondary path is configured but is not in an Up state. The ingress router signals and establishes the secondary path, moves traffic onto it, and tears down the primary path. If the ingress router has no secondary paths defined, it examines the TED to locate a new primary path meeting the constraints. If one is found, the ingress router creates a new primary path and moves the traffic onto it. This process occurs in one of two fashions:; either the ingress router creates the new path, moves traffic, and tears down the old path or the ingress tears down the old path, creates the new path, and moves the traffic. The actions of the ingress router in this situation are controlled by the `adaptive` command, which we discuss in the "Controlling LSP Behavior" section, later in this chapter. The ingress router might encounter one final possibility during a failure mode. There may be no secondary paths defined and the CSPF algorithm might not find a new primary path that meets the LSP constraints. When this occurs, the ingress router continues using the existing path and the detours to forward traffic across the network.

The JUNOS software performs fast reroute actions in one of two modes—node protection and link protection. Let's explore each in further detail.

Node Protection

In a *node protection* fast reroute environment, each router along the LSP path builds a detour path from itself to the egress router. This path is calculated using the information in the TED, and a strict-hop ERO is created for the detour. By default, the detour path inherits the administrative group settings of the main LSP to provide a limit as to which links the detour may use. In addition, you can apply a bandwidth reservation to the detour as well as a limit on the number of hops the detour can use. The main purpose of the detour path is to protect against the failure of the next downstream node in the LSP path. By default, this protection scheme also protects against the network link connecting the two neighbors. You enable fast reroute node protection with the `fast-reroute` command within the LSP itself:

```
[edit protocols mpls]
user@Sherry# show label-switched-path Sherry-to-Char
to 192.168.32.1;
fast-reroute;
primary via-Chablis;
```

FIGURE 8.7 Fast reroute sample network

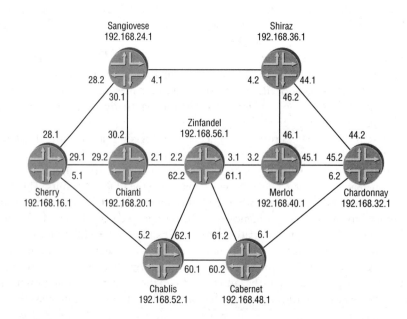

Figure 8.7 displays the network used to construct the **Sherry-to-Char** LSP. After the configuration we just described is committed to the router, Sherry begins sending `Path` messages along the LSP path that contain the Fast Reroute object. This object alerts each node along the path that it should create a detour path once the main LSP is established in the network. By examining the output of the `show mpls lsp extensive` command, we can see the establishment of the detour paths from the ingress router:

```
user@Sherry> show mpls lsp ingress extensive
Ingress LSP: 1 sessions

192.168.32.1
  From: 192.168.16.1, State: Up, ActiveRoute: 0, LSPname: Sherry-to-Char
  ActivePath: via-Chablis (primary)
  FastReroute desired
  LoadBalance: Random
  Encoding type: Packet, Switching type: Packet, GPID: IPv4
 *Primary    via-Chablis       State: Up
    Computed ERO (S [L] denotes strict [loose] hops): (CSPF metric: 30)
          10.222.5.2 S 10.222.60.2 S 10.222.6.2 S
    Received RRO:
          10.222.5.2(flag=0x9) 10.222.60.2(flag=0x1) 10.222.6.2
    8 Jun  7 11:26:46  Record Route:  10.222.5.2(flag=0x9) 10.222.60.2(flag=0x1)
    7 Jun  7 11:26:46  Record Route:  10.222.5.2(flag=0x9) 10.222.60.2 10.222.6.
    6 Jun  7 11:26:46  Fast-reroute Detour Up
    5 Jun  7 11:26:43  Selected as active path
    4 Jun  7 11:26:43  Record Route:  10.222.5.2 10.222.60.2 10.222.6.2
    3 Jun  7 11:26:43  Up
    2 Jun  7 11:26:43  Originate Call
    1 Jun  7 11:26:43  CSPF: computation result accepted
  Created: Sat Jun  7 11:26:37 2003
Total 1 displayed, Up 1, Down 0
```

NOTE   Some lines in the output extend beyond 80 characters and have been truncated for readability.

Within the attributes of the LSP itself, the `FastReroute desired` output tells us that the object was included in the `Path` messages for the LSP. This allows Sherry to select the primary path as the active path for the LSP and then establish a detour path to avoid Chablis. While we don't know how the detour was established, we can see that it is operational through the `Fast-reroute Detour Up` output. The next two entries in the history buffer inform us that the two transit routers, Chablis and Cabernet, have also established their detour paths. The Chablis router, 10.222.5.2, includes the flag=0x9 notation in its Record Route object (RRO) within the Resv message. This informs the upstream routers that a successful detour is established that protects both the downstream node and the downstream link. The Cabernet router, 10.222.6.2, includes the flag=0x1 notation in its RRO, which states that a detour is established to protect the next downstream link. While it might seem unusual for Cabernet to not protect the downstream node, a quick look at the network map reveals that the egress router of Chardonnay is the next downstream node. It is impossible for Cabernet to avoid the egress router, so only the downstream link is protected by the Cabernet router.

To see the actual links used by the detour paths, we need to use the show rsvp session detail command. As we move around the network, this command provides us with complete knowledge of the main LSP and all the detour paths in the network. From the perspective of the Sherry router we see the following:

```
user@Sherry> show rsvp session ingress detail
Ingress RSVP: 1 sessions

192.168.32.1
  From: 192.168.16.1, LSPstate: Up, ActiveRoute: 0
  LSPname: Sherry-to-Char, LSPpath: Primary
  Suggested label received: -, Suggested label sent: -
  Recovery label received: -, Recovery label sent: 100256
  Resv style: 1 FF, Label in: -, Label out: 100256
  Time left:    -,  Since: Sat Jun  7 11:26:43 2003
  Tspec: rate 0bps size 0bps peak Infbps m 20 M 1500
  Port number: sender 1 receiver 11185 protocol 0
  FastReroute desired
  PATH rcvfrom: localclient
  PATH sentto: 10.222.5.2 (at-0/1/1.0) 56 pkts
  RESV rcvfrom: 10.222.5.2  (at-0/1/1.0) 58 pkts
  Explct route: 10.222.5.2 10.222.60.2 10.222.6.2
  Record route: <self>  10.222.5.2  10.222.60.2  10.222.6.2
    Detour is Up
    Detour PATH sentto: 10.222.28.2 (at-0/1/0.0) 55 pkts
    Detour RESV rcvfrom: 10.222.28.2  (at-0/1/0.0) 55 pkts
    Detour Explct route: 10.222.28.2 10.222.4.2 10.222.44.2
    Detour Record route: <self>  10.222.28.2  10.222.4.2  10.222.44.2
    Detour Label out: 100240
Total 1 displayed, Up 1, Down 0
```

Within the context of the RSVP session representing the main LSP, we see that the detour path is established by the Detour is Up notation. The physical path of the detour is displayed by the Detour Explct route: output and uses Sangiovese and Shiraz as transit routers before reaching the egress router of Chardonnay. When we examine the session data on the first transit router of Chablis, we see some similar information:

```
user@Chablis> show rsvp session transit detail
Transit RSVP: 1 sessions

192.168.32.1
  From: 192.168.16.1, LSPstate: Up, ActiveRoute: 1
  LSPname: Sherry-to-Char, LSPpath: Primary
  Suggested label received: -, Suggested label sent: -
  Recovery label received: -, Recovery label sent: 100240
  Resv style: 1 FF, Label in: 100256, Label out: 100240
  Time left:  140,  Since: Fri Sep 28 13:54:33 2001
  Tspec: rate 0bps size 0bps peak Infbps m 20 M 1500
  Port number: sender 1 receiver 11185 protocol 0
  FastReroute desired
  PATH rcvfrom: 10.222.5.1  (at-0/2/0.0) 237 pkts
  PATH sentto: 10.222.60.2 (so-0/1/0.0) 237 pkts
  RESV rcvfrom: 10.222.60.2  (so-0/1/0.0) 238 pkts
  Explct route: 10.222.60.2 10.222.6.2
  Record route: 10.222.5.1  <self>  10.222.60.2  10.222.6.2
    Detour is Up
    Detour PATH sentto: 10.222.62.2 (so-0/1/1.0) 236 pkts
    Detour RESV rcvfrom: 10.222.62.2  (so-0/1/1.0) 236 pkts
    Detour Explct route: 10.222.62.2 10.222.3.2 10.222.45.2
    Detour Record route: 10.222.5.1  <self>  10.222.62.2  10.222.3.2
    10.222.45.2
    Detour Label out: 100176
Total 1 displayed, Up 1, Down 0
```

The detour created by Chablis is designed to avoid the Cabernet router as well as the link connecting Chablis to Cabernet. The detour is currently in an Up state and uses Zinfandel and Merlot as transit routers before reaching the egress router of Chardonnay. In fact, this is the exact same detour path used by Cabernet to avoid its downstream link to the egress router:

```
user@Cabernet> show rsvp session transit detail
Transit RSVP: 1 sessions

192.168.32.1
  From: 192.168.16.1, LSPstate: Up, ActiveRoute: 1
  LSPname: Sherry-to-Char, LSPpath: Primary
  Suggested label received: -, Suggested label sent: -
```

```
Recovery label received: -, Recovery label sent: 3
Resv style: 1 FF, Label in: 100240, Label out: 3
Time left:  126,  Since: Sat Jan  5 13:59:04 2002
Tspec: rate 0bps size 0bps peak Infbps m 20 M 1500
Port number: sender 1 receiver 11185 protocol 0
FastReroute desired
PATH rcvfrom: 10.222.60.1  (so-0/1/2.0) 243 pkts
PATH sentto: 10.222.6.2 (so-0/1/1.0) 243 pkts
RESV rcvfrom: 10.222.6.2  (so-0/1/1.0) 243 pkts
Explct route: 10.222.6.2
Record route: 10.222.5.1  10.222.60.1  <self>  10.222.6.2
  Detour is Up
  Detour PATH sentto: 10.222.61.1 (so-0/1/0.0) 242 pkts
  Detour RESV rcvfrom: 10.222.61.1  (so-0/1/0.0) 242 pkts
  Detour Explct route: 10.222.61.1 10.222.3.2 10.222.45.2
  Detour Record route: 10.222.5.1  10.222.60.1  <self>  10.222.61.1
  10.222.3.2  10.222.45.2
  Detour Label out: 100160
Total 1 displayed, Up 1, Down 0
```

Because the detour paths from Chablis and Cabernet use Zinfandel as a transit router, the fast reroute specification allows Zinfandel to merge the detour paths together. After all, they belong to the same main RSVP session and they are both sending packets to the same egress router. So, there's no harm in combining them into a single flow between Zinfandel and Chardonnay. As we look at the show rsvp session transit detail output on Zinfandel, we see the merge operation take place:

```
user@Zinfandel> show rsvp session transit detail
Transit RSVP: 1 sessions, 1 detours


192.168.32.1
  From: 192.168.16.1, LSPstate: Up, ActiveRoute: 1
  LSPname: Sherry-to-Char, LSPpath: Primary
  Suggested label received: -, Suggested label sent: -
  Recovery label received: -, Recovery label sent: 100224
  Resv style: 1 FF, Label in: 100176, Label out: 100224
  Time left:  120,  Since: Sat Jun  7 11:26:16 2003
  Tspec: rate 0bps size 0bps peak Infbps m 20 M 1500
  Port number: sender 1 receiver 11185 protocol 0
  Detour branch from 10.222.62.1, to skip 192.168.48.1, Up
    PATH rcvfrom: 10.222.62.1  (so-0/1/3.0) 247 pkts
    PATH sentto: 10.222.3.2 (so-0/1/1.0) 247 pkts
```

```
  RESV rcvfrom: 10.222.3.2  (so-0/1/1.0) 248 pkts
  Explct route: 10.222.3.2 10.222.45.2
  Record route: 10.222.5.1  10.222.62.1  <self>  10.222.3.2  10.222.45.2
  Label in: 100176, Label out: 100224
Detour branch from 10.222.61.2, to skip 192.168.32.1, Up
  PATH rcvfrom: 10.222.61.2  (so-0/1/2.0) 247 pkts
  PATH sentto: 10.222.3.2 (so-0/1/1.0) 0 pkts
  RESV rcvfrom: 10.222.3.2  (so-0/1/1.0) 0 pkts
  Explct route: 10.222.3.2 10.222.45.2
  Record route: 10.222.5.1  10.222.60.1  10.222.61.2  <self>  10.222.3.2
  10.222.45.2
  Label in: 100160, Label out: 100224
Total 1 displayed, Up 1, Down 0
```

The first thing to note is that both detours appear without the output of the same session, which includes the ingress address, the egress address, and the name of the LSP. We then see the detour path arrive from the Chablis router as noted by the Detour branch from 10.222.62.1 output. This also informs us that Chablis is attempting to avoid Cabernet (to skip 192.168.48.1). A similar set of data appears from Cabernet (10.222.61.2) to avoid the link connecting it to the egress router (192.168.32.1). The actual merge functionality that Zinfandel is performing can be seen by the label used to send traffic along the detour. Both detours have the same Label out: 100224 notation identified. This means that whether Zinfandel receives traffic from Chablis with a label of 100,176 or from Cabernet with a label of 100,160, it forwards the packet to Merlot with a label value of 100,224. When we look at Merlot's view of the detour, we see only a single set of information:

```
user@Merlot> show rsvp session transit detail
Transit RSVP: 1 sessions

192.168.32.1
  From: 192.168.16.1, LSPstate: Up, ActiveRoute: 1
  LSPname: Sherry-to-Char, LSPpath: Primary
  Suggested label received: -, Suggested label sent: -
  Recovery label received: -, Recovery label sent: 3
  Resv style: 1 FF, Label in: 100224, Label out: 3
  Time left: 140,  Since: Sat Jun  7 11:27:31 2003
  Tspec: rate 0bps size 0bps peak Infbps m 20 M 1500
  Port number: sender 1 receiver 11185 protocol 0
  Detour branch from 10.222.62.1, to skip 192.168.48.1, Up
  Detour branch from 10.222.61.2, to skip 192.168.32.1, Up
    PATH rcvfrom: 10.222.3.1  (so-0/1/1.0) 257 pkts
    PATH sentto: 10.222.45.2 (so-0/1/2.0) 259 pkts
    RESV rcvfrom: 10.222.45.2  (so-0/1/2.0) 257 pkts
```

```
    Explct route: 10.222.45.2
    Record route: 10.222.5.1  10.222.62.1  10.222.3.1  <self>  10.222.45.2
    Label in: 100224, Label out: 3
Total 1 displayed, Up 1, Down 0
```

Both the ERO of the detour and the `Label out:` information tell us that Merlot is the penultimate router for the detour path. We can tell that the detour was merged at some point upstream since multiple `Detour branch` statements appear before the `Path` and `Resv` message information.

When we finally reach the egress router of Chardonnay, we see information pertaining to the main LSP path as well as the two detours through the network:

```
user@Chardonnay> show rsvp session egress detail
Egress RSVP: 1 sessions, 2 detours

192.168.32.1
  From: 192.168.16.1, LSPstate: Up, ActiveRoute: 0
  LSPname: Sherry-to-Char, LSPpath: Primary
  Suggested label received: -, Suggested label sent: -
  Recovery label received: -, Recovery label sent: -
  Resv style: 1 FF, Label in: 3, Label out: -
  Time left: 146,  Since: Sat Jun  7 11:25:20 2003
  Tspec: rate 0bps size 0bps peak Infbps m 20 M 1500
  Port number: sender 1 receiver 11185 protocol 0
  FastReroute desired
  PATH rcvfrom: 10.222.6.1  (so-0/1/2.0) 263 pkts
  PATH sentto: localclient
  RESV rcvfrom: localclient
  Record route: 10.222.5.1  10.222.60.1  10.222.6.1  <self>
  Detour branch from 10.222.28.1, to skip 192.168.52.1, Up
    PATH rcvfrom: 10.222.44.1  (so-0/1/0.0) 262 pkts
    PATH sentto: localclient
    RESV rcvfrom: localclient
    Record route: 10.222.28.1  10.222.4.1  10.222.44.1  <self>
    Label in: 3, Label out: -
  Detour branch from 10.222.62.1, to skip 192.168.48.1, Up
  Detour branch from 10.222.61.2, to skip 192.168.32.1, Up
    PATH rcvfrom: 10.222.45.1  (so-0/1/1.0) 264 pkts
    PATH sentto: localclient
    RESV rcvfrom: localclient
    Record route: 10.222.5.1  10.222.62.1  10.222.3.1  10.222.45.1  <self>
    Label in: 3, Label out: -
Total 1 displayed, Up 1, Down 0
```

Link Protection

Although the purpose of *link protection* fast reroute remains the continued forwarding of traffic using MPLS in a failure mode, the actual mechanics used by link protection are quite different. When we examined a node-protection scheme in the previous section, we found that each node along the LSP generated a detour path that was associated with the main RSVP session. During a failure, the next upstream router, officially referred to as the *point of local repair* (PLR), performed a label swap operation for all incoming data packets and forwarded them along the detour path. In a link-protection environment, we create bypass LSPs from one router to its neighbor that avoid the interconnecting link. This is a function of RSVP and is enabled through the `link-protection` command on each RSVP interface requiring protection. The bypass LSPs are established when the ingress router for the main LSP configures the `link-protection` command to request that each node along the path use the bypass LSPs to protect the traffic flow.

When a failure occurs, the PLR performs a label swap operation to place the label advertised by the downstream node in the bottom MPLS header. The PLR then performs a label push operation to add the label corresponding to the bypass LSP and forwards the packet along the bypass. The penultimate router along the bypass pops the top label value and forwards the remaining data to the router that is downstream of the point of local repair. The received label value is known to this router since it originally allocated it for the main LSP. As such, it performs the appropriate label function and forwards the traffic along the path of the main LSP. Through this process, a bypass LSP can officially support repair capabilities for multiple LSPs in a many-to-one fashion.

Using the network in Figure 8.7, we first verify that the Cabernet router has no current knowledge of any LSPs or RSVP sessions:

```
user@Cabernet> show mpls lsp
Ingress LSP: 0 sessions
Total 0 displayed, Up 0, Down 0

Egress LSP: 0 sessions
Total 0 displayed, Up 0, Down 0

Transit LSP: 0 sessions
Total 0 displayed, Up 0, Down 0

user@Cabernet> show rsvp session
Ingress RSVP: 0 sessions
Total 0 displayed, Up 0, Down 0

Egress RSVP: 0 sessions
Total 0 displayed, Up 0, Down 0

Transit RSVP: 0 sessions
Total 0 displayed, Up 0, Down 0
```

We then configure each of the interfaces on Cabernet for link protection, which establishes bypass LSPs to protect the interfaces to Chablis, Zinfandel, and Chardonnay:

```
user@Cabernet> show configuration protocols rsvp
interface all {
    link-protection;
}

user@Cabernet> show rsvp session ingress detail
Ingress RSVP: 3 sessions

192.168.32.1
  From: 192.168.48.1, LSPstate: Up, ActiveRoute: 0
  LSPname: Bypass_to_10.222.6.2
  Suggested label received: -, Suggested label sent: -
  Recovery label received: -, Recovery label sent: 100240
  Resv style: 1 SE, Label in: -, Label out: 100240
  Time left:     -,  Since: Sat Jan  5 18:06:34 2002
  Tspec: rate 0bps size 0bps peak Infbps m 20 M 1500
  Port number: sender 1 receiver 4464 protocol 0
  Type: Bypass LSP
  PATH rcvfrom: localclient
  PATH sentto: 10.222.61.1 (so-0/1/0.0) 4 pkts
  RESV rcvfrom: 10.222.61.1  (so-0/1/0.0) 4 pkts
  Explct route: 10.222.61.1 10.222.3.2 10.222.45.2
  Record route: <self>  10.222.61.1  10.222.3.2  10.222.45.2

192.168.52.1
  From: 192.168.48.1, LSPstate: Up, ActiveRoute: 0
  LSPname: Bypass_to_10.222.60.1
  Suggested label received: -, Suggested label sent: -
  Recovery label received: -, Recovery label sent: 100224
  Resv style: 1 SE, Label in: -, Label out: 100224
  Time left:     -,  Since: Sat Jan  5 18:06:34 2002
  Tspec: rate 0bps size 0bps peak Infbps m 20 M 1500
  Port number: sender 1 receiver 4465 protocol 0
  Type: Bypass LSP
  PATH rcvfrom: localclient
  PATH sentto: 10.222.61.1 (so-0/1/0.0) 4 pkts
  RESV rcvfrom: 10.222.61.1  (so-0/1/0.0) 4 pkts
  Explct route: 10.222.61.1 10.222.62.1
```

```
Record route: <self>   10.222.61.1   10.222.62.1

192.168.56.1
  From: 192.168.48.1, LSPstate: Up, ActiveRoute: 0
  LSPname: Bypass_to_10.222.61.1
  Suggested label received: -, Suggested label sent: -
  Recovery label received: -, Recovery label sent: 100288
  Resv style: 1 SE, Label in: -, Label out: 100288
  Time left:    -,  Since: Sat Jan  5 18:06:34 2002
  Tspec: rate 0bps size 0bps peak Infbps m 20 M 1500
  Port number: sender 1 receiver 4463 protocol 0
  Type: Bypass LSP
  PATH rcvfrom: localclient
  PATH sentto: 10.222.60.1 (so-0/1/2.0) 4 pkts
  RESV rcvfrom: 10.222.60.1  (so-0/1/2.0) 4 pkts
  Explct route: 10.222.60.1 10.222.62.2
  Record route: <self>   10.222.60.1   10.222.62.2
Total 3 displayed, Up 3, Down 0
```

The first critical piece of information to note is the creation of three separate RSVP ingress sessions, one for each interface. Each session is described as a bypass LSP via the `Type:` output, and each has an LSP name automatically created for it. By default, the name appears as `Bypass_ to_interface-address`, where the interface address is the next downstream router's interface. For example, Cabernet established the ***Bypass_to_10.222.61.1*** LSP between itself and Zinfandel (192.168.56.1) to protect their interconnected network link. The `Explct route` for the session displays Chablis as the transit node for the bypass and Zinfandel as the egress node.

To take advantage of the established link-protection bypasses, the ***Sherry-to-Char*** LSP also configures the `link-protection` command:

```
[edit protocols mpls]
user@Sherry# show label-switched-path Sherry-to-Char
to 192.168.32.1;
link-protection;
primary via-Chablis;
```

This adds an RSVP transit session on the Cabernet router:

For ease in interpreting the output, only the outgoing interfaces along the ***Sherry-to-Char*** path have been configured with `link-protection`.

```
user@Cabernet> show rsvp session detail
Ingress RSVP: 1 sessions
```

```
192.168.32.1
  From: 192.168.48.1, LSPstate: Up, ActiveRoute: 0
  LSPname: Bypass_to_10.222.6.2
  Suggested label received: -, Suggested label sent: -
  Recovery label received: -, Recovery label sent: 100272
  Resv style: 1 SE, Label in: -, Label out: 100272
  Time left:    -,   Since: Sat Jan  5 18:19:23 2002
  Tspec: rate 0bps size 0bps peak Infbps m 20 M 1500
  Port number: sender 1 receiver 4466 protocol 0
  Type: Bypass LSP
  PATH rcvfrom: localclient
  PATH sentto: 10.222.61.1 (so-0/1/0.0) 5 pkts
  RESV rcvfrom: 10.222.61.1  (so-0/1/0.0) 5 pkts
  Explct route: 10.222.61.1 10.222.3.2 10.222.45.2
  Record route: <self>  10.222.61.1   10.222.3.2   10.222.45.2
Total 1 displayed, Up 1, Down 0


Egress RSVP: 0 sessions
Total 0 displayed, Up 0, Down 0


Transit RSVP: 1 sessions

192.168.32.1
  From: 192.168.16.1, LSPstate: Up, ActiveRoute: 0
  LSPname: Sherry-to-Char, LSPpath: Primary
  Suggested label received: -, Suggested label sent: -
  Recovery label received: -, Recovery label sent: 3
  Resv style: 1 SE, Label in: 100288, Label out: 3
  Time left:  156,   Since: Sat Jan  5 18:20:19 2002
  Tspec: rate 0bps size 0bps peak Infbps m 20 M 1500
  Port number: sender 3 receiver 11196 protocol 0
  Link protection desired
  Type: Link protected LSP
  PATH rcvfrom: 10.222.60.1  (so-0/1/2.0) 3 pkts
  PATH sentto: 10.222.6.2 (so-0/1/1.0) 3 pkts
  RESV rcvfrom: 10.222.6.2  (so-0/1/1.0) 4 pkts
  Explct route: 10.222.6.2
  Record route: 10.222.5.1  10.222.60.1  <self>  10.222.6.2
Total 1 displayed, Up 1, Down 0
```

Within the transit RSVP section for the ***Sherry-to-Char*** LSP, we see the `Link protection desired` output requesting protection from the ingress router. Since Cabernet has a bypass LSP in place to protect the downstream link, it associates this LSP with the bypass. This is indicated by the `Type: Link protected` LSP notation.

When we examine the output of this command on the transit router of Chablis, we see different information. Although the LSP is requesting link protection, no bypass LSP is established from Chablis to any of its neighbors. As such, the LSP is not actually link protected:

```
user@Chablis> show rsvp session detail
Ingress RSVP: 0 sessions
Total 0 displayed, Up 0, Down 0

Egress RSVP: 0 sessions
Total 0 displayed, Up 0, Down 0

Transit RSVP: 1 sessions

192.168.32.1
  From: 192.168.16.1, LSPstate: Up, ActiveRoute: 1
  LSPname: Sherry-to-Char, LSPpath: Primary
  Suggested label received: -, Suggested label sent: -
  Recovery label received: -, Recovery label sent: 100288
  Resv style: 1 SE, Label in: 100336, Label out: 100288
  Time left:  122,  Since: Fri Sep 28 18:15:48 2001
  Tspec: rate 0bps size 0bps peak Infbps m 20 M 1500
  Port number: sender 3 receiver 11196 protocol 0
  Link protection desired
  PATH rcvfrom: 10.222.5.1  (at-0/2/0.0) 10 pkts
  PATH sentto: 10.222.60.2 (so-0/1/0.0) 10 pkts
  RESV rcvfrom: 10.222.60.2  (so-0/1/0.0) 10 pkts
  Explct route: 10.222.60.2 10.222.6.2
  Record route: 10.222.5.1  <self>  10.222.60.2  10.222.6.2
Total 1 displayed, Up 1, Down 0
```

Controlling LSP Behavior

The JUNOS software also provides you with various methods for controlling how your LSPs establish themselves and operate within your network. These include the sharing of bandwidth reservations between paths of the same LSP, the advertisement of a 0 label by the egress router, the ability to hide the physical connectivity of your network, and the use of your LSPs for forwarding traffic for non-BGP learned routes. While I would agree that these topics don't necessarily have a natural fit with one another, they are important nonetheless. So, let's discuss each in turn.

Adaptive Mode

The default bandwidth reservation style in the JUNOS software is *fixed filter* (FF). This style allocates a unique bandwidth reservation for each sender (LSP ID) and receiver (Tunnel ID) pair. The opposite reservation style is known as *shared explicit* (SE), which allocates a single reservation for each unique RSVP session. This reservation can be shared among multiple sending ID values from the ingress router. The SE reservation style is enabled by configuring the adaptive keyword within your LSP.

Using *adaptive mode* in your network provides you with two unique qualities. The first of these is the establishment of a standby secondary path, which shares physical links in common with the LSP's primary path. As an example, suppose that an LSP is requesting 75Mbps for a bandwidth reservation for both the primary and secondary paths. At some point between the ingress and egress router, the two paths must share a Fast Ethernet segment that has not been oversubscribed. When the primary path is established in the network using the default FF reservation style, the 75Mbps reservation on the Fast Ethernet link is allocated solely for its use. This means that the ingress router can't establish the secondary path of the LSP since the available bandwidth of the Fast Ethernet is below 75Mbps. Such an example is shown in Figure 8.8.

FIGURE 8.8 Adaptive mode

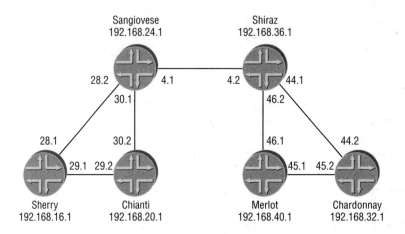

The **Sherry-to-Char** LSP is configured for a 75Mbps bandwidth reservation. The primary path is configured to use Sangiovese as a transit router, while the secondary path is configured to use Chianti as a transit router. The physical link between the Sangiovese and Shiraz routers is a Fast Ethernet segment that hasn't been oversubscribed. To allow both the primary and secondary paths to be established, the adaptive keyword is configured within the LSP:

```
[edit protocols mpls]
user@Sherry# show label-switched-path Sherry-to-Char
to 192.168.32.1;
```

```
bandwidth 75m;
adaptive;
primary via-Sangiovese;
secondary via-Chianti {
    standby;
}
```

WARNING The placement of the adaptive keyword at the global LSP level is quite critical here. This is what keeps the RSVP session information the same for the primary and secondary paths. If the adaptive command is placed within the primary and secondary paths themselves, the Tunnel ID values are not identical. This causes the paths to be viewed as separate RSVP sessions, which may not share the same bandwidth reservation.

Both the primary and secondary paths are established in the network and are in an Up state:

```
user@Sherry> show mpls lsp ingress extensive
Ingress LSP: 1 sessions

192.168.32.1
  From: 192.168.16.1, State: Up, ActiveRoute: 0, LSPname: Sherry-to-Char
  ActivePath: via-Sangiovese (primary)
  LoadBalance: Random
  Encoding type: Packet, Switching type: Packet, GPID: IPv4
 *Primary   via-Sangiovese   State: Up
    Bandwidth: 75Mbps
    Computed ERO (S [L] denotes strict [loose] hops): (CSPF metric: 30)
        10.222.28.2 S 10.222.4.2 S 10.222.44.2 S
    Received RRO:
        10.222.28.2 10.222.4.2 10.222.44.2
    6 Jun  7 18:01:18  Selected as active path
    5 Jun  7 18:01:18  Record Route:  10.222.28.2 10.222.4.2 10.222.44.2
    4 Jun  7 18:01:18  Up
    3 Jun  7 18:01:18  Originate Call
    2 Jun  7 18:01:18  CSPF: computation result accepted
    1 Jun  7 18:00:49  CSPF failed: no route toward 192.168.32.1
  Standby   via-Chianti      State: Up
    Bandwidth: 75Mbps
    Computed ERO (S [L] denotes strict [loose] hops): (CSPF metric: 40)
        10.222.29.2 S 10.222.30.1 S 10.222.4.2 S 10.222.44.2 S
    Received RRO:
```

```
            10.222.29.2 10.222.30.1 10.222.4.2 10.222.44.2
     4 Jun  7 18:01:18  Record Route:  10.222.29.2 10.222.30.1 10.222.4.2 10.222
     3 Jun  7 18:01:18  Up
     2 Jun  7 18:01:18  Originate Call
     1 Jun  7 18:01:18  CSPF: computation result accepted
  Created: Sat Jun  7 18:00:32 2003
Total 1 displayed, Up 1, Down 0
```

While both the paths are using the Sangiovese-Shiraz link, only a single 75Mbps bandwidth reservation is in place:

```
user@Sangiovese> show rsvp interface
RSVP interface: 3 active
                 Active Subscr- Static     Available    Reserved   Highwater
Interface   State resv   iption BW         BW           BW         mark
fe-0/0/2.0  Up        1   100%  100Mbps    25Mbps       75Mbps     90Mbps
at-0/1/0.0  Up        0   100%  155.52Mbps 155.52Mbps   0bps       0bps
so-0/2/0.0  Up        0   100%  155.52Mbps 155.52Mbps   0bps       0bps
```

The second major advantage to using adaptive mode comes into play when an established path attempts to reroute itself onto new network links. In this situation, the adaptive setting allows the ingress router to establish the new path and move traffic to it before removing the old path from the network. This action is referred to as a *make-before-break* operation. In addition, adaptive mode allows the establishing path to not double-count bandwidth reservations on links shared with the path being torn down.

Explicit Null Advertisements

Before we discuss the advertisement of the explicit null label by the egress router, it is helpful to quickly talk about how class of service is handled within the JUNOS software. Within the scope of a single router, the information in the packet header determines how the packet is queued on the outbound interface. In the default operating environment, the ingress router classifies the incoming packet and an outbound queue is determined. The ingress router may also specify the value of the experimental bits in the MPLS header, which allows the first transit router to classify and queue the packet differently. This process continues until the penultimate router is reached. In this case, the incoming packet contains an MPLS header and the experimental bits in that header classify the packet. Since the penultimate router was signaled a label value of 3, the implicit null value, the penultimate router pops the MPLS header and forwards the native IPv4 packet to the egress router. The egress router then performs its class of service operations on the IP Precedence bits in the IP packet. The contents of these bits may or may not allow for the proper class of service processing on the egress router.

In this situation, it may be advantageous to allow the egress router to advertise a label value of 0, the explicit null value, to the penultimate router. This allows the penultimate router to forward packets to the egress router with an MPLS header attached. Assuming that each router in the network has maintained the settings within the experimental bits, the egress router now has the ability to classify the packet using information set by the ingress router.

You enable this functionality by configuring the explicit-null command at the global MPLS level on the egress router. We see this configuration on the Chardonnay router in Figure 8.8:

```
user@Chardonnay> show configuration protocols mpls
explicit-null;
interface all;
```

When the *Sherry-to-Char* LSP is established in the network, Chardonnay signals a label value of 0 to Shiraz. In addition to ensuring that the LSP is established, we check on Shiraz and Chardonnay to verify that the correct label was advertised:

```
user@Sherry> show mpls lsp ingress
Ingress LSP: 1 sessions
To              From           State Rt ActivePath      P       LSPname
192.168.32.1    192.168.16.1   Up    0                 *       Sherry-to-Char
Total 1 displayed, Up 1, Down 0


user@Shiraz> show mpls lsp transit detail
Transit LSP: 1 sessions


192.168.32.1
  From: 192.168.16.1, LSPstate: Up, ActiveRoute: 1
  LSPname: Sherry-to-Char, LSPpath: Primary
  Suggested label received: -, Suggested label sent: -
  Recovery label received: -, Recovery label sent: 0
  Resv style: 1 FF, Label in: 100384, Label out: 0
  Time left: 156,  Since: Sun Jun  8 17:59:03 2003
  Tspec: rate 0bps size 0bps peak Infbps m 20 M 1500
  Port number: sender 1 receiver 11216 protocol 0
  PATH rcvfrom: 10.222.4.1  (fe-0/0/2.0) 4 pkts
  PATH sentto: 10.222.44.2 (so-0/1/0.0) 4 pkts
  RESV rcvfrom: 10.222.44.2  (so-0/1/0.0) 4 pkts
  Explct route: 10.222.44.2
  Record route: 10.222.28.1  10.222.4.1  <self>  10.222.44.2
Total 1 displayed, Up 1, Down 0


user@Chardonnay> show mpls lsp egress detail
Egress LSP: 1 sessions


192.168.32.1
```

```
    From: 192.168.16.1, LSPstate: Up, ActiveRoute: 0
    LSPname: Sherry-to-Char, LSPpath: Primary
    Suggested label received: -, Suggested label sent: -
    Recovery label received: -, Recovery label sent: -
    Resv style: 1 FF, Label in: 0, Label out: -
    Time left: 146,  Since: Sun Jun  8 18:01:18 2003
    Tspec: rate 0bps size 0bps peak Infbps m 20 M 1500
    Port number: sender 1 receiver 11216 protocol 0
    PATH rcvfrom: 10.222.44.1  (so-0/1/0.0) 4 pkts
    PATH sentto: localclient
    RESV rcvfrom: localclient
    Record route: 10.222.28.1  10.222.4.1  10.222.44.1  <self>
Total 1 displayed, Up 1, Down 0
```

Controlling Time-to-Live

The default operation of the JUNOS software with respect to time-to-live (TTL) is to copy the value from the IP packet to the MPLS header after decrementing it b y 1. The LSP routers decrement the value by one at each hop, and the value is rewritten to the IP header when the label is popped by the penultimate router. This default operation allows each hop in the LSP's path to become visible to devices outside the MPLS domain.

FIGURE 8.9 Time-to-live sample network

Figure 8.9 displays a network with the Chianti, Zinfandel, and Merlot routers participating in an MPLS network. The **Chianti-to-Merlot** LSP is established and operational in the network:

```
user@Chianti> show mpls lsp ingress
Ingress LSP: 1 sessions
To              From           State Rt ActivePath      P   LSPname
192.168.40.1    192.168.20.1   Up    1                  *   Chianti-to-Merlot
Total 1 displayed, Up 1, Down 0
```

The Sherry router is receiving the 192.168.32.0 /24 route via BGP, which allows reachability to the loopback address of Chardonnay:

```
user@Sherry> show route protocol bgp terse
```

```
inet.0: 15 destinations, 15 routes (15 active, 0 holddown, 0 hidden)
+ = Active Route, - = Last Active, * = Both

A Destination         P Prf   Metric 1   Metric 2  Next hop      AS path
* 192.168.32.0/24     B 170       100               >10.222.29.2  2 3 I
```

When the Sherry router performs a traceroute to a host within that subnet, each of the MPLS routers is visible in the output:

```
user@Sherry> traceroute 192.168.32.10 source 192.168.16.1
traceroute to 192.168.32.10 (192.168.32.10) from 192.168.16.1, 30 hops max
 1  10.222.29.2 (10.222.29.2)  0.731 ms  0.547 ms  0.488 ms
 2  10.222.2.2 (10.222.2.2)  0.792 ms  0.730 ms  0.704 ms
     MPLS Label=100288 CoS=0 TTL=1 S=1
 3  10.222.3.2 (10.222.3.2)  0.575 ms  0.563 ms  0.538 ms
 4  10.222.45.2 (10.222.45.2)  0.604 ms !N  0.584 ms !N  0.560 ms !N
```

Using the *no-decrement-ttl* Command

The first option available in the JUNOS software for hiding the details of an LSP's path is the no-decrement-ttl command. This option requires each router in the LSP to understand a special Label Request object, which signals the ingress router's desire to alter the default TTL processing rules. Once the LSP is established, the ingress router doesn't copy the IP TTL value into the MPLS header. Instead, it places a value of 255 in the MPLS header and forwards the packet to the first transit router. When the packet arrives at the penultimate router, the value in the MPLS header is not written back to the IP packet. Instead, the top label is popped and the remaining packet data is forwarded to the egress router.

The **Chianti-to-Merlot** LSP in Figure 8.9 is configured with the no-decrement-ttl command. This establishes the LSP in the network where we see the results in the output of the show mpls lsp detail command:

```
user@Chianti> show mpls lsp ingress detail
Ingress LSP: 1 sessions

192.168.40.1
  From: 192.168.20.1, State: Up, ActiveRoute: 1, LSPname: Chianti-to-Merlot
  ActivePath:  (primary)
  LoadBalance: Random
  Encoding type: Packet, Switching type: Packet, GPID: IPv4
 *Primary                      State: Up, No-decrement-ttl
    Computed ERO (S [L] denotes strict [loose] hops): (CSPF metric: 20)
        10.222.2.2 S 10.222.3.2 S
```

```
    Received RRO:
            10.222.2.2 10.222.3.2
Total 1 displayed, Up 1, Down 0
```

When we trace the route to the 192.168.32.0 /24 subnet from the Sherry router, we lose our ability to view some details of the LSP path:

```
user@Sherry> traceroute 192.168.32.10 source 192.168.16.1
traceroute to 192.168.32.10 (192.168.32.10) from 192.168.16.1, 30 hops max
 1  10.222.29.2 (10.222.29.2)  0.751 ms  0.552 ms  0.480 ms
 2  10.222.3.2 (10.222.3.2)  0.574 ms  0.563 ms  0.538 ms
 3  10.222.45.2 (10.222.45.2)  0.627 ms !N  9.542 ms !N  0.563 ms !N
```

More specifically, the Zinfandel router doesn't appear in the router output. Since the LSP is using penultimate hop popping, the Merlot router receives a native IPv4 packet. The TTL of the IP packet is set to a value of 1 as the ingress router decremented it prior to adding the MPLS header. This prompts Merlot to discard the packet and return an ICMP message back to the source of the packet.

Using the *no-propagate-ttl* Command

The second option available to hide the details of an LSP's path is the no-propagate-ttl command, which is configured at the [edit protocols mpls] global hierarchy level. This option doesn't signal any information in a Path message, which makes it interoperable with all other router vendors. As before, the ingress router doesn't copy the IP TTL value into the MPLS header and instead puts a 255 value in its place. When the packet arrives at the penultimate router, the TTL value is not written back into the IP packet, which is forwarded natively to the egress router.

Each of the routers in the path of the **Chianti-to-Merlot** LSP is configured with the no-propagate-ttl command. The configuration on Chianti looks like this:

```
user@Chianti> show configuration protocols mpls
no-propagate-ttl;
label-switched-path Chianti-to-Merlot {
    to 192.168.40.1;
}
interface all;
```

When we trace the route to 192.168.32.1 with this configuration, we no longer see the egress router in the path:

```
user@Sherry> traceroute 192.168.32.10 source 192.168.16.1
traceroute to 192.168.32.10 (192.168.32.10) from 192.168.16.1, 30 hops max
 1  10.222.29.2 (10.222.29.2)  0.735 ms  0.542 ms  0.496 ms
 2  10.222.45.2 (10.222.45.2)  0.605 ms !N  0.580 ms !N  0.557 ms !N
```

This output is caused by the ingress router not decrementing the IP TTL before pushing the MPLS header onto the packet. When the egress router receives the native IPv4 packet, the TTL is set to a value of 2. Merlot routes the IP packet to Chardonnay, which is the end device in the path.

FIGURE 8.10   Controlling LSP interactions

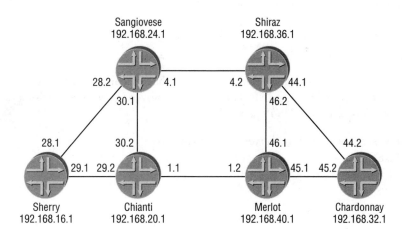

LSP and Routing Protocol Interactions

The default use of an established LSP is the forwarding of BGP transit traffic across your domain. The router accomplishes this by matching the egress address of the LSP, in the inet.3 routing table, to the address specified in the BGP Next Hop attribute. The JUNOS software provides multiple methods for altering or controlling this default selection process.

Advertising an LSP to the IGP

One convenient method for allowing the domain's IGP to forward traffic over an LSP is to advertise the connection into the link-state database as a point-to-point link. This *forwarding adjacency* is advertised within the routing advertisement by the ingress router with a defined metric value. As with a regular IGP adjacency, a bidirectional relationship must be established between the ingress and egress routers. As such, an LSP needs to be established in the return direction for the forwarding adjacency to become active.

Two LSPs are established between the Sangiovese and Chardonnay routers within the network in Figure 8.10. One LSP in each direction easily solves our bidirectional requirement:

```
user@Sangiovese> show mpls lsp
Ingress LSP: 1 sessions
To              From         State Rt ActivePath         P      LSPname
192.168.32.1    192.168.24.1 Up    0                     *      Sangio-to-Char
Total 1 displayed, Up 1, Down 0


Egress LSP: 1 sessions
To              From             State Rt Style Labelin Labelout LSPname
```

```
192.168.24.1    192.168.32.1    Up     0  1 FF      3         - Char-to-Sangio
Total 1 displayed, Up 1, Down 0

Transit LSP: 0 sessions
Total 0 displayed, Up 0, Down 0
```

Using the `label-switched-path` command within the IGP configuration, IS-IS in our case, we assign a metric value of 5 to the LSP. This allows Sangiovese to begin advertising the LSP as a point-to-point link within the IS-IS network:

```
user@Sangiovese> show configuration protocols isis
level 1 disable;
level 2 wide-metrics-only;
interface all;
interface fxp0.0 {
    disable;
}
label-switched-path Sangio-to-Char {
    level 2 metric 5;
}
```

```
user@Sangiovese> show isis adjacency
Interface          System          L State        Hold (secs) SNPA
Sangio-to-Char     Chardonnay      0 One-way              0
at-0/1/0.0         Sherry          2 Up                  19
fe-0/0/2.0         Shiraz          2 Up                   7   0:90:69:68:c8:2
so-0/2/0.0         Chianti         2 Up                  21
```

```
user@Sangiovese> show isis database Sangiovese.00-00 detail
IS-IS level 1 link-state database:

IS-IS level 2 link-state database:

Sangiovese.00-00  Sequence: 0x2bb, Checksum: 0xc97c, Lifetime: 1119 secs
    IS neighbor:                    Sherry.00   Metric:       10
    IS neighbor:                    Chianti.00  Metric:       10
    IS neighbor:                  Chardonnay.00  Metric:        5
    IS neighbor:                    Shiraz.02   Metric:       10
    IP prefix:            10.222.4.0/24 Metric:       10 Internal Up
    IP prefix:           10.222.28.0/24 Metric:       10 Internal Up
    IP prefix:           10.222.30.0/24 Metric:       10 Internal Up
    IP prefix:          192.168.24.1/32 Metric:        0 Internal Up
```

Because only Sangiovese has advertised the forwarding adjacency, it is not currently usable in the network. The adjacency state between Sangiovese and Chardonnay is set to One-way and no IS-IS routes are using the LSP for forwarding traffic:

```
user@Sangiovese> show route protocol isis terse

inet.0: 23 destinations, 23 routes (23 active, 0 holddown, 0 hidden)
+ = Active Route, - = Last Active, * = Both

A Destination        P Prf   Metric 1   Metric 2  Next hop        AS path
* 10.222.44.0/24     I  18       20                >10.222.4.2
* 10.222.45.0/24     I  18       30                >10.222.4.2
                                                    10.222.30.2
* 10.222.46.0/24     I  18       20                >10.222.4.2
* 192.168.32.1/32    I  18       20                >10.222.4.2
* 192.168.36.1/32    I  18       10                >10.222.4.2
* 192.168.40.1/32    I  18       20                 10.222.4.2
                                                    >10.222.30.2
```

 We know that the LSP is not being used since all metric values are multiples of 10 and the LSP is not listed as a valid next hop. In addition, some routes have been removed for readability.

Once the forwarding adjacency is advertised by Chardonnay, the adjacency changes to an Up state and the LSP is used for forwarding traffic in the network:

```
user@Sangiovese> show isis adjacency
Interface            System        L State       Hold (secs) SNPA
Sangio-to-Char       Chardonnay    2 Up                    0
at-0/1/0.0           Sherry        2 Up                   20
fe-0/0/2.0           Shiraz        2 Up                    7  0:90:69:68:c8:2
so-0/2/0.0           Chianti       2 Up                   26

user@Sangiovese> show route protocol isis terse

inet.0: 23 destinations, 23 routes (23 active, 0 holddown, 0 hidden)
+ = Active Route, - = Last Active, * = Both

A Destination        P Prf   Metric 1   Metric 2  Next hop        AS path
* 10.222.44.0/24     I  18       15                >10.222.4.2
```

```
*  10.222.45.0/24      I   18          15          >10.222.4.2
*  10.222.46.0/24      I   18          20          >10.222.4.2
*  192.168.32.1/32     I   18           5          >10.222.4.2
*  192.168.36.1/32     I   18          10          >10.222.4.2
*  192.168.40.1/32     I   18          15          >10.222.4.2
```

For further proof that the LSP is being used to forward traffic, we trace the route to Chardonnay's loopback address from the Sherry router:

```
user@Sherry> traceroute 192.168.32.1
traceroute to 192.168.32.1 (192.168.32.1), 30 hops max, 40 byte packets
 1   10.222.28.2 (10.222.28.2)  1.232 ms  0.917 ms  0.896 ms
 2   10.222.4.2 (10.222.4.2)  0.993 ms  0.841 ms  0.917 ms
       MPLS Label=100416 CoS=0 TTL=1 S=1
 3   192.168.32.1 (192.168.32.1)  1.377 ms  0.979 ms  0.921 ms
```

Providing LSP Access to Just the Ingress Router

The default action of placing the egress router address in the inet.3 routing table can be altered within the JUNOS software in multiple ways. Using various options within the traffic-engineering command, you can move the contents of the inet.3 table into inet.0, or you can copy the contents into inet.0. To complicate matters further, the copy functionality can have multiple effects on the router itself. Let's discuss how each of the functions works and provide some rationale for using each.

Using *traffic-engineering bgp-igp*

When you use the bgp-igp option within your MPLS configuration, the router moves the contents of the inet.3 table into inet.0. The movement of these addresses doesn't alter the default BGP recursive lookup functionality as the protocol inspects both the inet.3 and inet.0 tables. What you gain as a benefit, however, is the ability for the ingress router to locate the LSP during a normal IP routing lookup.

The Sherry router in Figure 8.10 has established the **Sherry-to-Char** LSP in the network. We see that the default action of placing the egress address in the inet.3 routing table has occurred:

```
user@Sherry> show route table inet.3

inet.3: 1 destinations, 1 routes (1 active, 0 holddown, 0 hidden)
+ = Active Route, - = Last Active, * = Both

192.168.32.1/32     *[RSVP/7] 00:00:05, metric 30
                     > via at-0/1/0.0, label-switched-path Sherry-to-Char
```

From the perspective of the ingress router, however, all IP packets with a destination address of 192.168.32.1 use the route installed by IS-IS. These packets do not use the LSP for forwarding across the network since all routing lookups are performed in the `inet.0` routing table:

```
user@Sherry> show route 192.168.32.1

inet.0: 29 destinations, 29 routes (29 active, 0 holddown, 0 hidden)
+ = Active Route, - = Last Active, * = Both

192.168.32.1/32    *[IS-IS/18] 00:04:35, metric 30
                    > to 10.222.29.2 via ge-0/2/0.0
                      to 10.222.28.2 via at-0/1/0.0

inet.3: 1 destinations, 1 routes (1 active, 0 holddown, 0 hidden)
+ = Active Route, - = Last Active, * = Both

192.168.32.1/32    *[RSVP/7] 00:01:15, metric 30
                    > via at-0/1/0.0, label-switched-path Sherry-to-Char
```

Sherry applies the `bgp-igp` knob to its MPLS configuration to move the `inet.3` routes into the `inet.0` routing table:

```
user@Sherry> show configuration protocols mpls
traffic-engineering bgp-igp;
label-switched-path Sherry-to-Char {
    to 192.168.32.1;
    primary via-Sangiovese;
}
path via-Sangiovese {
    192.168.24.1 loose;
}
interface all;

user@Sherry> show route 192.168.32.1

inet.0: 29 destinations, 30 routes (29 active, 0 holddown, 0 hidden)
+ = Active Route, - = Last Active, * = Both

192.168.32.1/32    *[RSVP/7] 00:00:46, metric 30
                    > via at-0/1/0.0, label-switched-path Sherry-to-Char
                    [IS-IS/18] 00:00:50, metric 30
                    > to 10.222.29.2 via ge-0/2/0.0
                      to 10.222.28.2 via at-0/1/0.0
```

Sherry now has the ability to use the LSP for traffic forwarding for packets address to the 192.168.32.1 address:

```
user@Sherry> traceroute 192.168.32.1
traceroute to 192.168.32.1 (192.168.32.1), 30 hops max, 40 byte packets
 1  10.222.28.2 (10.222.28.2)  1.425 ms  1.215 ms  1.163 ms
     MPLS Label=100448 CoS=0 TTL=1 S=1
 2  10.222.4.2 (10.222.4.2)  1.293 ms  0.924 ms  1.126 ms
     MPLS Label=100448 CoS=0 TTL=1 S=1
 3  192.168.32.1 (192.168.32.1)  0.836 ms  0.957 ms  1.169 ms
```

Using *traffic-engineering bgp-igp-both-ribs*

While some administrators find it advantageous to place the LSP egress address in the inet.0 table, one possible downside does exist. Specifically, the use of the MPLS network to support virtual private networks (VPN) requires the egress address to be located in the inet.3 routing table. To resolve this issue, the JUNOS software provides the bgp-igp-both-ribs option for the traffic-engineering command. This command copies the egress addresses into the inet.0 routing table instead of moving them.

The Sherry router is operating in a default mode for the 192.168.32.1 egress address of the **Sherry-to-Char** LSP:

```
user@Sherry> show route 192.168.32.1

inet.0: 29 destinations, 29 routes (29 active, 0 holddown, 0 hidden)
+ = Active Route, - = Last Active, * = Both

192.168.32.1/32    *[IS-IS/18] 00:00:04, metric 30
                    > to 10.222.29.2 via ge-0/2/0.0
                      to 10.222.28.2 via at-0/1/0.0

inet.3: 1 destinations, 1 routes (1 active, 0 holddown, 0 hidden)
+ = Active Route, - = Last Active, * = Both

192.168.32.1/32     *[RSVP/7] 00:00:04, metric 65535
                       > via at-0/1/0.0, label-switched-path Sherry-to-Char
```

The configuration of the traffic-engineering bgp-igp-both-ribs command on Sherry copies the address into the inet.0 routing table:

```
user@Sherry> show configuration protocols mpls
traffic-engineering bgp-igp-both-ribs;
label-switched-path Sherry-to-Char {
    to 192.168.32.1;
```

```
      primary via-Sangiovese;
}
path via-Sangiovese {
    192.168.24.1 loose;
}
interface all;
```

```
user@Sherry> show route 192.168.32.1
```

```
inet.0: 29 destinations, 30 routes (29 active, 0 holddown, 0 hidden)
+ = Active Route, - = Last Active, * = Both
```

```
192.168.32.1/32     *[RSVP/7] 00:00:41, metric 30
                    > via at-0/1/0.0, label-switched-path Sherry-to-Char
                    [IS-IS/18] 00:00:46, metric 30
                       to 10.222.29.2 via ge-0/2/0.0
                    > to 10.222.28.2 via at-0/1/0.0
```

```
inet.3: 1 destinations, 1 routes (1 active, 0 holddown, 0 hidden)
+ = Active Route, - = Last Active, * = Both
```

```
192.168.32.1/32     *[RSVP/7] 00:00:41, metric 30
                    > via at-0/1/0.0, label-switched-path Sherry-to-Char
```

As before, IP packets with a destination address of 192.168.32.1 are forwarded by the Sherry router across the LSP:

```
user@Sherry> traceroute 192.168.32.1
traceroute to 192.168.32.1 (192.168.32.1), 30 hops max, 40 byte packets
 1  10.222.28.2 (10.222.28.2)  1.303 ms  1.393 ms  1.071 ms
     MPLS Label=100448 CoS=0 TTL=1 S=1
 2  10.222.4.2 (10.222.4.2)  1.310 ms  1.465 ms  1.146 ms
     MPLS Label=100448 CoS=0 TTL=1 S=1
 3  192.168.32.1 (192.168.32.1)  0.828 ms  0.966 ms  1.160 ms
```

Using *traffic-engineering mpls-forwarding*

The main disadvantage to using the `bgp-igp-both-ribs` command is how the router views the LSP addresses in the `inet.0` routing table. By default, these routes have a better (lower) JUNOS software protocol preference value than the version of the route placed there by the IGP. This makes the LSP version of the address active in the routing table. As only active routes are eligible for routing policy processing, the placement of the LSP addresses might cause existing routing policies to not perform as expected. This is especially true when the routing policy is exporting the IGP routes into another protocol, like BGP.

To combat this issue, you can configure MPLS with the `traffic-engineering mpls-forwarding` command. This allows the LSP egress addresses to be copied to the `inet.0` routing table, but only marks them as active for purposes of forwarding packets. The IGP versions of these same addresses are left active for routing purposes. In effect, this command provides the best of all possible situations.

The Sherry router is currently configured with this command. From the router's output we can see that the different versions of the 192.168.32.1 route are notated differently in the routing table:

```
user@Sherry> show configuration protocols mpls
traffic-engineering mpls-forwarding;
label-switched-path Sherry-to-Char {
    to 192.168.32.1;
    primary via-Sangiovese;
}
path via-Sangiovese {
    192.168.24.1 loose;
}
interface all;

user@Sherry> show route 192.168.32.1

inet.0: 29 destinations, 30 routes (25 active, 0 holddown, 4 hidden)
@ = Routing Use Only, # = Forwarding Use Only
+ = Active Route, - = Last Active, * = Both

192.168.32.1/32     @[IS-IS/18] 00:00:08, metric 30
                        to 10.222.29.2 via ge-0/2/0.0
                      > to 10.222.28.2 via at-0/1/0.0
                    #[RSVP/7] 00:00:04, metric 30
                      > via at-0/1/0.0, label-switched-path Sherry-to-Char

inet.3: 1 destinations, 1 routes (1 active, 0 holddown, 0 hidden)
@ = Routing Use Only, # = Forwarding Use Only
+ = Active Route, - = Last Active, * = Both

192.168.32.1/32     *[RSVP/7] 00:00:04, metric 30
                      > via at-0/1/0.0, label-switched-path Sherry-to-Char
```

As we would expect, IP packets use the LSP for forwarding on the Sherry router:

```
lab@Sherry> traceroute 192.168.32.1
```

```
traceroute to 192.168.32.1 (192.168.32.1), 30 hops max, 40 byte packets
 1   10.222.28.2 (10.222.28.2)  1.531 ms  1.345 ms  1.109 ms
     MPLS Label=100464 CoS=0 TTL=1 S=1
 2   10.222.4.2 (10.222.4.2)  1.369 ms  0.895 ms  1.152 ms
     MPLS Label=100464 CoS=0 TTL=1 S=1
 3   192.168.32.1 (192.168.32.1)  0.901 ms  0.915 ms  1.160 ms
```

Summary

In this chapter, we examined how the JUNOS software constructs a traffic engineering database (TED) in the network. Information specific to MPLS, such as current reservations and available bandwidth, is propagated within the interior gateway protocols. OSPF uses a Type 10 Opaque LSA for this purpose, whereas IS-IS uses the Extended IS Reachability TLV, number 22. We discussed the steps of the Constrained Shortest Path First (CSPF) algorithm, which evaluates the information in the TED to compute a path from the ingress router to the egress router. User-defined constraints, including administrative groups and priority values, can be applied to the CSPF algorithm, and we discussed those next.

We then explored some methods available within the JUNOS software for protecting LSP traffic flows in the network. This discussion centered on the creation of primary and secondary paths for a single LSP. We further found that the secondary path could be placed into a hot-standby mode to quickly move traffic in the event of a failure. We examined the operation of fast reroute to further protect user traffic already contained within the LSP. We saw that both node protection and link protection created alternate paths through the network to quickly alter the traffic flows on a transit router should a failure occur.

We concluded the chapter with a discussion of various ways to control the behavior of the LSPs in your network. We first talked about adaptive mode, which establishes bandwidth reservations using the shared explicit style. This allows multiple paths within the main RSVP session to share the single reservation instead of double-counting the bandwidth. In addition, adaptive mode allows the ingress router to create a new LSP before tearing down the existing LSP in a make-before-break mode. After a quick look at having the egress router advertise a label value of 0, we saw two methods for hiding the topology of the LSP. We accomplished this by changing the ingress and penultimate router's default behavior with regard to the time-to-live value in the MPLS header. We then discussed methods for allowing other protocols to access the LSP for traffic forwarding. The first of these was the advertisement of the LSP as a point-to-point link within the IGPs themselves. The second was the use of the traffic-engineering command on the ingress router to allow IP route lookups to access the LSP.

Exam Essentials

Be able to describe how information is placed into the traffic engineering database. Both OSPF and IS-IS have been extended to carry traffic engineering specific information within their protocol updates. The Type 10 Opaque LSA and the Extended IS Reachability TLV contain bandwidth, administrative group, and addressing information. These advertisements are then placed into the TED on each IGP router.

Know the steps used by the CSPF algorithm to locate a path for the LSP. The algorithm first removes all links from the TED that don't meet the bandwidth requirements of the LSP. Then all links that do not contain any included administrative group information are removed. If the LSP is configured to exclude any administrative group information, those links are then removed by the algorithm. Using the remaining links, the algorithm locates the shortest path through the network from the ingress to the egress router.

Be familiar with methods available to the ingress router for protecting MPLS traffic flows. An individual LSP may be configured for both a primary and a secondary path through the network. When the primary path is available, it is used for traffic forwarding. In a failure mode, the ingress router establishes the secondary path and begins forwarding traffic using MPLS labels once again. The failover time on the ingress router can be shortened by allowing the secondary path to be established in the network prior to the primary path failure. This is accomplished through the use of the `standby` command.

Be able to describe how user traffic within an LSP is protected from failures. Once the ingress router has begun forwarding traffic along the LSP, a network failure in the path can cause those packets to be dropped from the network. To alleviate this problem, the LSP can be configured for either node or link protection fast reroute. These methods allow all routers in the LSP to preestablish paths in the network to avoid the next downstream link or node. During a failure mode, the device that notices the failure immediately begins using the temporary paths to continue forwarding traffic within the LSP.

Be able to describe how multiple LSP paths share bandwidth reservations. By default, all newly established paths in the network reserve unique and distinct bandwidth reservations using the fixed filter style. Within a single RSVP session, multiple paths can share a reservation when the shared explicit style is used during the path establishment. Within the JUNOS software, the `adaptive` command accomplishes this goal. In addition, adaptive mode allows the ingress router to use a make-before-break system for rerouting an LSP in the network. The new path is established and traffic is moved before the old path is torn down.

Understand methods used to provide LSP visibility to non-BGP learned routes. Advertising the LSP to the IGP link-state database is one effective method for accomplishing this goal. Each router in the network then sees the LSP as a point-to-point link with some metric value attached. This information is used in the SPF calculation on the router, which may result in the LSP being used for traffic forwarding.

Review Questions

1. How is traffic engineering information propagated in an OSPF network?

    A. Type 8 Opaque LSA

    B. Type 9 Opaque LSA

    C. Type 10 Opaque LSA

    D. Type 11 Opaque LSA

2. How is traffic engineering information propagated in an IS-IS network?

    A. IS Reachability TLV

    B. Internal IP Reachability TLV

    C. Extended IS Reachability TLV

    D. Extended IP Reachability TLV

3. Which CSPF constraint is carried in a 32-bit vector?

    A. Bandwidth

    B. Administrative groups

    C. Named path ERO

    D. Load-balancing configuration

4. What is the default JUNOS software setting for RSVP priority values?

    A. A setup of 0 and a hold of 7

    B. A setup of 7 and a hold of 0

    C. A setup of 0 and a hold of 0

    D. A setup of 7 and a hold of 7

5. What is the maximum number of primary paths allowed on an LSP?

    A. 0

    B. 1

    C. 2

    D. 3

6. What JUNOS software command allows an LSP path to be established before it is needed for a failure condition?

    A. `admin-group`

    B. `optimize timer`

    C. `standby`

    D. `traffic-engineering`

7. What fast reroute mode permits each router in the path to create a detour path to the egress router?

    A. Node protection

    B. Link protection

    C. Detour protection

    D. Bypass protection

8. What fast reroute mode permits each router in the path to create a bypass path to the next downstream router?

    A. Node protection

    B. Link protection

    C. Detour protection

    D. Bypass protection

9. What RSVP reservation style results from configuring `adaptive` on an LSP?

    A. Fixed filter

    B. Wildcard filter

    C. Shared explicit

    D. Wildcard explicit

10. Which JUNOS software configuration command copies entries from the `inet.3` routing table to the `inet.0` routing table while leaving the previous `inet.0` entries active for routing purposes?

    A. `traffic-engineering`

    B. `traffic-engineering bgp-igp`

    C. `traffic-engineering bgp-igp-both-ribs`

    D. `traffic-engineering mpls-forwarding`

Answers to Review Questions

1. C. OSPF uses the Type 10 Opaque LSA to propagate traffic engineering information to the network. This LSA has an area flooding scope that results in each area having a separate and distinct TED.

2. C. The Extended IS Reachability TLV is used by IS-IS to propagate traffic engineering information to the network. This TLV is flooded within a specific level that results in each level having a separate and distinct TED.

3. B. MPLS administrative groups are each assigned a value between 0 and 31. These values are each represented by a bit in a 32-bit vector propagated by the IGPs.

4. B. By default, each LSP is established with a setup priority value of 7 and a hold priority value of 0.

5. B. While an LSP can be configured without a primary path, it can contain only one. When the constraints of this path are met, it is used by the LSP for forwarding traffic.

6. C. The `standby` command is configured on a secondary path to establish the path in the network before the primary path fails.

7. A. The node-protection version of fast reroute allows each LSP router to create and establish a detour path to the egress router. During a failure mode, the point of local repair swaps the incoming label for the detour label and forwards the packet.

8. B. The link-protection version of fast reroute allows each LSP router to create and establish a bypass path to the next downstream router. During a failure mode, the point of local repair swaps the incoming label for the label advertised by the downstream router and pushes the bypass label onto the stack.

9. C. The shared explicit (SE) reservation style is used when an LSP is configured with the `adaptive` command.

10. D. All route entries in the `inet.3` routing table are copied to `inet.0` when the MPLS process is configured with the `traffic-engineering mpls-forwarding` command. Additionally, the existing `inet.0` entries are marked for routing use only while the new entries are marked for forwarding use only.

Chapter

9

Layer 2 and Layer 3 Virtual Private Networks

JNCIS EXAM OBJECTIVES COVERED IN THIS CHAPTER:

- ✓ Identify the differences between a CPE and a provider-provisioned VPN
- ✓ Describe the operation of the control plane in a Layer 3 VPN environment
- ✓ Describe the operation of the data plane in a Layer 3 VPN environment
- ✓ Identify the steps involved in configuring a Layer 3 VPN
- ✓ Identify the differences between a Layer 2 and a Layer 3 VPN
- ✓ Describe the steps involved in configuring a Kompella Layer 2 VPN
- ✓ Describe the steps involved in configuring a Martini Layer 2 VPN

In this chapter, we begin our discussion of virtual private networks (VPNs) by discussing the terminology used within the JUNOS software for configuring and deploying a VPN. We then focus our attention on the type of VPN that interacts with the customer's routing domain using Layer 3 routing protocols. We see how the control plane and the data plane of the VPN work within this constraint. After configuring a basic Layer 3 VPN using different routing protocols for the customer communications, we examine methods for providing Internet access to customer sites.

We then continue our examination of VPNs by focusing our attention on Layer 2 protocols transported across a provider network. After discussing the two types of Layer 2 VPNs available within the JUNOS software, we examine each of the varieties in further detail. Within the context of each method, we discuss the advertisement of Layer 2 connection information between the provider edge (PE) routers. We then see how the actual data is transmitted across the provider network using each of the Layer 2 VPN methods.

From a conceptual standpoint, a VPN is quite simple. It's the operation of a network over a common physical infrastructure. The provider of the infrastructure allows each customer to remain segregated within their own virtual connections. In fact, we've been running VPNs to interconnect locations for quite some time now. Three examples of these "traditional" VPNs include leased lines, Frame Relay, and Asynchronous Transfer Mode (ATM) circuits. In today's nomenclature, however, this type of connectivity is usually not associated with VPNs. This mainly arises from the fact that all access to the Internet, as well as remote locations, is driven from a connection to a provider that often uses Frame Relay or ATM for access. As such, we normally consider a VPN to connect multiple locations together using an IP-based technology. In fact, we're going to make that assumption for our discussion and focus on the methods used for connecting those locations.

VPN Basics

Before discussing either Layer 3 or Layer 2 VPNs, we first need to examine some terms that relate to both technologies as well as some terms that are specific to one or the other. Unfortunately for us, the use of a VPN within a provider network is filled with multiple terms and acronyms. So, let's see what they all mean.

Customer edge router   The *customer edge* (CE) router is the device physically located in the customer's location. It connects to the provider network using a Layer 2 technology such as

Frame Relay, ATM, or Ethernet. Within a Layer 3 (L3) VPN, the CE router forms a protocol relationship with the provider router to exchange routing knowledge. The CE router may be the only device in a particular customer location, or it might participate in a routing domain based in that location. For a Layer 2 VPN, the CE router transmits frames to the provider network that are destined for a remote customer location. The CE router may have a single static route that points at the provider, or it may be communicating via a routing protocol with other CE routers in remote locations.

Provider edge router   The *provider edge* (PE) router is located in the provider's network and communicates directly with the CE router. In addition, it maintains relationships with other routers inside the provider's network. For an L3VPN environment, the PE router communicates with its attached CE router to receive routing updates. This information is then advertised to a remote PE router that is connected to another of the customer's sites. When the PE router receives data packets destined for a remote site, it forwards the packets using a Multiprotocol Label Switching (MPLS) LSP across the provider's network. When the PE router is participating in a Layer 2 VPN, it simply receives a Layer 2 frame from the local CE router, which it forwards to a remote PE router using an MPLS LSP.

Provider router   The *provider* (P) router is located within the core of the provider's network. The P routers do not maintain any knowledge of the customer's VPN information but simply forward MPLS packets from one PE router to another.

VPN routing and forwarding table   In a Layer 3 VPN, each PE router maintains a separate *VPN routing and forwarding* (VRF) table for each customer connected to that local PE. Each VRF table contains routing knowledge specific to the customer's network. When the attached CE router advertises routes from that location, the PE router places them into that customer's VRF table. The routes are then advertised to the remote PE routers, which also service this particular customer. Each remote PE router places the received routes in that customer's VRF table and advertises them to their locally attached CE routers.

VPN forwarding table   A *VPN forwarding table* (VFT) is used in a Layer 2 VPN environment. Each PE router creates a separate VFT for each customer connected to that PE router. The VFT contains information that describes the local PE-CE connection, such as encapsulation type, local logical interface, a local site identifier, and some MPLS label information. Each VFT contains knowledge of the remote locations connected across the provider's LSPs.

VPN connection table   The information contained in a Layer 2 VFT is transmitted to the remote PE routers in a *VPN connection table* (VCT). Each VCT is a subset of the information contained in the VFT for that particular customer. This allows each PE to forward the received Layer 2 frames to the appropriate remote PE router.

Figure 9.1 displays a typical provider network that is supporting VPNs. The Sangiovese, Sherry, Shiraz, and Chablis routers are all CE routers, whereas the Chianti, Chardonnay, and Cabernet routers are PE routers. The only P routers in the network are Merlot and Zinfandel.

FIGURE 9.1 Provider-provisioned VPN environment

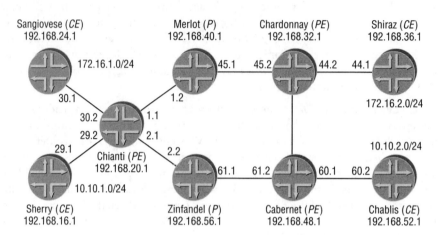

Layer 3 VPNs

Within a Layer 3 VPN, the customer advertises IP routing knowledge to the provider network. The ISP then advertises this routing information across its network to the other customer locations. This simple concept requires quite a bit of coordination between the provider and the customer. In addition, the provider network must be configured to support the advertisement of these routes. To accomplish this, we first need a method for ensuring that the customer routes remain segregated. This is the function of specially designed *Network Layer Reachability Information* (NLRI), which we discuss next.

VPN Network Layer Reachability Information

One of the core principles of operating a VPN is maintaining separation between the customer networks. The normal rules of Border Gateway Protocol (BGP) routing make this a difficult task since multiple versions of the same route are parsed through the route selection algorithm and a single best path is selected. It is only this single best path that is readvertised to all other BGP peers.

To better understand why this is an issue, let's assume that a provider is offering VPN services to both Customer A and Customer B. Each of the customers is using the Request for Comments (RFC) 1918 address space of 192.168.0.0 /16 within their network. When either customer sends routes to the local PE router, the routes are placed into the VRF table associated with that customer. In our example, the 192.168.1.0 /24 route arrives from Customer A on Router A within the provider's network while the same 192.168.1.0 /24 route from Customer B arrives on Router B. Both Router A and Router B advertise the 192.168.1.0 /24 route to Router C in the provider's core. From Router C's perspective, it receives the same route with different attributes from different peers. It then runs the route selection algorithm and selects the route from Router A as the local active route. This is readvertised to Router D on the far edge of the network, where both Customer A and Customer B have VPN connections. Router D sends the route to both of the customer routers, which install it in their local routing tables. The main problem, of course, is that when devices in Customer B's network send packets destined for the 192.168.1.0 /24 network, they are all delivered to Customer A. Since this version of the route was selected by BGP, the physical next hops for that destination were also installed in the routing table. This means that all traffic flows to that same destination. Clearly, this scenario doesn't work for a VPN environment.

To alleviate the issue we just outlined, a Layer 3 VPN uses a special format for representing customer routes within the provider's network. This format allows each provider router to uniquely view routes from different customers as separate, even when they advertise the same IPv4 prefix. Figure 9.2 displays this format, which includes the following fields:

Mask (1 octet)   This field displays the total length of the NLRI advertised within the BGP Update message. The value of the mask varies from 88 to 120.

MPLS Label (3 octets)   Each route advertised in a Layer 3 VPN is associated with an MPLS label, which is contained in this field. This label value is allocated by the PE router which first advertises the route into the provider's network. It is used for forwarding data packets to the appropriate CE router.

Route Distinguisher (8 octets)   The Route Distinguisher field is critical to the operation of a Layer 3 VPN. Within this field lies a specific value unique to each customer VPN or customer site. It is the route distinguisher (RD) that allows each provider router to view the customer IP addresses as separate and unique entities.

IPv4 Prefix (Variable)   This field displays the customer route being advertised between the PE routers.

Of course, the advertisement of specialized NLRI requires the establishment of multiprotocol BGP (MBGP) sessions between the PE routers. These sessions are established between individual peers based on the settings within the `family` command at the global, group, or neighbor level. (We discuss MBGP in Chapter 5, "Advanced Border Gateway Protocol (BGP)".) The PE routers of Chianti, Chardonnay, and Cabernet are configured to advertise the VPN-IPv4 NLRI to each other. For example, the configuration of Chianti is as follows:

```
user@Chianti> show configuration protocols bgp
group Internal-Peers {
    type internal;
    local-address 192.168.20.1;
    family inet-vpn {
        unicast;
    }
    neighbor 192.168.32.1;
    neighbor 192.168.48.1;
}
```

FIGURE 9.2 The VPN-IPv4 NLRI format

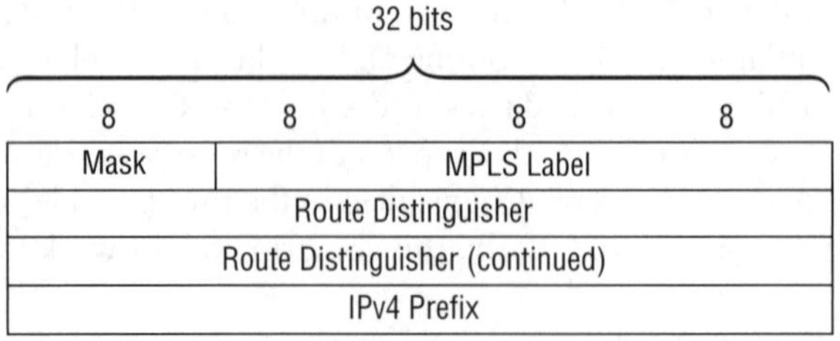

Once the sessions are established, the received NLRI appears in the bgp.l3vpn.0 routing table:

```
user@Chianti> show bgp summary
Groups: 1 Peers: 2 Down peers: 0
Table           Tot Paths  Act Paths Suppressed   History Damp State   Pending
bgp.l3vpn.0            5          5          0         0     0      0         0
Peer               AS      InPkt     OutPkt     OutQ   Flaps Last Up/Dwn State
192.168.32.1    65432     13974      14002        0       4 3d 19:56:13 Establ
  bgp.l3vpn.0: 2/2/0
  VPN-A.inet.0: 2/2/0
192.168.48.1    65432     13984      14019        0       0 4d 19:57:37 Establ
  bgp.l3vpn.0: 3/3/0
  VPN-B.inet.0: 3/3/0
```

Suppose the Chianti and Chardonnay routers are communicating routes for a VPN customer connected to each of them. On Chardonnay the VPN-IPv4 routing information appears within the bgp.l3vpn.0 table:

```
user@Chardonnay> show route table bgp.l3vpn.0

bgp.l3vpn.0: 1 destinations, 1 routes (1 active, 0 holddown, 0 hidden)
+ = Active Route, - = Last Active, * = Both

192.168.20.1:3:10.222.30.0/24
                    *[BGP/170] 01:24:05, localpref 100, from 192.168.20.1
                      AS path: I
                    > via so-0/1/1.0, label-switched-path Char-to-Chianti
```

The customer prefix being announced by Chianti is 10.222.30.0 /24. The leading information in the router output (192.168.20.1:3) is the RD appended by Chianti to provide unique routing information. Let's discuss that next.

Route Distinguishers

The *Route Distinguisher* is an 8-octet field that actually consists of three portions; the Type, the Administrator, and Assigned Number fields. The first 2 octets of the Route Distinguisher contain the type of RD being used, which determines the length of the remaining fields. A type code of 0 represents an Administrator field that is 2 octets long, whereas the Assigned Number field is 4 octets in length. A type code of 1, on the other hand, means that the Administrator field is 4 octets long and the Assigned Number field is 2 octets long.

FIGURE 9.3   Route distinguisher formats

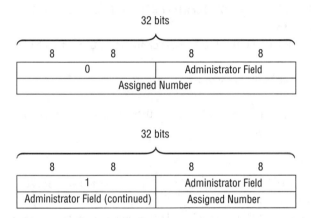

Figure 9.3 displays the two possible formats for RDs. The actual RD used within a Layer 3 VPN is entirely up to the discretion of the VPN's network administrators. The only requirement for assigned RD values is to keep them unique throughout the network, on either a per-VRF basis or a per-VPN basis. There are, however, some common best practices in use today. When the RD is using a 2-octet Administrator field, place the global Autonomous System value in this field. The router ID of the originating PE router should be used when the Administrator field is 4 octets long. In either case, the value placed in the Assigned Number field is left to the discretion of the administrator.

Within the JUNOS software, there are two main methods for assigning an RD to a particular VRF table—automatically or manually. When you use the `route-distinguisher-id` command within the [`edit routing-options`] configuration hierarchy, the PE automatically generates an RD for each unique VRF table enabled on that router. This process uses the router ID of the advertising PE router within the Administrator field and generates an assigned number automatically. As an example, the Chianti router in Figure 9.1 is currently advertising routes for two customers. We've entered Chianti's router ID within the `route-distinguisher-id` command:

```
user@Chianti> show configuration routing-options
route-distinguisher-id 192.168.20.1;
autonomous-system 65432;
```

This allows Chianti to advertise routes from each customer with a different RD to its established PE peers. We see one route appear on Chardonnay, whereas another arrives at the Cabernet router:

```
user@Chardonnay> show route table bgp.l3vpn.0

bgp.l3vpn.0: 1 destinations, 1 routes (1 active, 0 holddown, 0 hidden)
+ = Active Route, - = Last Active, * = Both

192.168.20.1:3:10.222.30.0/24
                    *[BGP/170] 01:54:16, localpref 100, from 192.168.20.1
                      AS path: I
                    > via so-0/1/1.0, label-switched-path Char-to-Chianti
```

```
user@Cabernet> show route table bgp.l3vpn.0

bgp.l3vpn.0: 1 destinations, 1 routes (1 active, 0 holddown, 0 hidden)
+ = Active Route, - = Last Active, * = Both

192.168.20.1:4:10.222.29.0/24
                    *[BGP/170] 00:07:44, localpref 100, from 192.168.20.1
                      AS path: I
                    > via so-0/1/1.0, label-switched-path Cab-to-Chianti
```

Although both values begin with the router ID of 192.168.20.1, the different Assigned Number fields provide a unique RD for each customer VRF table.

Of course, the JUNOS software also provides you the ability to manually control the RD value. Some administrators prefer to use an AS-based RD, whereas others would like more control over the value placed in the Assigned Number field. Either way, you configure a manual RD value within the [edit routing-instances] configuration hierarchy corresponding to the VRF table of a particular customer. For example, the Cabernet router assigns a manual RD as so:

```
user@Cabernet> show configuration routing-instances
VPN-B {
    instance-type vrf;
    interface so-0/1/2.0;
    route-distinguisher 65432:8989;
    vrf-target target:65432:2222;
}
```

This value appears within the bgp.l3vpn.0 routing table on the Chianti router:

```
user@Chianti> show route table bgp.l3vpn.0

bgp.l3vpn.0: 2 destinations, 2 routes (2 active, 0 holddown, 0 hidden)
```

```
+ = Active Route, - = Last Active, * = Both

192.168.32.1:3:10.222.44.0/24
                    *[BGP/170] 00:50:48, localpref 100, from 192.168.32.1
                      AS path: I
                    > via so-0/1/0.0, label-switched-path Chianti-to-Char
65432:8989:10.222.60.0/24
                    *[BGP/170] 00:50:48, localpref 100, from 192.168.48.1
                      AS path: I
                    > via so-0/1/0.0, label-switched-path Chianti-to-Cab
```

Other important commands to use in the configuration of a Layer 3 VPN include instance-type, interface, and protocols. The instance-type command informs the router what type of VPN service to operate for the customer while the interface command places the customer's interface into the VRF table. Finally, the specific routing protocol operating between the PE and CE routers is configured within the protocols section of the routing instance.

Basic Operational Concepts

When you are using a Layer 3 VPN, you need to be aware of the operation of both the control plane (route advertisements) and the forwarding plane (packet forwarding). We examine both topics within this section; let's begin with route advertisements. After all, you can't forward packets when you don't have a route for the destination.

The Control Plane

Customer routes in a Layer 3 VPN environment are advertised between PE routers within the provider's network. To ensure that the routes are delivered to each appropriate customer site, the provider has two main choices. The first option involves the PE router forming only a protocol relationship, BGP in our case, with the other PE routers connected to that particular customer. This approach has the main disadvantage of requiring a new BGP connection for each new customer site added to a different PE router. The second option uses a full mesh of BGP connections between the PE routers and routing policy to control which routes are accepted within each customer VRF table. Because this option carries with it the ability to easily change the logical topology, many real-world networks adopt this model. Therefore, we'll focus our attention in this direction.

The routing policies used by the PE routers in a Layer 3 VPN rely on a *route target* to identify routes belonging to a specific VRF table. The route target takes the form of a BGP extended community and is assigned to all routes advertised out of a particular VRF table. (We discuss extended communities in Chapter 4, "Border Gateway Protocol (BGP).") When the receiving PE router sees the route target associated with a local VRF table, it accepts the route advertisement and places the route into the customer's VRF table. Using the routers in Figure 9.1, let's examine each step in the process:

1. The Chardonnay router receives routes in the customer's VRF table that belong to that particular customer. In our sample network, these are direct and static routes but may also include routes received from a routing protocol operating between the PE and CE routers. The JUNOS software currently supports BGP, OSPF, and RIP for use as CE-PE routing protocols.

```
user@Chardonnay> show route table VPN-A.inet.0

VPN-A.inet.0: 3 destinations, 3 routes (3 active, 0 holddown, 0 hidden)
+ = Active Route, - = Last Active, * = Both

10.222.44.0/24      *[Direct/0] 2d 00:49:16
                     > via so-0/1/0.0
10.222.44.2/32      *[Local/0] 2d 00:49:18
                       Local via so-0/1/0.0
172.16.2.0/24       *[Static/5] 1d 20:00:29
                     > to 10.222.44.1 via so-0/1/0.0
```

2. Chardonnay then consults the export policy applied to this VRF table to determine which routes should be advertised to the other PE routers in the network. This policy also applies the appropriate route target to the advertised routes. Because Chardonnay is configured with the vrf-target command, it automatically advertises all active routes that belong to this particular VRF table. In addition, the route target of target:65432:1111 is applied to the advertised routes:

```
user@Chardonnay> show configuration routing-instances
VPN-A {
    instance-type vrf;
    interface so-0/1/0.0;
    vrf-target target:65432:1111;
    routing-options {
        static {
            route 172.16.2.0/24 next-hop 10.222.44.1;
        }
    }
}
```

Using this configuration, Chardonnay advertises the direct and static routes within the VRF table to Chianti:

```
user@Chardonnay> show route advertising-protocol bgp 192.168.20.1 detail

VPN-A.inet.0: 5 destinations, 5 routes (5 active, 0 holddown, 0 hidden)
* 10.222.44.0/24 (1 entry, 1 announced)
```

```
BGP group int type Internal
     Route Distinguisher: 192.168.32.1:3
     VPN Label: 100128
     Nexthop: Self
     Localpref: 100
     AS path: I
     Communities: target:65432:1111

* 172.16.2.0/24 (1 entry, 1 announced)
 BGP group int type Internal
     Route Distinguisher: 192.168.32.1:3
     VPN Label: 100144
     Nexthop: Self
     Localpref: 100
     AS path: I
     Communities: target:65432:1111
```

You can manually apply an export policy to the VRF table with the `vrf-export` command. Use this command when a subset of routes should be advertised to remote PE routers.

3. The receiving PE router, Chianti in our example, examines the incoming routes and compares them to the import policy applied to the VRF table. This policy matches on all routes that contain the route target assigned to the customer's VRF table. Chianti is configured in a similar manner to Chardonnay in that it uses the `vrf-target` command to assign a route target of `target:65432:1111` to the VRF table:

```
user@Chianti> show configuration routing-instances
VPN-A {
    instance-type vrf;
    interface so-0/1/2.0;
    vrf-target target:65432:1111;
    routing-options {
        static {
            route 172.16.1.0/24 next-hop 10.222.30.1;
        }
    }
}
```

Routes that match the import policy are placed into the bgp.l3vpn.0 routing table on the local PE router:

```
user@Chianti> show route table bgp.l3vpn.0
```

```
bgp.l3vpn.0: 2 destinations, 2 routes (2 active, 0 holddown, 0 hidden)
+ = Active Route, - = Last Active, * = Both

192.168.32.1:3:10.222.44.0/24
                    *[BGP/170] 1d 20:23:19, localpref 100, from 192.168.32.1
                      AS path: I
                    > via so-0/1/0.0, label-switched-path Chianti-to-Char
192.168.32.1:3:172.16.2.0/24
                    *[BGP/170] 1d 20:22:54, localpref 100, from 192.168.32.1
                      AS path: I
                    > via so-0/1/0.0, label-switched-path Chianti-to-Char
```

By default, routes that don't match a local route target are not installed in the Adjacency-RIB-In table by the JUNOS software.

You may also manually apply an import policy to a VRF table using the `vrf-import` command. Use this command when you want to accept only a subset of routes from remote PE routers.

4. The receiving PE router examines the received routes to determine the address listed in the BGP Next Hop attribute. For the routes advertised by Chardonnay, this value is the local BGP peering address of 192.168.32.1 (Self):

```
user@Chardonnay> show route advertising-protocol bgp 192.168.20.1 detail

VPN-A.inet.0: 5 destinations, 5 routes (5 active, 0 holddown, 0 hidden)
* 10.222.44.0/24 (1 entry, 1 announced)
  BGP group int type Internal
      Route Distinguisher: 192.168.32.1:3
      VPN Label: 100128
      Nexthop: Self
      Localpref: 100
      AS path: I
      Communities: target:65432:1111

* 172.16.2.0/24 (1 entry, 1 announced)
  BGP group int type Internal
      Route Distinguisher: 192.168.32.1:3
      VPN Label: 100144
```

```
Nexthop: Self
Localpref: 100
AS path: I
Communities: target:65432:1111
```

Chianti, the receiving router, then determines if the BGP Next Hop is available in the `inet.3` routing table. This ensures that an MPLS LSP is established from the local PE router to the remote PE router for forwarding user traffic within the VPN:

```
user@Chianti> show route table inet.3

inet.3: 2 destinations, 2 routes (2 active, 0 holddown, 0 hidden)
+ = Active Route, - = Last Active, * = Both

192.168.32.1/32     *[RSVP/7] 2d 23:15:46, metric 20
                    > via so-0/1/0.0, label-switched-path Chianti-to-Char
192.168.48.1/32     *[RSVP/7] 2d 23:15:46, metric 20
                    > via so-0/1/0.0, label-switched-path Chianti-to-Cab
```

5. The label value used to reach the remote PE router is associated with the routes received from that router. For the ***Chianti-to-Char*** LSP, Chianti pushes a label value of 100,448:

```
user@Chianti> show route 192.168.32.1 table inet.3 detail

inet.3: 2 destinations, 2 routes (2 active, 0 holddown, 0 hidden)
192.168.32.1/32 (1 entry, 1 announced)
        State: <FlashAll>
        *RSVP   Preference: 7
                Next hop: via so-0/1/0.0 weight 1, selected
                Label-switched-path Chianti-to-Char
                Label operation: Push 100448
                State: <Active Int>
                Local AS: 65432
                Age: 2d 23:19:27        Metric: 20
                Task: RSVP
                Announcement bits (1): 0-Resolve inet.3
                AS path: I
```

The MPLS label advertised with the route, the VPN Label, is also associated with the received routes in the `bgp.l3vpn.0` table. It is placed in a label stack along with the label used to reach the remote PE router:

```
user@Chianti> show route table bgp.l3vpn.0 detail

bgp.l3vpn.0: 2 destinations, 2 routes (2 active, 0 holddown, 0 hidden)
```

```
192.168.32.1:3:10.222.44.0/24 (1 entry, 0 announced)
        *BGP    Preference: 170/-101
                Route Distinguisher: 192.168.32.1:3
                Source: 192.168.32.1
                Next hop: via so-0/1/0.0 weight 1, selected
                Label-switched-path Chianti-to-Char
                Label operation: Push 100128, Push 100448(top)
                Protocol next hop: 192.168.32.1
                Push 100128
                 Indirect next hop: 8522000 325
                State: <Active Int Ext>
                Local AS: 65432 Peer AS: 65432
                Age: 1d 20:39:55      Metric2: 20
                Task: BGP_65432.192.168.32.1+179
                AS path: I
                Communities: target:65432:1111
                VPN Label: 100128
                Localpref: 100
                Router ID: 192.168.32.1
                Secondary Tables: VPN-A.inet.0

192.168.32.1:3:172.16.2.0/24 (1 entry, 0 announced)
        *BGP    Preference: 170/-101
                Route Distinguisher: 192.168.32.1:3
                Source: 192.168.32.1
                Next hop: via so-0/1/0.0 weight 1, selected
                Label-switched-path Chianti-to-Char
                Label operation: Push 100144, Push 100448(top)
                Protocol next hop: 192.168.32.1
                Push 100144
                 Indirect next hop: 8522150 362
                State: <Active Int Ext>
                Local AS: 65432 Peer AS: 65432
                Age: 1d 20:39:30      Metric2: 20
                Task: BGP_65432.192.168.32.1+179
                AS path: I
                Communities: target:65432:1111
                VPN Label: 100144
                Localpref: 100
                Router ID: 192.168.32.1
                Secondary Tables: VPN-A.inet.0
```

6. The received routes are placed into the VRF table corresponding to the appropriate customer. They are installed as BGP routes since they were received via that protocol:

```
user@Chianti> show route table VPN-A protocol bgp

VPN-A.inet.0: 5 destinations, 5 routes (5 active, 0 holddown, 0 hidden)
+ = Active Route, - = Last Active, * = Both

10.222.44.0/24      *[BGP/170] 1d 20:42:18, localpref 100, from 192.168.32.1
                       AS path: I
                     > via so-0/1/0.0, label-switched-path Chianti-to-Char
172.16.2.0/24       *[BGP/170] 1d 20:41:53, localpref 100, from 192.168.32.1
                       AS path: I
                     > via so-0/1/0.0, label-switched-path Chianti-to-Char
```

7. The PE router forwards the received routes to the attached CE router using the routing protocol operating between the two routers. In our case, Chianti and Sangiovese are using static routes for reachability, so no protocol advertisements are necessary.

The Data Forwarding Plane

Once the appropriate routes are advertised and received by the CE routers, the customer can begin forwarding data packets through the provider network. Suppose that the Sangiovese router in Figure 9.1 sends an ICMP echo request packet to the 172.16.2.1 address. The forwarding of the packet follows these basic steps:

1. The CE router of Sangiovese performs a route table lookup to locate a route to 172.16.2.1. It finds a locally configured static route for that destination with a next-hop value of 10.222.30.2. It then forwards the packet to Chianti across its so-0/2/0.0 interface:

```
user@Sangiovese> show route 172.16.2.1

inet.0: 13 destinations, 13 routes (13 active, 0 holddown, 0 hidden)
+ = Active Route, - = Last Active, * = Both

172.16.2.0/24       *[Static/5] 1d 20:47:47
                     > to 10.222.30.2 via so-0/2/0.0
```

2. Chianti receives the packet on the interface configured within the VRF table associated with the CE router. It performs a route table lookup within that VRF table to locate a route to 172.16.2.1:

```
user@Chianti> show route 172.16.2.1 table VPN-A

VPN-A.inet.0: 5 destinations, 5 routes (5 active, 0 holddown, 0 hidden)
+ = Active Route, - = Last Active, * = Both
```

```
172.16.2.0/24      *[BGP/170] 1d 20:50:59, localpref 100, from 192.168.32.1
                      AS path: I
                    > via so-0/1/0.0, label-switched-path Chianti-to-Char
```

The result tells Chianti to forward the packet out its so-0/1/0.0 interface along the *Chianti-to-Char* LSP. A more detailed examination of the routing table contents reveals important information concerning this forwarding action:

user@Chianti> **show route 172.16.2.1 table VPN-A detail**

```
VPN-A.inet.0: 5 destinations, 5 routes (5 active, 0 holddown, 0 hidden)
172.16.2.0/24 (1 entry, 1 announced)
        *BGP    Preference: 170/-101
                Route Distinguisher: 192.168.32.1:3
                Source: 192.168.32.1
                Next hop: via so-0/1/0.0 weight 1, selected
                Label-switched-path Chianti-to-Char
                Label operation: Push 100144, Push 100448(top)
                Protocol next hop: 192.168.32.1
                Push 100144
                 Indirect next hop: 8522150 362
                State: <Secondary Active Int Ext>
                Local AS: 65432 Peer AS: 65432
                Age: 1d 20:53:20        Metric2: 20
                Task: BGP_65432.192.168.32.1+179
                Announcement bits (1): 0-KRT
                AS path: I
                Communities: target:65432:1111
                VPN Label: 100144
                Localpref: 100
                Router ID: 192.168.32.1
                Primary Routing Table bgp.l3vpn.0
```

Chianti actually performs a double push operation on the forwarded packet. The VPN label of 100,144 is placed on the bottom of the stack, and the 100,448 label is placed on the top of the stack.

3. The Merlot router, a P router, receives an MPLS packet from Chianti. It examines the top label value of 100,448 and performs a switching table lookup for that label value. The result tells Merlot to pop the top MPLS label and forward the remaining data out its so-0/1/2.0 interface to Chardonnay.

4. Chardonnay now receives an MPLS packet with a top label of 100,144, which it originally allocated from its label space for routes belonging to the VRF table. The table lookup tells Chardonnay to pop the top label and forward the remaining data, an IP packet in this case, out its so-0/1/0.0 interface to Shiraz:

```
user@Chardonnay> show route table mpls.0 label 100144

mpls.0: 8 destinations, 8 routes (8 active, 0 holddown, 0 hidden)
+ = Active Route, - = Last Active, * = Both

100144             *[VPN/170] 1d 21:00:48
                    > to 10.222.44.1 via so-0/1/0.0, Pop
```

5. Shiraz, the remote CE router, receives the IP packet and finds that the 172.16.2.1 address is a local address, which makes it the destination of the packet. An ICMP echo reply message is formed by Shiraz and forwarded back to Chardonnay, where the same MPLS forwarding process occurs in reverse:

```
user@Shiraz> show route 172.16.2.1

inet.0: 11 destinations, 11 routes (11 active, 0 holddown, 0 hidden)
+ = Active Route, - = Last Active, * = Both

172.16.2.1/32      *[Direct/0] 1d 21:03:35
                    > via lo0.0
```

To see the end result of the forwarding process, we use the ping command on Sangiovese to generate some traffic within the VPN:

```
user@Sangiovese> ping 172.16.2.1 source 172.16.1.1
PING 172.16.2.1 (172.16.2.1): 56 data bytes
64 bytes from 172.16.2.1: icmp_seq=0 ttl=253 time=1.522 ms
64 bytes from 172.16.2.1: icmp_seq=1 ttl=253 time=1.254 ms
64 bytes from 172.16.2.1: icmp_seq=2 ttl=253 time=1.261 ms
^C
--- 172.16.2.1 ping statistics ---
3 packets transmitted, 3 packets received, 0% packet loss
round-trip min/avg/max/stddev = 1.254/1.346/1.522/0.125 ms
```

The use of the source option alters the source IP address of the ICMP packets. This is critical in our example because Shiraz has a route for the 172.16.1.0 /24 subnet only and not the 10.222.30.0 /24 subnet.

Using BGP for PE-CE Route Advertisements

While our sample Layer 3 VPN in Figure 9.1 works quite well using static routes, many network administrators prefer the dynamic nature of a routing protocol. The JUNOS software allows us to use RIP, OSPF, and BGP as routing protocols for the CE-PE connection. Within this section, we focus our attention on BGP. In our sample network, we migrate the current configurations from static routes to BGP. The CE router of Sangiovese is configured within Autonomous System 65000 and forms an EBGP peering session with its connected PE router of Chianti:

```
user@Sangiovese> show configuration routing-options
static {
    route 172.16.1.0/24 reject;
}
autonomous-system 65000;
```

```
user@Sangiovese> show configuration protocols bgp
group VPN-Connectivity {
    type external;
    export send-statics;
    peer-as 65432;
    neighbor 10.222.30.2;
}
```

```
user@Sangiovese> show bgp summary
Groups: 1 Peers: 1 Down peers: 0
Table          Tot Paths  Act Paths Suppressed    History Damp State    Pending
inet.0                 1          1          0          0         0            0
Peer              AS     InPkt    OutPkt     OutQ   Flaps Last Up/Dwn State
10.222.30.2    65432        15        17        0       0       5:38 1/1/0
```

The other CE router, Shiraz, is configured in a similar manner. Each of the CE routers advertises a static route to its EBGP peer. This route represents connectivity throughout its site to its remote CE partner:

```
user@Sangiovese> show route advertising-protocol bgp 10.222.30.2 172.16/16

inet.0: 14 destinations, 14 routes (14 active, 0 holddown, 0 hidden)
  Prefix                 Nexthop            MED    Lclpref   AS path
* 172.16.1.0/24          Self               0                I
```

```
user@Shiraz> show route advertising-protocol bgp 10.222.44.2 172.16/16
```

```
inet.0: 12 destinations, 12 routes (12 active, 0 holddown, 0 hidden)
  Prefix                    Nexthop            MED     Lclpref   AS path
* 172.16.2.0/24             Self               0                 I
```

To ensure that the VPN is working correctly, let's focus on just the 172.16.1.0 /24 route advertised from Sangiovese. This route is received by Chianti within the VRF table and is currently an active route:

```
user@Chianti> show route table VPN-A 172.16.1/24

VPN-A.inet.0: 5 destinations, 5 routes (5 active, 0 holddown, 0 hidden)
+ = Active Route, - = Last Active, * = Both

172.16.1.0/24        *[BGP/170] 00:10:08, MED 0, localpref 100
                        AS path: 65000 I
                     > to 10.222.30.1 via so-0/1/2.0
```

Because Chianti is using the automatic export of all VRF routes via the vrf-target command, the route is allocated a VPN label and advertised to Chardonnay with a route target of target:65432:1111:

```
user@Chianti> show route advertising-protocol bgp 192.168.32.1 detail

VPN-A.inet.0: 5 destinations, 5 routes (5 active, 0 holddown, 0 hidden)
* 10.222.30.0/24 (1 entry, 1 announced)
 BGP group int type Internal
     Route Distinguisher: 192.168.20.1:3
     VPN Label: 100384
     Nexthop: Self
     Localpref: 100
     AS path: I
     Communities: target:65432:1111


* 172.16.1.0/24 (1 entry, 1 announced)
 BGP group int type Internal
     Route Distinguisher: 192.168.20.1:3
     VPN Label: 100416
     Nexthop: Self
     MED: 0
     Localpref: 100
     AS path: 65000 I
     Communities: target:65432:1111
```

The listing of Nexthop: Self within the router output tells us that the BGP Next Hop is set to 192.168.20.1, which is a valid address within the inet.3 routing table on Chardonnay:

```
user@Chardonnay> show route table inet.3 192.168.20.1

inet.3: 2 destinations, 2 routes (2 active, 0 holddown, 0 hidden)
+ = Active Route, - = Last Active, * = Both

192.168.20.1/32    *[RSVP/7] 3d 02:40:50, metric 20
                    > via so-0/1/1.0, label-switched-path Char-to-Chianti
```

The Chardonnay router is also configured to accept all routes with a route target of target:65432:1111, which installs the 172.16.1.0 /24 route in both the bgp.l3vpn.0 and the VPN-A.inet.0 routing tables:

```
user@Chardonnay> show route table bgp.l3vpn.0

bgp.l3vpn.0: 2 destinations, 2 routes (2 active, 0 holddown, 0 hidden)
+ = Active Route, - = Last Active, * = Both

192.168.20.1:3:10.222.30.0/24
                    *[BGP/170] 00:15:27, localpref 100, from 192.168.20.1
                      AS path: I
                    > via so-0/1/1.0, label-switched-path Char-to-Chianti
192.168.20.1:3:172.16.1.0/24
                    *[BGP/170] 00:15:27, MED 0, localpref 100, from 192.168.20.1
                      AS path: 65000 I
                    > via so-0/1/1.0, label-switched-path Char-to-Chianti

user@Chardonnay> show route table VPN-A 172.16.1/24

VPN-A.inet.0: 5 destinations, 5 routes (5 active, 0 holddown, 0 hidden)
+ = Active Route, - = Last Active, * = Both

172.16.1.0/24      *[BGP/170] 00:15:40, MED 0, localpref 100, from 192.168.20.1
                      AS path: 65000 I
                    > via so-0/1/1.0, label-switched-path Char-to-Chianti
```

The presence of a valid EBGP peering session between Chardonnay and Shiraz allows the advertisement of the 172.16.1.0 /24 route to Shiraz:

```
user@Chardonnay> show route advertising-protocol bgp 10.222.44.1
```

```
VPN-A.inet.0: 5 destinations, 5 routes (5 active, 0 holddown, 0 hidden)
  Prefix                   Nexthop              MED    Lclpref    AS path
* 10.222.30.0/24           Self                                   I
* 172.16.1.0/24            Self                                   65000 I
* 172.16.2.0/24            10.222.44.1                            65000 I
```

An examination of the routing table on the Shiraz router reveals a problem, however. The route is no longer visible:

```
user@Shiraz> show route 172.16.1/24

user@Shiraz> show route 172.16.1/24 all

user@Shiraz> show route receive-protocol bgp 10.222.44.2

inet.0: 12 destinations, 12 routes (12 active, 0 holddown, 0 hidden)
  Prefix                   Nexthop              MED    Lclpref    AS path
* 10.222.30.0/24           10.222.44.2                            65432 I
```

While we've experienced this problem before in our discussion of BGP, it's helpful to revisit the behavior we're seeing. It appears as if the Chardonnay router is advertising the route but the Shiraz router is not receiving it. A closer examination of the routes advertised by Chardonnay reveals an important clue:

```
user@Chardonnay> show route advertising-protocol bgp 10.222.44.1 detail

VPN-A.inet.0: 5 destinations, 5 routes (5 active, 0 holddown, 0 hidden)
* 10.222.30.0/24 (1 entry, 1 announced)
 BGP group Shiraz-CE type External
     Nexthop: Self
     AS path: I
     Communities: target:65432:1111

* 172.16.1.0/24 (1 entry, 1 announced)
 BGP group Shiraz-CE type External
     Nexthop: Self
     AS path: 65000 I
     Communities: target:65432:1111

* 172.16.2.0/24 (1 entry, 1 announced)
 BGP group Shiraz-CE type External
     Nexthop: 10.222.44.1
     AS path: 65000 I
```

When Chardonnay advertises the route across its EBGP peering session with Shiraz, it prepends its local AS value of 65432 to the AS Path attribute. However, the attribute currently contains the AS value of 65000, which Sangiovese placed there during its advertisement to Chianti. When Shiraz receives the route with an AS Path of 65432 65000, it rejects the route as a routing loop prevention mechanism. The resolution most commonly applied in this situation is the configuration of the as-override command within the routing instance configuration of the PE routers. We update Chardonnay's configuration like this:

```
user@Chardonnay> show configuration routing-instances protocols bgp
group Shiraz-CE {
    type external;
    peer-as 65000;
    as-override;
    neighbor 10.222.44.1;
}
```

This configuration allows Chardonnay to examine the contents of the AS Path attribute to determine if its peer's AS value appears within the path. If it finds the peer's AS value, the local router replaces it with its own local AS value. This allows Shiraz to receive the 172.16.1.0 /24 route with an AS Path of 65432 65432 and accept the route:

```
user@Shiraz> show route 172.16.1/24

inet.0: 13 destinations, 14 routes (13 active, 0 holddown, 1 hidden)
+ = Active Route, - = Last Active, * = Both

172.16.1.0/24      *[BGP/170] 00:03:27, localpref 100
                     AS path: 65432 65432 I
                   > to 10.222.44.2 via so-0/1/0.0
```

After applying the as-override command on Chianti, the Sangiovese router is able to receive and install the 172.16.2.0 /24 route:

```
user@Sangiovese> show route 172.16.2/24

inet.0: 15 destinations, 16 routes (15 active, 0 holddown, 1 hidden)
+ = Active Route, - = Last Active, * = Both

172.16.2.0/24      *[BGP/170] 00:00:05, localpref 100
                     AS path: 65432 65432 I
                   > to 10.222.30.2 via so-0/2/0.0
```

With each of the CE routers installing a route to its partner, we can verify connectivity with a simple `ping` command:

```
user@Sangiovese> ping 172.16.2.1
PING 172.16.2.1 (172.16.2.1): 56 data bytes
64 bytes from 172.16.2.1: icmp_seq=0 ttl=253 time=1.474 ms
64 bytes from 172.16.2.1: icmp_seq=1 ttl=253 time=1.234 ms
64 bytes from 172.16.2.1: icmp_seq=2 ttl=253 time=1.229 ms
^C
--- 172.16.2.1 ping statistics ---
3 packets transmitted, 3 packets received, 0% packet loss
round-trip min/avg/max/stddev = 1.229/1.312/1.474/0.114 ms
```

Using OSPF for PE-CE Route Advertisements

When a customer is replacing an existing set of wide area links for a Layer 3 VPN, it often wishes to continue using the IGP in place before the switchover. One very popular customer routing protocol is OSPF, so let's see how this operates within our environment.

Within Figure 9.1, we now examine the operation of a VPN on the other half of our provider network. The Sherry and Chablis routers are CE devices using OSPF as their IGP for inter-site connectivity. Zinfandel is acting as a P router to connect the PE routers of Chianti and Cabernet. Both of the PE routers are using the automatic policy available through the `vrf-target` command. As an example, the Chianti router's configuration is

```
user@Chianti> show configuration routing-instances VPN-B
instance-type vrf;
interface ge-0/2/0.0;
route-distinguisher 65432:2222;
vrf-target target:65432:2222;
protocols {
    ospf {
        area 0.0.0.0 {
            interface ge-0/2/0.0;
        }
    }
}
```

The route target for the VRF is set to `target:65432:2222`. This AS-based value is also manually set as the RD within the routing instance. While this commonality is not a requirement, it makes operating and troubleshooting the VRF table easier.

At this point, each of the CE routers is maintaining a Full OSPF adjacency and is advertising their loopback address to their peer. To illustrate the VPN operation, let's focus on the 192.168.16.1 address of the Sherry router. This appears within the VRF table on Chianti as an OSPF route:

```
user@Chianti> show route protocol ospf table VPN-B.inet.0

VPN-B.inet.0: 6 destinations, 6 routes (6 active, 0 holddown, 0 hidden)
+ = Active Route, - = Last Active, * = Both

192.168.16.1/32    *[OSPF/10] 00:21:35, metric 1
                    > to 10.222.29.1 via ge-0/2/0.0
224.0.0.5/32       *[OSPF/10] 00:21:50, metric 1
                    MultiRecv
```

The automatic VRF export policy configured on Chianti allows for the allocation of a VPN label. This label, as well as the route target, is advertised to the remote PE router of Cabernet:

```
user@Chianti> ...rotocol bgp 192.168.48.1 192.168/16 detail

VPN-B.inet.0: 6 destinations, 6 routes (6 active, 0 holddown, 0 hidden)
* 192.168.16.1/32 (1 entry, 1 announced)
  BGP group int type Internal
       Route Distinguisher: 65432:2222
       VPN Label: 100448
       Nexthop: Self
       MED: 1
       Localpref: 100
       AS path: I
       Communities: target:65432:2222 rte-type:0.0.0.0:1:0
```

The BGP Next Hop is currently set to 192.168.20.1. This address is visible within the inet.3 routing table on the Cabernet router:

```
user@Cabernet> show route table inet.3

inet.3: 2 destinations, 2 routes (2 active, 0 holddown, 0 hidden)
+ = Active Route, - = Last Active, * = Both

192.168.20.1/32    *[RSVP/7] 01:04:03, metric 20
                    > via so-0/1/0.0, label-switched-path Cab-to-Chianti
192.168.32.1/32    *[RSVP/7] 3d 04:11:40, metric 10
                    > via so-0/1/1.0, label-switched-path Cab-to-Char
```

The automatic VRF import policy on Cabernet installs the route in the VPN-A.inet.0 routing table:

```
user@Cabernet> show route 192.168.16/24 table VPN-B.inet.0

VPN-B.inet.0: 6 destinations, 7 routes (6 active, 0 holddown, 0 hidden)
+ = Active Route, - = Last Active, * = Both

192.168.16.1/32    *[BGP/170] 00:27:09, MED 1, localpref 100, from 192.168.20.1
                      AS path: I
                    > via so-0/1/0.0, label-switched-path Cab-to-Chianti
```

When we look at the routing table on the Chablis router, however, we find that the route doesn't exist:

```
user@Chablis> show route 192.168.16/24


user@Chablis> show route 192.168.16/24 all


user@Chablis>
```

In fact, this situation is quite normal when combining routing knowledge from multiple protocols. The only method for advertising routes from Cabernet to Chablis is via OSPF, but the route is currently installed within the VRF table on Cabernet as a BGP route. This sounds like a job for route redistribution and a routing policy, so let's create the ***bgp-to-ospf*** policy on Cabernet and apply it within the routing instance:

```
user@Cabernet> show configuration policy-options
policy-statement bgp-to-ospf {
    term advertise-remote-routes {
        from protocol bgp;
        then accept;
    }
}


user@Cabernet> show configuration routing-instances VPN-B protocols
ospf {
    export bgp-to-ospf;
    area 0.0.0.0 {
        interface so-0/1/2.0;
    }
}
```

This allows Cabernet to advertise the 192.168.16.1 /32 route within an OSPF link-state advertisement to Chablis. The route then appears within the routing table on the CE router:

```
user@Chablis> show ospf database netsummary

    OSPF link state database, area 0.0.0.0
 Type       ID              Adv Rtr          Seq       Age Opt  Cksum  Len
 Summary  192.168.16.1    10.222.60.2     0x80000001   65  0x82 0x7ebb 28

user@Chablis> show route 192.168.16.1

inet.0: 16 destinations, 17 routes (16 active, 0 holddown, 0 hidden)
+ = Active Route, - = Last Active, * = Both

192.168.16.1/32    *[OSPF/10] 00:01:27, metric 2
                    > via so-0/1/0.0
```

Once we configure a similar policy on the Chianti router, the loopback address of Chablis (192.168.52.1) appears in the routing table on Sherry:

```
user@Sherry> show route 192.168.52.1

inet.0: 12 destinations, 12 routes (12 active, 0 holddown, 0 hidden)
+ = Active Route, - = Last Active, * = Both

192.168.52.1/32    *[OSPF/10] 00:00:04, metric 2
                    > to 10.222.29.2 via ge-0/2/0.0
```

We've now established connectivity between the loopback addresses of the two CE routers:

```
user@Sherry> ping 192.168.52.1 source 192.168.16.1
PING 192.168.52.1 (192.168.52.1): 56 data bytes
64 bytes from 192.168.52.1: icmp_seq=0 ttl=253 time=1.129 ms
64 bytes from 192.168.52.1: icmp_seq=1 ttl=253 time=0.903 ms
64 bytes from 192.168.52.1: icmp_seq=2 ttl=253 time=0.897 ms
^C
--- 192.168.52.1 ping statistics ---
3 packets transmitted, 3 packets received, 0% packet loss
round-trip min/avg/max/stddev = 0.897/0.976/1.129/0.108 ms
```

Domain ID

You might have noticed in the previous section that Sherry received the 192.168.52.1 /32 route in a Summary Type 3 LSA from Chianti. In a normal route redistribution environment, the **_bgp-to-ospf_** policy on Chianti injects routes into OSPF as AS External Type 5 LSAs. Within a VPN environment, this behavior of injecting external routes may not be desirable. For example, suppose that a customer is migrating from an existing WAN infrastructure to a Layer 3 VPN. The customer wants to bring up the VPN links between sites individually and begin using them for data transport before removing the existing connectivity. In this environment, the two sites are exchanging routes across the existing infrastructure using Summary LSAs. The same routes are also advertised across the VPN link but are advertised as AS External LSAs. Since internal OSPF routes are always more preferred to external routes, the remotes sites continue to communicate across the existing links.

To alleviate this dilemma, the JUNOS software assigns a *domain ID* value to each routing instance running OSPF. By default, this 32-bit value is set to all zeros (0.0.0.0). The domain ID allows the receiving PE router to advertise routes as either Type 3 or Type 5 LSAs. The format of the domain ID is shown in Figure 9.4.

Type (2 octets)   This field displays the type of extended community advertised with the route. The valid type codes for the OSPF domain ID are 0x0005, 0x0105, and 0x0205. The high-order byte in this field technically determines the format of the remaining octets, but is irrelevant in our case since all the remaining octets compose the domain ID value.

Domain ID (6 octets)   This field contains the domain ID value advertised by the PE router.

FIGURE 9.4   The OSPF domain ID

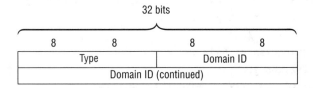

Before we examine the use of the domain ID in further detail, we also need to examine a BGP extended community called the *OSPF route type attribute*. This attribute is included automatically by the JUNOS software in all advertised OSPF routes and interacts with the domain ID on the receiving PE router to determine the type of route advertised. Figure 9.5 displays the format of the OSPF route type attribute, which includes the following fields:

Type (2 octets)   This field displays the type of extended community advertised with the route. The OSPF route type attribute uses a constant value of 0x0306 as its type code.

OSPF Area (4 octets)   This field contains the OSPF area value operating on the advertising PE router that received the original OSPF route. For received external routes, this field is set to all zeros (0.0.0.0).

Route Type (1 octet)   The route type field displays the LSA type of the route being advertised. It represents the method by which the advertising PE router learned the OSPF route. The possible values include

- 1—Intra-area routes from a Router LSA
- 2—Intra-area routes from a Network LSA
- 3—Inter-area routes from a Summary LSA
- 5—External routes from an AS External LSA
- 7—External routes from an NSSA LSA

Options (1 octet) This field is used only when the route type is set to a value of 5 or 7. The least significant bit in the field is set to a 1 (0x01) when the external route has a type 2 metric. This bit is set to a 0 (0x00) when the external route has a type 1 metric.

FIGURE 9.5 The OSPF route type attribute

32 bits

8	8	8	8
Type		OSPF Area	
OSPF Area (continued)		Route Type	Options

An OSPF route advertised across a VPN connection always contains the route type attribute but may not contain a domain ID. The absence of an ID value is interpreted by a receiving PE router as a null domain ID (0.0.0.0), the default JUNOS software value. We see these conditions on the Chianti router in Figure 9.1 as it receives the 192.168.52.1 /32 route from Cabernet:

```
user@Chianti> ...ute table bgp.l3vpn.0 source-gateway 192.168.48.1 detail

bgp.l3vpn.0: 4 destinations, 4 routes (4 active, 0 holddown, 0 hidden)
65432:2222:10.222.60.0/24 (1 entry, 0 announced)
        *BGP    Preference: 170/-101
                Route Distinguisher: 65432:2222
                Source: 192.168.48.1
                Next hop: via so-0/1/0.0 weight 1, selected
                Label-switched-path Chianti-to-Cab
                Label operation: Push 100368, Push 100464(top)
                Protocol next hop: 192.168.48.1
                Push 100368
                 Indirect next hop: 85222a0 336
                State: <Active Int Ext>
                Local AS: 65432 Peer AS: 65432
                Age: 1:20       Metric2: 20
                Task: BGP_65432.192.168.48.1+4403
                AS path: I
                Communities: target:65432:2222
                VPN Label: 100368
                Localpref: 100
                Router ID: 192.168.48.1
                Secondary Tables: VPN-B.inet.0
```

```
65432:2222:192.168.52.1/32 (1 entry, 0 announced)
      *BGP    Preference: 170/-101
              Route Distinguisher: 65432:2222
              Source: 192.168.48.1
              Next hop: via so-0/1/0.0 weight 1, selected
              Label-switched-path Chianti-to-Cab
              Label operation: Push 100416, Push 100464(top)
              Protocol next hop: 192.168.48.1
              Push 100416
               Indirect next hop: 85223f0 344
              State: <Active Int Ext>
              Local AS: 65432 Peer AS: 65432
              Age: 1:20       Metric: 1       Metric2: 20
              Task: BGP_65432.192.168.48.1+4403
              AS path: I
              Communities: target:65432:2222 rte-type:0.0.0.0:1:0
              VPN Label: 100416
              Localpref: 100
              Router ID: 192.168.48.1
              Secondary Tables: VPN-B.inet.0
```

The attribute value tells us that Cabernet received the route on an area 0 interface as a Router LSA (Type 1). The absence of a domain ID community means that Cabernet is using the default null ID value of all zeros. As the route contains the proper route target for the VPN, Chianti needs to advertise the route to its CE router of Sherry. It uses the route type and domain ID values in the following manner to determine if the route should be advertised as a Summary or an AS External LSA:

1. When the received route has an internal route type (1, 2, or 3) but does not contain a domain ID attribute, it is advertised as a Type 3 Summary LSA.

2. When the received route has an internal route type and a domain ID value equal to the locally configured domain ID, it is advertised as a Type 3 Summary LSA.

3. When the received route has an internal route type and a domain ID that doesn't equal the locally configured domain ID, it is advertised as a Type 5 AS External LSA.

4. When the received route has an internal route type and a domain ID value attached, but the local router has no configured ID value (the default null ID), it is advertised as a Type 5 AS External LSA.

5. When the received route has an external route type (5 or 7), it is always advertised as a Type 5 AS External LSA. This occurs regardless of the domain ID values contained on the local router and the received route.

Let's see how the JUNOS software interacts with these advertisement rules using the routers in Figure 9.1. The PE routers are each configured with a domain ID value of 1.1.1.1. Cabernet now looks like this:

```
user@Cabernet> show configuration routing-instances VPN-B protocols
ospf {
    domain-id 1.1.1.1;
    export bgp-to-ospf;
    area 0.0.0.0 {
        interface so-0/1/2.0;
    }
}
```

We create a routing policy called ***vpn-b-export***, which accepts all OSPF routes within the VRF table on Cabernet and applies the appropriate route target as well as the OSPF domain ID of 1.1.1.1. The policy also accepts all direct routes (the CE-PE link) and applies the route target while rejecting all other routes:

```
user@Cabernet> show configuration policy-options
policy-statement vpn-b-export {
    term send-local-ospf-routes {
        from protocol ospf;
        then {
            community add ospf-domain-id;
            community add vpn-b-route-target;
            accept;
        }
    }
    term send-direct-routes {
        from protocol direct;
        then {
            community add vpn-b-route-target;
            accept;
        }
    }
    term reject-all-else {
        then reject;
    }
}
community ospf-domain-id members domain:1.1.1.1:0;
community vpn-b-route-target members target:65432:2222;
```

The policy is applied to the routing instance on Cabernet using the vrf-export command. While this supersedes the settings within the vrf-target configuration for exported routes, we leave the vrf-target in the instance to accept all received routes with the appropriate route target:

```
user@Cabernet> show configuration routing-instances VPN-B
instance-type vrf;
interface so-0/1/2.0;
route-distinguisher 65432:2222;
vrf-export vpn-b-export;
vrf-target target:65432:2222;
protocols {
    ospf {
        domain-id 1.1.1.1;
        export bgp-to-ospf;
        area 0.0.0.0 {
            interface so-0/1/2.0;
        }
    }
}
```

The 192.168.52.1/32 route now appears on the Chianti router with multiple BGP extended communities attached:

```
user@Chianti> ...ute table bgp.l3vpn.0 source-gateway 192.168.48.1 detail

bgp.l3vpn.0: 4 destinations, 4 routes (4 active, 0 holddown, 0 hidden)
65432:2222:10.222.60.0/24 (1 entry, 0 announced)
        *BGP    Preference: 170/-101
                Route Distinguisher: 65432:2222
                Source: 192.168.48.1
                Next hop: via so-0/1/0.0 weight 1, selected
                Label-switched-path Chianti-to-Cab
                Label operation: Push 100368, Push 100464(top)
                Protocol next hop: 192.168.48.1
                Push 100368
                 Indirect next hop: 85222a0 336
                State: <Active Int Ext>
                Local AS: 65432 Peer AS: 65432
                Age: 9:30      Metric2: 20
                Task: BGP_65432.192.168.48.1+4403
                AS path: I
                Communities: target:65432:2222
                VPN Label: 100368
```

```
                        Localpref: 100
                        Router ID: 192.168.48.1
                        Secondary Tables: VPN-B.inet.0

65432:2222:192.168.52.1/32 (1 entry, 0 announced)
        *BGP    Preference: 170/-101
                        Route Distinguisher: 65432:2222
                        Source: 192.168.48.1
                        Next hop: via so-0/1/0.0 weight 1, selected
                        Label-switched-path Chianti-to-Cab
                        Label operation: Push 100432, Push 100464(top)
                        Protocol next hop: 192.168.48.1
                        Push 100432
                         Indirect next hop: 85223f0 344
                        State: <Active Int Ext>
                        Local AS: 65432 Peer AS: 65432
                        Age: 8:02      Metric: 1      Metric2: 20
                        Task: BGP_65432.192.168.48.1+4403
                        AS path: I
                        Communities: target:65432:2222 domain-id:1.1.1.1:0
                                     rte-type:0.0.0.0:1:0
                        VPN Label: 100432
                        Localpref: 100
                        Router ID: 192.168.48.1
                        Secondary Tables: VPN-B.inet.0
```

The 192.168.52.1/32 route has an OSPF route type of 1 and a matching domain ID to the local router. This allows Chianti to advertise the route as a Summary LSA, which we see in the link-state database on the Sherry router:

user@Sherry> **show ospf database lsa-id 192.168.52.1**

```
    OSPF link state database, area 0.0.0.0
 Type       ID            Adv Rtr        Seq        Age  Opt  Cksum  Len
 Summary   192.168.52.1   10.222.29.2    0x80000002 373  0x82 0xc86b 28
```

We now change the domain ID configured on the Chianti router to a value of 2.2.2.2:

user@Chianti> **show configuration routing-instances VPN-B protocols**
```
ospf {
    domain-id 2.2.2.2;
    export bgp-to-ospf;
```

```
    area 0.0.0.0 {
        interface ge-0/2/0.0;
    }
}
```

The local domain ID on the receiving PE router no longer matches the value attached to the route—domain-id:1.1.1.1:0. Although the OSPF route type of the route is set to an internal value of 1, the domain ID mismatch causes Chianti to advertise the route as a Type 5 LSA. We again verify this advertisement by using the database on the Sherry router:

```
user@Sherry> show ospf database lsa-id 192.168.52.1
```

```
    OSPF AS SCOPE link state database
 Type      ID              Adv Rtr         Seq        Age  Opt  Cksum  Len
Extern   192.168.52.1    10.222.29.2     0x80000001   137  0x2  0x3d05  36
```

In fact, we see this same Type 5 LSA when Chianti has no domain ID value configured. In essence, the default null value of 0.0.0.0 doesn't match the received domain ID of 1.1.1.1 attached to the route:

```
user@Chianti> show configuration routing-instances VPN-B protocols
ospf {
    export bgp-to-ospf;
    area 0.0.0.0 {
        interface ge-0/2/0.0;
    }
}
```

```
user@Sherry> show ospf database lsa-id 192.168.52.1
```

```
    OSPF AS SCOPE link state database
 Type      ID              Adv Rtr         Seq        Age  Opt  Cksum  Len
Extern   192.168.52.1    10.222.29.2     0x80000001   264  0x2  0x3d05  36
```

The CE router of Chablis now advertises the 10.222.55.0 /24 route to Cabernet as an external OSPF route. We see this appear in the link-state database associated with the VRF table on Cabernet:

```
user@Cabernet> show ospf database instance VPN-B extern
```

```
    OSPF AS SCOPE link state database
 Type      ID              Adv Rtr         Seq        Age  Opt  Cksum  Len
Extern   *10.222.29.0    10.222.60.2     0x8000009d   693  0x2  0x6837  36
Extern    10.222.55.0    192.168.52.1    0x80000001    36  0x2  0xd728  36
```

This route is advertised with an OSPF route type of 5, an external route, to Chianti:

```
user@Cabernet> show route advertising-protocol bgp 192.168.20.1 detail

VPN-B.inet.0: 7 destinations, 8 routes (7 active, 0 holddown, 0 hidden)
* 10.222.55.0/24 (1 entry, 1 announced)
 BGP group int type Internal
      Route Distinguisher: 65432:2222
      VPN Label: 100432
      Nexthop: Self
      MED: 20
      Localpref: 100
      AS path: I
      Communities: target:65432:2222 domain-id:1.1.1.1:0 rte-type:0.0.0.0:5:1

* 10.222.60.0/24 (2 entries, 1 announced)
 BGP group int type Internal
      Route Distinguisher: 65432:2222
      VPN Label: 100368
      Nexthop: Self
      Localpref: 100
      AS path: I
      Communities: target:65432:2222

* 192.168.52.1/32 (1 entry, 1 announced)
 BGP group int type Internal
      Route Distinguisher: 65432:2222
      VPN Label: 100432
      Nexthop: Self
      MED: 1
      Localpref: 100
      AS path: I
      Communities: target:65432:2222 domain-id:1.1.1.1:0 rte-type:0.0.0.0:1:0
```

The presence of this route type automatically prompts Chianti to advertise the route using an AS External Type 5 LSA, which is placed in the link-state database on Sherry:

```
user@Sherry> show ospf database extern

    OSPF AS SCOPE link state database
  Type      ID            Adv Rtr           Seq        Age  Opt  Cksum   Len
  Extern    10.222.55.0   10.222.29.2    0x80000001   260  0x2  0x2508  36
  Extern    10.222.60.0   10.222.29.2    0x80000075   205  0x2  0x3c8b  36
  Extern    192.168.52.1  10.222.29.2    0x80000002   505  0x2  0x3b06  36
```

The VPN Route Tag

Internal OSPF routes have inherent routing loop prevention mechanisms in place on the area border routers, which we discussed in Chapter 2, "Open Shortest Path First." Unfortunately, no such process exists for Type 5 external routes because they are flooded to all possible routers by default. This domain-wide flooding process presents a problem in a Layer 3 VPN environment. Suppose that both Router A and Router B are PE routers that connect to different CE routers in a single customer site. When Router A receives an external route from a remote PE neighbor, which is not Router B, it redistributes that route to the customer site as a Type 5 LSA. Its neighboring CE router receives the LSA and floods it throughout the customer site, where it arrives at the CE router connected to Router B. By default, Router B receives the LSA within its VRF table and forwards it across the VPN to neighboring PE routers. This advertisement by Router B can potentially cause a routing loop in the network. To avoid such occurrences, each PE router using OSPF as a CE-PE routing protocol generates a unique *VPN route tag* value and places it within the Type 5 LSA. When a PE router receives an external advertisement from a CE router with a tag value matching the local tag value, the router doesn't advertise that route across the VPN. This prevents potential routing loops from forming in the network.

The JUNOS software automatically computes a VPN route tag for each routing instance running OSPF. The tag value is based on the Autonomous System value configured on the PE router using the format shown in Figure 9.6. The tag's fields include:

Flags (4 bits)   The Flags field contains three attributes and is set to a value of 1101 by default. The most significant bit is set to a value of 1 to indicate that the route tag has been automatically calculated. The next bit in the field is also set to a value of 1 and informs all PE routers that this is the complete route tag information. The last 2 bits in the field are used to indicate the number of the AS values contained within the tag. These bits are set to a value of 01.

FIGURE 9.6   The OSPF VPN route tag

Arbitrary Tag (12 bits)   This field is set to all zeros (0x000) when the PE router automatically calculates the VPN route tag.

Autonomous System (2 octets)   The PE router places its own AS number in this field.

The Chianti router, which is within AS 65432, automatically generates a VPN route tag of 0xd000ff98 for the routing instance belonging to the Sherry router. When we change this hexadecimal value to a dotted decimal format, we find that the VPN route tag for the instance is 208.0.255.152. This value is placed within the Type 5 LSAs generated by Chianti:

```
user@Chianti> show ospf database instance VPN-B extern extensive
    OSPF AS SCOPE link state database
```

```
  Type        ID              Adv Rtr           Seq      Age  Opt  Cksum  Len
Extern   *10.222.55.0     10.222.29.2      0x80000003    71   0x2  0x210a  36
   mask 255.255.255.0
   Type 2, TOS 0x0, metric 20, fwd addr 0.0.0.0, tag 208.0.255.152
   Gen timer 00:48:48
   Aging timer 00:58:48
   Installed 00:01:11 ago, expires in 00:58:49, sent 00:01:09 ago
   Ours
Extern   *10.222.60.0     10.222.29.2      0x80000076   971   0x2  0x3a8c  36
   mask 255.255.255.0
   Type 2, TOS 0x0, metric 0, fwd addr 0.0.0.0, tag 208.0.255.152
   Gen timer 00:10:03
   Aging timer 00:43:48
   Installed 00:16:11 ago, expires in 00:43:49, sent 00:16:09 ago
   Ours
Extern   *192.168.52.1    10.222.29.2      0x80000004   371   0x2  0x3708  36
   mask 255.255.255.255
   Type 1, TOS 0x0, metric 1, fwd addr 0.0.0.0, tag 208.0.255.152
   Gen timer 00:43:48
   Aging timer 00:53:48
   Installed 00:06:11 ago, expires in 00:53:49, sent 00:06:09 ago
   Ours
```

The JUNOS software allows you to set a separate VPN route tag for each customer through the configuration of the domain-vpn-tag. This is configured within the routing instance for the customer and contains a 32-bit value used as the route tag. The Chianti router is configured with a tag value of 2,071,690,107. This translates to a dotted decimal format of 123.123.123.123, as seen in the OSPF database on the PE router:

```
user@Chianti> show configuration routing-instances VPN-B protocols
ospf {
    domain-vpn-tag 2071690107;
    export bgp-to-ospf;
    area 0.0.0.0 {
        interface ge-0/2/0.0;
    }
}
```

```
user@Chianti> show ospf database instance VPN-B extern extensive
    OSPF AS SCOPE link state database
  Type        ID              Adv Rtr           Seq      Age  Opt  Cksum  Len
Extern   *10.222.55.0     10.222.29.2      0x80000004    24   0x2  0xfda7  36
   mask 255.255.255.0
```

```
Type 2, TOS 0x0, metric 20, fwd addr 0.0.0.0, tag 123.123.123.123
Gen timer 00:49:35
Aging timer 00:59:35
Installed 00:00:24 ago, expires in 00:59:36, sent 00:00:22 ago
Ours
Extern  *10.222.60.0      10.222.29.2      0x80000078   24  0x2  0x152b  36
mask 255.255.255.0
Type 2, TOS 0x0, metric 0, fwd addr 0.0.0.0, tag 123.123.123.123
Gen timer 00:49:35
Aging timer 00:59:35
Installed 00:00:24 ago, expires in 00:59:36, sent 00:00:22 ago
Ours
Extern  *192.168.52.1     10.222.29.2      0x80000005   24  0x2  0x14a5  36
mask 255.255.255.255
Type 1, TOS 0x0, metric 1, fwd addr 0.0.0.0, tag 123.123.123.123
Gen timer 00:49:35
Aging timer 00:59:35
Installed 00:00:24 ago, expires in 00:59:36, sent 00:00:22 ago
Ours
```

The JUNOS software also uses the VPN route tag to prevent routing loops.
When a PE router receives a Type 5 LSA from a CE router, it examines both the
LSA ID and the tag value. If the LSA ID is not the local router but the tag values
match, the local PE router assumes that a possible loop is forming. To avoid
this, the PE doesn't include that LSA in its SPF calculation.

Internet Access for VPN Customers

When a provider's customer is using a Layer 3 VPN for intra-site connectivity, the customer
often wants to use the provider's network for Internet access. There are three main categories
for providing this type of service: access outside the confines of the VRF table, distributed access
to each VPN site, and centralized access from a single VPN site. Generally speaking, each of the
main access categories also has multiple variations included within it.

Independent Internet Access

The main point to remember concerning *independent Internet access* is that the routing tables
on the PE router are never consulted for packet forwarding. This means that the CE router
either forwards traffic directly to the Internet or uses the PE router as a Layer 2 forwarding
device to an Internet-aware router.

Figure 9.7 shows the first of these examples, with the CE routers of Sangiovese and Shiraz
each maintaining its own connections to the Internet. In this environment, Sangiovese sends all
VPN packets to Chianti for forwarding to the remote CE router of Shiraz. All packets whose

destination address does not fall within the VPN are forwarded by Sangiovese directly to the Internet. Of course, this type of connectivity doesn't provide any revenue to the provider. If a customer wishes to control its access in this manner, the provider can offer a Layer 2 logical circuit to the customer, as we see in Figure 9.8.

Within this independent Internet access example, the network provider is providing two logical circuits to the customer. One of the circuits is configured within the VRF table and is used by the customer for forwarding traffic within the VPN. The second logical circuit passes through the PE router at Layer 2 and terminates at another router in the provider's network—Merlot in our case. The customer sends Internet-bound traffic on this second logical circuit, and Merlot forwards that traffic based on its routing knowledge of Internet destinations.

FIGURE 9.7   Independent Internet access (1 of 2)

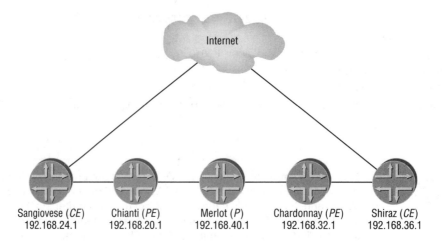

FIGURE 9.8   Independent Internet access (2 of 2)

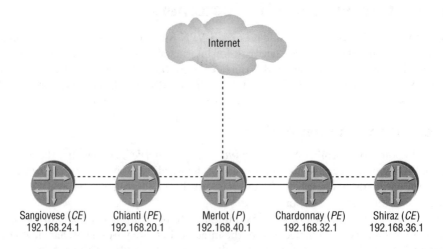

Distributed Internet Access

In a *distributed Internet access* model, each and every PE router provides connectivity to the Internet for its connected CE router. Within this environment, the provider has three main options for forwarding traffic through the PE router.

The first option (Figure 9.9) involves two logical circuits between the PE and CE routers. One of the circuits is configured within the VRF table on Chianti and is used for connectivity within the VPN. Sangiovese uses this circuit for forwarding traffic to Shiraz. The second circuit is configured as a normal interface, and Sangiovese uses this connection for forwarding packets to the Internet. While the customer may choose to operate a routing protocol across the non-VRF interface, many providers use a static routing model in this situation.

FIGURE 9.9   Distributed Internet access (1 of 3)

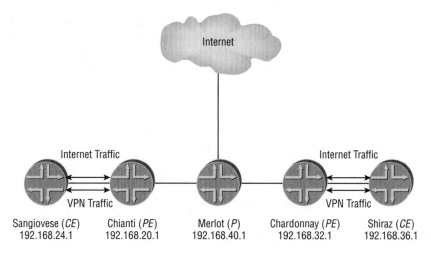

The Sangiovese router has the following operational interfaces:

```
user@Sangiovese> show interfaces terse so-0/2/0
Interface              Admin Link Proto Local             Remote
so-0/2/0               up    up
so-0/2/0.0             up    up    inet  10.222.30.1/24
so-0/2/0.1             up    up    inet  10.222.100.1/24
```

The so-0/2/0.0 interface is communicating via a BGP peering with Chianti as part of the VRF table. This allows the VPN routes to appear in the routing table with a physical next-hop of 10.222.30.2:

```
user@Sangiovese> show route terse protocol bgp

inet.0: 18 destinations, 20 routes (18 active, 0 holddown, 2 hidden)
+ = Active Route, - = Last Active, * = Both
```

```
A Destination        P Prf  Metric 1  Metric 2  Next hop      AS path
* 10.222.44.0/24     B 170    100               >10.222.30.2  65432 I
* 172.16.2.0/24      B 170    100               >10.222.30.2  65432 65432 I
```

All Internet-bound traffic uses a next hop of 10.222.100.2 over the so-0/1/0.1 interface:

```
user@Sangiovese> show route 0/0 exact

inet.0: 18 destinations, 20 routes (18 active, 0 holddown, 2 hidden)
+ = Active Route, - = Last Active, * = Both


0.0.0.0/0            *[Static/5] 00:02:29
                     > to 10.222.100.2 via so-0/2/0.1
```

While this route forwards traffic to Chianti and the Internet at large, we also need to be concerned about return traffic from the Internet. This reachability is easily solved by a static route on Chianti, which represents the customer's address space of 172.16.0.0/16. This route is redistributed to BGP and sent to the provider's network, where it is eventually advertised to the Internet:

```
user@Chianti> show route 172.16/16 exact

inet.0: 17 destinations, 17 routes (17 active, 0 holddown, 0 hidden)
+ = Active Route, - = Last Active, * = Both


172.16.0.0/16       *[Static/5] 00:01:15
                     > to 10.222.100.1 via so-0/1/2.1
```

FIGURE 9.10   Distributed Internet access (2 of 3)

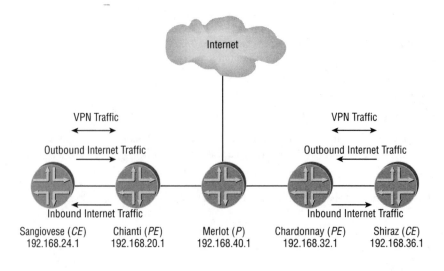

The second option for providing distributed Internet access to a customer (Figure 9.10) also involves two logical circuits between the PE and CE routers. The CE router sends both VPN and Internet traffic to the PE router across the same logical circuit. Return traffic from the Internet uses the second non-VRF logical circuit. From the perspective of Sangiovese, the CE router, both VPN and Internet routes have a next hop of 10.222.30.2 across the so-0/1/2.0 interface:

```
user@Sangiovese> show route terse

inet.0: 18 destinations, 19 routes (18 active, 0 holddown, 1 hidden)
+ = Active Route, - = Last Active, * = Both
```

A Destination	P	Prf	Metric 1	Metric 2	Next hop	AS path
* 0.0.0.0/0	S	5			>10.222.30.2	
* 1.1.1.0/24	D	0			>fxp0.0	
* 1.1.1.2/32	L	0			Local	
* 10.222.4.0/24	D	0			>fe-0/0/2.0	
* 10.222.4.1/32	L	0			Local	
* 10.222.28.0/24	D	0			>at-0/1/0.0	
* 10.222.28.2/32	L	0			Local	
* 10.222.30.0/24	D	0			>so-0/2/0.0	
* 10.222.30.1/32	L	0			Local	
* 10.222.44.0/24	B	170	100		>10.222.30.2	65432 I
* 10.222.100.0/24	D	0			>so-0/2/0.1	
* 10.222.100.1/32	L	0			Local	
* 10.250.0.0/16	D	0			>fxp0.0	
* 10.250.0.132/32	L	0			Local	
* 172.16.1.0/24	S	5	0		Reject	
* 172.16.1.1/32	D	0			>lo0.0	
* 172.16.2.0/24	B	170	100		>10.222.30.2	65432 65432 I
* 192.168.24.1/32	D	0			>lo0.0	

The main difference in this scenario is apparent on the PE router of Chianti. Since Internet-bound packets from the customer are arriving in the VRF table, the PE router needs a route in that table that allows the destination to be found. All Internet destinations can be placed within the VRF table itself, but this presents a large scalability problem when many customers are connected to the same PE router. In addition, those destinations are most likely already present in the inet.0 routing table on the PE router. This provides an interesting solution to our dilemma; now we need only a default route in the VRF table that allows for a second lookup in the main routing table. The JUNOS software uses a static route next-hop value of next-table to permit this "double lookup" on the router. The configuration of the routing instance on Chianti now looks like this:

```
user@Chianti> show configuration routing-instances VPN-A routing-options
static {
    route 0.0.0.0/0 next-table inet.0;
}
```

This allows the VRF table to contain a default route for matching destinations within the Internet:

```
user@Chianti> show route table VPN-A 0/0 exact

VPN-A.inet.0: 6 destinations, 7 routes (6 active, 0 holddown, 1 hidden)
+ = Active Route, - = Last Active, * = Both

0.0.0.0/0            *[Static/5] 00:01:16
                        to table inet.0
```

Of course, Chianti still requires a route for the customer's address space in inet.0 for advertisement to BGP and to the Internet. This allows return traffic from the Internet to reach the customer routers:

```
user@Chianti> show route 172.16/16 exact

inet.0: 17 destinations, 17 routes (17 active, 0 holddown, 0 hidden)
+ = Active Route, - = Last Active, * = Both

172.16.0.0/16        *[Static/5] 00:22:22
                        > to 10.222.100.1 via so-0/1/2.1
```

FIGURE 9.11 Distributed Internet access (3 of 3)

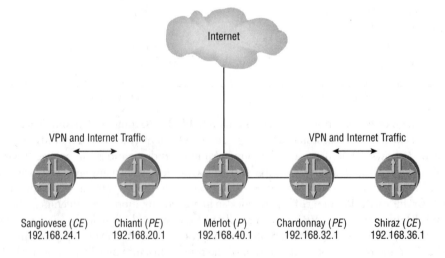

The final option for providing distributed Internet access for a customer uses just a single logical circuit between the CE and PE routers. In Figure 9.11, the CE router sends all traffic to the PE router, where route lookups are performed within the VRF table. This requires a static default route in the VRF table for Internet traffic that points to the `inet.0` routing table using the `next-table` command. On the PE router, no static routes are used for advertising the customer routes to the Internet or for routing traffic back to the CE router. Instead, all of the routes received by the PE router in the VRF table are copied to `inet.0` using a routing table group.

The configuration of Chianti is altered to support this Internet access scenario:

```
user@Chianti> show configuration routing-options
rib-groups {
    vpn-a-into-inet-0 {
        import-rib [ VPN-A.inet.0 inet.0 ];
    }
}
route-distinguisher-id 192.168.20.1;
autonomous-system 65432;
```

```
user@Chianti> show configuration routing-instances VPN-A
instance-type vrf;
interface so-0/1/2.0;
vrf-target target:65432:1111;
routing-options {
    static {
        route 0.0.0.0/0 next-table inet.0;
    }
}
protocols {
    bgp {
        group Sangiovese-CE {
            type external;
            family inet {
                unicast {
                    rib-group vpn-a-into-inet-0;
                }
            }
            peer-as 65000;
            as-override;
            neighbor 10.222.30.1;
        }
    }
}
```

This allows the 172.16.1.0 /24 route to appear in inet.0 with a next-hop value of 10.222.30.1, the interface address of Sangiovese:

```
user@Chianti> show route terse 172.16.1.0/24 table inet.0

inet.0: 18 destinations, 18 routes (17 active, 0 holddown, 1 hidden)
+ = Active Route, - = Last Active, * = Both

A Destination        P Prf   Metric 1   Metric 2  Next hop         AS path
* 172.16.1.0/24      B 170       100           0 >10.222.30.1      65000 I
```

Of course, the VRF table still contains the static default route referencing the inet.0 routing table:

```
user@Chianti> show route table VPN-A.inet.0

VPN-A.inet.0: 6 destinations, 7 routes (6 active, 0 holddown, 1 hidden)
+ = Active Route, - = Last Active, * = Both

0.0.0.0/0           *[Static/5] 00:19:35
                       to table inet.0
10.222.30.0/24      *[Direct/0] 00:47:56
                     > via so-0/1/2.0
10.222.30.2/32      *[Local/0] 00:47:56
                       Local via so-0/1/2.0
10.222.44.0/24      *[BGP/170] 00:04:02, localpref 100, from 192.168.40.1
                       AS path: I
                     > via so-0/1/0.0, label-switched-path Chianti-to-Char
172.16.1.0/24       *[BGP/170] 00:03:50, MED 0, localpref 100
                       AS path: 65000 I
                     > to 10.222.30.1 via so-0/1/2.0
172.16.2.0/24       *[BGP/170] 00:04:02, MED 0, localpref 100, from 192.168.40.1
                       AS path: 65000 I
                     > via so-0/1/0.0, label-switched-path Chianti-to-Char
```

We can also see from Chianti's router output that packets destined for customer sites within the VRF table are forwarded across the provider network to the remote CE router of Shiraz. An example of this is the 172.16.2.0 /24 route, with a forwarding next hop of the ***Chianti-to-Char*** LSP.

Centralized Internet Access

An ISP also has the option of providing its customers with access using a *centralized Internet access* model. The various methods for providing this service are identical to the distributed Internet access models we discussed in the previous section. The main difference between the two models is that just one CE-PE router pair is configured for Internet access. This central CE router advertises a 0.0.0.0 /0 default route to the other CE routers within the VPN. This route advertisement attracts Internet-bound traffic to the central CE router, which then forwards it to the Internet.

Using Figure 9.9 as a guide, we designate the CE router of Sangiovese as the central site that has Internet access configured. This router has a static default route installed that uses the non-VRF interface of so-0/2/0.1 for forwarding Internet traffic to the PE router:

```
user@Sangiovese> show route 0/0 exact

inet.0: 18 destinations, 20 routes (18 active, 0 holddown, 2 hidden)
+ = Active Route, - = Last Active, * = Both

0.0.0.0/0          *[Static/5] 00:10:12
                    > to 10.222.100.2 via so-0/2/0.1
```

In order to attract traffic from the other CE routers in the VPN, Sangiovese advertises the default route to the PE router as a VPN route. This is in addition to the locally reachable address space of 172.16.1.0 /24:

```
user@Sangiovese> show route advertising-protocol bgp 10.222.30.2

inet.0: 18 destinations, 20 routes (18 active, 0 holddown, 2 hidden)
  Prefix                  Nexthop           MED     Lclpref    AS path
* 0.0.0.0/0               Self                                 I
* 10.222.44.0/24          10.222.30.2                          65432 I
* 172.16.1.0/24           Self              0                  I
* 172.16.2.0/24           10.222.30.2                          65432 65432 I
```

Shiraz, the other CE device in the VPN, now has a default route for forwarding Internet-bound packets:

```
user@Shiraz> show route 0/0 exact

inet.0: 14 destinations, 15 routes (14 active, 0 holddown, 1 hidden)
+ = Active Route, - = Last Active, * = Both

0.0.0.0/0          *[BGP/170] 00:13:39, localpref 100
                    AS path: 65432 65432 I
                    > to 10.222.44.2 via so-0/1/0.0
```

When the packets reach the PE router connected to Shiraz, which is Chardonnay, they are forwarded to Chianti across the ***Char-to-Chianti*** LSP:

```
user@Chardonnay> show route 0/0 exact

VPN-A.inet.0: 6 destinations, 6 routes (6 active, 0 holddown, 0 hidden)
+ = Active Route, - = Last Active, * = Both

0.0.0.0/0          *[BGP/170] 00:14:38, localpref 100, from 192.168.40.1
                     AS path: 65000 I
                   > via so-0/1/1.0, label-switched-path Char-to-Chianti
```

The packets are received by Sangiovese on its so-0/2/0.0 interface and are passed back to Chianti on the non-VRF interface of so-0/2/0.1. Chianti then forwards them to the Internet using information in its inet.0 routing table.

Transporting Layer 2 Frames across a Provider Network

The concept of a Layer 2 VPN has been around for quite some time. Traditional X.25, Frame Relay, and ATM networks are prime examples of this connectivity paradigm. Each technology transfers Layer 2 frames that are unique to an individual customer across a common provider infrastructure. Of course, many providers built separate infrastructures to transport these different Layer 2 technologies across their networks. What modern Layer 2 VPNs bring to the table is the ability to transport all Layer 2 technologies across a common IP network using MPLS labels.

Within the JUNOS software, two main varieties of these VPNs exist. To help differentiate between the different Layer 2 VPNs, we'll use the configuration syntax as our guide. The first type of VPN is based on a draft specification by Kireeti Kompella. It uses the Border Gateway Protocol (BGP) as the mechanism for PE routers to communicate with each other about their customer connections. We'll refer to a Kompella-based configuration as a Layer 2 VPN. The second main form of a VPN is based on a draft specification by Luca Martini and uses the Label Distribution Protocol (LDP) between PE routers. Every router establishes a unique connection for each customer using the VPN. The Martini-based VPN is known as a Layer 2 Circuit within the configuration.

Figure 9.12 displays a provider network that we'll refer to throughout the remainder of the chapter to illustrate the operation of Layer 2 VPNs as well as Layer 2 circuits. This particular network is using IS-IS as its internal routing protocol, and each of the P and PE routers are advertising information to the network. We see this with a quick examination of the IS-IS database on the Zinfandel router:

```
user@Zinfandel> show isis database level 2
IS-IS level 2 link-state database:
```

LSP ID	Sequence	Checksum	Lifetime	Attributes
Chianti.00-00	0xdb	0xe634	1195	L1 L2
Sangiovese.00-00	0xdb	0x29f9	509	L1 L2
Chardonnay.00-00	0xd9	0x349a	627	L1 L2
Merlot.00-00	0xdc	0xa077	442	L1 L2
Chablis.00-00	0xdc	0xab3e	921	L1 L2
Zinfandel.00-00	0xda	0xcff2	612	L1 L2

 6 LSPs

Layer 2 VPN

A Layer 2 VPN within the JUNOS software utilizes the same provider infrastructure as the Layer 3 VPNs we discussed earlier in the chapter. This means that the PE routers use MBGP to advertise information between them concerning their connected customers. These advertisements contain a VPN connection table (VCT) that describes label information used to connect the customer sites. In addition, the MBGP advertisements contain route target extended community values, which enforce the logical topology of the VPN.

FIGURE 9.12   Layer 2 VPN provider network

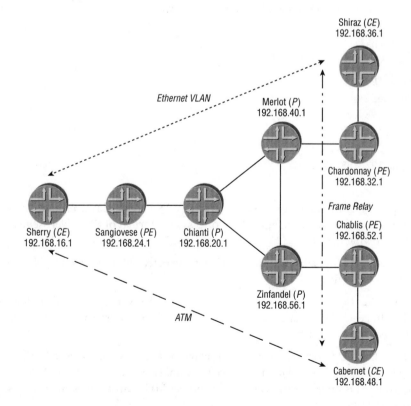

Each of the PE routers in Figure 9.12 has an active RSVP LSP from itself to other routers on the network. The Chardonnay router, for example, contains three LSPs:

```
user@Chardonnay> show mpls lsp ingress
Ingress LSP: 3 sessions
To               From           State Rt ActivePath       P     LSPname
192.168.20.1     192.168.32.1   Up    0                   *     Char-to-Chianti
192.168.24.1     192.168.32.1   Up    0                   *     Char-to-Sang
192.168.52.1     192.168.32.1   Up    0                   *     Char-to-Chablis
Total 3 displayed, Up 3, Down 0
```

 A Layer 2 VPN can also use LDP to provide MPLS connectivity between the PE routers.

To properly advertise the Layer 2 VPN information, each PE router is configured with the `family l2vpn unicast` command. This enables the negotiation of the Layer 2 VPN address family (196) as well as the labeled VPN unicast subsequent address family (128). The MBGP configuration of the Chardonnay router looks like this:

```
user@Chardonnay> show configuration protocols bgp
group internal-peers {
    type internal;
    local-address 192.168.32.1;
    family l2vpn {
        unicast;
    }
    neighbor 192.168.24.1;
    neighbor 192.168.20.1;
    neighbor 192.168.52.1;
}
```

This allows the PE routers to advertise the Layer 2 VPN network layer reachability information (the VCT) to each of its peers. Figure 9.13 displays the format of this advertisement, which includes the following fields:

Length (2 octets)   This field displays the total length, in octets, of the Layer 2 VPN information advertised by the PE router.

Route Distinguisher (8 octets)   As we saw with a Layer 3 VPN, the Route Distinguisher field uniquely identifies each customer connection and allows the PE routers to maintain separation between the customer networks.

Local Customer Edge ID (2 octets)   This field displays the *local customer edge ID* value assigned by the PE router to the customer connection. Each site within a particular customer VPN is assigned a unique ID value. This value is used to ensure that proper MPLS label values are used to send and receive traffic for a site.

FIGURE 9.13   Layer 2 VPN NLRI format

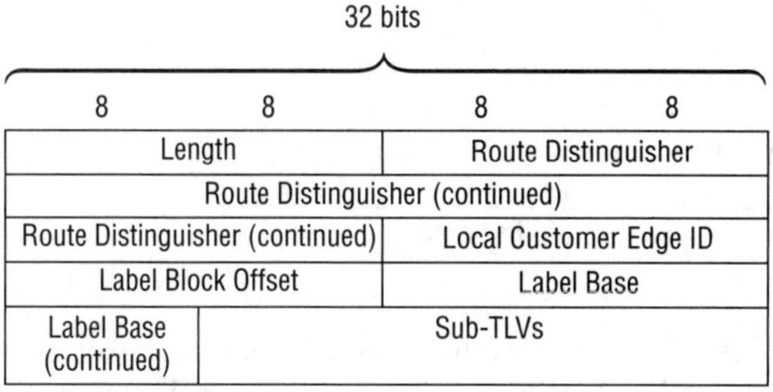

32 bits

8	8	8	8
Length		Route Distinguisher	
Route Distinguisher (continued)			
Route Distinguisher (continued)		Local Customer Edge ID	
Label Block Offset		Label Base	
Label Base (continued)	Sub-TLVs		

Label Block Offset (2 octets)   A PE router has the ability to advertise multiple sets of labels to its remote PE peers. In this situation, each receiving PE router requires knowledge as to how the separate label blocks are sequenced. This field, the *label block offset*, provides this information. It contains a 16-bit value that allows the receiving routers to sequence the multiple advertised label blocks.

Label Base (3 octets)   The Label Base field is used by PE routers to determine the exact MPLS label to use for forwarding and receiving traffic on a particular customer connection.

Sub-TLVs (Variable)   This variable-length field contains sub-TLVs that further describe the customer connection. Each sub-TLV contains a 1-octet type field, a 2-octet length field, and a variable-length value field. Only a single sub-TLV, the circuit status vector, is currently defined.

The circuit status vector is a bit-vector system in which each of the configured customer connections is assigned a bit. In addition to allowing the PE routers to infer the range of labels used for the VPN, it is used to monitor the status of the virtual connection. Each PE router is aware of its local circuit and the LSP to the remote PE router. When both of these connections are operational, the local PE sets the appropriate bit in the vector to the value 0. When either of these connections stops working, the bit for that logical circuit is set to the value 1. This system allows the two PE routers to monitor the end-to-end customer circuit and notify the customer when the circuit is down. This notification comes in the form of a Layer 2 management mechanism, such as the Local Management Interface (LMI) for Frame Relay.

In addition to the route target community advertised along with the connection information, the Layer 2 VPN specifications define an additional community value. The *Layer 2 information community* provides a method to ensure that the two PE routers are connecting a logical circuit that is compatible between the customer connections. After all, if one customer is transmitting frames using a Frame Relay Data-Link Connection Identifier (DLCI), it doesn't do much good if the remote customer connection is expecting ATM cells. The fields of the Layer 2 information community are shown in Figure 9.14 and include:

Extended Community Type (2 octets)   This field displays the type of extended community being advertised by the PE router. For the Layer 2 information community, a constant value of 0x800a is used.

FIGURE 9.14 Layer 2 information community

32 bits

8	8	8	8
Extended Community Type		Encapsulation Type	Control Flags
Layer 2 MTU		Reserved	

Encapsulation Type (1 octet) This field encodes the specific Layer 2 encapsulation used between the advertising PE router and its locally connected CE router. The possible values are as follows:

- 0—Reserved
- 1—Frame Relay
- 2—ATM AAL5 virtual circuit connection transport
- 3—ATM transparent cell transport
- 4—Ethernet virtual LAN
- 5—Ethernet
- 6—Cisco high-level data link control
- 7—Point-to-Point Protocol
- 8—Circuit emulation
- 9—ATM virtual circuit connection cell transport
- 10—ATM virtual path connection cell transport
- 11—IP Interworking
- 19—Virtual private label switching

Control Flags (1 octet) This field is a bit-vector that allows the advertising PE router to set parameters for the connection. The various bit definitions include:

Bits 7 through 4 These bits are not currently defined and must be set to a value of 0.

Bit 3 The Q bit is currently reserved and must be set to a value of 0.

Bit 2 The F bit is currently reserved and must be set to a value of 0.

Bit 1 The C bit defines the use of a *control word* within the provider network. The control word allows for the advertisement of Layer 2 management information between the customer sites by transporting it across the provider network. This is accomplished by adding a 4-byte header between the MPLS labels and the Layer 2 PDU at one edge of the provider network and further removing the control word at the other edge of the network.

When the C bit is set to a value of 1, the control word is required across the provider network. When it is set to a value of 0, it is not required.

Bit 0   The S bit defines whether a sequenced delivery of the Layer 2 frames is required. When the bit is set to a value of 1, the PE routers must ensure the sequencing of the transmitted frames. When it is set to a value of 0, sequenced delivery is not required.

Layer 2 MTU (2 octets)   Each advertising PE router has the ability to set the current MTU, excluding the Layer 2 header information, of the customer connection in this 2-octet field. In addition, the field may be set to a value of 0 when the MTU information is not required. In either case, the MTU values must match between the two PE routers in order for the connection to become operational.

Reserved (2 octets)   This field is not used and must be set to a constant value of 0x0000.

As you might expect, the configuration of a Layer 2 VPN is similar to a Layer 3 VPN. The main difference between the two is that the physical and logical interfaces connecting the PE router to the CE router requires some additional encapsulation information. We examine the specific details of the configuration within the context of a Frame Relay connection, but we cover both ATM and Ethernet configurations for completeness.

Frame Relay as the PE-CE Connection

One Layer 2 encapsulation that is currently popular as a wide area network technology is Frame Relay. This popularity makes it a leading candidate for migration to a Layer 2 VPN provider network. In addition to the establishment of the provider core network, which we discussed earlier in the chapter, the steps for enabling a Layer 2 VPN involve the encapsulation on the physical interfaces and the assignment of identifier values to the customer sites within the VPN.

Physical Interface Encapsulation

The end result of a Layer 2 VPN is the communication of two customer sites over a Frame Relay circuit. As such, the CE routers are configured to support Frame Relay and are assigned appropriate DLCI values by the network provider. Figure 9.12 shows a Frame Relay connection between Shiraz and Cabernet across our sample provider network. The interface configuration of these two routers currently looks like this:

```
user@Shiraz> show configuration interfaces so-0/1/0
encapsulation frame-relay;
unit 600 {
    dlci 600;
    family inet {
        address 10.222.100.1/24;
    }
}

user@Cabernet> show configuration interfaces so-0/1/2
encapsulation frame-relay;
unit 600 {
    dlci 600;
```

```
    family inet {
        address 10.222.100.2/24;
    }
}
```

The PE routers of Chardonnay and Chablis are responsible for receiving packets from and sending packets to the CE routers. As such, they also require some special interface configuration to support a Layer 2 VPN. Here's how they are configured:

```
user@Chardonnay> show configuration interfaces so-0/1/0
dce;
encapsulation frame-relay-ccc;
unit 600 {
    encapsulation frame-relay-ccc;
    dlci 600;
}

user@Chablis> show configuration interfaces so-0/1/0
dce;
encapsulation frame-relay-ccc;
unit 600 {
    encapsulation frame-relay-ccc;
    dlci 600;
}
```

 For simplicity we've used the same DLCI value of 600 on both sides of the VPN, but this is not required. Only the PE and its connected CE need to agree on the DLCI used.

 When you're using the `frame-relay-ccc` encapsulation, the DLCI values must be greater than or equal to 512.

The use of the `frame-relay-ccc` encapsulation on the PE routers allows the Layer 2 frames to be placed directly into an MPLS label-switched path for transmission across the network. It also provides the capability for the PE router to receive an MPLS packet and forward the encapsulated Layer 2 frame to the CE router.

After each PE-CE router pair begins exchanging the correct DLCI information, the interfaces transition to an Up state:

```
user@Chardonnay> show interfaces so-0/1/0 terse
Interface               Admin Link Proto Local                   Remote
```

```
so-0/1/0                    up    up
so-0/1/0.600                up    up   ccc


user@Chablis> show interfaces so-0/1/0 terse
Interface               Admin Link Proto Local               Remote
so-0/1/0                    up    up
so-0/1/0.600                up    up   ccc
```

Configuring Site Identifiers

You may have noticed that the NLRI advertised in a Layer 2 VPN doesn't contain an explicit VPN label for use by the remote PE router. In its place are an advertised label base and a label offset value. This allows the receiving PE router to automatically calculate the VPN label used to reach the remote site based on its local configuration. This local configuration centers on the *site identifier* for the customer.

Each customer site connected to a PE router is assigned a site ID within the VPN using the `site-identifier` command. This 16-bit value is required to be unique only within the particular customer network. In our sample network the Shiraz router is assigned a site ID of 1, whereas the Cabernet router is assigned a site ID of 4. The configuration of the Chardonnay router, which is connected to Shiraz, looks like this:

```
user@Chardonnay> show configuration routing-instances
FR-Customer {
    instance-type l2vpn;
    interface so-0/1/0.600;
    vrf-target target:65432:1111;
    protocols {
        l2vpn {
            encapsulation-type frame-relay;
            site Shiraz-CE {
                site-identifier 1;
                interface so-0/1/0.600 {
                    remote-site-id 4;
                }
            }
        }
    }
}
```

We see this ID value appear in the NLRI advertised to the remote PE router of Chablis:

```
user@Chardonnay> show route advertising-protocol bgp 192.168.52.1
```

```
FR-Customer.l2vpn.0: 2 destinations, 2 routes (2 active, 0 holddown, 0 hidden)
  Prefix                   Nexthop              MED     Lclpref   AS path
  192.168.32.1:2:1:3/96
*                          Self                         100       I
```

The Chablis router has a similar configuration that references a site ID of 4 for its CE router. As you would expect, this value also appears in the NLRI advertised by Chablis:

```
user@Chablis> show configuration routing-instances FR-Customer protocols
l2vpn {
    encapsulation-type frame-relay;
    site Cabernet-CE {
        site-identifier 4;
        interface so-0/1/0.600;
    }
}


user@Chablis> show route advertising-protocol bgp 192.168.32.1

FR-Customer.l2vpn.0: 2 destinations, 2 routes (2 active, 0 holddown, 0 hidden)
  Prefix                   Nexthop              MED     Lclpref   AS path
  192.168.52.1:2:4:1/96
*                          Self                         100       I
```

You may notice that the configuration of the Chardonnay router includes the `remote-site-id` command while it isn't present on the Chablis router. The use of this command is predicated by the default JUNOS software behavior for Layer 2 VPNs. Within the configuration of the customer site, each local interface connected to the CE router is listed. The PE router then makes a default assignment of local interfaces to remote site ID values. This default value assignment begins with a value of 1 and increments by 1 for each configured interface, skipping the local site ID value in the process. For the Chardonnay router, whose local site ID is 1, the `so-0/1/0.600` interface is automatically associated with a remote site of 2. Unfortunately, the Chablis router is using a site ID value of 4. This mismatch prevents the Layer 2 VPN from forming a connection and forwarding user frames across the network. When the Chardonnay router configures `remote-site-id 4` within that interface, the automatic value assignment is not used.

Once the correct site ID is determined for each remote customer site, each PE router chooses the VPN labels for receiving and sending traffic across that connection. The VPN label is the result of adding the label base advertised by the remote PE router to the site ID of the local customer connection. The label block offset advertised by the remote PE router is then subtracted from this total value to arrive at the VPN label. As a formula, we represent this calculation as: VPN label = *label-base-remote* + *local-site-id* − *label-offset-remote*. We can utilize this formula to determine the VPN labels used in our sample network.

The Chardonnay router is advertising a label base value of 800,000, a local site ID of 1, and a label offset value of 3:

```
user@Chardonnay> show route advertising-protocol bgp 192.168.52.1 detail

FR-Customer.l2vpn.0: 2 destinations, 2 routes (2 active, 0 holddown, 0 hidden)
* 192.168.32.1:2:1:3/96 (1 entry, 1 announced)
 BGP group internal-peers type Internal
    Route Distinguisher: 192.168.32.1:2
    Label-base: 800000, range: 2, status-vector: 0x80
    Nexthop: Self
    Localpref: 100
    AS path: I
    Communities: target:65432:1111
                Layer2-info: encaps:FRAME RELAY, control flags:2, mtu: 0
```

The relevant information from the Chablis router shows a label base value of 800,000, a local site ID of 4, and a label offset value of 1:

```
user@Chablis> show route advertising-protocol bgp 192.168.32.1 detail

FR-Customer.l2vpn.0: 2 destinations, 2 routes (2 active, 0 holddown, 0 hidden)
* 192.168.52.1:2:4:1/96 (1 entry, 1 announced)
 BGP group internal-peers type Internal
    Route Distinguisher: 192.168.52.1:2
    Label-base: 800000, range: 1, status-vector: 0x0
    Nexthop: Self
    Localpref: 100
    AS path: I
    Communities: target:65432:1111
                Layer2-info: encaps:FRAME RELAY, control flags:2, mtu: 0
```

From the perspective of Chablis, the label base advertised by Chardonnay (800,000) is added to the local site ID value of 4. This new value of 800,004 then has the label offset value advertised by Chardonnay (3) subtracted from it to arrive at a final label value of 800,001. In other words, VPN label = *label-base-remote* + *local-site-id* – *label-offset-remote* = 800,000 + 4 – 3 = 800,001.

We see this calculated value in the output of the show l2vpn connections command, which displays the status of each Layer 2 VPN configured on the local router:

```
user@Chablis> show l2vpn connections
Connections:
```

Legend for connection status (St)

OR -- out of range	WE -- intf encaps != instance encaps
EI -- encapsulation invalid	Dn -- down
EM -- encapsulation mismatch	VC-Dn -- Virtual circuit down
CM -- control-word mismatch	-> -- only outbound conn is up
CN -- circuit not present	<- -- only inbound conn is up
OL -- no outgoing label	Up -- operational
NC -- intf encaps not CCC/TCC	XX -- unknown
NP -- interface not present	

Legend for interface status
Up -- operational
Dn -- down

Instance: FR-Customer
Local site: Cabernet-CE (4)

connection-site	Type	St	Time last up	# Up trans
1	rmt	Up	Nov 6 12:50:09 2001	1

    Local interface: so-0/1/0.600, Status: Up, Encapsulation: FRAME RELAY
    Remote PE: 192.168.32.1, Negotiated control-word: Yes (Null)
    Incoming label: 800000, <u>Outgoing label: 800001</u>

In addition, we see the VPN label value used by Chardonnay (800,000) for forwarding traffic to Chablis.

Once each PE router receives an NLRI from its remote peer and calculates the VPN label to use for forwarding traffic, we can verify the final end-to-end connectivity using an ICMP ping:

```
user@Shiraz> ping 10.222.100.2 rapid
PING 10.222.100.2 (10.222.100.2): 56 data bytes
!!!!!
--- 10.222.100.2 ping statistics ---
5 packets transmitted, 5 packets received, 0% packet loss
round-trip min/avg/max/stddev = 0.745/0.819/1.083/0.132 ms
```

ATM as the PE-CE Connection

A second Layer 2 encapsulation that can be transported across a Layer 2 VPN is ATM. One main difference occurs in this environment, however, that sets it apart from a native ATM network. When the PE routers are configured with the atm-ccc-vc-mux encapsulation, which is the most basic ATM type of Layer 2 VPN encapsulation, the JUNOS software reassembles the ATM cells received from the CE router and forms an AAL5 protocol data unit before transporting it across the provider network. The remote PE router then segments the PDU back into ATM cells for transmission to the remote CE router.

The sample network in Figure 9.12 is supporting an ATM connection between the Sherry and Cabernet routers. The interface configurations of the PE and CE routers are:

```
user@Sherry> show configuration interfaces at-0/1/0
atm-options {
    vpi 0 {
        maximum-vcs 1000;
    }
}
unit 800 {
    vci 0.800;
    family inet {
        address 10.222.150.1/24;
    }
}


user@Sangiovese> show configuration interfaces at-0/1/0
atm-options {
    vpi 0 {
        maximum-vcs 1000;
    }
}
unit 800 {
    encapsulation atm-ccc-vc-mux;
    vci 0.800;
}


user@Cabernet> show configuration interfaces at-0/0/0
atm-options {
    vpi 0 {
        maximum-vcs 1000;
    }
}
unit 800 {
    vci 0.800;
    family inet {
        address 10.222.150.2/24;
    }
}


user@Chablis> show configuration interfaces at-0/2/1
atm-options {
```

```
        vpi 0 {
            maximum-vcs 1000;
        }
    }
    unit 800 {
        encapsulation atm-ccc-vc-mux;
        vci 0.800;
    }
```

The configuration of the routing instances on the PE routers shows a similar setup to what we saw with Frame Relay:

```
user@Sangiovese> show configuration routing-instances
ATM-Customer {
    instance-type l2vpn;
    interface at-0/1/0.800;
    vrf-target target:65432:2222;
    protocols {
        l2vpn {
            encapsulation-type atm-aal5;
            site Sherry-CE {
                site-identifier 1;
                interface at-0/1/0.800;
            }
        }
    }
}
```

```
user@Chablis> show configuration routing-instances ATM-Customer protocols
l2vpn {
    encapsulation-type atm-aal5;
    site Cabernet-CE {
        site-identifier 2;
        interface at-0/2/1.800;
    }
}
```

Since the provider core is already operational, we see the appropriate NLRI advertised between the PE routers:

```
user@Sangiovese> show route advertising-protocol bgp 192.168.52.1 detail
```

```
ATM-Customer.l2vpn.0: 2 destinations, 2 routes (2 active, 0 holddown, 0 hidden)
* 192.168.24.1:3:1:1/96 (1 entry, 1 announced)
 BGP group internal-peers type Internal
     Route Distinguisher: 192.168.24.1:3
     Label-base: 800000, range: 2, status-vector: 0x80
     Nexthop: Self
     Localpref: 100
     AS path: I
     Communities: target:65432:2222
                  Layer2-info: encaps:ATM AAL5, control flags:2, mtu: 0
```

```
user@Chablis> show route advertising-protocol bgp 192.168.24.1 detail
```

```
ATM-Customer.l2vpn.0: 2 destinations, 2 routes (2 active, 0 holddown, 0 hidden)

* 192.168.52.1:4:2:1/96 (1 entry, 1 announced)
 BGP group internal-peers type Internal
     Route Distinguisher: 192.168.52.1:4
     Label-base: 800002, range: 1, status-vector: 0x0
     Nexthop: Self
     Localpref: 100
     AS path: I
     Communities: target:65432:2222
                  Layer2-info: encaps:ATM AAL5, control flags:2, mtu: 0
```

The Layer 2 VPN connection is operational, and each PE router has calculated the appropriate VPN label to use for transmitting information to the remote router:

```
user@Sangiovese> show l2vpn connections
Connections:

Legend for connection status (St)
OR -- out of range            WE -- intf encaps != instance encaps
EI -- encapsulation invalid   Dn -- down
EM -- encapsulation mismatch  VC-Dn -- Virtual circuit down
CM -- control-word mismatch   -> -- only outbound conn is up
CN -- circuit not present     <- -- only inbound  conn is up
OL -- no outgoing label       Up -- operational
NC -- intf encaps not CCC/TCC XX -- unknown
NP -- interface not present
```

```
Legend for interface status
Up -- operational
Dn -- down


Instance: ATM-Customer
Local site: Sherry-CE (1)
    connection-site        Type  St    Time last up         # Up trans
    2                      rmt   Up    Jul 16 14:32:58 2003          1
        Local interface: at-0/1/0.800, Status: Up, Encapsulation: ATM AAL5
        Remote PE: 192.168.52.1, Negotiated control-word: Yes (Null)
        Incoming label: 800001, Outgoing label: 800002
```

We can now verify the end-to-end connectivity from the CE routers:

```
user@Sherry> ping 10.222.150.2 rapid
PING 10.222.150.2 (10.222.150.2): 56 data bytes
!!!!!
--- 10.222.150.2 ping statistics ---
5 packets transmitted, 5 packets received, 0% packet loss
round-trip min/avg/max/stddev = 1.832/2.026/2.397/0.193 ms
```

Ethernet VLANs as the PE-CE Connection

Many end users are familiar with the operation and configuration of an Ethernet VLAN. Therefore, the support for transporting these Layer 2 frames across a provider network is a critical
component of any technology. While the JUNOS software supports the transport of both
tagged and untagged Ethernet frames, we'll focus on interfaces configured with VLAN information. Figure 9.12 displays a Layer 2 VPN employing VLAN-tagged Ethernet frames between
the Sherry and Shiraz routers. The interface configurations of the respective routers are:

```
user@Sherry> show configuration interfaces fe-0/3/3
vlan-tagging;
unit 900 {
    vlan-id 900;
    family inet {
        address 10.222.200.1/24;
    }
}


user@Sangiovese> show configuration interfaces fe-0/0/3
vlan-tagging;
encapsulation vlan-ccc;
unit 900 {
```

```
    encapsulation vlan-ccc;
    vlan-id 900;
}


user@Chardonnay> show configuration interfaces fe-0/0/0
vlan-tagging;
encapsulation vlan-ccc;
unit 900 {
    encapsulation vlan-ccc;
    vlan-id 900;
}


user@Shiraz> show configuration interfaces fe-0/0/0
vlan-tagging;
unit 900 {
    vlan-id 900;
    family inet {
        address 10.222.200.2/24;
    }
}
```

WARNING The VLAN ID must be greater than or equal to 512 for the Layer 2 VPN connections. In addition, the values must match on both sides of the provider network. This is a difference from what we saw with Frame Relay and ATM, where the Layer 2 identifier could be different on the CE routers.

The configurations of the routing instances on the PE routers look like this:

```
user@Chianti> show configuration routing-instances VLAN-Customer protocols
l2vpn {
    encapsulation-type ethernet-vlan;
    site Sherry-CE {
        site-identifier 1;
        interface fe-0/3/0.900;
    }
}


user@Chardonnay> show configuration routing-instances VLAN-Customer protocols
l2vpn {
    encapsulation-type ethernet-vlan;
    site Shiraz-CE {
        site-identifier 2;
```

```
        interface fe-0/0/0.900;
    }
}
```

Our established provider core network allows the PE routers to advertise the appropriate NLRI:

```
user@Sangiovese> show route advertising-protocol bgp 192.168.32.1 detail

VLAN-Customer.l2vpn.0: 2 destinations, 2 routes (2 active, 0 holddown, 0 hidden)
* 192.168.20.1:3:1:1/96 (1 entry, 1 announced)
 BGP group internal-peers type Internal
     Route Distinguisher: 192.168.20.1:3
     Label-base: 800000, range: 2, status-vector: 0x80
     Nexthop: Self
     Localpref: 100
     AS path: I
     Communities: target:65432:3333
                 Layer2-info: encaps:VLAN, control flags:2, mtu: 0


user@Chardonnay> show route advertising-protocol bgp 192.168.24.1 detail

VLAN-Customer.l2vpn.0: 2 destinations, 2 routes (2 active, 0 holddown, 0 hidden)

* 192.168.32.1:4:2:1/96 (1 entry, 1 announced)
 BGP group internal-peers type Internal
     Route Distinguisher: 192.168.32.1:4
     Label-base: 800002, range: 1, status-vector: 0x0
     Nexthop: Self
     Localpref: 100
     AS path: I
     Communities: target:65432:3333
                 Layer2-info: encaps:VLAN, control flags:2, mtu: 0
```

Once the NLRI is received and processed by the PE routers, the appropriate VPN labels are selected and the Layer 2 VPN connection is established:

```
user@Chianti> show l2vpn connections
Connections:

Legend for connection status (St)
OR -- out of range             WE -- intf encaps != instance encaps
EI -- encapsulation invalid    Dn -- down
```

```
EM -- encapsulation mismatch    VC-Dn -- Virtual circuit down
CM -- control-word mismatch     -> -- only outbound conn is up
CN -- circuit not present       <- -- only inbound  conn is up
OL -- no outgoing label         Up -- operational
NC -- intf encaps not CCC/TCC   XX -- unknown
NP -- interface not present


Legend for interface status
Up -- operational
Dn -- down
```

```
Instance: VLAN-Customer
Local site: Sherry-CE (1)
    connection-site       Type  St     Time last up         # Up trans
    2                     rmt   Up     Jul 17 09:44:15 2003           2
       Local interface: fe-0/3/0.900, Status: Up, Encapsulation: VLAN
       Remote PE: 192.168.32.1, Negotiated control-word: Yes (Null)
       Incoming label: 800001, Outgoing label: 800002
```

As a final step, we verify connectivity between the CE routers:

```
user@Shiraz> ping 10.222.200.1 rapid
PING 10.222.200.1 (10.222.200.1): 56 data bytes
!!!!!
--- 10.222.200.1 ping statistics ---
5 packets transmitted, 5 packets received, 0% packet loss
round-trip min/avg/max/stddev = 0.772/0.859/1.152/0.148
```

Using Different Encapsulations for the PE-CE Connection

At this point in our discussion of Layer 2 VPNs, we've gained independence at the network layer by requiring the same Layer 2 encapsulation on both ends of the virtual connection. This occurs since the PE routers forward all received frames across the network without examining the contents of the network layer. A Layer 2 VPN, however, also has the ability to gain independence at the data link layer by requiring that the Layer 3 protocol be IPv4. This concept, known as *IP Interworking*, allows each PE-CE connection to use separate Layer 2 encapsulations.

A simple Layer 2 VPN using IP Interworking is shown in Figure 9.15. The connection between Shiraz and Chardonnay is using Frame Relay for its Layer 2 encapsulation, whereas ATM is used between Chablis and Cabernet. From the perspective of the CE routers, the configuration of the interfaces is no different from any other Layer 2 VPN setup:

```
user@Shiraz> show configuration interfaces so-0/1/0
encapsulation frame-relay;
```

```
unit 600 {
    dlci 600;
    family inet {
        address 10.222.222.1/24;
    }
}

user@Cabernet> show configuration interfaces at-0/0/0
atm-options {
    vpi 0 {
        maximum-vcs 1001;
    }
}
unit 0 {
    vci 0.1000;
    family inet {
        address 10.222.222.2/24;
    }
}
```

FIGURE 9.15 IP Interworking Layer 2 VPN

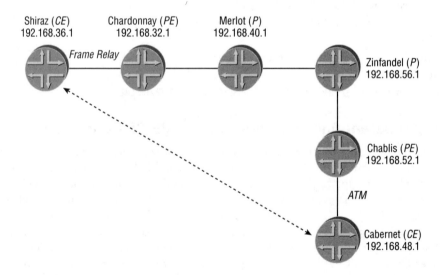

The knowledge of the IP Interworking connection is contained solely within the PE routers. Slight configuration changes appear in both the [edit interfaces] and the [edit routing-instances] hierarchies. The PE router of Chardonnay is configured like this:

```
user@Chardonnay> show configuration interfaces so-0/1/0
dce;
encapsulation frame-relay-tcc;
unit 0 {
    encapsulation frame-relay-tcc;
    dlci 600;
}


user@Chardonnay> show configuration routing-instances
IP-Interworking {
    instance-type l2vpn;
    interface so-0/1/0.0;
    vrf-target target:65432:4444;
    protocols {
        l2vpn {
            encapsulation-type interworking;
            site Shiraz-CE-Frame-Relay {
                site-identifier 1;
                interface so-0/1/0.0;
            }
        }
    }
}
```

On the PE interface, the encapsulation of frame-relay-tcc is configured. This allows the interface to remove the Layer 2 header from the incoming packet and forward the remaining IP information to the remote PE across the provider network. In addition, this encapsulation type provides the ability for Chardonnay to append the appropriate Layer 2 header to all received IP packets from the remote PE router.

Within the routing instance configuration, we also see some different information. In this case, the Layer 2 VPN encapsulation is set to interworking. This allows the PE routers to advertise and verify that the remote ends of the connection both support IP Interworking. We see this in the Layer 2 Information community advertised by Chardonnay:

```
user@Chardonnay> show route advertising-protocol bgp 192.168.52.1 detail

IP-Interworking.l2vpn.0: 2 destinations, 2 routes (2 active, 0 holddown, 0
hidden)
* 192.168.32.1:5:1:1/96 (1 entry, 1 announced)
```

```
BGP group internal-peers type Internal
    Route Distinguisher: 192.168.32.1:5
    Label-base: 800000, range: 2, status-vector: 0x80
    Nexthop: Self
    Localpref: 100
    AS path: I
    Communities: target:65432:4444
                Layer2-info: encaps:INTERWORKING, control flags:0, mtu: 0
```

The remote PE router of Chablis is also configured in a similar manner to Chardonnay:

```
user@Chablis> show configuration interfaces at-0/2/1
atm-options {
    vpi 0 {
        maximum-vcs 1001;
    }
}
unit 0 {
    encapsulation atm-tcc-snap;
    vci 0.1000;
}
```

```
user@Chablis> show configuration routing-instances
IP-Interworking {
    instance-type l2vpn;
    interface at-0/2/1.0;
    vrf-target target:65432:4444;
    protocols {
        l2vpn {
            encapsulation-type interworking;
            site Cabernet-CE-ATM {
                site-identifier 2;
                interface at-0/2/1.0;
            }
        }
    }
}
```

In the routing instance configuration, we see the same `encapsulation-type interworking` statement applied. There is a special encapsulation configured on the interface as well. In this case, it is `encapsulation atm-tcc-snap`.

The presence of the appropriate VRF target communities and the Layer 2 Information community allows the Layer 2 VPN connection to become established:

```
user@Chablis> show l2vpn connections
Connections:

Legend for connection status (St)
OR -- out of range              WE -- intf encaps != instance encaps
EI -- encapsulation invalid     Dn -- down
EM -- encapsulation mismatch    VC-Dn -- Virtual circuit down
CM -- control-word mismatch     -> -- only outbound conn is up
CN -- circuit not present       <- -- only inbound  conn is up
OL -- no outgoing label         Up -- operational
NC -- intf encaps not CCC/TCC   XX -- unknown
NP -- interface not present


Legend for interface status
Up -- operational
Dn -- down



Instance: IP-Interworking
Local site: Cabernet-CE-ATM (2)
    connection-site       Type  St     Time last up            # Up trans
    1                     rmt   Up     Nov 16 14:37:07 2001              1
        Local interface: at-0/2/1.0, Status: Up, Encapsulation: INTERWORKING
        Remote PE: 192.168.32.1, Negotiated control-word: No
        Incoming label: 800000, Outgoing label: 800001
```

As we would now expect, the CE routers can communicate with each other. We verify this using the ping command from the Shiraz router:

```
user@Shiraz> ping 10.222.222.2 rapid
PING 10.222.222.2 (10.222.222.2): 56 data bytes
!!!!!
--- 10.222.222.2 ping statistics ---
5 packets transmitted, 5 packets received, 0% packet loss
round-trip min/avg/max/stddev = 1.330/3.182/10.028/3.425 ms
```

Layer 2 Circuit

The main difference between a Layer 2 VPN and a Layer 2 Circuit lies in the control plane and the methods used to set up the virtual connection across the provider network. The configuration of the physical interfaces as well as the actual forwarding of traffic doesn't change. In fact, both a Layer 2 VPN and a Layer 2 Circuit encapsulate the incoming customer packet in the exact same manner.

As you might expect, we spend the majority of this section discussing Layer 2 Circuit control plane issues. We follow this with a quick examination of some sample configurations using Frame Relay, ATM, and Ethernet VLAN customer connections.

Control Plane

Customer circuit information is advertised in a Layer 2 Circuit environment using the Label Distribution Protocol (LDP). The two PE routers use targeted LDP Hello messages to form a session with each other. Once the session is established, the peers exchange Forwarding Equivalence Class (FEC) information, which advertises available prefixes with an MPLS label mapping. The PE routers use this FEC advertisement to establish the virtual connection by including a new TLV that contains circuit specific information. Figure 9.16 shows the format of this TLV, which contains the following fields:

FEC Element Type (1 octet)   This field displays the type of information advertised in the TLV for the FEC. A Layer 2 Circuit uses a constant value of 128 in this field.

C Bit and VC Type (2 octets)   The most significant bit in the field, bit 15, is called the C bit and determines whether the virtual connection should use the optional control word. When the bit is set to the value 1, the control word should be included in all packets. It should be omitted, however, when the bit is set to the value 0.

The remaining 15 bits in this field represent the type of virtual connection being established across the provider network. Possible values include:

- 0x0001—Frame Relay DLCI
- 0x0002—ATM AAL5 virtual circuit connection transport
- 0x0003—ATM transparent cell transport
- 0x0004—Ethernet virtual LAN
- 0x0005—Ethernet
- 0x0006—Cisco high-level data link control
- 0x0007—Point-to-Point Protocol
- 0x8008—Circuit emulation
- 0x0009—ATM virtual circuit connection cell transport
- 0x000a—ATM virtual path connection cell transport

VC Information Length (1 octet)   This field displays the length, in octets, of the Virtual Circuit ID and Interface Parameters fields. The JUNOS software uses a constant value of 4 in this field, which means that no parameters are included in the TLV.

FIGURE 9.16   Layer 2 Circuit FEC advertisement

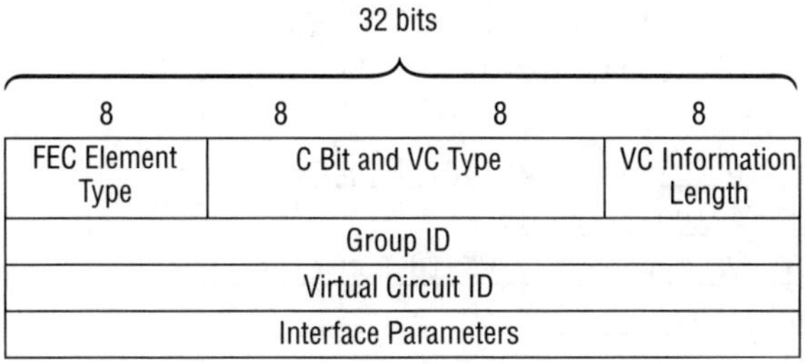

32 bits

8	8	8	8
FEC Element Type	C Bit and VC Type		VC Information Length
Group ID			
Virtual Circuit ID			
Interface Parameters			

Group ID (4 octets)   The group ID is a 32-bit value that represents a grouping of virtual circuits advertised by a PE router. This group concept is not used by the JUNOS software, and this field is set to a constant value of 0.

Virtual Circuit ID (4 octets)   The *virtual circuit ID* is a 32-bit value that uniquely identifies, when combined with the VC type, a particular circuit in the network. The two PE routers must agree on the virtual circuit ID value to establish the Layer 2 Circuit in the network.

Interface Parameters (Variable)   This variable-length field contains information that describes the properties of the customer-facing interface, such as the maximum transmission unit (MTU). The JUNOS software doesn't use this field, and it is not included in any FEC advertisements.

Please refer to Chapter 7, "Multiprotocol Label Switching (MPLS)," for a complete discussion on the FEC announcement message format.

Our sample network in Figure 9.12 shows multiple operational Layer 2 Circuits that connect the remote customer sites together. Each of the PE routers (Sangiovese, Chardonnay, and Chablis) has directly connected customers. These customer sites are using Frame Relay, ATM, and Ethernet VLANs to provide connectivity between themselves. Before advertising the virtual circuit information, the PE routers form targeted LDP neighbor relationships, as we see from the perspective of Chardonnay:

```
user@Chardonnay> show ldp neighbor
Address              Interface         Label space ID       Hold time
192.168.24.1         lo0.0             192.168.24.1:0          13
192.168.52.1         lo0.0             192.168.52.1:0          11
10.222.45.1          so-0/1/1.0        192.168.40.1:0          12
```

Once established, the LDP peers advertise virtual circuit information to each other using LDP Label Mapping messages. The output of a `traceoptions` file allows us to see Chardonnay send VC information to Sangiovese:

```
Jul 28 17:24:18 LDP sent TCP PDU 192.168.32.1 -> 192.168.24.1 (none)
Jul 28 17:24:18 ver 1, pkt len 214, PDU len 210, ID 192.168.32.1:0
```

```
Jul 28 17:24:18    Msg LabelMap (0x400), len 24, ID 9506
Jul 28 17:24:18     TLV FEC (0x100), len 8
Jul 28 17:24:18       Prefix, family 1, 192.168.32.1/32
Jul 28 17:24:18     TLV Label (0x200), len 4
Jul 28 17:24:18       Label 3
Jul 28 17:24:18    Msg LabelMap (0x400), len 32, ID 9512
Jul 28 17:24:18     TLV FEC (0x100), len 16
Jul 28 17:24:18       L2CKT, VC Type 32772 VC Id 800 Group 0
Jul 28 17:24:18     TLV Label (0x200), len 4
Jul 28 17:24:18       Label 100080
```

The L2CKT notation informs us that this FEC is for a virtual connection whose virtual circuit ID is 800. The VC Type field shows a decimal value of 32772, which we convert to a hexadecimal value of 0x8004. This means that the most-significant bit is set to a value of 1, which requires the use of the control word as part of the physical encapsulation. The remaining bits in the field (0x0004) represent an Ethernet VLAN virtual connection.

In a similar fashion, Chardonnay receives a Label Mapping message from Sangiovese, which also advertises an Ethernet VLAN virtual circuit connection using an ID of 800:

```
Jul 28 17:24:18 LDP rcvd TCP PDU 192.168.24.1 -> 192.168.32.1 (none)
Jul 28 17:24:18 ver 1, pkt len 214, PDU len 210, ID 192.168.24.1:0
Jul 28 17:24:18   Msg LabelMap (0x400), len 24, ID 185177
Jul 28 17:24:18    TLV FEC (0x100), len 8
Jul 28 17:24:18      Prefix, family 1, 192.168.24.1/32
Jul 28 17:24:18    TLV Label (0x200), len 4
Jul 28 17:24:18      Label 3
Jul 28 17:24:18   Msg LabelMap (0x400), len 32, ID 185183
Jul 28 17:24:18    TLV FEC (0x100), len 16
Jul 28 17:24:18      L2CKT, VC Type 32772 VC Id 800 Group 0
Jul 28 17:24:18    TLV Label (0x200), len 4
Jul 28 17:24:18      Label 100080
```

Both PE routers now have the ability to match virtual circuit ID values, connection types, and control word parameters for this customer. This allows for the establishment of a Layer 2 Circuit between these routers using the advertised label values as the inner VPN label.

Frame Relay as the PE-CE Connection

The Shiraz and Cabernet routers in Figure 9.12 have a Frame Relay circuit established between themselves across the provider network. The CE routers connect to Chardonnay and Chablis, respectively, in the provider network. The interface configurations of the Shiraz and Chardonnay routers are:

```
user@Shiraz> show configuration interfaces so-0/1/0
encapsulation frame-relay;
```

```
unit 600 {
    dlci 600;
    family inet {
        address 10.222.100.1/24;
    }
}
```

```
user@Chardonnay> show configuration interfaces so-0/1/0
dce;
encapsulation frame-relay-ccc;
unit 600 {
    encapsulation frame-relay-ccc;
    dlci 600;
}
```

On the PE routers, the configuration of the Layer 2 Circuit occurs within the [edit protocols l2circuit] configuration hierarchy. The local PE associates the remote PE router with the customer interface as well as the virtual circuit ID designated for the connection. Chardonnay is configured like this:

```
user@Chardonnay> show configuration protocols l2circuit
neighbor 192.168.24.1 {
    interface fe-0/0/0.800 {
        virtual-circuit-id 800;
    }
}
neighbor 192.168.52.1 {
    interface so-0/1/0.600 {
        virtual-circuit-id 600;
    }
}
```

Because LDP is required to advertise the virtual circuit information, we also use LDP as the signaling mechanism for packet forwarding across the provider core. This allows each of the PE routers to learn what MPLS label to use for forwarding between the PE routers. This allows the Layer 2 connection to transition to the Up state:

```
user@Chardonnay> show l2circuit connections
Layer-2 Circuit Connections:

Legend for connection status (St)
EI -- encapsulation invalid    NP -- interface not present
MM -- mtu mismatch             Dn -- down
```

```
EM -- encapsulation mismatch     VC-Dn -- Virtual circuit Down
CM -- control-word mismatch      Up -- operational
OL -- no outgoing label          XX -- unknown
NC -- intf encaps not CCC/TCC


Legend for interface status
Up -- operational
Dn -- down


Neighbor: 192.168.24.1
    Interface              Type  St    Time last up          # Up trans
    fe-0/0/0.800 (vc 800)  rmt   Up    Jul 26 13:13:50 2003           1
      Local interface: fe-0/0/0.800, Status: Up, Encapsulation: VLAN
      Remote PE: 192.168.24.1, Negotiated control-word: Yes (Null)
      Incoming label: 100080, Outgoing label: 100080
Neighbor: 192.168.52.1
    Interface              Type  St    Time last up          # Up trans
    so-0/1/0.600 (vc 600)  rmt   Up    Jul 26 13:16:18 2003           1
      Local interface: so-0/1/0.600, Status: Up, Encapsulation: FRAME RELAY
      Remote PE: 192.168.52.1, Negotiated control-word: Yes (Null)
      Incoming label: 100096, Outgoing label: 100096
```

Finally, we verify the end-to-end connectivity from the CE routers:

```
user@Shiraz> ping 10.222.100.2 rapid
PING 10.222.100.2 (10.222.100.2): 56 data bytes
!!!!!
--- 10.222.100.2 ping statistics ---
5 packets transmitted, 5 packets received, 0% packet loss
round-trip min/avg/max/stddev = 0.749/0.825/1.095/0.135 ms
```

 Just as we saw with a Layer 2 VPN, the MPLS connection between the PE routers can be established with either LDP or RSVP.

ATM as the PE-CE Connection

The Cabernet and Sherry routers are using ATM as their Layer 2 connection in Figure 9.12. These routers are physically connected to the PE routers of Chablis and Sangiovese. The current interface configurations of Cabernet and Chablis look like this:

```
user@Cabernet> show configuration interfaces at-0/0/0
atm-options {
```

```
    vpi 0 {
        maximum-vcs 1001;
    }
}
unit 700 {
    vci 0.700;
    family inet {
        address 10.222.150.2/24;
    }
}
```

user@Chablis> **show configuration interfaces at-0/2/1**
```
atm-options {
    vpi 0 {
        maximum-vcs 1001;
    }
}
unit 700 {
    encapsulation atm-ccc-vc-mux;
    vci 0.700;
}
```

The Layer 2 Circuit configuration of the Chablis router is currently:

user@Chablis> **show configuration protocols l2circuit**
```
neighbor 192.168.24.1 {
    interface at-0/2/1.700 {
        virtual-circuit-id 700;
    }
}
neighbor 192.168.32.1 {
    interface so-0/1/0.600 {
        virtual-circuit-id 600;
    }
}
```

The remote PE router of Sangiovese has a similar Layer 2 Circuit configuration, which allows the connection to become established on Chablis:

user@Chablis> **show l2circuit connections**
```
Layer-2 Circuit Connections:
```

```
Legend for connection status (St)
EI -- encapsulation invalid        NP -- interface not present
MM -- mtu mismatch                 Dn -- down
EM -- encapsulation mismatch       VC-Dn -- Virtual circuit Down
CM -- control-word mismatch        Up -- operational
OL -- no outgoing label            XX -- unknown
NC -- intf encaps not CCC/TCC


Legend for interface status
Up -- operational
Dn -- down


Neighbor: 192.168.24.1
    Interface              Type  St     Time last up           # Up trans
    at-0/2/1.700 (vc 700)  rmt   Up     Nov 16 15:45:48 2001            1
      Local interface: at-0/2/1.700, Status: Up, Encapsulation: ATM AAL5
      Remote PE: 192.168.24.1, Negotiated control-word: Yes (Null)
      Incoming label: 100080, Outgoing label: 100096
Neighbor: 192.168.32.1
    Interface              Type  St     Time last up           # Up trans
    so-0/1/0.600 (vc 600)  rmt   Up     Nov 16 15:45:48 2001            1
      Local interface: so-0/1/0.600, Status: Up, Encapsulation: FRAME RELAY
      Remote PE: 192.168.32.1, Negotiated control-word: Yes (Null)
      Incoming label: 100096, Outgoing label: 100096
```

Connectivity between the CE routers is also operational, which we verify with the ping command:

```
user@Cabernet> ping 10.222.150.1 rapid
PING 10.222.150.1 (10.222.150.1): 56 data bytes
!!!!!
--- 10.222.150.1 ping statistics ---
5 packets transmitted, 5 packets received, 0% packet loss
round-trip min/avg/max/stddev = 1.460/1.831/2.488/0.346 ms
```

Ethernet VLANs as the PE-CE Connection

The Sherry and Shiraz routers in Figure 9.12 are using Ethernet VLANs for their Layer 2 connection and physically connect to Sangiovese and Chardonnay. The interface configurations of the Sherry and Sangiovese routers are:

```
user@Sherry> show configuration interfaces fe-0/3/3
vlan-tagging;
unit 800 {
```

```
    vlan-id 800;
    family inet {
        address 10.222.200.1/24;
    }
}
```

```
user@Sangiovese> show configuration interfaces fe-0/0/3
vlan-tagging;
encapsulation vlan-ccc;
unit 800 {
    encapsulation vlan-ccc;
    vlan-id 800;
}
```

The Sangiovese router has a Layer 2 Circuit configuration to Chardonnay, which looks like this:

```
user@Sangiovese> show configuration protocols l2circuit
neighbor 192.168.32.1 {
    interface fe-0/0/3.800 {
        virtual-circuit-id 800;
    }
}
neighbor 192.168.52.1 {
    interface at-0/1/0.700 {
        virtual-circuit-id 700;
    }
}
```

The connection between Sangiovese and Chardonnay is now in the Up state:

```
user@Sangiovese> show l2circuit connections
Layer-2 Circuit Connections:

Legend for connection status (St)
EI -- encapsulation invalid     NP -- interface not present
MM -- mtu mismatch              Dn -- down
EM -- encapsulation mismatch    VC-Dn -- Virtual circuit Down
CM -- control-word mismatch     Up -- operational
OL -- no outgoing label         XX -- unknown
NC -- intf encaps not CCC/TCC
```

```
Legend for interface status
Up -- operational
Dn -- down

Neighbor: 192.168.32.1
    Interface              Type  St     Time last up          # Up trans
    fe-0/0/3.800 (vc 800)  rmt   Up     Jul 26 12:23:53 2003           1
      Local interface: fe-0/0/3.800, Status: Up, Encapsulation: VLAN
      Remote PE: 192.168.32.1, Negotiated control-word: Yes (Null)
      Incoming label: 100080, Outgoing label: 100080
Neighbor: 192.168.52.1
    Interface              Type  St     Time last up          # Up trans
    at-0/1/0.700 (vc 700)  rmt   Up     Jul 26 12:26:16 2003           1
      Local interface: at-0/1/0.700, Status: Up, Encapsulation: ATM AAL5
      Remote PE: 192.168.52.1, Negotiated control-word: Yes (Null)
      Incoming label: 100096, Outgoing label: 100080
```

As we would expect, the CE routers have end-to-end connectivity:

```
user@Sherry> ping 10.222.200.2 rapid
PING 10.222.200.2 (10.222.200.2): 56 data bytes
!!!!!
--- 10.222.200.2 ping statistics ---
5 packets transmitted, 5 packets received, 0% packet loss
round-trip min/avg/max/stddev = 0.808/0.886/1.163/0.139 ms
```

Summary

In this chapter, we examined Layer 3 Virtual Private Networks (VPN) in some detail. We began the chapter with a discussion of the terminology used within a provider-provisioned VPN. We saw the difference between a customer edge router, a provider edge router, and a provider router. Once the basic information concerning a VPN was established, we explored how the PE routers exchange routing information with each other using multiprotocol BGP sessions to exchange VPN-IPv4 network layer reachability information. The routes are kept separate within the provider's network through the use of an 8-octet route distinguisher. In addition, the routes contain a BGP extended community value called the route target, which ensures that the correct PE routers accept the routes for the VRF tables they support. We then discussed configuration options for establishing a basic Layer 3 VPN. This included a look at using BGP or OSPF as a routing protocol between the PE and CE routers. The next topic in our exploration was a look at providing Internet access to VPN customers. This usually requires multiple logical circuits between the PE and CE routers and the advertisement of the customer's address space to the Internet at large.

We concluded the chapter with a discussion of transporting customer Layer 2 frames across the provider network. We saw that the JUNOS software supports both a Layer 2 VPN as well as a Layer 2 Circuit. The main difference between the technologies was the method used to advertise the customer virtual connection information. We used MBGP within a Layer 2 VPN, whereas the Layer 2 Circuit used LDP.

Exam Essentials

Be able to describe the basic concept of a VPN.   A virtual private network (VPN) is the operation of a common physical infrastructure where each customer remains segregated within its own virtual connections. Some common examples of "traditional" VPNs include leased lines, Frame Relay, and ATM.

Be able to describe the functions of the CE, PE, and P routers.   The CE router advertises routes from the customer site to its connected PE router using a Layer 3 routing protocol. The PE receives these routes and assigns both an RD and a route target to the routes. They are then advertised to remote PE routers over MBGP sessions. The routes are then readvertised to the CE routers. The P routers, on the other hand, are solely responsible for forwarding MPLS packets between the PE routers.

Be able to identify the format of a VPN-IPv4 NLRI.   The routes advertised between PE routers over their MBGP sessions use a specialized format. This format includes an MPLS label allocated by the originating PE router, an RD, and the actual customer route. This combination of information allows the PE routers to keep the customer VPNs separate as well as forward traffic appropriately within each VPN.

Be able to describe the use of a route target.   VPN route targets are BGP extended communities that the PE routers use to logically build the VPN for each customer. The advertising PE router assigns a route target to the customer routes before advertising them to the remote PE routers. Each receiving PE router uses its locally configured route targets to determine which inbound MBGP routes to accept. The route targets further determine which specific VRF table the received routes are placed in.

Be able to describe the advertisement of Layer 2 VPN information.   Once the interface configurations and physical encapsulations are configured correctly, knowledge of this connection is advertised between PE routers. This advertisement uses MBGP to send virtual circuit data between the PE routers.

Be able to describe how a connection is established for a Layer 2 Circuit.   The two PE routers on either end of the Layer 2 Circuit form an LDP neighbor relationship between themselves using targeted Hello messages. Once they further establish an LDP session, each PE router advertises the customer circuit information in a Label Mapping message.

Review Questions

1. In a Layer 3 VPN, what are the roles of the CE router? (Choose two)

   A. Assign an MPLS label for the routes.

   B. Forward traffic using MPLS labels.

   C. Advertise routes from a site to the provider network.

   D. Receive routes from the provider network about remote sites.

2. What is the correct order for the fields in a VPN-IPv4 NLRI?

   A. Mask, Route Distinguisher, MPLS Label, IP Prefix

   B. Mask, MPLS Label, Route Distinguisher, IP Prefix

   C. MPLS Label, Route Distinguisher, Mask, IP Prefix

   D. Route Distinguisher, MPLS Label, Mask, IP Prefix

3. Which JUNOS software command automatically assigns a route target of `target:64512:1234` to routes in a particular Layer 3 VRF table?

   A. `vrf-import target:64512:1234`

   B. `vrf-export target:64512:1234`

   C. `vrf-target target:64512:1234`

   D. `vrf-route-target target:64512:1234`

4. In a Layer 3 VPN environment using RSVP for MPLS reachability, how many labels are placed on a data packet by the ingress PE router?

   A. 1

   B. 2

   C. 3

   D. 4

5. When a CE and PE router are exchanging routes via EBGP sessions, which JUNOS software command on the PE router is useful for ensuring that the advertised routes are received by the CE routers?

   A. `as-loops`

   B. `as-override`

   C. `local-as`

   D. `peer-as`

6. In a Layer 3 VPN environment using OSPF between the PE and CE routers, what attribute is always advertised to the remote PE router?

    A. Route type

    B. Domain ID

    C. VPN route tag

    D. Route origin

7. Which JUNOS software configuration command allows PE routers to exchange routes in a Layer 3 VPN environment?

    A. `family inet unicast`

    B. `family inet any`

    C. `family inet-vpn unicast`

    D. `family inet-vpn vpn-nlri`

8. Which protocol is used to advertise customer circuit information for a Layer 2 Circuit?

    A. LDP

    B. IS-IS

    C. BGP

    D. MBGP

9. Which JUNOS software configuration command allows PE routers to exchange routes in a Layer 2 VPN environment?

    A. `family inet-vpn unicast`

    B. `family inet-vpn vpn-nlri`

    C. `family l2vpn unicast`

    D. `family l2vpn vpn-nlri`

10. Which Layer 2 VPN access technology requires the data-link identifier to match on both sides of the provider network?

    A. Frame Relay

    B. ATM

    C. Ethernet VLAN

    D. IP Interworking

Answers to Review Questions

1. C, D. The CE router operates a Layer 3 routing protocol and communicates with its attached PE router. It advertises and receives routes specific to its own network environment.

2. B. The VPN-IPv4 NLRI first contains a mask to advertise the number of bits contained in the NLRI. The MPLS Label and Route Distinguisher fields follow, which are used to uniquely identify the VPN routes. Finally, the IP prefix is the actual route advertised by the CE router.

3. C. The `vrf-target` command is used to automatically assign a route target to all routes in a VRF table. Both the `vrf-import` and `vrf-export` commands apply routing policies to the VRF table. Although these routing policies may assign route targets to the advertised routes, it is not an automatic functionality.

4. B. The ingress PE router adds two MPLS labels to data packets received from a local CE router. The top label value is used to reach the remote PE router, whereas the bottom label is used by the remote PE router to forward the packet to the appropriate CE router.

5. B. By default, a PE router appends its local AS to a route and advertises it to the CE router. The CE router, in turn, sees this as a looped route as its local AS is already in the AS Path. The `as-override` command allows the advertising PE router to replace the CE router's AS number with its own before the default prepend action takes place. This keeps the CE router from rejecting the route due to an AS Path loop.

6. A. The OSPF route type attribute is a BGP extended community that contains information about advertised OSPF routes. It describes the type of LSA advertisement that was received by the CE router as well as the area configured on the PE router. Receiving PE routers use this value, in conjunction with other VRF attributes, to determine if the route is advertised in a Type 3 or Type 5 LSA.

7. C. In order for two PE routers to communicate over an MBGP session and advertise NLRI for a Layer 3 VPN, the `family inet-vpn unicast` command must be applied to the BGP configuration.

8. A. While the formation of the MPLS connection between the two PE routers can be formed in multiple ways, the advertisement of customer circuit information must occur using LDP.

9. C. Two PE routers use MBGP to advertise customer circuit information when the `family l2vpn unicast` command is configured within BGP.

10. C. Only Ethernet VLANs require that the VLAN ID match on both sides of the provider network. The remaining Layer 2 access technologies of Frame Relay and ATM allow different identifiers on each side of the network.

Glossary

Numbers

1X First phase of third-generation (3G) mobile wireless technology for CDMA2000 networks.

1XEV Evolutionary phase for 3G for CDMA2000 networks, divided into two phases: 1XEV-DO (data only) and 1XEV-DV (data and voice).

2-Way Adjacency state for OSPF that shows bidirectional communication between two neighbors has been established.

3GPP Third-Generation Partnership Project. Created to expedite the development of open, globally accepted technical specifications for the Universal Mobile Telecommunications System (UMTS).

A

accept JUNOS software syntax command used in a routing policy or a firewall filter. It halts the logical processing of the policy or filter when a set of match conditions is met. The specific route is placed into the routing table. An IP packet is forwarded to the next hop along the network path.

Access-Accept message Message sent from a RADIUS server to a router that positively authenticates a user.

Access-Reject message Message sent from a RADIUS server to a router that denies authentication to a user.

Access-Request message Message sent to a RADIUS server from a router that asks for validation of a user's identity.

action Within a routing policy or firewall filter, an action denotes a specific function to perform on a route or IP packet.

active node In LDP, the peer with the higher router ID that initiates the establishment of the session.

active route Route chosen by a router from all routes in the routing table to reach a destination. Active routes are installed in the forwarding table.

adaptive mode Operational MPLS mode that allows multiple LSPs within a single RSVP session to share bandwidth reservations in the network.

add/drop multiplexer (ADM) SONET functionality that allows lower-level signals to be dropped from a high-speed optical connection.

Address Family Identifier In BGP, a value that defines the major address family advertised as an NLRI to a peer.

address match conditions The use of an IP address as a match criterion in a routing policy or a firewall filter.

Address Resolution Protocol (ARP)   Protocol for mapping IP addresses to MAC addresses.

adjacency   Link-state network neighbor status that represents two neighbors who have exchanged their link-state database information with each other.

Adjacency-RIB-In   Logical software table that contains BGP routes received from a specific neighbor.

Adjacency-RIB-Out   Logical software table that contains BGP routes to be sent to a specific neighbor.

administrative groups   Logical value assignment to a network interface that supplies a constraint when establishing an RSVP-based LSP.

aggregation   The combination of groups of routes that share the same most significant bits into a single entry in the routing table.

aggregator   BGP attribute that advertises the router ID and AS number of a router that has aggregated prefixes into a single route.

allow   JUNOS software command that prevents a local router from sending an Open message to a peer. Further, the remote peer doesn't need to be explicitly configured on the local router.

allow-commands   JUNOS software command that allows a network administrator to add operational commands to the user's assigned class.

allow-configuration   JUNOS software command that allows a network administrator to add configuration commands to the user's assigned class.

Alternate Priority Queuing (APQ)   Dequeuing method that has a special queue, similar to SPQ, which is visited each time the scheduler moves from one low-priority queue to another low-priority queue. The packets in the special queue still have a predictable latency, although the upper limit of the delay is higher than that with SPQ. Since the other configured queues share the remaining service time, queue starvation is usually avoided. See also *Strict Priority Queuing (SPQ)*.

always-compare-med   JUNOS software command that always uses the MED attribute for evaluating BGP routes using the route selection algorithm.

American National Standards Institute (ANSI)   The United States' representative to the ISO. See also *International Organization for Standardization (ISO)*.

anycast address   The shared IP address used by RP routers in a single PIM domain operating Anycast-RP.

Anycast-RP   A method of using multiple RP routers in a single PIM domain where each router equally participates as an operating RP device.

application-specific integrated circuit (ASIC)   Specialized processors that perform specific functions on the router.

area   Routing subdomain that maintains detailed routing information about its own internal composition and that maintains routing information that allows it to reach other routing sub-domains. In IS-IS, an area corresponds to a Level 1 subdomain. In IS-IS and OSPF, an area is a set of contiguous networks and hosts within an Autonomous System that have been adminis-tratively grouped together.

area address TLV   IS-IS TLV that allows each router to advertise the areas it is configured to support.

area border router   Router that belongs to more than one area. Used in OSPF. See also *Open Shortest Path First (OSPF)*.

ASBR Summary LSA   OSPF link-state advertisement sent by an ABR to advertise the router ID of an ASBR across an area boundary. See also *Autonomous System boundary router*.

AS confederation   In BGP, another way to reference the global AS assigned to a provider net-work. It is also the collection of sub-AS networks when operating a confederation network.

AS confederation ID   In BGP, the value assigned to the global confederation network.

AS confederation sequence   An ordered list of member-AS values in the AS Path attribute when operating a confederation network.

AS confederation set   An unordered list of member-AS values in the AS Path attribute when operating a confederation network.

AS external-link advertisements   OSPF link-state advertisement sent by AS boundary routers to describe external routes that they know. These link-state advertisements are flooded throughout the AS (except for stub and NSSA areas).

AS path   In BGP, the path to a destination. The path consists of the AS numbers of all routers a packet must go through to reach a destination.

AS path group   A JUNOS software policy framework option that allows multiple AS Path regular expressions to be referenced as a single entity.

AS sequence   An ordered list of AS values within the AS Path attribute.

AS set   An unordered list of AS values within the AS Path attribute.

as-override   JUNOS software command that allows an EBGP router to replace the peer's AS value with its own local AS value in the AS Path attribute.

Asynchronous Transfer Mode (ATM)   A high-speed multiplexing and switching method utilizing fixed-length cells of 53 octets to support multiple types of traffic.

ATM adaptation layer (AAL)   A series of protocols enabling various types of traffic, including voice, data, image, and video, to run over an ATM network.

ATM Line Interface (ALI)   Interface between ATM and 3G systems. See also *Asynchronous Transfer Mode (ATM)*.

atomic   Smallest possible operation. An atomic operation is performed either entirely or not at all. For example, if machine failure prevents a transaction from completing, the system is rolled back to the start of the transaction, with no changes taking place.

atomic aggregate   BGP attribute that signals to other ASs that a less specific prefix was chosen over a more specific one.

attempt   OSPF adjacency state seen in a Non-Broadcast Multi-Access (NBMA) network that means the local router is to send a unicast hello packet to a neighbor for which it has not yet received any protocol packets.

authentication center (AUC)   Part of the Home Location Register (HLR) in 3G systems, the AUC performs computations to verify and authenticate the user of mobile phones.

Authentication Header (AH)   A component of the IPSec protocol used to verify that the contents of a packet have not been changed, and to validate the identity of the sender. The actual packet data is not protected. See also *encapsulating security payload (ESP)*.

authentication TLV   IS-IS TLV that contains either a plain-text password or a calculated MD5 hash.

Automatic Protection Switching (APS)   Technology used by SONET ADMs to protect against circuit faults between the ADM and a router and to protect against failing routers. See also *add/drop multiplexer (ADM)*.

Autonomous System (AS)   A set of routers under a single technical administration. Each AS normally uses a single Interior Gateway Protocol (IGP) and metrics to propagate routing information within the set of routers. Also called *routing domain*.

Autonomous System boundary router   In OSPF, routers that import routing information external to the protocol into the link-state database.

Autonomous System external-link advertisements   OSPF link-state advertisement sent by Autonomous System boundary routers to describe external routes that they know. These link-state advertisements are flooded throughout the Autonomous System (except for stub and NSSA areas).

Autonomous System path   In BGP, the path to a destination. The path consists of the Autonomous System numbers of all the routers a packet must pass through to reach a destination.

auto-RP   One of three methods of electing and announcing the rendezvous point to group address mapping in a multicast network. A vendor-proprietary specification supported by the JUNOS software.

B

B bit   The B bit is set in a router LSA when the router is configured as an ABR.

backbone area   In OSPF, an area that consists of all networks in area ID 0.0.0.0, their attached routers, and all area border routers.

backbone router   An OSPF router with all operational interfaces within area 0.0.0.0.

backplane   On an M40 router, a component of the Packet Forwarding Engine that distributes power, provides signal connectivity, manages shared memory on FPCs, and passes outgoing data cells to FPCs. See also *flexible PIC concentrator (FPC)*.

backup   Denotes a Routing Engine in a dual Routing Engine chassis that is not currently controlling the router's operations.

backup designated router   An OSPF router on a broadcast segment that monitors the operation of the designated router and takes over its functions in the event of a failure.

bandwidth   The range of transmission frequencies a network can use, expressed as the difference between the highest and lowest frequencies of a transmission channel. In computer networks, greater bandwidth indicates faster data-transfer rate capacity.

base station controller (BSC)   Key network node in 3G systems that supervises the functioning and control of multiple base transceiver stations.

base station subsystem (BSS)   Composed of the base transceiver station (BTS) and base station controller (BSC).

Base Station System GPRS Protocol (BSSGP)   Processes routing and quality-of-service (QoS) information for the BSS.

base transceiver station (BTS)   Mobile telephony equipment housed in cabinets and co-located with antennas. Also known as a *radio base station*.

behavior aggregate   Class of service classification method that utilizes information in the header of an incoming data packet.

Bellcore   Bell Communications Research. Research and development organization created after the divestiture of the Bell System. It is supported by the regional Bell holding companies (RBHCs), which own the regional Bell operating companies (RBOCs).

Bellman-Ford algorithm   Algorithm used in distance-vector routing protocols to determine the best path to all routes in the network.

BGP route selection algorithm   Defined process that allows a BGP router to select a single best route for every unique destination.

bit error rate test (BERT)   A test that can be run on a T3 interface to determine whether it is operating properly.

bit field match conditions   The use of fields in the header of an IP packet as match criteria in a firewall filter.

bootstrap message   Packet sent to a PIM-SM network that elects a bootstrap router and advertises RP-to-group address mappings.

bootstrap router   The single router in a multicast network responsible for distributing candidate rendezvous point information to all PIM-enabled routers.

Border Gateway Protocol (BGP)   Exterior Gateway Protocol used to exchange routing information among routers in different Autonomous Systems.

broadcast   Operation of sending network traffic from one network node to all other network nodes.

Building Integrated Timing Source (BITS)   Dedicated timing source that synchronizes all equipment in a particular building.

bundle   Collection of software that makes up a JUNOS software release.

C

call detail record (CDR)   A record containing data (such as origination, termination, length, and time of day) unique to a specific call.

candidate configuration   A file maintained by the JUNOS software containing all changes to the router's active configuration. It becomes the active configuration when a user issues the `commit` command.

candidate database   A logical data structure used by the link-state protocols when running the shortest path algorithm. The candidate database contains the total cost to each node from the root of the tree.

candidate-RP-advertisements   Information sent by routers in a multicast network when they are configured as a local rendezvous point. This information is unicast to the BSR for the multicast domain.

CDMA2000   Radio transmission and backbone technology for the evolution to third-generation (3G) mobile networks.

cell tax   Describes the physical transmission capacity used by header information when sending data packets in an ATM network. Each ATM cell uses a 5-byte header.

CFM   Cubic feet per minute. Measure of air flow in volume per minute.

Challenge Handshake Authentication Protocol (CHAP)   A protocol that authenticates remote users. CHAP is a server-driven, three-step authentication mechanism that depends on a shared secret password that resides on both the server and the client.

channel service unit/data service unit (CSU/DSU)   The channel service unit connects a digital phone line to a multiplexer or other digital signal device. The data service unit connects a DTE to a digital phone line.

chassis daemon (chassisd)   JUNOS software process responsible for managing the interaction of the router's physical components.

checksum TLV   IS-IS TLV that places a checksum hash value within the TLV to assist in troubleshooting a physical network link that experiences a transmission error.

circuit cross-connect (CCC)   A JUNOS software feature that allows you to configure transparent connections between two circuits, where a circuit can be a Frame Relay DLCI, an ATM VC, a PPP interface, a Cisco HDLC interface, or an MPLS label-switched path.

Cisco-RP-Announce   Message advertised into a multicast network by any router configured as a local rendezvous point in an auto-RP network. It is advertised in a dense-mode fashion to the 224.0.1.39 multicast group address.

Cisco-RP-Discovery   Message advertised by the mapping agent in an auto-RP network. It contains the rendezvous point to multicast group address assignments for the domain. It is advertised in a dense-mode fashion to the 224.0.1.40 multicast group address.

class of service (CoS)   The method of classifying traffic on a packet-by-packet basis using information in the type of service (ToS) byte to provide different service levels to different traffic. See also *type of service (ToS)*.

classless interdomain routing (CIDR)   A method of specifying Internet addresses in which you explicitly specify the bits of the address to represent the network address instead of determining this information from the first octet of the address.

client peer   In a BGP route reflection, a member of a cluster that is not the route reflector. See also *nonclient peer*.

cluster   In BGP, a set of routers that have been grouped together. A cluster consists of at least one system that acts as a route reflector, along with any number of client peers. The client peers mainly receive their route information from the route reflector system. Routers in a cluster do not need to be fully meshed.

cluster ID   In BGP, the unique value assigned to a cluster in a route reflection network.

cluster list   BGP attribute that details the sequence of route reflection clusters a route has traversed in a network.

Code Division Multiple Access (CDMA)   Technology for digital transmission of radio signals between, for example, a mobile telephone and a base transceiver station (BTS).

command completion   Function of the router's command-line interface that allows a user to enter only the most significant characters in any command. Users access this function through the spacebar or Tab key.

command-line interface (CLI)   The user's interface to the JUNOS software through a console, Telnet, or SSH session.

common language equipment identifier (CLEI)   Inventory code used to identify and track telecommunications equipment.

community   In BGP, a group of destinations that share a common property. Community information is included as one of the path attributes in BGP update messages.

Competitive Local Exchange Carrier (CLEC) (Pronounced "see-lek") Company that competes with the already established local telecommunications business by providing its own network and switching.

complete sequence number PDU (CSNP) Packet that contains a complete list of all the LSPs headers in the IS-IS database.

confederation In BGP, a group of small Autonomous Systems that appears to external Autonomous Systems to be a single Autonomous System.

confederation BGP In BGP, the method of communication used between member-AS networks within the confederation.

configuration mode JUNOS software mode allowing a user to alter the router's current configuration.

Connect BGP neighbor state where the local router has initiated the TCP session and is waiting for the remote peer to complete the TCP connection.

connection collision Process that occurs during the establishment of a BGP peering session. Each peer opens a TCP session to its neighbor and one of those sessions is then torn down.

Connectionless Network Protocol (CLNP) ISO-developed protocol for OSI connectionless network service. CLNP is the OSI equivalent of IP.

Connector Interface Panel (CIP) On an M40e or M160 router as well as on a T320 or T640 routing node, the panel that contains connectors for the Routing Engines, BITS interfaces, and alarm relay contacts.

constrained path In traffic engineering, a path determined using the CSPF algorithm. The ERO carried in the RSVP packets contains the constrained path information.

Constrained Shortest Path First (CSPF) An MPLS algorithm that has been modified to take into account specific restrictions when calculating the shortest path across the network.

context-sensitive help Function of the router's command-line interface that allows a user to request information on the JUNOS software command hierarchy. It is accessed in both operational as well as configuration modes.

Continue message Message sent from the router to a TACACS+ server that contains the user's password.

contributing routes Active IP routes in the routing table that share the same most significant bits and are more specific than an aggregate or generate route.

Control Board (CB) On a T640 routing node, part of the host subsystem that provides control and monitoring functions for router components.

control word In a Layer 2 Circuit network, this packet header field contains Layer 2 local management information pertaining to the PE-CE link.

core The central backbone of the network.

craft interface   Mechanisms used by a Communication Workers of America craftsperson to operate, administer, and maintain equipment or provision data communications. On a Juniper Networks router, the craft interface allows you to view status and troubleshooting information and perform system control functions.

customer edge device (CE device)   Router or switch in the customer's network that is connected to a service provider's provider edge (PE) router and participates in a Layer 3 or Layer 2 VPN.

customer premises equipment (CPE)   Telephone or other service provider equipment located at a customer site.

Customized Application of Mobile Enhance Logic (CAMEL)   ETSI standard for GSM networks that enhances the provision of Intelligent Network services.

D

daemon   Background process that performs operations on behalf of the system software and hardware. Daemons normally start when the system software is booted, and they run as long as the software is running. In the JUNOS software, daemons are also referred to as *processes*.

damping   Method of reducing the number of update messages sent between BGP peers, thereby reducing the load on these peers without adversely affecting the route convergence time for stable routes. The protocol accomplishes this by not advertising unstable routes.

data circuit-terminating equipment (DCE)   An RS-232-C device, typically used for a modem or printer, or a network access and packet switching node.

data-link connection identifier (DLCI)   Identifier for a Frame Relay virtual connection (also called a *logical interface*).

data service unit (DSU)   A device used to connect a DTE to a digital phone line. Converts digital data from a router to voltages and encoding required by the phone line. See also *channel service unit/data service unit (CSU/DSU)*.

Data Terminal Equipment (DTE)   The RS-232-C interface that a computer uses to exchange information with a serial device.

Database Description packet   OSPF packet type used in the formation of an adjacency. It sends summary information about the local router's database to the neighboring router.

dcd   The JUNOS software interface process, called the Device Control Daemon.

deactivate   A method of modifying the router's active configuration. Portions of the hierarchy marked as inactive using this command are ignored during the router's commit process as if they were not configured at all.

default interface address   Router address that is used as the source address on unnumbered interfaces.

dead interval   The amount of time an OSPF router maintains a neighbor relationship before declaring that neighbor as no longer operational. The JUNOS software uses a default value of 40 seconds for this timer.

default route   Route used to forward IP packets when a more specific route is not present in the routing table. Often represented as 0.0.0.0 /0, the default route is sometimes referred to as the *route of last resort.*

denial of service (DoS)   System security breach in which network services become unavailable to users.

dense mode   A method of forwarding multicast traffic to interested listeners. Dense-mode forwarding assumes that the majority of hosts on the network wish to receive the multicast data. Routers flood packets and prune back unwanted traffic every 3 minutes.

dense wavelength-division multiplexing (DWDM)   Technology that enables data from different sources to be carried together on an optical fiber, with each signal carried on its own separate wavelength.

deny-commands   JUNOS software command that allows a network administrator to remove operational commands from the user's assigned class.

deny-configuration   JUNOS software command that allows a network administrator to remove configuration commands from the user's assigned class.

designated router   In OSPF, a router selected by other routers that is responsible for representing the local segment to the remainder of the network, which reduces the amount of network traffic and the size of the routers' topological databases.

Destination Options header   IPv6 extension header that allows the source node to send special packet-handling instructions to the destination node.

destination prefix length   The number of bits of the network address used for the host portion of a CIDR IP address.

deterministic MED   In BGP, routes from the same neighboring AS are grouped together and evaluated against each other using MED as a tie-breaking rule for selecting the best route. This is the default operational mode of the JUNOS software.

Detour object   RSVP object used by a router along the LSP's path that is used to establish a fast reroute detour path.

Differentiated Services Codepoint (DSCP)   The use of the first 6 bits of the IPv4 Type of Service byte. The use of the DSCP for classifying traffic allows an administrator to have 64 unique service levels in the network.

Diffie-Hellman   A public key scheme, invented by Whitfield Diffie and Martin Hellman, used for sharing a secret key without communicating secret information, thus precluding the need for a secure channel. Once correspondents have computed the secret shared key, they can use it to encrypt communications.

Diffserv   Differentiated Service (based on RFC 2474). Diffserv uses the ToS byte to identify different packet flows on a packet-by-packet basis. Diffserv adds a Class Selector Codepoint (CSCP) and a Differentiated Services Codepoint (DSCP).

Dijkstra algorithm   See *shortest path first (SPF)*.

direct routes   See *interface routes*.

disable   A method of modifying the router's active configuration. Portions of the hierarchy marked as disabled (mainly router interfaces) cause the router to use the configuration but stop the pertinent operation of the configuration.

discard   JUNOS software syntax command used in a routing policy or a firewall filter. It halts the logical processing of the policy or filter when a set of match conditions is met. The specific route or IP packet is dropped from the network silently. It may also be a next-hop attribute assigned to a route in the routing table.

distance-vector   Algorithm used in Bellman-Ford routing protocols to determine the best path to all routes in the network. Each router determines the distance (metric) to the destination as well as the vector (next hop) to follow.

Distance Vector Multicast Routing Protocol (DVMRP)   Distributed multicast routing protocol that dynamically generates IP multicast delivery trees using a technique called reverse path multicasting (RPM) to forward multicast traffic to downstream interfaces.

Distributed Buffer Manager ASICs   Juniper Networks ASIC responsible for managing the router's packet storage memory.

domain ID   In a Layer 3 VPN network using OSPF as a PE-CE protocol, the domain ID allows PE routers to advertise routes as either Type 3 or Type 5 LSAs.

Down   OSPF adjacency state that is the starting state for the protocol.

downstream on demand   In MPLS, a method for advertising labels where the upstream node explicitly requests a label allocation.

downstream unsolicited   In MPLS, a method for advertising labels where the downstream node allocates a label upstream without an explicit request.

drop profile   Drop probabilities for different levels of buffer fullness that are used by random early discard (RED) to determine from which queue to drop packets.

dual inline memory module (DIMM)   A 168-pin memory module that supports 64-bit data transfer.

Dynamic Host Configuration Protocol (DHCP)   Allocates IP addresses dynamically so that they can be reused when they are no longer needed.

dynamic host name TLV   IS-IS TLV that contains the ASCII hostname of the local router. This allows other IS-IS routers to perform NET ID to hostname mappings.

dynamic label-switched path   An MPLS network path established by signaling protocols such as RSVP or LDP.

dynamic random access memory (DRAM)   Storage source on the router that can be accessed quickly by a process.

E

E bit   The E bit is set in a router LSA when the router is configured as an ASBR.

edge router   In MPLS, a router located at the beginning or end of a label-switching tunnel. When at the beginning of a tunnel, an edge router applies labels to new packets entering the tunnel. When at the end of a tunnel, the edge router returns to forwarding the packets using the destination IP address. See also *Multiprotocol Label Switching (MPLS)*.

editor macros (Emacs)   Shortcut keystrokes used within the router's command-line interface. These macros move the cursor and delete characters based on the specific sequence specified.

egress router   In MPLS, the last router in a label-switched path (LSP). See also *ingress router*.

electromagnetic interference (EMI)   Any electromagnetic disturbance that interrupts, obstructs, or otherwise degrades or limits the effective performance of electronics or electrical equipment.

Electronic Industries Association (EIA)   A United States trade group that represents manufacturers of electronic devices and sets standards and specifications.

embedded OS software   Software used by a Juniper Networks router to operate the physical router components.

encapsulating security payload (ESP)   A fundamental component of IPSec-compliant VPNs, ESP specifies an IP packet's encryption, data integrity checks, and sender authentication, which are added as a header to the IP packet. See also *Authentication Header (AH)*.

end system   In IS-IS, the network entity that sends and receives packets.

End-of-RIB marker   A BGP Update message that contains no routing information. This is used to signal to the remote peer that the local router has advertised all of its routing knowledge.

Equipment Identity Register (EIR)   Mobile network database that contains information about devices using the network.

Established   BGP neighbor state that represents a fully functional BGP peering session.

exact   JUNOS software routing policy match type that represents only the route specified in a route filter.

exception packet   An IP packet not processed by the normal packet flow through the Packet Forwarding Engine. Exception packets include local delivery information, expired TTL packets, or packets with an IP option specified.

Exchange OSPF adjacency state that means the two neighboring routers are actively sending Database Description packets to each other to exchange their database contents.

Exchange Carriers Standards Association (ECSA) A standards organization created after the divestiture of the Bell System to represent the interests of interexchange carriers.

EXP bits Three bits in the header of an MPLS packet that a router can evaluate for class-of-service processing.

explicit path See *signaled path*.

Explicit Route Object (ERO) Extension to RSVP that allows an RSVP Path message to traverse an explicit sequence of routers that is independent of conventional shortest-path IP routing.

export To place routes from the routing table into a routing protocol.

ExStart OSPF adjacency state where the neighboring routers negotiate who is in charge of the synchronization process.

Extended community In BGP, a group of destinations that share a common property. Community information is included as one of the path attributes in BGP update messages. An extended community uses 8 octets to store information, which provides greater flexibility over a standard community.

extended IP reachability TLV IS-IS TLV that advertises local IP subnet information using a 3-octet metric field.

extended IS reachability TLV IS-IS TLV that advertises connectivity to neighboring IS-IS nodes using a 3-octet metric field.

Exterior Gateway Protocol (EGP) The original exterior gateway protocol used to exchange routing information among routers in different Autonomous Systems. EGP was replaced by BGP as the size and complexity of the Internet grew.

External BGP (EBGP) BGP configuration in which sessions are established between routers in different ASs.

external metric A cost included in a route when OSPF exports route information from external Autonomous Systems. There are two types of external metrics: Type 1 and Type 2. Type 1 external metrics are equivalent to the link-state metric; that is, the cost of the route, used in the internal Autonomous System. Type 2 external metrics are greater than the cost of any path internal to the Autonomous System.

F

far-end alarm and control (FEAC) Signal used to send alarm or status information from the far-end terminal back to the near-end terminal and to initiate loopbacks at the far-end terminal from the near-end terminal.

fast reroute   Mechanism for automatically rerouting traffic on an LSP if a node or link in an LSP fails, thus reducing the loss of packets traveling over the LSP.

Fast Reroute object   RSVP object used by an ingress router to signal to the network that the LSP should be protected by detour paths.

field-replaceable unit (FRU)   Router component that customers can replace onsite.

figure of merit   A value assigned to BGP routes when damping is used to limit the effect of route flapping in the network.

firewall   A security gateway positioned between two different networks, usually between a trusted network and the Internet. A firewall ensures that all traffic that crosses it conforms to the organization's security policy. Firewalls track and control communications, deciding whether to pass, reject, discard, encrypt, or log them. Firewalls also can be used to secure sensitive portions of a local network.

first in, first out (FIFO)   Queuing and buffering method where the first data packet stored in the queue is the first data packet removed from the queue. All JUNOS software interface queues operate in this mode by default.

fixed filter   Reservation style where each unique sender and receiver pair is allocated its own set of resources.

flap damping   See *damping*.

flapping   See *route flapping*.

flexible PIC concentrator (FPC)   An interface concentrator on which PICs are mounted. An FPC inserts into a slot in a Juniper Networks router. See also *physical interface card (PIC)*.

floating static route   A route that should be used only when all dynamically learned versions of that same route are no longer in the routing table.

flood and prune   Method of forwarding multicast data packets in a dense-mode network. This process repeats itself every 3 minutes.

flow control action   JUNOS software syntax used in a routing policy or a firewall filter. It alters the default logical processing of the policy or filter when a set of match conditions is met.

flow label   In an IPv6 header, a 20-bit field that allows multiple packets in a traffic stream to be treated the same by the network.

forwarding adjacency   The advertisement of an established LSP to the link-state database of either OSPF or IS-IS.

forwarding class   Internal router designation that represents the queuing service offered to IP packets matching some set of criteria. The forwarding class is assigned to a packet when it enters the router and can be modified by a routing policy or a firewall filter.

Forwarding Engine Board (FEB) In M5 and M10 routers, provides route lookup, filtering, and switching to the destination port.

Forwarding Equivalence Class (FEC) In LDP, the advertisement of a prefix to label mapping to the network.

forwarding information base See *forwarding table*.

forwarding state bit In BGP, this bit is set during a graceful restart operation to signal that the router has retained its ability to forward packets.

forwarding table JUNOS software forwarding information base (FIB). The JUNOS routing protocol process installs active routes from its routing tables into the Routing Engine forwarding table. The kernel copies this forwarding table into the Packet Forwarding Engine, which is responsible for determining which interface transmits the packets.

Fragment header IPv6 extension header that is included in all fragmented packets. Each sending node is responsible for performing Path MTU discovery and fragmenting all packets that are too large to send to the destination.

Frame Relay Layer 2 encoding and addressing mechanism that uses a DLCI to segment logical circuits on a physical transmission media.

from JUNOS software command syntax that contains match criteria in a routing policy or a firewall filter.

Full OSPF adjacency state that represents a fully functional neighbor relationship.

fxp0 JUNOS software permanent interface used for out-of-band network access to the router.

fxp1 JUNOS software permanent interface used for communications between the Routing Engine and the Packet Forwarding Engine.

fxp2 JUNOS software permanent interface used for communications between the Routing Engine and the Packet Forwarding Engine.

G

Garbage Collection timer Timer used in a distance-vector network that represents the time remaining before a route is removed from the routing table.

Gateway GPRS Support Node (GGSN) Router that serves as a gateway between mobile networks and packet data networks.

G-CDR GGSN call detail record. Collection of charges in ASN.1 format that is eventually billed to a mobile station user.

General Packet Radio Service (GPRS) Packet-switched service that allows full mobility and wide area coverage as information is sent and received across a mobile network.

generated route   A summary route that uses an IP address next hop to forward packets in an IP network. A generated route is functionally similar to an aggregated route.

GPRS Tunneling Protocol (GTP)   Protocol that transports IP packets between an SGSN and a GGSN.

GPRS Tunneling Protocol Control (GTP-C)   Protocol that allows an SGSN to establish packet data network access for a mobile station.

GPRS Tunneling Protocol User (GTP-U)   Protocol that carries mobile station user data packets.

grace LSA   In OSPF, a link-local opaque LSA that allows a router to notify its neighbor of graceful restart operations.

graceful restart   Operational setup that allows the routing process on a router to restart while the device continues to forward packets.

graceful restart TLV   IS-IS TLV that allows the local router to perform a restart operation. In addition, this TLV allows the local router to assist in a neighboring router's restart operation.

group   A collection of related BGP peers.

group address   The IP address used as the destination address in a multicast IP packet. It functionally represents the sender and interested receivers for a particular multicast data stream.

group operator   Within a policy expression, the group operator allows for the alteration of the default evaluation order.

H

half-life   Value used when damping BGP routes. It decreases the figure of merit by exactly half within a defined time period. The JUNOS software uses a default value of 15 minutes.

hash   A one-way function that takes a message of any length and produces a fixed-length digest. In security, a message digest is used to validate that the contents of a message have not been altered in transit. The Secure Hash Algorithm (SHA-1) and Message Digest 5 (MD5) are commonly used hashes.

Hashed Message Authentication Code (HMAC)   A mechanism for message authentication that uses cryptographic hash functions. HMAC can be used with any iterative cryptographic hash function—for example, MD5 or SHA-1—in combination with a secret shared key. The cryptographic strength of HMAC depends on the properties of the underlying hash function.

hello interval   The amount of time an OSPF router sends a hello packet to each adjacent neighbor. The JUNOS software uses a default value of 10 seconds for this timer.

Hello mechanism   Process used by an RSVP router to enhance the detection of network outages in an MPLS network.

Hello PDU   Packets that establish and maintain an IS-IS adjacency.

helper mode   A process within graceful restart that allows a router to actively assist a neighboring device to perform a restart operation.

hierarchical route reflection   In BGP, a network design where a route reflector in one cluster is a client in a different cluster.

High-Level Data Link Control (HDLC)   An International Telecommunication Union (ITU) standard for a bit-oriented data link layer protocol on which most other bit-oriented protocols are based.

High-Speed Circuit-Switched Data (HSCSD)   Circuit-switched wireless data transmission for mobile users, at data rates up to 38.4Kbps.

hold down   Timer used by distance-vector protocols to prevent the propagation of incorrect routing knowledge to other routers in the network.

hold priority   Value used by RSVP to reserve resources at different priority levels.

hold time   Maximum number of seconds allowed to elapse between the time a BGP system receives successive Keepalive or update messages from a peer.

Home Location Register (HLR)   Database containing information about a subscriber and the current location of a subscriber's mobile station.

Hop-by-Hop Options header   IPv6 extension header that allows the source node to send special packet handling instructions to each network device along the path to the destination.

Host Membership Query   IGMP packet sent by a router to determine whether interested receivers exist on a broadcast network for multicast traffic.

Host Membership Report   IGMP packet sent by an interested receiver for a particular multicast group address. Hosts send Report messages when they first join a group or in response to a Query packet from the local router.

host module   On an M160 router, provides routing and system management functions of the router. Consists of the Routing Engine and Miscellaneous Control Subsystem (MCS).

host subsystem   On a T640 routing node, provides routing and system-management functions of the router. Consists of a Routing Engine and an adjacent Control Board (CB).

I

Idle   The initial BGP neighbor state where the local router is refusing all incoming session requests.

import   To install routes from the routing protocols into a routing table.

inet.0   Default JUNOS software routing table for IPv4 unicast routes.

inet.1   Default JUNOS software routing table for storing the multicast cache for active data streams in the network.

inet.2   Default JUNOS software routing table for storing unicast IPv4 routes specifically used to prevent forwarding loops.

inet.3   Default JUNOS software routing table for storing the egress IP address of an MPLS label-switched path.

inet.4   Default JUNOS software routing table for storing information used by the Multicast Source Discovery Protocol (MSDP).

inet6.0   Default JUNOS software routing table for storing unicast IPv6 routes.

infinity metric   A metric value used in distance-vector protocols to represent an unusable route. For RIP, the infinity metric is 16.

ingress router   In MPLS, the first router in a label-switched path (LSP). See also *egress router*.

init   OSPF adjacency state where the local router has received a hello packet but bidirectional communication is not yet established.

insert   JUNOS software command that allows a user to reorder terms in a routing policy or a firewall filter. It may also be used to change the order of a policy chain.

Institute of Electronic and Electrical Engineers (IEEE)   The international professional society for electrical engineers who set standards for networking technologies.

Integrated Drive Electronics (IDE)   Type of hard disk on the Routing Engine.

Integrated Services Flowspec object   RSVP object that contains the bandwidth request for the LSP in a Resv message.

Integrated Services Sender-Tspec object   RSVP object that contains the bandwidth request for the LSP in a Path message.

inter-AS routing   Routing of packets among different ASs. See also *External BGP (EBGP)*.

intercluster reflection   In a BGP route reflection, the redistribution of routing information by a route reflector system to all nonclient peers (BGP peers not in the cluster). See also *route reflection*.

interface cost   Value added to all received routes in a distance-vector network before placing them into the routing table. The JUNOS software uses a cost of 1 for this value.

interface routes   Routes that are in the routing table because an interface has been configured with an IP address. Also called *direct and local routes*.

Interior Gateway Protocol (IGP)   A routing protocol designed to operate within the confines of an administrative domain. Examples include the Routing Information Protocol (RIP), Open Shortest Path First (OSPF), and Intermediate System to Intermediate System (IS-IS).

intermediate system   In IS-IS, the network entity that sends and receives packets and that can also route packets.

Intermediate System-to-Intermediate System (IS-IS)   Link-state, interior gateway routing protocol for IP networks that also uses the shortest path first (SPF) algorithm to determine routes.

Internal BGP (IBGP) BGP configuration in which sessions are established between routers in the same ASs.

Internal Ethernet Another name for the `fxp1` and `fxp2` interfaces that provide communications between the Routing Engine and the Packet Forwarding Engine.

International Electrotechnical Commission (IEC) See *International Organization for Standardization (ISO)*.

International Mobile Station Equipment Identity (IMEI) A unique code used to identify an individual mobile station to a GSM network.

International Mobile Subscriber Identity (IMSI) Information that identifies a particular subscriber to a GSM network.

International Organization for Standardization (ISO) Worldwide federation of standards bodies that promotes international standardization and publishes international agreements as International Standards.

International Telecommunications Union (ITU) Formerly known as the CCITT, group supported by the United Nations that makes recommendations and coordinates the development of telecommunications standards for the entire world.

Internet Assigned Numbers Authority (IANA) Regulatory group that maintains all assigned and registered Internet numbers, such as IP and multicast addresses. See also *Network Information Center (NIC)*.

Internet Control Message Protocol (ICMP) Used in router discovery, ICMP allows router advertisements that enable a host to discover addresses of operating routers on the subnet.

Internet Engineering Task Force (IETF) International community of network designers, operators, vendors, and researchers concerned with the evolution of the Internet architecture and the smooth operation of the Internet.

Internet Group Management Protocol (IGMP) Multicast protocol used for router-to-host communications. Hosts use IGMP to request multicast data streams from the network. Routers use IGMP to determine whether group members are still present on the local segment.

Internet Key Exchange (IKE) The key management protocol used in IPSec, IKE combines the ISAKMP and Oakley protocols to create encryption keys and security associations.

Internet Processor ASIC Juniper Networks ASIC responsible for using the forwarding table to make routing decisions within the Packet Forwarding Engine. The Internet Processor ASIC also implements firewall filters.

Internet Protocol (IP) The protocol used for sending data from one point to another on the Internet.

Internet Protocol Security (IPSec) The industry standard for establishing VPNs, IPSec comprises a group of protocols and algorithms that provide authentication and encryption of data across IP-based networks.

Internet Security Association and Key Management Protocol (ISAKMP) A protocol that allows the receiver of a message to obtain a public key and use digital certificates to authenticate the sender's identity. ISAKMP is designed to be key exchange independent; that is, it supports many different key exchanges. See also *Internet Key Exchange (IKE)* and *Oakley*.

Internet service provider (ISP) Company that provides access to the Internet and related services.

intra-AS routing The routing of packets within a single AS. See also *Internal BGP (IBGP)*.

I/O Manager ASIC Juniper Networks ASIC responsible for segmenting data packets into 64-byte J-cells and for queuing result cells prior to transmission.

IP external reachability TLV IS-IS TLV that advertises routing information that is not native to the IS-IS domain.

IP interface address TLV IS-IS TLV that sends local router addressing to the network. By default, the JUNOS software advertises the local router ID in this TLV.

IP internal reachability TLV IS-IS TLV that advertises routing information that is local to the IS-IS domain.

IP interworking In a Layer 2 VPN, the ability of one PE-CE encapsulation to differ from the remote PE-CE encapsulation.

IP precedence bits Three most significant bits in the Type of Service header of an IP packet that a router can evaluate for class-of-service processing.

IPv4 Error-Spec object RSVP object in a `PathErr` or `ResvErr` message that contains the specific error condition.

IPv4 RSVP-Hop object RSVP object that contains the physical interface address of the upstream or downstream router.

IS neighbors TLV IS-IS TLV in a Hello PDU that details the neighboring devices from which the local router has received packets.

IS reachability TLV IS-IS TLV that advertises adjacent nodes to the network.

J

jbase JUNOS software package containing updates to the kernel since the last `jbase` package.

jbundle JUNOS software package containing all possible software package files.

J-cell A 64-byte data unit used within the Packet Forwarding Engine. All IP packets processed by a Juniper Networks router are segmented into J-cells.

jdocs JUNOS software package containing the documentation set.

jitter Small random variation introduced into the value of a timer to prevent multiple timer expirations from becoming synchronized.

jkernel   JUNOS software package containing the basic components of the software.

Join message   PIM message sent hop by hop upstream to a multicast source or the RP of the domain. It requests that multicast traffic be sent downstream to the router originating the message.

jpfe   JUNOS software package containing the Embedded OS software for operating the Packet Forwarding Engine.

jroute   JUNOS software package containing the software used by the Routing Engine.

K

keepalive   BGP packet used to maintain a peering session with a neighbor.

kernel   The basic software component of the JUNOS software. It operates the various daemons used to control the router's operations.

kernel forwarding table   See *forwarding table.*

L

label   In MPLS, a 20-bit unsigned integer in the range 0 through 1,048,575, used to identify a packet traveling along an LSP.

label base   In a Layer 2 VPN, the lowest advertised label in a set of labels that allows remote PE routers to know which label is used to forward traffic across the network.

label block offset   In a Layer 2 VPN, a value that allows remote PE routers to correctly sequence multiple advertised label sets.

Label Distribution Protocol (LDP)   A signaling protocol used to establish an MPLS label switch path. LDP uses the IGP shortest-path cost to each egress router in the network and is not capable of utilizing traffic-engineering concepts.

label multiple push operation   Function performed by an MPLS router in which more than one label is added to the top label of the data packet.

Label object   An RSVP message object that contains the label value allocated by the next downstream router.

label pop operation   Function performed by an MPLS router in which the top label in a label stack is removed from the data packet.

label push operation   Function performed by an MPLS router in which a new label is added to the top of the data packet.

Label Request object   An RSVP message object that requests each router along the path of an LSP to allocate a label for forwarding purposes.

label space   In LDP, the concept of a node and its method of allocating labels.

label swap operation   Function performed by an MPLS router in which the top label in a label stack is replaced with a new label before forwarding the data packet to the next-hop router.

label swap and push operation   Function performed by an MPLS router in which the top label in a label stack is replaced with a new label. In addition, another label is added to the data packet before it's forwarded to the next-hop router.

label-switched path (LSP)   Sequence of routers that cooperatively perform MPLS operations for a packet stream. The first router in an LSP is called the *ingress* router, and the last router in the path is called the *egress* router. An LSP is a point-to-point, simplex connection from the ingress router to the egress router. (The ingress and egress routers cannot be the same router.)

label switching   See *Multiprotocol Label Switching (MPLS)*.

label-switching router (LSR)   A router on which MPLS is enabled and is thus capable of processing label-switched packets.

label values   A 20-bit field in an MPLS header used by routers to forward data traffic along an MPLS label-switched path.

Layer 2 information community   In a Layer 2 VPN, the community advertised between PE routers that ensures the physical encapsulations match.

LDP address message   Message that advertises the local interfaces address of an LDP router.

LDP database   Logical data structure that contains the advertised label-to-FEC mappings for each LDP session.

LDP Hello message   Message that establishes a neighbor relationship between two LDP routers.

LDP initialization message   Message exchanged between LDP neighbors that establishes the session between them.

LDP keeplive message   Message that maintains the LDP neighbor relationships and sessions in the network.

LDP label mapping message   Message that contains the FEC-to-label mapping the local router is advertising to the network.

LDP label withdraw message   Message that contains the FEC-to-label mapping the local router is withdrawing from the network.

LDP tunneling   The ability to form an LDP session over an RSVP-based LSP.

Lightweight Directory Access Protocol (LDAP)   Software protocol used for locating resources on a public or private network.

line loopback   A method used to troubleshoot a problem with a physical transmission media. A transmission device in the network sends the data signal back to the originating router.

link   Communication path between two neighbors. A link is up when communication is possible between the two end points.

link hello   In LDP, Hello messages that are sent on all interfaces to all peers using UDP.

link protection   Operational fast reroute system that protects just the network link between the local router and the next downstream router.

link-state acknowledgment   OSPF data packet used to inform a neighbor that a link-state update packet has been successfully received.

link-state advertisement (LSA)   OSPF data structure that is advertised in a link-state update packet. Each LSA uniquely describes a portion of the OSPF network.

link-state database   All routing knowledge in a link-state network is contained in this database. Each router runs the SPF algorithm against this database to locate the best network path to each destination in the network.

link-state PDU (LSP)   Packets that contain information about the state of adjacencies to neighboring systems in an IS-IS network.

link-state request list   A list generated by an OSPF router during the exchange of database information while forming an adjacency. Advertised information by a neighbor that the local router doesn't contain is placed on this list.

link-state request packet   OSPF data packet that a router uses to request database information from a neighboring router.

link-state update   OSPF data packet that contains one or multiple LSAs. It is used to advertise routing knowledge to the network.

link TLV   Traffic engineering extension used by OSPF to advertise the type of link on the local router.

loading   OSPF adjacency state where the local router is sending link-state request packets to its neighbor and is awaiting the appropriate link-state updates from that neighbor.

local preference   Optional BGP path attribute carried in internal BGP update packets that indicates the degree of preference for an external route.

local significance   Concept used in an MPLS network where the label values are unique only between two neighbor routers.

local-as   JUNOS software command that allows a router to form a peering session using an AS value that is different than the configured value within the [edit routing-options] hierarchy.

Local-RIB   Logical software table that contains BGP routes used by the local router to forward data packets.

logical AND   In the policy framework, allows two policies to be evaluated as a single entity for a true or false result. Both policies must evaluate as true for the expression to be true.

logical NOT   In the policy framework, allows the logical evaluation of a single policy to be reversed. A true evaluation returns a false result while a false evaluation returns a true result.

logical operator   Characters used in a routing policy to represent a Boolean AND or OR operation.

logical OR   In the policy framework, allows two policies to be evaluated as a single entity for a true or false result. Either of the policies may evaluate as true for the expression to be true.

longer   JUNOS software routing policy match type that represents all routes more specific than the given subnet, but not the given subnet itself. It is similar to a mathematical greater-than operation.

loose   In the context of traffic engineering, a path that can use any route or any number of other intermediate (transit) points to reach the next address in the path. (Definition from RFC 791, modified to fit LSPs.)

loose hop   Router in an MPLS named-path that is not required to be directly connected to the local router.

loss priority   JUNOS software internal value assigned to all packets that the router uses to evaluate which packets to drop based on configured RED settings.

LSP entry TLV   IS-IS TLV that sends LSP header information to the network. It is used to synchronize the link-state databases in the network.

LSP-Tunnel Session Attribute object   RSVP object that contains the setup and hold priority values as well as fast reroute flags for a particular LSP.

LSP-Tunnel-IPv4 Filter-Spec object   RSVP object in a Resv message that is used to uniquely identify a sender for a particular LSP.

LSP-Tunnel-IPv4 Sender Template object   RSVP object in a Path message that is used to uniquely identify a sender for a particular LSP.

LSP-Tunnel-IPv4 Session object   RSVP object that contains the egress router's address and the tunnel ID for the LSP.

M

make before break   Method used by an ingress router to establish a new LSP and move traffic prior to removing an old LSP from the network.

management daemon (mgd)   JUNOS software process responsible for managing all user access to the router.

Management Ethernet   Another name for the fxp0 interface that provides out-of-band access to the router.

Management Information Base (MIB)   Definition of an object that can be managed by SNMP.

mapping agent A router used in an auto-RP multicast network to select the rendezvous point for all multicast group addresses. This information is then advertised to all other routers in the domain.

Martian address Network address about which all information is ignored.

Martian routes Network routes about which information is ignored. The JUNOS software doesn't allow Martian routes to reside in the inet.0 routing table.

mask See *subnet mask*.

master The router in control of the OSPF database exchange during an adjacency formation.

match A logical concept used in a routing policy or a firewall filter. It denotes the criteria used to find a route or IP packet before performing some action.

match type JUNOS software syntax used in a route filter to better describe the routes that should match the policy term.

max-suppress Value used when damping BGP routes. It specifies the longest amount of time that a route is damped and removed from the routing table. The JUNOS software uses a default value of 60 minutes.

MaxAge The maximum amount of time, 3600 seconds, that an OSPF LSA may exist in a network.

maximum transmission unit (MTU) Limit on segment size for a network.

MBone Internet multicast backbone. An interconnected set of subnetworks and routers that support the delivery of IP multicast traffic. The MBone is a virtual network that is layered on top of sections of the physical Internet.

mean time between failure (MTBF) Measure of hardware component reliability.

member AS In a confederation BGP network, each of the subdivisions of the global confederation.

member AS number In a confederation BGP network, the AS value assigned to each of the member AS networks that make up the global confederation.

mesh Network topology in which devices are organized in a manageable, segmented manner with many, often redundant, interconnections between network nodes.

mesh group A collection of IS-IS or MSDP nodes that are connected in a full-mesh network and that limit the redundant forwarding of protocol information between themselves.

message aggregation An extension to the RSVP specification that allows neighboring routers to bundle up to 30 RSVP messages into a single protocol packet.

Message Digest 5 (MD5) A one-way hashing algorithm that produces a 128-bit hash. It is used in AH and ESP. See also *Secure Hash Algorithm (SHA-1)*.

metric-out   JUNOS software command that sets the MED value on advertised BGP routes. In addition to setting the value itself, you may associate a local IGP cost with the advertised MED value.

midplane   Forms the rear of the PIC cage on M5 and M10 routers and the FPC card cage on M20, M40e, M160, and T640 platforms. Provides data transfer, power distribution, and signal connectivity.

Miscellaneous Control Subsystem (MCS)   On the M40e and M160 routers, provides control and monitoring functions for router components and SONET clocking for the router.

mobile network access subsystem (MAS)   GSN application subsystem that contains the access server.

mobile point-to-point control subsystem (MPS)   GSN application subsystem that controls all functionality associated with a particular connection.

mobile station   A mobile device, such as a cellular phone or a mobile personal digital assistant (PDA).

Mobile Station Integrated Services Digital Network Number   Number that callers use to reach a mobile services subscriber.

Mobile Switching Center (MSC)   Provides origination and termination functions to calls from a mobile station user.

mobile transport subsystem (MTS)   GSN application subsystem that implements all the protocols used by the GSN.

multicast   Operation of sending network traffic from one network node to multiple network nodes.

multi-field classifier   Class of service classification method that utilizes multiple pieces of information in the data packet. This can include destination and source IP addresses as well as destination and source port values.

multicast distribution tree   The data path between the sender (host) and the multicast group member (receiver or listener).

multicast scoping   The restriction of forwarding multicast traffic on the basis of an individual interface.

Multicast Source Discovery Protocol (MSDP)   Protocol that advertises multicast source information between RP routers in different domains as well as a single domain.

Multiple-Exit-Discriminator (MED)   Optional BGP path attribute consisting of a metric value that is used to determine the exit point to a destination when all other factors in determining the exit point are equal.

multihop   JUNOS software command that allows an EBGP peer to not be directly connected to the local router.

multipath   JUNOS software command that allows a BGP router to use next hops from multiple equal-cost BGP routes.

Multiprotocol BGP (MBGP)   An extension to BGP that allows you to exchange non-IPv4 routing knowledge within and between BGP ASs.

Multiprotocol Label Switching (MPLS)   Mechanism for engineering network traffic patterns that functions by assigning to network packets short labels that describe how to forward them through the network. Also called *label switching*. See also *traffic engineering*.

multiprotocol reachable NLRI   BGP attribute that advertises routing knowledge other than IPv4 routes.

multiprotocol unreachable NLRI   BGP attribute that withdraws routing knowledge from the network that had been advertised by the multiprotocol reachable NLRI.

N

named-path   JUNOS software syntax that specifies a portion or the entire network path that should be used as a constraint in signaling an MPLS label-switched path.

neighbor   Adjacent system reachable by traversing a single subnetwork. An immediately adjacent router. Also called a *peer*.

network entity title (NET)   Network address defined by the ISO network architecture and used in connectionless network service–based networks.

network layer reachability information (NLRI)   Information that is carried in BGP packets and used by MBGP.

network-link advertisement   An OSPF link-state advertisement flooded throughout a single area by a designated router (DR) to describe all routers attached to the DR's local segment.

network LSA   OSPF link-state advertisement sent by the DR on a broadcast or NBMA segment. It advertises the subnet associated with the DR's segment.

network service access point (NSAP)   Connection to a network that is identified by a network address.

Network Summary LSA   OSPF link-state advertisement sent by an ABR to advertise internal OSPF routing knowledge across an area boundary.

Network Time Protocol (NTP)   Protocol used to synchronize computer clock times on a network.

Next Hop   BGP attribute that specifies the router to send packets to for a particular set of routes.

no-advertise   Well-known BGP community value that prevents a neighboring BGP peer from readvertising a route sent from the local router.

node protection   Operational fast reroute system that protects both the network link between the local router and the next downstream router as well as the next downstream router itself.

no-export   Well-known BGP community value that prevents a neighboring AS network from readvertising a route sent from the local AS.

no-export-subconfed   Well-known BGP community value that prevents a neighboring sub-AS network from readvertising a route sent from the local sub-AS when the global AS is operating a confederation network.

nonclient peer   In a BGP route reflection network, a BGP peer that is not a member of a cluster. See also *client peer*.

notification cell   JUNOS software data structure generated by the Distributed Buffer Manager ASIC that represents the header contents of an IP packet. The Internet Processor ASIC uses the notification cell to perform a forwarding table lookup.

Notification message   BGP message that informs a neighbor about an error condition and then possibly terminates the BGP peering session.

not-so-stubby area (NSSA)   In OSPF, a type of stub area in which external routes can be flooded.

n-selector   Last byte of an ISO Network Entity Title (NET) address.

NSSA external-link advertisements   OSPF link-state advertisement sent by AS boundary routers to describe external routes that they know. These LSAs are flooded only within a not-so-stubby area.

null AS Path   In BGP, an AS Path with no entries. These routes originate within the local AS.

Null Register message   A PIM message sent by the first hop router to the RP. It informs the RP that the local source is still actively sending multicast packets into the network should future interested listeners send a Join message to the RP.

numeric range match conditions   The use of numeric values (protocol and port numbers) in the header of an IP packet as match criteria in a firewall filter.

O

Oakley   A key determination protocol based on the Diffie-Hellman algorithm that provides added security, including authentication. Oakley was the key-exchange algorithm mandated for use with the initial version of ISAKMP, although various algorithms can be used. Oakley describes a series of key exchanges called "modes" and details the services provided by each; for example, Perfect Forward Secrecy for keys, identity protection, and authentication. See also *Internet Security Association and Key Management Protocol (ISAKMP)*.

opaque ID   Within an opaque LSA, the final three octets of the link-state ID field make up the unique ID value for the LSA.

opaque LSA   OSPF link-state advertisement that each router may use to advertise information into the network. There is a link-local, an area-local, and a domain-local version of the LSA. The JUNOS software uses link-local opaque LSAs to support graceful restart. Traffic engineer capabilities are advertised using area-local opaque LSAs.

opaque type Within an opaque LSA, the first octet of the link-state ID field is defined as the type of opaque LSA being advertised.

Open message BGP message that allows two neighbors to negotiate the parameters of the peering session.

OpenConfirm BGP neighbor state that shows a valid Open message was received from the remote peer.

OpenSent BGP neighbor state that shows an Open message was sent to the remote peer and that the local router is waiting for an Open message to be returned.

Open Shortest Path First (OSPF) A link-state IGP that makes routing decisions based on the shortest path first (SPF) algorithm (also referred to as the Dijkstra algorithm).

Open System Interconnection (OSI) Standard reference model for how messages are transmitted between two points on a network.

operational mode JUNOS software mode allowing a user to view statistics and information concerning the router's current operating status.

Optical Carrier (OC) In SONET, Optical Carrier levels indicate the transmission rate of digital signals on optical fiber.

origin BGP attribute that describes the believability of a particular route. The router that first places the route into BGP should attempt to accurately describe the source of the route.

originator ID BGP attribute that details the first router that advertised a particular route to a route reflector.

orlonger JUNOS software routing policy match type that represents all routes more specific than the given subnet, including the given subnet itself. It is similar to a mathematical greater-than-or-equal-to operation.

OSPF Hello packet Message sent by each OSPF router to each adjacent neighbor. It is used to establish and maintain the router's neighbor relationships.

overlay network Network design seen where a logical Layer 3 topology (IP subnets) is operating over a logical Layer 2 topology (ATM PVCs). Layers in the network do not have knowledge of each other, and each requires separate management and operation.

overload bit Bit in an IS-IS link-state PDU that signals to the network that the local router does not have a complete database due to memory limitations.

P

package A collection of files that make up a JUNOS software component.

packet data protocol (PDP) Network protocol, such as IP, used by packet data networks connected to a GPRS network.

Packet Forwarding Engine   The architectural portion of the router that processes packets by forwarding them between input and output interfaces.

Packet Loss Priority (PLP)   Internal router designation that represents a greater probability of dropping a particular IP packet based on configured class-of-service settings. The priority is assigned to a packet when it enters the router and can be modified by a firewall filter.

padding TLV   IS-IS TLV that allows a router to increase the length of Hello PDUs to form adjacencies with neighboring systems.

partial sequence number PDU (PSNP)   Packet that contains only a partial list of the LSPs in the IS-IS link-state database.

passive   JUNOS software command that prevents a local router from sending an Open message to a configured peer.

passive node   In LDP, the peer with the lower router ID that waits for the active node to establish the session.

path attribute   Information about a BGP route, such as the route origin, AS path, and next-hop router.

Path message   RSVP message that initiates the establishment of an LSP.

PathErr message   RSVP message that indicates an error has occurred along an established LSP. The message is advertised upstream to the ingress router and it doesn't remove any RSVP soft state from the network.

PathTear message   RSVP message indicating that the established LSP and its associated soft state should be removed by the network. The message is advertised downstream hop-by-hop to the egress router.

Path State Block   RSVP logical database structure that each router creates upon the receipt of a Path message for a new RSVP session.

path-vector protocol   A routing protocol definition that describes the direction to the destination and the network path used to reach the destination. This often describes the functionality of BGP.

peer   An immediately adjacent router with which a protocol relationship has been established. Also called a *neighbor*.

peer-RPF flooding   Process used by MSDP routers to ensure that the flooding of SA messages are bounded.

penultimate hop popping (PHP)   A mechanism used in an MPLS network that allows the transit router prior to the egress to perform a label pop operation and forward the remaining data (often a native IPv4 packet) to the egress router.

penultimate router   The last transit router prior to the egress router in an MPLS label-switched path.

per-prefix load balancing   The default operation of BGP within the JUNOS software that assigns each unique destination a physical next hop from a list of equal-cost paths.

Perfect Forward Secrecy (PFS)   A condition derived from an encryption system that changes encryption keys often and ensures that no two sets of keys have any relation to each other. The advantage of PFS is that if one set of keys is compromised, only communications using those keys are at risk. An example of a system that uses PFS is Diffie-Hellman.

Peripheral Component Interconnect (PCI)   Standard, high-speed bus for connecting computer peripherals. Used on the Routing Engine.

permanent virtual circuit (PVC)   A logical Layer 2 connection between two network devices. The network path is preengineered and configured on each device in the network supporting the PVC.

Personal Computer Memory Card International Association (PCMCIA)   Industry group that promotes standards for credit card–size memory or I/O devices.

Physical Interface Card (PIC)   A network interface–specific card that can be installed on an FPC in the router.

PIC I/O Manager ASIC   Juniper Networks ASIC responsible for receiving and transmitting information on the physical media. It performs media-specific tasks within the Packet Forwarding Engine.

PLP bit   Packet Loss Priority bit. Used to identify packets that have experienced congestion or are from a transmission that exceeded a service provider's customer service license agreement. This bit can be used as part of a router's congestion control mechanism and can be set by the interface or by a filter.

point of local repair   In fast reroute, the router that notices a network failure and utilizes the protection path to continue forwarding traffic.

point-to-point adjacency TLV   IS-IS TLV used on point-to-point links that allows the local router to detail the remote systems it has received PDUs from.

policing   Applying rate limits on bandwidth and burst size for traffic on a particular interface or IPv4 prefix.

Policing Equivalence Classes (PEC)   In traffic policing, a set of packets that is treated the same by the packet classifier.

pop   Removal of the last label, by a router, from a packet as it exits an MPLS domain.

Point-to-Point (PPP)   Link-layer protocol that provides multiprotocol encapsulation. It is used for link-layer and network-layer configuration.

poison reverse   Method used in distance-vector networks to avoid routing loops. Each router advertises routes back to the neighbor it received them from with an infinity metric assigned.

policy chain   The application of multiple routing policies in a single location. The policies are evaluated in a predefined manner and are always followed by the default policy for the specific application location.

policy expression   The application of multiple routing policies as a single entity in a policy chain. The policies are evaluated using a logical AND, OR, or NOT.

policy subroutine   The use of a routing policy as a match criterion within a completely separate policy.

possible helper mode   A process within graceful restart that allows a router to assist a neighboring device to perform a restart operation when that neighbor requests it.

precedence bits   The first three bits in the ToS byte. On a Juniper Networks router, these bits are used to sort or classify individual packets as they arrive at an interface. The classification determines the queue to which the packet is directed upon transmission.

preempt   In MPLS, the process of a new LSP being established in place of an existing LSP.

preference   Desirability of a route to become the active route. A route with a lower preference value is more likely to become the active route. The preference is an arbitrary value in the range 0 through 4,294,967,295 that the routing protocol process uses to rank routes received from different protocols, interfaces, or remote systems.

preferred address   On an interface, the default local address used for packets sourced by the local router to destinations on the subnet.

prefix-length-range   JUNOS software routing policy match type representing all routes that share the same most significant bits. The prefix length of the route must also lie between the two supplied subnets in the route filter.

prefix list   A list of routes that is used as a match criterion in a routing policy. Each route in the list is evaluated as an exact match by the policy.

primary address   On an interface, the address used by default as the local address for broadcast and multicast packets sourced locally and sent out the interface.

primary contributing route   The contributing route with the numerically smallest prefix and smallest JUNOS software preference value. This route is the default next hop used for a generated route.

primary interface   Router interface that packets go out when no interface name is specified and when the destination address does not imply a particular outgoing interface.

primary path   In MPLS, the preferred path for an LSP. This path is always used if it is available.

priority queuing   The ability to assign a specific queue a priority value for preferential service when an interface is transmitting packets.

protocol address   The logical Layer 3 address assigned to an interface within the JUNOS software.

protocol data unit (PDU)   The basic data structure used by the IS-IS routing protocol to form adjacencies and exchange routing information.

protocol families   The grouping of logical properties within an interface configuration. The JUNOS software supports the `inet`, `iso`, `mpls`, and `inet6` families.

Protocol Independent Multicast (PIM) A protocol-independent multicast routing protocol. PIM sparse mode routes to multicast groups that might span wide-area and interdomain internets. PIM dense mode is a flood-and-prune protocol.

protocol preference A 32-bit value assigned to all routes placed in the routing table. It is used as a tiebreaker when multiple exact routes are placed in the table by different protocols.

protocols-supported TLV IS-IS TLV that advertises the Layer 3 protocols the local router can support.

provider edge (PE) router A router in the service provider's network that is connected to a customer edge (CE) device and that participates in a virtual private network (VPN).

provider router Router in the service provider's network that does not attach to a customer edge (CE) device.

Prune message PIM message sent upstream to a multicast source or the RP of the domain. It requests that multicast traffic stop being transmitted to the router originating the message.

public land mobile network (PLMN) A telecommunications network for mobile stations.

push Addition of a label or stack of labels, by a router, to a packet as it enters an MPLS domain.

Q

quad-wide A type of PIC that combines the PIC and the FPC within a single FPC slot.

qualified next hop A next hop for a static route that allows a second copy of a static route to have different metric and preference properties than the original.

quality of service (QoS) Performance, such as transmission rates and error rates, of a communications channel or system.

querier router PIM router on a broadcast subnet responsible for generating IGMP Query messages for the segment.

R

radio frequency interference (RFI) Interference from high-frequency electromagnetic waves emanating from electronic devices.

radio network controller (RNC) A device that manages the radio part of the network in UMTS.

Random Early Discard (RED) Gradual drop profile for a given class that is used for congestion avoidance. RED tries to anticipate incipient congestion and reacts by dropping a small percentage of packets from the head of the queue to ensure that a queue never becomes congested.

rate limiting See *policing*.

rate policing   See *policing*.

receive   A next hop for a static route that allows all matching packets to be sent to the Routing Engine for processing.

Record Route object (RRO)   An RSVP message object that notes the IP address of each router along the path of an LSP.

recursive lookup   A method of consulting the routing table to locate the actual physical next hop for a route when the supplied next hop is not directly connected.

regional Bell operating company (RBOC)   (Pronounced "are-bock") Regional telephone companies formed as a result of the divestiture of the Bell System.

Register message   PIM message unicast by the first hop router to the RP that contains the multicast packets from the source encapsulated within its data field.

Register Stop message   PIM message sent by the RP to the first hop router to halt the sending of encapsulated multicast packets.

regular expression   Allows for matching community and AS Path values using a series of terms and operators.

regular expression operator   Within a regular expression, an operator that allows a single term to appear multiple times within the community or AS Path.

regular expression term   Within a regular expression, a term that is the value being matched by the expression. In a community, the term is each individual digit. In an AS Path, the term is a complete AS value.

reject   A next hop for a configured route that drops all matching packets from the network and returns an ICMP message to the source IP address. Also used as an action in a routing policy or a firewall filter.

Remote Authentication Dial-In User Service (RADIUS)   Authentication method for validating users who attempt to access the router using Telnet.

remove-private   JUNOS software command that allows an EBGP router to remove private AS values from the AS Path attribute prior to advertising the route to a peer.

rename   JUNOS software command that allows a user to change the name of a routing policy, a firewall filter, or any other variable-character string defined in the router's configuration.

rendezvous point (RP)   For PIM-SM, a router acting as the root of the shared distribution tree.

Reply message   Message sent from a TACACS+ server to the router that authenticates a user positively or negatively.

Request for Comments (RFC)   Internet standard specifications published by the Internet Engineering Task Force.

Request message   RIP message used by a router to ask for all or part of the routing table from a neighbor.

resolve   A next hop for a static route that allows the router to perform a recursive lookup to locate the physical next hop for the route.

Resource Reservation Protocol (RSVP)   Resource reservation setup protocol designed to interact with integrated services on the Internet.

Response message   RIP message used to advertise routing information to a network.

restart candidate mode   A process within graceful restart that defines the capabilities of a local router to perform a restart operation.

restart state bit   In BGP, this bit is set during a graceful restart operation to signal that the router has performed a graceful restart operation.

result cell   JUNOS software data structure generated by the Internet Processor ASIC after performing a forwarding table lookup.

Resv Message   RSVP message that allocates resources in the network for a newly establishing LSP.

ResvConf message   RSVP message that allows the egress router to receive an explicit confirmation message from a neighbor that its Resv message was received.

ResvErr message   RSVP message that indicates an error has occurred along an established LSP. The message is advertised downstream to the egress router, and it doesn't remove any RSVP soft state from the network.

ResvTear message   RSVP message that indicates the established LSP and its associated soft state should be removed by the network. The message is advertised upstream to the ingress router.

Resv State Block   RSVP logical database structure that each router creates upon the receipt of a Resv message for a new RSVP session.

reuse   Value used when damping BGP routes. It specifies the figure of merit value at which time a damped route is returned to the routing table. The JUNOS software uses a default value of 750.

reverse path forwarding   Method used in a multicast routing domain to prevent forwarding loops.

reverse path multicasting (RPM)   Routing algorithm used by DVMRP to forward multicast traffic.

revertive   In MPLS, the process of returning an LSP to its primary path after a failure.

rewrite rule   The ability to alter the class-of-service information in the header of a data packet before it is retransmitted to the network.

rib-group   A mechanism that allows protocols to place routing knowledge in multiple routing tables. Also known as a *routing table group*.

route damping   The process where BGP routes that are continually advertised and withdrawn are removed from use in the network.

route distinguisher   Value added to a VPN NLRI that guarantees the uniqueness of the advertised prefix within the provider network.

route filter   JUNOS software syntax used in a routing policy to match an individual route or a group of routes.

route flapping   Situation in which BGP systems send an excessive number of update messages to advertise network reachability information.

route identifier   IP address of the router from which a BGP, IGP, or OSPF packet originated.

route leaking   In IS-IS, the ability of a router to advertise information between Layer 1 and Layer 2, or vice versa.

route redistribution   A method of placing learned routes from one protocol into another protocol operating on the same router. The JUNOS software accomplishes this with a routing policy.

route reflection   In BGP, configuring a group of routers into a cluster and having one system act as a route reflector, redistributing routes from outside the cluster to all routers in the cluster. Routers in a cluster do not need to be fully meshed.

route target   Extended community that allows PE routers to ensure that a VRF contains only routes belonging to that VRF.

router address TLV   Traffic engineering extension used by IS-IS to advertise the router ID of the local router.

Router ID   An IP address used by a router to uniquely identify itself to a routing protocol. This address may or may not be equal to a configured interface address.

router-link advertisement   OSPF link-state advertisement flooded throughout a single area by all routers to describe the state and cost of the router's links to the area.

router LSA   OSPF link-state advertisement sent by each router in the network. It describes the local router's connected subnets as well as their metric values.

Router Priority   A numerical value assigned to an OSPF or an IS-IS router that is used as the first criterion in electing the designated router or designated intermediate system, respectively.

routing domain   See *Autonomous System (AS)*.

Routing Engine   Architectural portion of the router that handles all routing protocol processes, as well as other software processes that control the router's interfaces, some of the chassis components, system management, and user access to the router.

Routing header   IPv6 extension header that allows the source node to source-route a packet across the network.

Routing Information Base (RIB)   A logical data structure used by BGP to store routing information.

Routing Information Protocol (RIP)   Distance-vector Interior Gateway Protocol that makes routing decisions based on hop count.

routing instance A collection of routing tables, interfaces, and routing protocol parameters. The set of interfaces belongs to the routing tables, and the routing protocol parameters control the information in the routing tables.

routing protocol daemon (rpd) JUNOS software routing protocol process (daemon). User-level background process responsible for starting, managing, and stopping the routing protocols on a Juniper Networks router.

routing table Common database of routes learned from one or more routing protocols. All routes are maintained by the JUNOS routing protocol process.

RP-Set Listing of all RP devices in a PIM domain and the group addresses each router supports.

RSVP Path message RSVP message sent by the ingress router downstream to the egress router. It begins the establishment of a soft-state database for a particular label-switched path.

RSVP Resv message RSVP message sent by the egress router upstream to the ingress router. It completes the establishment of the soft-state database for a particular label-switched path.

RSVP session Combination of RSVP objects that uniquely defines and identifies a connection in the network.

RSVP signaled LSP A label-switched path that is dynamically established using RSVP Path and Resv messages.

S

scheduler Method employed by the JUNOS software for assigning resources to individual queues.

secondary path In MPLS, one of multiple possible paths for an LSP. These paths may be used in the event of a failure or the nonexistence of a primary path.

Secure Hash Algorithm (SHA-1) A widely used hash function for use with Digital Signal Standard (DSS). SHA-1 is more secure than MD5.

secure shell (SSH) Software that provides a secured method of logging into a remote network system.

security association (SA) An IPSec term that describes an agreement between two parties about what rules to use for authentication and encryption algorithms, key exchange mechanisms, and secure communications.

Security Parameter Index (SPI) A portion of the IPSec Authentication Header that communicates which security protocols, such as authentication and encryption, are used for each packet in a VPN connection.

segmentation and reassembly (SAR) Buffering used with ATM.

Serving GPRS Support Node (SGSN) Device in the mobile network that requests PDP contexts with a GGSN.

Session Announcement Protocol (SAP)   A protocol used with multicast protocols to handle session conference announcements. It advertises SDP packets to network neighbors.

session attribute object   RSVP message object that is used to control the priority, preemption, affinity class, and local rerouting of the LSP.

Session Description Protocol (SDP)   A protocol used with multicast protocols to handle session conference announcements.

setup priority   Value used by RSVP when evaluating whether enough bandwidth is available at different priority levels.

shared explicit   Reservation style where multiple senders within a common RSVP session are allowed to share a single set of resources.

shared tree   The multicast forwarding tree established from the RP to the last hop router for a particular group address.

shim header   The name used to describe the location of the MPLS header in a data packet. The JUNOS software always places (shims) the header between the existing Layer 2 and 3 headers.

Short Message Service (SMS)   GSM service that enables short text messages to be sent to and from mobile telephones.

shortest path first (SPF) algorithm   An algorithm used by IS-IS and OSPF to make routing decisions based on the state of network links. Also called the Dijkstra algorithm.

shortest-path tree   The multicast forwarding tree established from the first hop router to the last hop router for a particular group address.

show route advertising-protocol   JUNOS software command that displays the routes sent to a neighbor for a particular protocol.

show route receive-protocol   JUNOS software command that displays the routes received from a neighbor for a particular protocol.

signaled path   In traffic engineering, an explicit path; that is, a path determined using RSVP signaling. The ERO carried in the packets contains the explicit path information.

Signaling System 7 (SS7)   Protocol used in telecommunications for delivering calls and services.

Simple Network Management Protocol (SNMP)   Protocol governing network management and the monitoring of network devices and their functions.

simplex interface   An interface that assumes that packets it receives from itself are the result of a software loopback process. The interface does not consider these packets when determining whether the interface is functional.

site identifier   In a Layer 2 VPN, identifies the specific PE-CE connection within the VPN. Each PE router uses the site identifier to select the proper label for forwarding to a remote site.

soft state   A database structure maintained by an RSVP router to store information about a particular label-switched path.

SONET Clock Generator (SCG)   On an M40e or M160 router as well as on a T320 or T640 routing node, the SCG provides a Stratum 3 clock signal for the SONET/SDH interfaces. It also provides external clock inputs.

source active message   In MSDP, a message that advertises active multicast sources known to a local RP to all established peers.

source-based tree   The multicast forwarding tree established from the source of traffic to all interested receivers for a particular group address. It is often seen in a dense-mode forwarding environment.

source-specific multicasting   As part of the IGMPv3 specification, this process allows an end host to request multicast traffic for a group address from a specific source of traffic.

sparse mode   A method of operating a multicast domain where sources of traffic and interested receivers meet at a central rendezvous point. A sparse-mode network assumes that there are very few receivers for each group address.

Split Horizon   Method used in distance-vector networks to avoid routing loops. Each router does not advertise routes back to the neighbor it received them from.

standby   In MPLS, the establishment of a secondary LSP in an Up state prior to a failure of a primary path.

Start message   Message sent from the router to a TACACS+ server that contains the user's name.

static label-switched path (static LSP)   See *static path*.

static path   In the context of traffic engineering, a static route that requires hop-by-hop manual configuration. No signaling is used to create or maintain the path. Also called a *static LSP*.

static route   A configured route that includes a route and a next hop. It is always present in the routing table and doesn't react to topology changes in the network.

static RP   One of three methods of learning the rendezvous point to group address mapping in a multicast network. Each router in the domain must be configured with the required RP information.

strict   In the context of traffic engineering, a route that must go directly to the next address in the path. (Definition from RFC 791, modified to fit LSPs.)

strict hop   Routers in an MPLS named path that are required to be directly connected to the local router.

Strict Priority Queuing (SPQ)   Dequeuing method that provides a special queue that is serviced until it is empty. The traffic sent to this queue tends to maintain a lower latency and more consistent latency numbers than traffic sent to other queues. See also *Alternate Priority Queuing (APQ)*.

stub area   In OSPF, an area through which, or into which, AS external advertisements are not flooded.

Style object   RSVP object that contains the type of request the ingress router would like for the LSP.

sub-AS   Another term describing the subdivisions in a global confederation BGP network.

Sub-Network Point of Attachment (SNPA)   The Layer 2 address of a node connected to a network link.

subnet mask   The number of bits of the network address used for the host portion of a Class A, Class B, or Class C IP address.

Subsequent Address Family Identifier   In BGP, a value that defines the particular type of NLRI within the major address family advertised to a peer.

summary-link advertisement   OSPF link-statement advertisement flooded throughout the advertisement's associated areas by area border routers to describe the routes that they know about in other areas.

suppress   Value used when damping BGP routes. It specifies the figure of merit value at which time a route is removed from the routing table and is considered damped. The JUNOS software uses a default value of 3000.

Switch Interface Board (SIB)   On a T320 or T640 routing node, an SIB provides the switching function to the destination Packet Forwarding Engine.

Switching and Forwarding Module (SFM)   On an M40e or M160 router, a component of the Packet Forwarding Engine that provides route lookup, filtering, and switching to FPCs.

Synchronous Digital Hierarchy (SDH)   CCITT variation of the SONET standard.

Synchronous Optical Network (SONET)   High-speed (up to 2.5Gbps) synchronous network specification developed by Bellcore and designed to run on optical fiber. STS-1 is the basic building block of SONET. Approved as an international standard in 1988. See also *Synchronous Digital Hierarchy (SDH)*.

Synchronous Transport Module (STM)   CCITT specification for SONET at 155.52Mbps.

Synchronous Transport Signal (STS) Level 1   Basic building block signal of SONET, operating at 51.84Mbps. Faster SONET rates are defined as STS-*n*, where *n* is a multiple of 51.84Mbps. See also *Synchronous Optical Network (SONET)*.

sysid   System identifier. A portion of the ISO Network Entity Title (NET) address. The sysid can be any 6 bytes that are unique throughout a domain.

syslog   A method for storing messages to a file for troubleshooting or record-keeping purposes. It can also be used as an action within a firewall filter to store information in the messages file.

System Control Board (SCB)   On an M40 router, the part of the Packet Forwarding Engine that performs route lookups, monitors system components, and controls FPC resets.

System Switching Board (SSB)   On an M20 router, the Packet Forwarding Engine component that performs route lookups and component monitoring and monitors FPC operation.

T

targeted hello   In LDP, Hello messages that are sent to just a specific peer.

TCP port 179   The well-known port number used by BGP to establish a peering session with a neighbor.

tcpdump   A Unix packet monitoring utility used by the JUNOS software to view information about packets sent to or received by the Routing Engine.

Terminal Access Controller Access Control System Plus (TACACS+)   Authentication method for validating users who attempt to access the router using Telnet.

terminating action   An action in a routing policy or firewall filter that halts the logical software processing of the policy or filter.

terms   In a routing policy or firewall filter, terms are used to segment the policy or filter into smaller match and action pairs.

through   JUNOS software routing policy match type representing all routes that fall between the two supplied prefixes in the route filter.

Time-Values object   RSVP object that contains the amount of time that an RSVP router should consider its neighbor available.

Timeout timer   Timer used in a distance-vector protocol to ensure that the current route is still usable for forwarding traffic. The JUNOS software uses a default value of 120 seconds.

token-bucket algorithm   The algorithm used in a rate-policing application to enforce an average bandwidth while allowing bursts of traffic up to a configured maximum value.

totally stubby area   An OSPF area type that prevents Type 3, 4, and 5 LSAs from entering the nonbackbone area.

traffic engineering   Process of selecting the paths chosen by data traffic in order to balance the traffic load on the various links, routers, and switches in the network. (Definition from www.ietf.org/internet-drafts/draft-ietf-mpls-framework-04.txt.) See also *Multiprotocol Label Switching (MPLS)*.

traffic engineering database   Data structure built by either OSPF or IS-IS that is used by RSVP for the establishment of LSPs in an MPLS network.

traffic engineering IP router ID TLV   IS-IS TLV that sends the router ID of the local router to the network for inclusion in the traffic engineering database.

transient interfaces   Interfaces that can be moved from one location in the router to another. All customer-facing interfaces are considered transient in nature.

transit area   In OSPF, an area used to pass traffic from one adjacent area to the backbone or to another area if the backbone is more than two hops away from an area.

transit router   In MPLS, any intermediate router in the LSP between the ingress router and the egress router.

Transmission Control Protocol (TCP)   Works in conjunction with Internet Protocol (IP) to send data over the Internet. Divides a message into packets and tracks the packets from the point of origin.

transport mode   An IPSec mode of operation in which the data payload is encrypted but the original IP header is left untouched. The IP addresses of the source or destination can be modified if the packet is intercepted. Because of its construction, transport mode can be used only when the communication end point and cryptographic end point are the same. VPN gateways that provide encryption and decryption services for protected hosts cannot use transport mode for protected VPN communications. See also *tunnel mode.*

tree database   A logical data structure used by the link-state protocols when running the shortest path algorithm. The tree database contains the final shortest path from the root of the tree to each leaf node.

triggered updates   Updates used in a distance-vector protocol to reduce the time for the network to converge. When a router has a topology change, it immediately sends the information to its neighbors instead of waiting for a timer to expire.

Triple-DES   A 168-bit encryption algorithm that encrypts data blocks with three different keys in succession, thus achieving a higher level of encryption. Triple-DES is one of the strongest encryption algorithms available for use in VPNs.

Tspec Object   RSVP message object that contains information such as the bandwidth request of the LSP as well as the minimum and maximum packets supported.

tunnel   Private, secure path through an otherwise public network.

tunnel mode   An IPSec mode of operation in which the entire IP packet, including the header, is encrypted and authenticated and a new VPN header is added, protecting the entire original packet. This mode can be used by both VPN clients and VPN gateways, and protects communications that come from or go to non-IPSec systems. See also *transport mode.*

Tunnel PIC   A physical interface card that allows the router to perform the encapsulation and decapsulation of IP datagrams. The Tunnel PIC supports IP-IP, GRE, and PIM register encapsulation and decapsulation. When the Tunnel PIC is installed, the router can be a PIM rendezvous point (RP) or a PIM first-hop router for a source that is directly connected to the router.

type of service (ToS)   The method of handling traffic using information extracted from the fields in the ToS byte to differentiate packet flows.

type, length, value (TLV)   A system for advertising and encoding information within routing protocols. IS-IS, BGP, RSVP, and LDP use this paradigm.

U

UMTS Terrestrial Radio Access Network (UTRAN)   The WCDMA radio network in UMTS.

unicast   Operation of sending network traffic from one network node to another individual network node.

unicast reverse path forwarding (uRPF)   Automated method for verifying that an incoming data packet is reachable from a particular router interface.

uninterruptible power supply (UPS)   Device that sits between a power supply and a router (or other piece of equipment) that prevents undesired power-source events, such as outages and surges, from affecting or damaging the device.

unit   JUNOS software syntax that represents the logical properties of an interface.

Universal Mobile Telecommunications System (UMTS)   Third-generation (3G), packet-based transmission of text, digitized voice, video, and multimedia, at data rates up to 2Mbps.

Update message   BGP message that advertises path attributes and routing knowledge to an established neighbor.

Update timer   Timer used in a distance-vector protocol to advertise routes to a neighbor on a regular basis. The JUNOS software uses a default value of 30 seconds.

upto   JUNOS software routing policy match type representing all routes that share the same most significant bits and whose prefix length is smaller than the supplied subnet in the route filter.

User Datagram Protocol (UDP)   Layer 4 protocol that provides an unreliable, connectionless service between two end IP hosts.

V

V bit   The V bit is set in a router LSA when the router is operating as an end point for a virtual link.

vapor corrosion inhibitor (VCI)   Vapor corrosion inhibitor. Small cylinder packed with the router that prevents corrosion of the chassis and components during shipment.

virtual circuit   Represents a logical connection between two Layer 2 devices in a network.

virtual circuit identifier (VCI)   A 16-bit field in the header of an ATM cell that indicates the particular virtual circuit the cell takes through a virtual path. Also called a *logical interface*.

virtual link   In OSPF, a link created between two routers that are part of the backbone but are not physically contiguous.

virtual local area network (VLAN)   A grouping of end hosts within a single IP subnet. These hosts usually reside on multiple physical segments and are connected through a Layer 2 Ethernet switched network.

virtual path   A combination of multiple virtual circuits between two devices in an ATM network.

virtual path identifier (VPI)   The 8-bit field in the header of an ATM cell that indicates the virtual path the cell takes. See also *virtual circuit identifier (VCI)*.

virtual private network (VPN)   A private data network that makes use of a public TCP/IP network, typically the Internet, while maintaining privacy with a tunneling protocol, encryption, and security procedures.

Virtual Router Redundancy Protocol (VRRP)   On Fast Ethernet and Gigabit Ethernet interfaces, a protocol that allows you to configure virtual default routers.

VPN forwarding table (VFT)   In a Layer 2 VPN, the VFT contains forwarding information from the local PE router to remote PE routers.

VPN routing and forwarding table (VRF)   In a Layer 3 VPN, contains routing information advertised by each CE router in the VPN.

W

wavelength-division multiplexing (WDM)   Technique for transmitting a mix of voice, data, and video over various wavelengths (colors) of light.

wide metrics   A common name for the advertisement of IS-IS metrics using a 3-octet field in the extended IS reachability TLV.

Wideband Code Division Multiple Access (WCDMA)   Radio interface technology used in most 3G systems.

weighted round-robin (WRR)   Scheme used to decide the queue from which the next packet should be transmitted.

wildcard filter   Reservation style where multiple senders from multiple RSVP sessions are allowed to share a single set of resources.

Index

Note to Reader: **Bolded** page references indicate definitions and main discussions of a topic. *Italicized* page references indicate tables and illustrations. References that include a letter, for example **B:10**, refer to the bonus chapters that are included on the accompanying CD.

C

G

J

O

R

TELL US WHAT YOU THINK!

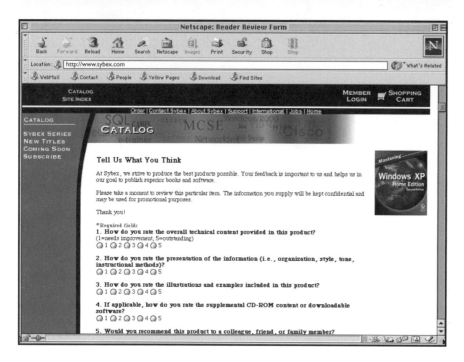

Your feedback is critical to our efforts to provide you with the best books and software on the market. Tell us what you think about the products you've purchased. It's simple:

1. Go to the Sybex website.
2. Find your book by typing the ISBN or title into the Search field.
3. Click on the book title when it appears.
4. Click **Submit a Review.**
5. Fill out the questionnaire and comments.
6. Click **Submit.**

With your feedback, we can continue to publish the highest quality computer books and software products that today's busy IT professionals deserve.

www.sybex.com

SYBEX Inc. • 1151 Marina Village Parkway, Alameda, CA 94501 • 510-523-8233

SYBEX®